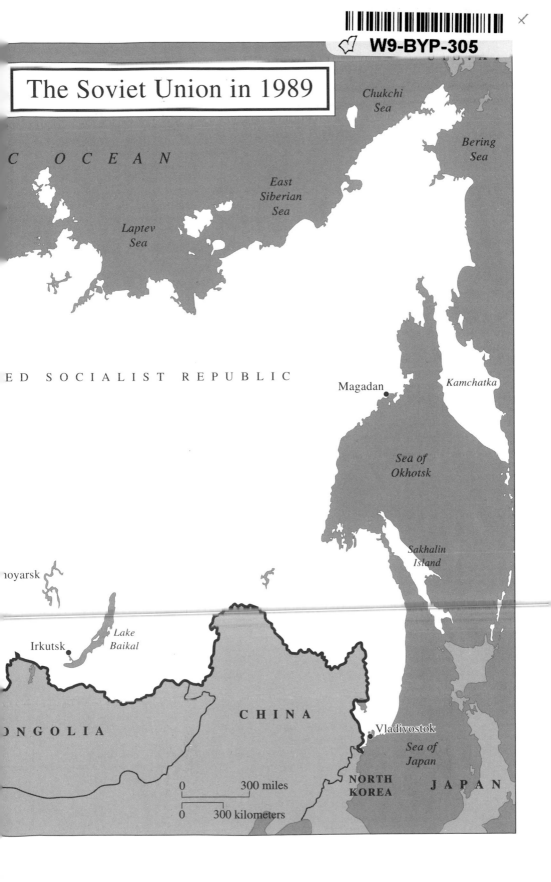

The Soviet Union in 1989

Chukchi Sea

Bering Sea

C   O C E A N

East Siberian Sea

Laptev Sea

E D   S O C I A L I S T   R E P U B L I C

Magadan

Kamchatka

Sea of Okhotsk

Sakhalin Island

noyarsk

Lake Baikal

Irkutsk

CHINA

Vladivostok

Sea of Japan

NGOLIA

NORTH KOREA

JAPAN

| 0 | 300 miles |
| 0 | 300 kilometers |

AUTOPSY ON AN EMPIRE

Jack F. Matlock, Jr.

AUTOPSY

ON

AN EMPIRE

—◆—

*The American Ambassador's Account
of the Collapse of the Soviet Union*

Random House   New York

Library of Congress Cataloging-in-Publication Data

Matlock, Jack F.
Autopsy on an empire: the American ambassador's
account of the collapse of the Soviet Union / Jack F.
Matlock, Jr.
p.   cm.
Includes index.
ISBN 0-679-41376-6 (alk. paper)
1. Soviet Union—Politics and government—1985–1991.
2. Soviet Union—Foreign relations—United States.
3. United States—Foreign relations—Soviet Union.
I. Title.
DK288.M386 1995   327.47073—dc20   95-13833

Book design by M. Kristen Bearse

Manufactured in the United States of America on
acid-free paper

4   6   8   9   7   5   3

*To the men and women
who served their country with skill and devotion
at the American Embassy in Moscow
and the Consulates General in Kiev and Leningrad
1987–1991*

Contents

List of Maps

AUTOPSY ON AN EMPIRE

How Did It Happen?

Russia is a country with an unpredictable past.
YURI AFANASIEV, May 1993[1]

Early in the evening of December 25, 1991, Mikhail Gorbachev walked across the hall from his Kremlin office and entered a room decorated with pecan-colored woodwork, light green damask wall coverings, and marquise curtains. Normally this room was used to receive visitors, but this time a television crew was waiting.

Gorbachev seated himself behind the table opposite the cameras, and when the Kremlin chimes had completed seven peals, began his final television address as president of the Union of Soviet Socialist Republics. In the past, most of his addresses had been taped in advance. This time, he went on the air live.

"I am ceasing my activity in the post of president of the USSR," he announced, and though the meaning of his statement was clear, his choice of words seemed strange. They implied that the position of president in a state called the Union of Soviet Socialist Republics was still in existence. It would have been more accurate if he had declared that the collapse of the state he headed had eliminated the job he had previously held.

Following his twenty-minute statement to the nation, he walked back to his office and was surprised to be told that the Soviet flag had already been lowered from the Kremlin. He had assumed that this would happen later, maybe at the end of the year, not within minutes of his resignation. The Russian tricolor of white, blue, and red horizontal stripes was on hand to be hoisted in its place, but there was a problem. The color guard had trouble fitting it to the harness and fumbled frantically before making a secure attachment and raising it, in convulsive jerks, to the top of the mast.

Thus the Union of Soviet Socialist Republics passed into history—precipitously, with hasty and careless preparation, but nonetheless conclusively.

The new flag marked the birth of a nation-state, but the transfer of authority was not yet complete. For centuries, Russian tsars had been crowned in the Uspensky Cathedral, located a few dozen paces from the Soviet president's office. The crown and scepter, symbols of imperial rule, had been held in custody in the Kremlin armory after Tsar Nicholas II was deposed and subsequently murdered. In 1991, however, the emblem of authority was more than symbolic. It was no less than the key to Soviet nuclear weaponry, which had a far greater destructive force than any Russian emperor could have imagined. The pomp and ceremony of a coronation were no longer necessary to underscore the ruler's power. Besides, the recipient, the president of Russia, was an impatient man.

Two days earlier, Presidents Gorbachev and Boris Yeltsin had agreed that they would meet in Gorbachev's office immediately after the resignation announcement to effect a transfer of the devices and codes which controlled the Soviet nuclear arsenal.

As with the flag replacement, the manner of the transfer failed to meet Gorbachev's expectations. When he returned to his office he was met not by Russian President Yeltsin but by the minister of defense. General Yevgeny Shaposhnikov explained that Yeltsin had been offended by some of the remarks in Gorbachev's farewell address and had refused to meet him as agreed. There was no point in arguing or prolonging the agony. Gorbachev directed that the briefcase with the infamous nuclear "button" be given to Shaposhnikov.

Other empires may have shattered under the pressure of war or revolution, but the Soviet Union expired quietly. Control over its nuclear weapons passed to a new master circuitously, almost casually. Within minutes, while most Americans were opening presents or preparing Christmas dinner, Russia replaced the Soviet Union as a nuclear power.[2]

The Russia that assumed control over all central Soviet institutions and would occupy the Soviet seat in the United Nations Security Council contained only slightly more than half the population of the previous Soviet Union. Henceforth, more than 140 million persons who were Soviet citizens when 1991 began would live in countries other than Russia. The three Baltic states—Estonia, Latvia, and Lithuania—had been recognized as independent four months earlier. Now the other twelve former union republics were also on their own.

As soon as Gorbachev had finished his television address, David Chikvaidze, an assistant who had helped make the arrangements with the television crew, returned to his office on the floor below and sank into his chair. He had known what was coming, of course, but now it had happened. For two hours he stared at the wall, deep in contemplation about the uncertain future.

Born and reared in Georgia, he was a brilliant young Soviet diplomat. Because of his cheery personality, his willingness to be helpful, and his perfect American English, he had become a favorite of Washingtonians during his earlier tour at the Soviet Embassy. Now he discovered that he no longer knew who he was. A proud and patriotic Georgian, he had served the Soviet government with loyalty and distinction. He regarded both Tbilisi and Moscow as home. He and his wife made sure their son spoke Georgian first and only then learned other languages.

Until that moment, this had been no problem. He was Georgian and he was Soviet, and there was no contradiction. Would he now be forced to choose? He was happy to be Georgian, but he also considered himself part of a larger country, and that country no longer existed. What now? Should he, could he, stay in Moscow and become a Russian citizen? Should he go home to Tbilisi and hope to find a job there? Should he try to stay on in Moscow as a "foreigner"? None of the alternatives was what he would have freely chosen.

My situation was totally different from David Chikvaidze's, but I too reacted to the news with shock and lengthy contemplation.

———

My wife, Rebecca, and I spent December 25 that year in two places. Having celebrated Christmas away from home for many years, we wanted to see as much of our family as we could. So for breakfast we went to our daughter's house in Alexandria, Virginia, where her family, two of our sons, and my brother had gathered. Then, after exchanging gifts, we flew to Fort Lauderdale to join my mother and our youngest son, who had come from Tennessee.

Christmas is an important day for our family, descended from southern Protestant stock. Nevertheless, my thoughts that day frequently strayed from religion and family. I knew that a decisive moment was approaching in the Soviet Union. I had seen Gorbachev in Moscow just a week earlier, when I had found him seemingly reconciled to the inevitable but not fully comprehending the forces about to engulf him. I knew Yeltsin and the other Russian leaders well and considered many of them personal friends. I also knew their opponents and had friends among them too. But most of all, there were literally hundreds of Soviet citizens, from hairdressers and domestic workers to poets, professors, bankers, and legislators, about whom we cared, and cared deeply. We had lived among them for years and shared, at least vicariously, their sorrows and hopes; they seemed part of our extended family. They, like David Chikvaidze, would bear the impact of what happened in Moscow that day.

When we had finished dinner and opened the last gifts, I retired to an upstairs bedroom and plugged my laptop computer into the telephone jack to check on the news reports from Moscow. They would give me more details than television. This is how I learned about Gorbachev's resignation speech and the events in Moscow, including the new flag that had been raised over the Kremlin.

The enormity of what had happened soon sank in. I had expected the outcome, but I also realized that, with all my acquaintance with the society and its politicians and my own participation in some of these events, I could not explain with confidence just how it had happened.

After all, the Soviet Union had possessed the largest military machine ever assembled on this planet by a single political authority. It had been governed by an apparently monolithic party with historically unparalleled instruments of compulsion. Tentacles of its elaborate bureaucracy had reached into every crevice of its subjects' lives. Its ideology had purported to reveal the secret of harnessing the very tides of history. How could such a state simply have destroyed itself?

If pressed for an answer, I could have said glibly that the system was inherently faulty, doomed to failure sooner or later; its leaders had been guilty of the most monstrous crimes against humanity, and history has a way of settling scores; the economic system was irrational and could not compete in the modern world; the ideology had lost its power to compel belief; the attempt to use military force to establish hegemony and to build "prestige" had been self-defeating—and on and on, for there were scores of plausible statements, each of which might well contain part of an answer but none of which would really explain how and why it had happened when it did.

I realized that while I probably knew as much about the political developments in Moscow during the past seven years as anyone not actually in the Soviet leadership, I could not give an honest answer to the questions the Soviet collapse raised. Why did it happen at the end of 1991, rather than years later—or months earlier? What were the decisive events that had brought it about? Had a different outcome ever been possible? Could the Soviet system have modified itself so as to last for decades to come?

These questions nagged. If I could not answer them, who could? Historians, maybe, but only after Soviet archives were opened, the participants had written their memoirs, and several generations of scholars had sifted and analyzed the records. Many details would doubtless come to light in the future. Whoever pronounced judgment hastily was bound to be wrong on many points.

But even with their fuller information, future historians would hardly agree on the meaning of the changes. After all, we were still debating the reasons for the decline and fall of the Roman Empire—to say nothing of the origins of the First World War. Such fateful convulsions have always produced a variety of interpretations.

Definitive answers might be impossible, but the questions remained important; if only to help us deal with the successor states.

But it was not such utilitarian considerations that nagged most insistently; here was a mystery I felt I *should* understand but couldn't. Any mystery is a challenge, but one so crucial to my own life and work was more than a challenge: solving it was an obligation. How could I make sense of my own life, devoted as it was to understanding the Soviet Union, if I could not understand the Soviet collapse?

———

If the Soviet Union had been merely the final post in my Foreign Service career, I might not have felt the same, but I had spent most of my adult life directly or indirectly dealing with the Soviet Union.

Many persons take a keen interest in the country of their ancestors, and that is natural. But I had no such excuse for what turned out to be a lifelong love affair with Russian culture. The first Matlocks came to North America in the seventeenth century from Derbyshire, England. They were Quakers who emigrated for the sake of religious freedom. When I was born in Greensboro, North Carolina, in 1929, the family could no longer remember how long we had been there, and my grandparents were not sure whether the family had originally been English or Scotch-Irish. They were no longer Quakers, though we had relatives who were.

As I grew up in the 1930s and 1940s, I had little direct contact with foreign cultures. Even so, I was fascinated by foreign languages and tried to learn some Russian on my own. But there was no one in Greensboro to tell me how to pronounce the letters, so I could not even memorize the alphabet.

Russian was not taught at Duke University when I entered in 1946, but my interest in the language increased when I read, not in class but on my own, Constance Garnett's translation of *Crime and Punishment* and other works by Dostoyevsky. It stirred my thoughts, imagination, and emotions as no other book had.

Later, when Duke added Russian to its curriculum, I registered for the first class. Rebecca and I were married before returning to Duke for our final year, and we both took courses in Russian history and literature. Duke at that time offered few such courses, but the quality of the teaching made up for the limited curriculum. John Curtiss, who taught the course on history, could convey the nuances of Russian historical development without skewing the evidence to fit some particular theory or national bias. In his first full-time teaching job, Tom Winner taught Russian language and literature with spellbinding gusto and introduced me to more than Russia. His dissertation was on Kazakh folklore, and I helped him proofread the final text. In this way I discovered the Kazakhs' tragic fate under Soviet colonialism, a topic that would eventually become one of my preoccupations.

By 1950, Rebecca and I had decided to go to graduate school and prepare for college teaching or the Foreign Service—or maybe both. After finishing the Russian Institute at Columbia University and teaching Russian language and literature at Dartmouth College, I entered the Foreign Service in 1956.

My first assignment was writing reports on internal Soviet developments. I was disappointed since I had hoped to go overseas, but the assignment turned out to be fortunate. I had a wider academic background in Soviet affairs than the more senior diplomats assigned to the office, and my work there brought a quick promotion and a favorable reputation with other Soviet specialists in the Service. After two years in Austria and one in Germany, I finally arrived at the American Embassy in Moscow in September 1961, thirteen years after I had registered for my first Russian course at Duke.

The Khrushchev "thaw" was just beginning, and some small cracks in the wall isolating Soviet citizens from foreign diplomats had appeared. Rebecca and I were determined to get outside the diplomatic ghetto and mix with Soviet citizens, at least to the degree we could without endangering them. We tried every approach we could think of to meet Russians, but usually after an encounter on a train or in a restaurant, say, the contact would terminate, sometimes with apologies that another meeting was just not convenient, more often without explanation. Obviously the KGB had warned our acquaintances not to see us.

Only two things worked. First, we began inviting American and other foreign students from Soviet universities (exchanges were just beginning) to come to our apartment for informal evenings, and as we got to know them we encouraged them to bring their Soviet friends. The Soviet students who came were usually either police informers or political nonconformists who subsequently became dissidents. The latter normally could spot the former, and we quickly learned to exclude the more obvious ringers.

We also learned that Soviet cultural figures eligible to visit to the United States would be allowed to meet us before and after the visit and prominent Americans who came to Moscow as part of an exchange would be allowed to meet their Soviet counterparts. Thus, we were able to meet and entertain writers and scholars, particularly during Robert Frost's visit in 1962.

By the time we left Moscow after a two-year tour, we had gotten to know several dozen people, including writers, artists, and theater directors, many of whom became friends for life. I had traveled to fourteen of the fifteen Soviet republics, and our family had grown from three children to five, one born in a Moscow hospital.

We spent the next seven years in Africa, but not because the State Department willfully disregarded area and language expertise. I had requested assignment to Africa because I wanted to witness the formation of new nations out of the colonial empires which were disbanding. I understood that the Soviet Union itself was an empire and sensed that what happened in Africa in the 1960s might someday be relevant to the Soviet Union itself. Furthermore, the Soviet rulers were certain to try to take advantage of the crumbling British and French empires. It would be interesting to witness the Soviet efforts to influence the fledgling nations.

We were sent first to Ghana, then Zanzibar, then mainland Tanzania, at a time when Soviet influence seemed to be growing. I made a point of getting to know most of the Soviet citizens sent out to those countries as diplomats, journalists, or teachers. Most of them, I found, were there to escape, if only for a time, the controls on their lives in the Soviet Union. Most were unhappy, and their relationship with the Africans was not close. I reported to Washington that their presence was more likely to be an inoculation against communism than a source of ideological infection.

In the 1970s I resumed working with the Soviet Union directly, first as director of Soviet affairs in the State Department in Washington, then as deputy chief of mission at our embassy in Moscow. It was the period of détente, and relations were easier than they had been in the 1960s. But they were by no means free. The KGB still tried to inhibit continuing contacts between us and Soviet citizens, and only some of the bravest (such as the poet Andrei Voznesensky and his novelist wife, Zoya Boguslavskaya) were willing to see us regularly. Nevertheless, our circle of acquaintances widened steadily before we returned to the United States in 1978.

In 1981 we were sent to Moscow again, this time for me to take charge of the embassy following President Ronald Reagan's inauguration. We stayed for most of the year, until Reagan's nominee, Arthur Hartman, arrived in the fall. This was a period of great tension in U.S.-Soviet relations: the Soviets had invaded Afghanistan a year before, the Senate had refused to ratify the treaty to limit strategic arms (SALT II), and polemics had become strident. Still we found that a remarkable number of friends seemed pleased to see us.

After two years in Prague as ambassador to Czechoslovakia, I was transferred to Washington to work on the National Security Council staff in Washington, responsible for relations with Europe and Canada, but with particular emphasis on the Soviet Union. I was asked to help devise a strategy to help lower tensions and reduce arms. When I was appointed, reporter Lou Cannon, who had never met me, wrote in *The Washington Post* that I was a "militant hard-liner."

The description was only partly true. I was indeed a hard-liner when it came to confronting the outrages of the Soviet imperial system and the false ideology of communism, which had been cynically imposed on a great people. I felt that we had no alternative but to demonstrate our determination and ability to thwart Soviet aggression. But I was not a hard-liner when it came to the Russian people and the other nations under the Soviet yoke. I thought their true interests were in harmony with ours, that they wanted to live in peace and freedom, and use their inherent creativity without the suffocating strictures of an omnipresent political machine. With a different political system, I was sure they would be friendly.

Unlike ideologues on both sides of the East-West divide, I believed that the Soviet Union could change and that we could encourage that change. President Reagan came to believe the same. The policy he approved combined firmness with a willingness to negotiate, and it placed respect for human rights at the top of the agenda.

Just before Christmas 1986, the president asked me to go to Moscow as ambassador when Arthur Hartman's tour ended. I now had an opportunity to implement the policy I had helped formulate.

When I arrived in Moscow in the spring of 1987 for my fourth tour of duty, perestroika was still in its infancy. The new Soviet leadership was dissatisfied with the economy and wanted change, but there was little evidence that reform would go beyond the earlier superficial "campaigns" that had flared periodically, only to disappear without a trace.

No matter how radical policy pronouncements might become, little would change if they were not put into practice. This meant that if I was to understand what was happening, I had to keep in touch with developments outside Moscow. I resolved to travel to both Russian and non-Russian areas of the Soviet Union as frequently as embassy duties would permit. I had already visited all but one of the union republics, but now I wanted to go to all I was permitted to visit (our own policy placed the Baltic states out of bounds for me) not just once but as often as possible.

This travel was strenuous. It was also immensely rewarding. Not only was it instructive, it gave me a chance to give an accurate account of the United States' position. The Soviet regime had justified its military buildup (never described in precise terms, lest the public balk at its enormous cost) to its own people as a response to U.S. threats: why not undercut this lie by showing us as the interested and caring nation we in fact are?

I was also aware that the various nationalities within the Soviet Union had proud and ancient traditions. They needed reassurance that we had not forgotten them. Many non-Russians were afraid of losing their ethnic identity within a homogeneous Soviet culture, Russian in language and Leninist in ideology. Members of these nationalities feared they would be forgotten by the world at large.

My trip in 1963 to the three Baltic states with embassy colleague Jack Perry, who later became our ambassador to Bulgaria, had made a deep impression. We had contrived as often as possible to elude the smothering embrace of the official tourist organization to roam the streets and go into theaters and restaurants, meeting as many ordinary people as we could and talking at length to those willing to risk talking to us. One theme had recurred so frequently in these conversations that it had become the leitmotif of the trip: "Please, don't think of us as *Russians.* We are *not* Russians. We are *Estonians* [or *Latvians* or *Lithuanians,* depending on the location]."

We had known this, of course, but now we understood the anxiety behind the assertion. The iron curtain had throttled the flow of accurate information in both directions. The Baltic states, like the other "national republics" claimed by Moscow, were increasingly considered by foreigners to be part of "Soviet Russia."

I did not, of course, pretend that all Americans knew what was going on within the borders of the Soviet Union. But I knew that the sympathy and understanding I showed for groups whose human rights had been infringed represented a tradition as old as our country.

As my interest in the Soviet Union deepened, I tried to learn as much as possible of its languages and cultures. Although I normally used Russian, when I was in non-Russian areas I always tried to use the local language as well. I wanted to show that I *did* know that the nation I was visiting was distinctive, that I respected its national identity, and that my interest and respect were sufficient for me to go to the trouble to learn enough of their language to address them, if only briefly, in it.

Our people at the Voice of America went out of their way to help me prepare speeches in Georgian, Armenian, and Uzbek, while friends in Moscow helped out with Ukrainian, Belarusian, Moldavian, Kazakh, and Chechen.

Each trip was a voyage of discovery, even in places I had already visited. As glasnost expanded, people became more frank. Taboo subjects became the center of conversation, and many people who could not have met us in the past were now allowed, and sometimes even encouraged, to talk to us.

Frequently Rebecca traveled not only with me but also on her own, as she was often invited to display her photographs and the tapestries she designed and made.

Our attention opened doors and hearts. People could sense that we were interested in them, and they responded with an interest in us and in America. We were candid with them, and they reciprocated. Consequently, we could sense mood changes and new attitudes as they evolved.

In communicating with Soviet citizens, we received crucial assistance from the Soviet media. Once virtually closed to foreign diplomats, particularly Americans, Soviet newspapers, magazines, and television and radio stations began to interview us, and by 1990 hardly a day passed that we were not mentioned in the media.

In Moscow, we found to our pleasant surprise that we were becoming a part of Soviet society. Visitors, mostly Soviet, gathered at our residence, Spaso House, a dozen or more times a week for concerts, films, art exhibits, luncheons, and dinners—and later for discussions of political and economic problems. When a new parliament was formed, the members frequently discussed issues at the dining tables in Spaso House before they reached the floor for formal debate.

As Soviet society relaxed and the tensions between our countries subsided, Soviet political leaders dealt with us more openly, discussing their plans, their hopes, eventually even seeking advice, particularly on democratic institutions and practices. With the help of the energetic diplomats in our embassy, we got to know virtually all the prominent politicians in Moscow and many of the most influential ones in regions outside the capital.

In 1989, President Bush asked me to extend my normal tour of duty. I agreed, but by the spring of 1991 I felt the time had come for me to turn to other things. The four years I had been in the Soviet Union as ambassador had been exhilarating but draining. I had witnessed the end of the cold war. Communism was clearly on its way out in the Soviet Union, which itself would either be transformed along more democratic lines or disintegrate. The tasks ahead for U.S. policy makers would differ greatly from those of the past.

It was time for a new hand at the helm of our embassy in Moscow and for me to leave public service and resume the life of writing and teaching I had started before I had entered the Foreign Service. In April, I told President Bush that I wished to leave Moscow that summer. Eventually, we set the date of August 11 for our departure.

A week after I left Moscow, a cabal of his own associates confronted Gorbachev, then on vacation in the Crimea, with a demand that he transfer power to them. When he refused, the final act in the drama of the Soviet Union's collapse began. I watched these events from the United States, but I knew the people who were making news, and it was easy to imagine the situation. In spirit, I stood with my Russian friends to protect their White House and was beside Boris Yeltsin when he climbed on a tank to shout defiance at the plotters.

As the Soviet Union passed into history, I wondered what an obituary might say. If a person of dubious character had died, I would say *"nil nisi bonum"* and eschew an objective appraisal. But a political system is not a person. The death of the Soviet empire was no cause for mourning.

Stalin had murdered more of his own citizens than the 20 million who perished as the result of Hitler's invasion and genocide. Millions of persons innocent of the slightest wrongdoing had been killed. Land had been seized from peasants and livestock from herders, crippling agriculture and creating famine. Successful farmers had been either executed or shipped to near-certain death in concentration camps for no other reason than that they had been successful and productive and thus bad examples for a collectivist society. Islands of autonomy in a totalitarian sea!

Whole nations had been deported on nothing more than the suspicion that they might have been disloyal or—in the case of the Koreans and Volga Germans—that they might someday be tempted to be disloyal.

The Soviet state had provided its functionaries with multiple instruments of coercion but no effective barrier to their arbitrary misuse. The only constraints had been those of practicality and calculations of political or economic utility.

Yes, it *was* an evil empire. But was this empire identical with the state that disappeared on December 25, 1991? Had not the old Soviet empire—the evil one—been so undermined that it had already given way in August 1991, with the dissolution of the Communist Party of the Soviet Union?

The treaty of association under negotiation subsequently aimed at a different state structure. Therefore, some—including many elected members of the Soviet parliament—would say that the choice in December 1991 was not between the Soviet empire and a group of independent republics but between a voluntary, democratic union and a congeries of independent states, many of them authoritarian or worse.

As I tried to compose the obituary in my mind, I realized that another question had arisen that I could not answer with confidence. What precisely was the state that had collapsed? The Soviet Union of old, which would have few mourners, or something else, which might have many?

One question did seem clear to me. That is, evil as the Soviet empire was, it was not an empire of evil people. The distribution of good and bad traits among Russians and other nations of the erstwhile Soviet Union was probably much like that among people of other nationalities and societies.

The Soviet system could bring out the worst in people but could not prevent remarkable acts of courage and nobility. While the Soviet system became an instrument of inhumanity in the hands of its leaders, it could not destroy a sense of justice and morality or the yearning for freedom. Few persons had the courage of Andrei Sakharov and Alexander Solzhenitsyn to confront the Communist rulers head on—though the number that did was remarkable, given the terrible risks. But even for the majority, who refused to run great personal risks for possibly quixotic goals, tacit resistance, an unspoken refusal to conform, was far more common than active support for the regime.

When the possibility of change became real, most, though not all, of the people who brought the Soviet system down had been participants in that system and beneficiaries of it, some at high levels. The questions posed earlier rise again: How could this be? How could a ruling party, with no effective opposition, destroy itself? How could a powerful military machine, without losing a major war, disintegrate?

Before sleep overcame me, in the early hours of December 26, 1991, I resolved to try to find the answers by retracing and re-examining the events that preceded the collapse.

Before I proceed, I should disclose my biases.

When I went to Moscow as ambassador, my first duty was to represent my own country and its interests. These interests conflicted with much in the Soviet system and the policies of the Soviet government at that time, but they did not conflict with the real interests of the Soviet peoples. Our goal was to prevent Soviet aggression and remove the causes, not just the symptoms, of East-West tension. A government in the Soviet Union that would be responsible to its own people and protect their rights was the best guarantee we could have of a peaceful future. I thought, and hoped, that the totalitarian Soviet empire would eventually pass from the world scene, but I did not see this as an immediate prospect.

From the late 1980s I was often asked by Soviet journalists if I had ever believed that the momentous changes we were witnessing would occur. I usually replied, "Yes, of course," and, after pausing to observe my questioner's surprise, added, "And I hoped my grandson would live to see them."

Throughout the perestroika period, I was intellectually and emotionally a supporter of democratic change in the Soviet Union. Such change was certainly in my country's interest, but it was even more in the interest of Soviet citizens. I thought it was important that the Baltic states be set free, since this was what their people wanted and since their annexation had violated international law and acceptable standards of international conduct. I did not feel that a Soviet Union based on consent rather than force would be a threat to the United States. Furthermore, I knew that a voluntary union could provide many benefits for its constituent parts.

With all my sympathy for the various nations trapped within the Soviet empire, I never rejected the idea of a union in and of itself. Independence is not necessarily the only way to realize a nation's potential and preserve its freedom. A voluntary union of limited powers, with democratic institutions and the checks and balances essential to an effective democracy, could have provided freedom and a framework for more effective economic development. This was as clear to me as it was to Soviet President Gorbachev, who toward the end defended the virtues of a voluntary union—at least in the abstract.

I felt, however, that such a union could come about only if the old state structure was replaced by a new one built by elected leaders at every geographical level. If the various nations that made up the Soviet Union were not convinced that a new union was in their interest, no amount of pounding by the old "Center" or cheerleading from abroad could forge a viable federation.

For me, the touchstone was democracy, defined not merely as free elections but also as a working system of government with limited powers, subject to the rule of law, that protects civil and minority rights. As an American, I had no doubt that such a country, whether a union of several nations or a smaller nation-state, would be a friend and a potential partner. An autocratic or totalitarian state, whether large or small, whether of the "left" or of the "right," would be a problem, for its own people most directly, but for us all eventually.

A goal is one thing; getting there is something else. I knew I had no sure answers, and I doubted anyone else did. We were all, directly or vicariously, experimenting. People change. Societies change. But never totally. Features of the past never disappear, either from individuals or from society. The most difficult and uncertain task in this maelstrom of change was to assess the strength of the new features as compared with the old. It was hard enough to do with individuals; it was much more difficult as one surveyed a whole nation, a whole society, a whole empire.

I also felt that the United States would benefit if a democratic Soviet Union, or a democratic Russia, was prosperous. I never agreed with those few observers who argued that it was in our interest to keep Russia weak. I doubted that we could do so even if we wished, but I also thought we would be stupid to wish for a weak Russia. If democracy could triumph, a strong Russia would be good for all of us. If democracy did not triumph, Russia would suffer from many of the weaknesses that had destroyed the Soviet Union. In any event, it was a choice Russians would make; Americans could not decide for them.

I do not aspire to write a definitive history of the Soviet collapse—that is manifestly impossible this close to the event, even if a history can ever be definitive. My account will also not try to trace in detail all features of perestroika or to chronicle U.S.-Soviet relations during that period. My focus will be on those events that are germane to a few fundamental questions: How did it happen that the Soviet empire collapsed when it did and as it did? What were the key events? Who, if anyone, bears the principal responsibility? Was it the Soviet empire that expired on December 25, 1991, or an embryonic successor? Was a democratic union ever a feasible possibility? And finally, are there lessons here for the future, or for the rest of the world?

My account will give scant attention to events and issues that do not bear on these questions, even though they may be important in other contexts. It will be an autopsy of the collapsed empire, not a biography. Since an autopsy is meant to fix the cause of death, the pathologist need not concern himself with every important facet of the deceased's life.

But even an autopsy should define what the patient's state of health was before the fatal illness ran its course or the fatal trauma took its toll. What can we say about the empire that fell to pieces in 1991? What held it together, and what sort of nations were in its thrall?

II

The Empire

The most democratic constitution in the world.
J. V. STALIN on the 1936 Soviet Constitution

Hypocrisy is the tribute vice pays to virtue.
LA ROCHEFOUCAULD

November 2, 1961. It was sunny and warm as I rode into Stalinabad, the capital of Soviet Tajikistan, a city nestled in a mountain valley not far from the point where the borders of China and Afghanistan touch. I was riding in the backseat of a black Chaika, the Soviet equivalent of a limousine, with Senator Allen J. Ellender of Louisiana.

Ellender was a tireless globetrotter, but this was not a pleasure junket. He insisted on a rigorous schedule of ten to twelve hours a day of visits to factories, farms, and offices. It was my duty, as the escort officer assigned by our embassy in Moscow, to make sure he was getting accurate translations (and sometimes relieving the interpreter) and to take notes of what we saw, whom we met, and what we were told. After each of his trips, the senator issued a lengthy report of his findings. This time his object was to familiarize himself with the agricultural and industrial development of areas that had been visited by few Westerners since the 1930s—and by not very many even before.[1]

A strange sight greeted us in Stalinabad. Though the sun was out and the temperature was in the seventies, from a distance it looked as if the city were under a blanket of snow, harmonizing with the upper reaches of the mountains surrounding us. As we entered town, I discovered that the white blanket was not snow. The huge central square, except for a strip barely wide enough for two lanes of traffic, was covered with four or five inches of soggy, unginned cotton.

Our hosts explained with some embarrassment that heavy rains had soaked much of the cotton harvest and that the city squares and every other open place had been taken into service as drying platforms in the warm autumn sun.

As we drove into the city, the Russian tourist guide explained that it had formerly been a mere hamlet named Dushanbe, but as it became an imposing city of 300,000 people and the capital of the Tajik Republic to boot, the old name had been deemed not commensurate with its new dignity. Luckily, Josef Stalin had graciously consented to allow it to bear his name.

Ten days later the name reverted to Dushanbe when Nikita Khrushchev's attacks on Stalin at the Twenty-second Party Congress were published.

Whatever the city was called at any given time, cotton was King . . . and Queen and—increasingly—Joker. It was also the dominant crop in neighboring and much more heavily populated Uzbekistan, and large parts of arid Turkmenistan to the west. In fact, the entire agricultural economy of Central Asia had been diverted to concentrate on cotton production at the expense of fruits and vegetables, which were in short supply in most of the Soviet Union.

Cotton production in these arid and semiarid lands required irrigation, and lots of it. In many places, the soil had a high salt content and had to be flushed each spring before planting. Water was used to flush out the salt, then more was used to grow the plants. Open canals had been built to supply this irrigation, and more and more water was being drawn from the rivers in the area. The giant Aral Sea was receiving less and less inflow and was already beginning to recede.

Water was not the only problem. Chemical fertilizers, insecticides, and defoliants were used with increasing abandon as these substances became more available. Both rivers and groundwaters were showing signs of serious pollution. One wondered, even in 1961, how much more punishment the environment could absorb without turning into a wasteland.

When we asked, we were assured that socialist governments were quite different from capitalist ones. Not to worry. Socialist governments always look out for the people. Practices that were not environmentally safe would simply not be allowed.

Most of the people we met in the cities of Central Asia were Russians or other Europeans. Very few were members of the indigenous nationalities. The rural areas, however, were almost exclusively populated by Central Asians.[2] Urbanization had been rapid, but it had resulted more from immigration than from a tendency of the local people to move to cities.

Did these population movements create friction? Absolutely not, our interlocutors assured us. We all live in perfect harmony because, you see, we do not allow any form of discrimination.

My mind was not a *tabula rasa* when I undertook that 1961 trip with Senator Ellender to Central Asia and the Transcaucasus. I had studied the Soviet Union for years and had taken an interest in its geography, its ethnic groups, and its history. I had read even more about its political system and official ideology. But it is one thing to read and absorb facts intellectually and another to see and experience a situation with one's own eyes.

As I reflected on what I had seen that autumn, it was obvious that I had witnessed a particular form of colonialism. Our official hosts would have denied this, but it was plain to any observer not blinded by ideological preconceptions. Economic and political decisions were made not in these republics by the people who lived there but by "planners" in Moscow. People on the spot, whether carpetbagger or native, simply carried out orders from above. "Above" was Moscow, and above Moscow was nothing. The regime was officially, and at that time, militantly, atheist. It answered only to "history" as Karl Marx and Vladimir Lenin had defined it.

The blanket of wet cotton that greeted us in a city then called Stalinabad served me personally as a powerful symbol of some of the characteristics of this empire.

It may have been in the interest of Central Asia to grow a modest amount of cotton to sell at world market prices or supply local mills. (We do not know for sure, since this was never tried.) But it was certainly not in the interest of the region to create a monoculture to provide cheap raw material for industry elsewhere. This would not have happened under a market economy that had to take into account capital expenditures and the comparative advantage of growing food.

It could have happened only in a command economy that treated its component parts as colonies. It could have happened to the degree it did only in a country without private ownership of land, since private owners would have had a vested interest in preserving their capital—the quality of the land itself—but state-owned property in theory belonged to everybody and in practice to nobody: least of all to the central planner, who was interested only in gross production.

Since the "system" set higher and higher goals for cotton production, it was necessary to divert a growing volume of scarce water for irrigation, again without regard to basic economic factors (such as an appropriate return on capital investment) or to the impact on the environment. Standards of living and health conditions in rural areas began to decline. Furthermore, the incessant demands for more and more production provided incentives to falsify the data, even as burgeoning corruption rendered fraud both possible and profitable.

The motivation for all this was the demand of the Soviet textile industry, mainly in Russia and Ukraine, for cotton, and a reluctance to use convertible currency to buy it abroad, where it could be produced more economically. Why spend real money when you can force people in your own "possessions" to produce raw materials on the cheap? Nobody was allowed to ask "On the cheap for whom?"

Two other features joined cotton as symbols for me: the name of many cities and their "face."

Claims that the Tajiks had spontaneously requested that their capital be named for Stalin or that the Kirgiz genuinely wished theirs to bear the name of General Mikhail Frunze, the commander of the Red Army unit that had conquered them, were patently absurd. Nor did it seem credible that the rapid and often forcible introduction of alien ethnic groups had reinforced the "friendship of peoples."

Ideology and political system entirely aside, all these characteristics are typical of absentee political rule, and the adjective we normally apply to that is "imperial." Whatever else the Soviet system may have been (and it had many other features), it was an empire.

Russian or Soviet?

IT WAS, HOWEVER, an empire with a difference. The Roman, British, French, and Spanish empires all resulted from one nation's conquest of others. The same is true of the Russian empire as it existed up to the 1917 revolution. The conquering nation became the "metropole," its colonies dependencies.

The Soviet empire, in contrast, was the result of conquest by a political party, the bureaucratic embodiment of an ideology. The metropole was the Communist ruling class, the *nomenklatura,* not a nationality. The Communist Party colonized Russia as surely as it did Ukraine, Georgia, and Uzbekistan.

Nevertheless, many continued to consider Russians colonizers, and with reason. Since Russians were much more numerous than any other nationality, and since they predominated in the central Communist Party apparatus and were often the principal immigrants into non-Russian national areas, many of those who were not Russian viewed Communist rule as a form of Russian rule. Furthermore, the Soviet empire appropriated the history of Russian imperial expansion as its own. It relied on the Russian language as a unifying factor, and the spread of Russian at the expense of other languages was for many indistinguishable from Russian national aggrandizement.

Many Russians, by contrast, viewed their state as having been seized by an international conspiracy that was as determined to snuff out traditional Russian values as those of other nations. Some Russians, aching for their shattered traditions, began to echo Alexander Solzhenitsyn's dictum that no one had suffered more from Communist rule than had Russians themselves.

This peculiar boast (readers of Dostoyevsky will recognize the effort to calibrate virtue by the degree of one's suffering) is difficult to substantiate. Russians, after all, had *not* been uprooted en masse, with enormous loss of life, as had the Crimean Tatars, Chechens, Ingush, Volga Germans, and some half-dozen other nationalities. They had not suffered from Stalin's collectivization of agriculture to the degree Ukrainians and Kazakhs did. Russians had not been deprived of the possibility of higher education in their native language, nor had they been discriminated against by Soviet authorities just because they were Russians. On the contrary, they enjoyed both protection and privileges when they migrated to areas of predominantly non-Russian population. Everyone was urged to learn their language and emulate them.

No, Russians did *not* suffer as much as some of the other nationalities, but they suffered quite enough. In Stalin's day, they were equally subject to arbitrary terror, and a so-called kulak or political suspect acquired no protection by just being Russian. Stalin's terror was indiscriminate. And so was the burden of real taxation to support the Communist bureaucracy and military industrial complex. It affected everyone, and since there were many more Russians than there were members of any other single nationality, more Russians suffered the ravages of communism than did any other single Soviet nationality.

Most Russians had an ambiguous attitude toward the Soviet empire. They considered the entire country their own but often resented the flow of resources out of Russia, particularly when the destination was Central Asia. They took pride in the size of the Soviet Union and the strength of the state, but when they learned about the sacrifices they had been forced to make to enable the Communist authorities to maintain the empire, they were resentful. They were keenly aware that Balts, Central Asians, and Caucasians were different, and many thought that shedding them would make Russia stronger. In contrast, they viewed Ukrainians and Belorussians as "little brothers" and had trouble conceding that they had any legitimate reason to part company with Russia.

Both colonizer and colonized, most Russians did not have a clearly defined attitude toward the Soviet empire. Until 1990, few gave much thought to whether the Soviet Union was a Russian empire or Russia a colony of the Soviet empire. From that year on, however, this question became one of the most fateful for the future.

The Russian Empire

THOUGH THEY MAY HAVE been a subject nation in the Soviet empire, the Russians had unquestionably once had their own empire. They had created it over centuries of intermittent but persistent expansion. Sometimes the expansion had been relatively peaceful, as when Russian peasant settlers and Cossacks moved east and settled sparsely populated lands. (Relatively, but not completely: some native peoples always suffered, just as the native North Americans did under the pressure of white settlement.) At other times, the expansion had been the result of military conquest.

The constant was expansion, the variable the method used. The result was a multinational empire that periodically tried to force its minorities into a uniform Russian nationality. Thus, for decades in the nineteenth century, it was illegal to print books in Ukrainian or Belorussian or to print the Lithuanian language using Latin characters. While some territories were annexed outright, others were absorbed more gradually: Georgia came under Russian protection in the early 1800s but was soon made an integral part of the empire. Finland initially had its own constitution but was reduced to the status of a mere province by a tsar who would brook no independent actors in his realm.

In short, the Russian empire was unabashedly an empire. There was no hypocritical pretense about constitutions, national rights, self-determination, and such. The tsar was an autocrat and intended to remain one.

When Tsar Nicholas II was deposed in February 1917, most of the non-Russian nations of the Russian empire immediately began to distance themselves from Moscow. The Ukrainian Central Rada, or council, was formed in March 1917, and demanded autonomy for Ukraine. The Belorussians formed a similar council in July, while most of the nations at the empire's periphery were doing the same. At this point they stopped short of demanding independence; what they wanted was a federation of nations rather than a Russian unitary state.

The provisional government in Petrograd, preoccupied with the war with Germany and growing social unrest, temporized, relegating the constitutional issue to a constituent assembly, which was to be elected when the war was over.

The Bolshevik seizure of power in November 1917, however, turned what had been tentative claims for autonomy into a stampede for full independence. Initially, the Bolsheviks' own statements encouraged this turn. One of their first acts was a Declaration of the Rights of the Peoples of Russia, which guaranteed "equality," "sovereignty," and "free self-determination including secession and the right to create independent states." Many non-Russians, to their subsequent pain, took the Bolsheviks at their word.

The Ukrainian Central Rada refused to recognize Lenin's government as "central" and prevented the local Bolsheviks from seizing the provisional government's agencies in Kiev. The Don Cossacks (Russian speakers who nonetheless considered their group an ethnically distinct part of the Russian nation) also refused to submit to Bolshevik rule. In December the Belorussian National Congress proclaimed autonomy.

The Baltic states were then occupied by the German army, but independence movements sprang up and the Caucasus and Central Asia witnessed developments analogous to those in Ukraine and Belorussia: in Tbilisi on November 15, the leading Georgian, Armenian, and Azeri national parties formed an incipient government called the Transcaucasian Commissariat.

Some three weeks later a Kazakh congress proclaimed the autonomy of the area now known as Kazakhstan, while Uzbek Muslims met in Kokand in December to proclaim autonomy for Turkestan—roughly, the area between Kazakhstan to the north and Iran and Afghanistan to the south. Several other nationalities followed suit in late 1917 and early 1918.

An Empire Reassembled

ON THE SURFACE, it would seem that the assurances given in the Declaration of the Rights of the Peoples of Russia were clear and unequivocal. But lurking in the shadowy annals of communist polemics there was a catch. To paraphrase, but not distort, Lenin's position, nations have the right to self-determination, but only the proletariat has the right to decide. And, as if that were not enough, only the Communist Party can speak for the proletariat.

This formula enabled the Bolsheviks to pose as liberators when it suited them (that is, when anyone else was in political control) and yet deny independence when they were strong enough to dominate. When "national liberation" movements declared their opposition to "imperialist" or "bourgeois" governments, they were deemed correct to do so and deserving of every support. But if national leaders should request the same of a Communist state—this merely proved that they did not speak for the proletariat and therefore their demands should be rejected and they themselves crushed as class enemies.

Debates among Communists on the "national question" before and just after the Bolshevik seizure of power amounted to an argument over the *presentation* of this formula, not its essence. Lenin stressed the propaganda value of the right of secession, confident that it would remain an academic question in fact. Stalin, on the other hand, was willing to be more forthright. In discussing the warnings in Lenin's "Testament" against Great Russian chauvinism, he stated:

> There are instances when the right to self-determination conflicts with another, higher right—the right of the working class to consolidate its power. In such cases—and one must be blunt—the right of self-determination cannot and must not be an obstacle to the working class in exercising its dictatorship.[3]

This "logic" came into play just as soon as nations began to break away from the shattered Russian empire. Attempts to move toward independence were met by military force whenever possible.

Only a few weeks after they seized power, the Bolshevik leaders in Petrograd used a tactic that would subsequently become standard practice in dealing with the authorities in territories they coveted. That is, they created a pretext for military intervention. In this initial instance it took the form of an ultimatum to the Ukrainian Central Rada demanding free passage of Russian Red Guards through Ukrainian territory to subdue the rebellious Cossacks. When the Rada balked, an invasion of Ukraine commenced, and just before the end of 1917 a Ukrainian People's Republic, led by Russians, was proclaimed in Kharkiv. That same week Russian Red Guards forcibly dispersed the Belorussian National Congress in Minsk.

In January 1918, Red Guards took Orenburg, a city east of the Volga that had been a center of separatist activity by Turkic-speaking political leaders, and disbanded the Kazakh and Bashkir assemblies. To the south, in February, Russian soldiers sent by the Bolshevik-dominated Soviet in Tashkent stormed Kokand, the seat of the provisional autonomous government of Turkestan, then massacred those Muslims who had been unable to flee and put the Old Town to the torch.

Events, however, began to place severe limits on the Bolsheviks' ability to achieve their ends by military force. In order to end the war with Germany, Lenin was forced to conclude the peace of Brest-Litovsk, by which Russia relinquished extensive territories in the west. Simultaneously, resistance to the Bolshevik seizure of power was developing, particularly in border areas.

The Bolshevik response was to sponsor nominally independent "national-Communist" regimes. If local Communists were too weak to take over, treaties were signed with national governments. This approach allowed the Bolsheviks to pose as champions of national independence and therefore to split their opponents. From the very beginning Bolshevik leaders considered the policy a temporary expedient.

The shortest-lived of these national Soviet republics was the Belorussian. It was formed in December 1917, but by the middle of the following month Communist Party officials in Moscow decided to merge it with the Russian Soviet Republic. Orders went out to the Belorussian "comrades" to begin the process of amalgamation at their next Congress of Soviets, scheduled for February. The Belorussians objected but subsequently gave in.

Even as the Bolsheviks attempted to turn national aspirations to their own ends, they made sure that the fictional independence of "state structures" did not extend to the Communist Party, where the real political power was lodged. When the Russian Communists met in their Eighth Congress in March 1918, they approved a resolution on the subject that was remarkable for its candor:

> All decisions of the Russian Communist Party and its leading organs are unconditionally binding on all elements of the Party, irrespective of their national composition. The Central Committees of the Lithuanian, Latvian, and Ukrainian Communists have the rights of regional committees of the Party and are completely subordinate to the Central Committee of the Russian Communist Party.[4]

A unitary, centrally directed Party standing behind an ostensible federation of "states" remained a cardinal principle of the Soviet empire, right up to its collapse in 1991. The unwillingness of the Communist leadership to change this principle when it was challenged in 1989 blocked all efforts to create a voluntary federation.

In 1918 and 1919, Ukraine was the scene of a struggle of bewildering complexity. Partly occupied by the Germans for several months, it was fought over by the non-Communist Ukrainian Nationalist Rada, two different Communist parties—one Bolshevik and one non-Bolshevik—and the Russian "White" Army, led by General Anton Denikin. When the dust settled, the Red Army was victorious and a Communist government was installed. Lenin had forced the two Communist factions to merge, and initially the Ukrainian Party was dominated by "national Communists."

National Communists, however, were not strong enough to form governments in all areas. Finland and the three Baltic states successfully asserted their independence even though Communists in each of the four fought to keep them under Soviet control. Moscow formally recognized them as independent when it became apparent that it lacked the military strength to occupy them—Finland in 1918 and the Baltic states in 1920.

In the Transcaucasus, independent governments were also formed in Armenia, Azerbaijan, and Georgia. Most Western countries recognized de facto the independence of all three, and twenty-two countries had extended de jure recognition to Georgia by January 1921. Nevertheless, all fell to invasions by the Red Army, which deposed their national governments.

Azerbaijan, with its oil fields, was the first target of Soviet aggression. In March 1920, Lenin ordered the seizure of Baku. A Red Army unit stationed north of the Caucasus range crossed the border of Azerbaijan on April 25 and captured its capital three days later.

The day Baku was captured, local Communists established an "Azerbaijan Soviet Independent Republic" and sent a telegram to Moscow asking for fraternal assistance. This device was destined to be used repeatedly in the future when Moscow deemed military intervention expedient. Local elements loyal to Moscow would be placed in power by military action, after which they would issue an appeal for assistance. The most recent use of this maneuver occurred in Kabul, Afghanistan, in December 1979, when the KGB's Alpha Detachment stormed the presidential palace, assassinated President Hafizullah Amin, then installed in his place Babrak Karmal, who promptly issued an appeal for Soviet "assistance."

Georgian forces managed to repel invaders from Azerbaijan in 1920, but independent Armenia was occupied in December. For a while, it appeared that Georgia might be left to its own devices since Russia signed a peace treaty with the Georgian government in May 1920 that recognized Georgian independence without any conditions. Nevertheless, this solemn commitment proved meaningless. A Soviet army from Azerbaijan conquered the independent republic in February of the following year.

As the Civil War raged in Central Asia, Siberia, and the Far East in 1918 and 1919, the Bolsheviks maneuvered, at times to exploit and at times to suppress, nationalist and localist movements. Once they had the upper hand, however, they invariably moved to assert control and to absorb these areas as integral parts of their empire.[5]

By 1922, when the USSR was officially founded, the Communist government had managed to reassemble most of the tsarist empire, with the important exception of a wide band of territory in the west running from Finland to Moldavia, where either independent states were recognized (Finland, Estonia, Latvia, Lithuania, and Poland) or territory was ceded to other countries (Romania).

For a while, governments of "union republics" were left in the hands of national Communists. The 1920s saw a rapid development of non-Russian languages and cultures, particularly in Ukraine and the Transcaucasus. The 1930s, however, brought first collectivization and resultant famine, and then a wholesale purge of national Communists and the national intelligentsia.

In Ukraine alone, millions of people died as the result of collectivization. In Kazakhstan, the population suffered even higher proportionate losses.[6] Stalin's purge of national Communists in the mid-1930s exterminated almost the entire Ukrainian Central Committee. More than a thousand non-Russian writers were executed or sent to the gulag, dealing a blow to the cultural development of many nations that has not been overcome to this day.

A Deal with Hitler

THOUGH IT HAD PREVAILED in an exhausting civil war, the Communist government in Moscow was, for a time, too weak to contemplate reassembling the empire in the west. Rebuilding from the ravages of war, then forced collectivization, pell-mell industrialization and a paroxysm of purges occupied the leadership through the twenties and thirties. To judge from subsequent events, however, Stalin never became reconciled to the "loss" of any part of the Russian empire. As soon as the possibility emerged to move the Soviet border westward, he seized it.

That opportunity materialized in 1939, when Hitler decided to attack France and Britain first and leave the Soviet Union for easy picking later. A flurry of secret diplomacy revealed that Stalin was ready to guarantee Hitler a peaceful "rear" for a price: a free hand to Moscow in dealing with its neighbors to the west. When the respective foreign ministers, Vyacheslav Molotov and Joachim von Ribbentrop, shocked the world by signing a nonaggression treaty in Moscow on August 23, 1939, they pointedly omitted mention of an even more significant secret protocol.

That protocol—to remain secret until the Allies captured a microfilm copy of it in 1945—in effect divided Eastern Europe between Hitler and Stalin. It divided Poland between Germany and the Soviet Union and allocated Estonia, Latvia, and Romanian Bessarabia to the Soviets. A few weeks later it was amended to add Lithuania to the Soviet sphere in return for material assistance to Germany and territorial concessions in Poland.[7]

Exactly a week after Ribbentrop left Moscow, Germany invaded Poland from the west, while on September 17 Soviet troops attacked from the east, quickly occupying the territory the Nazis had conceded to Stalin. During the autumn, Soviet troops also moved into the independent Baltic states. The following June, the three hapless countries were forced, literally at gunpoint, to "petition" for inclusion in the Soviet Union. In August 1940, Soviet troops moved into the Bessarabian region of Romania, which shortly thereafter was also absorbed into the Soviet Union.

On the night of the 1941 summer solstice, Hitler turned on Stalin and rapidly overran all these areas and many more, but when Hitler was defeated, Stalin managed to regain them all, except for part of Poland, and even to add to them. Poland was moved westward at German expense, and much of what had been eastern Poland was incorporated into Belorussia, Lithuania, and Ukraine. Part of East Prussia became Kaliningrad Oblast, a province of the Russian Federation, though separated from the rest of Russia by Lithuania. Czechoslovakia ceded its easternmost tip, a region known as Subcarpathian Rus, which was absorbed into a much-enlarged Ukraine. The Moldavian Soviet Socialist Republic was reestablished to perpetuate the seizure of Bessarabia from Romania. As a defeated German ally, Romania had no choice but to agree to the transfer.

The United States and most of the Western powers, even though allied with the Soviet Union during the war against Hitler, never recognized the legality of the Soviet annexation of the Baltic states. The United States did not, however, contest the other territorial transfers in

Europe which were eventually incorporated into peace treaties or other international agreements.

Stalin and all his successors (including Gorbachev) shrugged off the Western policy of nonrecognition as an insignificant trifle, an anachronism of Western policy that harmed only Western interests and eventually would have to be changed when it became clear that these borders had been fixed for all time.

It probably never crossed Stalin's mind, as he greedily stuffed country after country into the empire he ruled, that the state he fashioned would be shattered by political shock waves from epicenters up and down the band of territory he received courtesy of Adolf Hitler.

Stalin's Heritage: Pseudonational States

THAT WAS NOT Stalin's only unwitting mistake. Another goes back much further, all the way to the foundation of the Soviet state.

As commissar of nationalities, Stalin exercised direct influence on the structure of the Soviet Union when it was officially established in 1922. He preserved this structure with changes only of detail in the Constitution of 1936, when all power was in his hands, so it is not unreasonable to attribute its principal features to him.

On paper, the Union of Soviet Socialist Republics was a voluntary federation of sovereign states. In theory, it was a looser federation than the United States of America because its founding republics reserved an explicit right of secession.

Unlike in the United States, however, its political units were based on specific ethnic groups. Every ethnic group living in a definable territory was granted its own political entity. The more numerous nationalities were organized as "union republics," with their own parliaments, councils of ministers, and a governmental apparatus reaching down to the local level.

As the next rung down the hierarchical ladder, the "autonomous republics" were organized much as were union republics (in fact, over time, some changed from the status of one to that of the other) but did not have the right of secession. Most of the autonomous republics, or ASSRs, were in the Russian Socialist Federated Soviet Republic (RSFSR).

Then, smaller in terms of population, there were autonomous oblasts and national districts, which had fewer rights but nevertheless bore the name of a given nationality.

The rationale for this structure was that each nationality had the right to autonomy and that the political entities organized in its name would act to protect its interests. Throughout the entire history of the Soviet Union, however, this theory remained a fiction. In fact, the country was ruled in unitary fashion, on principles that did not take into account ethnic and local interests.

This occurred because actual political power did not reside in these constitutional entities. All political power was vested in the Communist Party of the Soviet Union (CPSU), which was organized in a highly centralized fashion. Although each union republic except Russia had its "own" Communist Party, these parties were treated by Moscow as provincial divisions of a single organization.

It was the unitary Communist Party that provided the reinforcing rods in the monolithic structure of the Soviet state. The borders of republics and other entities were like decorative lines on the surface of a concrete slab, there for appearance but with no structural function.

Nevertheless, these entities existed. Though they were controlled by the Party, each had its own structure of government that was formally identified with a specific national group. As the USSR began to open to the outside world and to develop some democratic institutions, the hypocrisy of national autonomy became obvious.

Divide and Rule

UNFORTUNATELY FOR THOSE who would like to see the world in neat, discrete territorial units, each belonging to a single ethnic group (a vision implicit in the theoretical Soviet model), the actual pattern of settlement in the Soviet republics—as in many other countries—did not conform. Major cities, particularly republic and regional capitals, were invariably home to a wide range of nationalities. Rural areas tended to be more homogeneous in individual settlements, but villages of different ethnic groups were often scattered over the landscape in patterns reminiscent of a patchwork quilt.

A drive through parts of Bashkiria (since 1991 Bashkortostan)—an area east of the Urals that is rich in oil and gas—for example, presents the alternating sights of a Bashkir village with its traditional Islamic-style buildings and Muslim cemetery and, a few miles away, a Russian village with its wooden houses ornamented with carved window and door frames painted bright colors and its Orthodox church next to a cemetery with crosses. Comparable patterns of mixed settlement prevail in many areas—and not just those along international borders.

Such patterns of settlement meant that boundaries could not be drawn with only ethnic factors in mind. At best, compromises had to be made, leaving minorities on both sides of the border. At worse, political calculations inspired the decisions and borders were drawn to stimulate local rivalries. Anything to inhibit local cooperation against rule from Moscow seemed to be the order of the day.

We see this particularly in borders drawn in the Caucasus and Central Asia, with Nagorny Karabakh a prime example. In this instance, an enclave with an Armenian majority was placed under the jurisdiction of Azerbaijan, not Armenia.

Another important instance of politically determined borders was the transfer of the Crimea from Russia to Ukraine in 1954. For reasons that have never been fully explained, Khrushchev ordered the transfer even though the Crimean peninsula, with its overwhelming majority of ethnic Russian residents, had been considered Russian since its conquest from the Tatars in the eighteenth century.

Central Asia provides the most flagrant examples of divide and rule. Historically, the area, when not united under a single ruler such as Alexander the Great or Tamurlane, had been divided into several khanates, which had not been organized along ethnic lines. When Central Asia was brought into the Russian empire, it was administered as a single unit known as Turkestan. Most of the indigenous people spoke cognate Turkic languages and used a single literary language, Chagatai. In the south there were many Persian speakers as well. Classical Persian had been the literary language of cities such as Samarkand and Bukhara, and many residents spoke both Turkic and Persian. What united them was not their language but their religion; all were Sunni Muslim.

Instead of creating a unified Turkestan when they reconquered the area in the early 1920s, the Communist leaders split it up along ethnic lines, creating in the process new "nations" on the basis of tribal and dialectical differences. In this manner the republics of Uzbekistan, Turkmenia, Tajikistan, Kirgizia, Kazakhstan, and Karakalpakia (the last an autonomous, not union, republic) were created.

These new nations did have individual ethnic identities before they were declared to be nations, and they eventually developed distinct national identities. But there can be no question that the initial impulse to divide them was to prevent their coalescence into a Muslim or Turkic bloc. In fact, for decades, the local leaders were forbidden to initiate regional groupings and scholars were forbidden to organize centers of Turkic studies, lest the pan-Turkic bacillus find fertile ground.

Divide and rule was evident even in such normally nonpolitical areas as orthography and language standards. Chagatai, the common literary language, was written in the Arabic script. The Soviets first defined several separate "national" languages and then introduced the Latin alphabet. Each of the new nations was assigned different letters for certain sounds that were the same in all. This made them look more different than they in fact were.

The process, however, did not stop there. Moscow soon decided that it would be dangerous to allow its Turkic peoples to use the Latin alphabet, which had come into use in Turkey. One had to erect as many barriers as possible to communication. Therefore, in the late 1930s, the Cyrillic alphabet was imposed, and once again different letters were often designated for the same sound so that these similar languages would look as different as possible.

To understand the impact of this linguistic divisiveness, one has only to think of what would have happened to the German speech area if a similar approach had been applied there before a standard literary language had become the common heritage of educated Germans. The various German dialects are not easily intelligible outside their native areas. The Bavarian dialect is hardly understood on the streets of Hamburg or Dresden, nor is the Berlin dialect on the streets of Munich. Yet Germans in fact understand one another and feel a common identity because they use the same literary language, the language of Luther's Bible translation.

If an occupying power in, say, the fifteenth or sixteenth century, had wished to ensure that the Germans would never form a unified nation, the most effective thing it could have done would be to promote numerous regional languages, each with its own orthography and grammatical standards, and to forbid teaching or writing in a supradialectical national language. Given sufficient time, such an approach could have produced separate Bavarian, Saxon, Rheinlandish, Prussian, and other "national" languages. Unity, in the future, would be most difficult to forge, since language, above all, defines one's sense of nation.

This is precisely what the Communists did in Central Asia, and from the standpoint of erecting barriers to future unity, they were successful.

They followed the same tactic in Moldavia after World War II, and for similar reasons. But this time it was not to divide the Moldavians among themselves but to separate them culturally from their Romanian cousins now across the border. The language spoken in Moldavia is, by any reasonable definition, Romanian. But there are some dialectical differences, comparable perhaps to the differences in the English spoken in Alabama and that in Massachusetts.

On the basis of these minor dialectical differences, a separate "Moldavian language" was declared to exist, and since it would have been difficult to perceive the difference if it were written in the Latin letters used by Romanian, the Cyrillic alphabet was imposed. That *did* make it *look* different. Try reading "Ай лав ю." If you don't know the Cyrillic alphabet, you may have trouble associating it with the English sentence "I love you."

The first step the Moldavians took, when they had the opportunity, was to revert to the Latin alphabet and resume calling their language Romanian, not Moldavian.

Tentacles to Hold . . . and Repel

BOUNDARIES AND CULTURAL policy were set with an eye toward preventing regional cooperation against Moscow's rule. Investment policy was implemented so as to deny any of the political units an economic superstructure that would permit autonomy.

Although Soviet planners had a propensity for building giant enterprises and concentrating production of items in one or a very few plants, they habitually scattered the facilities in various regions and republics. An automobile assembly plant in Moscow, for example, might get all its carburetors from a plant in Ukraine. A tire plant in Yaroslavl might get an essential chemical from Tajikistan. Only the most primitive plants making the simplest products relied entirely on local factors of production.

This practice led to many economic absurdities. A steel mill might get coking coal or ore from sources thousands of miles away when closer sources existed. But the design had a rationale: let nobody feel that he can survive without Moscow's all-too-visible guiding hand.

One of my friends ran a large mining concern on Russia's Pacific coast, north of Vladivostok. He mentioned to me that all the ore extracted at his mines had to be shipped thousands of miles to Siberia and the Urals for processing. When I asked why smelters and refineries had not been built on the Pacific coast, he said simply, "If they did that, we could get along without Moscow. More to the point, we could get along without the Ministry of Nonferrous Metallurgy."

Politics and bureaucracy make a formidable combination.

Another process that provided links, but also grounds for tension, was the dispersal of national groups, particularly Russians and Ukrainians, throughout the union.

Whenever new industries were built, people were brought into the area to operate them. More often than not, these tended to be Russians or Ukrainians. In some areas, such as the "Virgin Lands" of northern Kazakhstan, there was organized large-scale immigration.

In February 1990, I hosted a dinner in Kishinev (now Chişinău) for Ion Hadîrcă and other leaders of the Moldavian National Front. One of their grievances was that Russians, and to a lesser degree Ukrainians, had most of the good jobs in industry. Moldavian graduates of technical schools had trouble finding jobs in the specialties for which they had been trained.

I asked them why this was. They attributed the problem to the standard procedures followed by central planners in Moscow. My Moldavian guests felt that there was probably no conscious policy to discriminate against the local people, but absentee control had that effect in practice.

"Let's say the Ministry of Communications decides to locate a plant here to produce switching equipment," one of our guests explained. "We would not have skilled workers on hand because we haven't had that industry before. So they build the plant and recruit workers from all over the Soviet Union to staff it. Meanwhile, we know the plant is being built, and we start training Moldavians to work there. But by the time they graduate, the jobs are already filled, and the workers who came from Russia don't want to go back. They've settled in, the climate is better, food is in better supply. So Moldavians are blocked from participating in their own country's development."

In this way, the ties produced by ethnic dispersal were counterbalanced by conditions giving rise to envy and resentment.

National in Form, Socialist in Content

THE SLOGAN MOST OFTEN used to describe the Soviet nationality policy was "National in form, socialist in content." Translated into everyday English, it means "As long as you say what we wish, you can say it
in any language."

This was one of the few slogans that described actual practice. In fact,
the various nationalities were allowed to preserve their languages, and
those without a writing system were provided with one. Elementary
schools in rural areas were normally taught in the local language, and
the government-subsidized publications and radio and television broadcasts in the non-Russian languages. The content, however, was subject
to a censorship even more rigid than that applied to publications in
Russian.

In particular, except for a few abnormal periods of leniency in the
mid-1920s and early 1960s, any theme that was considered "nationalistic" was suppressed. Any treatment of history that suggested that the
Russian role had been anything other than progressive was labeled
unacceptably nationalistic.[8] National leaders who had resisted Russian
expansion became historical unpersons or, worse, traitors. Atrocities
committed during the tsarist period, such as the massacre of Kirgiz in
1916 when there was resistance against the military draft, became non-
events.

While development of non-Russian languages was permitted and in
some respects supported, increasing emphasis was given to the Russian
language as the language of the "new Soviet man" that the regime was
determined to create. Russian thus became the language of advancement, whatever the field one might choose. In many republics, ambitious parents would send their children to Russian-language schools
rather than those offering instruction in their own language, hoping to
provide a professional advantage later in life.

Russian emigrants to national areas, with rare exceptions, did not
bother to learn the local language, not even the rudimentary polite
phrases. Russian increasingly became the language of the elite and the
local language that of subordinates. In most republics, the best schools
and most advanced scholarly work were conducted in Russian. Russian
was a compulsory subject even in those schools taught in the local lan-

guage. Outside the Baltic states, Georgia, and Armenia, very little higher education was available in any language other than Russian.

The Soviet Union had a system of universal military service for young men (although some sons of the Party elite escaped), and the language of the army and navy was Russian. This meant that virtually every male citizen was forced to acquire at least a rudimentary knowledge of Russian while in military service.

Such practices disturbed national-minded intellectuals, but when they called attention to the problem, the official reaction was to treat them as dangerous dissidents. In the 1960s, for example, the Ukrainian scholar Ivan Dzyuba submitted several memoranda to the Party leadership pointing out practices that violated what he considered Leninist norms of national policy. He was subjected to a campaign of vilification and pressure to recant. Simultaneously, many who had protested more vigorously were arrested and sentenced to lengthy terms in prison.[9]

Aside from linguistic Russification, myriad pressures tended to denationalize non-Russian cultures. Some, such as urbanization and industrialization, were endemic to the twentieth century—though Soviet practices often intensified the disruptive effect on traditional culture. Others were specific to the Soviet empire.

The Soviet state was officially atheist, and during extended periods militantly so. Religion was suppressed and its teaching and practice subjected to severe limits. For example, it was a criminal offense to teach religion to a minor. Anyone professing a religion would not be allowed into the Communist Party (effectively precluding most careers) and could encounter considerable pressure at school or work. Many churches and most mosques and synagogues were closed. The open practice of religion was increasingly limited to the elderly.

The antireligious policy most affected those nationalities whose culture was intertwined with the traditional religion. Islamic peoples were largely cut off from their cultural roots. Jews became almost totally secularized and Russified. For a time, even teaching Hebrew was treated as a crime. Protestant and Catholic churches barely survived in Estonia and Latvia. Only Lithuania, Armenia, and Georgia managed to preserve strong national churches, and here, as elsewhere, great efforts were made by the Communist authorities to bring the clergy under control through KGB penetration.

While the regime was officially atheist, it did favor some religious groups that could serve a political purpose. In Ukraine and Belorussia, for example, the Russian Orthodox Church received official, including police, support against churches not subordinate to the Moscow Patriarchate, especially the Ukrainian Catholic ("Uniate") Church and the Ukrainian Autocephalous Orthodox Church, both of which were legally banned because they were considered potential supporters of separatism.

"Socialism," of course, was the obligatory economic system. This meant that, no matter what the national tradition, all republics had a collectivized agriculture and all were part of a unionwide economy based on central planning and management. Each union republic, to be sure, had its own State Planning Committee (Gosplan), but they operated as subsidiaries of the All-Union Gosplan in Moscow. Republic governments could not generate funds on their own, nor did they have the right to set prices or standards at variance with those imposed by Moscow.

The central bureaucracy's insistence on uniformity regardless of local conditions went to absurd lengths. In 1990, well after perestroika had in theory empowered local governments to make more decisions on their own, the mayor of Ashkhabad, the capital of Turkmenistan, complained to me of the inflexible requirements imposed by Moscow. Natural gas was plentiful in the area, and he wished to build a gas distribution pipeline to supply it to households in the city for cooking and heating. But Moscow was unwilling either to allocate the capital necessary for the development or to allow the city government to raise the money itself.

The city operated buses and streetcars at the cost of seven kopeks a passenger. Moscow, however, had set a fare of five kopeks, which it applied everywhere in the Soviet Union. The mayor wanted to raise the fare to ten kopeks and use the profit, along with the money otherwise used to subsidize transportation, to finance the gas distribution system. The city council supported this project, but Moscow refused to approve it. In principle, there was no ideological reason to deny city governments the right to use resources allocated to them as they saw fit. In practice, however, local initiative was normally prohibited simply because some ministry in Moscow was unwilling to permit others to intrude on its domain.

The attitude of the industrial ministries in Moscow, in fact, went beyond struggles for bureaucratic market share. Within the branch of industry they controlled, the top officials considered facilities throughout the country the property of the ministries—that is, themselves—to dispose of as they wished. Legally, of course, this was not the case. The property belonged to the state, and the ministries were merely the organizations designated by the state to manage its property. But the managers conveniently forgot that basic principle, just as American corporate officers sometimes forget that not they but the shareholders own the company.

During a reception at Spaso House in 1990, I mentioned Lithuania's demand for independence to the Soviet minister of communications. The minister reacted with great passion. "These people are extremists," he stormed. "They are claiming all the property in Lithuania. But it is not theirs. Why, my ministry has three plants there. We paid for them with our own money, and they belong to us!"

I observed that I was not a Marxist, but I presumed Soviet officials were, and I wondered how he could reconcile his attitude toward the plants with the socialist principle that the property belongs to the people. Ministries merely hold it in trust for the people, who presumably have a right to take it back if they choose.

"What does Marxism have to do with it?" he asked angrily. "The fact is, we paid our money for those plants and they belong to us!"

He was right on one point. His attitude had absolutely no connection with Marxism. But one can immediately grasp the implications of this attitude—universal among the ministries in Moscow—for people in the republics and provinces. As they saw it, and saw it accurately, all significant industry was being managed from Moscow as if it were the private property of bureaucrats in the ministries.

The absentee owners paid little heed to the impact of their projects on the environment. Nuclear power plants were built with unsafe designs, and some were even constructed on geological fault lines. Steel mills, chemical plants, and paper mills were not equipped to clean up their emissions and effluents. Tree harvesting and reforestation came under separate organizations, and it takes only one guess to determine which was adequately funded. In 1989, Ukraine alone released eight times the volume of pollutants into the air as did the entire United States—whose record in this respect is hardly unblemished.

One could fill volumes with the environmental atrocities committed by the Soviet command economy, operated by the USSR ministries in Moscow.[10] As facts about the assault on the environment became better known, they played a major role in creating national resentment against the Soviet empire and all its works. It was the people on the spot, after all, not the bureaucrats in the Moscow high-rises, who felt the effects in their daily lives.

The arbitrary system of administered prices, a prominent feature of Soviet-style "socialism," also provided fertile ground for national grievances. Primary commodities, the main products of many republics, were priced extremely low, while the industrial goods they received, mainly from Russia, seemed to have higher price tags—though still below world market prices. Nevertheless, in Central Asia in particular, the feeling was very strong that the price system was used to bilk them and that investment policy favored Russia over the peripheral areas.

Control in non-Russian areas, as in Russian ones, was exercised by the Communist Party. To make sure that local officials did not become soft on "nationalist tendencies," it was normal practice to assign an ethnic Russian as second party secretary whenever the first secretary was a local national. The second secretary acted as a watchdog, just in case. Actually, most non-Russian Communist officials acted in slavish conformity to Moscow's dictates. They knew that the slightest suspicion of disloyalty could bring an end to their careers.

Nevertheless, this did not prevent a cadre of non-Russian officials from gradually arising in many union republics. Indeed, during the Brezhnev period and its system of "mutual favors," Communist leaders in a number of republics managed to develop local "mafias" under the cover of the Communist Party. As long as they kept their superiors in Moscow happy with frequent gifts and favors and submitted to Moscow's political and economic dictates, they were allowed to develop networks of supporters who fed off state largess.

The position of the Party leaders in the republics and provinces was a lot like that of medieval barons: as long as they were loyal to the general secretary in Moscow (their king) and paid lip service to Moscow's policies, they had a free hand in their own baronies.

The Soviet state was nothing more than the instrument of the Communist Party. Until the last two years of perestroika, Party positions always took precedence over those of the government, however high sounding.

When the posts were not combined, the general secretary (at times first secretary) of the Communist Party took clear precedence over the chairman of the Supreme Soviet Presidium (the titular chief of state) and the chairman of the Council of Ministers (the head of the government). And this pattern was replicated at every level, down to the county and precinct.

Except at summit meetings, when we were told to give the general secretary all the honors due a chief of state, official protocol rarely mentioned Communist Party positions. It did not have to, because the pecking order was drummed into every Soviet citizen by life's experience. Rebecca and I had occasion to observe this, sometimes to our consternation and sometimes to our amusement, as we traveled about the country.

While traveling, we tried to meet a cross section of society and often hosted a reception, lunch, or dinner in a local hotel. We would always invite local Party and government officials—without whose approval few ordinary citizens would have dared attend—but we always tried to include a wide range of people.

Local habits often thwarted us, despite our efforts to reach out to the average citizen. In Irkutsk, capital of a province larger than Texas, though with fewer people, not a single Soviet guest dared cross the threshold of the reception room until the Party chief arrived and led them in. Even in places where guests could be coaxed into the reception hall, they would not touch food or drink until the senior Party official arrived and we had exchanged official toasts. It was not that they were indifferent to the buffet table: as soon as the local Party leader had answered our welcoming toast, the tables were stripped. But they all knew how to defer to political power.

"National Question Solved"

THE COMMUNIST PARTY'S GRIP on the empire seemed so strong that many observers doubted that the national tensions lurking beneath the surface could shake the system. Even if surface cracks should appear here and there, the reinforcing rods would prevent a collapse.

The official view, circa 1985, was that nationality issues formed a comparatively minor and easily manageable problem. The system's political leaders were convinced that a denationalized, "new Soviet man" was well along in development, and that this new type, Russian in language but *Soviet* in nationality, would steadily replace Ukrainians, Latvians, Moldavians, Kazakhs—and Russians as well. In their eyes, the future belonged to this new "international" type, even if, from time to time and for tactical reasons, some concessions had to be made to the emotional appeal of old-style national cultures. Even if this process of ethnic engineering took longer than they hoped, there were adequate instruments at hand to deal with those cranks who continued to resist the tidal wave of history.[11]

Gorbachev himself subscribed to this view. Even after two years in office as general secretary, and even while describing perestroika as a "revolutionary transformation," he wrote with smug confidence that "the USSR represents a truly unique example [of preventing national strife] in the history of human civilization. These are the fruits of the nationality policy launched by Lenin."

Gorbachev's only prescription at that time was more of the same: "Our entire experience shows that nationalist attitudes can be effectively countered by consistent internationalism, by internationalist education."[12] That was primarily for foreign audiences. When he addressed his countrymen, he made the same argument but added a pointed warning. For example, in January 1987, he informed the Party Central Committee:

> People's national feelings deserve respect, and we must not ignore them. But they should not be exploited either. Let those inclined to play on nationalist and chauvinist prejudices entertain no illusions and expect no weakening.[13]

As long as the Party's control of the country was assured, as long as the reinforcing rods kept the concrete from shattering, the confidence that national sentiments could not gain the upper hand was justified.

Most observers of the Soviet political process—and, for that matter, virtually all the participants in it—assumed that Party control was unshakable for the foreseeable future.

III

The Torch Passes

[Gorbachev] started by climbing a mountain whose summit was not even visible.
BORIS YELTSIN, 1989[1]

In 1985, I still believed the system could be improved.
MIKHAIL GORBACHEV, 1992[2]

*[T]here is nothing more difficult to plan or more uncertain of success or more
dangerous to carry out than an attempt to introduce new institutions . . .*
NICCOLÒ MACHIAVELLI, 1514[3]

S oviet media did not interrupt their programs the evening of March
10, 1985, when Konstantin Chernenko died. The death of the Soviet leader should have been the day's top news story the world over. It
was not. The masters of the Kremlin decided to withhold any announcement of Chernenko's death until a successor was selected.

The Politburo gathered the same evening, made its choice, and called
for an emergency meeting of the Party Central Committee the next day
to ratify it. Planes were dispatched from all over the Soviet Union that
night to bring the party oligarchs to Moscow for their conclave. One
senior Politburo member, Vladimir Shcherbitsky, the Ukrainian Party
boss, had to come all the way from California. He was the only member
of the group to travel part of the way courtesy of the U.S. Air Force,
which flew him from San Francisco to New York, where an Aeroflot
plane was sent for him.

In fact, the need to organize urgent transportation for Shcherbitsky
gave us in Washington the first tip that Chernenko had died. His health

had been poor and we had picked up rumors from time to time that he had died, but all had turned out to be without foundation. I was then responsible for Soviet and European affairs on the National Security Council staff at the White House, and just two days earlier, on March 8, I had written a memo to the president's assistant for national security pointing out that, while the latest rumor did not appear to be true, it was not too early for the president to decide whether he would go to Moscow for the funeral when the time came. Rebecca and I then went off for a weekend seminar on U.S.-Soviet relations at the Aspen Institute conference center at the Wye Plantation on Maryland's eastern shore.

When we got home on Sunday afternoon, the telephone was ringing. It was Mark Palmer, the brilliant and energetic deputy assistant secretary of state, who covered the Soviet Union and Eastern Europe. His news was that we had a request to help Shcherbitsky return immediately to Moscow. I agreed to ask the White House to authorize the Air Force to bring him to New York, where his Aeroflot plane could pick him up, and we discussed the obvious implications. Both of us then packed our bags for a quick trip to another Moscow funeral.

Despite our help, Shcherbitsky arrived too late for both meetings. Dinmukhamed Kunayev, the Party boss in Kazakhstan, also failed to make it in time. The absence of these two conservative Party officials from these crucial meetings led to subsequent speculation that Gorbachev had been selected by the Politburo by a hairline margin of five to four over Moscow Party boss Viktor Grishin.[4]

Tantalizing as this report was for Kremlinologists, it is probably untrue. At any rate, Gorbachev himself and other direct participants deny it.[5] It was not that all the members of the Politburo were solidly for Gorbachev, simply that his opponents did not have the votes on March 10.

Grishin had in fact intrigued in 1984 and early 1985 to be named Chernenko's successor. If he had succeeded, the inertia of the Brezhnev era might have persisted another few years. But Grishin had lost the tactical battle for the succession in 1984, when he had failed to enlist the support of Dmitri Ustinov, the powerful minister of defense. Ustinov died in December, which revived Grishin's hopes sufficiently that he attempted to obtain Chernenko's endorsement, employing to that end a flagrant campaign of flattery in the sections of the media under his influence.

Gorbachev, however, outmaneuvered Grishin at every point. Yegor Ligachev, then the Central Committee secretary responsible for personnel, systematically installed potential Gorbachev supporters as Party chiefs in provinces throughout the country; if the Politburo had been split on its choice, their votes could have been decisive in the Central Committee. Chernenko was either too infirm to notice Grishin's efforts to ingratiate himself or sufficiently responsible to reject them: he did nothing to block Gorbachev's effective control of the central Party apparatus and failed to suggest a successor other than Gorbachev. Such a suggestion might not have been decisive, but it would have made Gorbachev's effort to win by a unanimous vote much more difficult. Even more important, Gorbachev managed to bring Foreign Minister Andrei Gromyko, the most senior Politburo member, to his camp.

Still, when Chernenko died, if the decision had not been made rapidly, Gorbachev's enemies in the Politburo, including Prime Minister Nikolai Tikhonov and Leningrad Party boss Grigory Romanov, along with Grishin, might have conspired to develop an alternate consensus. Gorbachev's quick action prevented any such attempt.

As de facto second secretary, Gorbachev was the first to get the news of Chernenko's death. He called a Politburo meeting immediately, insisted that a decision be made without delay, and kept the members in the room until he had what he wanted: chairmanship of the Funeral Commission (traditionally held by the heir apparent) and the Politburo's recommendation that the Central Committee elect him general secretary.

The hurried meeting of the Party Central Committee the next day could only endorse the Politburo's recommendation, since no one had prepared the ground for a challenge. Realizing that a challenge would not only be futile but would bring an immediate and probably less-than-comfortable retirement, Grishin and his friends voted with the others.

Ghosts of Leaders Past

CHERNENKO, WHOSE LEADERSHIP ABILITY was as slight as his health was tenuous, had turned out to be an embarrassment—the third in a row, in fact, following Leonid Brezhnev's extended disability and Yuri Andropov's acute illness during most of his short incumbency. By all objective standards, the advent of a new and different sort of political leader was long overdue.

For a decade, the country had witnessed an aging, self-satisfied political leadership incapable of any originality and determined to suppress anyone with new ideas.

Brezhnev was a plodding oligarch even in his prime. Appreciative of adulation, luxury, fast cars, and young women, he ruled by propitiating the Party bureaucracy with the spoils of power. The armed forces and military industry had stood first in line behind the Communist hierarchs, and each powerful interest group had gotten its share. Stalin's terror and Khrushchev's rash experimentation had given way to a reeking morass of corruption. Personal connections among the rulers had decided everything.

Andropov, the empire's top "enforcer" for fifteen years as head of the KGB, had used his knowledge of corruption to weaken the Brezhnev faction and to claw his way to power. But then his kidneys had failed, and he had passed from the scene in just over a year.

Andropov had groomed Mikhail Gorbachev to succeed him, but when he died the Brezhnevites had taken their revenge and passed over Gorbachev for Brezhnev's crony Chernenko.

I first met Chernenko in Washington in the early seventies.

I was director of Soviet affairs in the State Department, and diplomats from the Soviet Embassy in Washington had contacted me to request special treatment for an upcoming visitor. When I failed to recognize Chernenko's name immediately, they explained that he was in charge of the files in the Central Committee, which would not have been particularly important if he had not been one of Brezhnev's close friends. He was interested in seeing how the State Department processed and distributed messages, since he was looking for ways to improve the Soviet system.

I doubted that State Department security officials would agree to show a Soviet official through the code room, but I agreed to ask.

To my astonishment, our people saw no problem with the tour. In fact, they tried to be as accommodating as they could, shutting down processing of classified messages during a slack period and arranging to demonstrate the distribution, filing, and retrieval procedures with an innocuous, unclassified document.

Chernenko arrived precisely as agreed, a broad smile on his round face, which looked like a kewpie doll's. His suit was new, and his shoes had such a bright shine I wondered if they were patent leather. Our communications specialists and I walked with him through the State Department facility under the watchful eyes of security officials. He listened closely to all that he was told, asked some questions about the way the distribution system and the computers worked, and left us with profuse thanks for the favor we had extended.

Subsequently, I saw him only at a distance. At public functions attended by the Politburo (such as sessions of the Supreme Soviet) he would invariably sit just behind Brezhnev and would occasionally be called out to receive a folder. He would always pass it to Brezhnev first, then to some of the other Politburo members present. Each would initial the document and give it back to him before it went to the next person. He was obviously custodian of the documents and apparently not much more. Thus it was a surprise when Brezhnev elevated him to the Politburo. He just did not seem to be a policy-oriented sort of person. But then, that's the way things were done under Brezhnev. Personal relations decided everything.

Chernenko was chosen by the Brezhnev crowd to postpone the changes they knew Andropov and his protégés had in mind. He was, without a doubt, a passive mediocrity in the top office. But, unlike some of his predecessors, he was not an evil man. And he refused to support those in the Politburo who wanted to sidetrack Gorbachev's candidacy to succeed him.

Chernenko's death was finally announced to the world in the early afternoon of March 11. A few hours later, in good time for the evening news broadcasts, TASS announced that Mikhail Sergeyevich Gorbachev had been elected general secretary of the Communist Party of the Soviet Union. The story of the day was Gorbachev's, not Chernenko's, and the point was driven home the next morning to Soviet newspaper readers, who found Gorbachev on page one and Chernenko's obituary on page four.

The funeral on March 13 seemed almost an afterthought—or, rather, a photo opportunity for world leaders, who used the obsequies as an excuse to rush to Moscow for an audience with the new general secretary. Vice President George Bush represented the United States, as he had at the Brezhnev and Andropov funerals,[6] but Prime Minister Margaret Thatcher, German Chancellor Helmut Kohl, and French President François Mitterrand all came in person. Following brief courtesy calls, all endorsed Mrs. Thatcher's earlier judgment (she had met Gorbachev in London the previous December) that here was a man, finally, with whom one could do business.

The New Chief

NO OTHER SOVIET LEADER had entered office basking in as much goodwill, both at home and abroad. Everyone was tired of watching the Soviet empire floundering under infirm incompetents. As American journalist Dusko Doder observed at the time, "He walks, he talks, and his suit fits." And thus he dazzled the world.

We in Washington knew a little more about him than we had about his predecessors when they had taken office. The Soviet media had long been prohibited from publicizing the private lives of political leaders. Intelligence organizations had to worm out such sensitive facts as how many children a political figure had and their names and occupations. When Andropov died, our White House staff had to do extensive research to find out whether he had a widow to whom condolences should be sent. We knew he had a son, but we did not know whether his wife was still alive.

Gorbachev was better known. We knew he was a graduate of Moscow University, the most prestigious institution in the country, and thus was presumably better educated than his predecessors (with the arguable exception of Lenin). He came from a rural background and had made his career in the Communist Party apparatus. He had somehow overcome the political liability of having been in charge of Soviet agriculture. He had traveled abroad more than his immediate predecessors had at the time they had taken office, which could be significant, since he also had a reputation for pragmatism. His wife, Raisa, an attractive, well-dressed, well-educated, and politically active woman, provided a sharp contrast to her predecessors as well.

Nevertheless, many aspects of Mikhail Gorbachev's background and personality were a mystery. Senior Communist Party officials, in the pre-glasnost days, generally avoided contact with foreigners; therefore few could say that they had even met him, much less knew him well.

In 1975, when our ambassador was away and I was temporarily in charge of the American Embassy in Moscow, I visited Stavropol and specifically requested a call on the regional Party leader, a young (we were almost contemporaries) official with a reputation as an experimenter and a political "comer." I hoped that he, unlike his stodgy counterparts in most other provinces, might make an exception to normal practice and receive an American diplomat. This, however, did not happen: I was relegated to the head of the provincial government, who arranged a highly selective tour of the region. I spent most of the time in the car or at banquets. Mikhail Sergeyevich did not then seem all that different from his colleagues in other provinces.

I finally met Gorbachev in May 1985, ten years after that first abortive attempt. The occasion was a visit to Moscow by U.S. Secretary of Commerce Malcolm Baldrige, an appealing ex-cowboy who still loved to ride in rodeos—and who, two years later, was tragically killed in a fall from a horse. Noting that Gorbachev also came from horse country, he brought a Western saddle as a gift. Gorbachev received it graciously, tactfully avoiding mention that he had been a tractor driver, not a horseman, in his early years.

The new general secretary spent more than two hours with us. I had observed several of his predecessors at close hand. By contrast, he was unusually articulate. He sat at the same long table used by Brezhnev and had a folder, presumably of prepared notes, before him. But he never referred to the notes. There were none of the awkward pauses there had been as Brezhnev peered intently at the script that had been placed before him, trying to make sense of letters that must have blurred before his eyes. There was no prompting by aides when the leader misspoke.

Gorbachev dominated the conversation; each question or comment by his guest would elicit a lecture. Nevertheless, he did seem to listen, and his responses were not always the ones we would have gotten from previous Soviet leaders.

He did not claim, for example, that they had the best system, and he spoke passionately of their need to improve management of the economy. But there was a defensive streak in his comment. He complained that U.S. Secretary of Defense Caspar Weinberger had recently commented that the Soviet Union could no longer feed its citizens.

As I recall his remarks, he protested vigorously. "Why do you constantly put us down? Do you accuse Britain or Germany of not being able to feed their people just because they import food? We do feed our people, and we, like they, import some food to do it. But we pay for it, cash on the barrelhead, and so far as I am aware, your farmers don't refuse to take the money. What's wrong with that? As far as production is concerned, we produce more wheat than you do, even per capita. Our problem is that we waste too much of it. That's our big problem, and we're working on it. If we solve it, your farmers will lose a major market—but that will be *your* problem and maybe we won't have to put up with demeaning jibes that we can't feed our people."[7]

This was typical Gorbachev: proud, defensive, clever in debate, and not totally oblivious to the facts. I subsequently remarked to my colleagues in Washington that U.S.-Soviet meetings might start being fun; perhaps the dreary, soporific experience of endlessly hearing and being forced to repeat the same old arguments would now be replaced by more spirited debate.

Mikhail Gorbachev was not only a man of different character from his immediate predecessors. He was also as determined to change the system as the Brezhnev clique had been to perpetuate it.

However, he was in no position to dazzle the country with a brilliant hundred days of change—first, because his political position was tenuous, and second, because his program was a limited one that did not get at the real problems the country faced. As he himself admitted later, in 1985 he still believed that the system could be fixed by tinkering with it.[8]

In the spring of 1985, the remnants of the Brezhnev clique were still in office. The Party Central Committee, which had not been elected since Brezhnev's days, was notoriously conservative. If Gorbachev moved too rapidly, his days as general secretary would be few.

Nikita Khrushchev, after all, had launched a series of reform initiatives. When they had begun to touch the prerogatives and comfortable habits of his colleagues, he had been unceremoniously dumped. This history was etched in the consciousness of every would-be reformer. The lesson was that no reform could be sustained unless the Soviet leader could avoid being ousted by a stand-pat Party leadership.

From the outside, Soviet leaders since Stalin have usually looked more powerful than they in fact were. Stalin, through a combination of guile and utter ruthlessness, had run the system as a one-man show. None of his successors managed to do the same, however. Scarred by their personal vulnerability to an unpredictable tyrant, Stalin's successors made certain that the Communist oligarchs could thenceforth hold a leader in check. This had nothing to do with democracy but was more like a mutual protection pact among gangsters.

The general secretary had no fixed term and no clearly delineated authority. His powers were as extensive as his ability to persuade, cajole, or coerce a majority of his colleagues. Normally, a "majority" was determined by a consensus rather than an up-and-down vote, and this usually required more acquiescence than merely 50 percent plus one. In theory, his tenure could be terminated at any plenary session of the Party Central Committee if a member stood up and proposed election of a different general secretary and a majority voted in favor. In practice, this could occur only with the connivance of a substantial faction in the Politburo, but Nikita Khrushchev's experience in 1964 proved it could happen.

Given these circumstances, Gorbachev's first moves were designed to gain a mastery of the Party high command. He would be able to lead only if he removed his principal opponents—or at least enough of them to give him a reliable majority—and promoted persons prepared to support him.

Gorbachev launched a campaign to dominate the Politburo as soon as he took office, and a year later his position was as firm as that of any of his predecessors, save only Stalin's at the height of his power. If he had not subsequently set out to change the system, he might have remained in power longer than Brezhnev.

Six weeks after he became general secretary, in April 1985, Gorbachev secured a working majority in the Politburo by engineering the election of Yegor Ligachev, Nikolai Ryzhkov, and KGB Chairman Viktor Chebrikov as full members. Subsequently, Gorbachev parted company with each of these three, but at the time they could be counted on for support.

By July, he was strong enough to remove from the Politburo the man considered most likely to challenge his leadership: Grigory Romanov, the Leningrad Party boss, noted for his imperious and autocratic crudeness. According to gossips, he took his surname, that of the last tsarist dynasty, seriously and made free use of the former tsarist collections in the Hermitage Museum. Rowdy guests at his daughter's wedding reception were said to have smashed some of the historic china "borrowed" from the museum for the occasion.

As Romanov was removed, important promotions were made: Boris Yeltsin to the Party Secretariat and Eduard Shevardnadze to full membership in the Politburo.

Simultaneously, Gorbachev signaled that he would take personal charge of foreign policy. Andrei Gromyko, whose twenty-eight years as foreign minister had given him a hammerlock on both the formation of foreign policy and its execution, was "kicked upstairs" to a prestigious but powerless position as titular head of state. Eduard Shevardnadze, the former Party chieftain in Soviet Georgia whom Gorbachev knew well from his long residence in nearby Stavropol Territory, was named foreign minister.

By fall, Ryzhkov had replaced one of Gorbachev's most persistent opponents, the septuagenarian Nikolai Tikhonov, as prime minister. By spring 1986, the remaining Brezhnevites in the top leadership had been removed, retired, or relegated to the political sidelines. A Party congress was held as scheduled in February 1986, and it brought major changes in the composition of the Party Central Committee. More than 40 percent of the full members were new, a magnitude of change much greater than had occurred at previous Party congresses. In fact, however, the change was less significant than the numbers suggested. In many instances, Tweedledum replaced Tweedledee. The Central Committee remained overwhelmingly conservative.

Reformers later commented that the Party congress had come a year too early. They felt that Gorbachev simply had not had time to "prepare" it properly and ensure that like-minded officials predominated. It seems more likely that Gorbachev had no clear idea of what reforms he wanted and therefore was in no position to seek out people who might be supportive. And even if he had known what direction his reforms would take, he would have had difficulty spotting people in the upper reaches of the Party who might be of help. The promotion filters of the old system had done their work.

Nevertheless, Gorbachev's consolidation of personal power during his first year was a stunning political maneuver. Even some of his sharpest critics conceded as much. Boris Yeltsin, for example, remarked in 1990 that "At that all-important first moment of his reforming initiative, he operated with amazing finesse."[9]

Team Members

BY THE END OF 1985, Gorbachev's two most important lieutenants for domestic policy were Nikolai Ryzhkov and Yegor Ligachev.

Ryzhkov, just a year and a half older than Gorbachev, was in his midfifties when he was named prime minister. Unlike most of his colleagues in the top leadership, who had spent most of their careers in the Party apparatus, he had risen as an industrial manager, with a speciality in heavy and military industry. For twenty-five years he had worked in and eventually managed one of the largest Soviet industrial enterprises, the giant Urals Machine Plant in Sverdlovsk. He had been brought to Moscow in 1975, the height of the Brezhnev era, to a top position in the ministry responsible for heavy machine building, then had been transferred to the State Planning Committee with responsibility for heavy industry and arms manufacture.

After Brezhnev died, Andropov brought Ryzhkov into a full-time Communist Party position, naming him the Central Committee secretary for economic questions in 1982. A decade later, Ryzhkov reminisced to me that he had been surprised by this transfer to "Party work," since he considered himself a practical manager rather than a typical Party bureaucrat. Andropov, however, insisted on the transfer since he was trying to put together a more pragmatic team, one that would improve efficiency and combat corruption.[10]

Ryzhkov and Gorbachev had not worked together until Ryzhkov was brought into the Party Secretariat, where Gorbachev had been serving since 1978 with responsibility for agriculture. Andropov called the two of them to his office and instructed them jointly to supervise a series of studies by specialists on the problems confronting the Soviet economy and ways in which management might be improved. This effort was to be carried out secretly, without discussion in the Politburo, until it was complete.

Andropov died before the project came to fruition, but by the time Gorbachev became general secretary, he and Ryzhkov had accumulated in their office safes some 120 studies they had commissioned. These formed the basis of the limited reform program unveiled at the April plenum in 1985.

I first met Ryzhkov in Stockholm. It was March 1986, and he was leader of the Soviet delegation to Swedish Prime Minister Olof Palme's funeral. He agreed to a meeting with Secretary of State George Shultz while both were in town.

A handsome man in a well-tailored suit, tastefully patterned tie, and light blue shirt, he would have seemed in place in the boardroom of any of our largest corporations. He possessed the easy affability of a person skilled in managing large bureaucracies. When we dealt with tendentious issues, he appeared to be more of a pragmatist than an ideologue. He exhibited a general familiarity with the Soviet position on key international issues but made it clear that Shevardnadze, not he, would deal with them in negotiations. His own interest and responsibility was in the Soviet economy and the development of foreign trade. He was eager to talk about the prospects for foreign investment in development projects and assured us that there would be a shift away from military production so that more capacity could be devoted to production of civilian goods. He gave no hint, however, that he foresaw fundamental changes in the system. He seemed to feel that the slowing Soviet economy could be reinvigorated by alterations of management style and a gradual shift in investment priorities.

While Ryzhkov was delegated to head the Soviet government bureaucracy, Yegor Ligachev assumed the de facto number two position in the Communist Party. (There was no formal position of deputy general secretary at this time, but Ligachev chaired meetings of the Secretariat, which gave him direct control over day-to-day operations.)

Ten years older than Gorbachev, he had a technical education like Ryzhkov but had made his career in Siberia as a Party apparatchik. His ruddy complexion and shock of white hair served as a reminder of his outdoor exposure in a cold climate. Just as Andropov had tapped Ryzhkov for a top party post to bring management expertise into the leadership, he had brought Ligachev into the Secretariat to take charge of personnel assignments as part of the effort to combat corruption. Ligachev had a clean reputation, and this appealed to Andropov. Ligachev also believed, as Andropov did, that reforms should be carried out only by the Communist Party. When Gorbachev subsequently demanded reform of the Party itself, Ligachev began to oppose him.

A third member of the initial Gorbachev team was one rung lower on the power ladder than Ryzhkov and Ligachev, being a candidate rather than full member of the Party Politburo, but he was destined to be by far the most important of the three. Boris Nikolayevich Yeltsin, the hard-driving former Party boss in Sverdlovsk, was placed in charge of the Moscow Communist Party organization on Christmas Eve 1985.

This was the organization that Gorbachev's putative rival Grishin had headed, the most important regional Party post in the entire country since it included the central bureaucratic apparatus that ruled the vast empire. Yeltsin's assignment was to clean out the corruption that had accumulated in this key Party organization under Brezhnev and

Chernenko. He set about that task with such energy, thoroughness, and flair for public attention that he soon became a hero to ordinary Muscovites and a power-hungry, potentially dangerous competitor to his colleagues in the leadership.

A Limited Program

IT BECAME HABITUAL in Communist Party circles to date perestroika, Gorbachev's reform program, from April 1985, the first plenary meeting of the Party Central Committee after his election as general secretary, known as the "April plenum." Actually, the program approved by this meeting was not the one that eventually became known to the world as perestroika, the program of fundamental political and economic reform, but a much more limited program. It would be more accurate to refer to it as the "Andropov platform," because it was, essentially, the approach worked out at his instigation.

Some supporters pressed Gorbachev to adopt more serious reforms from the outset, but he refused. Barely in office, he assigned the initial drafting of the "April program" to two reform-minded associates, Alexander Yakovlev and Mikhail Poltoranin. They were sent out to a suburban dacha to work undisturbed for several weeks, a technique used repeatedly by Gorbachev. According to Poltoranin, when Gorbachev saw their draft, he "X-ed out" all passages calling for political reforms. "That's for later," Gorbachev observed. "First, we'll have to maneuver."[11]

Gorbachev initially adopted the slogan "acceleration"—in other words, speeding up trends already present. It was to be achieved by greater discipline, tighter management, less corruption, more sobriety, and some adjustment of traditional management procedures.

The average citizen felt the new policy in two ways: pressures increased to work harder, and alcoholic beverages became harder to get and more expensive.

Shortages of many consumer goods were endemic, and supervisors normally turned a blind eye if employees spent two or three hours away at "lunch." Most used the time to stand in lines and obtain daily necessities. Attempts were made to curtail this practice by tightening personnel supervision and even sending inspectors into stores during normal work hours to verify that shoppers were not playing hookey from work. The campaign for greater discipline might have worked if it had been accompanied by an increase in consumer goods. When the shortages got worse, however, the pressure to work harder merely enraged the public. The campaign was discontinued after a few months.

The antialcohol campaign, announced in May 1985, made an even more profound impression on the populace. Alcohol abuse was a serious problem, but the tactic used to deal with it—reducing the availability of spirits, wine, and even beer—made matters worse. Vodka has deep roots in Russian culture. More than a millennium ago, Prince Vladimir of Kiev decided to adopt Christianity rather than Islam as the state religion because he judged that his subjects could not live without strong drink. Furthermore, opportunities for more healthful recreation were scarce and in some areas almost nonexistent. For many Soviet citizens, there wasn't much else to do but drink.

The antialcohol policies were pushed to self-defeating extremes. Ordered to make alcoholic beverages less accessible, in many areas bureaucrats decided to go one better and eliminate all production of potable alcohol. In the south, whole vineyards were plowed up, even though consumption of wine had not presented a major problem and wine had an important niche in many of the non-Russian cultures.

According to Ryzhkov, within one year the amount of vodka distilled officially was cut in half, wine production reduced to little more than a third of what it had been, and beer output by a third.[12]

When legal sources of alcoholic beverages were restricted, most tipplers simply turned to moonshine or even more dangerous concoctions. Within two years, sugar consumption had risen by 14 percent, and, as Gorbachev noted ruefully in one of his public speeches, "We all know what it is being used for."

One result of the antialcohol campaign was the government's loss of billions of rubles in revenues and the appearance, for the first time, of a budget seriously in deficit. Ryzhkov estimates the lost revenue over the three years from 1986 to 1988 as 67 billion rubles, $100 billion at the then-official exchange rate. The demand for vodka provided an opportunity for criminal elements, and the policy brought a sudden growth in organized crime.

Even though the restrictive policy on alcohol was quietly reversed in 1988, its effects were long felt. Vodka production was quickly restored, but production of wines lagged for years. Even in 1992, it was difficult to obtain wine in Russian restaurants: often the only choice was vodka or brandy, hardly an encouragement to moderation.

The campaign against corruption appeared, at the outset, to be more effective. From the winter of 1985, Gorbachev and his allies conducted an extensive purge of senior Party officials in many republics and provinces, using charges of corruption as the excuse. In non-Russian areas, however, these campaigns were often mishandled, for the dismissal of non-Russians, even when they were crooked, was likely to be interpreted as a purge of the local nationality in favor of Russian replacements.

In fact, the new team stumbled badly in December 1986, when it replaced the Kazakh Party leader, whom it considered corrupt, with a Russian. This led to a serious ethnic riot, some casualties, and many arrests. At the time, both the Soviet leaders and most outside observers considered it an aberration.

Reform Goes Political

BY THE SUMMER OF 1986, it was clear that the limited "reforms" adopted in 1985 were getting nowhere. Gorbachev began to sound more radical. In June he attacked the powerful State Planning Commission (Gosplan), and by late summer he was speaking of restructuring the *political* system. Until then, the word "perestroika" had been used rarely, and only in the limited context of "restructuring the system of economic management."

Another code word that came into vogue that summer was "glasnost," literally "giving voice," or publicizing the facts. The Russian word has no exact counterpart in English, and this led to confusion in the United States about what the policy really meant. It did *not* mean freedom of speech or freedom of the press, as some foreign observers tended to assume. It did mean that official bodies should operate with a degree of openness and thus is related to our concept of "transparency." Its aim was not to free the media but to create more effective propaganda for a policy of change. Gorbachev initially saw glasnost as a lever against officials opposed to his reform program.

Vitaly Korotich, for several years editor of the weekly magazine *Ogonek* (The Flame), commented subsequently that when Gorbachev proclaimed glasnost as a part of perestroika, he had in mind "giving an old trollop a sponge bath and putting clean clothes on her, assuming that this would restore her virginity."[13]

Though outsiders did not know it at the time, the key figure who tidied up the trollop was the former Soviet ambassador to Canada, Alexander Yakovlev. One of Gorbachev's early recruits for his team, Yakovlev was in charge of the Party's Propaganda Department in 1986, which gave him principal responsibility for selecting media executives. He still had to get the approval of the Politburo for major appointments, but he was able to take the initiative in promoting those persons he chose.

In the spring of 1986, the tragic mishandling of the accident at the nuclear power plant in Chernobyl gave Yakovlev the chance to put some life into the moribund Soviet media. When the radioactive dust began to settle and some glimmer of the magnitude of the disaster penetrated the Kremlin, it became obvious that the hypersecrecy of the past could not be sustained if reform was to occur. The Soviet leaders' international position was also at stake. By failing to level with the world, they had lost credibility just when they needed it most.

Chernobyl merely highlighted what had long been obvious to most observers: even as a propaganda tool, the Soviet media no longer counted. Newspapers and television had become so dull and uninformative that Soviet citizens ceased to pay attention; if they wanted to know what was going on, they tuned in to foreign radio broadcasts. Those who did not listen to foreign stations had to wait days before they got a coherent explanation for Chernobyl, and even then it was incomplete.

The way Korotich was brought in to *Ogonyok* is instructive. Although trained as a doctor, he had, like Anton Chekhov before him, drifted from medicine to literature. At first he had written poetry, in Ukrainian rather than Russian. Gradually he had turned to journalism and in the eighties had been given the editorship of a Ukrainian youth magazine published in Kiev, his hometown.

A few days after Chernobyl, Korotich received a call from the Party Central Committee in Moscow. This was most unusual, since his publication came under the tutelage of the Ukrainian Communist Party in Kiev, not the Moscow Center. An old acquaintance, Alexander Yakovlev, newly ensconced in his office on Staraya Square, was on the line.

Yakovlev asked if Korotich would consider coming to Moscow to take over the editorship of the weekly magazine *Ogonyok*. *Ogonyok* was a venerable magazine, the oldest Russian-language weekly in continuous publication. At one time it had been very popular; in the 1930s it seemed to be modeled on the American *Life* and *Look* magazines: it carried human interest articles, short fiction, some poetry, and a lot of pictures. For many years, however, it had been run by two of the most meretricious hacks in the entire Soviet propaganda stable and its popularity had plummeted. Yakovlev knew that Korotich had an independent mind and would try to make the magazine more responsive to real public interests if given the opportunity.

Korotich did not want to leave Kiev and equivocated, but within days he received a summons he could not ignore. He was instructed to present himself at Ligachev's office in Moscow at 11:00 A.M. two days hence.

Ligachev at the time was responsible for personnel appointments, and it was his custom to interview candidates before presenting their names to the Politburo for formal approval. The interview with Korotich was short and almost cryptic; Ligachev mentioned that they had checked on Korotich and had verified that he had not built up a "personal mafia." He seemed independent enough from extraneous influence to do the job. When Korotich wondered aloud if his health would stand up under the pressure, Ligachev assured him that they had checked his medical record and were convinced that he was robust. Obviously, Ligachev's office did thorough background checks.

Following their brief conversation, Ligachev ushered Korotich in to a meeting of the Politburo, introduced him as the person selected to edit *Ogonyok,* and asked if there were any objections to the proposal. When there were none, he told Korotich, "Fine. That will be all," and pointed to the door.

The procedure used for appointing Korotich illustrates how appointments were made under the Party's *nomenklatura* system. Candidates for positions of "All-Union" importance would be vetted by the relevant section of the Central Committee Secretariat (in this case, the Propaganda Department), reviewed by the secretary responsible for personnel (or "cadres," as it was known in Party jargon), then formally agreed to by the entire Politburo. This would have been the procedure for appointing not just editors to major publications but also members of the USSR Council of Ministers, directors of large industrial combines, "governors" of provinces, first secretaries in national republics, ambassadors, rectors of major universities, and commanders of military districts. The Communist Party controlled *all* appointments to jobs involving supervision of others. The more important the job, the higher the level of approval required. If an institution was considered of "All-Union" significance, this meant the Politburo itself.

When it was decided that the media required reanimation, the traditional approach was used: the people who had been in charge were simply replaced. But while the procedure was the traditional one, the faces were truly new. Alexander Yakovlev obviously intended to create a more independent press. He knew the individuals involved better than Ligachev and Gorbachev did. As things turned out, the new editors took reform more seriously than their Party masters did, but by the time the latter found this out, they were unable to continue operating in the traditional way.

Korotich was not the only editor brought in from outside the circle of propagandists who had presided over the decay of the Soviet media. During 1986, new editors were also named to the weeklies *Moscow News* and *Literaturnaya gazeta,* the government daily *Izvestiya,* and the prestigious monthly journals *Novy mir* and *Znamya.*

Though I was still in Washington when these appointments were made, I took an interest in them because I knew most of the people involved, some personally and others by reputation. I could not be sure what they would be able to do, but all seemed relatively independent types, potential mavericks who had not previously been given scope to show what they could do.

I had met Korotich in the 1970s, when he had traveled to the United States with a group of Soviet writers. After his trip, he would sometimes accept invitations to lunch or dinner when he came to Moscow. We rarely talked about political subjects, but when we did, he was guarded (who wasn't, in those days?) but honest.

When he subsequently wrote articles and a book focusing on ethnic and racial hatreds in the United States, I was dismayed but not as shocked as some of my colleagues. He was paying his dues for the privilege of traveling abroad, and he usually got his facts right—he exaggerated them and took them out of context, but he did not invent them. It seemed to me that his character was more evident in his poetry. (I was probably the only U.S. government official who had read it.) It revealed a sensitive and fundamentally honest personality. That would not necessarily make him a great editor, but it offered hope that he would be more daring than his predecessors if he thought he could get by with it.

Fyodor Burlatsky, who was placed in charge of *Literaturnaya gazeta,* was well known to diplomats in Moscow. He had worked closely with Khrushchev, which had placed a low ceiling on his career during the Brezhnev years. Still, he continued working as a journalist and managed from time to time to sneak Aesopic articles into the Soviet press. These usually included a cryptic message that the Soviet Union might also bear some responsibility for its problems with other countries. In particular, his articles warned of the dangers of using military power with abandon.

One of Burlatsky's dramatic skits, for example, portrayed imagined conversations in Washington during the Cuban missile crisis, in which President John Kennedy rejected demands by the U.S. military to attack Cuba and instead, on the advice of his brother Robert, made a deal with Khrushchev. The informed reader knew he was referring to Moscow and the Soviet military and not to Washington and the Pentagon and that he had switched the scene to get his piece past the censors. In case we Americans were too obtuse to understand what he was doing, Burlatsky made a point of taking diplomats aside at receptions and setting them straight.

So—one couldn't be sure what Fyodor would do with *Literaturnaya gazeta,* but presumably he would not have been named to the job if someone in the Party leadership did not want more "daring" articles to appear.

I had also met the new editors of *Novy mir* and *Znamya,* but I knew them better by their works than personally. *Novy mir*'s Sergei Zalygin, at seventy-three the oldest of the group, had a passionate interest in environmental protection. Would he go after future Chernobyls and Aral Seas?

Grigory Baklanov, assigned to *Znamya,* was also a noted novelist. His genre, the war novel, was an overworked theme in Soviet literature, but Baklanov knew how to portray real people. His characters were not the cardboard stereotypes that infested most Soviet fiction set during the war but believable human beings who struggled with real problems. I had read some of his work during the 1970s, and its honesty had impressed me. Baklanov could not tell it all, but what he told was true to life. In his characters one could experience vicariously the real problems of Soviet life and the moral dilemmas the Communist system created. One could be sure that, unless Baklanov's hands were tied, *Znamya* would become a major forum for dealing with society's spiritual malaise.

I did not know the new editors of *Izvestiya* and *Moscow News,* Ivan Laptev and Yegor Yakovlev, and therefore had no idea what to expect. While *Izvestiya* was the central government daily and had great potential, nobody paid much attention to *Moscow News.* It was considered a propaganda organ for foreigners (it had editions in English, French, German, Spanish, and several other languages) and was little read by

Russians, though there was a small Russian-language edition, presumably produced so the monoglot officials in the Party propaganda apparatus could see what was being fed to outsiders.

It was not long, however, before both these papers were making a splash, and when one referred to "Yakovlev," he or she would be asked, "Which one, Alexander or Yegor?" They were not related, but each became a key feature of glasnost.

Filmmakers threw out the Party stalwarts who had maintained "discipline" in the Cinematographers' Union and replaced them with some of their most talented colleagues, who also were reform activists. Soviet television viewers were occasionally startled by the appearance of a foreign spokesman expressing ideas at variance with the official line. Long-suppressed works began to be published and performed on the stage.

As glimmers of once-prohibited topics appeared in the media, the gates of prison camps were sporadically opened to release a political prisoner or two. Andrei Sakharov, by far the most prominent of the regime's critics, still languished in exile in a city on the Volga River that was then called Gorky but had previously been—and would soon again be—known as Nizhny Novgorod. On December 15, KGB agents arrived at Sakharov's apartment late in the evening and hurriedly reinstalled the telephone they had removed to reinforce his isolation. The next day, a call came in from Gorbachev personally, informing Sakharov that he could return to his apartment in Moscow.

In late 1986 Soviet leaders, wrestling with concepts that had been absent from Communist practice since the 1920s, postponed a planned session of the Party Central Committee three times when agreement eluded them. The issues were basic: Could the economy be fixed without political reform, and could one speak of political reform without betraying all that the system stood for?

The plenum finally convened at the end of January 1987, and Gorbachev surprised observers with his radicalism. He described the country's stage of development as one of "developing socialism," rather than repeating the familiar Brezhnevian formula, "developed socialism." He even spoke approvingly of "real elections" and secret ballots. Only a few years back, talk like that could have cost a Party official his job and, if repeated, landed him in a prison or insane asylum.

When Gorbachev presented these still very general ideas to the Central Committee in January, they were received more with astonishment than with outright opposition. The old habit of deferring to the general secretary and avoiding direct questions about his proposals was still very much alive. Many probably assumed that the proposals were intended to boost Gorbachev's image with the public as a reformer and were not meant to have concrete manifestations in practice. If that was all there was to them, there was no harm in humoring the general secretary.

Still, Gorbachev continued to develop the ideas throughout the spring and returned to the topic at the next full meeting of the Central Committee in June. Now the public began to take notice: Was this more than the periodic campaigns of the past? Among the Party faithful, the question began to be asked: Could he really be serious? And if he was, did he not realize that such ideas could undermine the authority of the Communist Party, the only reliable instrument for governing the country?

On the Threshold of Perestroika

WE FOREIGN OBSERVERS also began to notice the difference. In 1986, we had high hopes that Gorbachev would prove to be a different sort of Soviet leader, one who took the real interests of his country more seriously than ideological abstractions, one who would be willing to bring more pragmatism to the negotiation process. Summit meetings in Geneva and Reykjavik had exposed us to his charm and his loquacity. His policies on arms control seemed to be shifting.

Domestically, however, his policies showed little difference from the sporadic "reform" periods of the past. Khrushchev's "thaw" had ended some excesses of Stalinism but had then itself ended even before its author was swept from office. In the 1960s, proposals to streamline management, called the "Liberman reforms," attracted much attention, only to be forgotten. A much-heralded program to improve food supplies in the 1970s had also fallen flat.

Were Gorbachev's domestic policies essentially different? Until January 1987, the answer was emphatically no. The policies of 1985 and 1986 were much like the earlier failures: attempts to apply superficial correctives to a system whose defects were inherent. They were like an attempt to tame a shark by pulling a tooth or two. Unless the system could be changed—or destroyed—it would simply devour piecemeal efforts to alter it.

But Gorbachev's proposals in 1987 were directed at the system itself. The experience of his first two years in power had convinced him that only pressure from below could guarantee the changes he was prescribing from above. He now saw that the system itself resisted change and that orders from the top were not enough. During meetings I attended in 1987 and 1988, he would at times ruminate on this problem.

"Throughout our history," he would say—I paraphrase from memory—"change has come from above. And it was always implemented by force. Now, I cannot use force or I will defeat the goal itself. You cannot *impose* democracy on people, you can only give them the possibility of exercising it. What we are trying to do is unprecedented. We have to turn Russian history upside down. We have to teach our people to rule themselves, something they have never been permitted to do throughout our history."

Radical and ambitious as these thoughts were, his proposals were, to say the least, incomplete. They pointed in the right direction, but contained both false premises and surprising gaps.

The worst of these was that the Communist Party of the Soviet Union could be an instrument of reform. When Gorbachev took office, he told the Central Committee, "If we are to solve the problems we face, we must continue to strengthen the Party and intensify its organizing and guiding role."[14]

Given what subsequently happened, this might be read as a cynical deceit, but on that day Gorbachev believed what he said. He had reform in mind and believed he could take the Party with him. He still believed that when he declared in June 1987, "We shall not succeed with the tasks of perestroika if we do not firmly and consistently pursue democratization."[15] He as yet saw no contradiction between Party control and democratization.

Aside from his reliance on an inappropriate vehicle for taking the country to democracy, his concept of democracy was vague and incomplete. While he argued in favor of real elections, representative assemblies with real power, a separation of powers, and protection for individual rights, he still defended "socialism" and opposed private property in land and in most industry. Rejecting Stalinist excesses, he wished to return to a "true Leninism," a concept he was unable to define.

He also ignored the interests of the subject nations of the vast empire he governed and believed that national differences had diminished to the point that they no longer required special attention.

Finally, in presenting his program for democratization, he failed to make it clear that reform would be lengthy and painful. The country was sufficiently dissatisfied with the old policies that candor on this point would have been appreciated and supported. However, Gorbachev left the impression that introducing elements of democracy would instantly bring more food and other goods into the shops. His failure to appeal for sacrifice at the outset of his program was to haunt him later, when the economy sharply declined.

Even though his proposals were general and incomplete, they aimed at significant changes in the system itself. To the degree that he pressed for practical implementation, resistance within the Party apparatus was certain to grow. Only time would tell whether he had the commitment to press forward with his program of political change or would yield to pressure from the system when it began to resist.

Not all the action of the first two years of Gorbachev's rule was confined to the domestic arena. He had also begun to change Soviet foreign policy. His chance of achieving his goals at home depended critically on ending the arms race and relieving the international tensions that had brought it about.

IV

Elbow Room for Reform:
Easing Pressures from Abroad

Ensuring security is taking the form more and more of a political task,
and it can be solved only by political means.
MIKHAIL GORBACHEV, 1986[1]

No matter where we turned, we came up against the fact that we would achieve
nothing without normalization of Soviet-American relations.
EDUARD SHEVARDNADZE, 1991[2]

I f you ever use those Pershing missiles in Germany, there won't be
enough warning for me to get to the men's room, much less a shelter. Our radar operators would still be looking for bugs in their equipment when the missiles hit!"

So said Vadim Zagladin, a top official in the Party's International Department, when we met in Moscow in the winter of 1984. For those who,
like him, worked in and around the Kremlin, the cold war had suddenly
become very personal.

I agreed that his position was unenviable but pointed out that our
friends in London, Paris, Bonn, Rome, and other European capitals had
faced the same potential terror when the Soviet Union deployed its SS-
20 missiles in the 1970s. The obvious solution was to eliminate these
weapons altogether, but Moscow was not ready for a step that, at the
time, seemed utterly visionary.

In fact, East-West tensions were high in 1983 and 1984. NATO's decision to base U.S. missiles in Europe if the Soviets refused to withdraw

their SS-20s evoked a furious attempt by the Soviet authorities to block their deployment. Straining to persuade Western parliaments to refuse the weapons, Soviet propagandists claimed that war was imminent. Despite mass demonstrations, Germany and the other Western European allies held firm and deployments began. The Soviet government used the deployments as a pretext to withdraw its diplomats from all arms control negotiations. But its failed propaganda campaign produced an unintended side effect in the Soviet Union itself. The Soviet authorities had inadvertently created a war scare at home.

It must have been clear to Gorbachev and his associates, even before they came to power, that internal Soviet reform would be impossible if East-West tensions were not eased. Additionally, it was obvious that no such improvement could occur without better relations with the United States.

Even before he became general secretary, Gorbachev used his influence to avoid a total breakdown of communication with the West. While he was still second secretary, the Politburo decided to resume a high-level dialogue with the United States by sending Gromyko to Washington in September 1984 to meet with President Reagan. Gorbachev then used an invitation to London in December 1984, to establish his personal foreign policy credentials. His conciliatory speech to the British Parliament signaled that he would be more flexible than his predecessors. A month later the Politburo, with Gorbachev's support, decided to resume negotiations with the United States on nuclear arms.

Thus, when Gorbachev replaced Chernenko, there were already signs that Soviet foreign policy was retreating from the rigid, shrill rejectionism of the previous year. In fact, from the time he took office, a dialogue was established that brought, by fits and starts, a gradual improvement of relations.

President Reagan had been eager throughout 1984 for a summit meeting, but first Soviet policy and then Chernenko's poor health (along with—in all probability—the Politburo's reluctance to let him face Reagan) precluded a meeting that year. Reagan, therefore, lost no time when a new, healthy Soviet leader emerged. When he sent Vice President Bush to congratulate Gorbachev—and, incidentally, attend Chernenko's funeral—he sent along a letter I had drafted inviting Gorbachev to meet him in the United States.

Within two weeks, Gorbachev replied, accepting a meeting in principle, but it took a few more months to settle on a time and place. Reagan had proposed a meeting in Washington, while Gorbachev suggested Moscow. Toward the end of June, they finally agreed that their first meeting would take place in Geneva in November.[3]

This gave them both time to prepare. In Gorbachev's case preparation meant continuing to consolidate his power, naming a new foreign minister, toning down bellicose propaganda, downgrading his hawks, and flirting suggestively with the United States' allies in Europe. Soviet arms negotiators remained as stubborn as ever, but at least they were back at the negotiating table.

New Faces

WHEN GORBACHEV BECAME general secretary, Andrei Gromyko was the "dean" of the world's foreign ministers. He had held the job for nearly three decades and had undergone a metamorphosis from Stalin's flunky to a senior member of the Politburo, the unchallenged architect and executor of Soviet foreign policy. Though he rarely became embroiled in contentious domestic issues, any rival suspected of poaching on his foreign policy domain faced the full fury of his territorial instinct. He had a particular aversion to the Party's International Department and declared it off bounds for diplomats from Western countries. Party apparatchiks there were relegated to dealing with "fraternal countries" in the Soviet bloc and foreign Communist parties, subjects that interested Gromyko only slightly, if at all. He was a big-league player, and he knew where the big league was.

It was he who had nominated Gorbachev for the top position in the Party, and his support had been critical in ensuring that no effective challenge to Gorbachev's candidacy could be mounted by Grishin, Romanov, or Tikhonov.

When Gromyko relaxed his facial muscles, the left side of his lower lip tended to sag, an expression that suggested indifference or even contempt. Not infrequently photographers caught just that expression. He was, to much of the public, "Mr. Nyet" incarnate. Gromyko in fact seemed more comfortable in confrontation than in problem solving. In private he could be gracious and sensitive to his visitor's personal concerns and even show flashes of humor, but on official questions he was always stern and rigid.

Even when he had decided—or been instructed—to concede a point, he would preface his concession with a defense of his earlier position and an attack on the logic and morality of his interlocutor's. Only then would he announce his willingness to compromise (moving perhaps a tenth of the way to a fair agreement) as a token of his government's magnanimity and proof of its willingness to go the last mile to ensure peace and tranquillity.

These habits doubtless stemmed from a lifetime of trying to defend Soviet policies that were transparently propagandistic. Adversaries with the facts on their side could be held at bay only by bluster and filibuster. Repetition replaced reason and "facts" were molded, sometimes even created, to fit the argument. Gromyko's formative years as a foreign policy professional coincided with some of Stalin's most callous acts. Anyone who could go, literally overnight, from campaigning for a united front against fascism to defending the Nazi-Soviet pact would have no trouble denying that Soviet missiles were deployed in Cuba when Washington already had proof, denouncing inquiries about Soviet bacteriological weapons as malicious provocation, or branding the United States the "aggressor" when his own air force shot down a Korean airliner with 269 innocent people aboard.

Two things must have been apparent to Gorbachev when he became general secretary. First, however beholden he might be to Gromyko for supporting his candidacy for the top post, he could never hope to bring Soviet foreign policy under his own control as long as Gromyko was foreign minister. Gromyko's decades in the job had given him an organization that was not only his instrument but in many respects had been formed in his image. His style of diplomacy infused the entire Soviet diplomatic corps. And, while he had had to kowtow to Stalin and defer to the self-willed Khrushchev, during the Brezhnev years he had managed to develop autonomy for his ministry. By 1985, a general secretary could either follow his lead or remove him.

The second relevant consideration was that Gromyko's long history of defending a Soviet policy based on confrontation made him ill suited for implementing a policy of cooperation. Not that Gromyko would necessarily have opposed such a turn: he was capable of understanding the need for a more benign international environment and would possibly have welcomed the task of improving relations with the West.

Nonetheless, he was not the man for the job. His personal credibility was crushed under the burden of the past. Other governments were unlikely to take seriously any professed change in Soviet foreign policy if

Gromyko remained in charge. Once Gorbachev agreed to a summit meeting with Reagan, we in Washington wondered if Gromyko would still be in office when the meeting occurred.

We soon learned the answer. On July 2, 1985, the day before the November summit meeting was announced, Gromyko was "elevated" to the prestigious but honorific position of chairman of the Supreme Soviet Presidium, the titular head of state who had no authority over policy. His replacement, Eduard Shevardnadze, was a surprise, both inside and outside the Soviet Union. Shevardnadze, the Party boss in what was then Soviet Georgia, had not been active in foreign relations before, aside from an occasional brief trip to a neighboring country as a member of a delegation.

I had not met Shevardnadze when he was named foreign minister, but I had heard a lot about him. In fact, he seemed to be one of the most able of the Party leaders in the union republics. He was the only one, to my knowledge, who had exhibited any signs of independence from Moscow.

For example, throughout the 1970s, when Jewish emigration from the Soviet Union began, those of us who followed the pattern of departures noticed that a disproportionate number of emigrants came from Soviet Georgia. This suggested that officials in Georgia were more lenient than their counterparts elsewhere in granting exit permission. After they arrived in Israel, many emigrants from Georgia reported that Shevardnadze had been responsible. He was reputed to support the freedom to emigrate and therefore had encouraged Georgian officials to permit people to leave if they wished.

Shevardnadze also had a reputation as a conciliator. When faced with demonstrations by Abkhazians, a minority nationality within the Georgian republic that wished more autonomy and more cultural and educational facilities, he met most of their demands rather than simply calling out troops and suppressing them. (The one key demand he opposed was that Abkhazia be transferred to Russian rather than Georgian jurisdiction.) When, two years later, Georgian students demonstrated in Tbilisi against a move to depose Georgian as the republic's official language and to require all doctoral dissertations to be written in Russian, Shevardnadze persuaded Moscow to relent.

Not everything we heard was complimentary. Dissidents had been arrested in Georgia in the 1970s, as they had been elsewhere. One of these

was Zviad Gamsakhurdia, son of one of Georgia's most famous novel-
ists. He had become an active dissident during the 1970s and made
friends with several American diplomats in Moscow. Was he arrested on
Shevardnadze's orders, or on Moscow's? We did not know, but we did
know that Shevardnadze presided over a republic where political oppression still existed, though perhaps to a lesser degree than in many
other Soviet localities, and that he himself had served as minister of the
interior when this was the top police job in the republic. That hardly fit
the curriculum vitae of a radical democrat.

In July 1985, Eduard Shevardnadze was a question mark to U.S.
officials.

It had become a tradition for the U.S. and Soviet foreign ministers to
meet whenever they found themselves in the same city for an international conference. Just four weeks after Shevardnadze replaced
Gromyko, European and North American foreign ministers gathered in
Helsinki to mark the tenth anniversary of the accord signed by participants in the Conference on Security and Cooperation in Europe
(CSCE). When the conference was conceived, we assumed that Gromyko would attend. As it turned out, this became the occasion for Shevardnadze's debut on the world political stage.

That first meeting between Secretary of State George Shultz and the
new Soviet foreign minister, which I attended as a representative of the
National Security Council, was memorable. Most of us on the American
side of the table (the custom was for the ministers to sit at the center of
each side of a long table facing each other, with their teams arrayed to
their sides) had clocked what seemed like endless hours in negotiations
with Gromyko (one marathon session in Geneva had gone on for six
hours without a break), and this had come to seem the norm in U.S.-
Soviet talks.

We were in for a pleasant surprise. A white-haired, cheery man with a
ready and winning smile came into the room, shook hands with the
Americans, and began the meeting by telling his aides in his accented
Russian, "I'm new at this. Be sure to correct me if I goof." With a
chuckle, he got down to business.

No major problems were solved at that meeting, but for the first time
the entire agenda suggested by both delegations was covered. Shevardnadze would state the Soviet position succinctly, and, if Shultz could not

agree (as was usually the case), he would simply say, "All right, think about it. We think it's a good idea. Maybe you can suggest a better one." Then he would turn to the next topic, and when Shultz made proposals he could not accept he would respond with something like "We have a different point of view on that, but we need to solve the problem. Think about what I've said, and we'll study what you've said. Maybe next time we can move closer."

There were no histrionics, no long lectures, no recriminations. The substance of Soviet policy had not yet changed, but the mode of presentation was totally different. Instead of indulging in oratory as if he were addressing an audience of thousands, as Gromyko had, Shevardnadze spoke in a voice so soft that one had to strain to keep from missing a word or phrase. As the meeting ended, he turned to his staff and asked, "Okay, fellows, how did I do? How many bloopers did you count?" Before they could reassure him, he laughed and said, "Hold on, tell me when we get out of the room," shook hands all around, and departed.

"Don't tell me that's a *Soviet* foreign minister!" exclaimed one of the American participants when Shevardnadze had departed. "We're in a whole new ball game!" And so we were.

The other new face on Gorbachev's foreign policy team entered the scene with less fanfare than Shevardnadze, but his influence was critical in giving Shevardnadze a foreign policy that would work. While Shevardnadze was responsible for managing the country's diplomacy, Alexander Yakovlev developed the theoretical justification for placing Soviet foreign policy on a new basis.

Born in a rural village near Yaroslavl, in the heart of historic Russia, Yakovlev had been seriously wounded during the war. He had come home on crutches and, to the dismay of his peasant mother, who doubted the value of formal education, had gone to Yaroslavl to complete his training as a teacher. For years, his career had alternated from teaching to journalism, from work in the Communist Party apparatus to occasional periods of graduate study. One of these had been in the United States.

In the fall of 1958, three of the many foreign students beginning graduate study at Columbia University attracted more attention than normal—from the university, the press, and the FBI. These three were in the first group of Soviet graduate students to study in the United States under the U.S.-Soviet Exchange Agreement concluded during the Eisenhower administration.

Alexander Yakovlev was the oldest and the informal leader of the group. He had the impression that the FBI considered him a KGB officer, judging from the attention it gave him, but, as he later observed, "One of us was in fact from the KGB, but I was not the one."[4]

While at Columbia, Yakovlev studied under Professor David Truman, a specialist in U.S. foreign policy. Yakovlev's area of interest was Franklin Roosevelt's foreign policy, and he once told me that Truman had been an ideal mentor, one who left him free to pursue his research as he wished but who gave shrewd advice as to which books and articles were worth attention and which could be ignored. Unfortunately, Yakovlev's public remarks about his study in the United States have rarely touched upon the satisfactions but have concentrated on his unpleasant experiences with the FBI.

Yakovlev's most extensive experience abroad came later, when he was posted for ten years in Ottawa as Soviet ambassador to Canada. For years, the Moscow rumor mill described this assignment as an "exile" from high politics, brought on by an article Yakovlev had written that criticized Great Russian chauvinism.[5] Yakovlev, however, has said that it was not quite that simple.[6] He was finding it harder and harder to do his job at the Party Central Committee. Among other things, he had tried to tone down what seemed to him excessive praise of Brezhnev, only to learn that it had originated with Brezhnev himself. When Party officials attacked him for not clearing his article in advance, he requested a transfer to work abroad, in an English-speaking country if possible.

His sojourn in Canada was fateful for him. He was there in 1983 when the secretary responsible for agriculture in the Party Central Committee, Mikhail Gorbachev, made an extended tour of Canada. They had met years earlier when Yakovlev had still been working in the Central Committee and had defended some of Gorbachev's proposals for innovations in farm management, but this time there was an opportunity for extended discussion. It was a diplomatic must for the ambassador to accompany his high-level visitor at all times.

As Yakovlev later recalled, he was struck by Gorbachev's "candor and clear positions."[7] The two of them agreed that "We can't continue to live like this." Within months, Yakovlev was reassigned to Moscow and placed in charge of the prestigious Institute for the World Economy and International Relations, usually known by its Russian acronym, IMEMO.

In December 1984, Yakovlev was one of the small party that accompanied not-quite-yet-Soviet-leader Gorbachev to London for his first foray into high-level diplomacy. If it was Yakovlev's advice that won Margaret Thatcher's praise for his boss ("A man we can do business with"), he earned his fare.

Though they did not know him well despite his long residence in North America, our officials knew more about Yakovlev than Shevardnadze. And what they knew in 1985 was not promising. Yakovlev had been sufficiently trusted by the Communist Party establishment to be sent to the West as one of its pioneer students in that hostile environment. During a decade of diplomatic service in Canada, he had exhibited no public inclination to challenge traditional Soviet policy. His published writings were virulently anti-Western.

In a book published in 1984, after his long stay in Ottawa and just before he traveled to London with Gorbachev, he described American foreign policy in the following terms:

> American monopolistic masters believe that their domination of the world would offer the best solution for all the problems of international politics. They consider war a peerless catalyst to achieve this goal. For the sake of the sickest idea that life has ever produced, that of world domination, the weapons makers and brass hats have formed an alliance with death. They are prepared to bury hundreds of millions of people in the ruins of cities just to bring the world to its knees.
>
> Postwar American leaders, in essence, have always behaved like fighting cocks with nuclear talons, straining to fight communism and the Soviet Union, proving thereby their "reliability," their "muscle power" and their "courage."[8]

Thus we can be forgiven for not immediately anticipating the contribution that Alexander Yakovlev would make in transforming the Communist ideology on which both foreign and domestic policy was based. After he moved into the Party Secretariat and, for a time, the Politburo, he became a champion of limiting the power of the Communist system, protecting human rights, and basing foreign policy on cooperation rather than class struggle. Furthermore, he and Eduard Shevardnadze were the sole members of Gorbachev's team who recognized that they needed to change Soviet policy toward the non-Russian nationalities.

The American Factor

POTENTIAL NATIONALITY PROBLEMS, however, were not the center of the Soviet leaders' attention in 1985 and 1986. Having decided that "We can't go on like this," Gorbachev had to create a more benign international environment if any program of internal reform, however modest, was to be successful.

The United States was not the only foreign policy problem he faced. Indeed, some irreverent Soviet observers used to joke in private that the USSR deserved particular sympathy since it was the only country in the world "surrounded by hostile Communist countries." Nevertheless, the key to relieving the tensions that had fueled the arms race was the United States. If relations with the United States became less strained, many other pressures could be attenuated; if the two countries remained in confrontation, it would be hard to solve problems anywhere.

The Reagan administration had positioned itself for just such an eventuality. The rapid growth of the U.S. defense budget (which started during the Carter administration) was designed in part to demonstrate to the Soviet leadership that the United States would not permit, by default, Soviet military superiority. At the same time, particularly from early 1984, the United States set forth an ambitious program to settle our differences. Working with Richard Burt, then assistant secretary of state for European affairs, and his deputy, Mark Palmer, I had been the principal drafter of President Reagan's speeches on the subject and his correspondence with the Soviet leaders.

From the time I joined the National Security Council staff in 1983, my main duty had been to devise a negotiating strategy for dealing with the Soviet Union. The president made it clear to his immediate staff that his purpose in building up U.S. military strength was to position the United States for successful negotiations with the Soviet Union. Many in his administration, particularly in the Department of Defense and the Central Intelligence Agency, doubted that the Soviet leaders would conduct negotiations in good faith, but Reagan was an optimist. For all his distaste for the Soviet system, he nevertheless believed that it could change if subjected to sufficient pressure and his personal negotiating skill. Secretary of State Shultz was convinced of the value of negotiations and eager to take on the task, but he felt stymied by a reluctant

National Security Council and the opposition of Defense Secretary Weinberger.[9]

In June 1983, when I moved into an office in the ornate Old Executive Office Building adjacent to the White House, relations with the Soviet Union seemed about as tense as they could be short of actual conflict. The war in Afghanistan was at its height, and the Soviet forces were actually escalating the level of violence. Soviet-backed insurgent movements or totalitarian regimes were conducting local wars in the Horn of Africa, Angola, Nicaragua, and Cambodia. Soviet clients in the Middle East, such as Iraq and Syria, were not only keeping military pressure on Israel but were suspected of backing terrorist groups. The numbers of Jewish and Armenian emigrants from the Soviet Union, which had grown to more than 50,000 a year in the 1970s, had been cut back drastically. Few Soviet citizens were allowed to travel outside the Communist bloc, and most of them were government officials sent on official duty abroad. Political dissidents continued to be held in labor camps or insane asylums or sent into internal exile, and the media were tightly controlled. Jamming made most foreign broadcasts incomprehensible in urban areas.

The Soviet and U.S. positions in the arms control negotiations were so far apart that our representatives in Geneva seemed to be marking time. The one attempt Paul Nitze and Yuli Kvitsinsky made on their own to bridge our differences regarding intermediate-range missiles in Europe had been rejected by both capitals, and the Soviets were threatening to quit all arms control negotiations if U.S. missiles were deployed in Europe to balance their SS-20s.

These tensions encouraged both sides to escalate the public rhetoric. Just a few weeks before I joined the White House staff, President Reagan, in a speech in Orlando, Florida, said that the Soviet Union was "the focus of evil in the modern world." For months, Soviet political leaders and propagandists had vilified Reagan as a warmonger.[10] They now accused him of seeking negotiations not to reach agreement but to mislead the public.

Despite these obvious frictions and the public impression in both countries that relations were at rock bottom and highly dangerous, I began the job in an optimistic mood. As I saw it, fundamental trends were moving unmistakably in favor of the West. The Soviet economy, rigid and inefficient under a convoluted bureaucracy and sapped by enormous military expenditure, was stumbling. The Soviet Union was overcommitted abroad, and insurgencies it had backed were meeting increasingly effective opposition on the ground. Concerns about the war in Afghanistan and the threat of nuclear war were growing among the Soviet public. The Communist ideology had ceased to be a motivating force among the Party faithful; in private, few concealed their contempt for it. Even those who ran the political system were beginning to question whether it could last in its current form.

It seemed to me that the worst was probably over in U.S.-Soviet relations. There might be a few more setbacks over the coming year, but once relations had bottomed out, the fundamentals would favor a period of steady improvement provided the United States had defined reasonable goals and was prepared for skillful negotiation. The Soviet plight was not so bad that its leaders would accept a public defeat. The U.S. agenda could be most effective if it took into account legitimate Soviet concerns even as it served Western interests.

Defining an Agenda

DESPITE PRESSURE FROM SHULTZ, the White House staff had, until the summer of 1983, given little thought to what a negotiating program with the Soviet Union might look like. During the spring, however, Reagan began to think more about how he could use the bargaining chips he was accumulating through his defense buildup and agreed that Shultz could outline a forward-looking policy in testimony to Congress. In a lengthy presentation, Shultz described our policy as one based on "realism, strength and dialogue."[11] "Realism" meant that we would not blink at describing Soviet reality as it was. "Strength" meant that we would maintain the wherewithal to protect our interests and to negotiate reasonable settlements. "Dialogue" meant that we would stay in communication and not break off contacts as some American administrations had done in the past during political crises.

Shultz's testimony was an important signal that we intended to negotiate seriously with the Soviet Union. However, the three principles he outlined defined an approach rather than a policy. In fact, the administration had not yet articulated a coherent policy toward the Soviet Union. It had a grab bag of individual policies, most with long histories, on arms reduction, on human rights, on trade boycotts, on the unacceptability of the division of Europe and Soviet military intervention outside its borders, and on many other topics. Instinctively, everyone knew that interrelationships existed, if not in policy, then certainly in practice. When the Soviet Union invaded Afghanistan, the Senate had refused to ratify the SALT II treaty signed by Jimmy Carter and Brezhnev; even earlier, in 1974, the Congress had imposed trade restrictions on the Soviet Union because of its refusal to permit free emigration. Nevertheless, the various policy strands had not been woven into a coherent whole.

In the past, whenever U.S.-Soviet relations had improved, U.S. policy had become excessively optimistic, at times euphoric; but after every setback we had refused for a time to do business at all. Our policy had moved by fits and starts, jerky and discontinuous when we needed steadiness to be effective.

When we had tried to improve relations in some areas, ignoring problems in others, we had failed. Richard Nixon's attempt to expand trade had failed when the Soviet authorities had limited Jewish emigration and committed other violations of human rights. The Carter administration's decision to give priority to arms control over opposing Soviet military adventures in third countries ended with a defeat for the SALT II treaty in the Senate when the Soviets invaded Afghanistan.

Of course it was imperative to avoid nuclear war, but I doubted that arms control alone would achieve this. The American people viewed our relations with the Soviet Union as an integral whole. They would object to arms control agreements if the Soviets had just invaded another country, instinctively recognizing that such behavior was more threatening than the level of arms was and also that governments guilty of aggression are poor risks when it comes to carrying out agreements they make. This meant that an American administration would be making a mistake if it tried to deal with one issue to the exclusion of the others. Relations with the Soviet Union would improve across the board or not at all, and the Soviet leaders needed to understand that.

The crux of the problem was that the Soviet Union would have to change before the U.S.-Soviet relationship could improve fundamentally. If the Soviet Union stayed as it was, we could hope only to manage the mutual hostility, not to harmonize policies. Despite the doubts of those who were convinced that the Communist Party would never loosen its grip, I thought that a U.S. strategy that encouraged internal

Soviet change made sense. Though I could not predict that the Soviet leaders would begin an internal revolution, signs were accumulating that the Soviet leaders recognized the need for reform. If we could devise policies to protect our interests while helping them over some of their problems, why not try? Even if the current leader failed to respond, a future one might, provided we held a steady course.

While I considered reform of the Soviet system essential, I recognized that it would be a mistake to state this aim openly. Soviet leaders, out of pride and much else, would refuse to respond to demands that they alter their system to obtain agreements with us. This would block negotiations. An indirect route had to be found.

The growing pressures on the Soviet leaders to open the country and decentralize controls made an indirect approach possible. I was convinced that open borders, the free flow of information, and the establishment of democratic institutions would produce a fundamental change in the Soviet system, but any Soviet leader who embarked on reform would probably assume that the system could adapt to more openness in order to improve production efficiency. Therefore, we should not assume that Soviet leaders would continue to refuse to raise the iron curtain and guarantee some human rights. Such reforms could become self-sustaining since, once started, they would be difficult to reverse without severe economic and political repercussions. Thus, the Soviet Union could eventually change even if this was not the intent of its rulers.

The challenge was to construct a policy that would encourage openness and democratization within the Soviet Union. We needed to make sure that our interests and security were adequately protected while at the same time supporting change in the Soviet Union. We had to aim high but be prepared to wait if at first the Soviet leaders failed to respond.

We were still discussing negotiating strategy on September 1, 1983, when a Soviet fighter shot down a Korean airliner which had strayed into Soviet airspace, killing 269 persons, including a member of Congress and many other Americans. The Soviet government first denied that it had anything to do with the crash, then claimed that the United States was responsible because it was using the airliner as a "spy plane."

The shootdown itself, though an unmitigated tragedy, would probably not have caused a serious disruption of U.S.-Soviet relations if the

Soviet government had admitted what had happened, apologized, paid damages, and taken steps to prevent a recurrence. It had previously—most recently in 1977—downed civilian aircraft that strayed off course, but with far fewer casualties. The fact that measures had not been taken to prevent such accidents increased the Soviet regime's culpability.[12]

The Soviet reaction, however, turned the accident into a serious diplomatic confrontation. President Reagan rewrote the draft his speechwriters and I had composed and called the incident a "massacre" on national television. A meeting a few days later in Madrid between Shultz and Gromyko, which we had hoped would create a more productive negotiating framework, turned into a shouting match when Gromyko reacted with fury to Shultz's demand that their meeting be confined to discussion of the aircraft shootdown.

Shortly thereafter, Andropov issued a grim statement that "if there had ever been illusions" that one could do business with the Reagan administration, it was now clear that this was impossible. A few weeks later, when the first Pershing missiles were deployed in West Germany to counter the Soviet SS-20s, the Soviet government carried out its threat and withdrew its negotiators from the talks in Geneva on reducing intermediate-range and strategic weapons. U.S.-Soviet relations were back where they had been after the invasion of Afghanistan.

The Soviet reaction to its error in shooting down the Korean airliner exemplified a troublesome aspect of Soviet policy. Soviet officials lied, covered up known facts, then attempted to shift blame and, when this was impossible, resorted to bluster and threats. In doing so, they handed the Reagan administration a heavy club to pound them with before world public opinion.

Reagan had already decided to activate negotiations, but he was blunt when the Soviet leaders refused to accept responsibility for the crash. His outrage was genuine, as was Shultz's and that of every other member of the administration. The American reaction, however, was not blind rage but calculated to convey two important messages: first, that the Soviet government's reaction to its own blunder was unacceptable and ultimately harmful to the Soviet Union; second, that the United States was still interested in negotiating our differences. While the Soviets were threatening to withdraw their negotiators from the arms control talks in Geneva, we sent ours back to the table.

Reagan Offers a Program

DESPITE OUR DESIRE to keep the channels of communication open, U.S.-Soviet relations remained frozen for several months. Andropov's health deteriorated rapidly in the fall of 1983, and Soviet policy seemed mired in a sulk. But thoughtful Soviet officials understood that their leaders had committed a series of grave mistakes and that the country was paying a heavy price as a result of the international isolation and hostility they had aroused.

In October 1983, Sergei Vishnevsky, a political commentator for *Pravda* whom I had known in Moscow, called from New York to request a meeting. He was in the United States as a temporary replacement for the regular *Pravda* correspondent, who was ill. He was not interested in an interview for *Pravda,* he said, but wanted to discuss the current situation. I assumed that he called me to pass an unofficial message to the administration—a technique the Soviets had used in the past when relations were tense.

I invited Vishnevsky to lunch at a restaurant across the street from the Old Executive Office Building. He did most of the talking. He described the Soviet leadership as aging and rigid, worried about the state of their economy and aware that they needed to reduce international tension to permit reform but at a loss as to how to do this. They had unwisely blundered into a policy dead end by mishandling the negotiations on intermediate-range nuclear forces (INF) and the Korean airliner shootdown. They now realized that President Reagan not only would get approval for a growing defense budget but would be able to deploy missiles in Western Europe despite Soviet opposition and would very likely win reelection in 1984. He predicted that the Soviet leaders would have to break off the negotiations to carry out the threats they had made and that several months of stalemate, accompanied by shrill propaganda, would follow. But he advised us not to conclude that we could do no business in 1984. By the fall of that year, the Soviet leadership would attempt gradually to move back into a negotiating position.

Vishnevsky presented these ideas as his own, but I doubted he would have taken the initiative to come to Washington simply to give me his personal view. Most likely, this was a message someone in the Soviet leadership wanted us to hear. In fact, I had already drawn much the same conclusions.

As winter approached, I felt the time had come for the United States to begin setting an agenda for negotiations. Given the truculent Soviet mood and Andropov's illness, we could not expect an immediate response, but we needed to start building a negotiating framework for the future. We also needed to reassure the American public and our allies that we were serious about constructive negotiations. Soviet prestige in world opinion had suffered greatly from the continuing war in Afghanistan, the termination of the arms control negotiations, the mishandling of the Korean airliner shootdown, and continuing human rights violations. Nevertheless, a significant segment of the Western public worried that the Reagan administration was risking nuclear war by its unwillingness to compromise. It would be useful, therefore, to make clear to our public as well as the Soviet leadership that we wanted to negotiate on a fair basis.

I suggested that the president deliver a speech with his ideas for improving relations with the Soviet Union. Robert McFarlane, whom we all called "Bud" and who had just replaced William Clark as the president's assistant for national security, agreed and asked me to prepare a draft. It was time to marshal the thoughts that had been churning in my head since spring and put them into coherent form.

I consulted Rick Burt and Mark Palmer in the State Department. Our views coincided in all important respects, and we agreed that I would do an initial, skeleton draft and they would amplify it. When I was unable to make time for it during the working day, I canceled dinner plans and worked all evening. By three the next morning, when fatigue finally overcame me, I had finished about 80 percent of the draft, with all of the core substantive proposals. I dropped it off at the White House Situation Room to be sent by courier to Palmer at the State Department for review and completion later that day and drove home, grateful for the prospect of three hours sleep before my first meeting was scheduled.

The speech draft incorporated the "realism, strength, dialogue" themes that Secretary Shultz had enunciated. It also proposed a framework for negotiation that concentrated on three areas: (1) reducing—and eventually eliminating—"the threat and use of force in solving international disputes"; (2) reducing "the vast stockpiles of armaments"; and (3) "establishing a better working relationship" by respecting human rights, complying with agreements, expanding contacts, and conducting a free interchange of information and ideas. Subsequently this third point was divided into two, by establishing human rights as a separate agenda item, and the issues became our "four-point agenda."

We had not grouped these issues this way before, nor had we explained earlier that the problems were interrelated: progress in one would facilitate progress in the others. While the problems were not rigidly linked and did not require any particular sequence of decisions, we made it clear that failure to deal with any of the issues would impede solution of others; progress was likely to occur across the board or not at all. This linked, without self-defeating rigidity, arms control and the use made of arms, and external behavior with "internal"[13] issues such as human rights and the free flow of information.[14]

Soviet propagandists had accused Reagan of blaming all the ills of the world on them. To make clear that this was incorrect, Reagan said in his speech that we did not accuse the Soviet Union of creating the conditions that gave rise to local conflicts but rather of seeking to take advantage of these disputes by arming one of the parties or intervening militarily. As a symbol of our intent to improve relations after a period of tension, Reagan quoted from John Kennedy's speech at American University in 1962, when he had eased the tension following the Cuban missile crisis by proposing a limited ban on nuclear testing.

I did not expect the Soviet leaders to remember Kennedy's speech, but I knew they would receive an analysis of what Reagan said and that their American specialists would point out the intended parallel. Furthermore, by quoting a Democrat, Reagan would suggest to our domestic audience that he was seeking a bipartisan consensus.

Reagan also needed to make it clear that the invective that had begun to dominate the U.S.-Soviet dialogue need not prevent constructive negotiation. I therefore wrote the following explanation for him:

> I have been forthright in explaining my view of the Soviet system and of Soviet policies. This should come as no surprise to the Soviet leaders, who have never been reticent in expressing their view of us. But this doesn't mean we can't deal with each other. . . . In fact, in this nuclear age, the fact we have differences makes it all the more imperative for us to talk.

We had hoped that Reagan could deliver the speech before Christmas, and—after much editing and discussion—a text was ready by mid-December, but White House schedulers postponed it several times without a clear explanation. Much later I learned that Nancy Reagan's astrologer in California was responsible for these delays. It was finally delivered on January 16, 1984.[15]

The delay caused no harm. The speech was meant to set forth a long-term policy, and we did not expect an immediate response from Moscow. The president's advisers had originally preferred December to minimize the tendency of the media to see it as a campaign document. They thought that speeches given in 1984, an election year, were more likely to be considered politically motivated than those delivered in 1983.

Many American commentators did in fact dismiss the speech as campaign rhetoric, but I suspect they would have done so even if the speech had been scheduled in December 1983. Over time, Nancy Reagan strongly influenced her husband to negotiate with the Soviet Union so that he would be known in history as a "peace president." And who knows? Maybe her astrologer was right. Eventually, the policy this speech set forth in capsule form was to work beyond our wildest dreams.

Preparing for Geneva

ALL THIS OCCURRED over a year before Gorbachev took office, but from January 16, 1984, we had proposals on record that remained valid right up to the time the Soviet Union collapsed. Nevertheless, there were many disputes in the Reagan administration about specific policies, particularly those relating to arms reduction and curbing Soviet military activity in third countries. There was much wider agreement regarding human rights and the need to press the Soviets for a more open society, but many doubted that the Soviets would respond to these pressures and some failed to understand how they were connected with issues such as arms reduction and Soviet aggressive behavior.

During 1984, the Soviets refused to negotiate arms reductions, and we looked for topics that could break the ice. Renewing a cultural and educational exchange agreement that the Carter administration had allowed to lapse following the invasion of Afghanistan seemed the best bet, and we pressed for a new agreement that would involve more persons and more extensive travel than before. In June, Reagan outlined our proposals in a speech to a conference of Americans interested in U.S.-Soviet exchanges, sponsored by the Carnegie Corporation of New York and the Woodrow Wilson Center in Washington.[16] His concluding words struck a note of optimism at a time when U.S.-Soviet relations seemed historically bleak:

It may seem an impossible dream to think there could be a time when Americans and Soviet citizens of all walks of life travel freely back and forth, visit each other's homes, look up friends and professional colleagues, work together in all sorts of problems, and, if they feel like it, sit up all night talking about the meaning of life and the different ways to look at the world.

. . . I don't believe it's an impossible dream, and I don't think you believe that either.

When Gorbachev agreed to meet Reagan in Geneva, I realized that we needed to be more specific about ending Soviet and U.S. involvement in local wars. We had made concrete proposals for arms reduction, increased contacts, and human rights safeguards, but we had never specified precisely how we envisaged reducing our military competition in third countries. In particular, we had not made it clear that we would withdraw military support to parties in Third World conflicts if the Soviet Union would do the same.

Public attention still seemed riveted on the arms control negotiations and the various hot wars in which the Soviets were directly or indirectly involved. Reagan's proposal for a space-based strategic defense shield that the administration called SDI (Strategic Defense Initiative) and critics labeled "Star Wars" seemed to some not only ill advised but even an obstacle to arms control agreements.[17] Those who were understandably alarmed about Soviet-backed insurgencies in the Third World generally thought only of ways they could be opposed on the ground—such as by supplying arms to the contras in Nicaragua or Jonas Savimbi in Angola. Most would have scoffed at the idea that, while making sure that the Soviet adventures could not succeed militarily, we should create a way for the Soviets to withdraw from their military involvement without humiliation.

Though officially we always emphasized in public statements that we did not consider arms control the central issue in the relationship but rather one of several matters of equal importance, many administration officials acted in fact as if it were. Nothing, except perhaps sex and espionage, aroused passions to the degree weapons systems could. Most of the disputes within the administration were over how our negotiators should deal with this or that system. Each specialist had a favorite and regarded any attempt to limit that particular system as tantamount to conniving in surrender. The same people who resisted any limitations on our systems would argue that our negotiators had to persuade the Soviets to eliminate all their advantages. Even with their growing weakness, there was no hope the Soviets would agree to such an obviously one-sided arrangement.

The Soviet leaders considered arms control to be the central issue and insisted repeatedly that a major arms control agreement be reached before other issues of importance could be addressed. It was clear why they wanted it that way: they hoped to moderate the arms race and thus relieve the pressure on their economy without being forced to undertake fundamental reforms.

Given these attitudes, our respective positions on arms control seemed irreconcilable in 1984 and 1985, even after the Soviets returned to the negotiating table in 1985. I would have despaired if I had thought that arms control was the central issue in our relationship. But I didn't. The quantity of armaments, though dangerous and costly, was a symptom rather than a cause of the hostility between our countries, I believed. If we could diminish the hostility, the quantity of arms would be reduced, with or without agreements. If we did not, arms reduction agreements would do little good. In fact, unless something was done to alleviate suspicion and hostility, arms control agreements would only create new issues for dispute as each side accused the other of circumvention or violation.

For that reason, it was important not to let arms control dominate the Geneva summit. Weapons would have to be discussed, of course, and seriously, but we had to make sure that, whether Gorbachev wanted it or not, the other important issues found a place on the agenda. As the president had pointed out in letters to Gorbachev, they were interrelated and interdependent.

In early September, I wrote a memorandum to Bud McFarlane recommending that the president be ready at Geneva to discuss concrete ways to end conflicts in third areas and expand people-to-people contacts, particularly by high school and college students. I also pointed out that it would be important to discuss new ideas privately with Soviet representatives before the meeting in Geneva. Gorbachev was likely to discount as propaganda any proposal made initially in public. Giving him time to think about the ideas and comment on them before they were discussed in public would build trust. Shevardnadze's planned visit to

Washington later that month would give us a chance to try them out before the summit.

I knew that if we entrusted the ideas to the normal interagency process they would not be ready in time for Shevardnadze's visit, bureaucrats would whittle them down to triviality, and leaks to the press would make it impossible to present them to Gorbachev before they were discussed in public. Therefore, I proposed to develop the ideas in small groups of four or five experts from the NSC staff and the State Department. We notified Defense Secretary Caspar Weinberger and Director of Central Intelligence William Casey what we intended to do, and they sent word that they had no objection. Weinberger was pleased with any proposals that would take the public's mind off arms control issues, and though Casey doubted that Gorbachev would accept the proposals, he had no objection to making them.

Within a few days, our small working groups produced comprehensive proposals on both subjects. Referring specifically to the fighting in Nicaragua, Angola, Afghanistan, the Horn of Africa, and Cambodia, the proposal on regional conflict envisaged a three-stage process to eliminate both Soviet and U.S. military involvement and promote settlements by the parties to the conflict:

1. Both countries would encourage parties to regional conflicts to start negotiations for a peaceful settlement.
2. Once negotiations took hold, U.S. and Soviet representatives would decide how to halt the flow of arms to the parties from the outside.
3. When peace was established in the area, the United States and Soviet Union would cooperate in assisting economic reconstruction.

For the first time the United States offered the Soviet Union a way to disengage from local conflicts without accepting military defeat. It did not blame the Soviet Union for causing the conflicts and made it clear that the first responsibility for solving them was with the local parties involved. It promised to end U.S. military involvement in these wars if the Soviet Union withdrew and supported a negotiated solution. It committed the United States to support peaceful Soviet involvement in the area if the conflict could be resolved. (Until then American policy had usually opposed any Soviet activity in the Third World.) By calling for negotiations among the warring factions first, the proposal tried to minimize suspicion that the superpowers were colluding to impose settlements on others. The goal was to eliminate the U.S.-Soviet military rivalry that was exacerbating the conflicts.

The proposals aimed at piercing the iron curtain contained concrete ideas for large increases in exchanges of citizens, particularly young people, access to each other's information media, and stepped-up cultural, sports, and professional contacts.

The president and Secretary Shultz presented these ideas to Shevardnadze when he visited Washington on September 26 and 27, and spelled out further details in correspondence and subsequent meetings between Shultz and Shevardnadze. Only then did Reagan describe them to the public. He announced the proposal for dealing with regional conflicts in an address to the U.N. General Assembly on October 24, 1985,[18] and some of the details of his proposals for expanding contacts in his radio address to the nation just before leaving for Geneva.[19]

While we were working on the agenda for the Geneva meeting and—we hoped—for U.S. policy over coming years and even decades, the American media paid far more attention to the administration's criticism of Soviet actions and to leaked reports of infighting over arms control policies than to the agenda that was actually under negotiation. This is one of the reasons why the subsequent end of the cold war seemed sudden and inexplicable to much of the public.

As the Geneva meeting approached, Gorbachev, too, began to modify Soviet policy, but more slowly and without spelling out comprehensive goals the way Reagan had done. During the spring and summer of 1985, he exchanged letters with Reagan every few weeks. The tone was invariably cordial, but both correspondents addressed key problems with blunt candor. In midsummer, Gorbachev made a sudden proposal for a moratorium on nuclear testing, which American officials considered a propaganda ploy since it was announced to the public at the same time it was conveyed officially—typical Soviet procedure when no agreement is expected.

Nevertheless, we began to notice new terminology creeping into Gorbachev's presentation of Soviet security policy. During a trip to France in early October (widely seen as a warm-up for his meeting with Reagan in November), Gorbachev had spoken of "reasonable sufficiency" as an appropriate basis for determining the size of armed forces and had rejected ideological differences as a relevant factor in foreign policy. These statements were intriguing but too cryptic for us to discern precisely what they might mean in practice.

Gorbachev's statement that the Soviet Union might conclude an agreement to reduce intermediate-range missiles without requiring simultaneous agreements on strategic weapons and space defenses attracted more attention. The United States and its allies had long felt that these complex negotiations were unlikely to succeed if the Soviet Union continued to insist on all or nothing. Gorbachev's statement in Paris gave us hope that the Soviet position had shifted for the better.

Steps Toward a Common Language

BOTH REAGAN AND GORBACHEV had reason to be pleased with the Geneva summit. Though they were still far from common positions, they began to find a common language based on the recognition that there was no rational alternative to peace and that peace could be achieved only by facing the issues. This seems self-evident and commonplace. In fact, it was not, given the history of the relationship and the ideological baggage that accompanied it.

Until that meeting, Soviet negotiators had insisted that any joint statement endorsing peace be expressed as an endorsement of "peaceful coexistence." To many outsiders, there was nothing to object to here. Who could be against "peaceful coexistence?"

In fact, the term concealed an ideological trap, for Soviet dictionaries defined "peaceful coexistence" as "the class struggle on the international plane, conducted by means short of war." In other words, peaceful coexistence meant cold war, not peace. It meant that the West should passively accept a cold war waged from the East without any response in kind.

And that was not the only problem. Soviet officials usually added the phrase "between countries of different social systems." In other words, "peaceful coexistence" did not apply to relations between countries with the same social system. The "Brezhnev Doctrine," held that "socialist" countries had the right and duty to intervene in other "socialist" countries if "socialism" should be threatened, as in Hungary in 1956, Czechoslovakia in 1968, and Afghanistan in 1979.

In the heyday of summitry in the early 1970s, Nixon and Kissinger had agreed to such terminology in joint documents over the objection of Soviet specialists like myself. Both Nixon and Kissinger seemed to believe that the words were meaningless and, since the American public was indifferent, they were cheap bones to throw to a dullard like Brezhnev, who might be persuaded to ease our way out of Vietnam if we were nice enough to him. Unfortunately, such terminology was not meaningless to the Soviet leaders, and our acceptance of it was one of the factors (along with a number of more important ones) that persuaded Brezhnev and his cronies that they could inject military force into Third World conflicts with impunity.

Reagan took ideology more seriously than Nixon had and was determined to avoid words that might mean different things to different people. He had been accused by Soviet propagandists of "warmongering" and was eager to put his commitment to peace on the record. But he wanted to make a straightforward, nonideological statement to convey the idea he had already used in some of his speeches: "A nuclear war cannot be won and must never be fought."

I doubted that the Soviets would accept a simple formulation at Geneva. If they refused it, we were prepared to have no statement at all. However, after initially pressing for the usual "peaceful coexistence," Soviet negotiators consulted Gorbachev and then accepted verbatim Reagan's direct statement that a nuclear war could not be won and must never be fought. This was a major reversal of Soviet policy.

Since the Soviet Union could attack Western Europe with conventional forces, we Americans also insisted that any joint statement exclude a conventional war as well. Traditionally, Soviet representatives had insisted that both countries pledge not to be the first to use nuclear weapons, but this would have prevented the United States from using nuclear weapons to defend Western Europe from conventional Soviet attack. To our pleasant surprise, Soviet negotiators at Geneva abandoned their previous position and agreed to a statement that it was necessary to prevent "any war between them, whether nuclear or conventional."[20] Thus, after decades of argument, we had spelled out a doctrine acceptable to both sides.

Normally, I am impatient with hairsplitting in declarations and joint statements. Often the issues are trivial, comprehensible only to specialists, and not worth the negotiating effort when the document has no legal force. But this time, the language was important, not so much for what it said (the statement reflected what had long been the actual policy of both countries) but for the way in which it was said. Gorbachev had demonstrated that he was prepared to deal with the central issue of war and peace without recourse to disingenuous formulas.

The Geneva summit also produced a number of agreements that had been negotiated in advance, including a much-expanded program of exchanges that included many of the ideas Reagan had proposed.

The Carter administration had refused to extend the previous exchange agreement following the Soviet invasion of Afghanistan. Although Soviet troops were still fighting in Afghanistan, we felt that these exchanges were important for the long-term influence they could exert in the Soviet Union. Refusal to support people-to-people contacts simply reinforced the iron curtain, which we should have been puncturing, not strengthening. The best way to get the Soviet Union out of Afghanistan, I felt, was to give concrete assistance to the resistance forces there. I was pleased that we were finally able to make a distinction between moves that bring real pressure to bear and those that are self-defeating in the long run.

Rocky Road to Reykjavik

DESPITE THE IMPROVED tone after the Geneva meeting, 1986 was not an easy year for Gorbachev's foreign policy. When Reagan proposed two subsequent meetings, one in Washington and one in Moscow, Gorbachev accepted with alacrity, but when we tried to schedule the Washington meeting, he equivocated, demanding assurance that a substantial arms control agreement would be signed. Reagan was not opposed to signing an agreement if one could be concluded, but did not want to risk the charge that he had made concessions just for the sake of a meeting. He therefore refused to give advance assurances or to make negotiating concessions opposed by his advisers.

This led Gorbachev to suspect that Reagan was using negotiations as an end in themselves, to lull the American public and U.S. allies without intending to reach an agreement. Nevertheless, Gorbachev began step by step to alter Soviet negotiating positions.

In January 1986, he made a well-publicized proposal to phase out all nuclear weapons by the year 2000 that impressed Reagan favorably. In contrast to most of his advisers, Reagan believed nuclear weapons could and should be abolished, and now, for the first time, a Soviet leader was making concrete proposals to that end. Nevertheless, many of the details were not acceptable to him, and the way Gorbachev made his proposal (in a letter released to the press as soon as it was delivered) raised suspicions that his intent was propaganda rather than agreement.

In the same letter, Gorbachev followed up on the hint he had dropped in Paris a few months back and abandoned the rigid linkage Gromyko had imposed on the three nuclear arms negotiations: the Soviet Union, he announced, would no longer require agreement in all three before any could be settled. It would now be possible to agree on intermediate-range missiles and on-site inspection even if strategic and defensive weapons remained under negotiation.

In February, Gorbachev addressed a second major foreign policy issue when he called the war in Afghanistan a "running sore." This ended the boast that Soviet troops in Afghanistan were merely doing their "international duty." Henceforth, Soviet military involvement in Afghanistan was to be treated as a problem that needed to be solved. Although it took two more torturous years before Gorbachev made an acceptable proposal and three years before the Soviet troops were actually out, the end was in sight from 1986.

Shevardnadze was also busy changing the Soviet approach to diplomacy. He began to reassign many senior Soviet diplomats in April 1986, and on May 23 he organized a conference of Soviet diplomats and foreign policy professionals to explain "new thinking." Henceforth, Soviet diplomats were expected to discard the old technique of bluster and nay-saying and instead cultivate the art of persuasion.

Western diplomats regarded "new thinking," with interest but caution. Most of us wanted something more tangible than words. But then we began to notice that many hard-line Soviet diplomats were being retired to vague consultancies in Moscow, while younger professionals with accomplished linguistic and social skills were moving up with unprecedented speed. Shevardnadze had begun to shape the Soviet diplomatic establishment in his own, rather than Gromyko's, image.

These changes did not immediately close the gap between the Soviet and U.S. positions on arms control, and Washington and Moscow continued throughout the summer of 1986 to dicker over the date of the next summit meeting. Gorbachev refused to come to Washington for a summit unless he could sign an arms control agreement, but the negotiations in Geneva made little progress.

In early fall, Gorbachev proposed in a secret message that a quick "preparatory" meeting be held in a third country. This was not to take the place of the next full U.S.-Soviet summit, which he agreed should be in Washington, but would be a short working meeting to settle on the agreements to be signed in Washington.

To prove that he was literally willing to meet Reagan halfway, Gorbachev suggested Reykjavik, Iceland, a location four to five hours' flying time for each. He ignored a factor that his predecessors would have considered important: Iceland was not a neutral country, as Switzerland had been, but one of America's NATO allies, and therefore, in a political sense, he would be traveling more than halfway.

Though Reagan wanted a full-scale summit in Washington—he was particularly eager to show Gorbachev the United States—he agreed to a more limited meeting, and the two met in Reykjavik on October 11 and 12, 1986.

Contrary to the public impression that the meeting was improvised, both leaders had prepared their positions carefully, though rapidly and with tight security. Their correspondence and diplomatic contacts had given each a reasonably accurate understanding of what the other sought. For Gorbachev, arms control was the key issue; for Reagan it was important, but only part of his broader agenda.

Since the meeting in Iceland had been planned as a working session and not a full-fledged summit, there were no frills and no social engagements. Reagan and Gorbachev met both days, with breaks for lunch with their own delegations, and two negotiating groups, one on arms reduction and the other on regional and bilateral issues, met through the night.

During a working breakfast on October 11 at the small but comfortable American ambassador's residence, we reviewed the key issues with the president and then held a mock session. I played Gorbachev, speaking in Russian through an interpreter. During a similar exercise just before the Geneva summit, I had accurately guessed Gorbachev's arguments; this time I did not attempt to predict his specific proposals but rather to capture his style of discussion and argumentation.

Subsequently, I took turns with Thomas Simons of the State Department as note taker in the private sessions, was a member of the negotiating team on regional and bilateral issues, and took part in the U.S. team's discussions of arms control issues.

During the morning session the first day, Gorbachev presented a detailed proposal for a comprehensive arms control agreement, which, despite its positive elements, was vague or unacceptable in several respects. Negotiating teams headed by Paul Nitze and Marshal Sergei Akhromeyev worked through the night to clarify the issues. Simultaneously, another group, led by Ambassador Rozanne Ridgway and Alexander Bessmertnykh, dealt with regional conflicts, human rights, and bilateral contacts.

By early Sunday morning, the Soviet approach became clear. Gradually, they were making major concessions on arms control issues but offering very little in other areas.[21] Hope rose that Reagan and Gorbachev could find a common approach for a weapons reduction treaty when they met later that day. Initially, the talks went well, with Gorbachev accepting the U.S. proposals for a 50 percent reduction in heavy Soviet land-based missiles, low numbers for intermediate-range missiles, and extensive on-site inspection. By noon, an agreement on intermediate-range missiles seemed so close that we sent out urgent messages to our ambassadors in Western Europe and Japan to seek out the heads of government to which they were accredited and brief them on the terms. Since it was a Sunday afternoon, that would not be easy in many capitals.

The afternoon session was punctuated by frequent breaks for team consultations and drafting. Both delegations were exhilarated by what promised to be the most comprehensive arms reduction pact in history. It seemed that only two issues of principle remained. First, Gorbachev had proposed to eliminate all nuclear weapons by the year 2000, while Reagan had offered to eliminate all ballistic missiles. Second, Gorbachev was insisting that all research on strategic defense be confined to laboratories, to which Reagan would not agree since he felt that testing outside laboratories would be essential to the program.

To the dismay of his aides, Reagan accepted Gorbachev's proposal for the eventual elimination of nuclear weapons but refused to budge on SDI testing. As a result, the meeting ended with both principals in a glum mood. By evening, the euphoria of midafternoon had turned into resentment. The summit in Washington, which the meeting in Reykjavik had been designed to prepare for, was not scheduled, and this alone would be sufficient cause for the media to label the meeting a failure.

What we all failed to appreciate in the hours just after the meeting ended was that Reagan and Gorbachev had solved more disputed questions than our leaders had at any previous U.S.-Soviet summit meeting. Our disappointment dominated the initial press briefings[22] and inhibited a clear explanation of what was actually achieved. In fact, the agreements had gone beyond the goals we had set for the meeting, aside from setting a date for Gorbachev to come to Washington. Gorbachev had offered to accept equal and low levels of intermediate-range missiles and to apply the quotas globally. He had also agreed to reduce the heavy intercontinental missiles in the Soviet arsenal by 50 percent, thus conceding a prime U.S. objective. After decades of Soviet resistance, he had espoused the idea of on-site inspection.

Gorbachev had come to Reykjavik with authority to accept the U.S. positions on condition that the agreement preclude sudden deployment of strategic defenses by the United States. Since laboratory work was more important than testing in space at that stage of research in both countries, the United States could have accepted some limitations without crippling the program. But this was not clear to President Reagan, who reacted as if he had been asked to toss his favorite child into an erupting volcano.

The Reykjavik meeting produced breakthroughs that cleared the way for subsequent treaties, and it is just as well that no final agreement was reached at that time. The INF treaty signed the following year was better than what was agreed at Reykjavik, since it eliminated intermediate-range missiles altogether rather than allowing each side to retain a hundred of them. Reagan's consent to a goal of eliminating all nuclear weapons by the year 2000 would have created major problems with Britain and France, which were still determined to maintain independent nuclear forces and which had not been advised that Reagan would make this concession. It was not desirable to signal such a fundamental change in U.S. policy without thorough prior consultation with our allies.

American agreement to a major arms reduction program in the absence of more movement on other issues on the agenda might also have delayed Gorbachev's acceptance of the full agenda. He had come to Reykjavik still believing that he could mend U.S.-Soviet relations by reaching arms control agreements alone. It was only after Reykjavik that he understood that relations could be normalized with the United States only if he dealt with the full agenda of issues, including human rights and raising the iron curtain.

These judgments are possible in retrospect, but at the time they were not obvious. For several months, a feeling of bitterness and betrayal weighed upon U.S.-Soviet contacts. The leaders had come tantalizingly close to agreement, and each blamed the other for failure. Gorbachev, embarrassed by returning empty-handed despite major concessions, lambasted Reagan to his Politburo colleagues. Military historian and Stalin biographer Dmitri Volkogonov,[23] who reviewed Communist Party archives after the Soviet collapse, told me that Gorbachev's words had been so sharp and insulting that he found it surprising that Gorbachev could face Reagan again.[24] Fortunately, as Gorbachev would later remark, he and Reagan were "doomed to cooperate."

Spies, Diplomats, and a Hostage

THOUGH THE TWO LEADERS dealt with other things at Reykjavik, their meeting took place when the two countries were in the midst of a quarrel over spying.

It started in August, when the FBI arrested a Soviet-citizen employee of the U.N. Secretariat, one Gennady Zakharov, on the charge that he had violated U.S. espionage laws. Unlike diplomats assigned to embassies, employees of the U.N. Secretariat do not enjoy immunity for their unofficial acts and therefore can be prosecuted if they break the law.

Even though Zakharov's arrest was based on solid evidence, the KGB was determined to spring its man. But it faced a problem: there was no American citizen within reach whom they could legitimately arrest for espionage. Therefore, they decided to pick up an innocent American and trump up charges against him. The victim, Nicholas Daniloff, was the Moscow correspondent of *U.S. News and World Report*.

This brazen action transformed a comparatively routine law enforcement action into a major political confrontation. It was not the first time Soviet authorities had tried to force the release of one of their intelligence agents by arresting an American. During the Kennedy administration the KGB had arrested Princeton professor Frederick Barghoorn under such circumstances, but Khrushchev had backed down and ordered his release when Kennedy had protested.

Subsequently, however, when less-prominent Americans had been seized, both the Nixon and Carter administrations had misguidedly negotiated a mutual release. As a result, Americans were put at risk whenever a Soviet citizen without diplomatic immunity was arrested in the United States on charges of espionage.

President Reagan was determined not only to secure Daniloff's release but to put an end to this outrageous practice. To do so, he had to make sure that Daniloff was released quickly without conditions or—failing that—to require the KGB to pay a high price in terms of its own interests.

In direct messages to Gorbachev, Reagan made clear that Daniloff was innocent of the charges brought and insisted that he be released. When Gorbachev equivocated for more than three weeks, Reagan ordered out of the country twenty-five Soviet officials at the United Nations, all of whom we considered likely intelligence agents.[25]

At the same time, American officials passed a stern private message to the Soviet government: if it continued to hold Daniloff, further action would follow, and the United States would not tolerate retaliation against the U.S. Embassy in Moscow. We could not allow our embassy to be subjected to reprisals for actions taken in respect to the much larger Soviet installations in the United States. There was no American counterpart in the Soviet Union to the Soviet Mission to the United Nations, and even if there had been one, it would not be proper to expel innocent Americans because of well-founded charges against Soviet intelligence agents in the United States.

Therefore, Soviet representatives were notified that we would insist that our diplomatic establishments be of the same size if there should be any attempt to move against our embassy in Moscow. This would mean a substantial reduction on their part.

Daniloff was allowed to leave the Soviet Union less than two weeks later, by a prior arrangement negotiated by Shultz and Shevardnadze. Zakharov was also permitted to leave the United States after pleading *nolo contendere,* but only on condition that Yuri Orlov, a prominent political prisoner, be released from prison and allowed to come to the United States with his wife.[26] By the end of September, it seemed that the matter was closed.

However, this was not to be. Shortly after the Reykjavik meeting, the Soviets did what we had explicitly warned them not to do: they ordered the departure of five U.S. diplomats in retaliation for the earlier expulsions of Soviets in New York. Two days later, in accord with our earlier warning, the Soviets were notified to remove another 55 "diplomats" (most, if not all, seemed to be intelligence agents) from Washington and San Francisco, and a ceiling of 225 was placed on the Soviet Embassy in Washington and one of 26 on the Soviet Consulate General in San Francisco.

These ceilings were set on the assumption that the Soviet authorities would withdraw Soviet citizens from employment at the American Embassy in Moscow and Consulate General in Leningrad. While the ceilings required the Soviets to reduce their staffs substantially, they allowed us to send enough Americans to perform the work of the Soviet employees, should they be withdrawn. Sure enough, the KGB acted true to form, withdrawing Soviet employees from U.S. installations literally overnight and expelling five more diplomats.

This resulted in a very difficult winter for American diplomats in Moscow and Leningrad, but they rose heroically to the challenge and by the end of the following year, when Americans had been sent to Moscow to perform essential services, embassy operations ran more smoothly than they had with Soviet employees.

Though our actions had caused temporary pain to our diplomats in the Soviet Union, the net result clearly favored U.S. interests: Soviet missions in the United States had been purged of the great majority of their professional intelligence agents, ceilings had been set to make impossible their full replacement by others, and the security threat to our own installations in the Soviet Union had been diminished by replacing Soviet citizen employees with cleared Americans.[27]

But most important, we demonstrated to the KGB that it placed its own interests in jeopardy if it chose to trump up charges against innocent Americans.

Gorbachev and the KGB

BUT WHAT DOES THIS have to do with Gorbachev and the unraveling of the Soviet Union?

More than may appear at first glance.

For now it was clear that Gorbachev was prepared to back KGB parochial interests even when they conflicted with his country's overall interests. In this instance, the KGB suffered the most in the end, but this was because the KGB itself miscalculated the American response, assuming that the Reagan administration would react as its predecessors had in comparable situations. While Khrushchev had been willing to overrule the KGB when Kennedy protested Barghoorn's arrest, Gorbachev tried to strong-arm Reagan, continuing to use Daniloff as a hostage even when he had received the most solemn personal assurances that Daniloff was not a U.S. agent.

Gorbachev's reaction was not calculated to build trust between the two leaders. Since he was normally skillful in establishing personal relations with foreign statesmen, it was obvious to me that he was in many respects a captive of the KGB, either inclined to accept its disinformation uncritically or afraid to take issue with it (its support was essential to his tenure as Soviet leader), or else he felt he had to defend even a mistaken policy. In any case—and his attitude could have combined elements of all three—he would not have been a free agent in matters affecting KGB interests.

I was not surprised. After all, Gorbachev had been close to the KGB throughout his career, and had been a protégé of its former head, Yuri Andropov. But his credulity in accepting misleading KGB reports and his blind trust in the loyalty of the KGB chief were destined to play a role in the breakup of his country and his own political downfall.

The Dialogue Goes Public

WHILE THE PUBLIC, and many officials, were mesmerized by the on-again, off-again arms control negotiations at Reykjavik and the dramatic arrests and expulsions, other things were happening that would have a much deeper long-term effect. As we have seen, political prisoners began to be released. Also, emigration began to rise and the Soviet information media cracked their door to foreign spokesmen.

Traditionally, foreigners had been allowed to appear in the Soviet media only when they could be counted on to support Soviet positions or on such formal occasions when debate of real issues would be out of place. The consequence was that the Soviet public never received from their own media a clear idea of other countries' policies. Everything in the Soviet press and on the radio and television had passed through a tendentious filter; journalists and editors were not merely censored but were given direct "guidance" from the Party's Propaganda Department as to what issues were to be mentioned and how they were to be treated.

A few weeks before the Geneva summit, Soviet authorities agreed to publish a lengthy interview of President Reagan by a team of Soviet journalists. The interview was reproduced accurately in the Soviet press, though it was accompanied by "comment" that attempted to refute some of Reagan's statements. No American president had been interviewed for the Soviet media since Khrushchev's son-in-law, Alexei Adzhubey, had interviewed John Kennedy for *Izvestiya* in 1961.

But appearances of Westerners, and Americans in particular, in the Soviet media were still rarities in 1986. Therefore, I was intrigued when John Wallach, the enterprising foreign editor of Hearst Publications, asked me to take part in a public debate with Soviet officials.

Wallach was speaking on behalf of the Chautauqua Institution of upstate New York and of other potential sponsors, including the Eisenhower Foundation in Washington. Chautauqua, which sponsors a regular series of meetings, lectures, and colloquia in idyllic surroundings every summer, had devoted a week to U.S.-Soviet relations during its 1985 season and had invited a number of Soviet officials to take part. Now there was an invitation from the Soviet "Friendship" Committee for a return engagement, during which American spokesmen would be invited to debate with Soviet spokesmen. The Soviet sponsors promised an audience of five to six thousand and full coverage in the Soviet media including television. As the senior Soviet specialist at the White House, I was invited to deliver the keynote speech and head the official delegation.

There was one potential catch. The Soviets wished to hold the meeting in the Latvian resort town of Jurmala, just outside Riga, but we did not recognize the Soviet annexation of Latvia. Would the presence of senior U.S. officials at a meeting in Latvia imply recognition that it was part of the Soviet Union? It seemed to me that it could not. After all, I had attended conferences in Britain, France, and Germany on U.S.-Soviet relations without any implication that those countries were part of either country we were discussing.

Not everyone agreed, but Mark Palmer of the State Department consulted the principal Latvian-American organization and convinced its leaders to support the project. The one condition was that some Latvian Americans be included in the American group. We explained this condition to the Soviet hosts, and after some hesitation they agreed.

We all understood that the conference was being organized with the approval of Soviet officials and perhaps even the KGB.[28] Their presumed motivation was to test whether they could control a process of limited opening to the West. They obviously thought they could.

Even so, I considered the proposal an opportunity to test glasnost, which had just become official Soviet policy. If the Soviet media ignored the meeting and all the participants were handpicked Communist activists, we would know that nothing had changed. But it we were given even limited access to the Soviet public and media, we would know that a process had started which might eventually escape the Soviet regime's control.

The meeting almost did not come off. Shortly before we were scheduled to leave for Jurmala, Daniloff was arrested. His wife made a direct appeal on CBS television for the American group to boycott the meeting while her husband was being held. It was difficult for me to understand what leverage this meeting (for which the Soviet risks were not insignificant) could have exercised on Gorbachev's decision regarding Daniloff. But none of us wished to leave the impression that we were ignoring his plight, when in fact we were working night and day to get him out. We suspended preparations for the meeting so long as Daniloff was held in a Soviet prison. When he was released in the custody of Ambassador Arthur Hartman just hours before the Americans were to leave Washington by chartered plane, the experiment in citizen-to-citizen communication was back on.

The Soviet hosts kept their word. A group of several thousand people assembled to hear and question the speakers. They were handpicked, but the speeches were fully covered by the local media and in more abbreviated form by Moscow's "central" media. Some three hundred Americans, including Latvian Americans, were issued visas to attend.

The American sponsors selected a panel of speakers who would expose the Soviet audience to the sort of frank criticism the Soviet media normally ignored. They saw no point in sending speakers who, out of a misplaced feeling of politeness, would avoid contentious issues. Many, such as Senator Charles Robb of Virginia, Ben Wattenberg, Helmut Sonnenfeldt, and Mark Palmer, were known to be highly critical of Soviet policy.[29]

Although I had prepared a rough draft of a speech in advance, I had not had a chance to put it into final form until our chartered plane left Dulles Airport. I was particularly concerned about the initial paragraphs, which had been translated into Latvian at the Voice of America, since I had not had the opportunity to rehearse my delivery.

Two Latvian-speaking members of our delegation came to my rescue: Ints Silins, a Foreign Service officer who had served at our consulate general in Leningrad, and Ojars Kalnins, a representative of the Latvian-American Association, huddled with me on the plane and drilled me in the unfamiliar sounds.

The *Newsweek* correspondent who covered the conference reported that I began my speech in "labored Latvian" and then switched to "fluent Russian." The adjective describing my Latvian was accurate, but even labored Latvian made a hit with the local audience. I reserved the real substance of my message for the portion in Russian. After protesting Daniloff's detention, I gave a blunt description of those Soviet practices that endangered the peace, especially the Soviet takeover of the Baltic states. I made it clear that the U.S. government had never recognized that illegal seizure and would continue to insist that only the peoples of Latvia, Lithuania, and Estonia had the right to determine whether they wished to be independent or part of a larger union.

Over dinner that evening, Russian officials told the American guests that I had offended our audience by talking about our nonrecognition policy. Latvians had never lived better, they argued, and were not about to turn their backs on a union that had improved their lives.

I had a different impression. When I returned from the meeting in Jurmala to our hotel in Riga, the young woman at the reception desk met me with a beaming smile and asked, "They say you started your speech in Latvian. Is that really true?" When I assured her it was, she shook my hand vigorously. "Thank you. Thank you. No foreigner has ever done that before. Thank you for remembering who we are."

Meanwhile, a few hotel employees had gathered around me. My speech had not yet been carried on television, though it would be that evening, but they had heard what I had said. "Is it really true that the United States does not consider Latvia part of the Soviet Union?" one asked. When I confirmed the report, he said, "We didn't know that," and another added, "Then Americans *do* understand. I never dreamed."

Six years later, when veterans of the meeting in Jurmala gathered in Chautauqua for a reunion, we were joined by Dainis Ivans, the leader of the Latvian National Front, which had led the Latvian drive for independence. In 1986, Ivans had been considered by the Soviet authorities to be too unreliable to be allowed into the meeting hall at Jurmala, but he and his friends had gathered outside to learn what was going on and to meet the visiting Americans.

"Chautauqua in Jurmala gave us our start," he explained. "Until then, it all seemed hopeless. But we learned that we were not alone."

A Prophet Comes Home

RELEASES OF POLITICAL PRISONERS also began to remove some contentious issues from U.S.-Soviet relations. Gorbachev's call to Andrei Sakharov in December 1986 to tell him that he could return to Moscow helped us repair feelings after the jolts of Reykjavik and the Daniloff arrest.

As early as 1968, Sakharov had written about the need for a foreign policy of peace and, internally, the protection of the right of free speech. In 1970, he warned the Soviet leaders that the economy would rapidly slip behind that of the West if steps were not taken to establish democracy. Annoyed by the attention he was receiving in the foreign press (which filtered back into the Soviet Union through radio broadcasts), Brezhnev had ordered him exiled to Gorky, a closed city where visits by foreigners were prohibited.

Sakharov spent nearly seven years in Gorky, much of the time under virtual house arrest, before he received Gorbachev's call. When he returned to Moscow, he was still treated as a pariah by Soviet officialdom. Only during the summer of 1987 did Soviet publications test the limits of glasnost by quoting him occasionally.

We considered Sakharov's exile an outrage, made worse by the KGB's inhumane treatment of Yelena Bonner, his courageous wife, whose only offenses were her unswerving loyalty to him and the tongue-lashings she gave her husband's tormentors. We pressed insistently for his release, on the ground that his exile violated the principles the Soviet leader had endorsed upon signing the Helsinki Final Act. I had personally delivered many of these démarches and considered Sakharov's release from exile a favorable omen for perestroika. I made a point of calling on him as soon as possible after I arrived in Moscow in the spring of 1987 as ambassador.

Lanky and awkward in his physical movements, Sakharov was obviously not in robust health, but his mind was still quick and supple. He spoke slowly, halting at times to find the most precise phrase to convey a nuance, but always displayed a mastery of the facts relating to the causes he espoused.

During our first meeting in 1987, he seemed surprisingly optimistic. He showed no rancor at the treatment he had received but concentrated his thoughts on the problems of others. He urged the United States not to relax its pressure on the Soviet authorities to release all remaining political prisoners, to establish the right of persons to choose their place of residence and travel freely, and to enshrine these principles in legislation so the policies could not be changed at the whim of officials.

He also expressed admiration for Gorbachev, who, he believed, had "studied and understood" Khrushchev's mistakes. He felt that Gorbachev wanted to transform society in the right way even though it was not yet politic for him to speak directly about his plans. Therefore, he advised us to keep the pressure on Gorbachev to do the right thing and also to support him as long as he moved in the right direction.

Without ever acknowledging them directly, Gorbachev over time responded positively to most of Sakharov's appeals on behalf of individuals. But Gorbachev ignored his advice on ethnic conflicts, which attracted more and more of Sakharov's attention, as well as his proposals for structuring a democratic Soviet Union.

Gorbachev's own fate might conceivably have been different if he had paid more attention to Sakharov's appeals for more rapid steps to bring the KGB under control and to replace Party rule with that by elected officials.

But Gorbachev did favor gradually opening the Soviet Union to the rest of the world. He understood that the country could not otherwise be modern, productive, and creative.

In January 1987, jammers were turned off the BBC frequencies and, over the next few months, off those of the Voice of America and the West German station Deutsche Welle.

When Margaret Thatcher visited Moscow in March 1987, her views—highly critical of Soviet human rights violations and the continued military involvement in Afghanistan—were given full exposure in the Soviet media. In April, just after I arrived in Moscow, both Secretary of State Shultz and House Speaker Jim Wright were interviewed for Moscow television.

Shultz was blunt about Afghanistan. (Wright failed to mention it on the mistaken assumption that this would be "impolite.") When the Soviet interviewer told Shultz that the Soviet troops had been invited by the Afghans, Shultz replied: "No. They don't want you there. They want you out!"

As spring turned into summer, talk shows on Moscow television began occasionally to present a Western European or American guest, for example, Volcker Rühe, the leader of Chancellor Kohl's party in the West German Bundestag, and other prominent German politicians. Soviet citizens now had direct access to Western views without having to outwit the jammers. One thing that became clear was that the West had some very substantial reasons to be concerned about Soviet policy.

By mid-1987 Gorbachev had forced a reluctant Party Central Committee to grant qualified approval for political reform. Reykjavik and the "Year of the Spy" had receded. Moscow looked forward to an autumn and winter of political change, and Washington was hoping for a summit meeting that would get rid of intermediate-range nuclear missiles. But Gorbachev's goals for internal reform were still vague. Despite the ethnic riots in Alma Ata in December 1986, the political elite in Moscow seemed oblivious to the restive national minorities.

In fact, the capital was preoccupied with a debate over whether to change the political system. Many Communist Party officials paid lip service to perestroika while resisting attempts to introduce concrete changes. Disputes over the direction of perestroika and the speed of change were soon to split the team Gorbachev had organized two years earlier.

V

A Fateful Rift

Talk that we are divided is nothing but empty words and prattle by foreign radio
stations. They want to set us against each other, Gorbachev versus
Ligachev, Yakovlev against Ligachev, and the like.
MIKHAIL GORBACHEV, October 21, 1987[1]

We have no factions, reformers, or conservatives, but some people would
very much like for there to be such factions.
YEGOR LIGACHEV, July 1, 1988[2]

My first open clash with Yakovlev goes back to the fall of 1987.
YEGOR LIGACHEV, 1991[3]

B y the summer of 1987, Gorbachev had won Central Committee
approval of a general outline for political change, which was
supposed to create conditions for reforming the economy. Many details
were unclear, but the new slogan of "democratization" seemed to be more
than the eyewash of the past. The idea of holding real elections with
a choice of candidates and a secret ballot, and of opening up the political process to debate, would mean change if it ever came to fruition.

When I went to Washington in July for my first consultations after
becoming ambassador, I reported that Gorbachev was meeting strong
resistance but seemed to come out on top each time. I saw no evidence
that his leadership position was in question, but I predicted that he
would have difficulty in implementing perestroika. Nevertheless, I
thought he would win the formal battles over policy, would start putting
a legal framework for reform into place, and would gradually weed out
the most recalcitrant of the old officials. But the prospects were not

bright that his reforms would improve the economy. The public was impatient, and I foresaw serious troubles ahead in three to four years.

From "Right" to "Left"

YEGOR LIGACHEV, Gorbachev's number two in the Communist Party, would soon be considered the nemesis of reform by Soviet intellectuals pushing for rapid change. Some critics accused him of neo-Stalinism.

This was not right. Ligachev was never a Stalinist in the sense that he wished to return to the days of terror. His own family had suffered from the purges. His father-in-law, a general on Mikhail Tukhachevsky's staff, had been summarily executed by the predecessor of the KGB in 1937, and in his early career he carried the stigma of being married to the daughter of a "repressed person."

Ligachev was not a Stalinist, and he was even a reformer within limits. He wished to bring more efficiency to the economy and to rid the Party of the corruption that had grown like a cancer in Brezhnev's day. He wanted a more effective propaganda apparatus to support those changes he approved.

Ligachev, however, believed that effective reform could be carried out only by the Communist Party. He was in favor of steps that would make the Party more efficient and honest but was opposed to anything that would weaken the Party's grip on society or lower its prestige. He insisted that the media stay within the confines of Party policy and avoid exposing embarrassing episodes from the past.

He was probably the only member of the Politburo in 1987 who still believed that policy, domestic and foreign, should be based on Karl Marx's "class struggle" concept.

He had a forceful personality and always argued his point of view in private Party meetings with vigor. Though he was increasingly at odds with Gorbachev from 1987 on, Gorbachev took his arguments seriously. After all, they represented a point of view that had been instilled in Gorbachev throughout his career.

Ligachev had infrequent contact with foreigners. However, in the spring of 1987 he was chairman of the Foreign Affairs Committee in the rubber-stamp Soviet parliament of that day and in that capacity received a U.S. delegation led by Speaker Jim Wright of the House of

Representatives. I had just come to Moscow as ambassador, and I went with our congressmen to the meeting.

It took place in a conference room in one of the buildings on Moscow's Staraya Square, where the staff of the Party Central Committee worked. The hall was obviously designed for note taking, since every seat was equipped with a desk—almost like a schoolroom.

Ligachev's presentation of the goals of perestroika was indistinguishable from Gorbachev's at that time. He denied that there was any serious difference of opinion in the upper reaches of the Party and stressed that perestroika was an objective necessity, not dependent on any one individual. Party officials who could not adapt to the change would be replaced, he insisted.

It was clear, however, that for Ligachev management reform *within the traditional "socialist" system* was the heart of perestroika. The concrete changes he mentioned, such as enterprise "self-financing," more independence for plant management, and increased investment in machine building sounded very much like some of the abortive campaigns of the past.

He spoke of the necessity of glasnost and democratization but observed that it was a mistake to think that democracy was just beginning to take root in the Soviet Union. The October Revolution had created genuine social and economic rights and remained the basis of Soviet "democracy." As far as ethnic groups were concerned, he considered the Soviet system the "best in history in this respect" since more than a hundred nationalities lived in peace and harmony. He did concede that there had occasionally been problems, such as the riots in Alma Ata the previous December, but these were caused not by a faulty nationality policy but by such social ills as corruption, cronyism, and "speculation."

Such problems could be corrected, he argued, by tighter Party control. He cited the "success" of the antialcohol campaign as an example of what could be done. Alcohol consumption, he said, had dropped by more than half in three years, and absenteeism from work was also down by half. Mortality statistics, he claimed, showed that 354,000 fewer people had died in 1986 than in 1985.[4]

Ligachev's remarks made clear that perestroika as he defined it would be led by a purified and strengthened Communist Party and would be carried out without any significant alteration in the official ideology. Essentially, his was the "Andropov program," without the political reforms Gorbachev had begun to outline. Though he would deny it to outsiders at that time, he had opposed the political steps Gorbachev had proposed in January 1987, and the rift between the two men widened as Gorbachev espoused ever more radical proposals that year.

By far the most active of Gorbachev's lieutenants in 1987 was the head of the Moscow Party organization, Boris Nikolayevich Yeltsin. He accepted the goals of political reform with enthusiasm and showed a flair for public relations that contrasted with the remote, regal style of the typical high-level Communist Party official. Traveling, at least occasionally, by subway, he made a habit of turning up unannounced in stores or factories. When he arrived, he would sometimes pitch in and help the workers load or unload a truck.

However, heaven help the hapless store manager if Yeltsin found bare shelves in the shop and a supply of goods in the back room. It was well known that personnel in state-operated stores would siphon goods onto the black market, where they could obtain higher prices than those fixed for regular sales. A manager could be fired on the spot if Yeltsin caught him or her keeping hoarded goods out of sight.

Word spread swiftly in Moscow about the new fellow running the city Party organization. Unlike any of his predecessors, he seemed "one of us"—unpretentious, not too proud to ride public transport and pitch in with manual labor, knowledgeable about common rip-offs and determined to put a stop to them. He quickly became a legend and to Muscovites was the most tangible proof that perestroika was not a sham.

Yeltsin's popularity received little support from the media, however. He was rarely mentioned, except when his appearance at formal events required it. Since the media were becoming more open in 1986 and 1987, this seemed strange. Why was Yeltsin's highly newsworthy behavior largely ignored?

Only the naïve would have asked such a question, of course, and if it had been asked, the average Soviet citizen would have answered without hesitation, "Because *they* don't want us to know about him."

They did not require definition. *They* were the rulers, the Party apparat. All of life was a struggle between *us* and *them*.

Insiders, however, could be more specific. Orders to keep Yeltsin's "antics" out of the media came from the top, from Mikhail Gorbachev himself.

Within a few months of Yeltsin's appointment as Moscow Party chief, *Pravda* editor Viktor Afanasiev told colleagues he had instructions from Gorbachev personally to downplay coverage of Yeltsin. The paper was not to give Yeltsin any incentive to continue his "pandering to populist sentiments."

Then the propaganda section of the Central Committee, which supervised the media, was given the task. Mikhail Poltoranin, a Yeltsin ally who was editor of *Moskovskaya Pravda,* the newspaper sponsored by Yeltsin's own organization, told me later that he had been called in repeatedly and scolded for giving Yeltsin too much attention.[5] The pressure became so great that, in August 1987 Poltoranin's *Moskovskaya Pravda* published the text of a long report Yeltsin delivered to the city Party organization without identifying Yeltsin as the speaker.

In 1986 and 1987 Soviet citizens, with good reason, had little trust in their own media. The media boycott may actually have helped Yeltsin's image with the public, since accounts of his activities spread by word of mouth and thereby took on a heroic, bigger-than-life quality. If it had appeared that the official media were promoting him, the public might have been more skeptical.

My first opportunity to speak to Yeltsin directly occurred in August 1987, when senators Daniel Patrick Moynihan, Terry Sanford, and Paul Sarbanes came to town. Yeltsin was one of the few Politburo members still in Moscow during that traditional vacation month and was delegated to be the senior official to receive the group. Throughout the two-hour meeting his unorthodox comments on a variety of topics riveted our attention.

Without direct prodding and without reference to notes, he listed for the senators nine "negative developments" that required immediate correction. More than half were political: restrictions on freedom of expression, a lack of democracy, a "gap" between the Party and the public, loss of collegial habits (i.e., team spirit) in political leadership, and rigidity in foreign policy. The others were economic: barriers to new technology, concentration on heavy industry rather than consumer goods, lack of incentives, and tolerance of mediocrity.

While his attention was predominantly on domestic affairs, he showed that he was familiar with the principal issues in the ongoing arms control negotiations with the United States. He was eager to move on and conclude the agreements under negotiation and commented that "Such agreements are necessary if perestroika is to be possible."

It struck me at the time that Ligachev would never have referred to a rift between the Party and the people, as Yeltsin had done, and Gorbachev would not have talked about the lack of collegial habits. Though all of Yeltsin's comments were in the context of making socialism work within a one-party system, of returning to "true Leninism," as he put it, he stressed elements that the others ignored or—at least in public and to foreigners—would have denied.

Gorbachev, for example, doubtless agreed that arms control agreements with the United States were necessary for perestroika, but at that point he would not have been so candid. His line was that both countries needed and could benefit from arms reduction but that the Soviet Union was perfectly capable of implementing perestroika on its own if the United States did not wish to cooperate.

The Team Splits

IN LATE SEPTEMBER 1987, diplomatic missions in Moscow, including ours, received a notice that ambassadors were invited to meet with the first secretary of the Moscow Party Organization in the Political Education House run by the City Party Committee. A modern building near Moscow's inner Boulevard Ring, it had been off limits to foreign diplomats—at least those from non-Communist countries—since it was opened. The opportunity to take a look at the place where the Party trained its faithful and to talk to Yeltsin once again was irresistible, and I accepted.

Although the occasion was formally meant to explain plans for future development of the city to a group responsible for resident embassies, Yeltsin chose to discuss the course of the country as a whole. He pointed out that it was going through a "critical phase of perestroika" that involved a transition from proposals to practical measures. He felt that pressures in society were building and the people were impatient for results. If economic managers and political leaders were unable to cope with the requirements of perestroika, they must be replaced, he noted, and he went on to describe the extensive changes he had already made in the Moscow Party Organization.

During chats in the corridor following the session, I discovered that some of my diplomatic colleagues felt that Yeltsin's use of terms like "critical phase" showed that he was given to exaggeration. In their view, the conditions were not sufficiently precarious to justify such language.

It seemed to me, however, that there was more than hyperbole here. After all, Gorbachev was telling the public that perestroika was very much on track, with the worst behind and positive results beginning to show. To Yeltsin, however, the crisis was still ahead since they were only then beginning to translate policy into reality. Yeltsin's analysis seemed to me the more accurate one.

What none of us in the hall—aside from Yeltsin himself—knew was that nearly a month earlier Yeltsin had written a personal letter to Gorbachev, then on a Black Sea vacation. According to the text he published subsequently in his memoirs, Yeltsin excoriated Ligachev's style of work in general and interference in Moscow Party affairs in particular. He also referred to the opposition of other, unnamed, Politburo members to real change, and predicted that all of this would lead back to a condition very much like the Brezhnevian "stagnation" they had tried to cure. He then concluded with a request to be relieved of his responsibilities as a candidate member of the Politburo and first secretary of the Moscow Party Committee.[6]

What happened next is a matter of dispute. Gorbachev claimed subsequently that Yeltsin had agreed to discuss the matter with him after the November 7 celebration of the seventieth anniversary of the Bolshevik Revolution. Yeltsin wrote in his memoirs, however, that there had been no agreement and that Gorbachev had simply told him that he would discuss the matter with him "later."

In any event, when "later" stretched out to more than a month and a plenary session of the Central Committee was convened in late October, Yeltsin decided without further consultation with Gorbachev to lay the matter before the Central Committee. Just before Gorbachev was to close the meeting, Yeltsin repeated to the gathering the charge that the Party Secretariat had not changed its style of work in accord with the latest decisions and for that reason people were beginning to lose faith in perestroika. He then repeated his request that he be relieved of his duties as a Politburo candidate member.

Gorbachev reacted with extreme hostility to this intervention, summarized Yeltsin's criticism in distorted form, accused him of unbridled ambition, and called for a discussion. Taking their cue from the boss,[7] delegate after delegate arose to castigate Yeltsin. Of twenty-seven who spoke, only one, Georgy Arbatov, head of the Institute for the Study of the USA and Canada, had even a mild word for Yeltsin.[8]

Even though Yeltsin took the floor again to reiterate his support for perestroika, to deny wishing to split the Central Committee, and to apologize for bringing the matter up at an inopportune time, Gorbachev pressed the campaign against him, persistently distorting what Yeltsin had said.

For example, when Yeltsin remarked that "certain members of the Politburo" had been insincere in praising Gorbachev and perestroika, Gorbachev interrupted him with the accusation that he was politically illiterate to accuse the entire Politburo of fostering a "cult of personality" (the code expression for Stalinism). Actually, Yeltsin had made no accusation against the Politburo as a whole. What he was saying was that *some* members of the Politburo had praised Gorbachev to his face and tried to scuttle his policies behind his back.

Gorbachev continued his tirade, not allowing Yeltsin to correct the misrepresentations, and when there were shouts from the floor that Yeltsin was thinking only of his own ambition, Gorbachev picked up the theme and said:

> I think so too. And the members of the Central Committee understand you. It's not enough for your ego that only Moscow revolves around your person. Do you think the Central Committee should also be preoccupied with you? That's what you wanted, isn't it? . . .
>
> What extreme egotism it must take to put personal ambitions above the Party's interests, above our common cause!

The session ended with a resolution that declared Yeltsin's intervention "politically faulty" and instructed the Politburo and the Moscow Party Committee to take action on his resignation in light of what had happened at the plenum.

This clash was kept out of the media, lest it mar the celebratory atmosphere of the November 7 anniversary of the Bolshevik Revolution.

When Secretary of State Shultz met with Gorbachev the day after the plenum to discuss plans for Gorbachev's trip to the United States, Gorbachev was uncharacteristically subdued, and the meeting ended with no agreement for the summit. Something seemed to have happened, and Shultz, a very keen judge of people, commented to me that Gorbachev had always reminded him of a boxer who had never been floored, cocky and self-assured. But that day it was different. That day Gorbachev seemed to be a man who knew what it was to hit the canvas.

Shevardnadze quickly got the plans for the summit back on track by coming to Washington and settling the issues Gorbachev had left open when he had met with Shultz in Moscow. Meanwhile, rumors of the clash in the Central Committee began to make the rounds. Within a few days the foreign press had the gist of the story, which then was fed back into the Soviet Union by foreign radio stations.

The Moscow public was aghast. Could it be true that Yeltsin was to be dumped? If so, what would this imply for Gorbachev's commitment to perestroika? Yeltsin appeared with the other leaders for the formal anniversary events but did not engage in small talk with them as was normal.

At the Kremlin reception for the diplomatic corps, where members of the Party Politburo and Secretariat gathered at one end of the hall, isolated from their guests, I studied the scene intently for clues, there being no possibility that year of speaking informally to the "leadership." Yeltsin stood somewhat apart from his Politburo colleagues, bore a rather sheepish smile, and periodically shifted his stance from one foot to the other, rather like a schoolboy who had been scolded by the teacher. When he spotted me, he waved demonstratively and flashed a boyish smile but made no attempt to come close enough to talk. I fully understood. If his troubles were what the rumors suggested, the last thing he needed was to have a private conversation with the American ambassador.

Two days later the rumor spread that Yeltsin was seriously ill—some said he had suffered a heart attack—but glasnost had not progressed to the point that the media were permitted to report what had happened. Finally, on November 13, *Pravda* confirmed officially that Yeltsin had been removed as head of the Moscow Party Committee. The transcript of the meeting was published so that all could read Gorbachev's accusations along with Yeltsin's almost incoherent but self-incriminating reply.

Subsequently, Yeltsin claimed that he had been summoned from the hospital by Gorbachev, who insisted that he attend the meeting. His doctors, who earlier had forbidden him to get out of bed, pumped him full of painkillers and shipped him off to the meeting on Gorbachev's orders. In this condition, he was hardly conscious of what he was saying.[9]

According to Yeltsin, Gorbachev told him flatly that he would never be allowed to play an active role in politics again. Gorbachev did not push him all the way into political oblivion, however. Though there were no demonstrations or protest marches, much of the public, particularly in Moscow, identified reform with Yeltsin. When he was removed from the leadership, newspapers were inundated with letters of protest. No hint of this was conveyed to the public, but it was duly reported to Gorbachev. If Yeltsin was made a martyr, it would be difficult to convince the public that Gorbachev meant what he said about perestroika. Therefore, a respectable but powerless position was found for him.

We were at dinner in the home studio of a popular Georgian artist, Zurab Tsereteli, when Yeltsin's appointment was announced. Word had gotten out that an announcement would be made, and the dinner guests gathered around the television set with the same anticipation Americans might feel if they left a sumptuous table to view the final inning of the seventh World Series game.

When the newscaster read the official statement that Boris Yeltsin had been appointed first deputy chairman of the State Committee on Construction, with the personal rank of minister, the guests looked at one another silently, their faces reflecting a strange mixture of relief and disappointment: relief that Yeltsin had been given *something* but disappointment that it was not something more substantial. After a pause, one grimaced and said, "Rank of minister. Could be worse, I guess."

Yes, it could have been worse. But the unvoiced question in the minds of my fellow guests that evening, and of many Soviet citizens throughout the country, was why Yeltsin had been removed from the top political leadership. What was wrong with what he was doing if the leadership was intent on political reform as it claimed?

The official transcript of the clash at the October plenum was not published for nearly a year and a half.[10] Purported transcripts or summaries circulated in manuscript, but it was impossible for a person not present at the meeting to judge their authenticity. The KGB was well known for fabricating evidence to "prove" a particular point of view.

Nevertheless, it was difficult to believe that Yeltsin's speech could have been so egregious as to justify Gorbachev's reaction. After all, the basic argument was over the *speed* of perestroika and to what degree the Party Secretariat should try to manage cities and provinces directly. Though Yeltsin might have pressed to move more rapidly than Gorbachev thought wise and might have lacked tact in dealing with colleagues, he had already become the preeminent symbol of perestroika and the principal public guarantee that it was not simply another "campaign" that would flare for a few months and then be forgotten. In disgracing Yeltsin, Gorbachev damaged the program he espoused.

In their attempts to put a good face on Yeltsin's fall, Gorbachev's associates spread the story that Yeltsin had broken an agreement with Gorbachev to postpone discussion of his situation until after the November 7 celebration and had insulted him to the degree that Gorbachev had had to remove him in order to demonstrate who was in charge. Some asserted that Gorbachev's decisive action had *strengthened,* not weakened, his political standing.

Most of the purported transcripts of Yeltsin's speech to the Central Committee that circulated at that time contained a paragraph that criticized Raisa Gorbacheva for meddling in Moscow Party affairs. If Yeltsin had made such remarks at the plenum, many would have considered Gorbachev's rage comprehensible. He would have considered criticism of his wife at a formal Party gathering as totally out of place.

The published transcript, however, does not contain the paragraph on Raisa, and several participants in the plenum have assured me that it was not in Yeltsin's presentation. The fact seems to be that Yeltsin directed his reproaches at neither Gorbachev nor his wife. Nothing in the published record provides an explanation for the vehemence with which Gorbachev attacked Yeltsin or for Gorbachev's malicious misrepresentations of Yeltsin's position.

If Gorbachev had wished to save Yeltsin, he could easily have done so, even though Yeltsin was not popular with the conservative apparatchiks who made up the majority of the Central Committee. Gorbachev could have said something like "Comrade Yeltsin has touched on a number of topics that we should think about. I don't agree with everything he says, particularly about personalities, but he is certainly right when he says we must move from words to deeds. I do not believe we should accept his resignation without further discussion and would propose that any decision on the matter be postponed until our next session."

If Gorbachev had chosen to follow such an approach, there is no reason to doubt that the Central Committee would have acquiesced. Yeltsin would have continued to be a problem, but a manageable one, and Yeltsin's energy could have provided a useful counterpoint to the laggard conservatives.

October 1987 marks the first of Gorbachev's major political blunders. He made it because envy blinded his judgment. He viewed charismatic associates as potential competitors rather than valuable allies. That same emotion would lead him not only to continue mismanaging his relations with Yeltsin but to pick weak—and ultimately disloyal—associates simply because he felt they could not compete with him.

The "Right" Makes a Lunge

HAVING OUTMANEUVERED YELTSIN (with some cooperation on Yeltsin's part), those bent on stopping major political reforms saw their opportunity to gain the upper hand. In March 1988, both Gorbachev and Alexander Yakovlev had plans for foreign travel, Gorbachev to Yugoslavia and Yakovlev to Mongolia. Ligachev was temporarily in charge of the Party Secretariat, which still had the responsibility for overseeing the press. Suddenly the daily newspaper *Sovetskaya Rossiya,* notorious for its close ties to "conservative" elements in the Party, published an article that chilled the blood of reformers.[11]

Ostensibly a "letter" from a Leningrad teacher, Nina Andreyeva, it covered an entire newspaper page and was filled with the sort of accusations and innuendo typical of the worst periods of Stalinism. In language reminiscent of that employed by Stalin's ideological henchman Andrei Zhdanov (also from Leningrad), Andreyeva attacked criticism of the past as disloyal, decried the tendency to debate "bourgeois" values such as the multiparty system and religious freedom, and staunchly defended a "class viewpoint" as the only acceptable anchor for public policy. She defended Stalin's record and argued that those gathered under the anti-Stalinist slogan were descendents of the classes overthrown by the Revolution. She peppered her "letter" with anti-Semitic code phrases taken directly out of Zhdanov's speeches during the notorious ideological crackdown in 1948.[12]

Reports indicated that the "letter" had been distilled from a much longer diatribe submitted by Andreyeva and rewritten on instructions from above by the *Sovetskaya Rossiya* staff.[13] Some rumors held that it had been published on Ligachev's direct instructions. Not only was he in charge of the Party Secretariat at the time, he had close ties to the editor of *Sovetskaya Rossiya* and praised the article in a meeting with editors when it appeared.

Ligachev, however, flatly denied that he had had anything to do with its publication, though he conceded that he had endorsed some of the ideas in it after it had been published.[14] What appealed to him particularly in the letter were its strictures on articles that put Soviet history in a bad light. He had been arguing for more controls on "muckraking" publications such as *Ogonyok* and *Moscow News,* which were making a specialty of exposing Stalin's crimes, publicizing environmental disasters, and calling attention to unjustified Party privileges.

As soon as the "letter" was published, Party organizations in a number of cities and provinces ordered that it be "studied." The Leningrad Party leadership showed particular zeal in this respect.

These reactions showed all the usual signs of coordination, and many read them as a signal to the Party faithful that they would be protected if they wished to express conservative views during the run-up to the Party conference scheduled for the summer.

Gorbachev, Yakovlev, and the reformers in general believed that the article was intended as the opening shot in a campaign to put political reform back into its pre-1987 bottle. As Gorbachev reminisced to me in a private conversation in 1992, he did not have the option of moving faster in 1988 and 1989. "They opposed me every step of the way," he remarked. "I managed to get formal approval for *partial* reforms in 1987. Then what happened? I turned my back, and they hit me with Nina Andreyeva!"[15]

Whoever was behind it, the Nina Andreyeva ploy backfired. As soon as Gorbachev returned from Yugoslavia, he insisted that the Politburo discuss the article on two successive days. According to a summary record of these meetings that Gorbachev published in 1993, he led off the meeting by asserting that "the article should be seen as an anti-perestroika platform" and also expressed doubt that Nina Andreyeva could have written it without help.[16] What bothered him, he said, was not that it had appeared but that it had been recommended by Party officials as authoritative.

The published transcript indicates that only Yakovlev and Shevardnadze flatly condemned the Nina Andreyeva article. Gromyko even tried to defend it by saying that it was in reaction to "slanders" that had appeared in the media. All those who spoke, however, agreed that the Politburo must, above all, act in unity, and for the sake of unity agreed that a reasoned refutation of the article would be issued for publication in the Party press. To judge from the minutes of the meeting, Ligachev either was absent or did not speak.

On April 5, *Pravda* carried out the Politburo decision by publishing an unsigned article (actually written by Yakovlev) rejecting the premises of the Andreyeva letter. A few days later *Sovetskaya Rossiya* was forced to issue an apology for running the letter to begin with.

Gorbachev had reasserted his dominance, but observers could not be certain whether he could control the upcoming Party conference. There had not been a Party conference since Stalin had called one in 1941. Since Stalin's death, Party congresses had been held every five years, and though the Party rules allowed the Central Committee to convene a conference whenever it wished, it was not clear how much authority such a conference would have.

Gorbachev had two major reasons for calling a conference: to obtain a more authoritative resolution in favor of his version of perestroika than the existing Central Committee would approve and to alter the membership of the Central Committee itself. He had first broached the idea of a Party conference at the Central Committee meeting in January 1987, but the proposal had not been approved until the June plenum, indicating that even the idea of holding the conference met opposition.

Once perestroika took a political turn, debates within the Central Committee were heated and Gorbachev rarely obtained all he wanted. If perestroika was to attain its goal of democratization, Gorbachev had either to obtain a more compliant Central Committee or to devise some means of bypassing the Party structure altogether. The Nineteenth Party Conference was a stab at the first.

As far as changing the membership of the Central Committee, Gorbachev lost an initial battle when it was decided that only a Party congress could elect new people to the Central Committee. The conference could make limited changes by promoting candidate members to full membership, but it could not bring new members in from the outside.

The program was something else again. Following the Andreyeva challenge, Ligachev was quietly shifted from responsibility for ideology and Alexander Yakovlev was given the job. This made it possible to complete the substantive proposals under his supervision. They were issued in May 1988 as "theses" for discussion at the conference.

I was in Helsinki to brief President Reagan for his upcoming Moscow summit when the theses were published. I received the Russian text by fax from Moscow and went to my hotel room to read it, relieved that it was unclassified and could be taken out of the restricted area. I assumed that a casual scan would suffice for my briefing, since I did not expect to be surprised by its contents. They would likely enumerate the reforms that had already been discussed at Central Committee meetings and in Gorbachev's speeches.

But as I read and discovered one new element after another, my excitement grew. Never before had I seen in an official Communist Party document such an extensive section on protecting the rights of citizens or such principles as the separation of powers, judicial independence, and presumption of a defendant's innocence until proven guilty.

Some of the "theses" seemed paraphrased from the U.S. Constitution. There was little hint of the *Communist Manifesto* or even of *Das Kapital,* despite the use of the word "socialism." What had passed for "socialism" in Soviet parlance had dropped from sight. What the "theses" described was something closer to European social democracy.

The next morning a small group assembled with President Reagan in a room with an acoustic seal that had been assembled by security specialists in the hotel where we were staying to permit conversations that could not be overheard. It was my job to review the current political scene in Moscow, and I started with the "theses" for the Party conference. After summarizing them, I told the president that if they turned out to be real, the Soviet Union could never again be what it had been in the past. Although the "theses" stopped short of democracy as we would define it, they contained the seeds of the liberation of the country. If freedom of speech, press, and assembly were really guaranteed, if multiple-choice elections and secret ballots were allowed, if principles of judicial independence were legally enacted, then I had no doubt that the Communist Party monopoly on political power would soon end.

Of course, setting these goals did not ensure that they would be met soon—or at all. But stating the goals officially was an important step toward establishing democratic procedures. The Communist bureaucracy would resist real change, but an informed public armed with a vote could be expected to exert powerful pressure to bring it about.

What I did not know at the time was that Gorbachev had attempted to go even further. He had pressed for an endorsement of political pluralism and for amending the Constitution to permit a multiparty system, but this had been rejected by the Politburo. Only Yakovlev, Shevardnadze, and Vitaly Vorotnikov voted with Gorbachev, according to Arkady Volsky, who attended the meeting as an observer.[17] Gorbachev had to wait two more years before the Communist Party would agree to end its legal monopoly on political power.

Nevertheless, even in the truncated form approved by the Politburo, the "theses" provided unmistakable evidence that Gorbachev had implicitly accepted our four-part agenda. The struggle to provide protection for human rights and to open up and democratize the country had become avowed components of perestroika.

Kissing Babies on Red Square

RONALD REAGAN'S TRIP to Moscow in 1988 was the first by a U.S. president since Nixon had met with Brezhnev in 1974. Reagan made a much deeper impression on the Soviet public than Nixon had. Here, after all, was the man who just five years back had called the Soviet Union an evil empire. But now he came with the message that it was on the right track and should keep going the way it had started.

Gorbachev needed Reagan's endorsement and Reagan's visit to prove that his foreign policy was bearing fruit. A successful summit would give him momentum for the Party conference, which, he hoped, would endorse a more radical course of reform than he had managed to wring out of his associates up to then.

The U.S. Senate ratified the INF treaty just as Reagan arrived in Moscow and thus permitted a ceremonial exchange of instruments of ratification. This provided welcome proof that U.S.-Soviet relations were now moving in a constructive direction and that eliminating weapons would increase, not undermine, Soviet security. Vadim Zagladin would no longer have to worry about a Pershing striking before he could get to shelter.

Implicitly, Reagan exacted a price for his endorsement: he came determined to push human rights and democratization to the forefront of the agenda. Even before he had a substantive meeting with Gorbachev, he met at Spaso House with a group of refuseniks and political dissidents, and in subsequent speeches he stressed the need to build democratic institutions and protect the rights of individuals.

At the Writer's Club, where he had lunch with intellectuals from many fields, he pointed out that Solzhenitsyn's works had still not been published. As we were leaving the club, Sergei Zalygin, the editor of *Novy mir,* pulled me aside and said, "Tell the president we agree with him. It's a scandal that we haven't published *The Gulag Archipelago* yet. But we will soon. I'll see to that." And so he did. Before the end of the year, Solzhenitsyn's masterpiece was appearing in installments in a journal with a circulation of more than a million.

At Moscow University, Reagan electrified the students with a paean to freedom. The key to progress, he told them, "is freedom—freedom of thought, freedom of information, freedom of communication." In order to relate the concept of political and economic freedom to the Russian tradition, he quoted the Russian philosopher Mikhail Lomonosov, a contemporary of Voltaire and Benjamin Franklin for whom Moscow University was named, as stating: "Explorers of the modern era are the entrepreneurs, men with vision, with the courage to take risks and faith enough to brave the unknown." As he concluded his address, he once again outlined his dream of a world without barriers that obstruct travel and the interchange of ideas, much as he had in Washington in the summer of 1984, when he had called for broadened U.S.-Soviet cultural contact.[18] His young listeners were visibly stirred by his message; their standing ovation continued for minutes.

During one of the breaks in his meetings with Gorbachev, the two strolled on Red Square. The crowd was sparse, since KGB security agents had kept most tourists at a distance, but Reagan greeted a couple with a baby and took it in his arms: a typical act by a politician when cameras are around, but in this case it seemed to symbolize much more. By going through a political campaign ritual in the symbolic center of the Soviet Union, the American president was demonstrating that there are human qualities that unite us. He was no longer dealing with a hostile adversary but with human beings struggling, as we were, to find the way to a peaceful and more prosperous life.

As Reagan's visit was drawing to a close, Rebecca and I looked in on a dinner party in California industrialist Armand Hammer's Moscow apartment. The mood was festive, among the Soviet guests in particular. Our friend the poet Andrei Voznesensky, whom I had introduced to Reagan in Washington in 1985, was effusive. "Reagan's visit is one of the greatest events in all of Russian history," he stated. I told him that the president would be flattered by his hyperbole, but he persisted. "I'm not exaggerating," he protested, going on to say that Reagan's words and gestures had emboldened reformers throughout the country. Russian intellectuals had habitually doubted the capacity of their own country to absorb democracy, but Ronald Reagan, a man who could not be accused of closing his eyes to Soviet reality, had faith in them. That would encourage Soviet citizens to put an end to their traditional political passivity and start taking their future into their own hands.

Andrei's words, spoken under the influence of euphoria, were indeed hyperbole. No single visit of a foreign statesman could have such a profound impact on a nation's self-confidence as to alter the course of its history. At the same time, there was something to what he said. Reagan's encouragement of democracy in the Soviet Union came at a critical time, and his earlier no-nonsense condemnation of communism gave his words of encouragement a credibility that less outspoken public figures could not command.

His impact was also a lasting one. In December 1989, a year after Reagan left office and eighteen months after his visit to Moscow, a poll of Soviet citizens found that 16.5 percent picked him as the man of the year. Only Gorbachev and Sakharov drew more votes; Reagan ran ahead not only of George Bush, who was president that year, but even of Boris Yeltsin, who had achieved a spectacular electoral victory in March.[19]

Reagan's 1988 visit to Moscow, however, had its most immediate effect on Soviet politics by strengthening Gorbachev's hand as he made the final preparations for the crucial Nineteenth All-Union Conference of the Communist Party of the Soviet Union.

The Party Conference

WHEN THE PARTY CONFERENCE OPENED, Gorbachev made a surprise proposal: that the same person occupy the senior Party position and the senior government position at each level of government, from the local district to the country as a whole. This idea seemed to run counter to the overall aim of dividing the Party's responsibilities from those of the government and the elected assemblies. Furthermore, it could hardly end the practice by which Party officials directly interfered in economic management.

For these reasons, many reformers opposed it. Some felt that the proposal was simply self-serving. If approved, it would permit Gorbachev to keep his position as general secretary of the Party even as he became chief of state as the elected head of parliament.

I could understand the objection. If reforms were to mean anything, the Communist Party would have to be forced to relinquish its stranglehold on the country. Real elections might in time provide the engine for such a change, but if the top Party and government positions were occupied *ex officio* by the same individual, the Party would obviously stay in power. In principle, therefore, it was a proposal that could block the movement to real democracy.

Gorbachev, however, was forced to deal with the Communist Party as it was. It would have been naïve to expect local and provincial Party officials to cooperate in a transfer of power to elected assemblies if they were left out of the picture.

Gorbachev's proposal was a blandishment to encourage the entrenched *apparat* to think they could have it both ways: the new soviets would operate independently of direct Party tutelage, but the Party chiefs could hold two offices and keep their personal position as "number one" in their province, city, or precinct.

But if this happened, what would become of reform, which would be meaningless unless a real shift of power occurred? This was a question Gorbachev answered only indirectly, but attentive listeners noticed that his proposal might have a catch in it. True, it would allow a Party chief to run for chairman of the corresponding assembly (soviet) and to hold both jobs if he[20] won. But if the Party chieftain could not secure election as soviet chairman, the Party would have to "draw the appropriate conclusions" about his suitability to head the Party organization. In other words, elected chairmen might replace those first secretaries of the Party who could not manage to get elected in their own right.

This prospect probably occurred to a few first secretaries when the proposal was made, but most Party officials dismissed the proposal as a bit of harmless posturing by the general secretary and felt much easier about the upcoming elections. They had always turned out a 99.73 percent "vote" in their districts and were not likely to have a problem garnering only 50 percent plus one!

I thought at the time that Gorbachev had either abandoned his plans for political reform or was setting the Party *apparat* up for one of the most breathtaking scams in political history. The proof would come with the elections themselves. Would they be fair and open enough to defeat prominent Party officials? And would the Party replace losers with people who won election on their own? If the answers to both turned out to be "yes," we would know that a new day was indeed dawning.

Delegates from the reform wing of the Party were most critical of this proposal. Yeltsin expressed doubts and proposed that it be made the subject of a nationwide referendum. But in the end Gorbachev prevailed.

While the most contentious issue at the Party conference was the question of "combining posts," the most dramatic moment occurred when Yeltsin and Ligachev confronted each other from the platform. When they had clashed in the Central Committee nine months earlier, the media had been instructed to ignore the episode. This time the speeches were carried on nationwide television—not live, to be sure, and with a subtle bias against Yeltsin—but on the evening of the day they were delivered.[21] Full texts appeared the next day in *Pravda* and *Izvestiya*.

The telecast of the speeches gave no hint that Yeltsin's intervention had not been planned. By Yeltsin's own account, however, he was permitted to speak only after he, in effect, stormed the podium. He had not been included in the roster of speakers, but on the final day of the conference, just before the midday break, he left his assigned seat in the balcony, came down onto the main floor, and strode down the center aisle, waving his delegate credentials as he demanded the floor. Gorbachev sent an emissary to persuade him to go to a room behind the podium or back to his regular seat to await a decision, but Yeltsin refused, fearing a trick. He sat ostentatiously in the front row until Gorbachev announced that his name had been added to the list of speakers.[22]

When he was finally allowed to go to the podium, he first replied to criticism that had been leveled at him at the conference, then launched a direct attack on the Party for lagging behind its basic goal of becoming more democratic. His charges made his critique of the year before seem mild.

He started with the conference itself, noting that in many places delegates had been selected "according to the old practices." This was evidence, he said, that the "upper layer" of the *apparat* was not restructuring itself.

He asked for more time to consider the proposal to combine the top Party posts with the chairmanships of the corresponding soviets but spoke out strongly in favor of new elections as long as they were universal, direct, and on the basis of a secret ballot, principles he thought should be applied to elections within the Party as well. He also argued for a limit of two terms in any office and obligatory retirement at the age of sixty-five. He considered these measures a more reliable guarantee against dictatorship than a two-party system and described them as a return to the true principles of Leninism.

Noting that many countries observe the principle that if a leader goes, his team goes with him, he rebuked those who had been in the Politburo ten years or more but had done nothing to correct past mistakes. He challenged them to explain their complicity in the country's current dismal condition and appealed to the conference to retire them. "That would be a more humane step than posthumous attacks and reburial after death," he observed.

He then pointedly attacked corruption in the Party, accusing Mikhail Solomentsev, the chairman of the Party Control Commission (responsible for members' ethics)—who was presiding at this session—of investigating trifles and ignoring massive corruption at high levels. He noted that the Party budget was maintained in strict secrecy, even from the Central Committee, which had the duty of managing it, and demanded that it be disclosed, then made a stinging attack on the special privileges of senior Party officials.

By the time he reached the end of this portion of his prepared text, he had spoken longer than the period allotted to most of the speakers. When he announced that he wished to raise a "ticklish question," there were audible groans from the audience. He paused, glared out over the podium, and explained, "I just wanted to address the question of my personal political rehabilitation following the October Central Committee plenum." The noise continued. He gathered up his papers as if to leave and muttered, "If you feel we don't have time, then that's all." At this, he turned and looked at Gorbachev, who was seated at the center of the "presidium," behind the speaker's rostrum.

Gorbachev motioned for him to continue and said, "Go on, Boris Nikolayevich. They want you to." The speeches at the Central Committee the previous fall had not yet been published, so Gorbachev added, "Comrades, I think it's time to strip the secrecy from the Yeltsin affair. Let Boris Nikolayevich say whatever he thinks he should. Then if any of us feel the need, we can too."

Yeltsin turned to the audience and continued his speech, still reading from notes. He noted that it was customary to rehabilitate someone fifty years later but that he would like to be rehabilitated while he was still alive. He recalled the resolution of the Central Committee the previous October labeling his views "politically erroneous" and said he believed his only error was timing: he should not have marred the seventieth anniversary of the Revolution by pointing out problems in implementing perestroika. In order to preserve openness of discussion in the Party and to "rehabilitate me in the eyes of Communists," he requested that the conference rescind the Central Committee resolution.

The earlier part of his speech had been strong and defiant, but now he was pleading. When he finished, the conference broke for lunch.

It was scheduled to resume in the afternoon to pass a series of resolutions, but instead a number of speakers were called to refute Yeltsin's message and request. The counteroffensive seemed well planned and coordinated. Only one of the eleven speakers who followed defended Yeltsin in any way. But the most vehement refutation came from Yegor Ligachev.

Ligachev mounted the rostrum, prepared text in hand. He read most of his reply, looking up frequently from his text, but with oratorical skill. His intonation, his pauses, his style of delivery in general were effective. But while his voice was carefully modulated, one could sense a swell of emotion underneath that was barely held in check.

His words conveyed even more emotion. He chose not to discuss Yeltsin's ideas in their particulars but to attack him personally, lapsing at times into defensive self-justification. All was crafted to appeal to the apparatchiks who made up the bulk of his audience.

He started by saying that it was painful for him to speak on the subject, but not because he had qualms about defending his own record. It was painful because it was he who had brought Yeltsin to Moscow in the first place, and he had committed a serious mistake when he had done so. He then accused Yeltsin of gross mismanagement even before he came to Moscow, when he had allegedly had to introduce rationing in Sverdlovsk (a charge later proven false), and he uttered a phrase that became famous: "Борис, ты не прав!" (Boris, you are wrong!) His choice of *ty,* the Russian intimate form of "you," while normally used in private conversations between Politburo members, seemed condescending and offensive on this public occasion.

What particularly agitated Ligachev, however, was Yeltsin's critique of the Party for resisting change and clinging to undeserved privileges. He indulged in a long, emotional boast about his own services to "socialism" and the loyalty he had shown under adverse Siberian conditions. He considered it "monstrous" that Yeltsin would make the charges he had when he had a record of sitting through Politburo meetings in silence.

When he returned to his seat, the applause in the hall was strong and prolonged. No one was surprised when the delegates rejected the proposal for Yeltsin's "rehabilitation."

Ligachev had obviously found strong support among delegates in the hall, but his presentation made a much less favorable impact on the public, which savored it in full on television that night. *They* knew Party apparatchiks had a lot of privileges, and who was this Ligachev who thought he could fool them? It was clear whose side Boris Nikolayevich was on and whom Yegor Kuzmich was trying to shield!

Soon, budding entrepreneurs were turning out lapel buttons that reversed Ligachev's laconic reproach. "Егор, ты не прав!" they read. "Yegor, you are wrong!"

Onward to Real Elections

LIGACHEV'S FORMAL VICTORY over Yeltsin at the Party conference did not arrest the slide of his own authority. His opposition to political reform led Gorbachev to maneuver him out of the de facto number two position in the Party.

By splitting his opponents, compromising on some of his proposals, and taking advantage of the Party tradition of always endorsing proposals made by the leaders, Gorbachev had won the Party conference's formal endorsement of political reform. A few delegates had spoken in opposition, but Gorbachev had controlled the final votes. Following the conference, Gorbachev pressed his advantage. In September, before getting down in earnest to planning for the Soviet Union's first real elections, he engineered a major reorganization of the top Party structures and a reassignment of duties.

The Party Secretariat stopped meeting regularly as a body, and Ligachev's duty as chairman of these meetings ended. Ligachev was assigned the dubious honor of supervising agriculture. Chebrikov was removed as KGB chairman and placed in charge of a Party commission to oversee the police and criminal justice system. The new jobs sounded important, and it was contrary to traditional Party "ethics" to refuse a post for which one was qualified.

The reorganization served two purposes: it became much more difficult for senior Party officials to interfere directly in the operations of government, and it removed much of the organizational base of those who were blocking reform. Despite a grandiose-sounding mandate, the new Party commissions never exercised real authority. Their work was largely ignored. Their chairmen had been politically marginalized.

Gorbachev, having failed to bring enough reformers into the Party leadership to push his reforms, had decided to weaken the Party instead. Of course, he could not announce this publicly without courting Khrushchev's fate. He had to pretend that he was preparing the Party for an even more effective role, one that would determine policy, leaving the grubby day-to-day management to lesser figures in the government structure.

I wondered if anyone was really taken in by this argument. I had been around bureaucracies long enough to know that a "policy-making" job that does not include authority over those who carry out the policy is a sham.

Throughout the fall and winter of 1988, preparations were made for the Soviet Union's first real elections. Committees drafted detailed election regulations on the basis of the decisions of the Party conference, and by early December they were enacted into law by the old, rubber-stamp Supreme Soviet.

They provided for a radically different structure of government. The most authoritative state body had been the USSR Supreme Soviet, which theoretically was, as its name suggested, "supreme." The chairman of its Presidium was the titular chief of state.

In practice, however, the Supreme Soviet was a stage set rather than a real institution. Its members all held other jobs (often important ones), and they normally met only twice a year for two or three days to approve routinely proposals drafted in advance. They were "elected" from a single slate of candidates, prepared in advance by the Communist Party machine.

The Supreme Soviet, therefore, had a purely formal function. The Party Politburo, using the Secretariat as a staff, made the real decisions and simply passed legislation to the Supreme Soviet for legal enactment. Since the great majority of Supreme Soviet deputies were members of the Communist Party and subject to its discipline, there was no possibility that the Supreme Soviet would act independently.

The new regulations provided for an entirely new body, the USSR Congress of People's Deputies, which would have 2,250 members. One third would be elected from geographical districts, comparable to congressional districts in the United States; another third from "national" districts in union republics and other formally autonomous entities; and the final 750 from "public organizations." Most important, elections were to be based on multiple candidacies and secret balloting.

This Congress of People's Deputies, normally expected to meet twice a year for a few days at a time, was to select from its ranks a smaller bicameral Supreme Soviet of 271 deputies in each house. These deputies would be full-time legislators, relieved of other duties, but they would be "rotated." Twenty percent would change every year, with new faces being brought in from the ranks of the Congress. It was probably no coincidence that the total number of Supreme Soviet deputies was to be roughly equivalent to the total number of representatives and senators in the Congress of the United States.

The chief of state, with the new title "chairman of the USSR Supreme Soviet,"[23] would be elected by the Congress of People's Deputies. He, in turn, would name a prime minister, subject to confirmation by the Congress. The prime minister would then propose candidates for ministerial posts, and they would have to be confirmed by the Supreme Soviet. In theory, this was analogous to the requirement for Senate confirmation of Cabinet and other senior appointments in the United States, except that confirmation would be by the entire Supreme Soviet and not simply its upper house.

We in the embassy followed preparations for the election with fascination and sent numerous reports to Washington describing the developments, which were totally novel for specialists in Soviet affairs. For once, it seemed we might be able to observe an election in the Soviet Union that would not have a totally predictable outcome.

As I pondered these new structures and regulations at the end of 1988, several thoughts came to mind.

First, this was a very complex system that, even in principle, was not totally democratic. To select a third of the deputies from "public organizations" that the Communist Party controlled would result in disproportionate Communist representation, even if all the other elections were conducted fairly, which was more than any realistic person could expect. This practice also violated the "one person, one vote" rule, since a citizen would have a vote in as many organizations as he or she belonged to. One friend noted to me after election day that he had managed to vote six times, all legally. He had cast his ballot as a citizen but previously had voted for slates in the Artists' Union, the Academy of Arts, the veterans' organization, the Friendship Society, and the Peace Committee.

Second, indirect election of the legislature offered additional possibilities for manipulation. The notorious Article VI of the Constitution, which designated the Communist Party as the "guiding and directing force of Soviet society and the core of its political system" was still on the books, and this would allow Party leaders to control the selection of legislators if they chose.

Nevertheless, if the new regulations were observed, even in part, the public might be enfranchised as it had never been throughout Soviet history. Even if most of the candidates came from the Communist Party, they would have to compete for votes, and if voting was secret and the ballots honestly counted, unpopular figures could lose.

Voters intent on opposing the "system" were given one powerful tool. Regulations required that a successful candidate obtain a majority of the votes cast, not a plurality, and voters could vote "no" to all the candidates. Therefore, if the Party controlled the nomination process and its candidates were unsatisfactory, they could be voted down. Soviet voters were to have an option many Americans only dream about: the right to vote "none of the above" and make it stick.

It was obvious that real change would depend on two as-yet-unanswered questions: whether the elections would be real or would continue to be controlled by the Communist Party apparatus as "elections" had been in the past; and whether the resulting institutions would be independent of the Party apparatus.

I was convinced that Gorbachev would see to it that some of the changes were real, but it was clear that the greatest barrier to his proposed reforms was the entrenched Party bureaucracy. If he wished to pursue his reforms and to retain a modicum of job security as he did so, he would need to create countervailing institutions.

The new Congress seemed designed with this purpose in mind; it would bring pressure on standpat Party officials by forcing them to submit to secret balloting. Given his popularity with the public at that time, there was no question that Gorbachev could win the chairmanship of the new Supreme Soviet no matter how democratic the voting on deputies. Having done so, he could not be removed as easily as Khrushchev had been by a hostile cabal in the Party leadership.

Reformers and the public at large deplored Yeltsin's rejection by the Party congress, but many intellectuals considered him a political schemer who could not be trusted. And they blamed Ligachev much more than Gorbachev for the anti-Yeltsin vote at the Party conference. In fact, Yeltsin had begun to fade from the public view as Gorbachev preempted the reform movement.

A poll at the end of 1988 found that 55 percent of the population thought that Gorbachev deserved the "Man of the Year" award. Only 4 percent voted for Yeltsin. It seemed that Gorbachev had finally gotten out in front of radical reform, had shunted conservatives like Ligachev and Chebrikov to the side (though not totally out), and had begun to implement his democratization program. While the economy was ailing and shortages had grown, the public blamed Ryzhkov's government and Party apparatchiks, not Gorbachev.

Agitation, some of it with a nationalist coloration, had begun to emerge on the empire's periphery, and this was an annoyance, but to Gorbachev, as 1988 ended, it seemed manageable.

In any event, foreign policy was turning out to be his strongest suit. Tangible achievements were beginning to accumulate, and that year they were still overwhelmingly popular at home.

VI

"The Common Interests of Mankind"

*We are fully justified in refusing to see in peaceful coexistence a special form
of the class struggle.*
EDUARD SHEVARDNADZE, July 1988[1]

*We proceed from the class character of international relations. . . . Active
involvement in solving mankind's common problems must not be a reason to apply
brakes to the social and national liberation struggle.*
YEGOR LIGACHEV, August 1988[2]

*It is obvious that the use or threat of force cannot and must not be
an instrument of foreign policy.*
MIKHAIL GORBACHEV to the United Nations, December 7, 1988[3]

I t was a balmy evening in late May 1987, and guests were mingling
under the massive chandelier in Spaso House's main reception hall.
One of them, an American journalist, came up to me and said, "I just
had the strangest experience. One of my Soviet friends called and asked
if it was true that a foreign plane had landed in Red Square. That
seemed crazy, but since I was passing by on the way over here, I stopped
to take a look, just for the hell of it. And you know, a Cessna is actually
sitting there, all cordoned off. The markings look to be German, but
when I asked the militiaman what kind of plane it was, he just said
'What plane?' and gave me a blank stare."

Thus, for the first time, I heard about the plane that a nineteen-year-
old West German, Mathias Rust, had flown from Hamburg to an improvised landing site alongside the Kremlin wall.

Life in Moscow for a foreigner has always tended to be rather grim,
even lugubrious. So the story of the young man who had had the audac-
ity to elude the vaunted Soviet Air Defense Forces—forces that had not

hesitated to shoot down stray passenger jets—made for innumerable cocktail-party jokes. And not only foreigners joined in the levity: many Soviet citizens appreciated the discomfiture felt by their uniformed military, who generally dealt with the public with a haughty self-importance that seemed to invite attempts to take them down a peg or two. Besides, a Cessna could hardly be considered a military threat.

So I was not surprised when, at our next reception, Viktor Sukhodrev, the acting head of the American section in the Foreign Ministry, well known to the public as the Soviet leaders' top English interpreter, greeted me with "Have you heard? They've renamed Red Square!"

"No kidding! What's the new name?"

"Why, Sheremetyevo III, of course." Sheremetyevo I and II are names of the two terminals near Moscow that handle international flights.

Taming the Military

WHETHER GORBACHEV INDULGED in jokes about Mathias Rust's escapade, I do not know. He could hardly have welcomed the evidence that his country's air defenses were porous. Nevertheless, this embarrassing incident came at an opportune time politically.

One of the principal barriers to a more cooperative foreign policy was the Soviet military. From the very beginning of his rule, Gorbachev had signaled that the military would not play as large a role as under Brezhnev and Chernenko: the minister of defense, Marshal Sergei Sokolov, was not granted full Politburo status, as had been traditional. In addition, Gorbachev was toying with new but as yet poorly defined concepts such as "defensive sufficiency."

Rust's escapade handed Gorbachev the chance to shake up the Soviet military command, and he did so quickly. The German plane set down on Red Square on May 28, and only two days later, on May 30, Defense Minister Sokolov was replaced. So was the head of the Air Defense Forces, along with a number of other generals. In selecting a new defense minister, Gorbachev employed a classic maneuver of a politician building a patronage network: he passed over the most senior officers and picked a general several notches down. Under the circumstances, he had every reason to assume that the unexpected promotion would ensure Dmitri Yazov's personal loyalty.

A rough-hewn, red-faced man of sixty-three, well over six feet tall, Yazov came across as a blunt, straight-talking, but personally affable soldier. Later, he told visitors that the accident at the nuclear power plant at Chernobyl had influenced his thinking fundamentally. Before April 1986, he had genuinely believed a nuclear war could be fought and won; Chernobyl, however, had convinced him that this was impossible. In fact, a nation could be devastated even if nuclear weapons were not used, since conventional bombing of nuclear power plants could make entire countries uninhabitable.

The other key Soviet military figure at this time was Marshal Sergei Akhromeyev, chief of the Soviet General Staff. Born the same year as Yazov, he was senior to him in military rank, having been promoted to marshal of the Soviet Union (equivalent to five-star general in the U.S. Army) while Yazov was still a three-star. Nevertheless, though he was subordinate to Yazov in the Ministry of Defense, he was closer to Gorbachev. Akhromeyev was normally the senior Soviet military official to attend high-level arms control meetings, where he played a key role in negotiating with U.S. American officials.

Akhromeyev was a soldier's soldier who had risen from the ranks. During table conversation, he recalled that his first combat experience had been as a marine corporal assigned to the defense of Leningrad at the beginning of World War II. He had spent the first winter literally in the trenches without a roof over his head a single night. He soon received a commission and rose rapidly, commanding a tank battalion before the war was over.

After the war he had been given progressively more important command assignments, including that of the Far East Military District, which seemed to have been a required stepping-stone to chief of the General Staff. Then he had served for more than a decade in top staff positions in Moscow, with a break in the early 1980s, when he had directed Soviet troops in Afghanistan.

Akhromeyev was a strong partisan of the Soviet state who opposed any weakening of central control. National movements in the republics were anathema to him since he considered them disloyal to the country as he defined it. He was comfortable with the Communist system and accepted the principle of civilian control of the military but was a passionate defender of military honor. When the Soviet army came under increasing attack in the press, his was the most vigorous voice that came to its defense.

In dealing with us, his principal concern seemed to be to ensure that any agreement was reciprocal. If the cuts proposed affected both sides equally, he could be reasonable. If, however, he was convinced that the Soviets were being called upon for greater sacrifices, he would object. Unfortunately, he did not always appreciate that the disproportionate Soviet military buildup would sometimes require them to destroy more weapons than the West if there was to be parity. However, if Gorbachev needed or wanted an agreement, Akhromeyev was willing to help him get it, at times suppressing his own judgment to do so.

Despite his views, which were hard-line even in the conservative Ministry of Defense, Akhromeyev made many friends among the Westerners who dealt with him. Personable and with a keen sense of humor, he never left you in doubt where he stood, but he was also willing to listen, and he could negotiate vigorously without personal acrimony. As a consequence, he developed easy personal relations with people on our side of the negotiating table.

For the next two or three years, the Yazov-Akhromeyev combination (the two had such different personalities that it is difficult to speak of them as a team) served Gorbachev well. On the one hand, their military credentials were impeccable as far as their fellow officers were concerned. On the other, they were both willing to suppress their emotions and accommodate Gorbachev as the country's constitutional political authority. No doubt they would argue strongly for policies popular with the Soviet military establishment—but when Gorbachev decided on a different course, they supported him and thus helped keep potential hotheads in the military from getting out of control.

Not that Soviet generals opposed perestroika in principle. They were not so blind that they could not see the problems the Soviet economy was encountering as it lagged behind the technological advances of the West. The arms race, in particular, had pressed the Soviet Union, and the generals faced the specter of falling still further behind. At a certain point, quantity simply cannot make up for quality, and they knew it, though they were not above pressing with all their might for as much quantity as they could obtain.

In the 1970s, I would sometimes ask my Soviet acquaintances why it was that their military commanders insisted on such a great superiority of numbers. They had deployed double the number of NATO's tanks and more than double the number of artillery pieces, and had many more men under arms. Didn't they see that the rest of the world could only consider this a threat? Was it not clear evidence that the intent was to use a preponderant military power to establish hegemony?

Cautious Soviet citizens in those days would answer such questions by simply denying the facts: "What do you mean, we have more than you do? You have deployed more arms than we have to bring pressure to bear on us and are threatening nuclear war to boot," and so on. More sophisticated analysts would not try to deny the facts but would instead offer an appealing excuse.

"Look, you have to understand that our psychology is rooted in our history. And that history is that we *always* lose battles when we have only as many forces as our enemy. Usually, when war has broken out, we have had an advantage of numbers and still have lost. Look how many more men Kutuzov had than Napoleon, yet the little squirt took Moscow. The Japanese beat us in 1905 with a fraction of our forces. In World War I we not only had more men than the Germans and Austrians, we also had more artillery. In World War II, our forces were more than double those of the Wehrmacht, and the preponderance of armor and aircraft was even greater, yet we damn near lost.

"The fact is, no Russian believes in his heart that our soldiers, and particularly our equipment, are a match for German or American—or foreign in general, except maybe Chinese. Therefore, we just cannot feel safe with mere parity."

When I heard this familiar argument, I always tried to explain that we didn't find it convincing given the quality of their equipment and their prevailing military doctrine, which was anything but defensive in essence.

Nevertheless, this apologia did have some elements of historical truth. Unquestionably, Soviet military leaders played upon the cost in the past of military weakness to enlarge their share of the budget. They had done so with brilliant success under Brezhnev, whose cohorts saw in the Soviet military the basis of their own prestige and authority and tended to be generous.

Nevertheless, even a large slice of a stale pie has limited attraction. Therefore, economic reforms might well enlist the support of Soviet generals, as long as reform did not mean less for the military.

Gorbachev's dilemma was that he could not avoid impinging on the military's prerogatives if he was to revitalize the economy, nor could he avoid a change in Soviet military doctrine if he was to relieve international tension so as to permit more attention to domestic reform. To put

it bluntly, he had to get the Americans and NATO off his back if reform
was to have a chance at home, and he could not do this as long as Soviet
policy and military strength were viewed as a threat to the West. Brezhnev had co-opted the generals—or maybe it would be more accurate to
say that the generals had spiritually co-opted Brezhnev and his cronies—but in either case they had lived together in a symbiotic relationship. Gorbachev had to find a way to break the habits thus formed
without permitting the generals to break him.

Yazov and Akhromeyev could be expected to respond to Gorbachev's
political leadership, but they were by no means puppets who merely executed orders from above. They proved to be staunch defenders of Soviet
military interests and stubborn negotiators. Nevertheless, when political
decisions were made to cut Soviet forces or to withdraw from bases
abroad, they went along without public protest—at least for a few years.

A series of reciprocal visits between U.S. and Soviet officers began in
1988 after Secretary of Defense Frank Carlucci met Soviet Defense Minister Yazov in Switzerland during the spring, then visited Moscow and
several Soviet bases in August. Marshal Akhromeyev made a tour of
U.S. installations during the summer as the guest of Admiral William
Crowe, chairman of the U.S. Joint Chiefs of Staff, and Crowe subsequently paid a return visit to the Soviet Union.

These contacts made a deep impression on the Soviet officers. When
he returned from the United States, Akhromeyev lunched with me at
Spaso House and told me how impressed he was both by the warm hospitality extended and by the high quality of the U.S. forces he had seen.
He stood in awe of the enormous firepower of the American aircraft car-
rier he had visited—something he had doubtless known in the abstract
but had not experienced directly, since the Soviet Navy had nothing
comparable. But the incident that impressed him most, he said, had occurred at Fort Bliss, Oklahoma.

A former tank officer himself, he had watched a tank exercise with
keen interest, and when it was over the crews had lined up for review.
Akhromeyev had passed down the line of soldiers and stopped in front
of a tank commander, still dusty from the field. "Major, do you know
who I am?" he had queried.

"Yes sir," had come the answer.

"And do you know why I'm here?" Akhromeyev had asked.

"No sir, but I think it's a good thing you came," the young officer had replied.

Not the words of an enemy, nor of an imperialist aggressor—but of a professional colleague.

This was not Akhromeyev's last trip to the United States, but it was the one that doubtless made the deepest impression on him. His successor, General Mikhail Moiseyev, continued the contacts begun in 1988 and also established close and friendly relations with General Colin Powell, who succeeded Admiral Crowe as chairman of the Joint Chiefs of Staff, and contacts became more frequent at successively lower levels of our military establishments.

It would be naïve to think that personal contacts between military leaders (or, for that matter, politicians) automatically ensure peace. Many conflicts in history, including our own Civil War, prove the contrary. Nevertheless, the familiarity and personal respect that quickly developed between the Soviet and Western military leaders acted as a lubricant to the arms reduction negotiations. The people on the other side were no longer shadowy, unknown individuals hiding behind terse "biographies" provided by military intelligence but flesh-and-blood human beings struggling with many of the same professional problems. Both sides found—not necessarily to their surprise but in a manner that erased all doubt—that their counterparts also considered a NATO–Warsaw Pact conflict the ultimate catastrophe, to be avoided at virtually any cost short of surrender or humiliation.

Once these convictions prevailed, the rest was negotiable, as long as politicians did not interfere. Gorbachev, as we have seen, had powerful reasons for seeking a temporary accommodation with the West. The question for the West was whether his desire for improved relations was a tactic to gain time and strength for later challenges or represented a fundamental shift in Soviet doctrine.

Soviet military doctrine had begun to change by 1988. Previously it had been based on the concept of "repelling aggression" by offensive action. In Europe, for example, this meant that Soviet forces would immediately head for the English Channel if war should break out. The fact that Soviet war planning was predicated on "aggression" from the West was small consolation. Nothing in the doctrine, nor in the training and deployment of forces, would hamper starting a war if the Soviet political authorities so decided.

Throughout 1988 and 1989, Soviet military planners began to flesh out the vague but suggestive terms Gorbachev had started using in 1986. "Reasonable sufficiency" gradually became "defensive sufficiency." This expression was further explained as the amount of force necessary to deter strategic attack and repel an aggressor to the border, but not beyond.

When Marshal Akhromeyev returned from his trip to the United States, he wrote an article in the army newspaper, *Krasnaya zvezda,* that charged that many in the Soviet military were still "prisoners of old concepts" and urged that the quality of weapons be improved to make up for reductions in quantity, that combat training be altered to fit a purely defensive doctrine, and that reductions in the Soviet military structure be carried out.[4]

Some changes in Soviet military training and exercises were soon evident, but unless the military forces were substantially reduced and their deployment radically altered, these developments could be quickly reversed. Nevertheless, by the end of 1988, the philosophical basis for accepting a parity of forces with putative enemies had been laid. Implicitly, the change in doctrine constituted an admission that it was dangerous to attempt to maintain a superiority of armed forces in the nuclear age. Without this change in attitude, the arms reduction agreements still to come would hardly have been possible.

The Class Struggle and History's Dustbin

CHANGES THAT WENT BEYOND military doctrine were needed before the West could be confident that Gorbachev was in fact prepared to end the cold war. The most important of these was the Marxist doctrine of the class struggle.

The theory of class struggle was a central concept for the development of the Leninist state structure and the conduct of the cold war with the West. Without it, the rationale for a single-party state disappears, as does the reason for cold war.

According to Marx, society was divided into classes on the basis of their relationship to the means of production. These classes were destined to struggle for domination, and ultimately the most numerous and deprived class, the proletariat, would win. Thereupon, it would establish its dictatorship over society, eliminate the other classes, and eventually create a Communist paradise on earth.

The Communist Party, as the only authentic representative of the proletariat, was empowered to exercise its dictatorship over society. Supposedly, this had all happened in the Soviet Union as a result of the 1917 Bolshevik Revolution, except that the stage of pure communism had not yet been reached: it always remained just over the horizon.

The implications of this doctrine for relations with countries not under the dictatorship of the proletariat were obvious. They would be under "bourgeois" or "feudal" rule, which was destined to be swept away by the victorious proletariat. Any alliances or cooperative arrangements with non-Communist governments, therefore, could be only temporary, to be discarded when their tactical rationale disappeared. Peaceful coexistence, required by the nuclear age, did not mean the end of the class struggle on the international plane, merely that it would be necessary for a time to conduct that struggle by means short of war.

During the 1970s, when the West entered into a fleeting détente with the Soviet Union, the Brezhnev leadership made it clear to the Soviet public that arms control agreements like the 1972 ABM treaty did not imply any change in the class struggle concept. "There can be no détente in the field of ideology" was the oft-repeated slogan. High officials hob-nobbed with "bourgeois" Westerners, but Soviet society as a whole was closed off from such contact, and steps were taken to prevent ideological contagion by severely restricting the possibility of travel abroad, controlling the media, and jamming foreign radio broadcasts.

Furthermore, the class struggle hypothesis lay at the basis of decisions to assist revolutions in Africa, Latin America, and Asia and to send Soviet forces into Afghanistan in December 1979. Though the reality did not fit the theory, these actions were viewed by the Brezhnev clique as legitimate acts of class solidarity, which—if successful—would increase their own power and prestige, since they had the mandate of history to exercise the will of the world proletariat.

Having experienced, in the 1970s and 1980s, the results of Soviet adherence to the theory of class struggle, I watched for signs that it was being modified or abandoned. Until it was genuinely and officially discarded, any changes for the better in our relationship could turn out to be illusory or, at best, temporary. The stakes for internal Soviet policy were also large: it was hard to imagine that the Communist Party could ever be induced to give up its monopoly on political power or to allow factions within the Party to compete, as long as it adhered to the class struggle concept.

At first, Gorbachev, Yakovlev, and Shevardnadze chipped away at this doctrine by implication, as if to avoid a direct debate. Changes in policy were covered by the vague term "new thinking." Just what that meant was subject to piecemeal explication. But by the summer of 1988, when tension was rising between Yakovlev and Ligachev on domestic issues, the debate over class struggle burst into the public view.

In July, Shevardnadze convened a conference of senior Soviet diplomats and scholars on international affairs to pass the word about changes in Soviet diplomatic style and substance. The meeting was closed to foreigners, but *Pravda* carried a summary of Shevardnadze's introductory remarks. When I opened my copy of *Pravda* at breakfast on July 26, I scanned the article quickly. The following paragraph virtually jumped out at me:

> [Foreign Minister Shevardnadze] noted in his report that the new political thinking considers peaceful coexistence in the context of the realities of the nuclear age. We are fully justified in refusing to see in peaceful coexistence a special form of the class struggle. Coexistence, which is founded on such principles as nonaggression, respect for sovereignty and national independence, noninterference in internal affairs, etc., must not be identified with the class struggle. The struggle of two opposing systems is no longer the decisive tendency of the contemporary age. At the present stage, our ability to increase the pace of producing material benefits and distributing them justly on the basis of advanced science, modern equipment, and high technology, and our ability to restore and protect those resources essential for the survival of mankind, have taken on decisive significance.

Finally I had before me what I had been looking for: an authoritative renunciation of class struggle as a basis of foreign policy. If this was generally accepted in the Soviet leadership, I could expect similar comments to be repeated by other Soviet officials, including of course Gorbachev, over the coming months.

What came next, though, was not a reinforcement of Shevardnadze's stand but a refutation. Only a few days after the conference in the Foreign Ministry, Ligachev traveled to Gorky, the ancient city on the Volga that had long been closed to foreigners because of the concentration of defense industry in the area. Its traditional name, Nizhny Novgorod, had not yet been restored. He picked that occasion to reject Shevardnadze's thesis. As *Pravda* reported on August 6, Ligachev defended traditional "class struggle" in the most direct language:

We proceed from the class character of international relations. Any other formulation of the question only introduces confusion into the consciousness of Soviet people and our friends abroad. Active involvement in solving the common problems of mankind must in no way be used as artificial justification for putting brakes on the social and national liberation struggle.

Ligachev wanted it both ways: cooperate to solve "common interests" when convenient, but pursue the cold war whenever possible.

Normally, a debate over ideology is not an appropriate topic for representations by foreign ambassadors. Although our embassy was careful to report to Washington on ideological disputes in Moscow, only specialists in Communist affairs seemed to pay attention. It was difficult for American politicians, who are pragmatists by nature, to grasp the significance of what seemed to them arguments over esoteric, theoretical questions that had no apparent relevance to real life. To them, these debates were like the arguments of medieval theologians: harmless time wasters that practical people had best ignore.

Given this attitude, it was not surprising that we never received instructions to discuss or clarify points of Communist doctrine with Soviet officials. Nevertheless, I felt that a lot depended on the outcome of this debate, and I wanted to let the Soviet leadership know that some of us were following it with keen interest and that its conclusion would affect our confidence in Gorbachev's sincerity. Therefore, I resolved to discuss the matter with Shevardnadze at the next available opportunity, not as an official inquiry but as a personal one.

As luck would have it, I obtained an appointment with Shevardnadze on August 8 to deliver some messages from Secretary of State Shultz. My appointment was in the evening, when Shevardnadze was less pressed for time than during normal working hours. (He was well known for working most evenings until close to midnight.) So when I had finished my official business, I brought up the subject, explaining that I had a duty to interpret events in Moscow for Washington and that I wanted to be as accurate as possible. I had reported his remarks on the class struggle as a favorable development, but now, reading what Ligachev had said in Gorky, I wondered whether his view was shared throughout the Soviet leadership. Could he help me understand the situation better?

Shevardnadze, never comfortable with convenient lies but still not yet accustomed to discussing internal disputes with us, shifted uneasily in his chair and assured me that Gorbachev's views were the authoritative ones and he had stated clearly that avoidance of nuclear war is the overriding task. The class struggle is something that occurs *within* countries, he observed, and this must have been what Ligachev was referring to.

I pointed out that, according to *Pravda,* Ligachev had referred explicitly to the class struggle as the "guiding principle of international relations." Shevardnadze then retreated and confirmed the dispute indirectly by observing, "Well, not every statement made by officials in your government is consistent, either. Weinberger doesn't always agree with Shultz." Then he concluded by assuring me that his government believed firmly in the peaceful settlement of disputes.

My objective in mentioning Ligachev's speech to Shevardnadze was not to embarrass him but to strengthen his position in the internal Soviet debate, should he choose to make use of my comments. I thought it would not hurt if Shevardnadze could point out to his colleagues that the Americans understood the implications of this issue and that continued espousal of the class struggle theory could make accommodation between the two countries more difficult.

I have no idea whether this occurred, but within a week Alexander Yakovlev answered Ligachev (without naming him) in a speech delivered in Vilnius, Lithuania. Couched in philosophical terms, at times in a convoluted syntax that requires repeated reading to grasp their full meaning, his comments marked a definitive reinterpretation of this cardinal Marxist principle.

Snippets will not do. Let me share with you the heart of his argument, which I have tried to render into English as precisely as possible:

> Prevention of the nuclear threat, disarmament in the name of peace, trust and cooperation in the name of security, and the survival of mankind—these are the tasks of the modern world. But if one

thinks in historical categories, this is only the primary, the most essential, precondition for approaching a just, democratic, rational solution of mankind's other problems: to feed the hungry; to preserve the planet's environment, without which life is impossible; to make rational use of the earth's far from inexhaustible resources.

The common interests of mankind do not form some abstract category posited speculatively by some thinker in an ivory tower. In our time, when the entire planet, it would seem, has contracted to incredibly small dimensions, when the fate and history of mankind can be broken off by pushing a button, when any event becomes the property of 5 billion people within hours, the common interests of mankind have taken on flesh and blood.

These are really the interests of all mankind. And that means that they are our interests as well, for we are part of mankind and one of the most important factors of its social progress. These are interests that unite mankind, and that means that they are capable of transcending the forces of disunity, contradiction, confrontation, and war that have already delayed the development of civilization for centuries. This is something that brings opposites together: one person's interests merge with those of all persons while philosophical, abstract, historical classifications merge with the purely practical, secular, everyday empirical reality.

Marxism as such is the interpretation of the common interests of mankind from the point of view of history and the perspective of the development of all mankind, not only that of individual countries or classes, peoples or social groups. In placing in the forefront the interests of the downtrodden and exploited and in singling out in the social structure of their time a class to be the bearer of the historical mission of liberating man and mankind, can it be said that the founding fathers of socialism placed the interests of that class against the interests of all the others? Of course not.

The thesis of the priority of the common interests of mankind is valuable because it embraces the objective tendency of development. It calls for a rejection of dogmatic views of the world, of one's country, and of each ethnic group. It helps us look realistically and soundly at the idea of the coexistence of countries with different political structures as a requirement of history and a manifestation of the internationalist tendencies of global development.[5]

Is this the Marxism of the *Communist Manifesto* and *Das Kapital*? To use Yakovlev's words, of course not. For Marx *did* place the interests of the "proletariat" above those of other classes. And many of his other mistakes flowed from that fundamental one. If the Soviet leaders were willing genuinely to discard that concept, it would matter little whether they continued to call their guiding philosophy "Marxism" or not. It would be a different "Marxism" in a different world, a world we could all recognize. Mankind does have common interests, and if the Soviet leaders were to recognize that they share them, the cold war would recede into history.

A Common Agenda

WHEN PRESIDENT REAGAN, in 1984, proposed a four-part agenda to improve relations with the Soviet Union, he pointed out that his four points were politically interrelated and that success in solving the problems of one would be affected by progress in the others. He had in mind the political reality that the U.S. Senate was unlikely to ratify a major arms reduction treaty if the Soviet Union invaded another country, just as Congress would refuse to eliminate barriers to trade if the Soviet regime seriously violated its citizens' human rights. If Soviet society remained closed, arms treaties would be much more difficult to verify.

In 1985 and 1986, as we have seen, the U.S.-Soviet dialogue had intensified on all these topics, and the two leaders came very close to reaching an unprecedented arms reduction agreement at Reykjavik. Consultations had begun on regional conflicts, but Soviet soldiers were still fighting in Afghanistan. Gorbachev agreed to expand the contacts of ordinary citizens with the West at the Geneva summit in 1985, but implementation was slow. He still resisted negotiating on human rights and rejected American attempts to discuss the problem as unacceptable interference, as Gromyko had always done. Even though his negotiators at Reykjavik had agreed that it was a legitimate topic, for months they continued to resist our appeals on behalf of political prisoners and those refused permission to leave the Soviet Union.

From late 1987, however, we began to register significant results in all parts of the U.S.-Soviet agenda. The speed of change was dizzying for those of us who had worked for decades on what had for long seemed the intractable problems of dealing with the USSR. The high points:

• *December 1987:* Gorbachev makes his first visit to the United States for a summit meeting with Reagan in Washington. They sign a treaty to eliminate a whole class of nuclear weapons, those carried by intermediate-range ballistic missiles. The threat of the Soviet SS-20s to Europe and Asia would end, in return for which the U.S. would withdraw and destroy its Pershing II and cruise missiles, which had been deployed in response to the SS-20s.

· *February 1988.* Gorbachev announces that the Soviet Union will withdraw its forces from Afghanistan, and an agreement to bring this about is signed in April.

· *May 1988:* Reagan visits Moscow and makes strong presentations to the Soviet public on democracy, freedom, and human rights.

· *June 1988:* Regulations are changed to make it easier for Soviet citizens to travel abroad; emigration and private travel begin an exponential growth.

· *July 1988:* Shevardnadze convenes a conference of Soviet diplomats to promulgate a policy based on common human values.

· Foreign officials, diplomats, and journalists are interviewed with greater frequency in the Soviet media; from spring, articles by Soviet scholars critical of past policy begin to appear.

· Contacts with Western European leaders intensify, with regular visits by foreign ministers and more frequent contacts by Gorbachev with chiefs of state and government.

· *December 1988:* Addressing the United Nations, Gorbachev announces a unilateral cut of half a million Soviet troops and endorses the "common interests of mankind" as the basis for Soviet foreign policy.

Ronald Reagan's agenda of 1984 became the unacknowledged framework for our interaction: arms reduction, withdrawing from military confrontation in third countries, building respect for human rights, and raising the iron curtain. As Gorbachev was persuaded of the need to democratize the Soviet Union and to base his foreign policy on mankind's common interests, he could view progress on these issues as *mutual* goals. We were no longer playing a "zero-sum" game in which one side automatically lost when the other won. Now we both could win.

Therefore, Gorbachev was not capitulating to U.S. "demands" when he began to negotiate the issues on the agenda we had suggested. He and his colleagues gradually came to understand that the agenda defined the key issues and that the American proposals would not be harmful to a peaceful Soviet Union.

Nowhere was the Soviet shift more dramatic than in the area of human rights. Throughout the 1970s and early 1980s, the Soviet regime's violations of accepted international principles had been a major barrier to improved relations. Its restrictions on the freedom of movement and emigration had led to the Jackson-Vanik amendment to the U.S. Trade Act of 1974, which denied the USSR normal trading status as long as it refused to allow freedom of emigration.

Although Brezhnev would, from time to time, modify Soviet practice in the hope of obtaining concrete concessions from the United States, he always refused flatly to consider human rights a legitimate subject for discussion and negotiation with foreign countries.

Gorbachev, after initially clinging to the old position, agreed to discuss the issue in 1987, and by 1988 human rights was firmly on both agendas. In August of that year, I called on Shevardnadze to request that several political prisoners be released. He immediately agreed to look into the cases and either resolve them favorably or explain why that was impossible. (What a contrast with the fulminations about interference in their internal affairs I would have gotten from Gromyko!) And then he said that he would do this not because we requested it but because it was in the Soviet interest. Since the Soviet leaders had decided to create a state based on the rule of law, it was important to them to strengthen the rights of individuals.

I told him that this was the best possible reason for doing something. We had long pressed the Soviet Union to give more respect to the human rights of its citizens, not because we wished to derive some advantage but because these principles are important if we are all to live in a peaceful world. The fact that the Soviet leaders now understood this augured well for our relations in the future.

Faces of Friends

GORBACHEV'S PERSONAL EXPOSURE to the United States also affected his willingness to come to terms with the American agenda. One incident, in particular, made a deep impression upon him.

The official activities on December 10, 1987, the third day of Gorbachev's stay in Washington, began with a breakfast at the Soviet Embassy on Sixteenth Street in honor of Vice President Bush. Following that breakfast, the plan was to have the American guests accompany Gorbachev in his motorcade to the White House to meet with President Reagan.

However, when breakfast was over, the vice president and the rest of us were asked to wait at the Soviet Embassy for a short time while Gorbachev touched base with Moscow. We knew we had proposed a statement regarding strategic arms that went beyond the previous Soviet position, and we assumed Gorbachev wished to clear it with his Politburo colleagues before signing on.

So we waited . . . and waited . . . and waited. We were not informed what the problem was but were told simply that Gorbachev was not yet ready to leave. I imagine he had to wait for the Politburo to be polled.

Finally, late in the morning, he emerged, and we set off for the White House. I was several cars back in the motorcade. Suddenly and unexpectedly, we stopped, literally screeching to a halt. Normally, for security reasons, these motorcades move at a rapid clip. Cross streets are cleared in advance, and the procession never stops until it reaches the appointed destination. But here we were on Connecticut Avenue, a few blocks from the White House, and the motorcade was standing stock still.

I jumped out of the car to see what was happening. Only six years earlier President Reagan had been shot just a few blocks from where we were. My alarm increased as I saw several "lead" cars from the Secret Service and KGB protective detail make rapid U-turns to surround Gorbachev's limousine. And then, to my immense relief, I saw Gorbachev step out of his car and walk over to the crowd which had lined the street to watch him pass. He had made the decision on the spot to press the flesh of his well-wishers.

The hand shaking lasted only a couple of minutes, and we soon resumed the short drive to the White House. Stopping to interact with a crowd is so habitual among American politicians, and was also something that Gorbachev had started to do at home, that I was initially inclined to assume that the incident had been designed primarily as a photo opportunity. (Indeed, the major newspapers featured it on their front pages the next day.)

It turned out, however, that it was more than that. During lunch at the White House that day, Gorbachev told us that it had made a deep impression on him.

"The people I saw this morning were not the people I had been told I would see in America," he observed, explaining that they had been friendly and open and had obviously wished him well. He knew this could not have been contrived because he had not indicated in advance his plan to stop there. Then, looking across the table at the president, he added, "I want you to know that I will never again think of America as I used to." Though he had been convinced intellectually that our countries could settle some of our problems in a limited way, he now knew deep inside that there was nothing to prevent us being friends.

This may sound naïve or contrived. But I am convinced it was neither.

Russian crowds are not demonstrative, unless they are angry, in which case they can become all too demonstrative. When Gorbachev mixed with them, they often had sharp questions for him, even when he was still popular.

The American crowd was different. He was greeted like a conquering hero or movie star, with cheers, smiles, and frantic efforts to grasp his hand. Curmudgeons may deplore this American habit of cheering celebrities, but there was something genuine behind it that Gorbachev accurately sensed: the American public was not made up of downtrodden slaves of capitalism yearning to throw off their shackles nor of belligerent jingoists sworn to do in the Soviet Union. The faces on Connecticut Avenue radiated freedom, well-being, and goodwill.

This encounter impressed Gorbachev not only because it did not fit the stereotype that had been implanted in his mind. He was, and is, a man who enjoys the pomp and circumstance of power and thirsts for public acclaim. At home, he was already beginning to bridle at indications that his popularity was less than universal and to "contain" politicians like Yeltsin, who exhibited more charisma than he with people on the street. In Washington, as later in the capitals of Western Europe, he found what he had been denied at home: the worship of adoring crowds.

Gorbachev's developing personal relationships with Reagan, Bush, Thatcher, Kohl, Mitterrand, and other Western leaders reinforced the important insight this brief encounter, and subsequent ones, gave him. From December 1987, he no longer dealt with us as a hostile or potentially hostile force that had to be managed, fended off, appeased—anything but befriended. The focus shifted to how we could serve our common interests.

It was particularly important for Gorbachev to trust the good faith of Western leaders, since the intelligence reports he received from the KGB continued to encourage suspicion of the "imperialist threat."

Both Viktor Chebrikov and his successor, Vladimir Kryuchkov, were given to making such charges in public, and both men were notorious among insiders for slanting reports to Gorbachev to maximize suspicion about the outside world in general and the United States in particular. Although he was a victim of KGB disinformation about Soviet internal affairs, Gorbachev developed a degree of objectivity about developments abroad and gradually came to depend on his own eyes and Western colleagues for unbiased information.

Not all of Gorbachev's associates shared the insight he gained in his brief December encounter with the crowd in Washington. Later, after the cold war had ended, Marshal Akhromeyev—who had provided valuable political support to Gorbachev for arms reduction he personally deplored—remarked to my wife, who was seated next to him at a formal dinner, that his head could understand that his country needed to change but his heart and feet refused to follow. In August 1991, his heart and feet prevailed over his head when he supported the disastrous coup attempt.

A New "Universal Principle"

THE RAPID HEALING of East-West relations took place against the background of the internal debate we have already examined. Gorbachev's decision to embark on political reform at home both required and facilitated a *rapprochement* with the West. After all, one could not espouse a law-based state and still hold to the primacy of the "class struggle," just as one could not end the cold war with that concept intact.

Ligachev, it seems, did not oppose most of the concrete steps to improve relations with the West, though he defended—and still defends— the "class struggle" concept. His split with Gorbachev occurred over Gorbachev's espousal of *political* reform and Gorbachev's demand that more radical steps be taken to restructure the economy. While Ligachev had won, for the time, his battle with Yeltsin, he was beginning to lose the one with Yakovlev.

Gorbachev's December 1988 speech to the United Nations was a culmination of that year's developments both inside and outside the Soviet Union. His announcement of unilateral troop reductions demonstrated that he had mastered the Soviet military. Only weeks earlier, top military officials, including Chief of Staff Akhromeyev, had insisted that force reductions could come *only* as a result of negotiated agreements that included reductions on both sides. His blanket endorsement of common human values as the basis of foreign policy implicitly abandoned the class struggle concept.

That speech contained another fateful sentence: "Freedom of choice is a universal principle; it should not be subject to any exceptions."[6]

And suppose Eastern Europe chose to bolt the Warsaw Pact? Suppose the Germans chose to unify their country? Suppose the Balts or Ukrainians or Georgians chose independence?

Were there really no exceptions?

VII

Stirrings in the Hinterland

The nationalities question inherited from the past has been successfully resolved in the Soviet Union.
TWENTY-SEVENTH CONGRESS OF THE CPSU, March 6, 1986[1]

Let those who would like to play on nationalist or chauvinistic prejudices entertain no illusions and expect no loosening up.
MIKHAIL GORBACHEV, to Central Committee plenum, January 27, 1987[2]

The claim has been made that there are no problems in interethnic relations. . . . This has led to public disaffection that now and then escalates into conflict.
NINETEENTH CONFERENCE OF THE CPSU, July 4, 1988[3]

Gorbachev had plenty on his mind without ethnic conflicts within the Soviet Union. He had to secure his own position as the head of the Communist Party and chief of state. He had to force his colleagues to agree to fundamental changes. He had to chart a painful course for economic reform. And, of course, he had to negotiate a more benign international environment and extricate his country from Afghanistan. The last thing he needed was a revolt in the hinterlands.

It was also the last thing he expected, so it should not surprise us that he did nothing to deal with the problem until it began to overwhelm him.

During his first year in power, Gorbachev in fact faced no serious nationality problems. In Ukraine, under hard-line Vladimir Shcherbitsky, courts continued to convict human rights activists. In April, Mykola Horbal of the Ukrainian Helsinki group was sentenced to eight years in prison camp, plus three years exile, and in August Iosyp Terelya was sentenced to seven years in prison plus five in exile for defending the rights of Ukrainian Catholics, whose church had been banned by Stalin.

By that time so many Ukrainians had been arrested for asserting national and religious rights that these reprehensible sentences were no longer shocking. They followed a pattern that had begun in the late sixties of sending into prison or mental asylums any who dared challenge the primacy of the Moscow-controlled institutions.

Later that year, however, the tide began to turn. One of the most famous of the incarcerated Ukrainian dissidents, Vyacheslav Chornovil, who had been imprisoned three times running on political or trumped-up criminal charges, was freed from a labor camp in Yakutia before the end of 1985. More releases occurred in 1986, as Gorbachev and Shevardnadze struggled to gain international acceptance.

The rapid growth of anti-Moscow sentiment in what Communist bureaucrats called "the periphery" was not just the result of releasing assorted "troublemakers" but of several major developments that permitted suppressed grievances to emerge.

The most important of these was glasnost, which gave courageous editors, journalists, and scholars an opening to deal with topics previously kept taboo. At first, only an occasional article questioned the usual Party dogma. When this did not bring down the house, the articles became ever more daring.

The slogan of these newly liberated journalists and scholars was "More Light," the title of an impressive 1987 film on the ravages of Stalinism. More light on the past. More light into the dark corners of Orwellian "memory," hitherto cordoned off from public discourse. More light on the crimes of the ruling Party and the system it operated.

Despite Ligachev's growing alarm and Gorbachev's sporadic efforts to bring them under control, a small number of determined editors, filmmakers, writers, and—increasingly—academics persisted. As these succeeded, others joined in.

I began to notice this changed tone with some amazement, since I had been conditioned to expect nothing positive from the Soviet news media.

When I was assigned to Moscow in the 1970s, I rarely bothered to read the press, except the occasional literary journal to get an idea of the sort of writing the censors were passing. If an important article appeared signaling some change in Soviet policy, our staff would call it to my attention. Otherwise, it was simply a waste of time to read the Soviet press. It didn't tell you anything you didn't already know, and most of what it told you was misleading and dull.

When I returned to Moscow in April 1987, I found, to my pleasant surprise, that things had changed. The Soviet press was neither the most objective nor the most comprehensive in the world, but it had enough of interest to be worth reading. By 1988 and 1989, it had become positively exciting in the variety and intensity of political and economic debate it carried.

This new openness carried glasnost beyond its intended bounds and began to provide ethnic and other interest groups with information that increased their anger with the existing system. Whole periods of history that had been left out of the textbooks were gradually opened to public view. Stalin's crimes were exposed with specifics that had never been offered in public before. The Nazi-Soviet pact of 1939 became a topic of debate and historical research, as did the environmental impact of officially sponsored industrial development and agricultural practices.

The Soviet nations, including the Russian nation, had begun to regain their past.

Alma Ata: Misunderstood Harbinger

THESE CHANGED ATTITUDES and the specific issues that were raised varied from republic to republic, but the common denominator was a growing willingness to resist Moscow's policies.

The first direct challenge to Moscow's practice of sending carpetbaggers to rule its minorities occurred in Alma Ata, the capital of Kazakhstan, in December 1986. Young Kazakhs rioted for two days when Dinmukhamed Kunayev, an ethnic Kazakh, was replaced as the republic's Party chief by Gennady Kolbin, an ethnic Russian who had no roots in the republic.

At the time, most Moscow officials failed to heed the warning and put it down to local resistance to the anticorruption drive then under way: Kunayev, they reasoned, had created a corrupt network within the Communist Party of Kazakhstan, and when an outsider was sent to clean up the mess, the culprits had stirred young people to take to the streets in protest. Thus the national element, though present, was seen as secondary to the larger problem of corruption.

Gorbachev's original team, inherited from Andropov, rightly saw that they could not reform the Party or the country if they failed to clean up the corruption which had infected the top Party elite during Brezhnev's tutelage. But they also believed that national differences were diminishing and that a "new Soviet man" had been fashioned from human clay purged of ethnic qualities.

At the Party congress in February 1986, Ligachev stressed the need for an "exchange of cadres among republics," which meant in practice sending ethnic Russians to non-Russian republics to occupy senior positions. The reason, as he put it euphemistically, was to combat "local cronyism," which had "gained the upper hand." There is no reason to think that Gorbachev differed from him on this issue: Ligachev spoke for the entire leadership as the official responsible for personnel policy.

What Gorbachev and his associates at that time failed to understand was that "local cronyism" and "corruption" would be seen locally as positive phenomena, a defense, as it were, against the overarching ambitions of an imperial center. For the fact is that many non-Russian Communist leaders had managed, under the complaisant Brezhnev regime, to rebuild local Communist Party machines along national lines.

These organizations, which bought off the Center with political loyalty and lavish gifts and in return were allowed to rule at home for the benefit of the local Party elite, would have been considered criminal in a state with the rule of law. The Soviet empire, however, was *not* a law-based state, and the national elites were certain to resent attempts by the distant and hated Center to replace their own crooks with alien ones, who would siphon off resources otherwise available for distribution within their regions. Furthermore, these national elites could, if they chose, easily stir up their "masses" by appeals to ethnic solidarity when Russians were sent in to replace corrupt locals.

This is what happened in Alma Ata in December 1986.

Kunayev, the longtime Party leader in Kazakhstan, was a quintessential Brezhnevite. A tall man with handsome features, he even cultivated a physical appearance that mimicked Brezhnev's, with heavy black eyebrows accentuated by kohl. The two had been linked by a friendship that went back to Brezhnev's service in Alma Ata in the 1950s. Kunayev had become Brezhnev's protégé, and when Brezhnev had become number one in the Soviet Union, he had been allowed to rule Kazakhstan as a personal barony.

I called on Kunayev in his spacious, lavishly outfitted Alma Ata apartment some six years after the 1986 events. He was proud of his "achievements" while in power and reeled off statistics indicating that industrial and agricultural output had risen rapidly during his tenure.

Sitting next to him in his study packed with sets of literary classics and embellished by a large collection of ornamental cigarette lighters (his friends doubtless knew the sort of gifts he appreciated), I could not resist the occasional illusion that I had been ushered into the presence of a miraculously preserved Brezhnev. Brezhnev's collections and taste in books would have been different, but there would have been proud displays of gifts received and full shelves of unread books. Brezhnev's Russian diction would have been sloppier than Kunayev's more elegant speech. But the drift would have been the same: the Gorbachev crowd never appreciated all we achieved, and when they cast us aside, they ruined the country.

Kunayev has always commanded respect from many in Kazakhstan, even from those who knew it was time for a change in 1986. During his tenure the Kazakh nation began its recovery from the successive shocks of collectivization, forced emigration, and the resettlement of millions of non-Kazakhs on their traditional lands.

Consider the figures: in 1926, Kazakhs made up more than 57 percent of the republic's population, but in the 1930s, one in three Kazakhs died as the direct result of collectivization, either of starvation or as a result of the massacres that ensued when the Red Army was called in to put down revolts.[4] Nearly 20 percent fled the republic to escape the atrocities, many to China. During and immediately after World War II, the non-Kazakh population of the republic grew by nearly 3 million, more than the total number of Kazakhs there.

By 1959 the ethnic Kazakhs were down to 30 percent of the population. Russians, with nearly 43 percent, outnumbered the Kazakhs by 1.2 million. Afterward, there was a steady recovery of "population share," and by the 1989 census the Kazakhs once again formed a plurality in their own republic: 40 percent as compared with the 38 percent of ethnic Russians. The higher fecundity of Kazakh families and the cessation of large-scale immigration into the republic accounted for the shift.

Kunayev presumably had little to do with these demographic changes, but he had a lot to do with the "Kazakhification" of the Kazakh Communist Party. While he maintained easy relations with resident Russians and held in check any overt tendency to assert Kazakh "nationalism," power in the republic Party organizations quietly but effectively passed to Kazakhs, who formed an absolute majority in the republic Party and held a majority of key positions.

When I first visited Alma Ata in 1961 and conferred with senior officials in the Sovnarkhoz, the council established by Khrushchev to manage the republic's economy, not a single interlocutor was an ethnic Kazakh. By the late 1980s, three quarters or more of the leading officials we dealt with were Kazakhs.

Kunayev's policy of developing Kazakh political leaders while pretending slavish loyalty to Moscow created new opportunities for energetic young Kazakhs. One who took spectacular advantage of these new possibilities was Nursultan Nazarbayev.

Nazarbayev was born into the family of a poor herdsman the year Hitler attacked the Soviet Union. He remembers from his childhood just after the war the arrival in his village of exiles from other parts of the Soviet Union who exposed him for the first time to languages other than Kazakh. Since his parents still moved to high pasture with the collective-farm sheep, he lived with an uncle while he attended elementary school.

After high school he decided to study chemistry at the university in Alma Ata but despite his high marks was passed over for entrance in favor of sons of high Party officials. He then chose metallurgy and was sent to a technical institute in Ukraine to learn steelworking, in preparation for assignment to the new steel complex being built at Temirtau in northern Kazakhstan—one of Khrushchev's gigantic "development projects."[5]

Nazarbayev worked for a time in the steel mill, but was soon recruited for full-time Party work. He was quickly promoted to head the Temirtau city Party committee and then was named second Party secretary of the province. He accompanied Kunayev on one of his trips to the area, after which Kunayev brought him to Alma Ata to serve as Party secretary for industry in the republic Central Committee.

During those years of "stagnation," promotions moved slowly; Nazarbayev's rapid rise was an exception. Though his talents are remarkable, he doubtless owed much to Kunayev's preference for ethnic Kazakhs. By 1986, having become the youngest of the USSR's republic prime ministers,[6] he was in a position to vie for the Party leadership in his republic.

He did not do so precipitously or directly, but took advantage of the reform spirit in 1986 to call attention to "serious shortcomings" in the Kazakhstan Party organization during the Party congress in Moscow.[7] Though he did not name Kunayev, his critique impugned Kunayev's leadership, since he had been in charge for more than twenty years. It is reasonable to assume that Nazarbayev was encouraged by Ligachev or Gorbachev—or perhaps both.

Kunayev's initial reaction was naïve for a man of his experience: he tried to convince Gorbachev to remove Nazarbayev, who had crossed the line from loyal protégé to undeclared challenger. When Gorbachev refused his request, he must have grasped the situation. In any event, both he and his friends say that he was prepared to retire voluntarily as Party first secretary.

In his memoirs, he states that he informed Gorbachev in November of his desire to retire.[8] His friends say that he was planning a retirement celebration for January 1987, to coincide with his seventy-fifth birthday, and in anticipation he had a bust of himself installed in the park next to the apartment house where he lived.

Gorbachev, however, decided to preempt his resignation to make a political point.

On December 11, 1986, the Politburo convened in Moscow without Kunayev in attendance, though he was a full member, and formally accepted his resignation. Simultaneously it selected a successor, apparently without consulting anyone in Kazakhstan. In typical imperial fashion, the Politburo despatched a representative to Alma Ata to convey its decision to the Kazakh Party. The new first secretary was to be Gennady Kolbin, a professional Communist Party official and ethnic Russian who had no previous ties to the republic.

The decision was announced in Alma Ata on December 16, and immediately demonstrators began to gather in the large square facing the grandiose new Party headquarters, situated at the top of a hill in the center of town. The demonstrators were young Kazakhs, mostly—it seemed—students. At first they just milled about, but as the day went on their numbers grew from a few score to several hundred, and hand-lettered signs began to appear.

Kunayev says he was summoned to Party headquarters and offered to speak to the students, but Kolbin decided not to permit this. (Kolbin, on the other hand, has been quoted as saying that Kunayev refused to address the demonstrators.) In any event, by afternoon the Party chiefs decided to send some of the younger Party secretaries out to talk to the students, and Nazarbayev was among them.

But the demonstrations continued, and the next day the crowd had swollen to the thousands, gradually becoming more violent as the demonstrators threw rocks and other missiles at the police sent to control them and at the windows of Party headquarters. Finally, orders were given to break up the demonstration, and while this was done many were injured and some were killed. The jails could not hold all those arrested, and hundreds were trucked forty or fifty miles out into the steppe and simply dumped. December is very cold in this part of Kazakhstan. Eventually, many demonstrators were given long prison sentences, and more than a thousand students were expelled from the university.

Since glasnost was not yet in full flower and there were no foreign correspondents stationed in Alma Ata, the world initially received only scanty and distorted information about the riot. The Soviet press carried brief reports of "disturbances" caused by "hooligans, parasites, and antisocial elements."

The facts only gradually filtered out by word of mouth, and more detailed stories began to appear in the foreign press only at the end of the year. These were necessarily based on hearsay and probably exaggerated the number of casualties.[9] *Izvestiya* carried an article in January denouncing the accuracy of foreign reports, but aside from it the Moscow press did its best to ignore the riot. When asked about the riot at a press conference during a trip to Finland, Prime Minister Ryzhkov dismissed it as a minor incident involving only a "couple of hundred people," joined subsequently by "youth from a degenerate class."[10]

The Moscow Party leadership obviously held Kunayev, not its own decision to send Kolbin to replace him, responsible for the riots. In 1987, he was attacked specifically for mismanagement and removed from both the Politburo and the Central Committee. Nevertheless, Moscow did learn something from the Alma Ata experience: Kolbin's appointment was its last attempt to impose an ethnic Russian as Party chief of a non-Russian republic. When decisions were made over the next few years to change the Party leadership in various republics, a member of the local nationality was invariably selected.

Kolbin, himself, also seems to have learned something—though not according to Kazakh politicians, who invariably picture him as ignorant of local conditions and overbearing.

In fact, when he went to Alma Ata he had had considerable experience in non-Russian areas, having served, *inter alia,* as deputy to Eduard Shevardnadze in Georgia. A tall man with a winning smile and mild manner, at least to outsiders like myself, he struck me as a person who would have been a superior Party official in the 1960s or 1970s, a definite improvement over the autocratic, blustering, finger-in-the-till types who were typical at that time. Kolbin was not insensitive to Kazakh national concerns and publicly lectured Kazakhstan's Russian residents on the necessity of respecting and learning the Kazakh language.[11] Unfortunately for him, he was sent to the wrong place at the wrong time, and though he stayed in the job for two and a half years, his appointment is still deeply resented by the Kazakhs.

Uzbekistan and "Corruption"

WHEREAS CHARGES OF CORRUPTION were implicit in the political changes in Kazakhstan in 1986 and 1987, they were pressed with unusual vigor and publicity in neighboring Uzbekistan.

The campaign against corruption there began before Gorbachev became general secretary. When longtime Party leader and Brezhnev friend Sharaf Rashidov died in 1983, evidence of extensive corruption began to come to light. Rashidov's successor, Inamzhon Usmankhodzhayev, attempted to deflect attention from himself by attacking his predecessor and ostensibly cooperating with law enforcement officials. The most notorious of the cases involved a network of hundreds of officials who had conspired to inflate cotton production figures and embezzle proceeds from commodities that did not exist. Usmankhodzhayev's efforts to run with the cops turned out to be in vain. In January 1988, he himself was removed and charged with various felonies.

Usmankhodzhayev's successor, Rafik Nishanov, announced in 1988 that since late 1983, 100 officials in Uzbekistan had been indicted for corruption, 3,000 had been demoted, and 18,000 Party members had been expelled. Two had been convicted of crimes so serious that they involved the death penalty.[12]

Whatever the validity of the charges (most seem to have been based on fact), the campaign in Uzbekistan eventually misfired. Uzbeks deeply resented being singled out as scapegoats for what they considered, at worst, to be failings of the system as a whole. After all, many recipients of the alleged graft were in Moscow, not Tashkent, but except for some charges against Brezhnev's relatives, no effort was made to bring the Muscovites to justice. Two of the most successful investigators (in terms of confessions and convictions) sent by Moscow, Telman Gdlyan, an ethnic Armenian resident in Moscow, and Nikolai Ivanov, a Russian from Leningrad, were accused of using improper methods to extract confessions and to implicate innocent persons. Their tactics were eventually to become an issue in Moscow when they started directing their accusatory fire at senior officials there.

Injury followed insult when outsiders (mainly Russians) were brought into Uzbekistan to fill the management positions left open when Uzbeks had been arrested. The outsiders had little knowledge of the area and its customs and none at all of its language. To many Uzbeks, the entire "anticorruption" drive was no more than an imperialist trick to bring the area under tighter control by Moscow.

When I visited Tashkent in February 1988, I found that little had changed in the atmosphere since the 1970s. The top Party officials were not yet accessible to foreign visitors. We Americans were treated to lavish meals and colorful dances, but when I made an outdoor speech to open an exhibit sponsored by the U.S. Information Agency, only guests specifically approved by the local authorities were allowed to gather and a sound truck some fifty yards away drowned out the words from our loudspeakers. The political leadership was obviously tense, and this was not surprising, since prosecutions in the "Uzbek affair" were at their height.

Nevertheless, I managed two memorable visits, one to the headquarters of the Religious Board of Muslims of Kazakhstan and Central Asia, the other to the university.

The mosque and its associated library, which holds three thousand bound manuscripts and perhaps ten times that many printed volumes, were well maintained but seemed passive, even sleepy. Both were almost deserted when I was shown through them. At that time, restrictions on religious activity were just beginning to be eased. Two or three years later, Islamic communities would be in the throes of mosque building and organizing new religious training schools, but in 1988 they were still uncertain of what the future would bring and very circumspect in discussions with outsiders.

The university was crowded, but it had much more of a European than Central Asian character—in architecture and particularly in the ethnic composition of the faculty. Even the student body seemed to have a higher proportion of non-Asian students than their share of the republic's population.

Two American graduate students were enrolled at the Uzbek State University in Tashkent University that year. Both were specialists in Turkic languages and culture and associated primarily with Uzbek and other Turkic students. They asked me to support their request to the university administration for a course in colloquial Uzbek, not yet available in the regular curriculum. I was happy to do so but could only marvel at the total insensitivity the university administrators were displaying to the culture of the nationality the institution was supposed to serve. After all, where was one to study the contemporary Uzbek language on an advanced level if not at Uzbek State University?

The political authorities in Tashkent still resisted the very idea of organizing a center for Turkic studies. Stalin's divide-and-rule policy was still in force: Moscow refused to countenance studies that would remind the Turkic-speaking nations of their kinship, since they feared it might set the stage for local cooperation at the expense of the imperial Center.

Communist officials also feared that attention to the common Turkic roots shared not only by Kazakhs and most Central Asians but also by several peoples within the Russian Federation, such as the Tatars, the Bashkirs, and the Yakuts, could stimulate interest in closer ties with Turkey, the only independent Turkic-speaking state. Not only was the Turkish Republic a member of NATO, its predecessor Ottoman Empire had been the Russian empire's principal adversary to the south. During the Civil War that followed the Bolshevik Revolution, some of the anti-Communist leaders had fought under pan-Turkic slogans. However, the affinities among these neighboring nations were so obvious that the official discouragement of Turkic studies did more to irritate Turkic intellectuals than to obscure their ethnic ties.

Violence in the Caucasus

AFTER THE FLARE-UP in Alma Ata in December 1986, the next two years passed relatively peacefully in Central Asia, though local attitudes were hardening on the past policies promoted by Moscow. It was a different story south of the Caucasus Mountains, however; here Armenians and Azeris came into conflict during 1988 and began a chain of violence that was to persist for years.

Armenians had long resented the borders that had been drawn when the Transcaucasian republics had been brought into the Soviet Union. At that time two areas had been included in Azerbaijan that Armenians considered rightfully theirs: the Nakhichevan enclave, located on the Turkish border but surrounded on other sides by Armenia, and a region called Nagorny Karabakh in Russian, totally surrounded by Azerbaijanian territory. Over time, Nakhichevan became predominantly Azeri in population, while Nagorny Karabakh contained an Armenian majority.

Over the decades of Soviet rule, Armenians complained from time to time, but Moscow ignored the appeals as if to say, what difference do these formal borders make?

Nevertheless, as glasnost began to take root and the fear of speaking out subsided, agitation in Nagorny Karabakh's Armenian areas and in Armenia itself grew. Leading Armenian intellectuals took up the cause, and during the winter of 1987–88 the Armenian community in the enclave sent delegations to Moscow on three occasions to press their case. Somehow they received the impression that their desire to unite with Armenia would receive Gorbachev's approval, and in February the enclave's parliament, dominated by Armenians, voted in favor of a transfer to Armenian jurisdiction.

In Moscow, the Politburo rejected the request and instructed the Communist parties in Azerbaijan and Armenia to "normalize" the situation. Then, and subsequently, Gorbachev reacted with extreme irritation to all Armenian requests; he was invariably harsher in dealing with the Armenians than with the Azeris, but for a while the Armenians continued to nourish the hope that he would eventually accept their position.

In the absence of any positive move by Moscow to defuse the situation, it rapidly slipped out of control: demonstrations in Armenia grew from day to day and soon came to involve hundreds of thousands of people. When reports (actually unfounded) circulated in Azerbaijan that two Azeris had been killed in Nagorny Karabakh, unruly elements went on a rampage in Sumgait, an industrial town just north of Baku. News of these disturbances was suppressed, but when rumors spread in Armenia of mass pogroms with hundreds dead, the Soviet news agency TASS finally issued a report that thirty-one people "of different nationalities" had perished. Weeks later, *Izvestiya* told its readers that twenty-six Armenians and six Azeris had died during the disturbances.[13] The shock in Armenia, still grieving from the massacre of Armenians in riots in eastern Turkey during World War I,[14] was overwhelming. Once again, the Armenians seemed to face genocidal forces.

In 1987, half a million Armenians lived in Azerbaijan, mainly in cities, except for Nagorny Karabakh, which had a rural Armenian population. More than 180,000 Azeris lived in Armenia, mainly in rural areas. After Sumgait, Armenians began to flee Azerbaijan en masse, and Armenian authorities reacted by forcing Azeris to leave Armenia, often sending trucks to a village and moving all its residents and their portable possessions across the border.

Moscow equivocated, sometimes trying to suppress information, then publishing news intended to deflate exaggerated rumors, criticizing Armenian "extremists" and then promising "justice" and the rectification of past wrongs. To take the heat off, a commission was established to study the situation and make recommendations.

In May, both Party first secretaries were replaced by persons not closely connected with the existing Party establishments. In choosing the new republic Party leaders, Moscow showed that it had learned from its 1986 gaffe in Kazakhstan: this time an ethnic Azeri was sent to Baku and an ethnic Armenian to Yerevan.

Abdulrakhman Vezirov had been Soviet ambassador to Pakistan and had no obvious ties to the Heidar Aliev machine that had ruled Azerbaijan for decades. An energetic man in his late fifties, Vezirov preferred persuasion to repression and followed a more lenient policy toward unofficial organizations and peaceful demonstrations than his old-style predecessors had. When I called on him, he struck me as a Gorbachev type: articulate, relatively candid, and skilled in developing personal rapport.

His Armenian counterpart, Suren Harutiunian (Arutyunyan in Russian), some nine years younger than Vezirov, was also an outsider to the Armenian establishment. His career had been in Moscow, where his children had grown up and gone through high school.

During one of my visits to Yerevan, Harutiunian mentioned to me that his son, then at Yerevan University, had not spoken Armenian well until he was drafted but had learned it quickly while in the service. I wondered how this could occur, since the Soviet army operated exclusively in Russian. Harutiunian replied that the Armenian soldiers stuck together and spoke Armenian among themselves, and this had given his son the practice he needed to bring his native language up to standard. As soon as the family came to Armenia, Harutiunian Junior became an activist in the Karabakh committee and participated in the demonstrations and sit-ins that went on almost continuously from the spring of 1988.

During the year, Andrei Sakharov became actively involved in trying to head off conflict between Armenians and Azeris. He sent several memoranda and letters to Gorbachev and conferred personally with Yakovlev and other senior officials. In December, at Yakovlev's suggestion, he and his wife, Yelena Bonner, went to Yerevan, Baku, and Stepanakert (the capital of Nagorny Karabakh) to talk to both sides in an effort at conciliation.

They returned deeply discouraged. Despite their efforts to find ways to bridge the differences—and though they were dealing with intellectuals, who presumably were more amenable to reason than those who had less education—they discovered a total polarization.

Sakharov took what he considered a principled approach. Since Armenians made up the majority of the population in Nagorny Karabakh, he felt that their wishes regarding their political status should be granted. If this upset the Azeris, it was the duty of the Soviet authorities to prevent violence by force.

With all my respect for Sakharov's integrity, I felt his proposed solution could be dangerous. Granting a formal transfer of territory, no matter how justified in principle (and of course there would be arguments over that), would almost certainly lead to violence and extensive loss of life. And it would not be such a simple matter to protect the people involved—unless the Soviet Union reverted to a police state, the last thing Sakharov would have wanted.

For that reason, I found Gorbachev's refusal to change the constitutional structure understandable. What was not understandable were his failure to do *anything* effective and his increasingly evident bias against the Armenians. If Nagorny Karabakh was to be left under the jurisdiction of Azerbaijan, there should have been explicit warnings to Baku that Armenian rights in the enclave must be protected if a future transfer was to be avoided, establishment of an appropriate monitoring mechanism, and steps taken to prevent both republics from expelling persons of the other nationality.

Left to their own devices, and with Moscow's backing, men like Vezirov and Harutiunian could probably have worked something out. But they had no freedom of action. They were trapped between Moscow's passivity and political passions at home. Attitudes in both Armenia and Azerbaijan continued to harden, and old hatreds took on new life.

In 1988, however, there was no substantial independence movement in either of these republics. Each was seeking Moscow's support for its territorial claims, and neither, at this point, questioned its status in the Soviet Union or its commitment to "socialism." Recognizing this, most Moscow officials who dealt with the issue considered it a unique, though acute, problem and not a symptom of failure of Soviet nationality policy in general.

The Balts Look to the Past

ON THE NORTHWEST BORDER of the Soviet Union, a different sort of challenge, one much more direct, was building up in the three Baltic republics, which in the 1920s and 1930s had been independent nations.

During the decades of Soviet rule, it was compulsory in public discourse to adhere to myths that reversed truth and falsehood. Elected parliaments, it was alleged, had voluntarily petitioned for the privilege of entering the Soviet Union. If there had been some arrests after the war, they had been directed only at "class enemies" who had collaborated with the Nazis and committed war crimes.

To gain control over their future, the Balts first had to resurrect the facts of their past, in particular the manner in which they had been forced into the Soviet Union by a cynical deal between Hitler and Stalin, a claim Moscow still insisted was imperialist propaganda.

On August 23, 1987, the anniversary of the Molotov-Ribbentrop agreement, Estonians, Latvians, and Lithuanians tested the limits of glasnost by organizing protest demonstrations. Crowds of more than a thousand persons were allowed to march without serious interference. A year later, there would be tens of thousands of demonstrators.

In 1988, the Baltic resistance to Moscow became more organized. At first, the Estonians were the most active. In January, they issued a program for a national independence party that set forth the issues that were to dominate political debate over the next three years, including the restoration of "historical truth" about Estonia's absorption into the Soviet Union and the acts of repression carried out against Estonians, restoration of the Estonian language and ethnic Estonians to "precedence" in the republic, defense of the environment, replacement of the planned economy by a free market, a guarantee of internationally recognized human rights, military service confined to Estonian soil, multiple-candidate elections, reopening of Estonian diplomatic posts abroad, and observance of Estonia's original independence day as a national holiday.

This declaration made clear that the resumption of Estonian independence was the goal, although the declaration's drafters were willing to "defend the interests of the Estonian people in the present political situation, acting as a national opposition party to the Communist Party of Estonia."[15]

At that time, the Communist Party was the only legal political party in the USSR, so it was decided in Estonia and elsewhere to organize "national fronts" instead of political parties as such. By calling their organization something other than a "party," the organizers hoped to avoid legal prosecution and also to attract support from within the national Communist parties. They also used another device to ease their way with Moscow: most were called "movements to support restructuring," or perestroika. They thus suggested that their movements were designed to support, not oppose, Gorbachev's policies.

This strategy was spectacularly successful. Estonians formed a "National [or People's] Front in Support of Perestroika" in April and within two months it claimed 40,000 members. In June, Lithuanians founded a comparable organization which subsequently became famous as Sąjūdis, "The Movement" in Lithuanian. The Latvians soon followed, and draft programs appeared in local newspapers in late summer and early fall. By October, all three held founding congresses and had adopted programs that resembled the one suggested by Estonian intellectuals in January.[16]

A remarkable feature of all three political movements was the significant participation of Communist Party members.

Concurrently, public demonstrations became not just occasional occurrences but a regular practice. On February 25, some 4,000 persons demonstrated in Tallinn to mark the seventieth anniversary of Estonian independence. In March and June, there were demonstrations in all three republics to commemorate those who had suffered and died in the deportations and purges. And in August, on that year's anniversary of the signing of the Nazi-Soviet pact, the demonstrators in each capital numbered in the tens of thousands.

Under burgeoning public pressure, first Estonia, then Lithuania restored the flags and anthems of their independent states. The Communist-enforced taboos were falling with every month that passed, increasingly with the support of the local Communist Party itself.

Gorbachev's reaction to the growing nationalism in the Baltic was confused. He considered "nationalist" demands, whether from Armenians or Balts, to be acts of treachery that could bring down perestroika by providing Ligachev and other conservative elements in the leadership a pretext for cracking down. If this happened, it would mean the end of perestroika as Gorbachev defined it. There could be no elections in 1989 to create a truly representative assembly, and the goal of creating a state based on the rule of law would become a mockery.

But he also had to consider the foreign factor. He was, after all, in the midst of ending the cold war and was to face Ronald Reagan in May and Mitterrand, Thatcher, and Kohl later in the year, then travel to New York at the end of the year to try to impress the world with a speech at the United Nations and make sure that President-elect Bush would keep Reagan's cooperative policy on track. A crackdown on independence movements, particularly in the Baltic area, would strain the contacts he had cultivated so carefully and put him back into a position of confrontation with the West.

Still, he had no sympathy for the separatists. He had not risen to the top of the Soviet political structure to preside over its dissolution. And he had not become Communist number one to reestablish capitalism.

So he equivocated, trying to find a way to make the problems go away.

First, he tried to give a new, more human face to the local Communist parties. Between June and October all three of the old-style first secretaries were replaced by men more suited to working with the burgeoning democratic forces. In all three republics, the new Communist leaders made strenuous efforts to co-opt the reform movement.

Additionally, in August, he sent Alexander Yakovlev to Latvia and Lithuania to try to calm the situation. It was during this trip that Yakovlev delivered his strong rebuttal to Ligachev's defense of the class struggle concept. Although Yakovlev specifically rejected the Baltic goals of establishing embassies abroad and issuing a separate currency, his overall approach to Baltic agitation for autonomy was understanding and benign. His visit, which the Balts took as tantamount to endorsement by Gorbachev of their aspirations, encouraged the democratic forces there.

In fact, Gorbachev did not sympathize with what was happening in the Baltic states. When Yakovlev returned from his trip and proposed privately that they be offered autonomy in the framework of a confederation, neither Gorbachev nor any other member of the Politburo supported him.[17]

Instead of making concessions to the Balts, Gorbachev attempted to constrain them by restricting their constitutional right to secede. In October, draft amendments to the Constitution were published in connection with preparations for new elections. The Balts noted to their horror that the new USSR Supreme Soviet was to be given the power to approve or disapprove of the secession of union republics, as well as to annul republic laws deemed to be in conflict with union laws.

The reaction in all three Baltic states proved the extent to which nationalist forces had penetrated the local establishments. The national fronts, of course, condemned the proposed draft, and within days literally millions signed protest petitions. (In Lithuania, the signatories made up two thirds of the entire voting population.) But what was remarkable was that the three Supreme Soviets, which had been under tight Communist control and still had overwhelming Communist majorities, also condemned the effort to negate the right of secession.

The Estonian Supreme Soviet went even further. On November 16, it adopted a sovereignty declaration that asserted its right to overrule *Soviet* laws held in violation of the *Estonian* constitution.

At this point Gorbachev drew the line, formally and officially. He called the USSR Supreme Soviet Presidium into session and demanded that the Estonian action be overruled. In his speech to that body he also lashed out against the efforts of the Estonian parliament to assume control over assets in Estonia and to reestablish private property.

> As is known, private property is the basis of exploitation of man by man, and our revolution was conducted in order to eliminate it and transfer all property to the people. The attempt to restore private property is retrogressive and would be a seriously mistaken decision.[18]

Gorbachev won the round with the Estonian parliament since the USSR Supreme Soviet Presidium dutifully nullified the Estonian act. But he was forced to delay his effort to restrict the right of secession since many republics opposed the attempt. Gorbachev's emotional comments attacking the concept of private property showed how far he was from accepting a concept fundamental to a workable market economy.

His attacks on nationalism and private property did not play well in either the Baltics or the Caucasus. The nationalists in fact gained strength from Gorbachev's opposition. They would soon win overwhelming victories in the very elections Gorbachev was organizing.

The Western Borderlands

FREE OF THE VIOLENCE that was rocking Armenia and Azerbaijan, and—so far—of the republicwide national movements that formed so quickly in the Baltic, the three western republics of Belorussia, Ukraine, and Moldavia nevertheless began to awake from the political torpor that had been created and perpetuated by periodic repression. Naturally, the areas most recently acquired by the Soviet Union tended to take the lead in demanding change.

Moldavia, along with western Ukraine and the western provinces of Belorussia, had been effectively absorbed into the Soviet Union only after World War II. Like the Baltic states, these areas had been allocated to the Soviet Union in the Nazi-Soviet pact, but, unlike the Baltic states, they had not been independent countries before they became Soviet territory.

In all three republics, demands to give the national language a more prominent place was the first issue that attracted wide support. In Belorussia, the discovery of mass graves of persons executed on Stalin's orders gave further impetus to the campaign to organize a national front on the Baltic model.

Moldavian writers and other intellectuals joined in a Democratic Movement in Support of Perestroika, which organized a rally in Kishinev during the summer that drew five thousand people. The movement favored declaring Moldavian the official language of the republic, restoring the Latin alphabet, and replacing the republic's Communist flag with the traditional Romanian tricolor.

In Ukraine, hard-line Vladimir Shcherbitsky did his best to inhibit political movements that might question Communist policy, but Moscow's new stance made it impossible to block the formation of some "informal groups" that operated on a purely local basis, primarily in Lviv and other parts of western Ukraine.

Vyacheslav Chornovil, released from prison in 1985, returned to his native Lviv and was given work as a stoker in a construction materials plant. He immediately resumed his political activity, but it was 1987 before he put together (mainly with other released political prisoners) a group that called itself the Ukrainian Helsinki Union. It resumed a publication called the *Ukrainian Herald,* which Chornovil had published underground before his arrest.

In 1988, he and his associates started assembling an umbrella organization to coordinate several small opposition groups. They held a founding congress in July that issued a strongly worded Declaration of Principles. It labeled current policies "outright genocide" of the Ukrainian people and called for the restoration of Ukrainian statehood and a confederation of independent states to replace the USSR.[19]

In response, the Shcherbitsky regime placed them, in Chornovil's words, "under siege" for the next six months.[20] The authorities broke up demonstrations in Lviv with fire hoses and police dogs. It was not until the following year that these groups were able to put together a Ukraine-wide organization. But agitation was growing in cultural organizations like the Ukrainian Writers' Union for more attention to the use and development of the Ukrainian language.

The Belorussian authorities also maintained a hard line when intellectuals in Minsk began to organize. Nevertheless, some of the republic's most prominent writers, artists, and scholars formed an association called Adradzhennye, meaning "Rebirth" or "Revival." Its main purpose, as the name suggested, was to lead a revival of Belorussian language and culture. Many of the same figures were also active in a society called Martyrology of Belorussia, which was devoted to investigation of Stalin's crimes against the Belorussian people. Mass graves had been found near Minsk at a location called Kuropaty Forest, where the NKVD, a predecessor of the KGB, had conducted mass executions on the eve of World War II. Although the government had established a commission to investigate the atrocity, a citizens' group was formed to do the same.

These informal groups organized a large demonstration for October 30. Although they had obtained an official permit to gather, the authorities called out the riot police and broke up the demonstration brutally—though without casualties. Since this was at a time when demonstrations were routinely authorized in Moscow, Leningrad, and the Baltic states, the organizers cried foul, and Vasil Bykov, a Belorussian writer whose works were well known in Moscow, wrote an article for *Moscow News* that accused the Belorussian Party leaders of undermining Gorbachev's policies.

Shortly after his article appeared, Bykov joined a group of prominent intellectuals who accompanied Gorbachev on his trip to New York and the United Nations. It was not clear whether he was included because he had criticized the Belorussian leaders or in spite of that fact. His prominence and that of his associates in the National Front movement offered a measure of protection from personal reprisals, but the Belorussian authorities continued to harass public meetings and resisted registering the National Front movement as a recognized public organization.

At the end of 1988, none of the three western republics had national front movements on the scale of the Baltic states', but a foundation had been laid that would permit rapid growth of these movements the following year.

Chebrikov's Xenophobia

THROUGHOUT 1987 AND 1988, Moscow seemed confused over how to respond to the growing assertiveness of the non-Russian nations. Some things were permitted, some were opposed but tolerated, some were forbidden and repressed. But there was no consistent pattern.

The KGB, however, had an answer. When the summer of 1987 brought a wave of demonstrations in a number of cities—an unprecedented situation, since previously demonstrations had occurred singly and infrequently—KGB Chief Chebrikov considered it necessary to offer a public explanation. This he did in September in a speech charging that Western intelligence agencies were stirring up the minority nationalities.[21] This comment, which was to be revived from time to time as the troubles intensified, had no foundation, but respect for the facts had never been a KGB specialty.

Chebrikov's allegations did, however, provide certain operational advantages for his organization. By placing the blame on outsiders, it relieved the chief of Soviet intelligence of the embarrassing duty of explaining that the Communist Party itself was the culprit. Also, by blaming Western intelligence, he served notice to those critical of the regime that they could be suspected of espionage if they persisted. Chebrikov was to repeat these charges in 1988, and his successor reverted to them on the eve of the Soviet Union's collapse.

Whatever the cause of national unrest, by the summer of 1988 the Soviet leaders realized that their smug judgment two years earlier at the Twenty-seventh Party Congress had not been justified. The "nationality question" had *not* been solved. Public disaffection was rife, and outbreaks of violence were becoming more common.

Observing these events from Moscow, I was not surprised that the Balts were taking advantage of glasnost to demand changes. Their specific grievances were familiar to me. There were developments, however, that I could not have predicted.

First, reformers from Moscow began to support the Baltic cause as a logical part of their program to democratize the Soviet Union. Prominent "liberals" such as historian Yuri Afanasiev and sociologist Tatyana Zaslavskaya encouraged the Balts to organize and demand their rights. Legal scholar Boris Kurashvili of the Soviet Institute of State and Law first suggested in public print that organizations to support perestroika be formed in the republics. I fully agreed with them that true democratic reform of the Soviet Union would require giving the Balts freedom of choice, and I was encouraged that they not only understood that Baltic freedom was not the enemy of Russian freedom but were willing to act on that assumption.

Second, the movements for autonomy attracted widespread support from members of the local Communist parties. This clearly created a dilemma for Gorbachev. Would he allow the local Communist parties to support demands for autonomy and, eventually, independence—in which case he would have to let them operate independently of the Party high command in Moscow? Or would he insist on the total subservience of republic Communist parties to the Central Committee in Moscow, as had been traditional since the times of Lenin and Stalin?

We would get answers to these questions only later. In 1988, Gorbachev seemed to want to have it both ways. At the United Nations he was talking of freedom of choice without exceptions, but at home he seemed to be looking for reasons to make exceptions.

VIII

Washington Fumbles

I think the cold war is not over.
BRENT SCOWCROFT, January 22, 1989[1]

B y January 1989, when George Bush took the oath of office as president of the United States, it was obvious to me that the Soviet Union was no longer capable of maintaining the empire outside its borders. Once the Eastern Europeans decided to throw off the Soviet yoke, there would be nothing Gorbachev could do but accept the outcome. Any attempt on his part to apply military force would have brought an end to perestroika and his own rule. Having just emerged from the bruising and unpopular war in Afghanistan, the Soviet people would not tolerate another Kremlin decision that would expose their conscript army to mortal danger abroad.

When I reviewed the situation at the beginning of the year, I came to the conclusion that 1989 could be a year of opportunity for the United States to bring its influence to bear on the evolving Soviet system. Our policies had already helped set the Soviet agenda on such matters as human rights and the free flow of information; now was the time to bring our economic might to bear, not as we had done during the cold war, with sanctions and punitive measures but by supporting steps to bring the Soviet Union into the community of free nations, to lead it into a partnership.

The four-part agenda we had forged during the Reagan administration had deliberately omitted economic relations. It seemed to us then that closer economic ties would have to await the end of Soviet intervention in Afghanistan, Soviet meddling in other Third World conflicts, and the division of Europe—in other words, the end of the cold war. We also wanted to test Soviet willingness to reduce arms substantially and to make sure that the Soviet leadership was ready to respect human rights and let its citizens have some control over their government.

By January 1989, the trends were obvious, and I believed that a more active American policy in the economic sphere could accelerate Soviet reforms in a direction consistent with our interests. Economic cooperation, of course, would have to depend on Gorbachev's willingness to continue the changes he had started, but the prospect of a payoff in more trade and investment—and ultimately, if needed, in some types of assistance—might help Gorbachev make the hard decisions that confronted him.

I was not thinking of pouring American taxpayers' money into the Soviet economy. This would have been impossible politically and unwise in itself. The Soviet economy could not be cured by infusions from the outside. A version of the Marshall Plan for the USSR would not have worked. In 1946, Europe had been exhausted by the war but the basic institutions needed for an economic revival had been in place, so that the Marshall Plan could prime an existing pump. The Soviet Union had no such pump, and trying to prime it would be like pouring water onto sand.

Nevertheless, I believed there were ways an American government could encourage moves toward a market economy in the Soviet Union and simultaneously serve American economic interests. Take energy, for example. The industrialized world had been shaken by the oil crisis of the 1970s caused by OPEC's sharp price increases. By 1989, the oil market had stabilized, but the world remained dangerously dependent on oil from the Middle East. The largest known reserves in the world, however, were in the Soviet Union, where production had nevertheless begun to fall because of poor management and antiquated technology.

If the Soviet government could be convinced to improve conditions for foreign investment in energy production, it could attract large amounts of foreign capital, not as foreign aid but as investment. The results would be beneficial to all: more efficient energy production and rising foreign exchange earnings for the Soviet Union, profits for the Western investors, and more stable energy prices, which would benefit consumers everywhere.

However, this could not happen as long as the Soviet government maintained centralized control over the oil and gas industry. The government would have to be persuaded to restructure the industry so that production, processing, and distribution would be managed by competing firms. At first they might be state owned, but if they were reorganized as joint-stock companies, they could be more easily privatized in the future.

Or take agriculture. Since the early 1970s, the United States had sold each year from 8 million to more than 20 million tons of grain—mainly wheat and corn—to the Soviet Union. Our farmers had come to depend upon this trade. When President Carter restricted it following the Soviet invasion of Afghanistan,[2] his move caused a political rebellion in the farm states. The grain trade was financed by short-term credits guaranteed by a U.S. government agency, the Commodity Credit Corporation. The Soviets had always paid their debts promptly, but, if they should ever default, the U.S. taxpayer would have to cover the loss.

This situation was fraught with danger. In the first place, all the trade was through centralized Soviet organizations, the very organizations that must be broken up if perestroika was to succeed. And the Soviet government was piling up so much foreign debt that it would soon exceed its ability to pay unless export earnings turned around quickly, but there was little prospect of this. Therefore, if the United States and Soviet Union continued to conduct the grain trade as they had for nearly two decades, both countries would suffer rude shocks. The Soviet Union would eventually default on its debt at great cost to the American taxpayer, and the American farmer would lose an important market. Meanwhile, the food shortages resulting in the Soviet Union not only would cause much human suffering but would create a major problem for the political leadership.

But I saw not only dangers ahead but also opportunities. The Soviet Union could not solve its food problem unless it reversed the ravages of Stalin's collectivization by taking production out of the control of bureaucrats and re-creating a class of private farmers. Also, it would never be able to distribute food efficiently unless it replaced the centralized, corrupt bureaucratic system of retail trade with a privately owned, open, competitive system. The "socialist" trade bureaucracy let 40 to 50 percent of produce spoil before it reached the consumer. A modern, privately operated wholesale and retail trade system could greatly improve the food supply, even if farm production did not increase.

Some might question whether it was in the United States' interest for the Soviet Union to solve its food problem. Isn't it better, they would ask, to have it dependent on the United States for food imports and let the American farmer profit from this than to encourage it to meet its own needs? If it were successful, we might lose an important market.

This attitude seemed to me shortsighted. In the first place, the Soviet economy was deteriorating so rapidly that it could not continue to pay for our grain much longer if reform failed. This meant that the current situation could not go on indefinitely. Second, even a productive, largely self-sufficient Soviet agriculture would require large imports of feed grains for the diet the consumer wanted. The Soviet Union simply does not have the right climate for adequate feed grain production, while the United States is the world's most efficient producer. This meant that even if the Soviet Union could become self-sufficient in bread grains and our wheat exports were to fall as a result, our exports of corn and soybeans to feed chickens and fatten livestock would likely increase.

The question, as I saw it, was not whether it was in the United States' interest to help reform Soviet agriculture but whether it could be done. The barriers to privatization of agriculture, food processing, and marketing were enormous. They were doctrinal, on grounds of Marxist principle; legal, since there could be no private ownership of land; fiscal, because of prohibitive taxes on profits; and institutional, since there was no banking system for a market economy, sources of investment capital, or operative market mechanisms. These barriers could not be swept away overnight, and Gorbachev had not even decided that it would be a good idea to remove some of them. But if someone could explain to him how a market might work, he might be persuaded.

One approach seemed to me worth considering. Instead of continuing to offer credit guarantees for loans to finance grain exports, why not offer an arrangement whereby the United States would sell agricultural products in the Soviet Union for rubles and then invest the rubles in an investment bank, run under American supervision, to finance farmers and entrepreneurs in the food-processing industry? The offer would have to be contingent on a firm commitment by the Soviet government to create a private sector for food production and distribution, but I thought we had enough leverage to give an impetus to thinking that was already beginning to move in this direction.

One difficulty, of course, was that U.S. farmers would have to be paid from the federal budget at a time when the deficit was growing ever larger. But it seemed to me that the advantages outweighed the disadvantages. The loan guarantees we were then offering—and were likely to continue to offer in the absence of an alternative program—would not be cost free in the long or even medium run. If we continued our current practices, the taxpayer would end up paying for the grain exports anyway, we would lose the market, and the U.S. government would have no equity in the Soviet Union that might eventually provide a return on the initial investment.

Or take space technology. The Soviets were interested in competing in the world market for space-lift capability. Specifically, they wanted to bid on contracts to put communications satellites into orbit. They were also interested in leasing their space station. We had traditionally tried to exclude them from the communications satellite market (though they had their own satellite system) for both security and commercial reasons.

I thought we should take another look at our traditional policy. If the Soviets agreed to major reductions in their ballistic missiles, joined us in an international regime to control the spread of missile technology, opened their own rocket industry to foreign inspection and even cooperation, would it not be in our interest to allow them to participate in civilian markets? Their competition in lifting satellites could cut costs to communications companies and ultimately consumers, and joint use of the space station they had already developed might save the American taxpayer billions in duplicating the same technology.

These were only a few examples of ways in which the United States and other developed countries might support the Soviet Union's entry into the world economy and derive tangible benefits from the process. Unless the United States offered proposals of the sort I have described, I doubted that Gorbachev or other reformers could successfully lead the Soviet Union to a free-market economy. They would need consistent, practical advice from the West, backed up by concrete offers to cooperate in making a painful transition more bearable. But it had to be cooperation, a partnership with mutual benefits, and not simply aid, if it was to be effective and sustainable.

I was not an expert in any of these areas, and I knew that they were highly complex and required careful examination by people more knowledgeable than I before responsible proposals could be made. I had no desire to press for half-baked, impractical projects that would only cause resentment when they failed. But what worried me was the fact that neither our own government nor those of our allies had begun to think about concrete ways in which we could all benefit from a demilitarized, democratized Soviet Union. The sad fact was that our bureaucracies were still dealing with issues that while the cold war was on had seemed vitally important but as it receded were becoming increasingly irrelevant or—at times—actually counterproductive.

A new administration would shortly take over in Washington, and I hoped it would explore how we might accelerate the encouraging trends that were now, I thought, obvious to all.

George Bush Takes Over

THERE WERE SEVERAL REASONS to be optimistic that the Bush administration would take a fresh, creative look at the U.S.-Soviet economic relationship. Both George Bush and his secretary of state, James Baker III, had extensive business experience and a network of friends in the business world. Both were pragmatists, and both seemed to understand the dangers of becoming a captive of government bureaucracy. The bureaucracy could not be safely ignored—policy implementation depended on it—but it required firm leadership when new policies were needed since its natural tendency was to keep doing what it had always done.

There was also a political consideration that I hoped would focus the new president's attention on innovative policies. Although George Bush had been Ronald Reagan's vice president and in that capacity had been closely involved in forging Reagan's policies toward the Soviet Union, he would wish to put his own stamp on his administration's foreign policy. He could not simply continue the Reagan policies without a change; he would have to do something important with his personal label on it.

But Bush would have a handicap in dealing with the Soviet Union that Reagan had not suffered: he was distrusted by many in the Republican right wing. Reagan could not be outflanked from the right.[3] But Bush could, particularly on treaty ratification votes in the Senate, where he would need to muster a two-thirds vote. His weakness with the right would tempt him to play the tough guy in order to please his potential critics.

The Soviet leaders had learned that they could do business with Ronald Reagan, and by 1988 they were comfortable with him. They would have liked to see him continue in office for a third term, but since this was impossible, they were pleased that Vice President Bush won the 1988 election. They hoped that this would mean policy continuity, a theme Gorbachev stressed in his meetings with both Reagan and Bush on Governors Island in New York in December 1988.

Even before Bush took office, I sensed that there would likely be a pause in U.S. policy momentum. Though Bush had been part of the Reagan policy team on U.S.-Soviet relations, he would look for a policy he could call his own and in doing so would have to allay fears of potential right-wing critics that he was being taken in by Soviet duplicity. Some were arguing that perestroika was a giant hoax, designed to strengthen the Soviet Union militarily while disarming the United States and the West. The facts gave no support to this interpretation, and it ran against logic since perestroika was weakening, not strengthening, the Soviet military, but the argument was a political factor in the United States and had to be dealt with.

For these reasons, I realized that we should expect a few months of hard-line rhetoric in Washington, coupled with a show of adjusting our policy toward the Soviet Union to make it more demanding. If these maneuvers freed the new president's hands to engage the Soviet Union more actively, they would be worth the small delay.

Though I had no instructions to discuss the question with the Soviets—and expected none—I considered it important to tell them that they should be prepared for some slowing of momentum in our relationship and should recognize that some of the new president's early statements would be designed to disarm his critics, not to signal a harder policy.

The best way to get the message to the leaders, I thought, would be to rely on a senior Soviet official who had some understanding of U.S. politics to explain our ways. Alexander Bessmertnykh, one of Shevardnadze's principal deputies in the Foreign Ministry, who had spent most of his career in Washington, seemed ideally placed. He would likely understand my point, would know how to explain it to Shevardnadze and Gorbachev, and was senior enough to have ready access to both.

Therefore, shortly after our presidential election, I invited Bessmertnykh to a private lunch at Spaso House. When the conversation turned to the Bush administration, I told Bessmertnykh that I wanted to speak personally. I said I was certain that, when he took office, President Bush would seek to expand cooperation. However, he might make some strong statements now and then to defuse the criticism that he was "soft." If this should happen, the Soviet leaders should not assume that Bush had lost interest in constructive negotiations but understand that he was preparing the way for closer relations. Meanwhile, I hoped the Soviet leaders would avoid actions that would seem confrontational to the American public, since this would make it more difficult for Bush to develop a forthcoming policy.

Bessmertnykh assured me that they had no thought of precipitating any sort of confrontation. On the contrary, improved relations were vital to them. He seemed to understand what I had said about the possibility of rhetoric but reminded me that Gorbachev, too, faced political problems at home and that incautious statements from our side would make it more difficult for him to reach agreements with us.

Nevertheless, throughout the spring of 1989, both Gorbachev and Shevardnadze worried about the direction U.S. policy was taking under President Bush.[4] Bush periodically gave Gorbachev general assurances, as in a telephone call a few days after taking office, but American policy tended to freeze and on some questions became more demanding. The Soviet leaders could have understood a hiatus of a few weeks while the new president took stock and set a course, but the wholesale replacement of the Reagan foreign policy team and the months of "policy review" in 1989 made them nervous. Bessmertnykh and other "Americanists" tried to reassure their superiors that Bush would resume Reagan's policy of accommodation, but skeptics about improved relations with the United States, such as KGB Chief Kryuchkov and the military high command, seized on "the pause," as it was known in Moscow, as proof that Bush had no intention of dealing fairly with the Soviet Union.

By January, it was clear that Bush would make an almost clean sweep of the Reagan foreign policy team. In terms of personnel, the transition would be like what happens when control of the presidency passes to the opposition party rather than the normal pattern when a candidate of the presidential party wins. This did not surprise me. Having worked in the White House for more than three years, I was aware of the tensions between the "Reagan people" and the "Bush people"—though, as a professional who stayed out of partisan politics, I was on good terms with both groups.

Nevertheless, while I expected Bush to replace most Cabinet and sub-Cabinet appointees, I was not prepared for his tactics, which resembled a hostile takeover much more than a cooperative transition. I visited Washington twice during the transition period but, aside from one call on President-elect Bush with Andrei Sakharov, was unable to schedule any meetings with the persons he had named to head his new foreign policy team. They were all experienced and well informed in general but could not have been fully aware of many things that were then occurring in the Soviet Union, and—in particular—the growing potential for American influence on developments there. I was frustrated not to have an opportunity to discuss these matters with the incoming policy makers.

When I returned to Moscow, I asked our embassy staff to do a comprehensive review of recent developments in the Soviet Union and to think about ways in which the United States might usefully respond. We had already sent several reports when President Bush announced that he would undertake a comprehensive policy review of our relations with the Soviet Union.

Since I had been unable to brief the incoming team in person, I decided I would offer my recommendations to the new administration in a series of personal messages, early enough to be used in the government-wide policy review. I had the best staff any ambassador could hope for, but I knew that there is no substitute for the judgment of the chief of mission. I also knew that no message would be truly mine, in substance, style, and nuance, if I did not draft it myself.

Since before World War II, our embassy in Moscow had maintained a staff retreat on a four-acre plot in a village called Tarasovka, nearly an hour's drive from the Kremlin. Rebecca and I liked the restful surroundings and had taken our children for weekends and special holidays there during my earlier tours in Moscow. When I was in charge of the embassy in 1981, we had been able to spend most Saturday evenings and Sundays there.

Since we had returned to Moscow in 1987, however, we had rarely had time to use the dacha. Duties in Moscow or travel elsewhere occupied virtually every weekend, and our work did not cease on holidays. Nevertheless, I realized that I had to get my recommendations to the new administration soon if they were to have any practical effect on policy decisions. I blocked my calendar the last weekend in January so that I could go out to the dacha and gather my thoughts amid the snow-covered pines and birches.

On Friday evening, Rebecca and I drove out to Tarasovka armed with provisions for two days, a supply of yellow legal pads, and a fountain pen. I took no documents and no other reading matter. If there was not enough in my head for my analysis and recommendations, it was too late to fill the void.

After dinner Friday evening, I began to jot down the major points I wanted to make. Then, from Saturday morning, I would work for two to three hours at a stretch, then take a break for a half hour or so, strolling on the snowy paths, hauling firewood to the cottage in a wheelbarrow, or just watching the flames in the makeshift fireplace, which decades before had been adapted by a Russian craftsman from a typical Russian stove. Most of my ideas came during the breaks.

By Sunday afternoon, I had made up detailed outlines for three lengthy telegrams and rough drafts of the first two. I returned to Moscow in the evening with a sheaf of thoroughly wrinkled yellow sheets, which I had stuffed into my parka during walks and crushed under my pillow when I slept. Though I doubted the Soviets could derive any advantage from reading my analysis, I was determined to keep it private.

The next day my secretary heroically deciphered my scrawl and produced a legible text. I then circulated the drafts and the outline of recommendations to my key officers. I wanted their corrections, suggestions, and additional ideas. At first we discussed the messages in the embassy's secure conference room; then each section head gave me a memorandum in writing. By the end of the week, two messages were ready to send to Washington. It took another ten days to finish the third. All were mine in style and substance, but I could not have written them without the many contributions from my colleagues.

———

The three messages dealt, respectively, with internal developments in the Soviet Union, the evolving Soviet foreign policy, and recommended policy approaches for the United States. I was convinced that the foreign policy of the Soviet Union grew out of its internal politics and therefore we needed first to understand what was happening inside the country before analyzing its external behavior.

What was happening inside the country was potentially nothing less than a revolution. The goals set by the Party conference in 1988 for establishing a government of limited powers, taking steps to create an elective assembly with real power to legislate, opening public discussion and the mass media to new ideas, and formally rejecting the ideological basis for a struggle with the West had set forces into motion that would undermine the old system irretrievably. The first real election campaign in Soviet history was in progress and provided daily evidence of the degree and depth of change. Gorbachev, I felt, was still firmly in charge, even though opposition to his policies was growing, and his political future depended on a continuation of the reform course.

Since good relations with the West were essential if perestroika was to succeed, I was confident that Gorbachev's foreign policy would continue to stress cooperation with the rest of the world. This would mean that if reform movements developed in Eastern Europe, Gorbachev could not use or threaten force to put them down without sacrificing his domestic policy and probably his own position.

Even if Gorbachev should be overthrown by hard-line forces—something I did not expect—they, too, would be unable to use force in Eastern Europe since that would bring widespread and probably uncontrollable disorders in the Soviet Union itself. Therefore, the Brezhnev Doctrine was dead because it could no longer be applied, whatever the desire of the ruling group in Moscow.

I was aware that some in Washington were predicting that Gorbachev would not last long and therefore the new administration should not waste time and effort dealing with him. I thought that this attitude was totally mistaken and pointed out that Gorbachev had demonstrated an ability to outmaneuver his critics and was likely to continue to do so in the foreseeable future. Rather than holding back, we should engage him in an effort to channel his reforms in a direction compatible with U.S. interests and those of the Soviet people, whose real interests were not in conflict with ours. Even if the doubters turned out to be right, we would lose nothing by solving as many problems as possible while Gorbachev was in office.

Another argument I rejected was that perestroika was a trick to lull the West while the Soviet Union revamped its economy and surpassed us in arms.[5] Of course, the goal of perestroika was to improve the Soviet economy, but the methods Gorbachev had chosen were undermining the power of the Communist Party and the military-industrial complex to control the country. Perestroika would succeed only if it transformed the country into an open society with a government controlled by its citizens. There was no chance that such a society would devote a quarter or more of its gross national product to armaments.

Although I was convinced that Gorbachev's goals were consistent with ours, I did not favor giving him political support as an individual. I felt we would be deluding ourselves if we thought we could pick and choose Soviet leaders; only the Soviet political process could do that. If we showed favoritism toward individuals, that could actually be harmful to them at home. What I wanted was to support specific goals and policies. If a Soviet leader, in his own interest, stood for the same things we did and thereby derived some advantage from the relationship with us, that was fine, but our support should be for policies, not persons.

I recommended that we continue to negotiate the four-part agenda that had proved itself during the Reagan administration but that we add two categories. The existing agenda included reducing arms, working to settle conflicts in third areas, protecting human rights, and eliminating the iron curtain by permitting persons and information to flow freely between West and East. There had been substantial progress in all these areas, but much remained to be done. However, the process could be accelerated, I felt, if we added economic cooperation and a closer partnership in dealing with transnational issues such as terrorism, drug trafficking, and environmental degradation.

I knew that the economic questions would be particularly complex. Our policy had been based on limiting trade and investment so as not to strengthen the Soviet military machine and on denying the Soviet Union normal trading status because it restricted the right of its citizens to emigrate. Any change in our economic policy had to be contingent on changes in the Soviet Union, but aside from the demand for free emigration, we had never defined what we would require to drop our trade and investment restrictions.

I recommended an urgent, comprehensive study of the steps necessary for the Soviet Union to become part of the world economy, followed by a consideration of what we might do to encourage a move to a consumer-oriented economy. I hoped we could use the study for consultations with our European and Asian allies in an effort to harmonize our approaches to what was becoming a major international problem. If we did our homework promptly, by fall we would be in a position to engage the Soviet leaders in discussing cooperative measures that we and they could take. If they were willing to reduce the potential military threat to us and our allies and to move in a realistic way to join the world, we could ease the process by providing support at critical points.

Another recommendation was to propose holding annual summit meetings. These would allow our leaders to keep in touch with each other's thinking and gave impetus to the negotiating process. Nevertheless, summits had at times been delayed because political leaders feared that if they did not reach a major agreement their public would consider the meeting a failure.

I understood the potential political problem for both sides but thought the best way to deal with it would be to meet routinely every year. If special circumstances required meetings at other times, they could be arranged, but one meeting a year should be considered normal. In time the public would learn not to expect an orgy of signing ceremonies whenever our leaders met and would accept summit meetings as a normal component of diplomatic relations.

A third recommendation resulted from the growing separatism in many regions of the Soviet Union. We were trying, from our embassy in Moscow and our consulate general in Leningrad, to keep abreast of developments in a country with more than a hundred nationalities that covered nine time zones and was showing increasing signs of ethnic and regional separatism. It was manifestly impossible to give this vast territory the attention it required with only one medium-sized embassy and a much smaller consulate. Therefore, I proposed that we open several small offices, staffed by four or five Americans each, in regional capitals. What we needed to do—follow developments and provide an U.S. presence—did not require classified materials, secure conference rooms, and coded messages. If our people needed to send a confidential report, they could travel to Moscow and send it from the embassy.

Our colleagues on the Soviet desk in the State Department told us that my messages had been well received and useful; they had contained the first comprehensive review of the key issues in our relationship with the

Soviet Union in the new administration. However, except for the proposal to add transnational issues to the agenda, the recommendations seemed to have little effect on the policy that gradually emerged over the coming months. In particular, there was strong resistance to using economic pressure to push Gorbachev more rapidly toward disarmament and market reforms.

Eastern Europe

WHILE I WAS WORKING on my recommendations for the new administration, I was informed by colleagues in the State Department that Secretary Baker was seriously considering proposing negotiations with Moscow on the future of Eastern Europe. This was an idea attributed to former Secretary of State Henry Kissinger, who, I was told, thought that in Eastern Europe rebellions could soon break out that would lead to chaos or Soviet intervention unless there was a U.S.-Soviet understanding.

Kissinger had recently visited Moscow and had met with Gorbachev. Although he had not discussed his idea with me, I assumed he had presented it to Gorbachev. If he had, he would likely have received encouragement. If Gorbachev could draw the United States into a discussion of the future of Eastern Europe, the talks could have a dampening effect on Eastern European "nationalists," whatever position the United States took.

For that reason, I was shocked when I learned of the proposal. Although I was sure that Kissinger's intent was not to legitimate the Soviet hold on Eastern Europe, the talks he had proposed would seem to do just that. They would be seen, at best, as a superpower effort to limit the freedom of the Eastern Europeans and, at worst, as an attempt to divide Europe anew.

I was aware of the arguments in favor of discussing the future of Eastern Europe with Moscow. The situation in the Warsaw Pact countries, particularly the "northern tier" of Hungary, Czechoslovakia, East Germany, and Poland, was becoming explosive under the surface of continued Communist rule. Should there be disorders in one or more of these countries that led to the same sort of Soviet intervention as we had seen in East Berlin in 1953, Hungary in 1956, and Czechoslovakia in 1968 or to Soviet-backed martial law declared by national Communist authorities, as had happened in Poland in 1981, the whole course of perestroika and eased East-West relations would be interrupted. There could be extensive loss of life, and international tensions would rise dangerously. Everything possible should be done to avoid this.

Nevertheless, I rejected negotiations with Moscow for two reasons. First, I thought it was obvious that there could be no repetition of the sort of Soviet-sponsored repression we had seen in the past. Although the Soviet Union still possessed enormous military power, it no longer had the political will to apply it in Eastern Europe. The experience in Afghanistan had proved costly in terms of public opinion, and Gorbachev had just managed to extricate the country from that failed adventure. He could not precipitate a military confrontation in the heart of Europe without abandoning his entire reform program and probably losing his job as well.

Second, I saw clear signs that Gorbachev would encourage the Communist leaders of Eastern Europe to reform along the lines he was attempting in the Soviet Union. If he did so, the forces unleashed would probably sweep the Communist regimes from power, but by the time the Soviet leaders understood this, they would have no choice but to accept the outcome. To do otherwise would undermine their rule at home.

Under these conditions, a proposal by the United States to negotiate the future status of Eastern Europe would lead inexorably to U.S. complicity in an attempt to limit the freedom of the Eastern Europeans. Such an effort would be doomed to failure, since the Eastern Europeans would not tolerate limits on their freedom of action once they gained control over their own countries. Even more important, I felt we had no moral right to do this and—in view of the position we had taken during most of the cold war—that we would be betraying the democratic forces in Eastern Europe if we tried.

This did not mean we should refuse any mention of Eastern Europe in our discussions with Soviet leaders. We needed to make it clear that we had no designs on the area and would not attempt to move NATO eastward if the Warsaw Pact countries sought independence. We also needed to make sure Gorbachev understood that the improvements in East-West relations would disappear overnight if he should attempt to apply Soviet force in order to block democracy in the area. But we did not need to propose specific negotiations on the future of Eastern Europe to do this: these were points that could be made during our normal contacts.

For these reasons, I joined my colleagues on the Eastern European and Soviet desks in the State Department in arguing against what had been dubbed the "Kissinger initiative." After I returned to Moscow in late April I was relieved to hear that Secretary Baker had decided against proposing negotiations with the Soviet Union on Eastern Europe.

Soviet Foreign Policy Reborn

WHILE THE BUSH ADMINISTRATION was still engaged in its comprehensive policy review, Gorbachev set off on a remarkably successful campaign to replace the force and threats with which the Soviet Union had traditionally dealt with other countries with cooperation and good-neighborliness.

He completed the final withdrawal of Soviet troops from Afghanistan by February 15, as promised, then stepped up his courtship of Western Europe. His campaign on behalf of a "common European home" took him to London in April, Bonn in June, Paris and Strasbourg in July, Helsinki in October, and Rome in November. Simultaneously, Gorbachev acted to speed up negotiations between NATO and the Warsaw Pact for a major reduction of conventional forces in Europe. In fact, he moved so rapidly to satisfy Western demands in these negotiations that he created coordination problems in the alliance. Some of the Western proposals had been made on the assumption that Moscow would never accept them. When it did, some of the allies began to wonder if they could live with their own proposals.

While European and East-West issues were at the center of attention, Gorbachev also found some time for other problem areas abroad. A visit to China in May put an end to the last vestiges of Soviet-Chinese polemics after nearly two decades. He also worked in visits to Cuba and East Germany during the year and received a constant stream of foreign visitors in the Soviet Union.

The markedly eased relations with Western Europe and the United States were the fruits of earlier policy changes. Nevertheless, as long as Europe was divided by the iron curtain, talk of the "common values of mankind" could not be totally convincing. Gorbachev had said at the United Nations the previous year that freedom of choice admitted of no exceptions. In 1989, Eastern Europe put that assertion to the test.

Eastern Europe on the Threshold of Freedom

DURING MEETINGS IN THE SPRING with Communist leaders from Hungary, Czechoslovakia, Poland, and East Germany, Gorbachev made it clear that he expected them to emulate the reforms taking place in the Soviet Union. Many wondered at the time if he grasped the implications of what he was doing.

My guess then, and now, is that he did not appreciate the fragility of the Soviet position in Eastern Europe. He knew, of course, that the Communist regimes there were as flawed as Moscow's. He regretted that the Soviet invasion of Czechoslovakia in 1968 had ended that country's attempt to establish "socialism with a human face" and had blocked any meaningful reform in the Soviet Union for two decades. But he still felt that communism could be reformed and that the result would be something like Alexander Dubček's version during the Prague Spring of 1968. This he was willing not only to tolerate but to welcome.

What he did not understand was that Communist regimes throughout Eastern Europe had lost all hope of winning the support of the majority, not only because they were Communist but because they were tools of Soviet imperialism. In fact, in the "northern tier" from Hungary to the Baltic Sea, they had been able to stay in power only because they were backed by Soviet tanks: withdraw or immobilize the tanks, and they would fall.

Gorbachev and the rest of the Soviet leadership failed to understand their vulnerability in Eastern Europe not only because they were psychologically unprepared to accept hostility toward the Communist Party as an objective fact but because they were woefully misinformed about actual conditions there.

Rarely have intelligence organizations had resources to gauge opinion abroad to match those available to Soviet analysts in regard to the Warsaw Pact countries. Each Communist regime had its carbon copy of the KGB, trained by Soviet officers and obedient to requests from colleagues in Moscow. Networks of paid and unpaid informers blanketed each country. Yet the system did not produce accurate information for the political leadership, either in the countries themselves or for their Soviet masters.

Why? Because the leaders asked the wrong questions and would have penalized anyone who told them the truth. They assumed that anyone who questioned their policies was disloyal—and were usually right to do so—but they also assumed that their opponents were few, and in this they were profoundly mistaken.

Self-serving assessments by puppet rulers were seldom corrected by Soviet representatives in Eastern Europe because they were themselves part of the same system. Soviet embassies in Warsaw Pact countries were usually staffed not by professional diplomats but by Communist Party functionaries—the equivalent of political appointees in U.S. diplomacy. They had bought their jobs not with campaign contributions but with political services. Some had been sent into comfortable exile when the Politburo found their presence at home awkward. Although many were able in their own sphere, they were not equipped to understand other societies. They had access to the top, and for them this was enough.

Alexander Bessmertnykh, the brilliant, hardworking professional diplomat who followed Shevardnadze as Soviet foreign minister, once told me what a shock the 1989 events in Eastern Europe had been for Moscow because of the failure of Soviet embassies to convey an accurate picture of the situation there. When the Foreign Ministry got news of public discontent and inquired, he explained, the Soviet ambassador had always come back with something like "I just saw Honecker [or Husák or Jaruzelski] yesterday, and he says everything is fine. We mustn't fall for Western propaganda."

It took some months for the people in Eastern Europe, scarred as they were by the Soviet interventions in 1956 and 1968 and the threats that had forced Poland to declare martial law in 1981, to realize they could now take their future into their own hands. But when Gorbachev began to press their Communist leaders to reform, as he did during visits in the spring of 1989, the people in the area saw their opportunity.

The first non-Communist government in the Warsaw Pact was formed in Poland in August 1989. The Soviet press reacted with remarkable objectivity, and some commentators actually welcomed the development. Shevardnadze soon traveled to Warsaw, and Tadeusz Mazowiecki, the new prime minister, was invited to Moscow, making it clear that the Kremlin no longer insisted that only Communist governments were acceptable in what had been the Soviet bloc. The Brezhnev

Doctrine, which held that it was the duty of the USSR to preserve "socialism" in other countries, implicitly passed into history.

Summitry Delayed

WHEN I DRAFTED MY RECOMMENDATIONS in January and February, I thought the idea of holding annual summit meetings would be approved without question. President Bush knew the difficulty we had experienced in arranging summits and had argued for frequent summits when Reagan was president. A meeting in late spring or early summer would give him time to conduct a policy review and yet reassure Gorbachev that he genuinely wished to keep up the momentum of improved relations that Reagan and Gorbachev had achieved in 1987 and 1988.

In March, when I was in Washington for consultations, I called on the president and, after briefing him on the Soviet elections, noted that it would be useful to set a summit date and to seek agreement to meet annually. To my surprise, he reacted as if the idea had not crossed his mind. Wouldn't the Soviets use a summit meeting to put pressure on us for concessions in arms control negotiations? he wondered. I told him that I did not see how: when they had tried in the past, we had resisted the pressure and presumably still could.

Brent Scowcroft, the new assistant for national security, thought that American public expectations could be a problem. If the meeting did not produce a major agreement, the media would term it a failure. I replied that we should make clear that the purpose of the meeting was to discuss issues, not to conclude agreements. If we could have annual summits, the public would accept them as normal diplomacy and not expect a major agreement every time. I also added that if we delayed too long, expectations would be raised, and at the same time we would be missing an opportunity to influence Soviet policy at a time when it was in flux.

The president ended the discussion by remarking, "Well, we'll take a look at it," but his voice indicated that he was not convinced of the need for an early summit.

I went to Washington again in June. My colleagues on the Soviet desk told me that they had detected no signs that the White House was giving any thought to an early summit. Therefore, when I met with Secretary Baker, I renewed the plea I had made in March. I told him that I sensed that Gorbachev and Shevardnadze were still puzzled by what was turning out to be an exceptionally long pause in the formulation of the administration's policy. He and the president had kept giving general assurances that we wanted perestroika to succeed and that there would be a continuity of effort to improve relations, but Moscow had seen little in the way of concrete proposals. It seemed to me that an opportunity existed to achieve a number of American goals and at the same time to give impetus to changes in the Soviet Union that would allow us to put the cold war behind us and develop a broadening partnership. But this would require the president's personal leadership and personal involvement with Gorbachev. The longer a meeting was postponed, the greater the possibility that opportunities would be missed.

Baker listened with apparent interest to my arguments, but as we left the State Department for the White House, where I was scheduled to brief the president, he asked me to confine my comments to the situation in the Soviet Union. However, during the brief trip over he changed his mind, and as we walked in the basement entrance to the West Wing, he told me, "On second thought, Jack, why don't you tell the president what you told me about a summit."

I did so, and this time my comments seemed to spark genuine interest. The president asked his staff to take a close look at the pros and cons and report back with a recommendation.

The reaction both in the White House and at the State Department to my proposal to expand the economic relationship, however, was less promising. Baker seemed to suspect that Gorbachev was mainly interested in worming his way into international organizations such as the General Agreement on Tariffs and Trade (GATT), in which he could play a spoiler role. There was also concern that any talk of expanded trade would stimulate right-wing opposition and expose the Bush administration to the charge of being soft on communism. Some in the White House feared that such talk would weaken support in Congress for the administration's defense budget.

Specialists on the Soviet desk in the State Department understood that we could now influence the evolving situation in the Soviet Union and that, in refusing to apply our economic strength, we were passing up an opportunity to promote U.S. interests, but their arguments were simply not accepted by the people who were making policy. Each policy maker seemed to have a favorite excuse for clinging to the cold war habit of restricting trade, investment, and the sale of technology. None seemed willing to risk even a study of how we might support the transformation of the Soviet economy from a state-run, military-oriented system to one operating on market principles and concentrating on production for consumers.

Meanwhile, in Moscow, Gorbachev was becoming increasingly concerned about what he saw as U.S. inaction on bilateral issues and insensitivity to his domestic problems. At the United Nations in December, he had announced major unilateral moves to reduce arms and adopt a defensive military posture, but instead of meeting him halfway the new U.S. administration seemed to be pocketing every concession he made and actually toughening its demands. Washington's signals were mixed: while Bush and Baker usually talked of their desire to improve relations with the Soviet Union and both had said that they wanted perestroika to succeed, others—including Scowcroft, his deputy, Robert Gates, and Defense Secretary Richard Cheney—stressed the need for the United States to keep up its guard and at times suggested in public that Gorbachev might not last much longer.

These comments were invariably noted in the Soviet media and fed the hard-line opposition to Gorbachev's attempts to scale back the Soviet military. Gorbachev's anxiety grew when Bush announced a trip to Hungary and Poland and began to talk of the need to remove Soviet troops from Eastern Europe. This was indeed a worthy and essential goal, but making a public issue of it when Gorbachev was under pressure from so many forces at home was likely to do more harm than good. Finally, in early July, Gorbachev took advantage of a social occasion to give me a message for President Bush.

In 1989, July 4 fell on a Tuesday, and since we planned a major reception for Soviet and diplomatic guests on our national holiday, we set aside the preceding Sunday, July 2, for our traditional Fourth of July picnic for the embassy staff and all other Americans in Moscow. In addition, we had a rare treat in store that Sunday: Van Cliburn was scheduled to give his first public concert in Moscow in nearly twenty years. Since winning the Tchaikovsky Competition in 1958, Cliburn had become a legend in the Soviet Union. The announcement that he would return to Moscow and perform in public after many years of silence caused great excitement among the Soviet public and in the American community.

Though they rarely attended public functions in the evening, other than obligatory ones for the chief of state or head of the Party, the Gorbachevs came to the concert. The audience considered their presence both a tribute to a great American pianist and a gesture in support of closer Soviet-American cultural ties. During the intermission, one of Gorbachev's assistants conveyed an invitation for Rebecca and me to join the Gorbachevs for a chat following the concert.

Subsequently, while applause was still echoing through the hall, we were led to a private reception room behind the presidential box, where the Gorbachevs received Van, his mother, and a few other members of his party. We were served champagne, caviar, and other snacks, and we toasted the warming relations between our countries. Van inquired about the possibility of buying an apartment in Moscow, and Gorbachev offered to put in a good word on his behalf with the Moscow City Council.

After thirty minutes or so of light conversation, Gorbachev announced that he and Raisa would have to leave because just before the concert they had learned that Andrei Gromyko had died. They wanted to call on the family before they returned home. As the guests filed out, Gorbachev took me by the arm and led me to a corner of the room.

"Jack," he said, "there's something I'd like you to pass on to the president." I agreed, of course, and he continued, remarking that they were going through "a very complex and difficult period." He was determined to push fundamental reform, but opposition was growing. He thought his reforms would pave the way for closer relations with the United States, and he believed President Bush understood this and agreed. However, some statements coming out of Washington recently had been creating real problems for him. "Tell the president," he concluded, "to please be a little more considerate. What he says has an effect here."

The word he used in Russian, *vnimatelny,* also means "attentive" and "thoughtful," but "considerate" seemed to fit the context best in English. I wasn't sure just what he meant, and I tried to pin him down. "I'll certainly pass this on," I said, "but could you be a little more specific? Could I give him some examples?" I asked.

"No, just let him know that some statements complicate things here. He should just try to be more considerate if he wants to help."

When I relayed Gorbachev's message, I confessed that I could not be certain just what action or statement had annoyed Gorbachev but speculated that, with the president's trip to Hungary and Poland coming up, Gorbachev might have been offended by talk about the withdrawal of Soviet troops from the area. However desirable the objective, public urging by Bush would make it harder, not easier, for Gorbachev to agree. Perhaps Gorbachev worried that there would be more such talk during the president's visit to the area.

When he received this message, President Bush reacted immediately with assurances that he would, indeed, be attentive to the implications of his public statements in the future. He authorized me to discuss the matter in more concrete terms if Gorbachev desired. However, when I offered, Gorbachev sent word through the Foreign Ministry that this would not be necessary. Bessmertnykh, who gave me Gorbachev's reply, speculated that he had been irritated by some statement he had read in the news summaries he received every day and had blurted out his frustration to me when he had the chance. By now, three days later, Gorbachev seemed to want to forget about the exchange.

However, Gorbachev's words had the effect I presume he had intended. While Bush was in Eastern Europe, his comments about the Soviet role were so circumspect that Shevardnadze made a point of sending word that they had been pleased with Bush's "responsible behavior" during his trip.

Shortly after his trip to Poland and Hungary, Bush was finally persuaded to propose a meeting with Gorbachev. He dispatched a private message to Gorbachev with the proposal, thoughtlessly using Marshal Akhromeyev, who happened to call on him in Washington, as a courier, since he feared a leak if he sent the invitation via the State Department. Shevardnadze was not immediately informed and was furious when he learned he had been bypassed.

Although this misstep left no lasting ill will since it was not repeated, it did illustrate an unfortunate tendency on Bush's part: he took a childish delight in springing "surprises" on the media and sometimes would go to such lengths to keep a trivial secret that his staff was unable to make thorough preparations. The most vital secrets of U.S. weaponry were given less protection than the information that Bush and Gorbachev were planning a meeting later in the year. Though I respected the president's wish to keep the meeting a secret until it was announced and did all I could to protect the information, I had trouble understanding what real damage would be done to American national interests if the public had learned earlier about his plans. As it turned out, the story leaked in Washington the day before it was scheduled for announcement.

———

By the end of the summer, Washington seemed to be moving out of its self-imposed lethargy. Plans were under way for a summit meeting later in the year, and the United States had made a major new proposal for a substantial reduction of conventional forces in Europe, which illustrated that leadership by the president could produce impressive results.[6] On most issues, however, that leadership was not apparent. Negotiations on strategic weapons were at a standstill because the Bush administration had not yet made up its mind what it wanted from the agreement—even though the issue had been studied during the entire eight years of the Reagan administration and Bush's appointees were thoroughly familiar with it. No senior policy maker was giving serious thought to activating the economic relationship. It would take a visit to the United States by Shevardnadze in September to give the Strategic Arms Reduction Talks (START) a push and the December summit in Malta to put economics onto the agenda.

While Washington was sorting out its policies, however, events in the Soviet Union had moved rapidly.

IX

A Vote That Counted

The Congress [of People's Deputies] and all that preceded it . . . are a convincing victory of perestroika and a new page in the history of our state.
MIKHAIL GORBACHEV to First Congress of People's Deputies, May 1989[1]

The Party lost the election.
NIKOLAI RYZHKOV to Politburo, 1989[2]

May 25, 1989, promised to be a historic day in Moscow. The new Congress of People's Deputies, the first representative assembly in Russia since 1918 to be selected even partially by an honest and secret ballot, was to convene in the Kremlin's Palace of Congresses.

Foreign ambassadors were invited to witness the event. My daily calendar was normally so jammed that I was lucky to make all my appointments on time—arriving early was out of the question—but this time I asked my secretary to clear my calendar from nine o'clock on. I wanted to get to the Kremlin early, not merely to get a good seat in the diplomatic gallery but to have a few minutes to meet and chat with arriving deputies and to savor the scene.

My discreetly armored Cadillac, with the Stars and Stripes fluttering over the right fender, was admitted through the Borovitsky Gate, and we drove past the ornate Grand Kremlin Palace and the majestic ensemble of fifteenth-century churches surrounding the Palace Square, turned left past the buildings housing Gorbachev's office and that of Prime

Minister Ryzhkov, and pulled up in front of the sheer marble-and-glass
walls of the all too obviously twentieth-century Palace of Congresses.

The brainchild of Nikita Khrushchev, the Palace of Congresses was a
controversial addition to the Moscow Kremlin. Rebecca and I had attended its inaugural opening in 1961 during our first tour in Moscow.
Russian intellectuals were still wringing their hands. How could the sa-
cred precincts of Russia's most historic spot be sullied by a structure so
assertively modern? Clumsy imitations of Mies van der Rohe and Eero
Saarinen have no place in this sanctuary of Russia's historic soul!

The opposition was understandable, even though the Kremlin architecture is not of one piece. The buildings there span the styles of five
centuries, but their designs combine in an esthetic harmony while this
brash rectangular block clashes with its surroundings. The twentieth
century, which brought Russia's capital back from Peter the Great's
"Window to Europe," Saint Petersburg, may have deserved a place in
these hallowed precincts, but it should have been one that embodied
more respect for the past, said the critics.

The objections of Russian patriots went beyond esthetics. If the twentieth century was to contribute a structure to the Moscow Kremlin, they
said, let it not be a monument to glorify the greatest tragedy that ever
befell the country, namely, the Bolshevik Revolution. After all, the congresses to which this palace was dedicated were congresses of the Communist Party of the Soviet Union.

That day, however, it was not a Communist Party congress that was
to convene but what was, in effect, a constitutional convention, a body
charged with creating an entirely new system of rule for the Soviet
Union.

I had assumed that diplomats would be seated in the upper balcony,
as they normally were when invited to celebratory events, but was pleas-
antly surprised when I was ushered into a row of seats in an elevated
area at the left of the auditorium that provided an excellent view both of
the stage, from which the formal speeches would be given, and of the
deputies, who were seated in the portion of the hall that would have
been called the "orchestra" in an American theater.

As I waited for the proceedings to begin at ten o'clock, I thought of an
event that had occurred eleven years before I was born, one I had long
considered to be a turning point in Russian history. That was the forcible dissolution of the Constituent Assembly in January 1918. The first
body in Russian history elected on the basis of universal suffrage, the

Constituent Assembly was supposed to write a new constitution for the posttsarist period. The Bolsheviks, who had seized power just before the election was conducted in November 1917, received less than a quarter of the votes. After a day of deliberation, during which it became clear that the majority would not obediently endorse Bolshevik rule, troops dispersed the assembly. Two of the deputies were beaten to death.

With his contempt for elections he did not win, Lenin put an end to all semblance of democratic procedure. He made it clear that he would insist on ruling whether he had popular support or not. The legitimacy of Bolshevik rule was to be based on Marxist theory, not on the sovereignty of the people, and that made a police state ruled by force inevitable.

Occasionally, I speculated about what might have happened to Russia and the world if Lenin had been a democrat. If he had been willing to accept that his Party, as a minority, was entitled to rule only if it could convince a majority of the population to vote for it, he could have cooperated in establishing a constitutional order that might have avoided a civil war, the hostility of Western Europe, a reliance on terror, and the autocratic structure that Stalin was able to convert to tyranny.

Whenever my thoughts began to wander in this direction, the words of our son David, uttered when he was fourteen and in a different context, brought me back to reality. At that time David had taken a great interest in military history and was particularly fascinated by World War II. Once, as we were discussing Hitler's invasion of the Soviet Union, I observed that if the Nazis had liberated the people from Communist rule without treating Ukrainians and Russians as *Untermenschen* and attempting genocide of the Jewish population, they might well have conquered the Soviet Union and won the war.

David looked at me quizzically and asked, "In other words, Dad, if the Nazis hadn't been Nazis, things would have been different?"

Precisely. If the Nazis hadn't been Nazis, if the Bolsheviks hadn't been Bolsheviks . . . the transcendent tragedy of the twentieth century had been that both the Nazis and the Bolsheviks had been true to themselves.

A Representative Government?

BUT NOW I WAS SITTING in a structure built by Bolsheviks to house the ruling body of the Party they had created but was witnessing a different sort of assembly: one that had, to a substantial extent, been elected by citizens of the country; one that had a formal mandate to establish a new constitutional structure; one that had been proposed by the head of the Communist Party and organized by that Party.

Could I be witnessing Gorbachev's atonement for Lenin's original sin against democracy? Was the leader of the Communist Party of the Soviet Union no longer a Bolshevik?

Such were the thoughts that swirled in my mind as I watched the deputies drift in to their seats, spotted familiar faces, and responded to waves of greeting when our eyes met. The mood was festive; everyone in the hall seemed to share the feeling that we were participating in one of history's turning points.

The assembly was gaveled to order at the stroke of ten, and the head of the Electoral Commission read his report on the results of the election. It was longer than necessary, and some deputies began to shuffle, impatient to get on with the substance of the session. When he finished, the first item on the agenda was approval of the Presidium, but a deputy from Latvia came forward and took the floor. He proposed a moment of silence for those who had died when a peaceful demonstration in Tbilisi was dispersed by troops on April 9. He then demanded that the Congress be informed officially who had given the order to use poisonous substances and what those substances were.

This did not seem to be in the original script; would the deputies really be allowed to take charge of this gathering? That seemed too much to expect. Gorbachev doubtless had his plan, and though he might allow occasional deviations, he could be expected to guide things to a predetermined conclusion.

The slate for the Presidium was duly approved, but before a vote was taken on the proposed agenda I spotted Andrei Sakharov, tall and bent, striding toward the podium. This too can't have been what the organizers had planned, I mused.

Of course I was curious about what Sakharov would say, the more so because formal debate had not even begun. However, it seemed to me that the fact that he was a deputy and was being allowed to participate actively in these proceedings was more important than what he said. If this first Congress of People's Deputies did nothing more than legitimate Sakharov's role in Soviet political life, it would be an important milestone.

Nearly two years had passed since I had called on Sakharov following his return from Gorky. Only occasionally mentioned by the Soviet media, he nevertheless had become very active politically, not only in Moscow but in trips to trouble spots outside the capital.[3]

Gorbachev still held Sakharov at arm's length, treating him like a capricious distant relative who could not be totally excluded from family gatherings but who was apt to make a scene and therefore should neither be encouraged to come nor embraced when he chose to. By 1989, the optimism Sakharov had expressed two years earlier regarding Gorbachev had begun to wane, but Sakharov consistently followed his own advice to keep the pressure on Gorbachev to do the right thing and, to the extent he did, to support him.

And now he was on the podium, a full-fledged member of that august assembly, ready to address his fellow deputies. Gorbachev's face betrayed a certain annoyance, but he held his tongue.

Speaking on behalf of "a group of Moscow deputies," Sakharov made two proposals on issues the group considered important in principle: first, that the Congress of People's Deputies, rather than the smaller Supreme Soviet that it would appoint, have sole legislative authority and second, that the election of the chairman of the Supreme Soviet, the new chief of state, should take place not at the beginning of the session, as had been planned, but at the end, following debate on the issues and consideration of all potential candidates. In making the proposal, he made clear that he favored Gorbachev's election to the position but considered it a bad precedent to hold the election before discussion.

The noise in the hall increased as Sakharov spoke, and toward the end his voice was almost drowned out. Gorbachev broke in to say that speeches should be limited to five minutes and Sakharov should conclude. Later, when votes were taken, Sakharov's proposals were overwhelmingly rejected.

Watching the scene, I had mixed emotions. It was most encouraging that Sakharov had been allowed to speak, even before debate was scheduled on the agenda. But the hostility in the hall was ominous; the mood among the deputies did not suggest open minds.

At the same time, I felt that Sakharov and the deputies allied with him had shown poor judgment in the issues they had selected for his maiden speech. No matter how liberal Gorbachev might have become, it was obvious that there would be a limit on the number of times Sakharov would be allowed to address the Congress. I doubted that these two issues were the most urgent and wondered why he could not have waited and used whatever time he might be given on subjects of more immediate import.

I understood the reasoning that had led him to propose that only the Congress of People's Deputies be empowered to approve legislation: it was the *elected* assembly. The Supreme Soviet chosen by it could, in theory at least, be more easily manipulated, and its members' responsibility to a specific body of electors would be more tenuous.

Nevertheless, I could not imagine that a body of 2,250 individuals, most holding other full-time jobs and therefore able to meet only sporadically, could be an effective legislative body. Nor was it clear to me that the smaller body would be more easily manipulated than the larger one. It was to be a group of full-time legislators. If they had to relinquish their other positions, would they not begin to defend the independence and prerogatives of the legislative body with more zeal than the occasional legislators in the Congress as a whole?

It seemed to me at the time that the weaknesses of the two-tiered structure, a Congress of People's Deputies selecting a subordinate Supreme Soviet, could best be corrected in the new Constitution that the Congress was expected to draft and enact. It was an issue that could best be debated in that context.

As far as Sakharov's second proposal was concerned, I thought he had a point, but it was largely theoretical. Gorbachev was going to be elected to the position in question. This was clear to all, and no amount of debate was going to change that. Even Sakharov favored his candidacy. Nevertheless, Sakharov was right that the procedure proposed would set a bad precedent, and I wondered why Gorbachev didn't see that. He could easily have accepted this proposal without any damage to his own position.

This brief exchange alerted me to some important things about both men. Just as with his views on Nagorny Karabakh, Sakharov's strength in discerning important principles was not matched by his grasp of political maneuver, the art of getting from the place you are to the place you want to be. Gorbachev, on the other hand, was stubborn; having made up his mind to do something a certain way, he would close it to other possibilities and employ all his manipulative skills to achieve something that was arguably not in his best interest. He would have made a bad chess player because he could not bring himself to sacrifice a pawn in order to capture a knight a few moves later.

But enough of my reflections on that morning in May. Before we go further in examining the new Congress, we should look at its members and how they got there. Most of them were Communists, but were they the same sort as those who had dominated the insipid rubber-stamp Soviet parliaments of the past? To answer that, we must go back and take a look at the campaign.

The 1989 Election Campaign

I DID NOT DOUBT that when the Party Central Committee approved the new election rules and the old Supreme Soviet enacted them into law in December 1988, most Communist Party officials were confident that nothing would really change. True, they would be expected to go through a nominating process and were strongly encouraged, though not absolutely required, to propose more than one candidate for a position. But these technicalities must have seemed manageable. Since the local Party organizations would control the election commissions, they would be able to guide the nominating process and choose a slate that would inevitably win, even with a secret ballot.

In a number of jurisdictions, particularly in rural areas, this is what happened. But in many others, especially in major cities, the apparatchiks were surprised.

The most spectacular reversal of Communist Party fortunes occurred in the capital itself, where Boris Yeltsin won the decisive victory that ensured his political comeback. To win it, he had to fight the Party apparatus as well as Gorbachev, who stood behind the Party's machinations, only occasionally showing his hand.

Ignored by the media since his ouster from the Politburo, Yeltsin sensed an opportunity to return to center stage through the new election procedures, which for the first time in Soviet history cracked the door to the possibility that the Communist Party could be overruled in a secret ballot.

If nominations depended only on the degree of popular support, he could have gotten onto the ballot in virtually any district in the country. The procedures, however, were not that simple: the electoral commissions that certified candidates were dominated by the local Communist Party organizations, which could be expected to employ almost any trick to ensure that their favorite candidate faced no serious opposition.

As a precaution, therefore, Yeltsin first secured a place on the ballot in the rural district in the Urals where he had grown up by turning up unexpectedly at a crucial meeting and thus taking the local Party officials unawares.

This was only a fallback, for the prize he sought was much more significant. He was aiming at the most politically visible district in the entire country, National Territorial District Number 1, which included the entire city of Moscow, with more than 6 million voters. The campaign there would receive national attention, and a Yeltsin victory, should it occur, could not be put down as merely a preference for a favorite son. Furthermore, a win in Moscow would be a sweet victory over the city's Party apparatus, which he once had dominated but which had rejected and humiliated him.

The final public meeting to certify the candidates was arranged for the Hall of Columns in a historic building just outside Red Square and the Kremlin. Originally the club building for the Moscow aristocracy, it had been turned over to the official trade union organization and given the name House of Unions but was often used for government-sponsored functions. It was the scene of the notorious purge trials of the 1930s, where Andrei Vyshinsky had ranted against Stalin's political opponents and secured death sentences on transparently false charges. It was where the bodies of many Soviet leaders, including most recently Andropov and Chernenko, had lain in state before their funerals. It was also where Rachmaninoff's *Vespers* had been performed in 1988, marking the first time since the 1917 Revolution that this magnificent choral composition had been offered to the public: its religious roots had been too deep for an atheist regime until glasnost.

The final nomination meeting was called for February 22, and the Moscow Party officials had arranged it with meticulous care so that there would be a show of democracy but a foreordained result. The ten candidates, including Yeltsin, would be given their say, but the delegates would be selected to ensure that the two receiving the most votes would be Yuri Brakov, manager of the ZIL auto plant, and Georgy Grechko, a popular cosmonaut. That way, the Party organization could certify two candidates and get credit for a contested election but not be embarrassed by a Yeltsin victory. The Communist managers were sufficiently confident of the outcome to allow the proceedings to be televised on the local Moscow channel. Yeltsin was being set up for another humiliating rejection.

To Muscovites watching television that evening, it appeared that the

Party apparatus would have its way. Yeltsin faced an audience that seemed packed with antagonistic delegates. Yeltsin himself contributed to this impression by selecting the most hostile questions, which had been passed to the podium in writing, to answer first. Many speakers excoriated him and demanded that he withdraw, but he stood his ground under an avalanche of critical comment. He would probably have done so anyway, but he knew something that the delegates and the television audience did not: Grechko had told him in advance that he would withdraw before the vote. Yeltsin had asked him to wait until the last minute so that the Party organizers would not have time to build up an alternate candidate.

And so, after a marathon twelve-hour meeting, in the wee hours of the morning after the television cameras had been turned off (either because the crews were exhausted or because the meeting's organizers realized that the proceedings were slipping out of control), a vote of the delegates was taken. Brakov, as expected, came in first, but Yeltsin, following Grechko's shock withdrawal, came in second, which gained him a spot on the ballot.

To remove Yeltsin at that point would have made a mockery of the whole election procedure, which Gorbachev could not afford.

The Party was still able to close most of the media to Yeltsin, but his supporters were resourceful in finding ways around the ban. Publicity began to appear in the most unexpected ways. One day, a friend brought me a copy of a publication I had never heard of. The masthead read *Propeller,* which means the same in Russian as in English, and all of its four pages were given over to Yeltsin's election platform. It turned out that Yuri Ryzhov, the head of Moscow's prestigious Aviation Institute (the alma mater not only of the top Soviet aviation designers but also of political figures such as Yegor Ligachev and Anatoly Dobrynin, longtime Soviet ambassador to the United States), had arranged for the institute's student newspaper, *Propeller,* to carry the program. Printers had contributed overtime work to produce tens of thousands of extra copies.

As it turned out, Yeltsin probably did not need to conduct a political campaign in the usual sense. As the Party's hostility became more evident, Yeltsin's popularity rose. The public attitude was that anybody the Communist apparatchiks detested must be a hero. The campaign the Party waged against Yeltsin was not merely futile; it was Yeltsin's strongest political asset.

Nevertheless, the extent of his victory came as a shock. After the first round of voting on March 26, 1989, the count stood at a stunning 89.4 percent in favor of Yeltsin and 6.9 percent for Brakov. The rout of the post-Yeltsin Moscow Party organization was total. When the vote was announced, I asked several Gorbachev intimates if they were surprised. Their replies were consistent: "We knew he would win, but we were astonished by how much."

As for me, I found Yeltsin's victory less astonishing than the fact that *the votes had been counted fairly.* Though Gorbachev could be accused of sanctioning any number of dirty tricks to impede Yeltsin's political rehabilitation, in the final analysis he demonstrated that he would not sacrifice his goal of reforming the Soviet political structure to win a personal vendetta. An important milestone on the road to Russian democracy had been passed.

Yeltsin's was not the only spectacular victory on that March 26, and Brakov's was not the only stunning defeat. Many districts, particularly in Moscow and Leningrad, elected candidates who had run against the Party apparatus. A number of prominent intellectuals, chafing at the Party leadership's ineptitude, challenged the system with successful campaigns.

Oleg Bogomolov, the longtime head of a research institute specializing in Eastern Europe, was one. Competing in a three-way race in a Moscow suburban district, he despaired at times during the campaign since the local Party chief, one of his opponents, not only mobilized the Party faithful in his personal behalf but indulged in a variety of dirty tricks to undercut Bogomolov. When Bogomolov received more than 60 percent of the votes on the first round, he observed, "I didn't realize what a great advantage it would be to run *against* the Party."

Historian Yuri Afanasiev, head of an institute that trained archivists, also won in a suburban Moscow district. Looking younger than his fifty-five years, he combined rugged good looks with the build of a football linebacker—a few years into retirement, perhaps. Though a member of the Communist Party himself, he was already known as one of the most radical of the reform intellectuals, arguing for an open, pluralistic political system, a thorough airing of past abuses, a free economy, and an end to police repression. His oratorical talents matched his imposing physique: he was particularly effective when addressing large groups of demonstrators in public squares.

Anatoly Sobchak, a university law professor, won in a largely work-ing-class district in Leningrad in the face of a campaign organized against him by the Party establishment that included fabricating slan derous rumors: that he was a philandering, wife-beating alcoholic and such. The public quickly grasped what was going on and paid no atten-tion. Like Afanasiev, Sobchak was tall and handsome and appeared younger than his fifty-two years. A passionate defender of the rule of law and scourge of corrupt practices, he became one of the most active members of the Congress and its Supreme Soviet.

Not all the winners were prominent; some were young and practically unknown to the public until their successful election campaign. Sergei Stankevich, a thirty-five-year-old specialist in American history, won in Moscow's working-class Cheryomushky district. Arkady Murashev, a thirty-two-year-old physicist whose first foray into politics had won him a seat in Moscow's City Council two years before, won easily in his home district. Ilya Zaslavsky, who carried the vote in Moscow's Octo-ber district—named for the Bolshevik Revolution itself—had not even reached the age of thirty, had never been in the Communist Party, and from childhood had had a physical handicap that made it impossible for him to stand for extended periods or to walk without support.

Stankevich, Murashev, and Zaslavsky distinguished themselves subsequently as major players in the democratic movement. Supporting, but not hiding behind, their more prominent elders, they provided much of the energy and organizational talent to put together an effective movement. Stankevich was to be the principal drafter of many opposi-tion declarations and publications, Murashev the organizer of demon-strations and public events, Zaslavsky the most consistent proponent of a free economy and more effective public support for the disabled. His experience with the existing Soviet system had taught him that a "social-ist" system that purports to care for all in fact cares only for the few who hold political power. Economic freedom, on the other hand, can bring the productivity that will permit a society better to care for those who really need it.

The Soviet political arena had always been dominated by males. Only once had a woman, Yekaterina Furtseva in Khrushchev's time, made it to the Politburo, and even then she had not been a member of the real inner circle of rulers. At the middle levels of politics and management women were more in evidence but were still denied a share anywhere near their proportionate numbers. The old Supreme Soviet had con-tained a substantial proportion of women, yet most were there to fill an informal quota of "milkmaids and female textile workers," and their presence neither gave them political power nor indicated that they occupied positions of influence.

The new Congress of People's Deputies contained even fewer women than the old one had, but most of those there had won their seats in competitive elections—sometimes against staggering odds. For example, ethnographer Yevdokia Gayer defeated General Viktor Novozhilov, the commander of the Far East Military District, for the Vladivostok counterpart of Yeltsin's Moscow seat. A widow in her mid-fifties who would not reach five feet in her stocking feet, Mrs. Gayer was from the tiny Nanai nation. Her electoral victory was as if an Aleut or Tlinkit woman had defeated a prominent member of the local political establishment for a U.S. Senate seat from Alaska—except that her constituents numbered in the millions rather than a hundred thousand or so, as would be the case in Alaska. Subsequently, when Party stalwarts mounted a hostile campaign against Andrei Sakharov in the Congress, Yevdokia Gayer was the only deputy to come forward, peer over a rostrum almost as high as she was, and cry shame on Sakharov's attackers.

While most candidates, both male and female, had conducted campaigns in their home districts or close to home—though residence in the district was not required—Galina Starovoitova was an exception. An ethnic Russian historian who worked in Moscow, specializing in nationality issues, she waged a successful campaign in Armenia and won a seat from a district in its capital, Yerevan. She would subsequently become one of the most active leaders of the reform group of deputies.

Sometimes the Party officials who schemed to set themselves up for an unopposed victory were ambushed by "none of the above" votes. This was the fate of Leningrad Party boss Yuri Solovyov, who garnered only 110,000 out of 240,000 votes cast and thus lost to a nonexistent opponent. Solovyov was the only member of the Politburo to suffer this indignity, but lower-ranking Party nominees failed in many other districts. As a Russian friend commented, it takes a special type of person to lose an election when there is no opponent, but this type was abundant in the upper reaches of the Party.

Under the new rules, a runoff election between the two top candidates was held when three or more candidates split the vote and none received a clear majority. When a single candidate was voted down—or neither finalist won in a runoff—new elections were held with nominations made from scratch and failed candidates ineligible to run.

Enough of the original candidates were turned down by the voters to provide additional opportunities for challengers during a second round of voting. That was the route followed by aspirants such as *Ogonyok* editor Vitaly Korotich, who had been forced off the ballot during the first round by a stacked meeting in a Moscow district. When the Communist Party candidates in Kharkiv failed, he was nominated for the second round of voting and won by a landslide. The poet Yevgeny Yevtushenko also won a seat during this follow-up round.

The victory of the fifty-five-year-old scientist Stanislav Shushkevich in the second-round election in a Minsk district was of far greater historical significance. The Party's candidate had been defeated in the first round, and Shushkevich, then a vice rector at the Belorussian State University, had been persuaded to run by friends. His election to the USSR Congress of People's Deputies initiated a meteoric political career that culminated two and a half years later in his becoming the first chief of state of independent Belarus.

Only 1,500 of the 2,250 seats in the new Congress of People's Deputies were selected in electoral districts. A third of the seats were allocated to representatives of "public organizations," such as the Communist Party and its various affiliates. This had the obvious purpose of allowing some of the top officials such as Gorbachev himself to enter the new assembly without having to solicit votes and risk losing. In theory, Gorbachev, through the Party Central Committee apparatus, should have been able to name all 750 of these deputies, since the Communist Party by law was the "leading core" of all the organizations permitted to "elect" deputies.

Tight Party control had already slipped from some of these organizations, however, and the stimulus of the election campaign impelled others to try to escape the Party shackles. An attempt by the presidium of the Academy of Sciences to select deputies in the old way set off a revolt that had repercussions far beyond the walls of its laboratories and institutes.

The slate of candidates proposed by the Academy's ruling board was remarkable not for the names on it but for those left off. Two of the omissions were among the most popular scientists in the Academy: Andrei Sakharov and space scientist Roald Sagdeyev. Both were known to be in favor of radical reforms, and both were hated by the Party hacks who still dominated the Academy's administrative structure. When the presidium made its slate public, there was immediate protest both within and outside the Academy.

The rules required that the presidium's nominees be endorsed by the membership as a whole, a step that in the past would have been a mere formality. Not this time. A campaign began within the Academy to reject the official nominees and force the presidium to come up with a list more acceptable to the membership, one that—at the very least—would include Sakharov and Sagdeyev.

Residents of several electoral districts also pressed Sakharov to run, and if he had been allowed on the ballot, there seems to be no question that he could have won without difficulty as long as he did not go up against a popular figure like Yeltsin. After some hesitation, Sakharov rejected seeking election outside the Academy, with which his entire adult life had been associated, and announced that if he went to the Congress at all, he would have to be sent there by his fellow academicians.

And so it was. The members of the Academy of Sciences rejected most of the initial nominees and forced a second round of voting, at which time Sakharov, Sagdeyev, and a number of other reformers received a majority vote.

The Academy of Sciences was not the only organization to go its own way in selecting deputies to the Congress. The Cinematographers' Union, for example, sent a slate made up entirely of radical reformers, who were also conspicuous in other groups dominated by intellectuals.

Gavriil Popov, the editor of the journal *Problems of Economics,* the principal academic publication in its field, was sent to the Congress by the Union of Scientific and Engineering Societies. A man of medium height with close-cropped, almost crew cut, hair and a small mustache, he had an aversion to neckties and usually appeared, even at formal meetings, in a sweater and open-necked shirt. Given to conceptual thinking, he had earlier written extensively on management issues but now was turning his attention to fundamental economic and political questions.

Similarly, the group of scientific societies and associations affiliated with the Academy of Sciences sent Tatyana Zaslavskaya to the Congress as one of its representatives. She was the most prominent Soviet sociologist and one of the Soviet Union's few specialists in public opinion polling. Most of her institute's work had been kept secret, lest the public learn something of its attitudes not flattering to the Party. But one effect of glasnost was that more and more polls could be published. They were used increasingly by reform forces to bolster their demands to move more rapidly in implementing perestroika.

The Central Committee of the Communist Party was allowed to fill 100 seats—the largest single allocation—and this is one that Gorbachev surely controlled. Gorbachev maintained a certain balance in putting it together: it contained several from the top Party leadership, including both Ligachev and Yakovlev, along with a small quota from each segment of society: managers, military officers, writers, farm chairmen, and the like. Collectively, they included a scattering of reformers and a much larger number of meretricious apparatchiks.

When the results were in, Gorbachev boasted that the elections had been a victory for the Communist Party, since 87 percent of the deputies elected were Party members. Ryzhkov recalls in his memoirs that he challenged Gorbachev's claim and reminded him that the Party had actually lost since thirty important regional leaders had failed to be elected and many of the Party members who had won had done so not because they belonged to the Party but in spite of it.[4] I was not aware of this exchange at the time, but my judgment coincided with Ryzhkov's.

Overall, the results of the election process were encouraging to those who hoped for democracy in the Soviet Union. Not that every election was conducted fairly—many, even most, were not. Not that the result was an assembly clearly dedicated to establishing a constitutional state based on the rule of law—most of the deputies were conservative Party stalwarts unwilling to contemplate any loss of power.

The outcome was heartening because the elections produced, for the first time in Soviet history, a significant body of representatives who had won a popular vote against the entrenched political forces. Equally important, a noticeable number of the more autocratic Communist Party leaders had lost ignominiously. This would not be the last election, and the lesson to the public as a whole was that you *could* defeat an official candidate if you really tried.

Another aspect of the campaign represented a profound change in public attitudes. Suddenly, *people lost their fear of speaking out.* This was remarkable in a country in which, a few decades back, the mere suspicion of dissidence could be fatal and until recently could lead to imprisonment or exile. Suddenly, the most devastating criticisms of the Communist regime seemed to be on everyone's lips.

This came to me forcefully as I watched the evening news on election day, March 26, 1989. The returns would not start coming in until the next day, but television crews interviewed people leaving the polling places, asking what they had voted for or against. Only a few short clips were selected for the program, but all those quoted said they had voted for change. One young woman put it crisply; "I voted against everything we have now and for everything we should have." An elderly man first expressed skepticism that they would put him on television and then, when assured that they would, said, "Well, I voted against *them,* all of them."

Wanting to throw the rascals out was not unique to the Soviet Union, nor did it surprise persons familiar with Soviet public opinion. What was new was that people were expressing these opinions openly, even on camera, and the media were broadcasting them.

A New Kind of Parliament

AFTER THE INITIAL DEVIATIONS from the announced program, the first Congress of People's Deputies proceeded generally within the bounds set by Gorbachev and his associates. The debates were vigorous and often dealt with basic issues. Decisive votes often required considerable backstage maneuvering, an exercise at which Gorbachev excelled.

The Congress nearly discredited itself on several occasions. An organized campaign to vilify Sakharov was unleashed. In words that echoed unbridled Stalinist invective, speaker after speaker accused him of having insulted the Soviet army. Gorbachev may not have inspired this disgraceful effort, but he did nothing to impede it.

A second occasion involved Yeltsin. One of the tasks before the Congress was to select from its ranks a Supreme Soviet that would serve as the continuing parliamentary assembly and include about one fourth of the deputies to the Congress, or 556 out of 2,250. Yeltsin announced his candidacy, and, given the overwhelming vote he had received, it was inconceivable that he would be passed over if the deputies wished to give the appearance of a democratic assembly. Yet this almost occurred.

The delegations of all the republics except Russia decided to present to the Congress a slate of candidates equal to the number of seats allocated to that republic. The assembly as a whole would be expected to ratify the choice of the deputies from the republic. The Russian deputies, as a matter of principle, decided that the number of nominees from

Russia should exceed the number of seats allocated, so that the Congress would be given a choice.

Yeltsin was one of the candidates from Russia, but when the vote was taken by secret ballot, he received too few votes to win a seat in the Supreme Soviet. Russia was entitled to eleven seats in the Chamber of Nationalities, but the votes in favor of Yeltsin placed him twelfth. This vote confirmed what was already obvious: a majority of deputies at the Congress was much more inclined to support the Party establishment than the sort of reforms that might weaken it. In this case, the rejection of Yeltsin threatened to discredit the new institutions Gorbachev had labored so long to bring into being.

Alexei Kazannik, a hitherto obscure forty-seven-year-old law professor from the west Siberian city of Omsk, whose striking beard, black on his cheeks and white on his chin, provided instant recognition for millions of television viewers, saved the day. He was the twelfth-ranking Russian candidate for the Supreme Soviet and had been included on the Russian slate only because Yeltsin and others had insisted that the deputies be given a choice. Kazannik announced that he could not face his voters at home if he appeared to be responsible for Yeltsin's exclusion from the Supreme Soviet and therefore would yield his seat.

The Congress elected Gorbachev chairman of the Supreme Soviet, and thus chief of state, in a manner reminiscent of the old days. In allowing this to happen, Gorbachev lost two opportunities to establish precedents for democratic procedure. First, he encouraged the Congress to reject Sakharov's suggestion that issues be discussed before the election was held. Second, he permitted the election to be conducted without an alternate candidate.

Gennady Burbulis, a philosophy teacher from Sverdlovsk who would later become a well-known figure in Yeltsin's Russian government, nominated Yeltsin, but Yeltsin refused to be a candidate. One deputy, however, Alexander Obolensky, a forty-five-year old engineer in a geophysical institute near Murmansk, was so eager to get onto the ballot that he nominated himself.

Gorbachev took no position on the question, and the deputies voted two to one against adding Obolensky to the ballot, a vote that would have gone the other way if Gorbachev had requested a contested election.

Gorbachev was encouraging other Party officials to allow competition in the voting, and many of them felt he should have insisted on a second candidate in his case as well. Apparently Gorbachev could not bear the thought that *some* deputies might vote for someone else in the secret ballot. As it turned out, 2,123 deputies voted for him and 87 against. It is unlikely that Obolensky would have gotten more than these 87 votes; conceivably, fewer than 87 might have been cast against Gorbachev if there had been another name on the ballot, since some "no" votes were probably to protest his running unopposed.

Gorbachev's candidacy was, however, not entirely traditional. Extensive and relatively unrestrained debate preceded the vote.

Marju Lauristin of Estonia, for example, asked him three questions: What provisions to guarantee the sovereignty of republics should be included in the new constitution, whether use of the army against civilian demonstrators was permissible in a democratic state, and who in the Politburo had known in advance about the bloody suppression of the demonstration in Tbilisi in April. One deputy asked if Gorbachev was using government money to build himself a vacation home in the Crimea. Some reminded Gorbachev that his popularity was slipping because of the slow progress of perestroika. Several demanded that he give up the position of general secretary of the Communist Party if he was to become chairman of the legislature. Gorbachev addressed most of these questions before the vote was taken but did not give clear answers to Lauristin's.

The end of the first session of the Congress of People's Deputies merged almost seamlessly with the initial session of the new Supreme Soviet. The public had grown attached (some would say addicted) to the unaccustomed delight of watching political debates, so that Supreme Soviet sessions, like those of the Congress, were broadcast in full—but at night, so that people would not continue to neglect their work in order to watch the proceedings live.

The new Supreme Soviet lost no time exhibiting an independent spirit. When Prime Minister Ryzhkov presented his nominations for ministerial posts, one after another was rejected. I lost count at eleven (there were about sixty ministerial posts in all), and deputies would joke at dinner that they were maintaining higher standards than the U.S. Senate, which rarely refused to confirm Cabinet appointments.

The debates in this first session were spirited. Since we were busy most evenings, I would set my videotape machine to record the day's session and then play it when I came in. This kept me up late but was worth it. Many of the questions the legislators took up were basic issues of a new constitutional order, and the new body had an abundance of orators. I could only marvel at how well they had been kept under wraps under the previous system and how quickly they were adapting to the hurly-burly of parliamentary debate.

At first, Gorbachev spent much of his day actually presiding at Supreme Soviet sessions, which did much to enhance the prestige of the body. Eventually, the press of other business was not to be denied, and he turned the task over to his deputy, Anatoly Lukyanov.

Lukyanov and Gorbachev had studied in the Law Faculty at Moscow University at the same time, and many assumed that they were close friends from their college days. It is true that they had known each other at that time and had worked together in the Communist youth (Komsomol) organization, but Lukyanov was two years older and their relationship was not close. But close or not as students, Lukyanov was Gorbachev's candidate for the position, and for a time they seemed to work well in tandem.

Lukyanov had most recently worked on the Central Committee staff, out of the public eye. Therefore, his Supreme Soviet position was the first job that gave him extensive exposure in the media. Television viewers soon grew accustomed to the sober expression on his elongated face and the gravelly voice he employed to keep the chamber in order. He exercised his authority firmly. Whether because they talked more than others or as a result of bias on his part, he was more often seen reining in the radical reformers than the more conservative deputies.

Though Lukyanov seldom smiled, he could occasionally come up with a memorable phrase. I once attended a meeting he held with a group of visiting American high school students from New Jersey and Maryland, part of an exchange program that grew out of a proposal I had drafted for the Geneva summit. I was delighted to be invited to join their meeting with Lukyanov.

I was even more pleased when I observed the facility with which the young Americans spoke Russian and the quality of their questions. The exchange program seemed to be working just as I had hoped it would. The students were well briefed and knew far more about the Soviet Union than the average U.S. congressman did.

Lukyanov fielded their questions about the new parliament and the current political situation capably, but then came a zinger. One of the Americans asked, "Why is it that the friends we made here can't get passports to visit us?"

Lukyanov paused, looked straight at the group, and said, "That illustrates the depth of stupidity human beings are capable of. But we are going to fix that. Before long, your friends will be able to get passports to travel abroad."

And then the follow-up: "And will they be able to exchange their rubles for dollars?"

"That I cannot promise you," Lukyanov replied. "We haven't solved that problem yet."

That day, at least, Lukyanov gave honest, straight answers. Over the coming months, however, it became apparent that his idea of reform was closer to Ligachev's than to Gorbachev's.

Opposition Party in Embryo

REFORMERS DID NOT DOMINATE the new Congress of People's Deputies or its subsidiary assembly, the Supreme Soviet, but they were not an insignificant minority. They had swept the elections in the city of Moscow, and their representation from a number of other large cities, including Leningrad and Yeltsin's Sverdlovsk, was heavy. They formed a majority among the deputies from the Baltic states and had scattered representatives from other areas such as the Caucasus, Ukraine, and the Far East. Also, many of the organizations dominated by scientists and intellectuals had chosen democratic activists.

Since these representatives were articulate and highly motivated, they made a public splash out of proportion to their numbers, thanks to television. Nevertheless, they were too few to prevail unless Gorbachev supported their positions and delivered the votes.

They obviously needed an organization to coordinate their political moves, but most were still Communist Party members and Party rules prohibited factionalism. Therefore, they cautiously spoke of "groups," not "factions" or—heaven forbid—"parties."

The deputies from Moscow took the lead. It was on their behalf that Sakharov had spoken at the opening of the Congress, and during the session they began networking with like-minded representatives who had come in from other parts of the country.

Well-known Moscow intellectuals such as Sakharov, Yuri Afanasiev, Tatyana Zaslavskaya, and Gavriil Popov joined forces with younger deputies such as Sergei Stankevich, Arkady Murashev, Galina Staro voitova, and Ilya Zaslavsky. As they began to find sympathetic deputies from other areas, such as Sobchak from Leningrad and Gayer from Vladivostok, they also firmed up their alliance with Boris Yeltsin.

Even after Yeltsin's landslide election in Moscow, many Moscow intellectuals did not trust his commitment to reform. Anything but an intellectual himself, he struck many as a typical Party boss who was fighting the establishment out of personal ambition rather than political commitment. The charges Gorbachev made in 1987 left their mark, and Yeltsin himself had been more intent on working the crowds than intellectual salons.

Nevertheless, the reformers and Yeltsin needed each other. Though they had not done badly at the polls themselves, the reform intellectuals needed allies with Yeltsin's proven vote-getting ability. As for Yeltsin, he had been something of a loner on the political scene since his ouster from the leadership in 1987. He operated with a handful of staffers headed by Lev Sukhanov, whom he had met at the State Committee on Construction, plus a few political allies such as Sverdlovsk academic Gennady Burbulis and Moscow journalist Mikhail Poltoranin, who provided advice on occasion. His own platform was still rudimentary and consisted mainly of opposition to the Communist Party machine and exhortations to speed up perestroika. If he was to make an impact on the legislature, he needed both policy and organizational support.

For a time, the Moscow reformers met in the Party's Political Education Building, but when the Supreme Soviet committees were allocated temporary office space in the Moskva Hotel, just off Red Square, much of the platform writing and position drafting took place in the suite assigned to Yeltsin as the chairman of the Committee on Construction and Housing. The deputies from out of town lived in the same hotel, and it provided an ideal spot for coalition building. For those who still thought of their task as returning the country to the true principles of Leninism, the view may also have provided some inspiration since the windows faced directly on the massive red brick Lenin Museum just across the street.

By summer, more than three hundred deputies had expressed interest in working with the group, and on July 19 Yeltsin announced to the Supreme Soviet that a coordinating body had been formed to organize an "Interregional Group of Deputies" and that a founding conference was scheduled for the end of the month. The aim of the Interregional Group would be to "speed up the process of perestroika" and pursue it "more decisively and consistently." Without using the word, he made it clear that the group, being a minority in the Supreme Soviet, would operate as an opposition, drawing up alternative proposals for legislation.

In this way, the first significant opposition movement that drew support from more than one republic used the same approach as that followed by the national fronts in individual republics: an organization in support of perestroika.

The founders also adopted a technique used effectively during the election campaign, especially in Moscow, Leningrad, and the Baltic republics: mass demonstrations. Outnumbered in parliament itself, they were able to attract tens of thousands of supporters to mass meetings in Moscow alone, and they began to do so regularly, particularly while the Supreme Soviet was in session. Since the principal "conservative" argument against radical reform was that society would not support it, the ability of the reformers to draw much larger crowds than their opponents could was a potent weapon that they used with increasing frequency in the coming winter and spring.

While the proponents of radical reform viewed themselves in opposition to the majority in the Supreme Soviet, they were very much a loyal opposition so far as Gorbachev was concerned. In fact, most still thought of themselves as Gorbachev's most consistent supporters, with the goal of mobilizing public support for reform so that Gorbachev could eventually shake free from the Communist Party diehards. Some who had resisted Party membership before Gorbachev came to power had decided to join the Party to provide support for him. Sobchak did so in 1987 and Stankevich in 1988.

Even Yeltsin still talked as if his major goal was to prod Gorbachev to do the right thing, not to challenge or oppose him. A few weeks after his victory in the March election, I asked him about his relations with Gorbachev. He replied that they had met privately for nearly an hour and that he hoped to establish a regular pattern of contact. "I think he is beginning to listen," Yeltsin added, "but he is still too beholden to Ligachev and the conservatives. Maybe the election will tell him something."

In case Gorbachev was slow to understand, Yeltsin had arranged for Gennady Burbulis to nominate him to oppose Gorbachev for the Supreme Soviet chairmanship, even though he intended to refuse to run. Yeltsin knew he would lose the vote at the Congress but wanted to signal Gorbachev that he would face a direct challenge later if he continued to exclude Yeltsin from his team.[5]

A few days after the first Congress ended, Yeltsin and his delightful wife, Naina Iosifovna, came to dinner at our residence. I asked him how he would assess the first session.

"Not too bad," he replied. "It accomplished half of what it should have." Then, as he recalled some of the questions still open, he revised his statement: "Well, maybe not really half, but a quarter for sure." When I asked whether it would have been realistic to expect much more, he said no, a realist should not be disappointed.

He was in an optimistic mood since he sensed that public opinion was moving in his direction. He noted how the mood of the Congress had become less hostile to him and his allies in the "Moscow group" during its second week and attributed this to the stream of telegrams backing the reformers that the voters were sending their representatives. While most of the deputies were still just watching how their local first secretary voted and followed suit (he mimicked a person casting a side glance and then raising his hand), he thought this would become less and less common in the future. Telecasts of the sessions had brought the debates into the homes of people everywhere, and most did not want their representatives simply to follow the Party lead.

Throughout the evening's conversation, there was not the slightest hint that Yeltsin thought of himself in competition with Gorbachev. He was still competing with those who were influencing Gorbachev to go slow on perestroika, and his stated aim was to convince Gorbachev that he could and should speed up the reform process and rely on Yeltsin as his principal lieutenant. Perhaps this would not have satisfied his ambitions in the long run, but his comments seemed sincere at the time. The intense personal hatred that developed over the next two years resulted from Gorbachev's repeated efforts to put him down.

The evening passed without a single disparaging remark about Gorbachev personally. This restraint did not apply to another member of Gorbachev's family, however. When we discussed the possibility of his visiting the United States, I urged him to take Naina when he went. His reaction was emphatic: "No. Absolutely not! I'll not have her acting like Raisa Maximovna!"

His statement was unfair to both ladies. Though he probably never changed his mind about Raisa, he was to learn that he needed Naina more than he thought.

Could Reform Prevail?

IT WAS LATE JUNE. The first session of the Congress of People's Deputies had passed into history, and the new Supreme Soviet had started its work. I was on a Pan American flight to Washington for routine consultations. Dinner was over and, instead of watching the movie, I took out my laptop and wrote some notes to myself. I doubted that the KGB had the plane bugged, and I knew I could leave the disk in a safe place in Washington. It might be helpful if I could think through some of the questions I would be asked when I made my Washington rounds. Here is what I wrote:

1. Turning Point? Gorbachev says the Congress of People's Deputies was. Is he right?

He may turn out to be right, but we really can't say at this time. My guess is that he *is* right, though, even if there is retrogression at some point. There is a movement toward representative government which will be hard to deny; if it is denied, will it not come back with renewed force later?

What *is* new? There have been abortive attempts to create representative institutions before—the dumas, the Constituent Assembly of 1918—and some common elements can be observed (e.g., corporate representation in the first Duma). But in the past, all attempts have essentially been efforts from below, resisted more or less successfully by the supreme political authority. Now we have the dominant figure in that supreme political authority pushing the constitutional process and trying to tap popular emotions and participation to give motive force and dynamism to the process. That is different.

2. How threatening are the negative tendencies (bare shelves in shops, budget deficit, ethnic and nationality unrest)? Some are now talking of the possibility of civil war in the next two to three years; others of the possibility of famine.

They are threatening, indeed, and will become critically so if social and economic protest begins to join hands with ethnic hatred. This may actually be beginning in Ferghana and Novy Uzen. If it were simply ethnic animosity, it could probably be contained by a sufficient application of force—enough to keep the parties at odds from going after each other with lethal force. But these various emotions tend to get mixed up in highly volatile combinations.

Worst-case scenario: prices continue their rise, shortages become more acute. Scattered small protests coalesce and become violent, going after the most convenient local target: a minority nationality, Party or police headquarters—or just on a general rampage. Attempts are made to put it down. They work only sporadically or not at all, and the protest movement grows, city after city. What then? Could they order a Tiananmen Square? Probably. Would it work? Probably, in the short term at least, but at the cost of the reform process itself. And confidence that it would work could not be high. Suppression is likely to occur only as a last, desperate resort. But it *could* occur, unpleasant as this thought is for me and as vigorously as I try to suppress it and rationalize my way out of it.

But that is a worst-case analysis, not necessarily the most likely outcome. And what might the most likely one be? Stumbling on, putting down isolated disturbances when they occur but propitiating the forces insofar as possible. Bobbing and weaving, so to speak, and avoiding a general uprising of protest. (The violence itself tends to create its antidote, in that the bulk of the population will come to fear the effects of violence and disorder more than they hate current conditions.) So one could have a good bit of turmoil, but also attempts to meet some of the grievances, and as things change, more and more groups might secure a vested interest in not threatening what they have achieved by violent methods. Pipe dream? Possibly. But I don't think this sort of future should be ruled out as a scenario with a substantial probability.

3. Is Gorbachev's position really secure for the next five years? If not, what could topple him?

I have trouble devising a *plausible* scenario which would result in Gorbachev's forcible ouster before his current term as chairman of the Supreme Soviet Presidium is over. Of course it could happen, as a theoretical proposition. But in reality, who could do it (assuming KGB loyalty)? I don't see a candidate on the horizon, except maybe Yeltsin eventually. But he probably couldn't make a move for at least five years. He is anathema to the Party *apparat,* which means that his only tool for a challenge would be via the electoral process, directly or indirectly. And that really means five years from now in the next Congress of People's Deputies. That would take a political turnaround which would be breathtaking, even by today's much revised standards.

But think again of the worst case. Strikes and disturbances all over;

split in Politburo as to how to deal with them. Either a charismatic leader (none currently in the Politburo except Gorbachev seems to meet that description) or a conspirator gathers strength and makes a challenge—public and open or covert and conspiratorial. The Central Committee makes a decision; other agencies are forced to salute and approve like in the old days. Probability on this is too substantial to dismiss.

4. What would happen if Gorbachev is removed?

My earlier judgment was that it would be a tragedy for the Soviet peoples but not for the United States. I still think that is true, since a successor regime would be so preoccupied putting down dissent and trying to keep things from falling apart that it would hardly be capable of moving against us or our allies in a military way. I see no reason to revise this basic judgment. (It will be relevant to notice what happens in China in this regard; will they become more aggressive? I doubt it.)

5. Is there an organized opposition against perestroika?

Yes and no. Yes in the sense that some "conservative" or reactionary groups are being formed. [The anti-Semitic] Pamyat and some of the organizations formed recently in Leningrad with a Nina Andreyeva philosophy are cases in point. But nationally no. And powerful enough to mount a practical challenge—also no. An organized opposition in this sense is still probably in the future, but I do not doubt that one will form eventually, particularly if the process of democratization proceeds. So the absence of one now does not provide much guarantee for the future.

6. Will the Party apparatchiks acquiesce in their own eclipse?

Not willingly, but they may not be given a choice.

By the time I left the plane in Washington, it had dawned on me that the empire's reinforcing rods might soon disintegrate.

X

The Balts Take the Lead

*The cornerstone of the election platform is the step-by-step transition from a
sovereign union republic of the Soviet Union to a state not dependent upon the
Soviet Union, an ally; the next aim is to become an independent state
in a demilitarized, neutral Balto-Scandinavia.*
Estonian National Front, election platform, October 1989[1]

*The consequences could be disastrous for these peoples if the nationalists
manage to achieve their goals. The very viability of the Baltic nations could be
called into question.*
CPSU Central Committee, statement, August 27, 1989[2]

While the new Supreme Soviet was still in session, I was asked
to meet with a group of deputies from Lithuania who represented Sąjūdis, the political movement that had dominated the March
elections there. As ambassador to the Soviet Union, I had always refused to meet with Baltic officials, since such meetings could imply that
the United States accepted the Soviet Union's forcible annexation of the
Baltic states.

This did not mean, of course, that I refused to meet people from the
Baltic states as individuals. In fact, we were eager to do so in order to
show our interest in their fate and to keep abreast of developments
there. Meetings with private citizens did not violate our nonrecognition
policy since they were not official meetings with persons who held office
in what the Soviet Union claimed to be a constituent republic.

The Sąjūdis request for an *official* meeting was explicit, and I thought
about the implications before I agreed. Although the persons in the
group were deputies to the USSR Supreme Soviet, they had not re-

quested the meeting in that capacity. They were to come as representatives of Sąjūdis, and I knew that this organization was genuinely popular in Lithuania. Even more relevant, my would-be callers had won in a free election. The decision, therefore, was an easy one. By meeting with them officially I would be showing support for the democratic process—and our respect for them as legitimate representatives of their occupied nation.

I invited the group to my residence, Spaso House, rather than to my office because I wanted to make sure that the Soviet authorities could see that we were meeting openly. There would be nothing suggesting surreptitious or covert activity—which might be used against my visitors if the situation were to change.

Sąjūdis did not profess to be a political party (political parties other than the Communist Party were still banned) but rather a movement in support of perestroika that included both Communists and non-Communists. It had been organized less than a year when it achieved its sweeping victory in the March elections, taking thirty-three of the thirty-six seats it contested, most by landslides. I was eager to meet some of the winners and hear what they would have to say.

The six delegates arrived as a group and filed into the parlor at Spaso House, which we called the music room. Their expressions were serious, even grave, as they introduced themselves. Professor Vaidotas Antanaitis, distinguished by his close-trimmed white beard, was an academic specialist in forest ecology and one of the founders of the movement of "Greens" in Lithuania. Kazimieras Antanavičius, just over fifty but looking younger, had a doctorate in economics and was a senior researcher in the Vilnius Institute of Economics. Professor Bronislavas Genzėlis, bald with just a fringe of gray hair though not yet sixty, taught philosophy at the Lithuanian State University. Kazimieras Motieka was the only lawyer in the group. A graduate of the Lithuanian State University, he practiced in Vilnius. Romualdas Ozolas, the vice president of Sąjūdis, stood out with his dark hair and black, bushy mustache. He had been an editor at a Vilnius publishing house when elected. Virgilijus Čepaitis, the secretary general of Sąjūdis, rounded out the group.

Ozolas took the lead, explaining that Sąjūdis President Vytautas Landsbergis had requested the meeting to apprise the U.S. government officially of their plans. But he had been called out of town and had asked this group to speak for him and for the movement as a whole.

With that introduction, the members took turns describing aspects of

their organization's current strategy, which was no longer merely to secure economic autonomy and defend Lithuanian culture from the onslaught of Russification but to achieve complete independence by
mid-1990.

Their plan would proceed by stages, with simultaneous moves to deal
with legal, economic, and political issues. They would remove the legal
basis of their inclusion in the Soviet Union by declaring the secret protocol to the 1939 Nazi-Soviet pact null and void and reversing the Act of
Accession, which had been forced at gunpoint out of a rump Lithuanian
parliament in 1940. They would take control of the economy by subordinating enterprises in Lithuania to the government in Vilnius or local
authorities from January 1, 1990. They would also insist upon election
of a new Lithuanian Supreme Soviet, if possible before the end of 1989
but in any case by early 1990. If Sąjūdis won a majority—which did not
seem in doubt—the Supreme Soviet would propose a new constitution
modeled on that of independent Lithuania and call for a referendum to
approve it no later than June 1990, after which a totally new parliament
called the Seimas—the name used in the twenties and thirties—would be
elected. No election held under Soviet auspices would be valid in the
independent state.

My first thought as I listened to this audacious plan was how much
things had changed. I could not imagine that Lithuania would be free
within a year. Two or even three years would be a miracle.

But the point was not whether my visitors' timing was realistic but
that here were serious, experienced people, who without any tradition or
tutoring had run effective political campaigns when, for the first time in
their lives, they had a chance to do so. They had suffered enough under
the Soviets to have no illusions about the system they were taking on.
Yet they clearly expected to win.

But this was not what made me reflect on the degree of change. I had
long known that most Balts wanted independence. *That* was not what
had changed. What was new was the fearlessness with which they discussed their goals. Only three or four years back, a prison camp or insane asylum would have awaited anyone who called openly for
secession. Forty years ago, it would have been a bullet at the base of the
skull.

Now the leaders of an organized political group, independent of the

Communist Party, not only dared speak and write of secession but were
staking their careers and perhaps their lives on that goal. What as-
tounded me most was that they had come to talk to the ambassador of
the United States and risk a charge of treason by telling a foreign power
what they had in mind.

These are acts of a psychologically free people, and from that day in
1989 I never doubted they would prevail, not in some far-off generation
of the next century but before the end of this one.

They would prevail, but at what cost? Would they provoke the Nean-
derthals in the Communist Party, the KGB, and the military to put them
down by force? Just a few weeks earlier the Chinese had demonstrated
how bloody repression can work at least temporarily. But if there were
attempts to crush Lithuania and the other Baltic states, it would likely
trigger a civil war and lead to a resumption of the cold war internationally. This increased the stakes for all of us.

"What do you think the Soviet reaction will be?" I inquired.

"Oh, they will do their best to block us. But we believe that if we do
not yield to provocation, we can succeed. They would have to kill thousands, maybe tens of thousands to stop us. And if they do that, it is the
end of perestroika, the end of Gorbachev. We think they know this."

"What do you mean by yielding to provocation?"

"Meeting force with force. They will try to goad us to react violently,
then use our reaction as a pretext to call out the troops. Our hardest task
is making our own people, particularly some of our young men, understand that we can win only if we keep it peaceful. Tolerating abuse, insults, and even violence is going to take more courage than grabbing a
gun and shooting at the nearest soldier."

"So you really think it's going to work?"

"Yes. At every step of the way Gorbachev will be confronted with the
choice of allowing us to edge closer toward our goal or bringing down
his whole policy and probably his own rule with it. For once *we* have the
initiative, and we don't intend to lose it."

My guests then asked me how the United States would react when
Lithuania declared its independence and whether they could expect U.S.
assistance if the Soviets attempted an economic blockade.

I explained that I could not give an official answer to their questions
and I doubted that Washington would be willing to answer them in the

abstract. Governments do not like hypothetical questions. I could give only my personal assessment.

On the first point, the United States government and virtually all Americans would sympathize with Lithuania if it declared independence. Nevertheless, immediate recognition would be unlikely since recognition involves a judgment that a government actually controls the territory it claims. If Lithuania remained under effective Soviet control, the American government could probably not recognize its government as independent, no matter how much it might sympathize.

I also told them that immediate recognition by the United States might encourage the Soviet hard-liners to use force. To them it would seem a direct challenge, and Moscow knew that, whatever its sentiments, the United States could not risk nuclear war by attempting military protection of Lithuania. Early recognition could also make it impossible for the Soviet moderates to negotiate independence, since they would be accused of capitulation to their cold war "enemy."

Regarding economic aid, I could only say that it would be impossible for outsiders, be they Americans, Germans, Swedes, or anyone else, to supply economic aid in the event of a Soviet blockade. Soviet forces controlled the borders of what they considered the Soviet Union, and if they refused to allow supplies to enter, it would take an act of war to deliver them. Lithuanians should under no circumstances assume that the United States or any other foreign country would be able to help them directly if their actions brought on military or economic sanctions from Moscow.

One of the guests (I have forgotten who) looked me in the eye and observed, "So we're on our own. You're for democracy and self-determination, but we're on our own."

The words stung.

"Spiritually and politically, you're not entirely on your own," I said to put things into perspective. "We do not recognize that you are legally part of the Soviet Union, and we never will unless that is what the people of Lithuania freely choose. If there should be attempts to use force against you or apply an economic boycott, our reaction will be strong, though nonviolent.

"I can't say in advance just what it would be since that would depend on circumstances, but it would certainly end the Soviet-American cooperation which is just beginning. Good relations with the United States and the West in general are vital to perestroika, and all that would go out the window if there is repression in Lithuania—or elsewhere in the Baltic states. Therefore, I am not saying that we would do nothing to support you. If you are able to carry out your plans successfully, it will be in no small part because Moscow knows it would face a very damaging reaction from the West if it uses force.

"But if things do go wrong and the Soviets use force, there is no way we can protect you. You will be as vulnerable as the Chinese students on Tiananmen Square. In this sense you *are* on your own. I wish it were otherwise, but I would not be telling the truth if I said anything else."

Silence. Ten seconds. Maybe twenty. It seemed longer. Then a voice: "When you put it that way, I guess we have to agree. It's not that we ever thought others could do our work for us."

We turned to lighter subjects. We needed to get to know one another, for my colleagues and I would stay in constant touch with these and other Sąjūdis leaders over the coming months.

Nationalists on a Roll

THOUGH GORBACHEV HAD SLAPPED the Estonians down when they had attempted to assert their sovereignty in 1987, they persisted, and their Lithuanian and Latvian neighbors began to do the same.

By February 1988, all three republics had made their own languages "state languages." Previously, both Russian and the republic languages had been official, but Russian residents had rarely learned the local language and therefore had dealt with Estonians, Latvians, and Lithuanians only in Russian. Now, after a transition period all persons and institutions that served the public would be required to conduct business in the local language if their clients so desired.

Then, in quick succession, the Supreme Soviets in all three republics declared economic autonomy and began attempts to limit immigration. In May, the Lithuanian parliament passed a declaration of sovereignty almost identical to Estonia's, which had been vehemently rejected by Moscow six months earlier. In July, the Latvians did the same.

Outrage over the Nazi-Soviet secret protocol continued to build. In its first session, the USSR Congress of People's Deputies appointed a commission to investigate the issue. Senior Soviet officials were no longer flatly denying that the secret agreement had ever existed but were claiming that the original could not be found and therefore its existence could not be proven. When the commission did not issue its report before the anniversary of the pact in August, the Lithuanian Supreme Soviet issued its own declaration that the secret agreement had been illegal and therefore had been null and void *ab initio*.

By 1989, the new leaders of the Baltic Communist parties began to cooperate more and more openly with the national fronts—particularly in Estonia and Lithuania. In February, Vaino Väljas, the new Estonian Party leader, attended the ceremony in which the flag of independent Estonia was raised over the ancient Tall Hermann tower in Tallinn to mark the anniversary of Estonian independence.

Algirdas Brazauskas was even more active in Lithuania. Having won public esteem by making significant concessions to the Catholic Church when he became Party leader in late 1988, he could not prevent an attempt by hard-liners at the Lithuanian Party plenum the following February to mount a counteroffensive against Sąjūdis. But these hard-liners lost every contest in the March election, and the next Party plenum, in June, brought a wholesale ouster of Moscow loyalists from the Lithuanian Central Committee. By July, the Lithuanian Communist Party was discussing a new program to eliminate its legal monopoly of power, transfer legislative authority to an elected assembly, and "create an independent, democratic, law-based Lithuanian state." Plans were made for a Party congress later in the year to approve these propositions, a heresy even by the revised standards of perestroika.

The Communist youth organization, the Komsomol, outdid the Party itself. The Lithuanian Komsomol officially withdrew from the All-Union Komsomol in June. In Estonia and Latvia, newspapers controlled by the republic Komsomol organizations became principal outlets for national front opinion.

Communist-dominated parliaments and Councils of Ministers in the Baltic republics began to adapt to the new public mood with the prospect of new elections. There had not been elections to the republic Supreme Soviets since 1985, and until 1989 these bodies fit the traditional mold of puppet assemblies that gathered for two or three days a year to give unanimous approval to legislation drafted by the Communist Party.

These transformations must have bewildered observers unable to recognize the effect of aroused voters on politicians facing a real election. First, the legislators supported autonomy in the face of stubborn opposition from Moscow, and as the year progressed, they took a sharp turn toward outright independence. By the fall of 1989, all three once-puppet parliaments had defected to their patriot brethren.

In Estonia, Arnold Rüütel, the chairman of the republic's Supreme Soviet, took the lead in pressing Estonia's case. In Latvia, Anatolijs Gorbunovs did the same.

Activists in the national fronts were named to senior positions in the republic governments, and many government officials began to espouse the national cause—particularly after the March elections revealed the strength of national sentiment in the public at large. For example, Kazimiera Prunskienė, an economist who was a member of the Sąjūdis council and had won a seat in the USSR Congress of People's Deputies, was named deputy prime minister of Lithuania in July. Public calls for secession, still rare in 1988, became routine.

The Empire Strikes Back

THE NATIONALIST FERVOR that won the hearts of most ethnic Balts alarmed not only the Communist authorities in Moscow but also the recent immigrants to these republics, most of whom were either employees of Moscow-run state industries or Soviet military personnel and their families.

The Baltic living standards, especially in Estonia and Latvia, were higher than those elsewhere in the Soviet Union, and it was easy for industrial enterprises to recruit Russians to move there. Military personnel stationed in the Baltic states frequently retired in place rather than return to Russia or other Soviet republics.

Such immigration, combined with a relatively low birthrate among the Baltic peoples, who had lost population in World War II to extensive emigration and afterward to the gulag, had caused a great demographic shift in Latvia and Estonia. Latvians, for example, who had once made up 77 percent of the population of independent Latvia, by 1989 held only a tenuous majority of 52 percent. If the trends continued, they would become a minority in their own country before the end of the century. In Estonia the picture was less bleak but still threatening: 38 percent of the population was non-Estonian, compared to less than 20 percent in the 1930s. Furthermore, some areas in the eastern part of Estonia were now populated predominantly by Russians. Lithuanians were still in an overwhelming majority in their republic, with 80 percent of its population, but they were also disturbed by what seemed a growing influx of outsiders.

Many, but by no means all, non-Balts living in the area were alarmed by the spreading nationalist sentiment. If the Balts did take charge of their countries and limit immigration, would the Russians be allowed to stay? If so, would they be treated as second-class citizens? Would they be forced to learn the local language, which they had so far been able to ignore?

Key officials in Moscow exploited these concerns. Bureaucrats in the economic ministries who considered the enterprises they had built in the Baltic their private property fanned anti-Baltic sentiments with the active help of the KGB, conservative apparatchiks in the Communist Party, and military officers. They began organizing opposition groups in the Baltic states that they could manipulate, in the hope that this would counter the Baltic drive for independence.

Their principal method was to create organizations, largely of ethnic Russians, called "International Fronts," or "Interfronts," which would organize demonstrations and strikes to protest moves by the national organizations. These activities were highly publicized by the central media in an effort to convince Russians and others outside the Baltic that the Baltic nationalists were dangerous extremists who had little support among the population as a whole. But these factions simply polarized local publics and led to increasing tensions between Baltic and non-Baltic communities.

Moscow intellectuals joked in the summer of 1989 that "A nationalist is a person who speaks two languages, his own and Russian." "So what is an internationalist, then?" "Why, someone who speaks only Russian."

Divide and rule was so ingrained in Soviet imperial practice that any efforts at regional cooperation not sponsored by Moscow were considered suspect. As the three Baltic nations began to push for more autonomy from Moscow, they also began to establish better means of cooperating with one another. All were essentially in the same boat, and it was clear to most patriots that none was likely to achieve independence if they continued to act alone.

In May, representatives of the Lithuanian Sąjūdis and the Estonian and Latvian National Fronts formed a Baltic Council, facilitated by the

significant presence of national front representatives in the three delegations to the Congress of People's Deputies. Their first public action was
to walk out of the Congress of People's Deputies to protest a proposal to
establish a Committee for Constitutional Oversight. They feared that
the committee, whose mandate was poorly defined, might overrule Baltic legislation and limit the constitutional right of secession. To avoid an
open split, Gorbachev compromised on the issue.

The most spectacular collective act occurred in August. To mark the
anniversary of the Nazi-Soviet secret agreement, the national fronts—
with the cooperation of the leaders of the Lithuanian and Estonian
Communist Parties—organized the "Baltic Way" on August 23, 1989.
This turned out to be the largest demonstration yet.

More than 2 million people responded to the appeal to form a human
chain by holding hands in an unbroken line running through the capitals
of Tallinn, Riga, and Vilnius. The total number of Estonians, Latvians,
and Lithuanians living in the three Baltic countries was somewhat in excess of 5 million, so that participants made up an astounding 40 percent
of the entire ethnic Balt population.[3]

It was a warm, sunny day (not always the case during Baltic sum-
mers), and the atmosphere was festive. Demonstrators traveled to designated places carrying flowers and singing songs. I did not observe the
scene directly since, as ambassador to the Soviet Union, I was prohibited by our own regulations from visiting the occupied Baltic states lest
our policy of nonrecognition be undermined. Accounts from participants and observers, however, agreed that the occasion was peaceful
and good-humored.

One Russian couple who was vacationing in Lithuania at the time
told me how they had been swept up in the emotion of the moment and
accompanied their Lithuanian acquaintances to the demonstration.
They felt no hostility whatever; the Lithuanians accepted them with
open arms and even showered them with flowers. They returned to Moscow convinced that the Baltic cause was righteous and that democracy
would never prevail in Russia until the Balts were given their independence.

To Gorbachev and the authorities in Moscow, however, the events of
the summer, and the human chain in particular, appeared insolent. The
reaction of Communist Party headquarters to the Baltic Way was swift.
On August 26, a strong warning was issued in Moscow in the name of
the Central Committee.[4]

I was far away, traveling on the island of Sakhalin, when I read the statement in the press. It struck me as emotional to the point of incoherence. It spoke of "nationalist, extremist groups" taking advantage of "democracy and glasnost" to delude the public. It accused the national fronts of creating organizations like those "at the time of fascist occupation" and railed at them for practicing "intimidation, sheer deception, and disinformation." It also noted that the "nationalist leaders" "abused the freedom of international relations by contacting foreign organizations and centers" (like the American Embassy?) and "treating them as consultants and advisers."

As far as the August 23 event was concerned, the organizers were accused of whipping up "nationalist hysteria" and foisting slogans on people with hatred toward the Soviet system, the Russian people, the CPSU, and the Soviet army. And then the clincher: "The fate of the Baltic peoples is in danger. . . . The consequences could be disastrous . . . if the nationalists manage to achieve their goals. *The very viability of the Baltic nations could be called into question.*"[5]

In other words; if you keep this up, you're going to be crushed.

This reminder of the bad old days misrepresented the facts and defied logic, since the demonstrators campaigning for secession were exercising a right guaranteed by the Constitution. Under the rule of law—one of the prime objectives of perestroika—exercising a right is hardly criminal incitement.

One could only wonder at what sort of "freedom of international relations" (also guaranteed in the Constitution) there could be if "contacting foreign organizations" was suspect.

The "facts" were as fallacious as the logic: there was no credible evidence that the national fronts had used intimidation, deception, or disinformation, techniques that had been employed in fact by the Moscow Center, the KGB and the military but were not characteristic of the independence movements, whose tactics were far from deceptive but direct and open.

It was the Central Committee that was employing intimidation and disinformation, and its evident panic would have been amusing if not for the transparent threat the statement conveyed. The mighty Communist Party of the Soviet Union quailing before a group of singing, flower-bearing, hand-holding demonstrators!

It is inconceivable that this statement was issued without Gorbachev's approval, even though he was not in Moscow when it was released to the press.

The Georgian Trauma

THE POLITICAL CHALLENGES in the Baltic were peaceful, but in 1989 there were violent outbursts in the southern borderlands of the Soviet empire. The confrontation between Armenians and Azeris over Nagorny Karabakh continued throughout the year, but fatal clashes were sporadic and on a small scale. It was in Georgia, Uzbekistan, and Kazakhstan that large numbers of people died in incidents that had little else in common.

The first occurred in Tbilisi, the capital of Georgia, on April 9, when military forces brutally broke up a peaceful demonstration, killing or fatally wounding at least nineteen people. The decision to use force against demonstrators occurred at a time when reformers throughout the Soviet Union were struggling to establish the right to demonstrate peacefully. Therefore, any forcible dispersal of peaceful demonstrators would have been a political issue, even if officials had avoided casualties. The suppression of the demonstration in Tbilisi was literally the first issue to be brought before the Congress of People's Deputies, and it was brought by a deputy from Latvia, not Georgia.

There had been sporadic demonstrations in Tbilisi from the fall of 1988 and a small group of young people, mainly women students, had announced a hunger strike during the winter. They were demanding more rapid movement toward Georgian autonomy and resistance to demands of some of Georgia's minorities for more freedom from Georgia. For several months, the local authorities had treated them with hostility but had not seriously interfered. April 8 was a Saturday, the weather was warm, and large numbers of people gathered in the central square in support of the demonstrators.

After midnight troops charged the crowd, wielding sharpened entrenchment shovels and gas canisters. Eyewitnesses described their actions as savage. Persons who had fallen to the pavement were beaten to death, and gas was sprayed directly into the faces of prostrate, unarmed individuals. Scores of people were hospitalized, many suffering from gas poisoning.

Inexplicably, the military authorities who had conducted the operation refused to identify the gas that had been used against the demonstrators. They either denied that they had used gas or said that it had been only tear gas. But the symptoms of those affected pointed to more poisonous substances. Georgian physicians did not have the means of identifying the chemical and thus could not treat their patients.

Andrei Sakharov flew to Tbilisi immediately after the incident to see what had happened and offer assistance. When he and others were unable to find out locally what sort of gas had been used, he telephoned me for assistance, asking whether doctors in the United States could help. I immediately contacted the Soviet desk in the State Department, which put the question to U.S. toxicologists. They sent some advice about possible types of gas that could have caused the symptoms described and offered to send specialists to Tbilisi to consult on the spot.

Washington's prompt and helpful response to Sakharov's request impressed me, but I was appalled by how the authorities in Moscow were dealing with what could only be considered criminal acts by forces brought in ostensibly to restore order. Instead of identifying the culprits, the initial reaction was a cover-up and then, when that turned out to be impossible, to dump all the blame on Georgian Party leader Dzhumber Patiashvili, who had been removed a few days after the massacre.

The Congress of People's Deputies debated the issue at length, established a commission to investigate, and demanded explanations from those in authority. Gorbachev, Ligachev, and other Politburo members denied that they had known in advance that troops were to be used. Patiashvili admitted that he had asked for troops to disperse the demonstration but insisted that the local military commander, General Igor Rodionov, had assured him that it could be done peacefully, without injury to anyone. Rodionov asserted that injuries had occurred only because the demonstrators themselves had been violent, a claim that eyewitnesses—and television films made at the time—refuted.

The determination of the "system" to protect those responsible for ordering the violence eventually became the key issue, and reform elements throughout the Soviet Union intensified their campaign for better legal guarantees of the right of assembly. In Georgia itself, the effect was even more profound. Nobody believed that local officials had acted without sanction from Moscow, and it was not lost on them that the general in command at the time was a Russian, as were most of his troops.

From April 1989, the political mood in Georgia swung from a desire to reinforce the republic's autonomy within the Soviet system to a full-scale drive for independence. There had always been some tensions between Georgians and Russians, but relations had been more harmonious than those between many other ethnic groups. They deteriorated rapidly. By fall, Georgia seemed headed in the same direction as the Baltic states, even though the Georgian opposition forces were not united in a national front but splintered among dozens of competing political groups.

Communal Violence in Central Asia

THE VIOLENCE IN UZBEKISTAN and Kazakhstan was even bloodier but had different origins. In June, more than a hundred people died in Uzbekistan's Ferghana Valley when Uzbeks went on a rampage against members of a small ethnic group called Meskhetian Turks. A few days later, there was a similar disturbance on the northeast shore of the Caspian Sea when Kazakhs attacked Chechens and other north Caucasians in the jerry-built oil town of Novy Uzen.

The Meskhetian Turks had been among the victims of Stalin's deportation frenzy. Until World War II they had lived in Georgia in a mountainous area on the Turkish border. Speaking Turkish and professing Islam in its Shi'ite version, they had held themselves aloof from the Christian Georgians in the valleys below. Stalin had moved them to Uzbekistan during the war because he considered them potentially disloyal. At first, the Uzbeks had accepted them hospitably, even sharing food with them during the difficult war years, but the Meskhetian Turks had kept to their ethnic neighborhoods and considered themselves exiles from their proper home—which, of course, they were. Khrushchev had eventually allowed some of the deported peoples to return to their homelands, but the Meskhetians had been left in Uzbekistan. Georgians had moved into the areas where they had once lived and refused to let them return.

The riots ended when the authorities evacuated the remaining Meskhetian Turks from Uzbekistan altogether, first to military bases, then to farms in Russia. But this solution did not suit the Turks; they wanted to return to their original homeland in Georgia. Throughout 1990 and 1991, their representatives mounted repeated demonstrations in Moscow, but to no avail.

Officials have never given a credible explanation of just how the riots started and why so many people were allowed to die. Rumors, never properly clarified, abounded that local Party officials and the KGB helped to instigate them, supposedly to demonstrate the risks of democratization, and to force Moscow to crack down. Whether or not there was truth to these rumors, it was obvious that neither the local nor central authorities did anything effective to stop the riots until they had run their bloody course.

The contrast between Tbilisi and Ferghana was telling: in the first the authorities had shed blood to suppress a peaceful demonstration; in the second they had failed or refused to prevent bloodshed by agitated mobs.

The riots in Novy Uzen were less serious but also showed the inflammatory combination of Soviet policies regarding nationalities and economic development. Industrial installations had been constructed in haste with little regard for their impact on the environment or attention to amenities for normal life. The high birthrates in Central Asia and the Caucasus had forced more and more young people off the land into cities in search of a livelihood. There, they lived in crowded slums with little chance for a better life. With many different nationalities competing for crumbs, small incidents suddenly escalated into full-scale riots.

The National Fronts Gather Strength

THE THREE REPUBLICS to the southwest, Belarus, Ukraine, and Moldavia, were beginning to look like the Baltics the year before.

In May, Shcherbitsky's hard-line Ukrainian regime attacked both Rukh and the Ukrainian Helsinki Union as "anti-Soviet." Nevertheless, demonstrations in the western areas, particularly Lviv, intensified. Partisans of the Uniate Church became more aggressive and were strongly backed by the Vatican, which let Gorbachev know that no meeting with Pope John Paul II would be satisfactory if the official ban on the Ukrainian Catholics continued.

Rukh, a counterpart of the Lithuanian Sąjūdis in conception (both words mean "movement," and both unified several informal groups in ostensible support of perestroika), finally managed to hold its inaugural congress in Kiev in early September and elected as chairman the poet Ivan Drach, the head of the Ukrainian Writers' Union. A heavyset man in his early fifties, Drach was well known not only for his poetry but also as an outspoken champion of the Ukrainian language. He once wrote after one of my speeches in Kiev that it was incomprehensible that Russian officials who lived in Ukraine would not take the trouble to speak Ukrainian, while the U.S. ambassador, who was only visiting, could do so.

Although Rukh now had a foothold in Kiev, most of its support was still in Ukraine's western regions, particularly the city of Lviv and areas nearby. There, Vyacheslav Chornovil and Mikhail Horyn, both former political prisoners, were leading a burgeoning movement for Ukrainian autonomy.

Shcherbitsky was finally forced to retire as head of the Ukrainian Party organization in late September. He was replaced by Vladimir Ivashko, an ethnic Ukrainian from Kharkiv, where Ukrainian national sentiment was weaker than in the west. Ivashko, whose views seemed close to Gorbachev's, introduced more permissive policies than Shcherbitsky's but was determined to align Kiev's policies with Moscow's.

Nationalist sentiment, however, was growing. Before the end of the year the Ukrainian Supreme Soviet made Ukrainian the state language as of January 1, 1990. New parliamentary elections were scheduled for the spring of 1990, and Rukh and its allies were campaigning vigorously. The ban on the Ukrainian Catholic Church was lifted just before Gorbachev visited Rome in late November, and Uniate congregations began taking over the churches that had been seized in 1946 and given to the Russian Orthodox Church.

Two developments in particular undermined the authority of the Ukrainian Communists. Three years after the Chernobyl accident, the media finally revealed that the resulting radioactive fallout was much greater than had been admitted and additional areas would have to be evacuated. Clearly the republic's Communist leaders had been part of a cover-up that had prevented an adequate response to the nuclear accident.

Then, in the Donets Basin, a major coal-producing area, the miners went on an extended strike. They threw out the local Party officials and the Party-sponsored trade unions and organized their own "workers' committees," which administered the area more effectively than the official authorities had managed. The myth that the Communist Party represented the working class was shattered. Gorbachev had to promise local elections soon, along with economic concessions.

But the nationalists in the west had not yet formed an effective alliance with the worker militants in the east. Those in the west wanted political reform and Ukrainianization; those in the east wanted better working conditions and a higher standard of living and were not greatly disturbed by the gradual Russification of the area.

Though Belorussian activists suffered even greater repression for most of the year, the revelations about Chernobyl had an even stronger effect there since it was located upwind from the power plant and had absorbed more fallout than Ukraine. The radioactive contamination of Belorussia was proportionately much more serious than that of Ukraine.

Intellectuals in Minsk continued to publicize the Stalinist atrocities, revive the Belorussian language and culture, and combat policies that were ruining the environment, but the Communist authorities harassed them continuously. Party members were forbidden to participate in Adradzhennye, the Belorussian counterpart of Sąjūdis and Rukh, and denied Adradzhennye leaders premises for their founding congress in Minsk. They were forced to hold it in Vilnius, in next-door Lithuania. Sympathetic newspaper editors were threatened with the loss of their jobs if they publicized the informal groups.

In the March elections for the USSR Congress of People's Deputies, the dissidents defeated several Party stalwarts, among them the head of the Party organization for the city of Minsk. Some Adradzhennye leaders, such as Vasil Bykov, had good connections with reformist Party officials in Moscow and spread the word about the hard-line policies in Minsk, which were clearly out of line with perestroika. These efforts resulted in a *Pravda* editorial in July criticizing the Belorussian Party leadership for being "out of touch."

Agitation over the Chernobyl cover-up grew as the year went by. A map was published showing that extensive areas had been affected by radioactive contamination, but no action had been taken to evacuate or even to warn many of the people living there. Almost 20 percent of the republic's cropland was affected. Residents from contaminated areas gathered in Minsk for a mass demonstration in September, and under intense public pressure the Belorussian Supreme Soviet approved a program that would resettle one hundred thousand people from the affected areas. The cost of the program, however, was nearly double the normal annual budget of the entire Belorussian government, and it was not at all clear where the money would come from unless Moscow was uncharacteristically generous.

The official hostility benefited Adradzhennye. By the end of 1989 the organization had a hundred thousand members, 60 percent of whom had joined after the organization had been forced to hold its congress in Lithuania.

Moldavians had better luck securing the support of the republic's Communist Party for a restoration of their cultural heritage than did the Ukrainians and Belorussians, but they had a different problem: ethnic minorities were increasingly opposing their efforts.

Support for the Moldavian National Front grew rapidly through the year, both before and after its founding congress in May. By late summer the National Front was drawing up to three hundred thousand persons for its demonstrations in favor of making Moldavian the official language and reverting to the Latin alphabet used in Romania. Under this pressure, the Supreme Soviet made Moldavian the state language and designated Russian as the "language of interethnic communication." In the parliament, deputies could use either Moldavian or Russian, with simultaneous translations available on earphones for those not proficient in both languages.

The growth of the Moldavian National Front stimulated a counterorganization led by ethnic Russians called Yedinstvo (Unity), which resembled the Baltic Interfronts. Smaller minorities of Gagauz (Christian Turks) and Bulgarians also formed ethnic-based organizations.

For several months the authorities delayed "registering" these organizations formally, but they finally did so in November. In the same month, Petru Lucinschi (Luchinsky in Russian) was named first secretary of the republic's Party organization, replacing conservative Semyon Grossu, who was spirited out of the country to fill the surprisingly junior diplomatic position of agricultural attaché at the Soviet Embassy in Mexico.

Lucinschi, an ethnic Moldavian despite his Slavic name, had been second secretary in Tajikistan. Not yet fifty, he was younger than Grossu and more in tune with perestroika. Like Vladimir Ivashko, his counterpart in Ukraine, his general approach was close to Gorbachev's in substance, which meant that in the end he pleased nobody but Gorbachev. He allowed the National Front a freer rein than his predecessor had, disappointing the Russian chauvinists in Yedinstvo, but opposed the more extreme national front positions. His attempts to head off separatist demands and mediate between the Moldavian nationalists and the very significant Russian minority fell victim to the irreconcilables in Yedinstvo, who were unwilling to concede even symbolic steps to mollify the Moldavian majority.

When the opposition movements in both Ukraine and Moldavia became increasingly demanding in 1990, Gorbachev brought both Lucinschi and Ivashko to Moscow to join him in a revamped Party Politburo.

Democracy or Independence?

JUST AS THEY WERE beginning to coalesce, the fledgling opposition groups in the Soviet Union exhibited two contrasting tendencies. While every group favored greater democracy, greater openness, and an end to one-party rule, the opposition in Russia emphasized individual freedoms. The national fronts, on the other hand, stressed autonomy or independence for their nations.

This divergence became apparent in the summer of 1989 as Yeltsin, Popov, Afanasiev, and the other founders of the Interregional Group tried to bring the national-minded Baltic deputies into their organization. Some—Professor Viktor Palm of Estonia, for example—became members from the start, but most of the Balts hesitated. They supported the aims of the Interregional Group of Deputies and could normally be counted on to vote with it in the Supreme Soviet, but they felt that their agenda came before that of democracy in the entire Soviet Union. They wanted to disengage from Soviet institutions as soon as possible and were wary of becoming too much a part of them, even as members of the opposition.

Most Russian reformers supported self-determination as a matter of principle and generally voted with the Baltic national leaders on Baltic questions, but they felt that only a democratic evolution of the Soviet Union would open the door to Baltic independence and that placing nationalism above democracy could eventually produce carbon copies of Soviet rule in the breakaway republics. Furthermore, as a minority in the Congress and Supreme Soviet, the "democrats" needed all the help they could get, but the Balts were showing an increasing tendency to opt out.

Though they were in earlier stages of development, the national fronts in other republics were showing the same tendency. After April, Georgian deputies were preoccupied with putting space between their republic and Moscow. Deputies from Armenia and Azerbaijan had already grown accustomed to concentrating on Nagorny Karabakh. Moldavians, faced with strong resistance from their Slavic minority as they attempted to recapture their Romanian cultural roots, also stressed developments at home.

This created a dilemma for Gorbachev, who genuinely intended to liberalize the system even as opposition grew within the Party apparatus, the military, and the police. But these "egotistical, power-mad nationalists"—as he would have termed them—made it harder to achieve the reforms he desired.

It was this attitude that pervaded the ominous Central Committee warning to the Balts in August.

Another factor that impelled Gorbachev to reject the course urged by the Interregional Group and exclude compromise with the Baltic national fronts was personal: the growing possibility that Boris Yeltsin might establish a base for challenging him.

During the summer of 1989, the alliance between Yeltsin and the reform forces had been forged. Yeltsin did not emerge the sole leader of the Interregional Group (some prominent members such as Sakharov still suspected him of being a crypto-apparatchik), but he was one of the cochairmen and the most popular figure in the group. If Gorbachev had bridled at the publicity Yeltsin had received in 1986, when his own position was beyond challenge and Yeltsin was a loyal ally, how much more vigorous would his reaction be now that he felt besieged and had evidence of Yeltsin's powerful way with the voters?

Nevertheless, in the summer of 1989, one could not be absolutely sure how Gorbachev would react. He had shown a remarkable ability to maneuver, and perhaps he could bring himself to do so again. Since it was now clear that he had failed to lick Yeltsin, he might see the wisdom of joining him again, while he himself could still be the senior partner.

Yeltsin, Gorbachev, and the KGB

EVENTUAL RECONCILIATION WITH GORBACHEV was the hope of those who had organized the Interregional Group. They thought they were providing essential political support for his goals. Most of them understood that he could hardly endorse their group outright for fear of suffering Khrushchev's fate. But they did hope that he would provide indirect protection while they gathered strength and could thus support him when it was time for a showdown with the Party conservatives.

Insofar as Yeltsin personally was concerned, these hopes were soon dashed. Gorbachev kept him at arm's length, and by fall there were unmistakable signs that a renewed campaign to discredit him had begun. The first evidence of this followed Yeltsin's first trip to the United States.

Yeltsin had mentioned to me in June that he would like to see the United States. I had already given some thought as to how we might arrange a trip for him. He had traveled abroad very little and had never been to the United States, and I believed it would be in the interest of both countries if he knew us better. However, as long as he was deputy chairman of the State Committee on Construction, protocol would require that his boss be invited first. We had an official agreement for cooperation in housing that included reciprocal visits, and I intended to arrange an invitation for Yeltsin as soon as the chairman of his State Committee had made the trip.

His election to the Supreme Soviet changed the situation. He was now chairman of its Committee on Construction and Housing, which solved the protocol problem. I requested the State Department to encourage an appropriate congressional committee to invite him, but nothing materialized during the summer. When I returned from an extended trip to Siberia and the Soviet Far East on Labor Day, however, I learned that he had already made arrangements for a trip with the assistance of James Garrison of the Esalen Foundation in California and would be leaving for the United States on September 9 for a lecture tour.

By this time I had gotten to know Yeltsin well, and the news worried me. He would doubtless expect a lot of official attention, but I was not sure that his tour organizers were in a position to arrange the sort of meetings he was sure to want. A quick check with the State Department confirmed that no appointments had been made. I immediately went to see him to find out what was going on.

We met in a reception room in the Moskva Hotel that had been provided for Supreme Soviet deputies to receive visitors in. He was set to fly to New York the next day and showed me the advance schedule that had been prepared by his American sponsor. I took one look at it and blanched. It had him making two, three—sometimes even four—

speeches a day, often in different cities. On one day, if memory serves, he was to give a noon address in Miami and then one after dinner in Minneapolis.

"Boris Nikolayevich," I said, handing the paper back, "you have remarkable stamina. But this schedule will kill you. I don't see how any human being could survive it. You've got to tell your sponsors to lighten it up."

He said he had wondered about that himself and added that he had been disturbed to read press reports that he was coming to the United States to make money from lectures. This was not his purpose, he stated emphatically. "The money from the lectures will go to our organization to combat AIDS," he said. "I plan to buy disposable hypodermic needles for our hospitals. [Soviet hospitals still routinely reused needles for inoculations, and a hospital in southern Russia had recently infected several infants with the fatal disease.] However, this is not my main purpose. My main goal is political, to consult your leaders, and also to see your country."

I assured him that I would do what I could to arrange appointments in Washington, but cautioned that some key people might not be available because time was so short. He then asked who would meet him at Kennedy Airport when he arrived in New York. I said I didn't know; presumably his sponsor would take care of that. "But Secretary of State Baker will come, won't he?" At first I thought he was joking, but then I realized that it was a serious question, and I explained that it was not our custom for senior officials to meet visitors, even the most prominent ones, when they arrived at airports, and furthermore Baker would be in Washington, not New York.

"Well, in that case, I am sure Governor Cuomo will be there," he continued. I had to disabuse him of this expectation as well, pointing out that the state capital was in Albany and that New York had so many prominent foreign visitors that the governor would have no time for anything else if he tried to meet even a fraction of the number at the airport. "Well, Albany can't be more than an hour or so by helicopter," he grumbled.

All this turned out to be preliminary to his main request: at the very least, he would expect a meeting with President Bush when he was in Washington.

This was one I had been anticipating. We had discussed the matter with officials in the State Department, who had reported that there was no chance that Yeltsin would get an appointment with the president, but Secretary of State Baker and General Brent Scowcroft, the president's assistant for national security, would probably receive him.

I tried to let him down as easily as possible, saying that he would undoubtedly be received at the White House and at high levels in the State Department but that he should not expect an appointment with the president. He persisted, saying that he would not have expected to see the president if he had gone to the United States before the recent election. Now, however, things were different. Didn't the president see opposition leaders from democratic countries?

This required an explanation that, while such meetings occur occasionally, they are not routine or obligatory. I refrained from adding that the Interregional Group was not an opposition group in the formal sense, that the Soviet Union was not yet a democratic state, and that he was not the sole chairman but only one of several cochairmen. He would doubtless have considered these inconsequential technicalities, and his comment would likely have been something like "If you want us to be a democracy, why don't you help by treating us like one?"

I left the meeting even more worried than I had been before. Yeltsin's expectations seemed to be so high that it would be difficult not to disappoint him. Also, if he tried to go through with a schedule as intense as the one he showed me, he would certainly be exhausted toward the end, with unpredictable results.

For the rest of the afternoon I was on the telephone with people in the United States to see what could be retrieved of the situation. Yeltsin had mentioned that Frederick Starr, the president of Oberlin College and one of the keenest American observers of the Soviet scene, was associated with the sponsors of his trip, and he expected Starr to accompany him for at least part of his itinerary. If Yeltsin was correct, I could rest easier. I knew Starr well and knew no one more skilled in dealing with Russians.

Fred was not in Oberlin, but my secretary tracked him down in New Orleans and put him on the line. I explained the situation and learned to my dismay that although he had been contacted by the organizers a few months back and had agreed to help with the Yeltsin trip, he had not been kept informed and was not part of the current plans.

Our next step was to press our colleagues in the State Department to obtain some higher-level appointments in Washington. I asked them to

reopen the question of a meeting with the president, not to please Yeltsin personally (we could deal with any disappointment on his part) but
because it would support the democratic process in the Soviet Union for
the president to be seen dealing with him.

My meeting with Yeltsin had confirmed my hunch that he wished to
use the trip to bolster his political prestige at home so he would be seen
operating as *the* opposition leader to Gorbachev.

I realized, of course, that the skittishness in the White House
stemmed precisely from that: there was a great reluctance to do anything
to offend Gorbachev. Nevertheless, I thought that the White House attitude was ill advised. If the Soviet Union was to evolve in a democratic
direction, it had to allow an opposition to develop, and its leaders had to
come to understand that it is perfectly proper for foreign governments
to maintain contact with opposition leaders. I considered it dangerous
to make policy on the basis of individuals. We should support principles, not persons.

Of course, if Yeltsin had been backing policies inconsistent with U.S.
interests, it would be prudent to avoid actions that seemed to endorse
them. This, however, was not the case: Yeltsin was in favor of more
rapid cuts in the Soviet military budget than Gorbachev was and was
urging Baltic self-determination. His policies were closer to ours than
Gorbachev's were. I thought it would not hurt at all to nudge Gorbachev toward cooperation with Yeltsin and his democratic allies. In the
long run, this would even be in Gorbachev's interest.

Before Yeltsin reached Washington, we had a compromise: there
would be no formal meeting with President Bush, but the president and
Vice President Dan Quayle would drop in on Yeltsin's meeting with
Scowcroft. This seemed to be a reasonable approach, but I was surprised to receive instructions to provide an explanation to Gorbachev
via the Foreign Ministry. I acted as instructed but felt that the action
was unnecessary and condescending. We did not consider it necessary to
explain to Prime Minister Thatcher why the president met with Labour
leader Neil Kinnock; why not take Gorbachev at his word that he
wished to create a democratic system of government? If he had questions about our actions, he could ask, and that would be the time to
explain.

As Yeltsin's visit to the United States progressed, I stopped worrying.
The press reports seemed positive. *USA Today* headlined one story
"Boris Yeltsin: A Star is Born" and noted: "Maverick Soviet legislator

'Just call me Boris' Yeltsin has taken the USA by storm—shaking hands, slapping backs, and posing with paupers, politicians and plumbers."[6]

Unfortunately, Yeltsin was beginning to show fatigue by the time he got to Washington and left a bad impression at the White House. As Robert Blackwill, who was in charge of European affairs on the White House staff, told me later, when Yeltsin entered the West Wing for the meeting with Scowcroft, he stopped, threw up his hands, and announced that he would go no further unless he was to see the president. I do not know why he had not been informed that the president intended to join the meeting, but his behavior was not endearing. The meeting itself reportedly went smoothly, but there was a feeling by staffers that he failed to describe a coherent program, and Scowcroft actually dozed off as he talked on. Those who attended the meeting were inclined to put him down as a bombastic political lightweight who would soon fade from the scene.

The Soviet press initially gave scant attention to Yeltsin's activities in the United States. *Pravda* carried a brief TASS report of his meeting with Scowcroft and the president that quoted the White House announcement that President Bush had spoken of his very positive relations with Gorbachev and support for perestroika during the meeting. The dispatch then cited an article in *The Washington Post* quoting unnamed "official circles" as saying that Yeltsin's proposals were very general and not practical.

Pravda suddenly took a greater interest in his visit when a lengthy article caricaturing Yeltsin appeared in the Italian newspaper *La Repubblica*. Its Washington correspondent, Vittorio Zucconi, portrayed Yeltsin as an inebriated buffoon, careening from one escapade to another, a constant embarrassment to his hosts. The picture he gave was not of the person I knew, though I was aware that Yeltsin was capable of occasional social faux pas, particularly when he was tired, ill, or annoyed. I also noticed some slips that indicated that Zucconi was not invariably precise. For example, he identified "Jack Daniel's" as "Kentucky whiskey," which was enough to put partisans of Tennessee sour mash on guard.

It was most unusual for Soviet newspapers, and *Pravda* in particular, to publish entire articles from the foreign press, but in this case the reason for the exception was obvious: the word was out to do everything possible to diminish Yeltsin's popularity. By citing a non-Communist newspaper, *Pravda*'s editors hoped to enhance the story's credibility with the Soviet leader.

The Zucconi story could have appeared in *Pravda* without any assistance from the KGB, having been transmitted to *Pravda* by the TASS bureau in Rome. Subsequent events, however, were plainly the work of the KGB. A few weeks after Yeltsin's trip to the United States, members of the Supreme Soviet began receiving copies of what purported to be a confidential letter from James Garrison, the American who had organized Yeltsin's trip, to his own board of directors. In less flowery style, it recounted many of the same alleged instances of misbehavior as those that had appeared in the Zucconi article.

Some Soviet politicians mentioned to me that a Russian translation of this "letter" had mysteriously appeared in their mail. One deputy from the Urals sent me a copy and asked whether it was authentic. I noticed that it had been produced professionally, probably by desktop publishing, in a polished Russian translation and mailed from Zurich, Switzerland, with no meaningful return address.

I wrote the deputy who had sent it to me that I had no way of determining the authenticity of what purported to be a translation of a private letter but that he might ask himself who would be able and motivated to obtain private correspondence, translate it, print it professionally, and mail it from abroad.

From the fall of 1989, there took place a series of strange events involving Yeltsin. He began receiving threats, sometimes anonymous, sometimes supposedly on behalf of the KGB. These he defied since he doubted that even the KGB would be stupid enough to make a martyr of him; its goal was to undermine his credibility with the public and intimidate him personally.

In 1992, after he had gained access to KGB records, Yeltsin told me that he had been under close surveillance from the time he was expelled from the Politburo in 1987. He was still a member of the Party Central Committee and thus supposedly exempt from such treatment, but even his kitchen (where most family conversation in Russian households occurs) had been bugged. The transcripts, he said, if stacked on top of one another, would make a pile twenty to thirty feet high![7]

It is difficult to believe that Gorbachev was not aware of this KGB activity.

Economic Woes

As an opposition to Gorbachev's Party machine formed, the economic news was uniformly gloomy. Shortages were growing, production was beginning to decline, crime was up. Perestroika was supposed to bring a better life, but people were living worse and had little confidence that the announced changes would improve their lives.

In fact, with all the talk about new policies and new approaches, bureaucrats resisted all meaningful change exactly at a time when shortcomings could no longer be concealed. Having more accurate information about life abroad, the public had lost its fear of speaking out, and the more flaws the media exposed, the more discontented the public became.

A Law on State Enterprises, passed in 1987, promised to liberate plant managers, stimulate competition and initiative, and lead eventually to a "regulated" market. Centrally planned goals were to be simplified, and plant managers were to be given the right to sell a portion of their production outside the central command system. Thus there would be a mixed system combining "state orders" (supply contracts to government agencies) with sales on the open market.

At the same time, Communist Party officials were told to stop second-guessing economic managers. The number of Party officials who supervised the economy was reduced, and this might have contributed to greater managerial independence had it been accompanied by a reduction of staff at Gosplan and in the central ministries. But this did not happen; instead, the central authorities, freed from petty Party supervision, became even more dictatorial.

In Moscow, economic problems were debated endlessly, and if one listened only to the speeches one would conclude that a revolution in industrial management was taking place. However, a trip to the provinces and a few conversations with managers revealed that nothing much had changed.

In Siberia and the Soviet Far East, I asked several executives about state orders and how they were using the freedom to enter the market with a portion of their output. In every case, state orders accounted for 90 percent of output or more.

The director of a large fishery on Sakhalin said that if he had his way all production would be covered by state orders. His right to sell 10 percent of his production on the market was useless to him because there was no open market for what he had to buy. He could obtain fuel and supplies for his fishing fleet only if he had state orders in hand. Therefore, he had to cut production by 10 percent.

The manager of a woolen mill in Ulan Ude told me proudly that her plant was 100 percent on state orders, and she would insist that it stay that way since there was no way she could find wool, fuel, or spare parts without Gosplan's allocation.

Clearly, the change of terminology from planned output to state orders altered nothing essential. Industrial managers, though freed to some degree from petty tutelage by local Party officials, were still as dependent on Gosplan and their ministries as ever. But the system, under attack and subject to tinkering, was working even more poorly than before.

A Law on Cooperatives, passed in 1988, that opened the door to cooperative-owned small enterprises, fared better than the Law on State Enterprises. The number of cooperatives, most in retail trade and personal services, quickly mushroomed. But this encouraging move toward a market economy was hobbled by the hostility of local officials, heavy taxation, and—soon—the penetration of criminal elements. Nevertheless, more than a million people were employed in the cooperative sector by the end of 1989, and their income was generally much higher than that of employees of state enterprises.

But the leadership, Gorbachev included, remained hostile to the concept of private ownership. He continued to hold that only collective ownership of the means of production was permissible, using words similar to those he had employed when he had condemned the Estonian parliament in 1988 for initiating tentative moves toward privatization.

From 1987, Gorbachev had equated perestroika with revolution, and in the political sphere the changes he espoused were potentially revolutionary. But his economic signals were confused: he repeatedly called for radical reform but never gave these appeals real content.

Prime Minister Ryzhkov, a firm believer in gradualism, had the principal responsibility for implementing economic reform. He recognized the need for change, and in particular the necessity of shifting production from military to civilian goods, but he thought this could be done gradually and by direction from above. He feared destroying the old system before a new one could be constructed, and did not see that there could be no new system as long as the old one was intact and could block it.

Throughout 1989, relations between Gorbachev and Ryzhkov were tense, but both tried to keep their differences out of the public view. Though Ryzhkov did not share Ligachev's ideological fervor, he increasingly sided with him on economic issues, while Gorbachev pressed for more rapid change. Neither, however, had endorsed a program that was likely to turn the economy around, as the reformers in the Interregional Group of Deputies persisted in pointing out.

XI

A Pivotal Year

*Perestroika really started, really dates from, 1989, when we actually began the
processes both to alter our economy and to change the political system.*
MIKHAIL GORBACHEV, January 1990[1]

*Federalist concepts are fundamentally unacceptable in the structure
of the Communist Party of the Soviet Union.*
CPSU CENTRAL COMMITTEE, declaration, September 20, 1989[2]

When Gorbachev returned to Moscow in September 1989 from his annual Crimean vacation, he faced an unprecedented array of problems. Relations with the rest of the world were improving, but that was the only bright spot in an otherwise dismal picture. The economy continued to deteriorate, with growing shortages in the shops and the resulting long lines and consumer frustration. A significant faction in the new parliament had set a course in opposition to the Party and government. Baltic politicians were beginning to talk of secession, and nationalists in many other republics were gathering strength. Eastern Europe was poised for reform, and it was not clear in Moscow whether the Warsaw Pact could survive the changes ahead. In the face of these pressures, the Communist Party was showing unmistakable signs of stress. Factions, still forbidden by the Party rules, were obvious, as was the fact that a growing number of senior Party officials had begun to question the course set by the general secretary.

The restive nationalities required the most urgent attention. In fact, Gorbachev had spent much of his vacation time thinking about them.

What Kind of Union?

FOR SEVERAL YEARS, there had been recurrent rumors that a plenary session of the Party Central Committee would be called to deal with the "nationalities question." Problems were multiplying, and in 1988 Party documents had begun, for the first time in decades, to acknowledge them, but solutions seemed so elusive and controversial that the session was postponed, postponed, and postponed again.

By the fall of 1989, it was clear that events had moved far ahead of the Party. If the Communist Party was to have any influence on the developing situation, it would have to make some fundamental choices. The long-awaited "nationalities plenum" finally convened on September 19 to address the problem.

The results pleased no one.

The lengthy document the plenum approved recognized serious flaws in the way ethnic groups had been treated and called for a "renewed federation." At the same time it specifically rejected changing the Party structure to permit a genuine federation.

There is a German proverb that may be loosely translated as "If you say 'A,' then you must say 'B' next." I recalled it when I read the Draft Nationalities Policy approved by the Central Committee. It seemed to me that the Central Committee managed to say "A" but gagged on "B." Instead, it vaguely suggested that there might be some "A prime" out there that would complete the alphabet.

After all, the document admitted that the "administrative command system" created by Stalin had "ignored the needs of national development" and "abridged the autonomy of republics" to the point that the sovereignty provided by the Constitution had become "largely formal." Furthermore, it pointed out that there had been "mass repressions," entire peoples had been forcibly resettled, and intellectuals had been "persecuted" on false accusations of nationalism. It admitted that economic decisions had been made without regard to their social and ecological consequences, which had seriously injured national values and traditions. It condemned the claim that differences among national groups were diminishing and the assertion that the nationality question had been resolved.

So far, so good. This was far from the complacent statement the Party congress had issued in 1986 and Gorbachev's judgment in his book *Perestroika,* which he had written in 1987. However, even the diagnosis of the problem was incomplete and potentially misleading because the document also asserted (twice, in fact) that the existing union was "completely voluntary."[3] The reason for this is clear. Since the document argued that things had gone wrong only *after* Lenin had died and called for a return to a genuine Leninist policy, it could hardly acknowledge that Lenin had erred when he had ordered the military conquest of many of these "republics."

Such dishonesty could have been dismissed as necessary doubletalk if the prescriptions for a cure had been sound. However, despite much talk about how the "renewed federation" should be different, the document rejected every concrete idea that might have made it so. Most important, it proclaimed that there could be no thought of federalism within the Communist Party itself.

The Soviet Constitution still contained the notorious Article VI, which established the Communist Party as the sole legitimate political organization in the country and provided for its "leading role" throughout society. Thus, any "federal" constitution would be a sham if the only legitimate political party could not be organized on federal principles.

In addition, the document specifically rejected the more important demands the republics were making: that the laws of the republics take precedence over the laws of the USSR and not be drawn up in accord with "basic principles" promulgated by the USSR and that immigration from other republics be restricted and residency requirements for voting be established. The document also continued the military draft with no provision for conscientious objection. Property in the republics could belong to either the republic or the USSR, but there could be no doubt which of those entities would claim the lion's share or which would have the means to enforce a claim.

Just as the nationalities plenum ended, Shevardnadze went to the United States for meetings in Washington and Wyoming and a speech at the United Nations. He seemed guardedly optimistic that the Party was finally facing the problem and felt that the constitutional right of secession would now have to be addressed. He predicted that procedures would be worked out to permit orderly secession but doubted that things would go that far if the authorities dealt more sensitively with the problem. He assured us that force would not be used either in Eastern Europe or the Baltic. The use of force in either area, he noted, would mean the end of perestroika and most likely the end of Gorbachev.

With the nationalities plenum out of the way, committee work started in earnest to define a new constitutional structure for the Soviet Union. Several scholarly articles appeared, a number of which indicated that a flexible union was being considered, in which constituent republics could define their relationship to the Center in different ways. Some authors recalled that in tsarist Russia areas such as Finland had had a constitutional status that differed from that of the provinces. They also noted that Puerto Rico and Micronesia had ties with the United States that differed from those of the states.

Such schemes seemed to me impractical as the basis for a union. Where they had worked, as with Finland in the nineteenth century or Puerto Rico in the twentieth, they were exceptions to constitutional principles that were uniform for most of the country. In other words, I could imagine a Soviet federation with a few territories granted special status but not one in which each constituent republic had a unique status, which could be changed at the will of the republic. Eventually, the idea of a flexible (or "multivariant," to translate the Russian term) federation was dropped as unworkable.

Entirely aside from disputes over the nature of a new Soviet federation, the committee process Gorbachev set into motion worked so slowly that events constantly ran ahead of it. Many observers later lamented that if a concrete and generous proposal for a federation had been offered the republics in 1989, it would have been accepted with gratitude and probably forestalled the burgeoning separatism—but who can say?

The "External Empire" Crumbles

JUST AS NATIONALIST PRESSURES built up within the Soviet Union, the Soviet "alliance system" in Europe (actually an empire in all but name) fell apart with breathtaking rapidity.

The first non-Communist government in the area was formed in Poland in August. The Hungarians and Czechoslovaks quickly emulated
the Poles, though the Communist leaders in Hungary were more flexible
than those in Czechoslovakia.

The Soviet public remained remarkably passive in the face of this momentous geopolitical shift. While some intellectuals followed with rapt
attention what was happening to the west, particularly in Poland, most
citizens were too busy coping with shortages and the mounting problems of everyday life to pay much attention. Most Soviet citizens simply
did not care much about the external empire, from which they derived
no personal benefit. Many were convinced that the Eastern Europeans
lived better than they because of Soviet subsidies; if so, good riddance.

The Soviet public would doubtless have felt different if it had been
convinced that the loss of Eastern Europe affected its security—if it still
had believed, in other words, that the United States and its allies were
potential aggressors. In that case, a retreat to the Soviet borders in
Europe might have produced a war scare. But this did not happen. The
"new thinking" pioneered by Shevardnadze and Yakovlev had taken
root, largely because the Soviet public was aware of the accommodating
Western response to the changes in Soviet policy and was better informed about former Soviet policies that the West had considered aggressive.

Four or five years earlier, the Soviet public had been told that the
United States had deployed missiles in Europe so it could deliver a nuclear strike on the Soviet Union, but in 1989 the atmosphere was totally
different.

Gorbachev had not expected the Warsaw Pact to unravel so quickly,
but his domestic politics gave him a remarkably free hand in dealing
with it. He wisely decided to make a virtue of necessity and accepted
with understanding, even grace, the choice the Poles, Czechs, Slovaks,
and Hungarians made.

Germany, however, was another matter. Though the Soviet public
might be largely indifferent to what happened in other Eastern and Central European countries, Germany was special. To the Soviet public—
and the military in particular—the division of Germany was the most
obvious proof of who had won World War II and at the same time the
most tangible guarantee that Germany could never again threaten the
Soviet Union or Russia.

Gorbachev could easily accept a "reform Communist" in East Berlin and—with greater difficulty—even a non-Communist government there so long as the German Democratic Republic remained intact. In the autumn of 1989, the illusion that this would happen, at least for a decade or so, eased Moscow's acceptance of the rapid changes then under way. German unity was to be a question for the future, preferably on somebody else's watch, so far as Gorbachev was concerned.

During a visit to Moscow in October, Zbigniew Brzezinski shocked his audience at the Soviet Diplomatic Academy when he observed that a divided Germany could exist in a divided Europe but not in a unified Europe. If the Soviets wanted a "common European home," they would have to face the question of German unity soon. The foreign policy professionals in attendance reacted as if this thought had never crossed their minds. If it had, they must have rigorously repressed it.

The year was nearly out before the Soviet leaders grasped the truth of Brzezinski's observation. In early December, just after we returned from the summit meeting on Malta, I discussed the situation in Eastern Europe with Shevardnadze. He reiterated that, whatever happened, force would not be used and seemed content with developments in the northern tier. He also predicted reforms in Bulgaria soon but was pessimistic about Romania, since Nicolae Ceauşescu had moved toward repression rather than reform. Regarding East Germany in particular, he said he was impressed by the commitment its new leaders had to their "statehood." In other words, German reunification would wait awhile.

Within a few weeks, however, Soviet policy makers began to grasp the awful truth that they were facing irresistible pressure for German unity. The breach of the Berlin Wall in November and the opening of the GDR borders with West Germany had produced such a flood of emigration that no one could any longer believe that a separate East German state with open borders would be viable. Just before the New Year I met with Valentin Falin, then head of the Communist Party's International Department and the "dean" of Soviet German specialists. "We had hoped German unification was a question for the future," he observed, "but now it is clear that it is upon us."

It was indeed, and it was to become one of the most delicate problems facing Gorbachev in 1990.

After Germany, the most traumatic event in the onetime Soviet bloc for the Communist Party and the KGB was the bloody revolution that took place in Romania at the end of the year. The violence directed at Ceauşescu and his family, and members of the hated Securitate secret police, was covered in great detail by the Soviet press, and television did not spare its viewers the scenes of violence. But when the anti-Ceaușescu forces invited Soviet intervention to support them, Moscow refused, signaling that the days of military intervention in Eastern Europe—even under conditions the West might have found tolerable—were over.

For many Soviet officials, Romania was a shock. But its lesson was ambiguous. Reformers would argue that it showed what could happen if the system resisted change. But the KGB and Party conservatives knew that in anti-Communist revolutions, secret policemen and Party bosses tend to end up swinging from lampposts.

Glasnost Under Fire

PUBLIC PRESSURE FOR REFORM grew in tandem with expansion of press freedom. *Moscow News,* a hitherto negligible propaganda sheet, had under Yegor Yakovlev become the organ of opposition forces throughout the country. Vitaly Korotich's *Ogonyok* described the full horror of Stalin's crimes and publicized wasteful defense expenditure. Fyodor Burlatsky's *Literaturnaya gazeta* carried thoughtful articles exposing past foreign policy blunders and human rights abuses. Sergei Zalygin ran a series of articles in *Novy mir* describing ecological atrocities and began publishing Solzhenitsyn for the first time since the latter's exile in the early 1970s. Ivan Laptev had turned *Izvestiya* into a respectable, objective newspaper, one that kept its readers reasonably well informed about developments throughout the country and made a strong push for private farming and entrepreneurship.

But these editors were not really free, and the more daring of them had running battles with the Party's Ideological Department. If their transgressions were considered particularly serious, they would be called in by Vadim Medvedev, who had taken over the ideology portfolio from Alexander Yakovlev, and at times Gorbachev himself would scold them, whereupon most would be circumspect for an issue or two, then return to their favorite themes. Pressure from the Party kept the editors on edge, but nobody was fired.

Korotich gradually concluded that Gorbachev would shout at them from time to time so as to tell Ligachev, Yazov, and Kryuchkov that he had called them to account, but that he did not really expect them to change, a supposition Ligachev indirectly supported when he noted in his memoirs that he could not understand how Korotich could repeatedly promise to "mend his ways" and then keep on doing the same muckraking he had sworn off. But others found Gorbachev increasingly threatening.

There was one subject Gorbachev found intolerable: articles that called into question his own popularity. In October 1989, *Argumenty i Fakty* carried a short article reporting that among its readers Sakharov was more popular than Gorbachev. This set off the last serious effort to bring the print media back under Party control.

The culprit was not one of the editors Alexander Yakovlev had promoted in 1986 and 1987 but a self-made crusader who had turned a little-noted newsletter into one of the country's most influential newspapers.

Argumenty i Fakty had existed for decades as a limited-circulation fact sheet designed for lecturers on the circuit sponsored by the Znanie (Knowledge) Society, a Party-controlled public organization devoted to adult education and propaganda. Subscriptions had not even been available to the average citizen until 1988. However, Vladislav Starkov, its longtime editor, was determined to abandon propaganda and provide objective facts about matters that interested the public. In 1981, he had managed to sneak past the censors the entire program issued by Poland's independent trade union, Solidarity, but the weekly's circulation was so limited that few people noticed.

When *Argumenty i Fakty* was made available to the general public, its circulation soared. It went above 20 million in 1989 and by 1990 was just short of 34 million. Physically, it was unimpressive. Just eight tabloid pages printed on a single sheet and folded twice without cutting, it took some practice to read the pages in the numbered order. So what was the secret of its popularity? In the first place, it provided what its title promised: arguments and facts. The former were plentiful in Soviet society, but the latter were scarce, and Starkov stressed the latter. In contrast to most Soviet journalism, which can be described charitably as the leisurely exposition of opinion, his articles were concise and to the point. In addition, the weekly was cheap. It cost 2 kopeks on the newsstand, and a year's subscription was only 1 ruble 4 kopeks, less than $2 at the then-inflated official exchange rate.

The difference in Starkov's approach came to my attention when I was interviewed by the paper in 1988. Soviet publications had just begun the daring exercise of interviewing the American ambassador (*Ogonyok* had been first) but had steered clear of controversial subjects. Starkov, however, went straight to the most contentious issues in the U.S.-Soviet relationship. His final question was the one which must have intrigued the Soviet reader most: "Did we really bug your embassy?" he asked. "And if so, have you seen proof of it?"[5]

"Yes you did," I replied. "And I have seen the evidence." His question and my reply were published verbatim. The public loved his paper because it asked the same questions they were asking and gave straight answers.

For all his boldness, Starkov did not attach himself to any particular political group. He was as likely to run an interview by Ligachev as by Sakharov. Data from public opinion polls were the sort of information that had been withheld from the public in the past, and as polls became more common *Argumenty i Fakty* made a specialty of covering them.

The October article that indicated that *Argumenty i Fakty* readers considered Sakharov the most popular political figure in the country infuriated Gorbachev. Fighting Party conservatives for a more open political system, he considered anything that called his leadership and popularity into question to be disloyal. He immediately called leading editors, journalists, and writers to the Party Central Committee on October 13 and berated them for undermining perestroika.[6]

The next day, Starkov was summoned to the Central Committee by Medvedev, who demanded that he resign as editor of *Argumenty i Fakty* and accept a different job. He was given the choice of editing a Soviet-sponsored journal published in Prague or the Supreme Soviet bulletin, where he would be under Lukyanov's supervision.

Traditionally, such a demand by the Politburo member responsible for the press could not be challenged, but Starkov refused to go quietly and referred the matter to his own editorial board, which voted 47–2 to support him. Formally he was an employee not of the Party but of the Znanie Society, whose directors rarely met.

For several weeks he and the reformers, who had a heavy stake in press freedom, waited anxiously for further steps to compel his removal. They never came. Gorbachev had apparently decided not to force the issue. The incident, however, convinced Soviet intellectuals that they needed legal protection against such pressures, and as a result they stepped up their campaign for legislation to guarantee editorial independence from Communist Party control.

Though Gorbachev failed to press the issue, he made an enemy quite unnecessarily. Starkov had been one of the strongest supporters of perestroika and continued to support reforms, but he could never forgive Gorbachev for trying to fire him. In 1992, Starkov warned me, "If you give Gorbachev credit for glasnost, you will insult all of us who had to fight him to get it. The Party Central Committee was always on our back, right up to August 1991. Gorbachev did not give us glasnost. We took it."

I asked whether he thought Gorbachev had really intended to remove him, or merely wished to scare him. He was absolutely convinced that Gorbachev had wanted to force him out. "Then why didn't he?" I asked. "Surely he could have if he had insisted."

"No, he couldn't," Starkov replied. "Things had changed." I did not ask who had been responsible for that change, since it was clear that Gorbachev's behavior in 1989 had closed Starkov's mind to that irony.

The Balts Press Ahead

JUDGING BY THE RESULTS, the Balts were stimulated rather than deterred by the resolutions on the "national question" issued by the Party plenum in September and the Central Committee's stern statement in August. The independence movement in all three countries gained momentum through the fall and winter, and hardly a day passed without a new move or countermove.

By late 1989 the Lithuanians had taken the lead from the Estonians as all three countries moved in the same direction, though using different tactics.

In August the three Baltic Communist parties met in emergency session to discuss the Central Committee's threatening blast. Officially they tried to be conciliatory without abandoning positions of principle, but the "ideology secretaries" in Estonia and Lithuania (traditionally the most conservative positions in the leadership) publicly denounced Moscow's declaration. The national fronts could afford to be even blunter: the one in Latvia, for example, called the statement "improper and high-handed" and compared it to Moscow's attitude fifty years earlier, when the Baltic states had been annexed.[7]

The Lithuanians did more than criticize the August statement. Their leaders challenged Moscow by calling a Party congress for December to consider withdrawing from the Communist Party of the Soviet Union if the latter refused to grant the Lithuanian Party autonomy.

Taking advantage of relaxed travel controls, people from the Baltic

stepped up their contacts with foreigners, including Baltic communities
in Scandinavia and Western Europe, and Estonians began to visit their
ethnic cousins in Finland as a routine matter. Many Americans of Baltic
origin were now visiting, and some stayed to help and advise.

In October, I received a request from a group of Estonian deputies to
the USSR Supreme Soviet for a formal meeting on behalf of the Estonian National Front. Two of the three I already knew. Igor Gräzin, a
thirty-seven-year-old law professor with a high forehead, small mustache, and ready smile, had become a regular guest at Spaso House social functions. He had been elected from a Pärnu rural district, though
he made his home in the university city of Tartu. The son of a Russian
father and an Estonian mother, he spoke Russian with an Estonian ac-
cent and preferred the Estonian spelling of his name to the Russian
Gryazin. Marju Lauristin, a philology professor at Tartu University
with close-cropped blond hair and a serious mien, had a famous name in
Estonia: her father had been a Communist in independent Estonia and
had chaired the parliamentary session that had "petitioned" for entry
into the Soviet Union, but she was one of the deputies who had posed
sharp questions for Gorbachev at the Congress of People's Deputies.
Gräzin and Lauristin were joined by Hardo Aasmee, a geographer with
a trade association in Tallinn, who would later be elected mayor of
the city.

Unlike the Lithuanians in July, they did not lay out a grand strategy
for independence but stressed their determination to press for an independent Estonia by all legal and nonviolent means. They felt that Estonia was an occupied country that had been deprived of its rights, but
they also knew that merely establishing that fact would not automatically bring independence. They would have to negotiate and be flexible.
Above all, they would have to avoid any resort to violence. Like the
Lithuanian visitors of the summer, they well understood that violence
could end their efforts to free themselves and would bring additional
tragedy to their people.

What they wanted from me was an explanation of U.S. policy. They
were aware of our nonrecognition policy but wanted to probe its implications. In particular, they wondered if their actions in negotiating with
the Soviet authorities and participating in some Soviet political institutions would undermine their claim that their absorption into the Soviet
Union had been illegal. They had probably been briefed by my Lithuanian visitors, though they did not mention this, wishing to hear the answers from me directly.

I explained our policies to them as I had to the Lithuanians in July, stressing that there was no possibility that we would change our non-recognition stance just because the Balts were forced to participate in Soviet institutions as they attempted to free themselves. As long as they did not vote in a free and honest election to be part of the Soviet Union, their participation in the "system" could not be used to prove that the Soviet takeover had been legal. At the same time, I explained that a declaration of independence would not be sufficient to obtain recognition as an independent country: independence had to be a reality before formal recognition would be possible.

It might have been mere chance that the Estonians who visited me were on average younger than the Sąjūdis group had been. The national front movements in all three Baltic countries involved many younger people. Perhaps Gräzin, Lauristin, and Aasmee had been chosen because they spoke English. But it was noticeable that all three had been born well after World War II—between 1949 and 1952. These were not people past middle age yearning for a lost, idyllic childhood. They were, in a generational sense, the products of "Soviet Estonia." What's more, all three were members of the Communist Party—though two would leave it shortly and the third not much later.

Closed societies rely on rumor. When normal sources of information are unreliable, people turn to friends, family, coworkers, and even casual contacts. Word of mouth, particularly from someone who knows someone who knows someone whose sister-in-law works in a government office, is more likely to be believed than what politicians and the mass media say.

Such was the conditioning of the public in the Soviet Union (not that other societies have not been known to question the veracity of politicians) that the growing openness of the Soviet press was insufficient to shake the presumption that facts were being withheld—or misrepresented—by authorities determined to mislead the public.

By the fall of 1989 Eastern Europe had begun its pell-mell escape from the Soviet embrace. The Communist Party had lost an election in Poland in the summer, the Hungarian Party was splitting badly and on the verge of collapse, in Czechoslovakia the Velvet Revolution was sweeping the country, Erich Honecker was ousted in East Germany, and Todor Zhivkov was removed in Bulgaria. Ceauşescu hung on in Romania, but before the end of the year he would be killed.

In the midst of these kaleidoscopic events, official spokesmen in both Moscow and Washington announced that Bush and Gorbachev planned to meet on Malta in early December.

Gorbachev had responded with enthusiasm to Bush's suggestion for a meeting. While in the past he had sometimes delayed summits until he could be certain of the outcome, he had been eager all year to have an official meeting with President Bush in order to make sure U.S. policy would continue along the lines Reagan had set. Furthermore, he was beginning to prefer touring foreign lands and dealing with foreign leaders to dealing with the increasingly tangled mess at home. A trip to Malta could easily be combined with a promised visit to Italy and a long-sought call on Pope John Paul II.

There were many good reasons for the Malta summit from both countries' point of view, but the announcement gave rise to a flood of rumors in the Baltic—and elsewhere in the Soviet Union—that Bush had made or would make a deal with Gorbachev to liberate Eastern Europe in return for tacit approval for Gorbachev to deal with Soviet nationalities as he wished. Reports earlier in the year about Henry Kissinger's recommendation to negotiate with the Soviet leaders on the future of Eastern Europe bolstered these suspicions.

The rumors aroused acute alarm among the new political leaders in the Baltic. A group of them asked to see me right away. This time all three countries were represented. The same three Estonians who had called on me in October were in the group, as well as two of the Lithuanians from July (Antanaitis and Motieka). The new faces included Egidijus Bičkauskas, a thirty-four-year-old lawyer from the prosecutor's office in Vilnius with dark hair, rimless glasses, mustache and a penchant for dark shirts. He would soon be named Lithuanian permanent representative (i.e., ambassador) in Moscow and become a valued colleague. And—the most articulate of the group—Kazimiera Prunskienė, the economist who had recently been named deputy prime minister of Lithuania and would shortly become prime minister.

Two Latvians joined the group: Ilmars Bišers and Mavriks Vulfsons. Bišers, a law professor at the Latvian State University, was a large man of my age (meaning nearing sixty) with a receding hairline and horn-rimmed glasses. We had met earlier, since he was a deputy chairman of the Supreme Soviet Council of Nationalities and had traveled to the United States with a group of deputies. Though his Russian was flawless, I realized when I met his wife that his family spoke Latvian at home; her Russian was heavily accented, and at times she would complain about the difficulty of finding the right Russian expression. Vulfsons, a white-haired septuagenarian, taught political science at the Academy of Arts in Riga and was an active member of the Supreme Soviet International Affairs Committee. He was Jewish and thus a reminder that not all political activists pressing for Baltic independence were ethnic Balts.

It was late in the day, so we sat at the table in Spaso House's large dining room, convenient for note taking and refreshments on the side.

My visitors came right to the point. Was it true that Bush and Gorbachev had made a deal as rumored? All eyes were fixed on me, but for once I welcomed the interrogation since I could give them good news.

"You have plenty of things to worry about," I said, "but this is not one of them. The answer is no, absolutely not. There has been no deal, and there will be none."

They weren't sure. Their anxiety was almost palpable. "But what will happen on Malta?" one inquired.

"I don't know for sure, though I expect a good discussion—on arms control, on Eastern Europe, on our future economic relationship. But I do know for sure what will *not* happen, and that is a change in our policy of refusing to recognize the Soviet annexation of the Baltic states."

"But what if Gorbachev demands that as the price of letting Eastern Europe go?"

"President Bush wouldn't agree. But I don't think Gorbachev will ask. He has dealt with us enough to know that it wouldn't work. Besides, how could he make a threat to intervene in Eastern Europe credible? He's in no position to use force there, and just about everybody understands that."

The conversation then shifted to the possibility of economic assistance, and here I was less reassuring. I pointed out that the U.S. budget deficit would probably preclude large-scale assistance, even if the Soviet government would permit it—which was far from certain. They would be on sounder ground, I suggested, if they assumed that foreign aid, even under the best of circumstances, would be limited and that they should find the bulk of resources internally for whatever policy they might adopt.

When the meeting ended, I was not sure that they were convinced that some U.S.-Soviet deal was impossible, but events soon confirmed what I had told them.

The Official View

THE BALTIC DRIVE FOR INDEPENDENCE became a frequent topic in many conversations, of which one of the most revealing occurred in October with Alexander Yakovlev, when Zbigniew Brzezinski was visiting. We posed a number of questions regarding Eastern Europe, and Yakovlev assured us that the Soviet Union would under no circumstances use force if the countries there ended Communist rule, which was exactly what we were hearing from Shevardnadze.

Brzezinski then asked what would happen if the Baltic states declared their independence. Yakovlev replied without hesitation, "That would be the end of perestroika." He then said that the Balts should try a "real federation" for five or six years and see if that would not suit them. They could, he added, have "political and economic sovereignty." He did not specify exactly why Baltic independence would end perestroika, but we understood him to mean that hard-line forces would take over if the Balts insisted on secession.

Yevgeny Primakov, whom I saw a few weeks later, took a different tack. A specialist on the Middle East, he had moved from his job as director of the Institute for the World Economy and International Relations (where he had replaced Yakovlev) to become chairman of the Council of Union in the new Supreme Soviet, a position roughly comparable to our speaker of the House of Representatives. He believed that the economic autonomy that had been granted to the three Baltic states from January 1, 1990, would have a salutary effect. The Balts would learn, he thought, that they could not get along without the rest of the union, and this realization would bring them to their senses and the clamor for secession would subside.

Most Soviet citizens found it hard to understand that even if the Baltic economies were to suffer as a result of independence (a far from certain proposition), their attitude might not change. They also found it hard to grasp that national independence did not necessarily mean breaking established trade ties or erecting barriers to the movement of people. The reason for this confusion was understandable: for decades the Soviet Union had lived behind an iron curtain that had blocked private travel to the outside world as well as all trade not conducted by the official Ministry of Foreign Trade. Many political leaders who should have known better imagined that independence was synonymous with isolation.

Partly because of these misconceptions, most Russians were unsympathetic to the Baltic cause and Central Asians even more so, since they believed—incorrectly—that the high Baltic living standards proved that the Balts had received more than their share of resources and investment.

The democratic forces that began to organize in Russia in 1989, however, took a different view and tried to make common cause with the Balts. While most would have preferred a democratic federation or confederation to a breakup of the Soviet Union, they understood that democracy was inconsistent with holding the Baltic states against their will.

Summit at Malta

By December 1, when President Bush arrived on Malta for his long-planned meeting with Gorbachev, he was finally convinced that he could and should support perestroika. Stung by criticism in the American press that he was lacking in initiative, vision, and leadership, he was determined to change his public image by announcing a series of proposals to improve relations. Many of these would be in the economic area.

His staff still worried that Gorbachev might use the meeting to seize a propaganda advantage by making sweeping proposals, but I thought this was a needless worry. We had repeatedly warned the Soviets to avoid a Reykjavik-type surprise, and they had assured us they would. I believed them since I thought that Gorbachev's interest dictated coming to terms with us, not jostling for public acclaim. He was doing very well in Western opinion without playing propaganda games. Furthermore, what he really needed was not more imagery but concrete American cooperation in reaching the goals he had set.

Bush had hoped for a basket of major proposals to put before Gorbachev, but his staff had generally taken the lowest common denominator from Washington's interagency process, which had produced a list of steps to remove some cold war barriers to trade. Most could easily have been proposed six or eight months earlier and should have been. Nevertheless, it was encouraging that we were finally moving to permit a more active economic relationship.

Gorbachev had come to Malta prepared to complain that the Bush administration had been too passive in developing a partnership. Bush, however, disarmed him by presenting his proposals for removing economic barriers at the outset of the first meeting. Gorbachev was obviously pleased. However, during a subsequent discussion of the Soviet economy, both Bush and Baker were struck by how poorly Gorbachev understood market economics. For example, he argued that much property in the West was held collectively: corporations, for instance.

It was true that Gorbachev had a very hazy and at times inaccurate understanding of capitalist economics, but Bush missed the import of his remark that corporate ownership was collective. What Gorbachev was doing was redefining the meaning of "socialist" property. Though he still gagged on the term "private property," he was prepared to consider corporations owned by stockholders an acceptable form of "collective" property. If he could make this definition stick, it would open an avenue to privatization of large state enterprises. Thus it marked a significant step forward in the evolution of his thinking.

Such misunderstandings were, however, the exception at this summit. Next to the Reagan-Gorbachev meeting at Reykjavik, it probably achieved more substantively than any other U.S.-Soviet summit meeting, even though no major agreements were signed. What was most significant at Malta, besides removing barriers to expanded trade, were the informal understandings reached regarding Eastern Europe, Germany, and the Baltic states. These were not negotiated "deals" behind the backs of third parties—which our allies and the Eastern Europeans understandably opposed—but rather mutual assurances growing out of a discussion of the situation.

Gorbachev assured the president that force would not be used in Eastern Europe, that he was aware that Soviet troops would have to be withdrawn, and that he would allow the Eastern Europeans freely to choose their political and economic system. He still hoped to keep the Warsaw Pact intact but would not use force or threats to do so. For his part, Bush told Gorbachev that, as long as force was not used, the United States would not attempt to take advantage of the changes in Eastern Europe and would not take action that would make it more difficult for Gorbachev to accept the changing situation.

Gorbachev's assurances in regard to the Baltic states were less categorical than those he gave for Eastern Europe. He was determined, he said, to avoid repression if at all possible, since using force would mean the end of perestroika. While he would look at virtually any form of association for the Baltic states, he could not permit unilateral secession; the Balts would have to act in accord with constitutional and legal requirements.

Bush reminded Gorbachev that the United States had never recognized the annexation of the Baltic states and would not do so. But he assured Gorbachev that if force was not used against the independence movements, the United States would do nothing to exacerbate the situation. However, he continued, if Moscow should ever resort to violence, anti-Soviet feelings would sweep the United States and block further improvements in our relations.

The discussion of the Baltic took place in a private meeting. When I was briefed on it, I thought the president had set just the right tone. He had made it clear that Soviet use of force in either Eastern Europe or the Baltic would end movement toward U.S.-Soviet cooperation but had reassured Gorbachev that he would not try to take advantage of the rapidly changing situation. At the same time, he had avoided any negotiation on the future status of the Eastern European and Baltic countries, insisting on the principle of free choice, to which Gorbachev had agreed.

Not all the conversations were so harmonious. Bush strongly criticized the supplying of Soviet arms to Latin America and Soviet support for Cuban military activities in the region. He told Gorbachev that these would be major irritants so long as they continued.

Gorbachev also voiced a major complaint: he objected to Bush's claim that "Western values" had triumphed. At first, Bush had trouble understanding Gorbachev's objection, pointing out that Western values embodied the same principles Gorbachev had endorsed, such as transparency and openness and, in the economy, incentives for progress and a free market. Yakovlev explained that the term implied that "Western values" were different from Eastern values—or Northern or Southern values—and therefore would strike many in the Soviet Union as Western ideological imperialism. On Baker's suggestion, all agreed that it would be acceptable to speak of "democratic values" as the basis of a common platform.[8]

The discussions on arms control were less productive than they might have been if Reagan had still been president. The Bush administration had still not determined its position on some key issues in the negotiations on strategic arms and therefore was not able to take advantage of

Shevardnadze's move in September to delink strategic arms reduction from defensive and space systems. Washington still seemed more concerned with getting congressional approval for new weapons systems than finding ways to reduce the dangerous overstock in both nations.

Arms control, however, was no longer the centerpiece of Soviet attention, as it traditionally had been. The Strategic Arms Reduction Talks (START), and those on conventional forces in Europe (CFE), were important to Gorbachev, but at Malta he needed other things more. With the Soviet position in Eastern Europe rapidly collapsing, he needed reassurance that the United States would not embarrass him by appearing to take advantage of his weakness. He needed to be seen dealing with Bush as an equal, not as a vanquished enemy. He needed the prospect of economic support from the United States as his reforms developed.

Gorbachev got all of that at Malta, but when he flew back to Moscow it didn't make much difference. A bruising session of the Congress of People's Deputies was awaiting him.

The Reformist Agenda

THE LEADERS of the Interregional Group of Deputies, spurred by the upcoming elections in the republics and the upcoming session of the Congress of People's Deputies, had by then developed a comprehensive platform. Their main political goal was to amend Article VI of the USSR Constitution, which provided the legal basis for Communist Party dominance of the state structure. Those who were members of the Communist Party—virtually all except Andrei Sakharov—were also pressing for a change in Party rules to allow factions to develop. As for the economy, the group opposed attempts by the Ryzhkov government to retain central control, arguing that the responsibility for management should be transferred to enterprises, localities, and republics, except for a few sectors critical to the entire country. In addition, they pressed for constitutional amendments and legislation that would permit farmers to own land and entrepreneurs to acquire businesses. Many felt that the Soviet Union had to become a confederation, with the Center in Moscow exercising only those powers delegated voluntarily by the republics.

Gorbachev opposed all these initiatives, either because he had been unable to secure Politburo approval (in the case of Article VI) or because he genuinely thought they were a bad idea (private property in land, for example). The debate came to a head at the second session of the Congress of People's Deputies in December. The tactics Gorbachev employed at that session to avoid a full discussion of these fundamental issues persuaded many reformers that Gorbachev was more interested in preserving his position as head of the Communist Party than in carrying out the reforms he had initiated.

The most dramatic confrontation occurred on December 12, the second day of the Congress, when Andrei Sakharov proposed that the agenda be amended to allow for debate on land and property ownership, enterprises, and Article VI—those provisions in the Constitution that were obstructing perestroika. The Congress, he argued, had to clear the way for the Supreme Soviet to pass appropriate laws on those questions by removing constitutional prohibitions.

Gorbachev, who was in the chair, reacted with extreme irritation and hounded Sakharov from the podium before he had time to explain his proposal. Subsequently, Gorbachev ordered a vote on the motion to add these questions to the agenda and it lost, but not by an overwhelming margin. If Gorbachev had backed the proposal, it would have won easily, but he was exhibiting the same stubbornness he had shown at the first session.

The spectacle of Gorbachev humiliating Sakharov as the latter tried to make an eminently reasonable proposal was shown on national television that evening. Reformist intellectuals were scandalized: to them Gorbachev's reaction was typical of a provincial Party boss (which, of course, Gorbachev had been for much of his career) and not what would be expected of a national leader bent on changing the country.

Two days later, when Andrei Sakharov died quietly in his sleep, many of his friends were convinced that Gorbachev's brutal treatment of him at the Congress had contributed to his fatal heart attack.

Congress's refusal to place Sakharov's proposals on the agenda did not prevent all debate on the issues. Regarding Article VI, Gorbachev argued that the question should be settled as a new constitution was drafted and pointed out that the one-party system had been established without sanction in the Constitution and could not be abolished simply by eliminating the constitutional provision.

The other issues were closely related to the government's proposal for a staged transition to "market relations," which was presented to the Congress by Prime Minister Ryzhkov on December 13. It called for a gradual transition in two stages of three years each, all carefully planned in Moscow. In one of his interviews, Ryzhkov ridiculed the demands to eliminate economic direction from the Center:

> Just imagine this. In 1990, we tell everybody from now on there will be no centralized distribution of resources, try to find them on your own. What will happen then? I am not going to frighten anybody, but that would be a real economic crisis. People would not be able to work for two or three years.[9]

Gavriil Popov, still the editor of the country's leading economic journal and a cochairman of the Interregional Group of Deputies, denounced Ryzhkov's center-directed gradualism:

> The past five years have shown that the concept of perestroika from "above" does not work, that a new approach is needed. The Center must be prepared not to rush in to save a drowning enterprise, but to hand over the salvage operation to others who are nearer and who are no less interested in saving it. That is, the republics and the local soviets. And, above all, the people who are actually drowning. Especially since our enterprises are often "drowning" not because they do not know how to swim but because the Center binds them hand and foot, puts a millstone around their neck, and then offers advice on how to keep above water.[10]

Popov then pointed out that a market system cannot be introduced piecemeal since one segment depends on the others. A starter cannot start an automobile engine if there is no carburetor, and thus the essential market institutions would have to be introduced simultaneously. By his analysis, five laws were needed: on ownership, land, the enterprise, economic independence of republics, and local self-management—essentially the ones Sakharov had mentioned—and he deplored the refusal to debate them at that session of the Congress. However, he devoted most of his eloquence to the need for empowering the people to make economic decisions:

> I recently discovered in the RSFSR statistical report that each hen laid an average of 182 eggs during the first nine months of 1987, while the average was 183 eggs during the same period of 1989. Maybe the time has come to stop and think and grasp that in countries where eggs are abundant governments don't decide how many eggs a hen should lay.[11]

The Congress, however, approved the government plan by an over-whelming majority and rejected calls for more economic independence for the republics. Many deputies went home from this session disillusioned. The Ukrainian Petro Palanchuk, head of a technical college in Kiev, made these bitter comments on a local radio broadcast:

> What the devil is this union when a republic works so hard and the Center then grabs everything, forcing it to go begging on its knees to the Center for this or that? . . . I do not believe that what the government has in mind can be carried out by the old ministries, by the very people who brought us this social catastrophe. . . . We need to dismantle the command-administrative system immediately. We must do away with the practice by which our republic works so hard, but in the end 95 percent of the output goes to the Center and only five percent stays here.[12]

A Martyr for Reform

REBECCA AND I were in Brussels for a conference of American ambassadors in Europe when we heard that Andrei Sakharov had died. The State Department asked me whether I thought President Bush should send a special representative to the funeral. I answered that protocol did not require a special emissary, but one would be entirely appropriate and in fact politically desirable. "Would Gorbachev be offended?" I was asked. I replied that he would likely prefer that no high-level representative be sent, but I felt that his attitude was not the most important factor in a decision. The important thing was that Sakharov had become not merely a spokesman for human rights and democracy in the Soviet Union but the very symbol of democratic change.

I hoped President Bush would name a high-level official or close associate to represent him at the funeral. I thought Sakharov should be honored for what he had represented and not for reasons of formal protocol. If honoring Sakharov made Gorbachev uncomfortable, that would be regrettable but also salutary, for if he too sought the acclaim of the world, he could do no worse than take more seriously than he had the causes Sakharov had espoused. Special attention to the Sakharov funeral would be a tactful way to bring this point home to Gorbachev.

A few hours later I was told that a decision had been made not to send an emissary from the United States but to designate me as the president's representative at the funeral. It was, of course, an honor I could only welcome, yet I could not help wondering whether the decision had not been made out of a misguided concern for Gorbachev's ego. Did I detect a dangerous tendency in Washington to bank too much on a single individual? I hoped not but could not entirely dismiss the thought.

We flew back to Moscow on Sunday, December 17, and went directly from the airport to the Youth Palace, where Sakharov's body lay in state. The temperature was well below zero Fahrenheit, but an enormous line of people, several abreast, stretched down Komsomolsky Prospekt for many blocks. Most would have to stand for hours before getting a glimpse of the bier inside. As official foreign representatives, we were admitted at the head of the line. A deeply moving scene awaited us.

Sakharov's casket was on a raised platform in the center of a large hall normally used for exhibitions. A dense thicket of flowers surrounded it on all sides, and each visitor added more to what was already an enormous but orderly heap. We walked past the open coffin, paused for a silent prayer, and uttered a few words of consolation to Yelena Bonner, his widow, and other members of the family. I then stepped back and paused to take in the scene.

People of all ages had come, of course, but the number of young people was truly remarkable. Whatever hatreds Sakharov's activities had inspired in the policemen, generals, and Communist Party hacks, it was clear that he had captured the hearts (and, I hoped, the minds) of those who counted most for the future of the country: the educated youth. Sobs mingled with the shuffle of feet moving slowly past the bier. Along with flowers, many were leaving off hand-lettered notes, some as large as placards. Almost all had a variant of one of three themes: "Forgive us, Andrei Dmitriyevich," "Never again!" and "Finest flower of the Russian intelligentsia."

The following morning Sakharov's body lay in state at the Academy of Sciences. Gorbachev and other senior Party and government officials came and signed the condolence book. So did I and other foreign representatives. The public funeral, however, was scheduled for the afternoon. Yelena Bonner had insisted on ceremonies at a location where everyone who wished could attend; no structure was large enough to contain all those likely to be interested, so the funeral was scheduled for the open fields near Luzhniki Stadium in Moscow, despite the below-zero temperature.

The public announcement was for funeral ceremonies from 1:00 to 2:00 P.M., followed by interment at Vostryakovskoye Cemetery, on the outskirts of Moscow, at 3:00. Yelena Bonner requested that only family and close friends go to the cemetery, since it was too small to accommodate a large crowd.

Rebecca and I, accompanied by Tatyana Volkov-Gfoeller, one of the embassy's most capable political officers, set off for the funeral just after noon. We knew there would be a large crowd and wanted to have plenty of time to get to the proper place. Still, we had not anticipated the waves of people who converged on Luzhniki. At first I thought the service would be held in the stadium—the announcement had been ambiguous—but we were directed across an open field, already filled with tens of thousands of people. We worked our way through the crowd, since I knew it was important for the family to know that I was present. As people recognized us, they graciously made way and directed us to a rectangle of perhaps a quarter acre that had been fenced off and supplied with a platform for the casket, a larger, more elevated one for speakers, and a few rows of chairs. As we approached the fenced area, I was surprised to see Marshal Akhromeyev, in full uniform, standing modestly in the crowd. Our eyes met and we exchanged nods of recognition, but he made no attempt to move closer.

To this day his presence at the Luzhniki funeral puzzles me. He had been one of Sakharov's bitterest public critics. If he had felt some gesture of respect to be necessary, he could simply have signed the condolence book at the Academy of Sciences that morning. But here he was, standing in the cold among a mass of Sakharov's most fervent supporters. Why? I later asked Yelena Bonner (who did not know that he had been there), and she speculated that he had just been curious about what would happen. However, I suspect it was more than that. His curiosity could have been satisfied by press stories or the report of a subordinate. My guess is that he was honoring Sakharov as the creator of the Soviet hydrogen bomb, not as the political activist he subsequently became. Or maybe he came out of respect for a person who defended his beliefs, no matter what. I regret that I failed to ask Akhromeyev why he was there when he was still alive. At the time I simply marveled at how complicated human relations can be and how often one confronts the unexpected.

Having reached the "inner circle," we had a long wait for the coffin and the funeral party—over an hour, in fact. We were wrapped in heavy coats, fur hats, and scarves, but the cold began to penetrate our clothing. Our feet, standing on frozen snow, were the first to feel it, and I regretted that the sturdy felt boots worn by Russian peasants, practically impervious to both moisture and cold, were not acceptable diplomatic attire. But the crowd around us kept growing. How many? A hundred thousand? Easily. Two hundred thousand? More than likely. Half a million? Probably not. But it was more than enough to shield us from the wind.

Finally the pallbearers arrived with the casket, and the family and speakers assembled on the platform. Those of us in the fenced-off area took turns standing with lighted candles at the four corners of the coffin, Russian Orthodox fashion, as the eulogies were pronounced. But it was not a religious ceremony.

There were eulogies, yes, but they did more than praise the deceased; most were also political speeches. All the leaders of the Interregional Group were there—Yeltsin, Afanasiev, and Popov, as well as representatives of many non-Russian nationalities. Sakharov was everybody's champion, and the grief at his death united ethnic groups as no political issue could have.

As speaker after speaker made direct appeals for political action, I began to wonder if it was seemly to turn a funeral into a political demonstration. But then I realized that in this instance, at least, it was appropriate. It is exactly what Sakharov would have desired: using his death to give impetus to a campaign for the goals he had set.

The short December day began to wane before we left for the cemetery. Yelena Bonner kindly removed any uncertainty as to whether Rebecca and I were considered "close friends and relatives" when she sought us out and urged us to accompany the family to the cemetery. There, under candlelight, we watched as she kissed the deceased and pallbearers closed the coffin and lowered it to its final resting place. Each of us took our turn casting handfuls of soil onto the grave. The man who, more than any other of his lifetime, had embodied the conscience of his nation was no more.

As we trudged back to our car through the paths in the cemetery, I realized that I was no longer feeling the cold. Unlike the afternoon's speeches, the rituals at the burial site had been human, not political. What Sakharov had left his nation—and the world—was not so much a political program, admirable as his might have been, but an attitude, a moral stance. I thought of the messages the people had brought to the

Youth Palace the day before and to that afternoon's funeral and tried to paraphrase and complete the slogans in my mind. "Forgive us, for we were silent when they tortured you." "Never again will we lack the courage to stand up to tyrants." "You showed us the duty of Russian intellectuals."

But no. That last sentence was not quite right. How could I translate terms so redolent of emotion as those Russian words—themselves borrowed from Latin—*intelligentsia* and *intelligent*? "Intellectual" just doesn't do. In English, there is something cold and clinical about "intellectual" when applied to a person. In Russian, *intelligent*—pronounced with a hard "g"—is different, because it carries obligatory moral overtones. An *intelligent* is not just an "intellectual" but a person of learning and culture who is devoted to the good of society. Not a "do-gooder" but a person with a moral compass.

It was Sakharov's unerring moral compass that left its mark on his countrymen. Their grief was obvious, their commitment clear. But I could not help wondering how they would really react if put to the test. It would be August 1991 before I received an answer.

The Lithuanian Communists Split

THE PRESSURES IN THE BALTIC continued to build up through the fall, stimulated further by the prospect of local elections early in 1990. It began to dawn on the republic Communist parties that they could be shut out in the upcoming elections if they did not do more to cultivate public opinion. The only move that might save them would be an endorsement of independence.

Secession fever was highest in Lithuania, where the Communist Party had first endorsed independence. More and more Party members demanded that the Lithuanian Party break with the Communist Party of the Soviet Union if the latter refused to reorganize along federal lines, with each constituent Party granted freedom of action. If chained to Moscow, the Party would surely drown in the electoral tide.

Gorbachev summoned the entire Lithuanian leadership to Moscow for an unprecedented joint meeting with the CPSU Politburo, but his attempt to browbeat the Lithuanians failed. Lithuanian Party leader Algirdas Brazauskas explained to Gorbachev that the Party could not survive as a political force in Lithuania unless it distanced itself from

Moscow. Gorbachev rejected this argument and along with it any thought of restructuring the Party along federal lines. It would remain unitary, under Moscow's control.

Faced with a choice of committing political suicide as a favor to Gorbachev or defying him and thereby surviving the coming elections, the Lithuanians persisted on their separatist course. When Brazauskas returned to Vilnius from the confrontation in the Politburo, he announced that the Lithuanian Party would proceed with its plans for a congress. Divorce was now inevitable. Polls showed that only 16 percent of Party members in Lithuania opposed the break. Since non-Lithuanians made up more than 16 percent of the republic's population, this meant that some ethnic Russians and Poles had joined their Lithuanian neighbors in favoring independence.

On December 20, 1989, a congress of the Communist Party of Lithuania, meeting in Vilnius, declared its independence from the Communist Party of the Soviet Union. Less than a fifth of the delegates disagreed, walked out, and pledged their continued allegiance to Moscow.

Gorbachev immediately called an emergency Central Committee plenum to deal with the crisis the Lithuanians had precipitated. Though the Lithuanian Party congress had the support of the overwhelming majority of Party members in Lithuania, Gorbachev persisted in opposing their move and categorically insisted on retaining a unitary Communist Party rather than restructuring the Party along federal lines as some, like Alexander Yakovlev, were pressing him to do. His words were dramatic:

> Isn't it clear that if we should cross this line [replacing the Party's unitary structure with a federal structure] you could say that we are consciously pushing things to a dismemberment of the USSR, and that would be a historical dead end for all the peoples of the Soviet Union?[13]

I was astonished when I read this argument in the press the following day. Although I could understand that Gorbachev might consider it impossible openly to espouse federalism in the Party at that point, I did not understand why he considered it necessary to condemn it in such categorical terms. After all, if he intended to create a real federation, he should leave open the possibility of a federal structure for the Party.

Furthermore, by insisting that Lithuania's status was like that of every other Soviet republic, he was closing the door to the possibility of treating the Baltic republics differently from the other twelve. Just the day before this speech, the Congress of People's Deputies had voted a resolution that declared the Nazi-Soviet pact illegal. I thought it would have been wise for him to hold in reserve the argument that the Baltic states should be treated differently from the other republics because of the historic injustice which had occurred, but his words seemed to exclude that possibility.

There was another aspect of Gorbachev's lengthy speech that disturbed me. In excoriating Sąjūdis and the secessionist Lithuanian Communists, Gorbachev accused them of trying to "internationalize" the question by "knocking on the doors" of the American Embassy in Moscow and the White House in Washington. Earlier statements had accused the Balts of seeking foreign advice, but this was the first time Gorbachev had alluded in public to the Balts' meetings with us. These contacts obviously disturbed him, and while I was determined to continue them, I wondered if Gorbachev was getting accurate information. His words raised the suspicion that the KGB had doctored its reports to "prove" that the Lithuanians and other Balts were acting at our instigation.

In fact, I would have considered advice from us to the Balts entirely proper, given our nonrecognition policy, had we chosen to give it. But we had not advised them, since we could not protect them if Moscow cracked down. If Gorbachev bought the KGB argument about outside agitation, this would not only reduce the possibility of his understanding the situation but increase the chances of his approving the use of force.

Despite Gorbachev's strong words, the plenum postponed final action on the attempt to create an autonomous Communist Party until Gorbachev could visit Lithuania in January. But Gorbachev's speech and the resolution by the plenum gave him little room for maneuver. His visit to Lithuania could be successful only if he managed to dissuade the Lithuanians from persisting on the course they had set.

Glasnost Triumphs

EDITORS AND, particularly, television producers still felt the attempts of political authorities to "guide" their work. The media were still not free, and conservatives in the Party apparatus were straining to bring public information back under their control. Nevertheless, by the end of the year reformers were breathing a little easier. Starkov had fought back the attempt to remove him from *Argumenty i Fakty,* and reformist editors still ran *Moscow News, Ogonyok, Izvestiya,* and *Literaturnaya gazeta.* Even *Pravda* was now under different leadership, its conservative editor, Viktor Afanasiev, having been replaced in October by philosopher Ivan Frolov, a personal friend of Gorbachev. The cumulative efforts of courageous journalists, editors, and scholars had succeeded in exposing many of the atrocities and scandals of the past that had previously been swept into an Orwellian "memory hole."

It had been a year when the Soviet military had seen disappear their cherished invulnerability to criticism. Publications like *Ogonyok* and *Moscow News* criticized mistakes of the past and current mismanagement. Georgy Arbatov, the head of the Institute for the Study of the USA and Canada, who had been well known to Americans as a spokesman for Soviet foreign policy in the 1970s and 1980s, published a series of articles charging that Soviet defense budgets had been inflated and military ranks bloated with manpower and equipment far in excess of defensive needs.

The Soviet high command, since World War II coddled in praise and adulation, reacted with fury. Marshal Akhromeyev responded sharply to Arbatov's charges, and the public was treated to a spectacle long familiar to Americans: a wide-ranging debate over defense expenditures. The Soviet public had never been told how many resources had been consumed in the name of "defense." As the truth began to sink in, the public was increasingly convinced that they had been bilked by their political and military leaders.

Dirty secrets from the past were exposed, half denied, then not contested, then finally admitted officially. Such was the case with the massacre of Polish officers by the NKVD (one of the KGB's aliases) at the Katyn Forest near Smolensk. For decades, the Soviet government had insisted that the Gestapo had murdered the Poles after the Germans overran the area and that the claims of NKVD culpability were simply anti-Soviet propaganda generated by the Nazis.

In 1989, *Moscow News* published an article with evidence pointing unmistakably to Stalin's culpability. Virtually the entire Polish officer corps captured by the Soviet army following the division of Poland with the Nazis had been executed on his orders, to prevent the revival of "bourgeois" Poland following the war. The Polish officers were, for the most part, not full-time professionals, but reservists: lawyers, doctors, businessmen. If Poland was deprived of its "bourgeoisie," it could be turned into a "workers' state" obedient to the Soviet Union when the time came. Such was the "logic" of the Marxist class struggle in Stalin's twisted mind.

The article in *Moscow News* was clearly intended to prod the authorities to admit what had happened. After all, the Polish Communists were on their way out. It would be much more difficult to establish normal, friendly relations with Poland if the Soviet Union continued to deny the obvious.

But the Soviet government hesitated. By late October, however, we received a signal that an official admission of what had happened might be imminent. Before his arrival in Moscow, Zbigniew Brzezinski had requested permission to visit the Katyn site where the murders had occurred. The Soviet Foreign Ministry unexpectedly agreed and in fact made arrangements for the visit. Brzezinski asked me to accompany him as a sign that the U.S. government had an interest in full disclosure. I, of course, readily agreed.

When we arrived at one of the burial sites where a monument had been erected, we witnessed a moving scene. Several busloads of Poles had arrived, many of them relatives of the murdered officers, to honor the deceased on All Souls' Day. The monument that had been erected by the Soviets stated that it marked the grave of Polish officers murdered by the Gestapo in 1941. Someone had covered "Gestapo" and "1941" with hand-lettered signs reading "NKVD" and "1940." The Soviet custodians had not removed the corrections from the monument.

A Catholic chaplain led the Polish visitors in prayer, and we stood, heads bowed, emotionally drained by the enormity of the crime that had been committed on that spot.

As we moved away from the grave site, a Russian television correspondent approached us and asked Brzezinski for an interview. He agreed and made an eloquent statement calling on the Soviet government to admit the atrocity. Both the Soviet Union and Poland had suffered from Stalin's policies, he pointed out, and a recognition of that fact could form the basis of Soviet-Polish reconciliation. I was asked to comment, and I could only echo Brzezinski's words and add that only by coming to grips with their past could the Soviet people ensure that such horrors would not recur.

That evening, Channel 1, broadcast throughout the Soviet Union, carried on its evening news scenes of the Polish visitors to Katyn, close-ups of the corrections on the monument, and the interviews with Brzezinski and me. A few weeks later, the Soviet government issued a statement admitting that the atrocity had been the responsibility of Stalin and the NKVD.

Still, I wondered why it had taken so long for the Soviet authorities to recognize that it was in their interest to admit Stalin's crimes. Clearly, powerful forces in the system were still attempting to conceal the truth. In 1992, I got an answer. I was visiting Moscow to interview officials for this book and had an appointment with Russian Vice President Alexander Rutskoy. When the appointed hour arrived, an assistant came to the anteroom to notify me that the meeting would start late. A delegation of Poles, relatives of the murdered officers, was then meeting with Rutskoy, and the meeting was running over its allotted time.

In fifteen minutes the Poles filed out and my party was ushered in. Rutskoy, a professional military man himself, seemed shaken by the meeting. "The relatives want some very simple and reasonable things," he volunteered, "and they are right to demand them. But I don't know if we can do what they want."

I asked him what, specifically, he had in mind. He said that the Polish relatives wanted the remains exhumed, identified if possible, and reburied properly, and this was being done. But they also wanted the full facts about the atrocity to be documented from KGB archives. It was this that he doubted would be possible. I asked why that was a problem.

"There is no statute of limitations on war crimes," he explained, "and people are still alive who took part in the massacre. President Yeltsin and I have both repeatedly tried to obtain the full documentation. I think Gorbachev also tried. But the 'organs' just will not produce the information. They want to protect their own, come what may. We'll keep trying, but I doubt if the full information will ever see the light of day."[14]

The KGB. It was a state within a state, even when its previous leadership had been disgraced and removed and the organization transformed into the Russian Ministry of Security. In 1989, it must have taken enormous pressure from people like Shevardnadze and Yakovlev, and the support of Gorbachev, to force an official admission of the obvious.

The Katyn Forest massacre was just one of the past misdeeds to be confirmed officially. On Christmas Eve, the Congress of People's Deputies finally passed a resolution declaring the secret protocol between Hitler and Stalin legally invalid from the time it was signed. This followed presentation of a lengthy report by the commission headed by Alexander Yakovlev that proved that the text of the agreement the Western Allies had found in Germany was authentic, even though the Russian original could not be found.[15]

Nor were all the publicized misdeeds those of the Stalin period: the Congress of People's Deputies also investigated the killing of demonstrators in Tbilisi in April and approved a resolution in December condemning the use of force and ordering consideration of further steps. But many considered the report less than satisfactory. It seemed, in particular, that the Soviet military was withholding information regarding responsibility for the decision to use force. Therefore, while the legislative investigation set a useful precedent, it was clear that the commission lacked adequate power to extract facts from a reluctant bureaucracy.

Disclosures regarding the Chernobyl nuclear plant disaster in 1986 had an even more profound effect on the public image of Communist Party officials, since it revealed that senior officials of the CPSU, as well as the Belorussian and Ukrainian Parties, had participated in a massive cover-up that had endangered the health of millions. An accurate map showing radiation levels was released for the first time in 1989, and it revealed that persons in some of the most heavily affected areas had been neither evacuated nor even warned. In fact, radiation dosimeters that had been distributed as part of the civil defense program had been collected to prevent residents from detecting the elevated radiation levels.

For many people, 1989 marked a turning point in their attitude toward the existing system. While most of the public was generally aware that there had been serious abuses in the past, the concrete evidence that came to light that year galvanized hatred for the regime throughout the country.

After Ukraine had declared independence, I asked President Leonid Kravchuk when he had turned from belief in communisn to a conviction that Ukraine must be independent. He replied, "In 1989." He then explained that, while he had known in general that there had been abuses and even atrocities in the past, he had not seen the concrete evidence until that year. What he had seen and learned in 1989 had convinced him that only independence could save his country from such horrors in the future.[16]

In one of his judgments, Yegor Ligachev was absolutely right. The

media campaign to expose the dark sides of Soviet history, along with
the country's existing shortcomings, was undermining the very foundations of the regime.

Gorbachev's Strategy

FROM THE SPRING OF 1988 I had been convinced that Gorbachev was
serious about pursuing genuine political reform in the Soviet Union and
that this would require a good-faith effort to come to terms with the
West. Events since then had reinforced this conviction. I was also fully
aware that he was meeting massive opposition in the Communist Party,
most of it still passive, to be sure, but that his opponents were now beginning to speak out more and more openly and one could expect a
more coherent opposition within the Party to develop. I understood that
no program of reform could be successful until the grip of the Party *apparat* was broken.

I was not sure, however, that Gorbachev understood that he would
have to break the power of the Party he headed if his reforms were to
have a chance. He still talked as if he could turn the Party into a vanguard of reform, but I did not know whether that was rhetoric to buy
time for maneuver or he really believed it. If he really believed the Communist Party could create a democratic system, reform would have no
chance.

Nevertheless, I thought Gorbachev's record in outmaneuvering his
opponents was impressive, as was his capacity for learning from his mistakes and changing his course when required. With that record in mind,
I pointed out in messages to Washington and in background briefings to
American journalists in Moscow that it would be risky to bet against
him in the bouts he was facing. Despite the growing criticism from both
conservatives and reformers, Gorbachev remained by far the most popular political leader in the country, and that popularity would be an irreplaceable asset if he could introduce more democratic procedures into
the country's political life.

While I thought Gorbachev would manage to stay on top of the Soviet political structure for the foreseeable future, I had no confidence
that his economic reform program would be successful. In fact, it
seemed doomed to failure, and the principal question in my mind was
whether Gorbachev would realize this in time to adopt a program of

more radical and fundamental change. He also seemed all but blind to the real force behind ethnic and nationalist agitation, and I wondered whether he would prove as adept in dealing with it as he had in persuading Party officials to participate in real elections. When it came to elections, he seemed to know what he wanted, even when he followed a devious course. As for the nationalities—Russians and non-Russians alike—either he did not know what he wanted, or he wanted something he could never have: imperial control voluntarily granted.

One of the criticisms that surfaced with increasing frequency was that Gorbachev did not know where he was going. He had—as both Ligachev and Ryzhkov charged in their memoirs—set policies into motion without defining or understanding the intended result. Just before he left Moscow for his state visit to Italy and the Vatican and his summit meeting with President Bush on Malta, he published a lengthy essay intended to meet this criticism.

Entitled "The Socialist Idea and Revolutionary Perestroika," it appeared on the first three pages of *Pravda* on Sunday, November 26, 1989. It was signed "M. Gorbachev," with no title, which indicated that the essay represented his personal view and had not been cleared by the Politburo. When I read it, I was struck by the distance he had traveled in the two years since his October Revolution anniversary speech in 1987 and his book *Perestroika*. While the article still professed adherence to "socialism," Gorbachev redefined the term in a manner much more compatible with Western social democracy than with the "socialism" inherited from Lenin and Stalin.

At the outset, he admitted that his views had changed since he had come to power in 1985. "We have begun to see many things differently," he stated, then explained:

> Whereas at first we thought it was basically a question only of correcting individual deformations in our social organism, of perfecting the system that had developed, we are now saying that we must radically remodel our entire social system, from the economic foundation to the superstructure . . . [including] reform of property relations, the economic mechanism, and the political system, along with changes in the spiritual and moral atmosphere of society.[17]

He then rejected both preservation of the existing command economy and the adoption of capitalism. Instead, he proposed creating a "humane, free, and rational society," which he claimed was "connected with the theory of Marxism-Leninism." Such a society, he suggested, would reject "bureaucratic centralism" in favor of management by "voluntary associations of labor collectives." Workers would own the means of production they used, and peasants would be the masters of their land.

In the political sphere, his goal was to establish a civil society and a law-based state, and he praised "democracy and freedom" as "great values of human civilization," which merely needed the addition of a "socialist content" to be a suitable goal. Anticipating the protest of hard-liners that what passes for democracy in the West is not real (that is, economic) democracy, he pointed out that though the aim was to create *real* democracy, experience had shown that *formal* democracy was also important.

This formulation indirectly but unmistakably rejected the traditional Communist argument that "bourgeois" democracy is not real democracy: democracy is democracy, Gorbachev seemed to be saying, and we must model our political institutions on those of the Western democracies if we are to have it. Then, as if to drive the point home, he stated that socialist ideas had to be combined with the "time-tested mechanisms" of representative democracy, including a clear separation of legislative and executive power and independent courts.

The Communist Party, he concluded, would have "a special role" in the "new social organism," since it was called upon to be the "political avant-garde" of Soviet society. But this would require it to stop trying to manage the economy and to restructure itself internally. He maintained that it was "expedient" to maintain the one-party system at the "present complex stage" of social change but warned that the Party itself must develop pluralism and competition of ideas and expand glasnost. Without giving credit to Yeltsin for an idea he had been expressing for the last two years, Gorbachev noted ruefully that up to now the Party had been lagging behind society as a whole in moving toward democracy.

As I pondered this article, I was much more encouraged than discouraged. An optimist by nature, I am normally more impressed by water filling a previously empty glass than by the amount left to be filled. I could not say whether Gorbachev had filled the glass of reform goals 20 percent or 40 percent or maybe even 60 percent. Certainly, a lot of room was left in the glass. But Gorbachev was showing that he was learning from experience. As a result of the difficulties he had encountered, his goals were becoming more radical rather than more cautious.

This essay totally omitted mention of the class struggle, and its concept of fundamental democratic institutions was no different from that in the West. However, Gorbachev's economic ideas seemed confused. The dogmatic Marxist formulas that had filled his "anniversary" speech in 1987 were absent; instead we find a vague preference for collective ownership and management and a continued insistence on defending "socialism" as a general concept. There was no indication of the importance of moving to a system of market relations and no recognition at all that political democracy is not feasible without the right to hold private property.

Of course, I would not have expected even the most clear-sighted Soviet leader to write an article in 1989 defending capitalism. If Gorbachev had done so, he would not have lasted much longer as Soviet leader. His quasi endorsement of Western social democracy was probably as far as he could go at that time. Nevertheless, I had the feeling that his defense of a redefined "socialism" was more than tactical; he really seemed to believe that collective ownership was superior to that of individuals. Unless these convictions were shaken by subsequent experience, such beliefs would hobble his thinking in the future.

His comments on the Party, by contrast, suggested to me that, despite his lip service to its "avant-garde role," he was preparing the way to loosen the Party's hold on the political process. The one-party system was no longer described as a necessary political institution: it was merely "expedient" at the given time. And though there was exhortation for it to act as society's avant-garde, Gorbachev also stated that society was changing faster than the Party. In other words, society was now the avant-garde and the Party the laggard. If the Party continued to hold the country back by resisting reform, what then?

Gorbachev did not say, but I thought I knew. His next logical step would be to create a power base for himself outside the Party. Then he would pressure the Party to follow him, and if it failed to do so, he could eventually dispense with it without automatically losing his job.

While I could surmise what Gorbachev's strategy might be for staying in power while he forced political change, I had less confidence that I understood his strategy regarding the economic and nationality problems that were nearing a crisis point. Evidence was accumulating that his understanding of these issues was faulty.

Most large and medium-sized factories throughout the Soviet Union were run from Moscow by central ministries and their huge bureaucracies. This was not only inefficient and wasteful; managers and workers on the spot resented the absentee control. This was bad enough in the provinces of Russia; in other republics it was considered an outrage, a clear manifestation of imperialism. There had been much talk throughout the perestroika period of transferring management responsibility to the enterprises, but it had never happened. As long as the central ministries were preserved, it could not happen. While Gorbachev at times seemed to understand this, he seemed unwilling or unable to force a concrete change.

The question of property ownership also had implications for the nationality question. As long as the state owned all means of production, political leaders in the republics would have a powerful incentive for breaking away from the Center if it ever became possible in practice. A declaration of independence would give them a claim not only to the governmental structure of the republic but also to its land and property. The apparent rewards of independence were therefore much higher than if the system had permitted a substantial amount of private property—or property owned by small, local collectives. Gorbachev, who periodically attacked attempts in the Baltic republics to restore private property, seemed oblivious to the threat to the union posed by centralized ownership.

Therefore, it seemed to me that, in resisting steps to private property and refusing to grant real economic autonomy to the republics, Gorbachev was creating problems for his policy. I could understand that he might be unable to get backing for immediate privatization, but I did not understand why he felt it necessary to denounce the concept so categorically. If he was unable to start the process of privatization throughout the country, he should at least allow decisions on economic reform to devolve upon elected republic leaders. Otherwise, if the economy continued to decline, economic pressures would fuse with nationalist emotions and the country would literally fly apart at the first sign that Moscow could no longer enforce its will.

As far as Lithuania and the other Baltic states were concerned, I felt that independence was now inevitable. If it were granted soon enough and a true federal system were offered to the other republics, Gorbachev might have constructed a "firebreak" between the Baltics and the others. The official admission that the Nazi-Soviet pact had never been legal provided a basis for restoring the sovereignty of the Baltic states without treating the other republics the same. It was probably true that Gorbachev could not immediately grant the Baltic republics independence and survive, but he could have done more to ease the process. Instead, his tactics throughout 1989 seemed to leave him no room to maneuver, even as they were destroying his credibility with the Baltic population.

At the end of 1989, I felt that Gorbachev would likely remain in power for a few years to come—probably to the end of his term in 1994 if the Soviet Union itself survived that long. However, I doubted he could accomplish his goals. While he was a fast learner and I expected his positions to evolve for the better, it seemed to me that he, like the Communist Party, was beginning to lag behind public opinion as a whole. Unless he could do something dramatic in 1990 to reverse current trends, he would be in serious difficulty by 1991.

Fatal Infections?

WITH THE ADVANTAGE of a pathologist's hindsight, I would say that 1989 was the year the Soviet Union contracted its fatal infections. Public confidence had plummeted just as the public was being allowed to express its views. Nationalism found sustenance in nutrients thrown off by the centrally controlled economy. Economic reform had been bungled— or rather had not been seriously attempted—and the stumbling economy was causing growing distress. The Communist Party control mechanism had been undermined.

This was serious but probably not yet terminal. It seemed to me that Gorbachev had two broad options. He could split the Communist Party, remove it from effective control, and attempt to use elected republic and provincial leaders and reform intellectuals to implement reforms—or he could turn his back on perestroika and attempt to restore as much as possible of the old system. This was, in effect, what Ligachev had been urging, and Ryzhkov would have agreed so long as it was carried out under the smoke screen of reformist rhetoric. There was no need to declare a change of policy since Moscow could reimpose controls simply by taking a series of small steps backward.

The problem with the first strategy was that Gorbachev would have risked Khrushchev's fate if he had adopted it. The problem with the second was that it would not work in the long run. Even if control could have been successfully reimposed, the country would emerge worse off than when perestroika had first been started, and it would be only a matter of time until another effort at reform would be required—but then it would be up to somebody other than Gorbachev, who would go down in history as an unmitigated failure.

XII

A Winter of Discontents

We now visualize our goal more clearly. It is a humane, democratic socialism,
a society of freedom and social justice.
MIKHAIL GORBACHEV, New Year's address, December 31, 1989[1]

A slave is not the one who is put in chains but the one who kisses his chains
in admiration. We will not kiss our chains.
KAZIMIERAS MOTIEKA, address to rally in Vilnius on the day Gorbachev arrived[2]

If [Gorbachev] is planning to rely on right-wing forces, he will lose.
If, instead, he cooperates with progressive forces, both the people and the Party
will support him without reservation.
BORIS YELTSIN, January 1990[3]

We can't go on like this.
YEGOR LIGACHEV, February 2, 1990[4]

I t was a long-standing Soviet custom for the top political leader to
address the nation just before the stroke of midnight on December
31. Normally, these speeches were filled with self-congratulation for the
outgoing year's achievements and predictions of even better things to
follow.

On December 31, 1989, however, the traditional approach was not
appropriate. The problems that had accumulated during the year were
so obvious that an attempt to pretend they did not exist would have outraged the public. Gorbachev understood this and addressed his countrymen with a sober countenance. He acknowledged that 1989 had been
"the most difficult year of perestroika" and admitted that economic reform had encountered "heavy weather," but he claimed that 1989, with
all its pain, had laid the foundation for future peace and prosperity. The
end of the cold war would permit the nineties to be "the most fruitful
period in the history of civilization." What would be needed most would
be "reason and kindness, patience and tolerance."

Rebecca and I watched the address in Spaso House's upstairs study with friends visiting from Kansas. I tried to give a running translation, which forced me to pay more attention to the speech than I might have otherwise. As soon as Gorbachev finished, the Kremlin chimes struck midnight and we uncorked the champagne. But I had felt something was missing from the speech.

When we had toasted the New Year, it suddenly occurred to me: Gorbachev had said nothing about Lenin, communism, or the Communist Party! These were normally obligatory themes for Soviet leaders in such speeches. Could this be the first year they were omitted?

When our guests went to bed, I rummaged among my videotapes and found the one I had recorded the year before. I played it and found that my memory had not betrayed me: on December 31, 1988, Gorbachev had spoken of "the resurrection of the Leninist conception of socialism" and of the "responsibility of the Leninist party."

That evening Lenin was out and religion was in. One of the television channels featured a roundtable of clergymen discussing the social and human values of faith and a sermon by a metropolitan of the Russian Orthodox Church. The contrast with the past, when the mass media had mentioned religion only to attack it, was striking. In fact, it had been habitual for the most popular entertainment programs to be scheduled for Easter, in the hope that this would keep young people out of church.

The television fare on New Year's Eve proved to be a harbinger of things to come. A week later, when the Russian Orthodox Church observed Christmas in accord with the Gregorian calendar, the entire three-hour service in one of Leningrad's cathedrals was televised, along with explanations of the rituals by a priest. It would be another year, however, before well-known political figures started attending church on holidays.

Holiday spirit was subdued as 1990 began and quickly evaporated. Gorbachev had no respite from the cares that developed in 1989. He faced a crisis in the Party brought on by the withdrawal of the Lithuanians and demands to end the Party's monopoly of power, a failing economy, growing opposition to perestroika, and, with Eastern Europe slipping away and Germany in the throes of unification, a foreign policy that for the first time was drawing criticism rather than applause. Large protest demonstrations, previously concentrated in the warm-weather months, had become a winter phenomenon in many republics, particularly those in the Baltic and the Transcaucasus. Violent clashes continued in Azerbaijan and had started in parts of Georgia.

Gorbachev's most pressing political commitment was to visit Lithuania. The Central Committee plenum of December 25 had condemned the efforts of the Lithuanian Communist Party to become independent but had postponed final action until General Secretary Gorbachev could visit the republic. It was obvious that he hoped to persuade the Lithuanian Communists to stay in the Communist Party of the Soviet Union and the people of Lithuania to give a "real federation" a try before insisting on secession.

The trip to Lithuania must have been one of the hardest tasks of a difficult political career. Gorbachev loved to travel and loved to mix with crowds when they were friendly. But this time his reception, though respectful, was fundamentally hostile. Most of the exchanges that occurred during the three-day visit were a dialogue of the deaf.

Sąjūdis organized a mass rally in Vilnius on January 11, the day Gorbachev arrived. The organizers had invited Gorbachev to come, but he chose the more friendly precincts of an industrial plant in the city for his main appearance. Meanwhile, Cathedral Square was filled to capacity, and people even jammed the side streets in their effort to participate in the independence rally. The Soviet central media concentrated their attention on Gorbachev and virtually ignored the larger gathering, but representatives of our consulate general in Leningrad were present, and the U.S. Foreign Broadcast Information Service translated the speeches broadcast on Lithuanian radio.

Kazimieras Motieka, one of the Lithuanians who had visited me the previous summer, opened the rally at two o'clock with the announcement that Lithuanians had gathered to declare that they would not live without independence. Vytautas Landsbergis, the Sąjūdis chairman, then came to the microphone and observed that most political leaders, in both the West and East, "advise Lithuanians not to hurry." These people should come and live in the Soviet Union to get an idea of what their advice meant. The crowd chanted "freedom, freedom" as Landsbergis continued. He said that Moscow was pretending not to hear the clear messages sent by the Lithuanian people: a petition with 1,800,000 signatures demanding that only Lithuanian laws should prevail in Lithuania, one with 1,500,000 signatures demanding that the Molotov-Ribbentrop pact be annulled, a letter six months ago from Lithuania's

Supreme Soviet deputies requesting negotiations on independence. "We have said everything there is to say, and Moscow cannot pretend to be an adolescent who doesn't get the point."

Landsbergis regretted that Gorbachev had not joined them in the square but said that he believed in Gorbachev's goodwill. "He is the head of a powerful though dangerous eastern state, a symbol of its new policy. We wish to have friendly and economically beneficial relations with that state on the basis of mutual respect and mutual advantage."

Not every speaker was willing to give Gorbachev this much credit. Nikolai Medvedev, an ethnic Russian from Vilnius, said, "I would like very much to believe in Mikhail Sergeyevich, but I know who is standing behind him. . . . I remember how Andrei Dmitriyevich Sakharov was booed. I remember how they did not want to admit that Bolshevism produced genocide in its own country. As long as they lie, we cannot believe in them. Holy Russia is still drugged by the frightful Marxist poison."[5]

Gorbachev spoke at an electrical equipment plant that afternoon, stressing themes he would repeat throughout his visit: the Soviet nationalities are bound together with ties so close that all will lose if they are severed; attempts at secession could lead to ethnic strife and bloodshed; Lithuanians can obtain all they want in a new, democratic federation. As for the Communist Party, it should retain a unitary structure to provide coherence in the new federation. The idea of autonomy for republic parties made as much sense, he argued, as removing load-bearing supports from a bridge.

It was obvious even from the official record of the visit that most Lithuanians were not accepting these arguments. Independence, they said, did not mean severing economic and human ties: they wanted close economic relations and open borders. There would be no bloodshed because there was no basis for ethnic strife. Furthermore, they had no confidence that Gorbachev could create a true federation, particularly if he refused to allow a federal structure in the Communist Party. His rejection of the request for autonomy by 80 percent of Lithuanian Party members was seen as proof that any future federation would be a sham.

When Gorbachev left Vilnius for Moscow on January 13, he tried to put the best face on a failed mission. "We have laid a good foundation for continuing the dialogue," he remarked, expressing the hope that the Lithuanian Communists who had broken with Moscow would reconsider their action and send representatives to the next Party Congress.

Brazauskas responded to this comment at the departure ceremony by reiterating politely but firmly that the withdrawal of the Lithuanian Party from the Communist Party of the Soviet Union was irrevocable.[6] The dialogue would not be continued on Gorbachev's terms.

Two days after Gorbachev left Vilnius, Algirdas Brazauskas was elected chairman of the Lithuanian Supreme Soviet. The rump Lithuanian Communist Party loyal to Moscow lost all political influence, despite the fact that Gorbachev had given it the Party's extensive assets in the republic.

I wondered why Gorbachev had undertaken a mission that was bound to fail. Anyone familiar with attitudes in Lithuania knew that his arguments would not sway the Lithuanian public. So why had he gone? One reason might have been to prepare for a change in policy. He could have gone, made the best case he could, then returned to Moscow to say that Lithuania had taught him that only a federated Party structure would be viable in the future. But this was not what he did; before he left he had ruled out the only concession that would have justified his trip.

He might also have had more Machiavellian tactics in mind. He could have planned to go to Lithuania, prove how "incorrigible" the Lithuanians were, and use this as an excuse for a subsequent crackdown. But this possibility also did not fit the facts. Throughout the entire trip, despite a steady stream of comments and questions he must have considered insulting, he did not once utter a threat. The bluster of the previous August was not repeated. And, besides, a crackdown in Lithuania would have meant the end of perestroika, which he seemed determined to accelerate, not abandon.

So why did he go and risk the damage to his authority that a public rejection of his pleas would inflict? I believe there were two reasons. First, he had been duped by the KGB's reports that the "nationalists" were in a minority. Therefore, he really believed that he could bring local pressure to bear on the "secessionists." And second, he took the trip to demonstrate to conservatives that he would not connive with those who would split the Party. He was preparing major proposals for changes in the Party and the governmental structure. They would at best be difficult to get through the Politburo and Central Committee; if he was suspected of being soft on nationalism, the worst might happen and he could suffer the fate of Khrushchev.

Gorbachev might also have feared that the local military authorities, supported by conservatives in the KGB and the Party, might be tempted to provoke violence in the hope of forcing him to intervene—as they tried to do a year later—or perhaps even of forcing him from office. The trip, therefore, could also have been an effort to buy time.

In fact, Party conservatives and most senior military officers considered opposition to Baltic independence a litmus test for loyalty to the country. As they watched the Soviet position in Eastern Europe crumble and Germany rushing to unify, their determination to resist any change of the Soviet Union's own borders intensified. Virtually all observers close to the Moscow political scene felt that no Soviet leader could let Lithuania, let alone all the Baltic states, secede and survive as leader. I have no doubt that this was also Gorbachev's assessment, and it would explain much of his subsequent maneuvering on the issue.

Azerbaijan's Abortive Revolution

WHILE GORBACHEV was still on his futile mission to Lithuania, arguing that separatism could lead to bloodshed, scores died when pogroms and riots broke out in Azerbaijan—as the result not of separatism but of ethnic hatreds that had festered over Nagorny Karabakh.

The dispute had continued to rage during 1989, with mass demonstrations taking place periodically in both Yerevan and Baku, but there had been few clashes that led to loss of life. During most of the year Nagorny Karabakh had been administered not by Azerbaijan but by veteran Party official Arkady Volsky, who had been dispatched to the enclave by the USSR Supreme Soviet as a special administrator. Neither the Armenians nor the Azeris were happy with this arrangement, but it was more acceptable to Armenia than to Azerbaijan. The Armenians could hope that it was the first step toward transfer of the territory to Armenia, while the Azeris could only view it as an infringement on their republic's territorial integrity.

In November 1989, I had visited both Yerevan and Baku. Tension in both cities was evident. Armenia was still reeling from the effects of the cataclysmic earthquake the previous year, but public attention seemed focused even more on the fate of Armenians in Nagorny Karabakh. Public demands to transfer the territory to Armenia had become so insistent that no politician could hope to stay in power without paying lip service to them. Nevertheless, it was obvious that Azeris would react violently to these moves. Suren Harutiunian, the new first secretary of the

Armenian Party, told me privately that the only feasible solution would be to keep Nagorny Karabakh under direct Moscow control, but he feared this would prove unacceptable not only to Azerbaijan but to Gorbachev as well.

Abdulrakhman Vezirov, Harutiunian's counterpart in Baku, took a different approach. Armenians, he said, had always lived in Azerbaijan and would always be welcome. The riots in Sumgait had been caused by riffraff and would not recur. He thought it unfortunate that so many Armenians had left in fear and was determined to keep their jobs and apartments for them in the hope they would soon return. The Azeris who had been expelled from Armenia should also be encouraged to return, he argued. But for this to work, the Armenians would have to renounce all claim to Nagorny Karabakh. The Armenian territorial claim, he argued, had enraged the public in Azerbaijan and could only lead to a de facto state of war between the two republics.

I left both republics with a heavy heart. The demands of public opinion in each—unfortunately inflamed by both nations' intellectual elites, which seemed bent on stirring emotions with tendentious and exaggerated versions of history—had left no room for compromise. Events were moving toward an explosion.

On November 28, a few days after I returned to Moscow, the USSR Supreme Soviet voted to end the special administration in Nagorny Karabakh and return it to Azerbaijan's jurisdiction. The reasoning in Moscow at the time was that this step would force each republic to take responsibility for coming to terms with the other. It turned out to be a tragic miscalculation.

Armenian demonstrators immediately gathered in Stepanakert, the capital of Nagorny Karabakh, to protest the decision to return them to Azerbaijani control. The Armenian Supreme Soviet condemned Moscow's action and, on December 1, voted to unite with Nagorny Karabakh. The Azerbaijan authorities, taking advantage of the fact that virtually all fuel and most goods from Russia were shipped to Armenia by rail lines across Azerbaijan, responded by imposing a blockade on Armenia.

Public agitation grew in both republics and reached mass proportions in Azerbaijan. The Azerbaijani National Front, which Party Secretary Vezirov had agreed to legalize a few months earlier, took advantage of the Nagorny Karabakh issue to gain a mass following and began to force out Communist officials in several cities. By January 11, 1990, the day Gorbachev arrived in Vilnius, demonstrators had blockaded government offices in Lenkoran, Azerbaijan's second largest city,[7] and were gathering in massive numbers in central Baku.

Two days later, the capital of Azerbaijan witnessed the bloodiest riots since the Bolshevik Revolution. Mobs attacked apartment houses in which Armenian families were living and massacred the occupants. Women and children were literally thrown from upper-story windows to their death on the pavement below.

The Azerbaijani National Front seized control of the republic. Party leader Vezirov fled to Moscow, and the National Front took control of all the key points in the city. On January 15, Moscow ordered troops into the area, but they did not enter Baku in force until the night of January 19. Gorbachev went on television the evening of the following day to urge calm and peace and accused Party and government officials in both republics of failing to cooperate. Vezirov was removed as Party chief in Azerbaijan, which suggested that he would be blamed for the violence.

By January 21 the Soviet army had secured control of Baku, but the city was not calm. The Azerbaijani Supreme Soviet passed a unanimous resolution to conduct a referendum on secession from the Soviet Union if the Soviet Army continued to occupy the city.

In Moscow, we followed the news reports of these shocking events with horror. Central Television did a creditable job of reporting the events, although announcers described the violent acts rather than showing them on the screen. After watching the television news on January 21, I jotted down the following observations:

Baku is said to be calm following the military action yesterday, but the population is seething. One general interviewed on TV described the situation as "tense to the limit." Official figures of those killed are less than 100, but everyone seems to believe that the count should be much higher. All this was covered in great detail this evening on *Seven Days,* the new Sunday-evening "week in review" program. BBC says that Nakhichevan has announced its secession from the Soviet Union. I notice that the Soviet media are not claiming that the situation is calm there. The Azerbaijan National Front has called a general strike for tomorrow, and memorial meetings. It seems obvious that the curfew is not being generally observed.

From here it would seem that the leadership had no choice but to introduce troops, and to give the order to fire when fighting and resistance continued. But it looks as if the action may not be a quick one, and if it drags on, or if there is extensive loss of life, this will only add to the general malaise of the population. . . .

Another thing seems clear: Party rule in the area has collapsed. To the degree there is order or disorder it is attributable to the National Front and to the Soviet army. So much for the "leading role."

Later, when I read a statement by Defense Minister Yazov in *Izvestiya* on January 26, I realized that my initial impression that military intervention was necessary had probably been wrong. Yazov announced that the army had arrested "about eighty" members of the National Front and of informal organizations and explained the arrests as follows:

> Our task is not to detain them all but to destroy the power structure that has been established at all enterprises and establishments.
>
> I did not misspeak. I mean literally power. They were preparing to seize it and were so certain of success that they themselves declared a state of emergency at 11:00 P.M. on January 18, a day before troops were introduced into Baku. Soviet and Party organs in fact ceased to function from that time in many districts of the city. A mass demonstration was called for January 20, at which time it was intended to announce that the National Front had assumed power.

So the primary reason for military intervention was not to save lives but to dislodge the National Front from power! Indeed, one might infer that the National Front had ended the rioting before the Soviet army intervened, since it had itself declared a state of emergency.

A few days later I pursued these questions with Andrei Girenko, a new secretary in the USSR Party Central Committee. I had previously met him in the Crimea, where he had headed the Party organization. He had recently been transferred to the Party Secretariat in Moscow and had been sent to Baku, along with Yevgeny Primakov, when the violence began. He said that they had gone to Baku on January 14, the day after the rioting had started, and had attempted to "find a political solution." However, they had found that "healthy elements" in the Azerbaijani National Front had "lost out" to "terrorists." On January 18, the National Front had declared a state of emergency, and the next morning it had seized all government and Party buildings. The following day, Moscow had declared martial law and sent troops.

Like Yazov, Girenko indicated that order had been restored before Soviet troops had intervened and that the intervention had been designed to return the Communist Party to power.

This was the conclusion most Azeris, and most Soviet Muslims, drew. Friends of the National Front maintained that the anti-Armenian riots on January 13 had been precipitated by homeless Azeris who had been expelled from Armenia with no possibility of resettlement. The Azerbaijani authorities had tried to avoid permanent resettlement, hoping that a mutual return of refugees to Armenia and Azerbaijan could be arranged. When the pogroms had started, the authorities had been paralyzed and the National Front had taken control and calmed the situation, its partisans maintained.

I did not find this explanation totally convincing, since the National Front had taken a hard line on Nagorny Karabakh and thus had helped create the conditions that had led to the January 13 pogroms. Nevertheless, it seemed clear in retrospect that the Soviet army's seizure of Baku had increased rather than reduced the loss of life and that political factors had outweighed humanitarian ones when the decision was taken.

The decision to remove the Azerbaijani National Front by force created a national grievance in the republic that could only bolster future calls for secession. It also produced some serious side effects in Russian public opinion. Demonstrations occurred in several Russian cities to protest the deployment of Soviet troops in Baku—not because there was sympathy for the Azerbaijani National Front but because the families of draftees did not want them exposed to danger. Russians began to realize that they, too, could be targets of ethnic violence. Hitherto, pogroms had been something that happened to minorities like Jews or Armenians. But when the Soviet army seized Baku, the families of servicemen stationed in Azerbaijan had to be evacuated to ensure their safety.

Military intervention as a future means of "bringing order" to the republics began to look more and more problematical. The Russian public was less and less willing to pay the price the Soviet empire was exacting.

A Platform for Imperialists

THE EMPIRE, however, had its defenders, and they were beginning to coalesce as they watched, first with concern and then with horror, the crumbling Soviet position in Eastern Europe, the assertiveness of non-Russian nationalities, and the weakening of central controls. In early January 1990, a young writer, Alexander Prokhanov, published an article in the conservative literary weekly *Literaturnaya Rossiya* that became both rallying cry and platform for those who wanted to preserve the empire at any cost.[8] Prokhanov attacked the Gorbachev leadership for undermining the foundations of Soviet unity, which he identified as socialist ideology, political control by the Moscow Center, and a planned economy. He predicted chaos and civil war, followed by foreign invasion, if these trends continued.

Even though it appeared in a publication of limited circulation, Prokhanov's article attracted much attention, since it provided a justification for the political union of Russians with a chauvinistic bent, most of whom were emotionally attached to the tsarist system and therefore anti-Bolshevik in principle, with the current Communist Party *apparat,* the military, and the police. The unifying theme was attachment to the empire, and if only the Communists could hold it together, the imperialists would support the Communists. This was the approach followed by the Russian Patriotic Bloc, which had been formed by twelve Russian "patriotic movements" toward the end of 1989 with the aim of promoting like-minded candidates in the upcoming republic elections.[9]

I read Prokhanov's articles and the pronouncements of the Russian Patriotic Bloc with alarm. They confirmed a belief I had held for years that communism, fascism, and imperialism were kindred political movements, all based on a single group's rule by force. Traditionally, Western intellectuals of both conservative and liberal bent had been mesmerized by an assumption that fascism was a movement of the "right" and communism of the "left" and that they were therefore antithetical. In the 1930s, many Western intellectuals had refused to condemn Stalin's purges for fear that this would help Hitler, and even the Nazi-Soviet pact had failed to shake this belief in many minds. Among French intellectuals this attitude had prevailed right up to the invasion of Hungary in 1956—and, for some, until the invasion of Czechoslovakia in 1968. "Conservatives," meanwhile, frequently apologized for right-wing tyrants since they considered them bulwarks against communism. Actually, a tyrant normally found it easier to adopt Communist ideology and backing than to build democratic institutions. The perceived "left-right" dichotomy simply obscured the real issue, the arrogance of untrammeled power.

The alarming aspect of the embryonic alliance of imperial partisans was the propensity of the self-proclaimed Russian "patriots" to embrace some of the most distasteful aspects of tsarist Russia. Most were xenophobic and anti-Semitic, though only the extremists said so openly. All assumed that Russia had a mission to rule the vast area from "Constantinople" to the Pacific Ocean, from the Baltic Sea to India, and to exercise hegemony over all borderlands. They considered the Russian state, in its most bloated imperial form, to be the principal touchstone of national identity, and preservation of that state, they felt, should take precedence over the rights of individuals and those of nations other than Russia. While they deplored the damage the Russian Orthodox Church had suffered from Bolshevism's militant atheism, the destruction of traditional rural life by Stalin's agricultural collectivization, and the rape of the environment by mindless industrialization, they were willing to make common cause with the perpetrators of these outrages to preserve the imperial state.

At first, Prokhanov and other prominent spokesmen for Russian chauvinism refrained from criticizing Gorbachev by name in their public statements, even though it was clear that their attacks were aimed directly at his policies. During the winter of 1989 and 1990, they still hoped to influence Gorbachev and in particular to block any inclination on his part to compromise with Baltic nationalism. Here, too, their interests coincided with those of the most retrograde elements in the Communist Party, the KGB, and the Soviet army.

The Party Reformers Organize

THE REFORMERS MOVED more rapidly than the "empire builders" to put their programs into organizational form. Between four hundred and five hundred Party members from seventy-eight cities held a weekend conference in Moscow on January 20–21, at which they founded the Democratic Platform of the CPSU. The organizers included the leaders of the Interregional Group from the Congress of People's Deputies as well as representatives of strike committees from mining areas.

The meeting called for the establishment of a multiparty system, conversion of the Communist Party into a normal political party, rejection of "democratic centralism," and election of Party officials from below, by secret ballot. Some of the organizers, such as Boris Yeltsin, argued that the group should concentrate on change from within the Communist Party, while others, such as economist Gavriil Popov and historian Yuri Afanasiev, wished to force a split in the Party if the upcoming Party elections were not conducted in democratic fashion. Alexander Yakovlev did not participate in this gathering, but he was widely considered to be a silent backer. His protégé, Vyacheslav Shostakovsky, the rector of the Higher Party School, was among the leaders and in fact drafted much of the program.

In retrospect, it may seem that the group's ostensible goal of "democratizing" the Communist Party was hopelessly quixotic. In fact, most of the group's leaders were not optimistic that they would be successful. Nevertheless, they felt that a show of strength at the upcoming Party congress was important, since Gorbachev was unlikely to move decisively against the conservatives in the Party until he was sure he could win. It was incumbent on the reformers, therefore, to demonstrate that there was sufficient support for reform in the country for Gorbachev to proceed. Second, they were aware that rank-and-file Party members resented the authority and privileges enjoyed by the full-time Party professionals. Truly democratic elections from below could be used to remove many Party officials who were there only because of their loyalty to their superiors. Sharply reducing the Party's bureaucratic apparatus would also weaken the ability of Party officials to control or override elective bodies. Finally, there was the issue of the Party's extensive property, particularly its ownership of much of the media. If the reformers simply left the Party, this property would fall under the control of the conservatives. A show of strength, however, might force a division of Party property following a future schism.

Essentially, however, the reformers were organizing in the hope of attracting, or forcing, Gorbachev's protection. It would have been premature for him to endorse them openly, yet his reform program could not succeed unless it took the sort of steps prescribed in the Democratic Platform.

Splitting the Difference

THROUGHOUT JANUARY, Gorbachev's advisers worked on a major policy paper to be presented to a Central Committee plenum scheduled for the end of the month. The issues turned out to be so contentious that the session was delayed a week, until February 5. The reformers on Gorbachev's staff, whose attitudes coincided with those of the Democratic Platform, pressed him to break definitively with the conservatives in the Party *apparat.* One of their documents made its way to French correspondent Bernard Guetta, who published extensive excerpts in the Paris daily *Le Monde* on January 31.[10] It pointed out that Party conservatives were now the principal obstacle to carrying out perestroika and that they were beginning to make common cause with the most reactionary and chauvinistic elements of society. Therefore, Gorbachev could no longer lead the country by occupying the center ground between reformers and Party conservatives. If perestroika was to succeed, Gorbachev would have to ally himself with the radical intellectuals and break with the Party conservatives, a step Yeltsin had been urging for nearly three years.

Although this document was not published in the Soviet media, it was no secret to Party conservatives that Gorbachev was considering breaking with them. As the debate within the Party became more intense, several political observers told me that conservatives, including Ligachev, were convinced that Gorbachev had strayed from Marxism-Leninism and had become a social democrat of the Western European variety. In rejecting the class struggle he had, in their eyes, abandoned the key ideological tenet on which the Communist regime rested. In retreating from Eastern Europe, he was betraying those who had paid with their blood for the defeat of Nazi Germany. In weakening the Communist Party's grip on society, he was threatening to plunge the country into chaos. He seemed unwilling even to defend the territorial integrity of the country since he refused to authorize the use of force to crush the separatist movements in the Baltic states and elsewhere.

As Ligachev told an Italian correspondent just before the February plenum, he feared that the Soviet Union was losing its deepest values and its faith in the future. The country was becoming ungovernable, and everything was being questioned. "We can't go on like this," he remarked, adopting without attribution a comment attributed to Gorbachev from the early 1980s. But Gorbachev had been talking of Brezhnevite "stagnation," while Ligachev was referring to Gorbachev's perestroika. Ligachev's solution to the problem was to reestablish unity in the country under Communist Party control; in other words, to reverse the course Gorbachev had taken since January 1987, when he had launched his program of political reforms.[11]

There was nothing surprising about Ligachev's views, which were familiar to close observers of Soviet politics. What struck me personally was his resort to an interview with a foreign newspaper to express them. After all, one of the major charges he had made against Yeltsin in 1988 and 1989 was that he had utilized the foreign media to criticize conditions in the Soviet Union. Increasingly, all sides of the internal Party struggle were carrying their cases to the public, both at home and abroad. I considered this a positive development and a step toward openness and political maturity. It was certainly in sharp contrast to the secrecy that had traditionally marked political struggles in the Soviet leadership.

In preparing for the plenum, Gorbachev did not depend primarily on public debate. In fact, he was careful not to reveal his plans. Instead, he maneuvered to ensure that he could dominate the Central Committee session despite the hostility to his policies expressed by a growing number of its members. Several steps seemed designed to head off a rebellion.

First, several provincial Party bosses were replaced just before the plenum convened. This served to remind Central Committee members that Gorbachev's displeasure could have painful repercussions.

Second, he met with a group of militant miners on February 2, allowed them to voice strong criticism of the Party *apparat,* and had his own critical comments published in *Pravda* the morning the plenary session opened.

Third, he did nothing to block a large demonstration in Moscow in support of reform on Sunday, February 4, the day before the plenum opened. The square around the Hotel Moskva, where most of the out-of-town delegates were staying, was filled with at least 200,000 demonstrators demanding a more rapid movement toward reform.

When the plenum opened, I felt that Gorbachev had set the stage with skill. While political gossips had been concentrating on the opposition to him, he had placed some high psychological hurdles in his opponents' path. In addition to the three steps already mentioned, he announced at the start of the plenum that the proceedings would be published in full. I made the following comment in my journal:

> So, what is a provincial Party secretary who comes into Moscow loaded for bear and raring to lash out at current policy to do? The removals provide a "there but for the grace of Gorbachev . . ." The

mob scene on Sunday will bring forth images of Bucharest. Gorbachev's words to the miners amounted to a declaration of war against the midlevel *apparat,* and then the (sudden?) realization that every word uttered on the floor will be in tomorrow morning's paper. So sound off against perestroika and go back home and see what happens. Or, just maybe . . . a more prudent course?

As for his overall strategy, I believe that that, too, is becoming more evident. His remarks at his speech yesterday regarding the need to study the advantages of a presidential system suggest that he does indeed intend to prepare for himself a post of sufficient power and authority that would allow him to relinquish his Party post later this year. In any event, if the Party goes into a rapid decline, why should he want to ride it into oblivion?

Rumors of Failure

EVER SINCE DIRECT OPPOSITION to Gorbachev's policies had surfaced at the Party conference in 1988, the Moscow rumor mill had periodically issued reports of Gorbachev's imminent political demise. I felt that these recurrent rumors were a distorted reflection of infighting in the Party and generally discounted them, since I believed that Gorbachev had demonstrated his ability to keep control of the Party machinery. However, when the Moscow correspondent of the Cable News Network reported such a rumor on January 30, 1990, it produced a sharp drop of share prices on the New York Stock Exchange and galvanized world attention.

I was not aware of the CNN report until I returned to Spaso House following a gala dinner hosted by the American publisher Malcolm Forbes. It had been a particularly full day, the sort that reminded me of Woody Allen's remark that 90 percent of life is just showing up. For an ambassador, showing up at appropriate occasions is a large part of the job. Sometimes it can be a bore, if ceremonial occasions drag on with numerous vapid speeches, but more often it is a pleasure.

That day, the events had been a pleasure: an exhibit featuring bejeweled Fabergé eggs from collections abroad had opened in the Kremlin's Bell Tower. This was the first exhibit with foreign sponsorship allowed inside the Kremlin in recent memory, and I commented in a television interview following the opening that it was a sign of the new trust that was growing between our societies.

A reception and lunch in honor of Malcolm Forbes and San Diego Mayor Maureen O'Connor, who had helped organize the exhibit, followed. The new Soviet minister of culture, actor and theater director Nikolai Gubenko, hosted these events, which gave me the opportunity to check with him on plans to bring Mstislav Rostropovich and Washington's National Symphony Orchestra to Moscow.

Rostropovich, considered by many the world's leading cellist and one of its great conductors, had been forced to leave the Soviet Union in the 1970s, when he had befriended Alexander Solzhenitsyn. When he left, he and his wife, singer Galina Vishnevskaya, had been deprived of their Soviet citizenship and stripped of their awards. He was then named music director of the National Symphony Orchestra, which he turned into one of the world's great orchestras. Now there were plans for him to return to Moscow for the first time since his expulsion. I had a special interest in the event, not only because an American orchestra was involved but also because Rostropovich was coming as our personal guest. He had told me, while I was still working at the White House, that he would return to the Soviet Union only when I was ambassador "to protect him" and he was allowed to bring his orchestra. Now both of these conditions had been met, and a visit had been announced.

I asked Gubenko about Rostropovich's citizenship. He had not made restoration of his Soviet citizenship a condition of his return, but it obviously was important for the current government to make amends for Brezhnev's petty vindictiveness. Gubenko told me proudly that he had persuaded Gorbachev to order the restoration of Rostropovich's and Vishnevskaya's citizenship and of all their awards.

From this lunch, we rushed to attend the ceremonial opening of the first McDonald's restaurant in the Soviet Union. It was a delight to observe the smiling, eager faces of the Russian staff. Service in Soviet restaurants was normally sullen; waiters and waitresses considered customers a nuisance who should not be encouraged to intrude upon their leisure. The success of McDonald's American management in training people to treat the customer as a welcome visitor confirmed my conviction that, given proper incentives and training, Russians could match workers anywhere. The Big Mac, produced entirely with local ingredients save only the ketchup, tasted just like one at home.

Then Rebecca and I returned to Spaso House to host a reception for the Americans who had sponsored the Kremlin exhibit. The Forbes family had been allowed to come to Moscow on the family jet named

"Capitalist Tool," and Malcolm Forbes had received a permit to send his hot-air balloon up near central Moscow.[12] Even a year earlier, Soviet officials would have turned pale at the thought of permitting such "bourgeois propaganda."

We went directly from the reception to a gala dinner at the refurbished Savoy Hotel, this one hosted by Malcolm Forbes. I was seated next to Mayor O'Connor, who filled me in on San Diego's experience with its American-Soviet Arts Festival the previous year. The greatest problem had occurred with the Georgian participants.

After the massacre of demonstrators in April, the Georgians had initially refused to participate in any festival that classified them as Soviet, even though they had earlier signed contracts to do so. I had intervened with the Georgian foreign minister to persuade them to send a dance troupe, which they finally did, but they still refused to send a museum exhibit as had been agreed earlier. The Georgian dancers refused to perform in San Diego until all Soviet flags were removed from the hall. Mayor O'Connor's account of the city's difficulty in holding the Georgians to their contract illustrated the strength of anti-Soviet sentiment following the massacre in Tbilisi, as well as the fact that some Soviet institutions had begun to act independently of Moscow.

Nevertheless, I came home in a happy mood. The day had been filled with evidence of substantial and encouraging change. The country was opening up, expanding its ties with the outside world, and making peace with the political and cultural dissidents who had fled. Free enterprise might be given a chance to demonstrate its viability. The Georgians' reaction to the atrocity they had suffered would reinforce pressures to create safeguards against abuses of power in the future.

It was about 10:30 when we walked in the front door of Spaso House, and the telephone was ringing. I picked up the receiver and found that James Dobbins, the acting assistant secretary of state for European affairs, was calling. He said that CNN was carrying a story that Gorbachev would resign as general secretary and asked if we could shed light on the report. I told him I had not heard the report (we did not at that time receive CNN in Moscow) and doubted that Gorbachev intended to resign but that I would investigate.

It was still early afternoon in Washington, and it was obvious that we could not wait until morning to provide some clarification. I called my deputy, Mike Joyce, and asked him to have our staff find out what we could about the report since I would probably have to talk to the presi-

dent or secretary of state shortly. Within five minutes our political counselor called to say that Moscow's CNN bureau had reported that Gorbachev was meeting at his dacha with close associates to consider
whether he should resign his Party position as part of a general reorganization. They had no information that he had made a firm decision.

I hardly had time to complete my sigh of relief (we in the embassy had
not, after all, been laggard in our information, since we were aware that
these meetings were taking place) when the telephone rang again. This
time it was Secretary of State Baker, and I was happy to tell him that the
resignation report seemed premature. I pointed out, however, that it
would not be surprising if Gorbachev gave up his Party post at some
time in the future. I doubted he would do so, however, until he felt that
he could lead the country effectively from a different position. I was confident he would not voluntarily abandon leadership of the country and
doubted that his opponents could remove him at that time.

When Gorbachev opened the Central Committee plenum a week
later, *New York Times* correspondent Bill Keller called attention to
Gorbachev's skill at political prestidigitation in an apt simile:

> Now Mr. Gorbachev, the Houdini of politicians, is back on the
> stage, ready for his next act. He has slipped out of those two perilously
> tight spots [Lithuania and Azerbaijan] and again confounded the
> credulous spectators who believe, each time the master is wrapped in
> chains and dropped into the river, that they are witnessing his final
> stunt.[13]

The Party's Monopoly Ends

THE DECEMBER 1989 SESSION of the Congress of People's Deputies
had refused even to debate a proposal by reformers to amend Article VI
of the Constitution, which provided the legal basis for the Communist
Party's monopoly of power in the country. This was the issue being debated on the day Gorbachev insulted Andrei Sakharov in refusing him
the floor. I wondered at the time why Gorbachev had rejected the proposal so categorically. When I discussed the question with persons close
to him, such as Alexander Yakovlev, I got explanations like "The time is
not yet right" or "In practice, we already have a multiparty system: just
look at the Baltic."

I learned only later that Gorbachev, Yakovlev, and Shevardnadze had tried in 1989 to gain Politburo support for dropping the Party's legal monopoly of power and had failed. Gorbachev's harsh treatment of Sakharov and the other reformers at the December Congress of People's Deputies may have stemmed from his frustration at having to defend a position against his better judgment. He probably knew those demanding an end to the Party's monopoly of power were right but resented their putting him on the spot publicly when he was bound by Party discipline to reject the proposal.

Hardly a month had passed after that sharp debate when indications appeared that Gorbachev's position might be changing. During his trip to Lithuania, when he was asked about Article VI, he hinted that he would no longer defend it, saying "I see no tragedy in a multiparty system . . . if it arises as a result of a normal historical process and answers the needs of society."[14] Political observers in Moscow interpreted this statement as a trial balloon; sentiment in favor of ending the Party's power monopoly was clearly building.

A few days before the February plenum convened, I called on Ivan Laptev, the editor of the government newspaper *Izvestiya.* Laptev's views were very close to Gorbachev's, but he was in a position to discuss them more frankly than government officials. A question would always evoke a detailed answer in rapid, clipped Russian that required my utmost concentration to avoid missing an important phrase. I had learned that careful attention to what he said was worth it; his judgments and predictions were usually remarkably accurate.

When I asked about Article VI, he said that it would be eliminated at the next session of the Congress. He was a strong supporter of establishing the rule of law and understood that this could not occur unless the Communist Party was deprived of its power to overrule the normal branches of government. As he put it, the "fourth branch of government," which was accustomed to dominating the other three, had to be converted into "a normal political party."

Laptev also said he favored creation of a presidential system, which would allow Gorbachev to become more independent of the Communist Party and to break the Party's administrative grip on the country. Others had been arguing in favor of a presidency—among them Fyodor Burlatsky, the former Khrushchev speechwriter who now edited *Literaturnaya gazeta,* a weekly newspaper very influential among intellectuals—but Gorbachev had rejected the idea as recently as the fall of 1989, commenting that it would concentrate too much power in the hands of one individual.

Gorbachev, in fact, waited until the Central Committee convened on February 5 to show his hand. The formal reason for the plenary session was to set a date for the next Party congress and to approve a draft Party program for the congress to consider. Only the congress had the authority to change the Party's structure, and Gorbachev had been impatient to convene one to carry through the changes he had in mind. The 1988 Party conference had produced some radical-sounding resolutions and some personnel changes but had not altered the Party's organization or mission. Party rules required a congress each five years but did not prohibit more frequent sessions. Nevertheless, the "conservatives" were aware that they were likely to lose at the next congress, so they had opposed convening one before it was required, that is, in February or March 1991.

Gorbachev overcame this opposition when, in December 1989, he secured a Central Committee resolution to advance the congress by six months. Now it was time to determine what the congress would consider. Key issues included whether the Party should relinquish its formal monopoly on power (Article VI), whether its "governing organs" should be reorganized and streamlined, whether a federal structure would be allowed, and whether a presidential system should be introduced in the state structure. The fundamental question for economic reform was that of private property: Should individuals be allowed to own land and productive assets such as stores and factories?

When Gorbachev gave the opening address at the plenum, he stressed the need for "revolutionary change" in the Party itself and formally proposed that the Party abandon its monopoly of power. As he put it, "In a society that is renewing itself, the Party can exist and fulfill its vanguard role only as a democratically recognized force. This means that its position should not be established by constitutional provisions."[15] He did not dwell on a companion proposal to establish a presidential system of government, but it was spelled out in the fine print of the draft Party program distributed to delegates. Once again, Gorbachev had offered a major proposal suddenly, without extensive public discussion, hoping to force acceptance before opposition to it could be organized.

The tactic worked. After three days of bruising debate, the Central

Committee approved the proposals by an overwhelming vote. They were truly revolutionary. If implemented, these steps would create a supreme political authority totally independent of the Communist Party, and the Party itself would be able to stay in power only by winning elections.

It was clear to me why Gorbachev had made these proposals. Though he could not say so publicly, the Party apparatus had become the major impediment to perestroika—just as Yeltsin had been pointing out. Gorbachev had been forced to curb his reform efforts to avoid ouster by an unsympathetic Central Committee. The start of real elections and creation of a Congress of People's Deputies had given him some protection that had not been available to Nikita Khrushchev, but not much. If it chose, the Central Committee could force his removal as chief of state by recalling him from his seat in the Congress, since he was there as a representative of the Party. As a president elected for a fixed term, he would not be vulnerable to such machinations. The creation of a presidential system would also provide Gorbachev with an incentive to weaken the Communist Party while remaining its general secretary.

How, then, did Gorbachev persuade the Politburo and Central Committee to approve measures that would doom them?

First, as I have noted, he set the stage to make opposition to his specific proposals psychologically difficult. The tradition of always supporting the general secretary still had force, especially among "conservatives," who understood that if they were on the losing side of the debate it could be the end of their careers. General criticism of the current situation would be tolerated, but not overt opposition to Gorbachev's specific proposals.

Second, public opinion, particularly in Moscow, where the plenum was held, had swung strongly in favor of radical reform, as evidenced by the large demonstration on February 4. Memories of Bucharest in December were still fresh in the minds of the senior apparatchiks who made up the Central Committee.

Third, Gorbachev was careful to compromise and to grant the Party "conservatives" some of the things they felt most strongly about: He continued his strong line against "separatism" in the republics and continued to support a centralized Party structure. He did not support legalization of factions in the Party. He continued to defend "socialism"—albeit redefined—and rejected the right to hold private property in land.

These compromises were eventually to cripple perestroika, but Gorbachev either did not understand that in January 1990 or felt that creation of a presidency and revision of the Constitution to permit a multiparty political system took precedence over the others. Until he could insulate his own position from the danger of removal by a hostile cabal in the Party's upper reaches, he could not press ahead on all fronts.

In fact, the debate at the February plenum was sharp and wide ranging. Speaker after speaker noted the crisis in the country and in the Party itself. There was an undercurrent in most speeches suggesting that the country needed stronger leadership to restore discipline, and even though the remarks were directed at Gorbachev, they made it difficult to reject his proposal for a presidency. Gorbachev was saying implicitly, "All right, you want a stronger hand at the helm. Here's your chance for one."

Ligachev doubtless spoke for many participants when he charged the Politburo and government with committing "serious omissions and mistakes" in carrying out perestroika. He opposed turning the Communist Party "into an amorphous organization, a political club" and lashed out at attempts to legalize private property. He also spoke with alarm at the movement toward German reunification and compared the "revision of post–World War II borders" to the appeasement of Hitler in Munich in 1938. Gorbachev had not yet come to terms with West German Chancellor Kohl on the conditions for German unification, and Ligachev was putting him on public notice that compromise on this issue would carry a heavy political price at home.[16] Nevertheless, Ligachev did not oppose the amendment of Article VI or establishment of a presidency, apparently because prior agreement on these points had been reached in the Politburo.

Yeltsin, on the other hand, was not bound by Politburo discipline and used the occasion to present a ten-point program for reform of the Communist Party—essentially a summary of the Democratic Platform. He called for the elimination of the principle of "democratic centralism" (which had become centralism without democracy), secret balloting in contested elections for all Party offices, elimination of professional Party officials and of the *nomenklatura* system, introduction of the right to form factions, grassroots control over Party expenditures, and adoption of a voluntary, federal structure for the Party.[17]

When most of his proposals were not accepted, he cast the lone vote against the proposed Party platform.

———

Lithuania was another piece of unfinished business. The December 25 Central Committee plenum had postponed a decision on the status of the breakaway Lithuanian Communist Party until Gorbachev could visit the country in January. Now the issue could no longer be postponed, and there was a replay of the exchanges that had marked the December session. Both sides held to their previous positions, with Gorbachev continuing to insist on a unitary Party structure and Brazauskas, the leader of the schismatics, refusing to reverse the withdrawal from the Communist Party of the Soviet Union voted by his Party's congress in Vilnius the previous December.

Following all the bombast that had occurred on this issue, the resolution approved by the plenum seemed mild. It condemned the majority of Lithuanian Communists for withdrawing from the All-Union Party and recognized the small minority of Lithuanian Communists who remained faithful to Moscow, thereby placing them in control of the extensive Party properties in Lithuania. At the same time, it invited the breakaway faction to return to the CPSU and to send delegates to the upcoming Party congress in Moscow.

"Democrats" Defect

I HAD NO MEANS of gauging the opposition to change in the Party, but I understood that it was massive. Therefore, I marveled at Gorbachev's feat in securing formal approval for steps that might free him from the deadweight of Party conservatism. If his ultimate intentions were what I thought they were, I was not inclined to second-guess his tactics. The domestic reformers, however, were not so charitable. They were appalled by Gorbachev's compromises on democracy within the Party, which they saw as giving Party conservatives the upper hand in selecting delegates for the upcoming Party congress. And while they were willing to support the idea of a presidential system in principle, they balked at Gorbachev's attempt to force approval with minimal discussion.

Just after the Central Committee plenum, two hundred members of the Moscow Party Club for Perestroika (essentially Moscow-based members of the Democratic Platform) met and issued a statement that the draft platform approved by the Central Committee was "muddled, contradictory, and totally inconsistent with existing desires and demands." It said that the plenum had raised but not resolved the question of the multiparty system and criticized its failing to abolish the principle of democratic centralism, and its voting in favor of a presidential system, "which under current conditions could take on an antidemocratic character."

The latter charge, clearly directed at Gorbachev personally, was just the sort of talk to arouse Gorbachev's hostility, and not without reason. Gorbachev, after all, as general secretary of the pre-perestroika Communist Party, enjoyed power unbounded by any constitutional or legal limits. He was now moving to break the Party's stranglehold on the country and to create a position of limited power independent of the Communist Party—a revolutionary change, without which all reform attempts would fail. And yet these reform "theorists" (as he would have put it) were proposing a lengthy debate on details that would give Party conservatives time to organize and block any real change.

Those hostile to reform had better insight into Gorbachev's psychology than the reformers did. KGB Chairman Kryuchkov exploited Gorbachev's sensitivity to personal criticism by highlighting critical remarks made at public rallies by the "democrats" or even distorting noncritical remarks to make them seem hostile.[18] For example, the large public demonstration on February 4 assisted Gorbachev in securing Central Committee approval to amend Article VI and establish a presidential system, but he came to regard it as hostile because the reports he received stressed critical remarks a few participants had made and misinterpreted Yuri Afanasiev's slogan, "Long Live the Peaceful February Revolution of 1990," as anti-Gorbachev. In fact, the demonstration had been largely pro-Gorbachev, but Kryuchkov's distorted reports left a different impression.

When the same organizers called for another, even more massive demonstration in Moscow on Sunday, February 25, Gorbachev panicked. Maybe it was the date: February 25 (on the old calendar) had been the day the tsar was overthrown in 1917, and Russians love historic anniversaries. Maybe it was the disinformation about the previous demonstration. Maybe it was false reports that the organizers planned to storm the Kremlin, which Kryuchkov peddled assiduously. Probably it was all of this, plus the irritation caused by Gorbachev's plans for a presidential system being questioned.

Whatever it was, instead of allowing the demonstration to go forward and using it as an argument for reform, Gorbachev tried to block it. Rumors were spread that violence was planned, and people were warned to stay away. The Supreme Soviet approved a statement that insisted that only authorized demonstrations in authorized locations be allowed. Prime Minister Ryzhkov went on television to urge citizens to stay home. Finally the demonstrators were allowed to assemble in Gorky Park and to march down Moscow's wide Garden Ring to a square in front of the Foreign Ministry, but troops were brought into the city to reinforce a police cordon to prevent the demonstrators from moving into the center of the city toward the Kremlin.

I normally stayed away from political demonstrations since it would not have been proper for a foreign diplomat to be seen supporting particular political factions, and I was too well known not to be noticed. Nevertheless, this demonstration was scheduled to pass just a couple of blocks from our residence, and Rebecca and I walked over to watch it from the sidelines, just to get a feel of it. We found that the official alarums and precautions were unnecessary. All was peaceful, and the atmosphere was rather like that of a holiday celebration. A hundred thousand or so demonstrators gathered in Gorky Park and moved peacefully down the Garden Ring to Smolensk Square, where a podium had been erected for speeches. No one tried to move into the center of town, much less storm the Kremlin. Nor were the speeches particularly revolutionary: they simply called for the same things the reformers in the Interregional Group and Democratic Platform had been seeking for months. One huge banner caught my attention. It read "Seventy-two Years on the Road to Nowhere." This was not much different from what Gorbachev had been implying of late.

Nevertheless, the official reaction to the plans for this demonstration embittered the democratic movement. Was Gorbachev's understanding of democracy so shallow that he would use force to block freedom of speech and assembly? Ordering troops into Moscow to prevent an attack on the Kremlin that had never been planned suggested at the very least faulty judgment, and who could welcome a strong executive president who had shown such irrational suspicion? Opposition to Gorbachev's plans for the presidency grew.

Two days after the demonstration, when the proposal to establish a presidential system of government was finally presented to the Supreme Soviet, many members of the Interregional Group criticized it as flawed. Most agreed that a presidential system should be established eventually but felt that the enabling legislation had been put together too hurriedly and gave too much authority to the president.

The criticism was led by Sergei Stankevich, who characterized the proposal as defining an "imperial presidency" since the legislation would allow the president to make decisions affecting the union republics without consulting those republics. He therefore recommended that further work be done on the draft before it was adopted.[19] Anatoly Sobchak echoed Stankevich's strictures and added some of his own, then proposed that Gorbachev be given temporary special powers as chairman of the USSR Supreme Soviet while the legislation for the presidency was revised to provide a more precise and limited definition of presidential power.[20]

I watched the proceedings on television that evening and noted that Gorbachev's face showed growing annoyance as speaker after speaker rose to find some fault in the draft he had presented. Just before he put it to a vote, Gorbachev took the floor to defend the proposal. His face was drawn with fatigue, and his remarks were more defensive and emotional than necessary. After all, he must have known that he had the requisite votes, and there seemed no need for him to do more than say that the suggestions offered would be given due consideration before the Congress of People's Deputies met to amend the Constitution.

His disjointed remarks, filled with innuendo and uncompleted sentences, reminded me more of an outburst during a lovers' quarrel than of a political debate. He accused the critics of "cheap demagoguery" and of trying to delay, and thus "bury," his proposal. He was wounded by the implication that he, of all people, was seeking excessive power. "What has this got to do with Gorbachev?" he asked rhetorically and illogically, as if nobody had any idea who would be "elected" president.[21]

It was not a convincing performance, but what Gorbachev said was not relevant to the outcome. The Supreme Soviet voted overwhelmingly to convene an extraordinary Congress of People's Deputies on March 12 and to accept the draft legislation to create a presidential system of government as the basis for a constitutional amendment.

Unlike many of his colleagues in the Democratic Movement, Boris Yeltsin voted in favor of Gorbachev's proposal. Was he trying to ingratiate himself with Gorbachev, or did he simply wish to have the office created so he could eventually occupy it himself? Only he knows for sure, but at the time he still said privately that he wanted nothing more than to be on Gorbachev's team.

Lithuania Spoils the Party

LITHUANIA DID NOT manage to arrange republic elections before the
end of 1989, as my Sąjūdis callers had hoped in July, but they were held
on February 25, 1990, somewhat earlier than the elections in most other
republics. As anticipated, Sąjūdis won an overwhelming majority. Runoff elections were conducted on March 4 and 8, and the first session of
the new Lithuanian Supreme Council (Lithuanians preferred not to use
the term "soviet" in Western languages) was scheduled for March 10.

Events seemed to be moving along the lines the Lithuanians had explained to me. More than two thirds of the members of their new parliament had been elected on an independence platform. One could assume
that one of their earliest acts would be to adopt a formal declaration of
independence, but it was not clear precisely when this might occur.

Shortly after the Lithuanian election we received a request for a meeting with Sąjūdis leaders on March 7, a day when they planned to be in
Moscow. The purpose of the call was to describe the situation in Lithuania following the election. I invited them to come to Spaso House at
eleven o'clock.

When I woke that day my head was throbbing and I had a fever; it
appeared to be the onset of a "twenty-four-hour flu" common in Moscow that time of the year. Its severity was usually matched by its brevity.
I wondered if I should not stay in for the day and try to head off the
illness with rest. But before I had a chance to check with our doctor,
word came from my office that Shevardnadze had asked to see me privately on an urgent matter at ten o'clock. The Foreign Ministry was
only three short blocks from Spaso House and I often walked over for
appointments, but this time I bundled up and took my car.

Normally when I met with Shevardnadze, there were at least two
other people in the room, each of us having a note taker to make a record of the matters discussed. Often there were more, since he frequently
invited a deputy or specialists in the topics to be discussed to join us.
This time, however, there were just the two of us.

He greeted me cordially but with a serious expression, apologized for
summoning me on such short notice, and offered me my usual seat, on a
couch next to his armchair. An assistant entered, put a cup of tea with
milk at his place and one of black coffee at mine, and left. My visits were

frequent enough that she knew my preference. Shevardnadze took a sheet with handwritten notes from a folder and laid them on a table before him. I noticed that they were written in his native Georgian, not in Russian. He had obviously prepared them himself.

He turned to me with a grave expression and said that he wished to convey a very important message. He wanted us to understand that the coming weekend, March 10 to 12, would be "decisive" for the future of the Soviet Union. It was Gorbachev's plan to establish a presidential system and a federation of sovereign states, but strong opposition had arisen. While the country's economic problems were serious, they were manageable. The nationality problems, in contrast, were much more difficult to solve.

He had already talked to us privately about the intractability of the nationality problems, so his opinion that these were more serious than the economic issues, which were still receiving more public attention, came as no surprise. I was also, of course, aware of Gorbachev's plans and knew that there was opposition to them. I was surprised, however, that Shevardnadze felt things were moving to a crisis as soon as the coming weekend. He proceeded to explain without my asking.

The internal situation, he said, had reached an explosive stage, particularly with the Soviet military. A misguided step could literally start a civil war, and bring a military dictatorship to power. The situation in Lithuania, he continued, was particularly delicate. If its new parliament should attempt to declare independence before the Congress of People's Deputies acted to establish a presidential system, a civil war could result. Without specifying precisely how a civil war might start, he pointed out that there were many defense plants and troops stationed in Lithuania, implying that the Soviet military might attempt to seize power there without Gorbachev's approval—or perhaps that they would even attempt to remove Gorbachev.

He was less concerned about the possibility of a declaration of independence following establishment of a presidential system in Moscow. If the Lithuanians waited until then, he observed, Gorbachev could deal with the situation without undue risk.

He then turned to the specific reason he had called me in. He said he understood that I had an appointment to meet with the Sąjūdis leaders. Of course, it was up to me to decide whom I talked to, but he felt it would be prudent to postpone the meeting until the following week to avoid any suspicion that the Lithuanians were acting on "instructions" from the United States should they proceed to declare independence during the weekend as they were threatening to do.

I glanced at my watch. It was nearly 10:30, and the Lithuanians were due at Spaso at 11:00. I doubted that postponing the meeting was the right thing to do, but even if it had been, it was too late. I could not notify my visitors that the appointment was changed before they got to my house, and to refuse to see them then would have been impossible to explain. My visitors would doubtless report it to the press, and many would conclude that U.S. policy toward the Baltic states had changed.

The meeting had to take place as planned, but I was not inclined to dismiss Shevardnadze's concerns; the situation might well be as delicate as he had described it. If so, there would be people who, without a shred of evidence, would assume that any contact between Lithuanians and the American Embassy meant that the United States was manipulating the situation to break up the Soviet Union. To such people, this would be a powerful argument in favor of putting down the Lithuanian and other Baltic independence movements by force.

I told Shevardnadze that I appreciated his candor and I would make sure my government understood his description of the situation. Although, as he was well aware, we had never recognized the forcible incorporation of the Baltic states into the Soviet Union, we had done nothing to encourage the Balts to take precipitate action. In fact, as he could confirm from his own sources (I had KGB listening devices in mind), I had consistently told the Balts that they should not expect U.S. recognition until they were actually independent, and furthermore that economic aid from the outside would be impossible if the Soviet government forbade it. Therefore, while we had given no advice and would give none, the explanations we gave of our policy amounted to a counsel of prudence.

So far as my meeting with the Sąjūdis leaders, I continued, it was scheduled to begin within minutes, and I did not see how it could be postponed. They would probably be at my residence when I returned, and if I refused to see them, it could become a public issue between our governments. However, I could assure him that I would say nothing to encourage hasty action on their part.

Shevardnadze's face fell when I explained that I could not postpone the meeting, but he did not protest. He simply asked if it could be kept as short as possible. I told him that I was feeling rotten and was not up to a long meeting, so he could be sure that I would not indulge in a lengthy discussion.

As my car approached the gate to Spaso House, the Lithuanians were entering. Vytautas Landsbergis, the chairman of Sąjūdis who seemed likely to be elected leader of Lithuania following its declaration of independence, led the group, which also included several others who were familiar faces at the residence, such as Romualdas Ozolas, Vaidotas Antanaitis, and Egidijus Bičkauskas.

I greeted them, explained that I was coming down with *grippe* and therefore could be with them only a short time but that they were welcome to continue the meeting with the embassy officers present after I left. Following Shevardnadze's request, I might have feigned illness, but I didn't need to: my head was pounding, I could sense the heat in my flushed cheeks, and my voice had begun to crack.

After putting them on notice that I would have to excuse myself soon, I observed (for the KGB listening devices as much as my visitors) that all of us must take particular care that this meeting and others like it not be misunderstood. We Americans would not be offering them advice about specific decisions or actions, and nothing we say should be construed as such. It was important to both our countries that they not seem to be acting at American behest. I added that political developments in the Soviet Union were moving at a rapid pace, which meant that all participants should act with the utmost care. Then I asked what was on their minds.

Landsbergis explained that they had come to inform us that the Lithuanian Supreme Council would convene over the weekend and would very likely declare independence. They had two questions: first, what the United States' reaction would be to the declaration of independence and, second, whether there was any understanding between the United States and Soviet Union regarding the nationalities question.

I replied that, as I had informed several in the group the previous summer, a declaration of independence would not evoke automatic recognition by the United States. The United States normally recognizes a specific government only when it is in effective control of its territory. A declaration of independence alone would not give them that control, and therefore they should not expect recognition.

As for their second question, I assured them that there was absolutely no U.S. "understanding" with the Soviet Union regarding nationalities. I explained that we sometimes discussed these problems, but only in the sense that we explain our respective policies to each other. We had constantly reiterated to the Soviet authorities our refusal to recognize the

Baltic states as part of the Soviet Union, and that policy had not changed.

Landsbergis observed that Lithuania got most of its oil from the Soviet Union and therefore would be vulnerable if the supply should be interrupted. Would the United States assist Lithuania if Moscow stopped oil deliveries? I answered that I did not see how the United States could help, since Moscow would control Lithuania's ports and airspace.

One of the guests raised the recognition question again: Why would the United States be unwilling to recognize a freely elected government of a country it still considered legally independent? I explained again that recognition of a specific government includes a determination that it controls the territory it claims. In addition, I added, it could be dangerous for the Lithuanians if the United States granted immediate recognition. Would our recognition not give the hard-liners an excuse to put them down by force? Only a few weeks earlier the Azerbaijani National Front had been removed from power by the Soviet army. Although the circumstances in Azerbaijan were quite different from those in Lithuania, the Soviet government had shown that it could restore its control of a republic by force if it decided to do so. If there should be military intervention in Lithuania, it would not be Americans who would pay the price.

After a pause, one of the group—I forget who—said he agreed. It would in fact be best if the United States delayed recognition, because the Soviet military would consider it a provocation and it could goad them into action. Landsbergis did not contradict him.

Before excusing myself, I asked why they were rushing to complete a declaration of independence that weekend. Landsbergis replied that the timing was crucial because they wanted it done before Gorbachev assumed the powers of the presidency. They were convinced that Gorbachev was seeking these extra powers in order to crush their independence movement.

I said that I was in no position to speak for Gorbachev, but they should know that this was not what Soviet officials were telling us. They were telling us that Gorbachev was determined not to use force but would consider a declaration of independence before Congress acted on the presidency as a provocative act that could lead to violence. I added that we could not vouch for this explanation but were unaware of any facts that would contradict it.

"We simply don't trust him," Landsbergis countered. "He wants the power so he can crush us!"

"Are you saying he doesn't have the power now to use force against you if he chose?" I inquired. Silence. "I don't see that the presidency is going to make it any easier for him to use force against you," I observed. Then I concluded by repeating that I was not attempting to give advice but they should know that my understanding of the situation was not the same as theirs.

After I had been with the group for about fifteen minutes, feeling worse and worse all the time, I excused myself, invited them to stay and continue their discussion with my colleagues, and retired to my upstairs study. Before taking the medicine the doctor had sent over, I dashed off reports summarizing the events of the morning and sent them to the embassy for transmission to Washington. Then I tried to get some rest, since I needed to recover before what promised to be a busy weekend.

By evening I was feeling better and was able to participate in a seminar we had organized for U.S. and Soviet scholars to discuss Dostoyevsky's meaning in the modern world. The discussion was lively and thought provoking—a Moscow literary journal subsequently published a transcript—but I had difficulty concentrating on the subject at hand. Shevardnadze's warning of the imminent possibility of a military coup d'état was sufficiently plausible to put me on edge. I had the feeling that the Lithuanians were not fully aware of the risk they were running, and I could not understand why they thought it was important to declare independence before Gorbachev became Soviet president. If he was determined to crush them, he would do so without regard for the timing of their declaration.

The idea that Gorbachev was seeking the presidency just so he could put the Lithuanians down did not make sense to me. It seemed much more likely that he saw the presidency as a means of freeing himself from Party tutelage and of gaining better control over the forces that were clamoring for a crackdown on the Baltic states. If so, the Balts should welcome the step rather than trying to preempt it. But this was only my opinion, and without some proof that I could cite, it was unlikely to sway our Baltic friends.

Just as the seminar ended and the guests dispersed, a call came in from Washington. It was my old friend Stapleton Roy, who was then executive secretary of the State Department (and subsequently became ambassador to China). He wanted to let me know that my messages were receiving the president's direct attention and that I would probably receive further instructions by morning.

His prediction was, as usual, accurate. He called again at 7:15 the next morning (11:15 at night in Washington) to let me know that I should seek an appointment with Shevardnadze to discuss the situation further. Although March 8 was a Soviet holiday and offices were officially closed, the Foreign Ministry's duty officer informed us that Shevardnadze would be pleased to see me later in the day. Subsequently, I was invited to come at 6:00 P.M.

My flu had passed and I was feeling almost normal, so I walked over to the ministry. There was no need to encourage speculation about why the American ambassador should be meeting with the Soviet foreign minister on a holiday, which might have happened if my official car with its American flag had been spotted in front of the ministry.

After a short delay, Shevardnadze received me. He was alone as he had been the day before. I told him that the president and secretary of state had taken careful note of his message the day before and would do nothing to add tension to the situation he had described. I then summarized for him what I had told the Lithuanians the day before. Although I assumed that he could obtain a transcript from the KGB if he wished, I was beginning to suspect that KGB reports were not always accurate and thought it would be a good idea if he and Gorbachev had a description of the meeting directly from me. It had, after all, not been a confidential one.

Shevardnadze heard me out, and though he did not express approval, he seemed satisfied with the way the meeting had gone. I told him that Landsbergis and colleagues seemed determined to proceed with their declaration over the coming weekend and I was not sure anyone could dissuade them. However, a thought had occurred to me that might be worth considering, if the situation was as desperate as he had described it.

It was clear to me, I said, that the primary reason for the Lithuanians' haste in declaring independence was their distrust of Gorbachev's motives in seeking a presidential system. I had questioned their judgment on this point but was not in a position to tell them that they were wrong. They might conceivably be willing to delay the declaration for a week or so if they could be convinced that Gorbachev would not use his position as president to move against them forcibly. It would not be easy to convince them, and there was little time left to do so, but I would be willing to recommend to President Bush that we privately urge Landsbergis and his colleagues to hold off a week or so, provided Gorbachev gave us his personal assurance that he would negotiate the terms of Lithuanian independence in good faith shortly after he became president. I added that there could be no assurance in advance, of course, that Landsbergis would agree. His suspicion was deep, and given some of Gorbachev's recent statements and actions, I could understand why it was. Nevertheless, I could think of nothing else that had any prospect of persuading the Lithuanians to wait.

Shevardnadze said the idea was an interesting one but raised a number of delicate issues. He could not approve it without checking with Gorbachev.

I told him that I fully understood the delicacy. To be persuasive, we would need to tell Landsbergis that we had a commitment from Gorbachev, and yet if it were known that he had made such a commitment, that could be used against him by his Soviet opponents. Therefore, I would understand if he was not interested. I just wanted to make the point that if it was as important as he had suggested that the declaration not take place until after the decision on the USSR presidency, it might be worth the risk.

He said he appreciated the offer and would check on it but that we should do nothing more unless he gave us a "go-ahead." I assured him I would be home over the long weekend and could be reached at any time by telephone.

I had the feeling he was less worried than he had been the day before and was therefore shocked when he looked me in the eye as he rose to accompany me to the door and said, "Jack, I'll tell you one thing. If I see a dictatorship coming, I'm going to resign. I'll not be part of a government with blood on its hands."

I stumbled out of his office, unbalanced by the sudden realization that at least one Politburo member thought that a reversion to dictatorship might be imminent. His words later came to mind when he surprised the world with his resignation speech in December.

No call came from Shevardnadze over the weekend, and matters proceeded in Vilnius just as Landsbergis had told me they would. In the wee hours of Sunday, March 11, exactly five years after Gorbachev had been elected general secretary of the Communist Party of the Soviet Union, the Lithuanian Supreme Council voted 124 to 0, with six abstentions, to declare the restoration of Lithuania's status as a democratic independent republic. The parliament established the name of the country as the "Lithuanian Republic" instead of the previous "Lithuanian Soviet Socialist Republic" and elected Professor of Musicology Vytautas Landsbergis its chairman and the country's chief of state.

The vote for chairman was by secret ballot, and Landsbergis received 92 votes. Algirdas Brazauskas, the chairman of the Lithuanian Communist Party, which had broken with Moscow, received 31. While the vote was not close, it showed that Brazauskas's gamble had worked: he and his Party had survived as a political force in Lithuania, though not the dominant one at this time. If he had followed Gorbachev's advice or yielded to his pressure, he would have been out of play in the political process that was unfolding in Lithuania. A few days later, when Kazimiera Prunskienė was named prime minister of Lithuania, Brazauskas was elected her first deputy.

XIII

—◆—

The Unelected President

*The law on the presidency should be introduced only if and when it is incorporated
into an integral, unified, organic text of a new democratic constitution. Outside such
an integral constitutional context, presidential power is dangerously unpredictable.*
YURI AFANASIEV to the Congress of People's Deputies, March 12, 1990[1]

*The presidential powers will be used by me for a truly decisive advancement
of all the processes of perestroika on a democratic basis.*
MIKHAIL GORBACHEV upon accepting the office of president, March 15, 1990[2]

From the time of the Central Committee's approval in principle, it
had been clear that Gorbachev would secure the constitutional
amendments to establish an executive presidency, provided he moved
fast enough to preempt attempts to organize opposition to the concept.
The lopsided vote in the Supreme Soviet in favor of a presidential system
demonstrated his control of that body—at least as long as he had formal
Central Committee approval of his approach. The vote at the Supreme
Soviet to convene an extraordinary session of the Congress of People's
Deputies, which alone had the power to amend the Constitution, was an
equally essential victory in his game plan.

The Third Congress convened in the Kremlin Palace of Congresses
on March 12, 1990, some two weeks after the Supreme Soviet decision
and the day following Lithuania's declaration of independence. I attended as an observer since the session promised to provide a historic
landmark, even if its outcome was predictable. In fact, I witnessed more
verbal fireworks than I had anticipated.

Reformers in Opposition

SPEAKING FOR THE Interregional Group of Deputies, historian Yuri Afanasiev called the "hasty attempt" to introduce the presidency "a gross and very serious political mistake" and demanded that consideration of a presidential system of government be delayed until a new union treaty had been concluded, a new legislature elected, and a multiparty system established. In addition, he insisted that the new Soviet president be elected by popular vote and not be allowed to occupy a high position in a political party at the same time. He rejected Gorbachev's claim that the country's problems had arisen because of weak executive authority and attributed them instead to Gorbachev's "erratic and dangerous" leadership, which had sapped public confidence. When he went on to call for rejection of "the outlived Communist idea" and to speak of Stalin's crimes and Brezhnev's corruption, implying that a presidential system would allow a repetition, he was informed that his time had run out. He requested an extra minute, but Gorbachev, who was presiding, refused it, and he was forced to leave the platform.

I had expected Afanasiev and other members of the Interregional Group to appeal for further discussion before establishing a presidential system, and their five conditions were not unexpected since they had discussed them at length in public. Afanasiev's intemperate personal attack on Gorbachev did surprise me, however, and I realized that Gorbachev's *ad hominem* criticism of the democratic reformers and his open hostility to the February 25 demonstration had created a degree of hostility that would be difficult to bridge. A few weeks earlier, the leaders of the Interregional Group (save perhaps Yeltsin) had still been willing to concede Gorbachev's good intentions, but now they seemed to be as estranged as Landsbergis, suspecting that Gorbachev sought additional power only to be able to move against them.

I deplored this split. I felt that Afanasiev and his fellow "democrats" were correct in principle but misguided in their tactics. Eventually, if the Soviet Union was ever to be a democracy, their five conditions would have to be met, but to demand that they be met before Gorbachev was permitted to establish his power independent of the Communist Party seemed to me self-defeating. To arrive at a democratic system, the Party's stranglehold on the political process had to be broken. There was no practical way to do this except by establishing a presidency or the same thing with a different name.

Gorbachev's plan included amending Article VI of the Constitution to eliminate references to the "leading role" of the Communist Party and to permit a multiparty political system. This *was*, in my view, an essential prerequisite to an executive presidency, and Gorbachev's success in securing Central Committee approval for it had to be considered a major achievement. However, Afanasiev and the democratic reformers seemed to give him no credit for achieving what had been their principal goal only a few weeks before.

If Gorbachev had taken their advice on all five points, it is most unlikely that he could have established a position for political leadership outside the Communist Party, particularly if he relinquished control of the Party while it was still able to block political change. Before he could bow out of Party leadership, he had to establish a system of governance outside the Party. A presidential system would provide a cover for doing so, and it seemed to me that his goal at the upcoming Party congress would be to restructure the Party so that it could not in the future rule the country directly by dominating the formal organs of government.

As I discussed these issues in private with Gorbachev's supporters as well as his critics, I sometimes wondered if I was being gullible and naïve. Gorbachev is a man of great personal charm—at least when he deals with foreigners—and he knows how to choose arguments that will appeal to a visitor. We were developing a personal relationship of increasing confidence, and this was certain to influence my attitude. I recalled that one of my most distinguished predecessors as ambassador to the Soviet Union, Lewellyn Thompson, had been so influenced by his relationship with Khrushchev that he had ignored the signs that Khrushchev's position was weakening and that he might be removed by his colleagues.

In fact, as a junior officer at the Moscow embassy in 1963 I had felt the brunt of Thompson's displeasure for reporting that a faction, most likely led by Brezhnev, was preparing to push Khrushchev aside. From his position as the senior adviser on Soviet affairs in the State Department, Thompson had dispatched the Soviet desk officer to Moscow with the message that we should cease indulging in "speculative Kremlinology" that might undermine Washington's confidence in Khrushchev's political durability. In October 1964, what we had described as a possibility became a reality when a faction led by Leonid Brezhnev removed Nikita Khrushchev from power.

My experience from the early 1960s reminded me of the danger of allowing personal likes and dislikes to influence judgment. I would periodically recount my earlier experience to my staff and ask them to set me straight if they detected a similar tendency on my part.

As I analyzed the situation, it was obvious to me that I had more confidence in Gorbachev's intentions than some of his own people did, people, furthermore, who were well informed and whose judgment I respected. I considered this a warning for me to rethink the reasons for my conclusions. I did, but however often I reviewed recent events I could rationally come only to the conclusion that Gorbachev was seeking the presidency to do what he had stated—speed up perestroika—as well as something he could not state—marginalize the Communist Party so that he could eventually dispense with it.

I did not base this conclusion primarily on his statements, public or private. I knew he could dissimulate when it suited him. But I based my conclusion on his actions and an analysis of the choices he was facing. Both his record, flawed and inconsistent as it was in some respects, and the logic of his position argued that he was serious about reform.

Unquestionably, he loved power. Unquestionably, he shuddered at the thought of losing it. Unquestionably, he had been too thin skinned in dealing with critics and had unwisely treated friendly criticism as betrayal. Nevertheless, his actions made no logical sense if his object was simply to enhance his own personal power. Why would he seek the presidency for the purpose of putting down the Lithuanians or turning on the reformers? If those were his primary aims, he could achieve them much more easily and more surely by using the existing Party, police, and military machinery. If power had been his sole or primary goal, he could have exercised it much more effectively without changing the system he had inherited. In attempting to reform the country, he was running a risk, and the only rational reason I could find to justify that risk was the goal he had set: a state based on the rule of law.

Furthermore, I did not see what the reformers had to lose by giving Gorbachev, for the time being at least, the benefit of the doubt. Though the initial legislation for a presidential system did not contain all the checks and balances necessary for a fully functioning democracy, it did provide some limits on executive authority, a clear advance over the existing system, which had none at all.

Most of all, I thought the reformers should have recognized that timing was critically important if Gorbachev was to have any hope of breaking the authority of the Party apparatus. The presidential system would not in itself do this, but no other course had been suggested that had any hope of success.

In short, I thought the reformers would have been wise to support the rapid introduction of a presidential system as an immediate step, while stating that, to be acceptable in the long run, certain further conditions would have to be met in the new constitution. As for Gorbachev's intentions, they could best be judged after the upcoming Party congress. If he did not use the Congress to undermine the conservative Party apparatus, he would deserve more forthright opposition, but premature opposition would only weaken his hand in dealing with those who wanted to block real change.

Avoiding a Direct Election

FOR THESE REASONS, I was distressed to observe the growing personal invective between the "democrats" and Gorbachev. If it continued, it would weaken both sides. However, one of the five conditions Afanasiev set forth seemed to me to make sense: the idea that the president should be elected by a direct vote.

Obviously, if the new president received a direct popular mandate, he would enjoy greater political authority than if he was chosen by the Congress of People's Deputies. It was clear that Gorbachev would need all the authority he could muster if he was to achieve the sort of reforms he sought. Nevertheless, the draft legislation presented to the Congress provided for an initial election by the Congress of People's Deputies for a five-year term, after which the president would be elected by popular vote.

Gorbachev's popularity was still extensive, particularly compared with other politicians', and the polls indicated that he could probably win a majority of the votes cast if an election were held soon. I wondered why he did not take advantage of this rather than avoiding an electoral test and thus weakening his mandate.

During the weeks preceding the Congress, I discussed this question with many Soviet politicians and journalists. Those hostile to Gorbachev felt that he was avoiding a direct election simply because he wanted to exclude the possibility of losing. Those who supported him pointed out that an election would be time consuming and distracting and time was of the essence if Gorbachev was to keep perestroika on track.

Nevertheless, the advantages of a popular mandate seemed so clear that I found the latter argument unconvincing. I began to get a clearer idea of why Gorbachev shied away from an electoral campaign in 1990, however, when the draft legislation was finally published. According to the draft, presidential elections would be decided by a majority vote *in a majority of the republics.* This provision was obviously designed to avoid Russian domination of the selection of a president. If a president could be elected by a majority of all votes cast, ethnic Russians could elect a president who did not receive majority support in any other republic. The non-Russian republics would not accept a constitution that made this possible.

The requirement of winning a majority of the republics in the Soviet Union must have seemed difficult to Gorbachev and his political advisers. Of the fifteen republics, seven (the three Baltics, the three in Transcaucasia, and Moldova) were already seriously estranged, and it would have been exceedingly difficult for Gorbachev to win any of them. That meant that he would have to win *all* the others, and a campaign would offer the temptation for each to escalate demands for autonomy as the price of its support.

Whatever his reasons, Gorbachev chose the easy course and proposed that the president initially be selected by the Congress of People's Deputies. Boris Yeltsin, who had voted in favor of establishing a presidential system in the Supreme Soviet in February, announced that he could only support a president who had been elected by the people. On the eve of the Congress, he told the Italian daily *Corriere della Sera:* "Gorbachev wants to be elected by the Congress of People's Deputies and not by the people, and this is a method I do not approve and will oppose." He then added, "This could change the day on which the president is elected by universal suffrage, perhaps in four years or maybe even in one. If Gorbachev does not change course, his replacement will become necessary."[3]

Debate on the presidency continued for the rest of the day on March 12 and was resumed the following morning. After two hours, however, debate was closed and a vote taken. The motion to establish a presidency passed by 1,817 in favor, 133 opposed, and 61 abstaining.

The next item on the agenda was selecting the first president. In addition to Gorbachev, Prime Minister Ryzhkov and Interior Minister Vadim Bakatin were nominated. Both withdrew their names, so that Gorbachev was unopposed on the ballot.[4]

In contrast to the vote on the law to establish the presidency, which was by roll call, voting for president was by secret ballot. The magnitude of opposition to Gorbachev, when the deputies voted in secret, was striking. He won by 1,320 to 495, but 313 deputies either did not vote or cast invalid ballots, which meant that Gorbachev received the votes of fewer than 60 percent of the deputies.

The number of "no" votes and abstentions was only one of several clouds on the horizon. Though the country was in for some stormy weather ahead, the overwhelming fact was that, in the period of just a few weeks from the time Gorbachev had first spoken publicly of the possibility, the constitutional structure of the Soviet empire had been altered fundamentally. The Communist Party no longer had a legal mandate for exclusive rule, and a structure of state and government had been prescribed that had no formal links to the previously omnipotent Party organs. The change was potentially revolutionary, but implementation was still a matter for the future.

The Lithuanian Challenge

LITHUANIA'S DECLARATION of independence did not bring on the coup d'état that Shevardnadze had feared, but it definitely put a strain on the Third Congress of People's Deputies, which Gorbachev had obviously hoped would resemble a coronation ceremony.

From the morning of the second day, delegates began demanding a discussion of the situation in Lithuania. Vaidotas Antanaitis had been sent from Vilnius to convey a message to the Congress from the Lithuanian parliament. He noted that the Lithuanian deputies were there as observers, not participants, announced that the Lithuanian Supreme Council had voted to restore Lithuania's independence, and appealed to the Congress to facilitate negotiations between Lithuania and the Soviet authorities.

Although the Estonians had not yet made a formal declaration of independence, their representatives in the Congress presented Gorbachev with a formal request for negotiations on Estonian independence and announced that they would not take part in the vote for president since that could affect the status of the republic.

Responding to the appeals for negotiation, Gorbachev stated categorically to the assembly that "there can be no question of any negotiations with Lithuania, or with Estonia or Latvia." Before the

Third Congress ended, it approved a resolution that invalidated the act of the Lithuanian Supreme Council restoring independence and instructed the USSR president, Supreme Court, and Council of Ministers to ensure the legal rights of all Soviet citizens in Lithuania and the union's property rights there.[5]

Landsbergis stood his ground with a letter to Gorbachev rejecting the Congress's resolution. In an uncharacteristic attempt to soften the blow, he said publicly, "We do not expect that tomorrow the Soviet Union will accept Lithuania's position, and they should not expect us to change our position." But then he added the bitter comment "The Third Congress . . . has proclaimed the right of an aggressor to govern its victims."[6]

That weekend, competing rallies were held in Vilnius and other Lithuanian cities. Russian residents were mobilized to demonstrate against the independence declaration, even as Lithuanians were celebrating it. The demonstrations were remarkably orderly, but this was not the impression the Soviet public got from Central Television.

I was traveling in Central Asia that weekend and made a point of watching the television news from Moscow. Previously, coverage of Baltic events, though biased against Baltic nationalists, had occasionally carried objective accounts of their activities and demands. An attentive viewer could obtain enough information to discount the bias and form a reasonably accurate picture of events. Now this had changed. Orders had obviously gone out in Moscow to carry only Moscow's view of events.

I was shocked by the distortions and vilification of the elected Baltic leaders. Only the demonstrations against independence were covered in detail, and the camera exaggerated their size. Viewers were fed fiery speeches by recent Russian immigrants accusing the Lithuanian authorities of violating their most elemental human rights, even though they were unable to cite any persuasive evidence that this had happened. (Subsequently we learned that many of the demonstrators had been bussed in from outside Lithuania!) Then "talking heads" in studios would gravely assure their audience that the "extremists" who had declared independence represented only a small minority of the Lithuanian people and in fact were spiritual descendents of the fascists who had collaborated with Hitler. Shocked by this display of old-style Soviet slander, I realized that the achievements of glasnost were quickly reversible in the electronic media, which were still under tighter central control than the press was.

The following week both Ryzhkov and Gorbachev issued decrees that ordered Lithuanians to turn in all firearms, law enforcement agencies to "ensure the rights and legitimate interests of Soviet citizens in Lithuania," border guards to "strengthen protection" of Lithuania's border, and security authorities to "end violations by foreign citizens."[7] If taken at face value, some of these orders seemed strange: there had been neither violent acts by Lithuanians nor evidence that possession of firearms was widespread (in contrast to the situation in the Transcaucasus); there was no evidence that the border was not still under the control of the Soviet authorities or that foreigners were entering without visas. The intent of the decrees was clearly provocative, to create pretexts for law enforcement authorities to search houses, take control of property, or expel foreigners. The Lithuanian government immediately declared the decrees invalid. The stage was set for legal skirmishes that could escalate into physical clashes if either side tried to enforce its claims.

In fact, the Soviet military forces in Lithuania began to flex their muscles by increasing the number of their flights and ground exercises. Prime Minister Prunskienė sent a message to Ryzhkov on March 21, complaining about this pattern of activity and pointing out that the status of the Soviet forces in Lithuania had not yet been determined.

By March 22, the threats from Moscow seemed so serious in Vilnius that the Lithuanian parliament issued an "Appeal to the Nations of the World." Noting that "it is becoming more apparent each day that another state is preparing to use armed force against the Lithuanian Republic," the legislators called on other nations "to bar, with their protests, the way to the possible use of aggression against Lithuania."[8]

On March 23, we received notice from the Soviet Ministry of Foreign Affairs that all diplomats in Lithuania should leave within twelve hours. Though we had no permanent office there, we had for weeks kept at least two diplomats on temporary duty in Vilnius to observe events. Simultaneously, journalists were "advised" that visits to Lithuania would "temporarily" not be approved. (Both diplomats and journalists were still subject to travel controls, though normally trips to the Baltic capitals were approved routinely.) The order expelling diplomats was so abrupt that those issuing it had not checked whether transportation would be available: our representatives from the consulate general in Leningrad were unable to book either plane or train travel and managed to meet the deadline only by renting a car and driving out.

The attempt to remove foreign diplomats, journalists, and citizens from Lithuania seemed to many to be the most ominous move Moscow had taken so far. It suggested that Moscow considered violence an imminent possibility, because it intended either to use force itself or to provoke it. Moscow's reasoning seemed to be that expulsion of foreigners from Lithuania would serve the dual purpose of eliminating both "outside agitators" and eyewitnesses to a crackdown.

We, and many other countries, immediately protested the expulsion order. Nevertheless, diplomats had no choice but to comply. As it turned out, however, Moscow did not manage to remove all journalists and foreign private citizens, some of whom remained in Lithuania under protection of the Lithuanian authorities.

I returned to Moscow from my trip to Central Asia on Saturday, March 24, and immediately met with the embassy's senior staff to discuss recent developments. I concluded that Gorbachev was trying to intimidate the Lithuanians but probably still hoped to avoid using force. The problem, however, was that the more the Lithuanians were challenged directly, the more truculent they would likely become. Though the Lithuanians would try to avoid violence, since they understood they could not win that way, Soviet officials might at some point not resist the temptation to save face by acting. I was particularly disturbed to hear that high-ranking military officers were demanding that force be used in Lithuania if necessary to prevent a breakaway. Though two weeks earlier Shevardnadze's fears had not materialized, this did not mean they were groundless.

Washington was worried that any outbreak of serious violence in Lithuania would stop the general improvement of U.S.-Soviet relations, upset our arms reduction negotiations, and complicate solving the remaining issues in Eastern and Central Europe. Some cynics might have suspected that the United States might "sacrifice" Lithuania and the other Baltic states to secure these "more important" objectives, but no American administration could maintain close relations with a Soviet government that used force to rein in the Baltic states. Congress would tie the hands of any U.S. president who tried to do business as usual following a crackdown there.

Although I assumed that the Soviet leaders realized that the American reaction to force in Lithuania would be sharply negative, I could not be certain that they grasped just how vehement our reaction was likely to be. Several senior officials had complained to me after their invasion of Afghanistan that they had had no forewarning of the United States' reaction. In 1981, one had commented, "When one government after another fell in Afghanistan, you acted as if you really didn't care, but then when we did what we considered necessary, your temper tantrum destroyed the entire relationship we both had been building for a decade."

In 1979, the Soviet leaders might not have been deterred by warnings, but in 1990 they had much more at stake in their improved relations with the United States and the West as a whole. It was important that Gorbachev have no illusions that a close relationship with the United States could survive a crackdown in the Baltic states. I thought it would be timely to give him a clear warning.

On this occasion, the thinking in Washington paralleled my own. I had no sooner drafted a recommendation that a high-level warning message be sent than I was informed that a letter was on the way from Secretary Baker to Shevardnadze. It arrived on Sunday morning, and we delivered it immediately since events were moving so fast I did not want to risk waiting for an appointment with Shevardnadze the next day.

Senator Edward Kennedy of Massachusetts arrived in Moscow the same day. His visits were infrequent but always useful. He left at home any political differences he might have with the administration, kept us fully informed of his activities, and always made sure that what he did supported our bipartisan goals in regard to the Soviet Union. He was particularly effective in pressing for resolution of human rights cases.

When I met him at the airport, I could see that he was deeply concerned. He asked me to brief him on the situation in Lithuania before he spoke to the journalists who had assembled. I told him that there had as yet been no serious incidents but tension was rising to a dangerous level. He then stepped before the cameras and stressed the need for a peaceful solution in Lithuania and pointed out the danger to U.S.-Soviet relations if there should be violence or repression.

This was important and helpful. Given the private representations we had made, it was useful to have a leading Democrat give the same message, particularly since he could give it in public without seeming threatening.

That weekend I began to see some indications that the Moscow media were easing off their hitherto unrelievedly anti-Lithuanian stance. The Friday-evening television news offered hostile coverage of events in Vilnius but then followed it with President Bush's statement on the need for dialogue and an interview with Professor Gail Lapidus, a leading American academic specialist on Soviet nationalities. She told her Soviet listeners that they could solve their nationality problems only by offering maximum freedom, and that Lithuania, in particular, would not be calm until it was free. They were wise words but not what Gorbachev and the other Soviet leaders were saying. Somebody at Central Television, it seemed, was trying to offer more objective comment on the Baltic events than we had been seeing of late.

The next day, *Izvestiya* carried a report from Lithuania that was somewhat more balanced than I had come to expect. It quoted accurately from the most recent Landsbergis message to Gorbachev, which denied that Lithuania was forming military units and characterized the current situation as a "war of nerves." It then went on to quote a Lithuanian legislator as saying that it was time to search for common interests and to negotiate on that basis. This was the first report I had noticed in the Moscow press since the Lithuanian independence declaration that portrayed the Lithuanian position in reasonable terms, and I wondered whether it was a sign that the official position was easing or merely a reflection of editor Ivan Laptev's liberal attitude. *Pravda,* I noted, did not carry the same story, although it had originated with the official news agency TASS.

In fact, however, the pressure on Lithuania did not ease and the comments I heard from Soviet officials the following week were not reassuring. Yevgeny Primakov, the chairman of one of the houses of the Supreme Soviet, hosted a lunch for Senator Kennedy on March 26, and Lithuania was naturally the center of our attention. When Kennedy and I pressed Primakov on the need to start negotiations with Lithuania, he said that the tactics used by the Lithuanian leaders had made this impossible. If their tactics changed, discussions might be possible, he said, but negotiations, never. I asked whether they were not entangling themselves in semantics: why the sharp distinction between "discussions" and "negotiations"? Primakov asked whether the president of the United States would negotiate with domestic groups, and I said that of course he would: his negotiations with Congress, with state governments, and with interest groups of all sorts are constant.

"But he wouldn't negotiate with a state governor who declared independence," he pointed out.

"Maybe not," I replied, "but our Constitution does not give states the right to secede."

Author with the Gorbachevs in Geneva,
November 1985.

Summit in Reykjavik, October 1986

The meeting begins. Clockwise from left: Gorbachev, Sergei Tarasenko, unidentified Soviet interpreter, Shevardnadze, the author, Reagan, Dimitri Zarechnak (U.S. interpreter), Shultz.

On Air Force One, en route to Washington following the meeting in Reykjavik. Left to right: author, Patrick Buchanan, speechwriter Anthony Dolan, Reagan, NSC staffer Steven Sestanovich.

Lunch at the White House during Gorbachev's first visit to Washington, December 1987, when Gorbachev told Reagan that he would never think of the United States as he had. Left side of table: Anatoly Dobrynin, Pavel Palazchenko (interpreter), Gorbachev, Alexander Yakovlev, Deputy Prime Minister for Foreign Trade Kamentsev, Chief of Staff Valery Boldin. Right side of table: author, Vice President Bush (obscured), Reagan, William Hopkins (interpreter). Jim Coon, Reagan's staff assistant, is standing on the right.

Top: Spaso House, the U.S. ambassador's residence in Moscow.
Bottom: Valeria Matlock with Andrei Sakharov at Spaso House.

Top: Shevardnadze and author in Shevardnadze's aircraft, en route to Irkutsk, August 1990. *Bottom:* Author opening an American trade exhibit in Moscow, 1989. In foreground: author, Prime Minister Ryzhkov, Gorbachev.

Author briefs President Bush in the Oval Office,
April 1991.

Top left: "Gorbachev was only a pimple on the skin of Russian history." Vladislav Starkov in his office at *Argumenty i Fakty*. *Top right:* Anatoly Sobchak signs a copy of his book in his office in St. Petersburg.

Meeting with Alexander Yakovlev in his office at Communist Party Central Committee headquarters on Staraya Square in Moscow. On left side of table, Charles Z. Wick, director of the U.S. Information Agency, author, Raymond Benson, counselor for public affairs at the U.S. Embassy in Moscow. Yakovlev is on the extreme right, opposite Wick.

Author's call on Vladimir Kryuchkov, chairman of the KGB, in January 1991.
Left to right: John W. Parker, first secretary, U.S. Embassy Moscow, author,
Kryuchkov's notetaker (not identified), Kryuchkov. The Soviet interpreter, who was
not used during the conversation, is at the end of the table, on the right.

USSR Vice President
Gennady Yanayev offers a
toast on board his plane returning to Moscow from Kiev
following President Bush's
visit on August 1, 1991.

Some Spaso House Activities

Top left: As author looks on, General Dmitri Volkogonov delivers a lecture on unanswered questions regarding Stalin. *Top right:* Guests listen to discussion following dinner.

Vitaly Korotich, editor of *Ogonyok,* at lunch. Rebecca Matlock is on the right.

Top: General Yazov comes to dinner at Spaso House, October 1990. Left to right:
U.S. Secretary of Defense Richard Cheney, author, Mrs. Cheney, General Yazov.
Bottom: Chiefs of defense staffs at Spaso House, 1991. Facing camera: General Colin
Powell, chairman of U.S. Joint Chiefs of Staff, Rebecca Matlock, General Mikhail
Moiseyev, chief of Soviet General Staff.

Top: Rebecca and Jack Matlock on balcony of Spaso House, Moscow. *Bottom:* Author's last press conference for Soviet journalists in Spaso House ballroom, August 1991.

Author's call on President Yeltsin, September 1992. The room is the one
from which Gorbachev gave his resignation address in December 1991.
David Matlock is on the right.

After the Fall ...

PHOTOGRAPH BY REBECCA MATLOCK

Author's call on Mikhail Gorbachev at the Gorbachev Institute,
Moscow, September 1992.

Top: Russian Parliament Chairman Ruslan Khasbulatov in the Russian "White House," March 1992. *Bottom:* Author with Russian Vice President Alexander Rutskoy, March 1992, in his Kremlin office.

Two of the Three Who Put an End to the Soviet Union

Top: Author with Belarusian Parliament Chairman Stanislav Shushkevich in his office in Minsk, September 1992. *Bottom:* Author with Ukrainian President Leonid Kravchuk in Kiev, September 1992.

PHOTOGRAPH BY JOE PINEIRO, COLUMBIA UNIVERSITY

Top: Matlocks with Kazakhstan President Nursultan Nazarbayev, Columbia University, 1994. *Bottom:* Author with Armenian President Levon Ter-Petrosian and Mrs. Ter-Petrosian, Columbia University, 1994.

"Ours have the right to secede, but only in accord with the law," Primakov commented.

Others changed the subject before I could ask how a "right" can be made subject to approval by others before it can be exercised. As he well knew, the draft of a secession law then being debated in the Supreme Soviet would make secession dependent on approval of the USSR Congress of People's Deputies.

Though Primakov was adamant in refusing to consider "negotiations," he did assure us that they did not intend to use force. Others, however, were less comforting on that score. When asked about Lithuania at a press conference with Admiral William Crowe, the just-retired chairman of the Joint Chiefs of Staff who was visiting Moscow, Marshal Sergei Akhromeyev stated that stability of the Soviet Union's borders was a prerequisite for perestroika and that while the primary task of the military was to defend the country against external threats, it had been and would be used to resolve internal matters "when necessary." His words seemed to substantiate Shevardnadze's fears.

The Soviet military, of course, had strong feelings about the three Baltic countries. They had bases there of some importance, particularly for air defense, but our defense attachés at the embassy—whose professional opinion I sought—believed that Soviet defensive strength would not be gravely impaired if the Baltic states became independent, as long as they did not fall under the control of a hostile power. Furthermore, if Moscow had been willing in 1990 to negotiate the terms of Baltic independence, it could probably have kept its most important military bases there.

The Soviet military attachment to the Baltic was probably more a matter of emotion than of military necessity. The Soviet army had been trained to defend *all* Soviet territory to the death, and to it the Baltic states were part of Soviet territory.

In Search of a Solution

PRESIDENT BUSH'S PUBLIC STATEMENT, followed by Secretary Baker's message to Shevardnadze, had been timely, but the parties seemed no closer to a dialogue that might relax the tension. Gorbachev was obviously under great pressure to "do something" and so far was refraining from the direct application of force but nevertheless, by increasing the psychological pressure, was running a high risk that a small confrontation would escalate into an uncontrollable situation.

I began to ask myself, then others, whether there was anything the United States or—for that matter—other outsiders could do to help the parties lower the tension and begin a dialogue. Generally our Baltic friends could think only of threats and Soviet officials only of advising the Lithuanians to nullify their declaration of independence and join the negotiations over a new union treaty. The second was certainly a non-starter, and we had done about all we usefully could to warn of our negative reaction to a crackdown. Still, some way needed to be found to finesse the "positions of principle" that prevented any effective dialogue.

The draft law on secession, although not yet adopted officially, provided a possible way out. While it contained a number of unacceptable provisions, it did concede that secession would be legal under certain conditions, and it provided that the process could be started by a referendum in a republic, which would require a two-thirds vote to be valid. It seemed to me that the referendum requirement, taken by itself, was not unreasonable. What if Lithuania could be persuaded to conduct a referendum, on the understanding with Moscow that negotiations would follow? They could surely obtain a two-thirds majority in favor of independence, and this would offer a face-saving solution to Moscow.

When I discussed the idea with Lithuanians and other Balts, they were initially dubious. First, they rejected the concept that they were seceding from the Soviet Union, since they felt (as did we) that they had never been legally part of the Soviet Union but rather an occupied country. Second, if they seemed to comply with a Soviet law, even in part, could it not be argued that they were acknowledging Soviet jurisdiction? Third, although the Lithuanians were confident that they could get the support of more than two thirds of their people, would they not be betraying their Baltic neighbors if they set the precedent of agreeing to a referendum? The Latvians, in particular, made up less than two thirds of their republic's population.

I pointed out to them that their problem was not so much one of legal niceties as of political reality. They could have an airtight legal argument and still not gain independence. Besides, they could conduct a referendum without officially conceding Moscow's legal interpretation. A referendum could be held of their own volition, to demonstrate to the world that Moscow's allegations that most Lithuanians did not want independence were false.

Their fear of undermining their legal position by implicitly acknowledging Soviet jurisdiction also seemed to me misplaced. They were in fact an occupied country, and whatever actions they took under duress to secure their independence could hardly be interpreted as voluntarily conceding Soviet jurisdiction.

And, finally, I argued that, with a bit of judicious political campaigning, all three Baltic countries should be able to win two-thirds majorities in favor of independence. I doubted that voting would be entirely along ethnic lines and was sure that many non-Balts would vote for independence. In Latvia, for instance, independence advocates could attain a two-thirds majority if they received support from 80 percent of the Latvians and 40 percent of the non-Latvians, targets a well-planned campaign should be able to reach.

Several conversations along those lines with Baltic representatives persuaded me that, despite their initial skepticism, the Lithuanians could probably be convinced to hold a referendum provided Gorbachev would agree to start negotiations in good faith if a two-thirds majority voted in favor of independence.

I felt that a proposal of this sort would be a useful supplement to our warnings of the dire consequences of repression in the Baltic states since it pointed to a way out of the dilemma both sides then faced. I was scheduled to leave for the United States at the end of the week to participate in meetings with Shevardnadze in Washington and to attend the weddings of two of our sons. I intended to try to get approval to make such a proposal.

The thinking in Washington continued to move parallel to ours in Moscow, and at the same speed. I flew to Frankfurt, Germany, on the evening of March 29, intending to proceed to the United States the following day. However, I was awakened after midnight by a call from Washington that informed me that I would be asked to return to Moscow in the morning to deliver an important message.

Mike Joyce, my deputy, who not only managed our overburdened embassy with great skill but also stayed prepared to take on my tasks when I was away, met me at the airport in Moscow. When my plane landed, we had barely time to drive to Alexander Yakovlev's office for the appointment scheduled for me, and Mike briefed me in the car on the way in. President Bush had sent Gorbachev a personal letter that Mike had delivered to Shevardnadze that morning. In it Bush had made it plain that he was coming under increasing pressure to do more about

Lithuania and suggested that a referendum might provide a way out of the current impasse if both sides could agree in advance to be bound by the result. There had been a meeting of the Council of Federation that afternoon, and Bush wanted Gorbachev to have his letter beforehand, since decisions might be made in the council regarding Lithuania. My task was to discuss the letter with Yakovlev and to provide more details on the background of the president's proposals.

My instructions could easily have been conveyed in two sentences: "Point out to Yakovlev the dangers of repression in Lithuania and get his reaction to the president's idea of settling the current impasse with a referendum. Make it clear that if repression should occur for any reason, the fruitful cooperation that has developed of late will no longer be possible." Any diplomat of minimal competence would know how to present these points in a manner most convincing to his interlocutor.

However, I found, more to my amusement than dismay, that I had been sent instructions that extended over two single-spaced pages: a good idea had virtually been smothered in banal verbiage. What faced me was a typical bureaucratic product from people trying to prove to their colleagues and superiors how much they knew. No matter how obvious, every point was belabored in excruciating detail. Although the document seemed to assume that the recipient was incompetent, I knew the "system" too well to draw that conclusion. All officials, including presidents, were treated that way by "interagency committees" determined to leave nothing to chance.

The lengthy paper had one advantage: I could read it to Yakovlev orally in Russian, then leave a copy with him in English. This would prove that my presentation was indeed official and I was not freelancing. Then we could begin our real discussion.

Knowing that Yakovlev, along with Shevardnadze, was the Politburo member most likely to have some understanding of the Lithuanian position, I had hoped to receive at least a glimmer of encouragement for a referendum. However, his condemnation of the recent Lithuanian actions was categorical. A dialogue had always been possible, he said, until the declaration of independence and subsequent acts had brought it to a halt. If the Lithuanians had wanted to open a dialogue, they could have done so at that day's meeting of the Council of Federation, but they refused to come. Their "defiant and provocative" stance made any attempt at dialogue useless.

Yakovlev conceded that a referendum could have started a process of secession if the Lithuanians had used it. But for it to work now, he said, the Lithuanians would have to restore the situation that had existed before their declaration of independence. He accused them of ignoring the many ties that had grown up with the rest of the Soviet Union and of distorting history. Although the secret protocol to the Nazi-Soviet pact had been illegal, the Lithuanian vote to join the Soviet Union in 1940 had been valid, and the current Lithuanian leadership could not simply sweep that away with a declaration.

The Lithuanian action, he added with feeling, was "a gift to conservative forces" and could derail perestroika. Demands that force be used were growing, he claimed, as were demands that the Lithuanians be required to pay hard currency for all goods sent there. Nevertheless, he assured me that trade would continue in rubles since the population as a whole would suffer if it was billed in convertible currency.

I remembered that Yakovlev had told me a few months earlier that a Lithuanian declaration of independence would be "the end of perestroika." I was also aware that conservatives in the Party were blaming him for the Lithuanian apostasy: they charged that his visit in the summer of 1988, when he had argued against the "class struggle" theory, had started the Balts on their separatist route. This was nonsense, but he doubtless had a sense of his own political vulnerability and had to make sure that he stuck closely to the current official line when he spoke to me.

I told him that I saw no point in debating the legal status of Lithuania since each of us was familiar with the position of the other. However, it seemed clear that the interests of both the Soviet Union and Lithuania would be served by lowering tensions in Lithuania. Obviously, no dialogue could begin if one side demanded surrender beforehand. But that was what the Soviet leaders were doing. Whether or not the Lithuanians were wise to declare independence when they did, they clearly could not reverse the decision just to get talks started.

Yakovlev simply repeated that a referendum would be acceptable only if the Lithuanians restored the status quo ante and "stopped their illegal acts."

Since he had mentioned the presence of close economic ties as an argument against independence, I pointed out that independence did not necessarily mean breaking the existing ties. He should think about his time in Canada: here was a country that was independent but maintained the closest economic and human ties with Great Britain, of which it formerly had been part.

He did not answer the point but grumbled that attempts to "frighten one another" were inappropriate. While the Soviet Union had criticized recent U.S. actions in Panama and the Philippines, it had never suggested that U.S.-Soviet relations would be affected. U.S. "threats" over Lithuania would be "counterproductive."

I replied that when we said that repression in Lithuania would make it impossible to continue to develop our relationship we were not issuing a threat. We were simply explaining a political fact of life. If we failed to do so and our position was misunderstood, we would be remiss.

We had come full circle, and it was clear that Yakovlev had been instructed to show no "give." I concluded the meeting with a final observation that Moscow's current tactics would not solve the problem. When this became apparent to Gorbachev, he might find that a referendum would give him a political rationale for negotiating the terms of independence.

The Lithuanian specter hovered over Shevardnadze's meetings in Washington the following week, but there was no further progress in our discussions of the issue. His visit, however, did achieve its main aim: a date was set for the next summit meeting. This time, Gorbachev would come to the United States at the end of May and early June. I welcomed this agreement. It was not only consistent with my conviction that annual summits are a useful practice but would also provide an incentive for Gorbachev to do all he could to avoid violence in Lithuania and the other Baltic states during the spring. He could have no doubt that bloodshed there would require cancellation of his planned meeting with President Bush.

Shortly after we returned to Moscow on April 9, 1990, we hosted a visit by seven American senators, led by Majority Leader George Mitchell. Their meeting with Gorbachev provided another opportunity to probe his thinking on the issue.

Gorbachev began the meeting with a long presentation on the importance of perestroika and the difficulties it was encountering. He said nothing directly about Lithuania, but as he concluded his opening presentation he commented that he had been "surprised by the reaction by the U.S. Congress to some developments here." Obviously, he was referring to the resolutions Congress had passed supporting Lithuania.

Senator Mitchell asked him about the prospects for a START agreement and for dealing with Lithuania. Gorbachev dealt with START briefly, noting that Secretary of State Baker would be visiting soon and he hoped the remaining questions would be solved, although the United States still seemed to be seeking some unilateral advantages. Then he turned to Lithuania and, despite his disclaimer that so much had been said recently that it was difficult to know what to add, spent nearly an hour setting forth his views.

Lithuania, he felt, was unlucky in its current political leadership. They were refusing to participate in a fundamental reform of the Soviet system. He did not know who was advising the Lithuanians, he remarked—looking straight at me—but perhaps their policies resulted from ignorance and political incompetence. They had decided to rush ahead and act before the presidential system was established in the USSR, but then they couldn't figure out what to do.

We are patient, Gorbachev asserted. If they are independent, we should cut them off and treat them like a foreign country. Then they would really have trouble managing. But the real problem is Landsbergis himself, not the Lithuanian people, and we do not want them to suffer.

Like Yakovlev, Gorbachev insisted that any negotiations on Lithuanian independence could begin only after the Lithuanians "restored the situation as it existed on March tenth," that is, before their declaration of independence. Even if that should happen, he observed, the negotiations were likely to be lengthy and difficult, since more than 800,000 non-Lithuanians were living there and many would leave. Then he added that if people understood how these negotiations would turn out, they would not support the "secessionists."

As for himself, he was coming under tremendous pressure to solve the problem. People were saying that he was indecisive and weak, but he was convinced that the situation required forbearance and patience. Nevertheless, he could not rule out harsh measures and the introduction of presidential rule if the situation should require it.

The last sentence galvanized our attention. It seemed to contradict what Shevardnadze and others had been saying about the continued determination not to use force. But Gorbachev persisted in his monologue without pausing for questions or comments. He was particularly sensitive to the actions of the U.S. Congress and was not about to pass up the opportunity to give this group of prominent senators a piece of advice.

The U.S. Congress, he said, should not appear to interfere in these questions or assume the role of teacher, which would only give offense. Besides, countries other than the Soviet Union were concerned over the precedent Lithuania's withdrawal from the Soviet Union might set: federations such as Brazil, India, Canada, and Yugoslavia could all be affected, he claimed.

Gorbachev himself seemed to be drifting further and further from reality, and I wondered if he was beginning to wind down. He seemed to be preparing to conclude but could not resist some final jabs. "Not everything depends on us," he observed, implying again that the Lithuanians would have to do the adjusting. "I told them when I was in Lithuania that if they thought it was just a matter of raising their hands and voting, they would be mistaken. The matter is much more serious than that. But many are looking for ways to change the current leadership, so maybe there is hope. By the way, they called on Ambassador Matlock before their declaration and may do so again. They seem to want his advice, but I don't know what he's telling them."

At this point, I interrupted his monologue without waiting for the interpreter to translate his words. I told him in Russian, "They didn't ask for advice, and they didn't get any."

Gorbachev chuckled as if to signal that his observation had not been hostile and observed, "Well, in the past month they have been passing laws as if they were frying pancakes." They would, he repeated, have to go back to the situation of March 10 if they wished divorce proceedings to start.

Finally he paused. Senator Mitchell tried to pin him down tactfully on a policy of not using force, saying that he wished to commend his commitment to nonviolent methods of dealing with the problem. Gorbachev immediately corrected him with the comment "I said nonviolent methods were *desirable*."

Mitchell denied any desire to lecture but reminded him of the longstanding U.S. policy of nonrecognition. This meant that for us the matter was not exclusively one of internal Soviet jurisdiction. But Americans hoped that dialogue would lead the way to a peaceful solution. Gorbachev groused a bit about some recent actions by the Lithuanian government and then brought the meeting to an end. It had gone on for nearly two hours, and he had done almost all the talking.

As we left the room, I paused to tell him that his comment about my giving advice had no foundation. The Baltic representatives had from time to time explained their policy to us, and I had cautioned them not to expect either automatic recognition or economic assistance. There-fore, though we had always made our nonrecognition policy clear, we had not acted to instigate specific moves on their part. Gorbachev grasped my arm, smiled, and said, "Don't worry. I know. I've been briefed."

"I'm sure you've been briefed," I replied. "I just want to make sure the briefing was accurate."

Tightening the Vise

GORBACHEV'S MONOLOGUE left me more concerned than comforted. Though he had said nothing strikingly new, his comments revealed that he had learned nothing since his trip in January. I had already noted that he was less willing than Shevardnadze to give categorical assurances that he would avoid the use of force, and this meeting had made it clear that he was preserving that as a possibility "if necessary to save lives." But any application of force would be publicly justified on those grounds, so the qualification provided little reassurance. The crackdown in Azerbaijan in January had been explained the same way.

Gorbachev still seemed to be laboring under the illusion that Lands-bergis did not command majority support. The personal antipathy the two men held for each other had been clear for some time, but the over-whelming support Landsbergis had received during and following the recent elections should have alerted Gorbachev that he was—to use one of Gorbachev's favorite expressions—"a political reality" that could not be avoided. Instead, Gorbachev seemed to believe that Lands-bergis's own people were trying to get rid of him. Such wishful thinking was most likely the result of false KGB reports designed to dissuade him from serious negotiation with the elected Lithuanian leadership.

The argument that other countries could be affected by the "prece-dent" set by Lithuania seemed totally contrived. I had occasionally heard comments from Ministry of Foreign Affairs officials that "other countries are concerned with the precedent we may set," but I could never discover any evidence that such concern had been expressed, ex-cept possibly by the Yugoslavs. Ambassadors from other federations had assured me that no representations had ever been made by their countries that suggested or implied that they opposed granting indepen-dence to the Baltic states because it might have an effect on their own internal problems. The Western countries, for the most part, had not recognized the Soviet annexation of the Baltic states, and it would have been illogical for them to consider a restoration of Baltic independence as a precedent for breaking up their own voluntary federations. The status of Lithuania was simply not relevant in any way to the status of Quebec or the Punjab.

I realized that Gorbachev was grasping at straws to reinforce his position, which—as a passionate advocate—he was inclined to do. But I wondered whether he really believed the argument. It is a short jump from a briefing paper that argues that "many countries with a federal system may be sensitive to this issue" to the assumption that "countries with a federal system are sensitive to this issue." If Gorbachev really did believe the latter, he would have trouble dealing with reality.

His apparent conviction that all of the non-Lithuanians living in Lithuania opposed the demand for independence also seemed to reflect a misunderstanding of the actual situation. In the recent election around half of the non-Lithuanians had voted for Sąjūdis, and the Russian Orthodox Church in Lithuania was actively campaigning for independence. Gorbachev seemed oblivious to this reality as well.

Though Gorbachev had repeatedly stressed the importance of a constitutional process, he ignored the inherent contradiction between a "right" guaranteed by the Constitution and a law that professes to implement that right but in fact circumscribes and potentially negates it. Logically, the constitutional right takes precedence. He also ignored the Baltic states' argument that they should not be required to secede from the Soviet Union since they had been illegally forced into it. Since Gorbachev had been trained as a lawyer himself, these points could hardly have escaped his notice, but, of course, he was acting not as a lawyer but as a politician prepared to ignore legal niceties when they were incompatible with political goals.

Gorbachev's comment about being under great pressure and having "little room for maneuver" provided one key to the reason for his one-sided presentation. In part he was misinformed; in part he willfully ignored factors that should have been obvious; but in very large part he was reacting to demands by the hard-liners to end the Baltic drive for independence by whatever means necessary.

For a month, Moscow's reaction to the Lithuanian declaration of independence involved psychological pressure rather than specific measures of compulsion. However, on April 15, Gorbachev decided to ratchet the pressure up.

I had spent the day in press briefings and meetings with the visiting senators. That evening Senators Mitchell and Bill Bradley and a few other guests were invited after dinner to a small gathering at Yevgeny Primakov's personal dacha. This was a sign both of the changed U.S.-Soviet relationship and of the degree to which senior Soviet political leaders were opening themselves to the outside world. Traditionally, foreigners would have been entertained only in restaurants or special "guest houses" maintained for that purpose. They would never have been invited into the homes of Soviet leaders.

A medium-sized bungalow in a grove of trees several miles from the city, Primakov's dacha was comfortable but not lavish. Primakov explained to us that he had constructed it, using personal funds, while he had been director of the Institute for the World Economy and International Relations (IMEMO) and that it had cost 30,000 rubles. Most senior officials used government-owned dachas provided as a fringe benefit, but Primakov was obviously more comfortable on his own property, and he showed us through the house with pride.

Long an academic specialist on foreign affairs, particularly the Middle East, Primakov was about to shift jobs again. He had been chairing one of the Supreme Soviet chambers (and thus had been the official host for our senators) but had just been named to Gorbachev's new Presidential Council. I had known him since the 1970s. Since the summit meeting in Reykjavik in October 1986, where he had been the principal Soviet negotiator on regional issues, he had acted more and more frequently as an unofficial foreign policy spokesman. He was obviously close to Gorbachev, and many thought he coveted Shevardnadze's job as foreign minister.

The evening at the dacha was relaxed and, in Soviet terms, bipartisan, since Anatoly Sobchak was included in the small group of guests. As one of the most vocal reformers who often criticized Gorbachev for half measures, Sobchak was already considered an opposition leader, even though as yet no opposition existed in the formal sense and he was still a member of the Communist Party.

Primakov's daughter acted as our hostess, and as we looked at photographs and family momentos we were reminded of the personal misfortunes that had befallen him: shortly after his wife had died, his only son, a teenager, had lost his life as well. His had been a close-knit family, and Primakov still bore the psychological scars of his bereavement. Showing us his late wife's photograph, he observed that although four years had passed since he had lost her, he had absolutely no interest in remarrying. He was now, it would seem, married to his job.

Despite these sad reminiscences, the evening was relaxed and there was much talk of ways in which the U.S. Congress and the Supreme Soviet might exchange information and work cooperatively. Earlier that day, however, Primakov had reinforced the uncertainty about Gorbachev's total commitment to a peaceful solution in the Baltic states. When pressed for a flat statement that force would never be used, he replied that while "no one" wants violence and there was no intention to use force, ultimately every country must "protect its vital interests" no matter what others think. Retaining Lithuania was obviously, in his mind, a "vital interest." Nevertheless, there was no hint at all that further steps to bring Lithuania into line were imminent.

Senators Mitchell and Bradley rode back into town with me. As we pulled up to their hotel entrance, I noticed television cameras and reporters gathered there. I wondered what was up. Suddenly, as the senators emerged from the car, the lights came on, the reporters came forward, and one called out, "What do you think about the economic boycott of Lithuania?"

Senator Bradley ducked and, in a feinting maneuver he had practiced many times on the basketball court, slipped off to the left and into the hotel. The lights were still on Mitchell and me. Mitchell threw me a quizzical glance, to which I replied with a shrug, since I knew no more than he about any "boycott." He then handled the question with practiced skill. He could not comment on an announcement he had not yet heard, he said, but he sincerely hoped that a dialogue could soon be initiated. It was important to settle the problem without pressure and violence.

The announcement had been made on Moscow radio while the senators were dining with their hosts. It reported that Gorbachev had sent Landsbergis a message threatening to "stop deliveries" of products normally sold abroad for foreign currency if the Lithuanian parliament did not annul a series of recent decisions, including the procedures for determining citizenship, the cessation of the Soviet military draft in Lithuania, and attempts to assume control of property claimed by Moscow. The Lithuanians had been given only forty-eight hours to comply.[9]

It was not immediately clear precisely which "products" would be considered those "normally sold abroad for foreign currency," but oil was an obvious candidate. Lithuania got practically all its natural gas and oil from other Soviet republics, and these commodities were also the largest sources of Soviet export earnings. As the Lithuanian leaders had already sensed, their greatest economic vulnerability was their dependence on Moscow for oil, and it was not surprising that Gorbachev was now exploiting this weakness.

Nevertheless, I was struck by the clumsiness, indeed brutality, of the timing. Gorbachev had issued an ultimatum on Good Friday to a country that was traditionally, and still largely, Roman Catholic, with a deadline on Easter Sunday! One could hardly imagine more inept timing. Landsbergis did not hesitate to call attention to this fact by replying that the Lithuanians would observe Easter and only then consider how to reply.

As I rode to the airport with the senators on Saturday morning, we discussed what the United States might do. I told them that I could not predict the administration's reaction: obviously the president would wish to do what he could to discourage such pressure on Lithuania but at the same time would want to avoid a confrontation that would strengthen the Soviet hard-liners. Nevertheless, I thought it would be a good idea to suspend negotiations with the Soviet government on a new trade agreement as long as economic sanctions were imposed on Lithuania.

Gorbachev had obviously been hoping to sign a trade agreement when he went to Washington in May. I thought we should refuse to do so if he was still applying economic pressure on Lithuania. It would be incongruous for us to try to expand trade with the Soviet Union while it was using trade as a weapon against the Lithuanians. I had long supported expanded economic ties under appropriate conditions, but one of the purposes was to create potential leverage in situations such as the one we were facing. If Gorbachev imposed an oil embargo on Lithuania, now would be the time to use it. The senators agreed that this would be an appropriate response. In any case, they felt that the Senate would refuse to ratify any trade agreement while Moscow was imposing economic sanctions on Lithuania.[10]

Though I thought we should react to Moscow's punitive economic measures against Lithuania, I also thought it was important to avoid overreaction. Worse things could happen there, such as mass arrests or a violent crackdown, and we needed to retain the ability to deter more serious acts of repression.

———

On Easter Monday, the Lithuanian Supreme Council began debating its reply to the ultimatum from Gorbachev and Ryzhkov. Its debate continued for three days, and a resolution was finally approved without a negative vote[11] on Wednesday. It ignored the demand to reverse previous legislation but selected a delegation to begin negotiations with Moscow and offered not to pass new legislation of political significance until May 1, provided negotiations began.

Moscow ignored the offer and began to limit supplies of oil and natural gas to Lithuania the following day, April 19. Crude oil supplied by pipeline to a refinery in Lithuania stopped flowing that morning, and gas supplies were cut by 85 percent. Although these moves caused panic buying of gasoline at service stations throughout Lithuania, they also called attention to the difficulty Moscow would have if it tried to punish Lithuania with economic sanctions. The refinery in Lithuania also served other republics, and virtually all the supplies to the Russian oblast of Kaliningrad (part of the former East Prussia, taken from Germany following World War II) passed over Lithuanian territory. A nuclear power station in Lithuania supplied electricity to parts of Latvia, Belorussia, and Russia itself. There was no way to deprive Lithuania of energy without penalizing other areas.

Nevertheless, the partial economic boycott continued for weeks and caused considerable hardship and even more nervousness in Lithuania. The Soviet army contributed to the tension by stepping up military activities, increasing the number of "maneuvers" and the movement of troops through cities. The Lithuanian parliament had ended the military draft, but this was one of the laws Moscow considered illegal, and the Ministry of Defense made it clear that it intended to enforce the spring call-up throughout the country. It had already reacted vigorously to apprehend Lithuanian "deserters" from the Soviet army, soldiers who had left their units and returned home after Lithuania declared its independence.

Moscow also began to order the seizure of buildings, a practice that eventually would lead to bloodshed. Just before the threat of an economic blockade was issued, armed policemen from the USSR Ministry of Internal Affairs seized the building containing the Lithuanian Communist Party archives, apparently to prevent it from falling into hands of the breakaway Lithuanian Party.

Estonia and Latvia Opt for Independence

THE ATTEMPTS TO INTIMIDATE the Lithuanians were also intended to deter the other Balts from moving toward independence, but they had the opposite effect—as anyone familiar with the Baltic character could have predicted. Although the Estonian and Latvian leaders delayed declarations of immediate independence, they moved toward that end with unmistakable determination.

Carrying out the warning its representatives had given the USSR Congress of People's Deputies, on March 30 the Estonian Supreme Soviet declared that Soviet rule in Estonia had been illegal from the time of its imposition and proclaimed a "period of transition" to the "restoration" of the prewar Republic of Estonia.[12] On April 12, it voted to discontinue service by Estonians in the Soviet military on the ground that Estonia was a country under foreign occupation.

In Latvia, as in the other two Baltic states, the National Front won control over the republic Supreme Soviet in the March elections. The new parliament was certain to move toward independence just behind Lithuania and Estonia, though it might adopt less confrontational tactics.

Gorbachev had repeatedly excluded the possibility of "negotiations" with any of the Baltic states and refused to provide interlocutors for the Lithuanian delegation sent to Moscow to open a dialogue. However, on April 19, the very day the oil and gas supplies to Lithuania were reduced, he met separately with delegations from Estonia and Latvia. His purpose was not to negotiate with them but to dissuade them from following the Lithuanian example. He pressed the Estonians to rescind their declaration of March 30 and informed both delegations that their republics had only two choices. If they wished complete independence, they must comply with the new USSR law on accession. However, if they were willing to negotiate the terms of a voluntary federation and stay in the restructured union, they could be granted a special status that would involve complete autonomy.[13]

The Balts were not buying. The Estonians refused to budge, and within two weeks the new Latvian parliament adopted a resolution that declared Latvia's accession to the Soviet Union invalid and restored much of its prewar constitution.

The pressures from Moscow stimulated cooperation within the Baltic region. Just before the economic sanctions were imposed on Lithuania, the three Baltic governments signed an agreement on economic cooperation with the goal of a unified Baltic market. A Baltic Cooperation Council would be established in Riga to coordinate work on a regional investment bank, a marketing association, and other institutions.[14] Real cooperation, however, would not be possible unless and until the republic leaders wrested control of their economies from Moscow. In 1989, the USSR Supreme Soviet had approved a law granting "economic autonomy" to the Baltic republics from January 1, 1990, but by spring it was clear that nothing had changed in practice. The Moscow ministries still considered the industrial facilities in the republics to be their property and resisted all attempts by the local governments to take control of them. This experience reinforced the Baltics' reluctance to take Gorbachev's promises at face value.

The law on secession, finally passed by the USSR Supreme Soviet and signed by President Gorbachev on April 3, provided further ground for skepticism. While theoretically allowing a union republic to leave the USSR, it prescribed a procedure so complex and so full of "catches" that it would be practically impossible to comply. A referendum, requiring a two-thirds majority, would only start a process of negotiation, which would be subject to approval by the USSR president, Supreme Soviet and Congress of People's Deputies at various stages. The USSR Congress of People's Deputies would determine the period of transition, which could last as long as five years and could be ended only by an act of the Congress. Throughout this period, USSR laws would prevail in the republic.[15]

The new law ostensibly to implement the constitutional right of secession was as hypocritical as the constitutional provision had been in Stalin's time. I could see why the Baltic leaders refused to comply.

By May, it seemed that relations between Moscow and the Baltic parliaments had reached a stalemate. Gorbachev continued to refuse any negotiations on independence that did not conform to the law on secession, and the leaders of all three Baltic states refused to withdraw the declarations they had made. Pressure on Lithuania, and to a slightly lesser degree on Estonia and Latvia, was stepped up, but that pressure stopped short of outright violence.

Even the economic sanctions were far from total. While they created some distress and much annoyance, they were insufficient to cause acute suffering. The saber rattling by the military and police was ominous but had not led to bloodshed. Gorbachev seemed to be tightening the pressure as a means of propitiating the hard-liners, who were insisting that he do *something* to bring the Balts into line. He also, however, wanted to "teach the Balts a lesson" about their ultimate economic dependence on the USSR. Whatever utility the first of these motivations may have had (and it is possible that the tough talk and firm decrees in fact deterred attempts to remove Gorbachev), the second was doomed to failure. The economic pressures were insufficient to bring the Balts to their knees but painful enough to reinforce their determination to become independent. The assumption Gorbachev and his advisers made that pressure would bring the Balts to terms was 180 degrees off course.

Organizing the Presidency

AT THE SAME TIME as he was fending off independence demands by the Balts, Gorbachev set to work to organize the presidency. The constitutional amendment he had pushed through the Congress of People's Deputies provided for two advisory bodies: a Council of Federation, made up of leaders of the union republic parliaments, and an appointive Presidential Council. The duties and authorities of these bodies were far from clear. It would seem that the president would be free to take or ignore their advice as he chose. However, they provided a semblance of collectivity to decision making.

I suspected that Gorbachev had devised the Council of Federation to give union republic parliaments the feeling that they had a voice and a stake in the central government. Whether it would serve that purpose would depend on whether it had an influence on decisions important to the republics. As for the Presidential Council, I assumed he would try to use it as a surrogate Politburo. If he could shift discussion of political and economic policy out of the Communist Party and into the office of the president, under his direct personal control, he would be in a position to distance himself from the Party machinery and eventually bypass it.

Two weeks after the presidency was created, Gorbachev announced appointments to his Presidential Council. It included several key government officials such as Foreign Minister Shevardnadze, KGB Chairman Kryuchkov, Minister of Defense Yazov, Minister of Interior Bakatin, and Gosplan Chairman Yuri Maslyukov. Gorbachev also named two close associates, Alexander Yakovlev and his staff assistant in the Central Committee, Valery Boldin. Three moderate reformers, physicist Yuri Osipyan, economist Stanislav Shatalin, and writer Chingiz Aitmatov, were balanced by three well-known "conservatives," Siberian writer Valentin Rasputin, Veniamin Yarin, a factory worker from the Urals whom conservatives considered a potential "Lech Wałęsa from the right," and Albert Kauls, a Latvian director of a farming enterprise.

In selecting the members of his Presidential Council, Gorbachev had obviously acted with more regard to political balance than to consistency of personality or policy. Only the radical reformers seemed left out entirely, since Academician Shatalin, who was later radicalized, was still considered a moderate. I could understand the political utility of reassuring major groups in the country that they were "represented" on the Presidential Council, but I did not see how this group was going to act as a cohesive body. In fact, it never did.

Nevertheless, Gorbachev did his best to give the Presidential Council prestige. He held his first meeting with the group the day after it was named and saw to it that the meeting was well publicized. He also moved the members into spacious offices in the Kremlin, a locale reserved for the most senior Soviet officials. By fall, the Presidential Council had replaced the Party Politburo as the senior body in terms of protocol. At the formal National Day reception in November, members of the Presidential Council received foreign dignitaries, standing in a place to which, in previous years, only members of the Politburo had been admitted.

When the presidency was established, the USSR Council of Ministers was retained, so that the structure was more similar to that in France, where the Council of Ministers is separate from the presidency—and indeed the prime minister is often of a different political party—than to the presidential Cabinet system in the United States. I suspected that Gorbachev had wished to bring the Council of Ministers more directly under his control but had decided not to in part because of massive resistance in the government bureaucracy and in part to avoid public humiliation of Prime Minister Ryzhkov, who had supported the creation of a presidency and had refused to be an opposing candidate for president. Nevertheless, many observers, including myself, expected Gorbachev to reduce the size of the Council of Ministers and to transfer the functions of most of the economic ministries to the republics as soon as this seemed politically feasible. Initially, however, the presidency brought no significant change to the structure or personnel of the Council of Ministers.

The events in April also seemed to run counter to some of the assumptions I had made about Gorbachev's intent to reduce the Party's grip on government at the upcoming Party congress. Radical reformers in the Party had issued, in full conformity with Party rules at the time, a "Democratic Platform" for the congress. I did not expect Gorbachev to endorse the platform, for it was opposed by the majority of Party officials, but I did expect him to encourage its sponsors to stay in the Party. Without them, reform would have no strong, consistent support in the congress debate. Influential members of his own staff had urged him in January to make common cause with these reform intellectuals, and though he had chosen to compromise the issues and to criticize the reformers for haggling over the terms of the presidency, I assumed that he understood he needed them—if for no other reason than to appear as a moderate to his conservative colleagues. Furthermore, the reformers were continuing to show they could win elections in key places. The Democratic Russia coalition swept Moscow, Leningrad, Sverdlovsk, and several other major cities during voting in March.

To my surprise, these victories—like Yeltsin's earlier—seemed to offend Gorbachev rather than convince him that the democratic movement could be useful to him. Instead of allowing the "democrats" to exert as much influence as possible on selection of delegates to the Party congress, Gorbachev tried to force them out of the Party before the congress met. On April 11, 1990, just as voting on delegates was to start in Party organizations throughout the country, *Pravda* carried an open letter from the Central Committee that, in effect, demanded that sponsors of the Democratic Platform leave the Party. It accused them of trying to "turn our Party into some kind of shapeless association with complete freedom for factions and groups." It then asked rhetorically whether it was possible "for such people to remain within the ranks of the CPSU" and, while denying that it was calling for a purge, did just that by inviting Party organizations to act against those "who organize factional groups."[16]

Yuri Afanasiev, whom Gorbachev had criticized personally, told me when the letter appeared that he saw no point in retaining his Party membership any longer. On April 18 he announced publicly that he had left the Communist Party.[17] Most of the other reformers, however, resolved to stay in the Party at least until the Party congress, so that the conservatives would not win by default.

The official pressure on proponents of the Democratic Platform did not, however, induce them to present a united front on key issues. There was soon a round of public bickering, often essentially on personal grounds. Writing in *Izvestiya,* Nikolai Shmelev accused Gavriil Popov of favoring rationing. Reform economist Larisa Piyasheva charged that she had been dropped as a candidate by Democratic Russia because she had criticized some of Ilya Zaslavsky's views.[18] In general, no sooner had a platform been issued by the "democrats" than quarrels over it ensued.

The supporters of Democratic Russia were also initially unsuccessful in uniting to support particular candidacies. When Gorbachev vacated the post of chairman of the Supreme Soviet to become president, the Congress of People's Deputies elected a successor. Gorbachev backed Anatoly Lukyanov, who had been his deputy, for the post, but there was widespread opposition to him, particularly among the reformers, who felt that he was more interested in preserving the Communist *nomenklatura* than promoting reform. Nevertheless, they were unable to agree upon a candidate and thus their votes were scattered among several, including law professors Konstantin Lubenchenko and Anatoly Sobchak, physicist Yevgeny Velikhov, Alexei Kazannik, the deputy from Omsk who had given his seat on the Supreme Soviet to Yeltsin, and Gennady Filshin, an economist from Irkutsk. Even with the opposition splintered, Lukyanov's majority was a slim 53.6 percent, which suggested that his opponents might have carried the day had they been united.[19]

This experience encouraged the reformers to unite behind Yeltsin when, a few weeks later, the new Russian parliament convened. I wondered at the time whether this would have happened if Gorbachev had thrown his support to a moderate like Lubenchenko rather than to Lukyanov. By favoring a candidate known to resist rapid political and economic change, Gorbachev inadvertently helped Yeltsin build his coalition in the new Russian Supreme Soviet and made it more likely that the two bodies would clash. But then Lukyanov, with his horse face and gravelly voice, made a poor impression on television viewers and would never compete with Gorbachev for popularity. One could not be sure about a person as handsome, vigorous, and eloquent as Konstantin Lubenchenko.

Benchmarks for Economic Reform

GORBACHEV'S UNWILLINGNESS or inability to reorganize the Council of Ministers, the central governmental bureaucracy, was both a symptom and cause of the deepening economic malaise. As I reviewed the situation that spring, I could see only dismal prospects for the Soviet economy the way things were going.

Delays in real economic restructuring were now chronic, and I felt that unless a way could be found to break the Moscow bureaucracy's grip on the economy, public morale and confidence in Gorbachev's leadership would enter a tailspin.

During my trips outside Moscow I searched in vain for evidence that authority to make economic decisions was being transferred out of Moscow. Despite talk about the virtues of a market economy, steps to create one were minuscule and ineffective. This stood in sharp contrast to the rapid and fundamental changes in the political system. There, forces had been unleashed that, willy-nilly, were exerting pressure toward democratization. But no such forces had been set into motion that might break the bureaucracy's stranglehold on the economy.

Though there had been frantic Supreme Soviet debates on economic issues, the legal basis for reform was still grossly deficient. For example:

- The property law failed to sanction genuine private property.
- The land law did not end the state and kolkhoz monopoly on land.
- The leasing law did not offer real incentives for increased use of leasing.
- Essential legislation on banking, competition, and the breaking up of monopolies was not yet even in sight, and new laws in all these areas would be required for successful reform.
- The tax rates imposed in the new tax laws were much too high. They would inevitably undercut wage and other incentives, stifle growth, and encourage corruption.
- There was no legal machinery in place to enforce whatever new system was put into place—and I detected very little understanding of how to fashion one.

Meanwhile, the entire country was laboring under the immense handicap that few persons really understood how a market works. Resentment of control by Moscow was building in the republics and regions, and this also contributed to ethnic tensions. Gorbachev still seemed to depend on Gosplan and the ministries to plan and execute his economic reforms, and this was tantamount to giving a fox responsibility for poultry security.

I feared that the piecemeal measures that were being introduced would actually worsen the situation, since they were not being accompanied by the systemic changes that would make them effective.

For example, "procurement prices" for agricultural products had just been raised, but since the system of food production and distribution had not been altered, this step was more likely to enlarge the budget deficit and cause inflation than to improve the food supply. Peasants would assume that this was simply the first of a series of price increases and therefore would hold on to their produce rather than selling it to the state. Furthermore, as long as consumer goods were scarce in rural areas, there was little incentive to acquire worthless rubles.

The emerging problems were so obvious that describing them was an easy task for our embassy—though I doubted that the "system" was providing Gorbachev with an objective description. Determining what steps might bring the Soviet economy successfully into the world market system was another matter. Every economist seemed to have his or her favorite formula, but these usually ignored the crucial element of political feasibility. The comprehensive study of "benchmarks" in a transition from a command to a market economy that I had recommended that the U.S. government undertake in 1989 had not, to the best of my knowledge, been done. There was no general agreement among specialists within or outside our government as to what we should be watching to assess the prospects for successful economic reform in the Soviet Union.

By 1990, it was clear to me that our embassy could not expect guidance from Washington to set goals for reporting on the Soviet economy. If our reporting was to have coherence and if we were to have reliable criteria on which to base our judgments, we would have to develop them ourselves. I asked our economic and political sections, led by two very able diplomats who knew the Soviet Union well, John Blaney and Raymond Smith, to do a systematic study of the critical issues. We met periodically for discussions, and our meetings often resembled a graduate seminar at a university, except on these occasions the "professor" was in fact the student.

The discussions with our embassy staff and my own observations of the deteriorating Soviet economy convinced me that the most effective step the Soviet leadership could take would be to eliminate the central economic ministries, forcing most of their functions to devolve upon enterprise management with perhaps some services performed by much smaller union republic ministries. This would be a first step aimed at ending the central, imperial control of the economy, breaking up monopoly producers, and creating a framework for eventual privatization.[20] In the short run, such a radical step would be painful and disruptive, but it would liberate forces that could create a competitive economy. It seemed to me that a rapid dismantling of central controls—cutting the umbilical cords from the central ministries to the enterprises—would have several inevitable effects:

- Enterprise managers would *have* to create markets to survive.
- Gorbachev could duck responsibility for future mistakes if republics and oblasts had direct supervisory authority over the economy.
- Economic incentives to declare independence would shrink, as would one source of ethnic tension.
- Given the opportunity, some republics would rapidly legitimize private property and other institutions essential to a market economy, creating competitive pressures on all to do so.
- Decentralization would permit the allocation of a reliable tax base to republics and municipalities, since Moscow would need much smaller revenues for the central government if it was not trying to subsidize inefficient industry throughout the country. Furthermore, bureaucrats who were blocking reform would have to find jobs in enterprises and local and regional government bodies, and this would change their perspective.

Steps as radical as those I felt necessary would certainly fail if they caused too much social dislocation. While no one could be sure how much would be too much, steps would have to be taken simultaneously to cushion the impact on the average citizen. The following seemed to me a minimal set of measures to accompany a thorough decentralization of economic decision making:

1. Strengthening the ruble as an economic measure by controlling the money supply and reducing the budget deficit, most of which had

been caused by production of unneeded armaments, subsidies to inefficient industries, and salaries of large bureaucracies. (One method of reducing the "ruble overhang" could be by selling assets owned by the state to private entrepreneurs.)

2. Breaking up monopolies and adopting strict antitrust legislation.

3. Encouraging development, largely outside the state structure, of institutions essential to a market economy: for example, commercial and investment banks, instruments to enforce commercial codes, and training centers to develop the new skills required.

4. Transferring essential social services from state enterprises to local and municipal governments—a precondition of successful privatization. The services could be financed by property taxes and a reallocation of funds from the central budget.

5. Creating a safety net, including unemployment compensation, indexing low fixed incomes such as pensions to the cost of living, and subsidizing the poorest people with programs such as food stamps. Providing support to targeted groups would be far less costly to the budget than subsidizing food and housing for everybody, as the current system did.

Obviously, such developments would take time, but I believed reform would fail unless it included rapid, concrete steps toward these goals. The bureaucracies would not change until they were forced to, and bureaucrats would not become entrepreneurs if they could continue being bureaucrats. But if they had no choice, many would quickly adapt to a different environment. If a person who is physically fit refuses to learn to swim, the only way to teach him may be to throw him into deep water.

I understood that outsiders, no matter how well informed and well intentioned, could not do these things for the Soviet peoples. Soviet citizens would have to do them for themselves. I did not intend to hector them or to try to "sell" my favorite ideas for reform. But by the spring of 1990 I finally had in mind a set of benchmarks against which I could measure the various reform programs that would be discussed in coming months.

As he organized his presidency, Gorbachev obviously felt that the political traffic would not bear the sort of radical economic reform I considered necessary. When he consolidated his position as president and reorganized the Party at the Party congress during the summer, would he be prepared to take these steps? I would have to wait at least until fall for the answer. The most critical question was whether he would be willing to dispense with the central institutions of economic control.

XIV

❖

Russia Makes a Choice

*Comrades, if you subject what he [Yeltsin] has said to a serious analysis,
you will see that, under the banner of restoring Russia's sovereignty,
he is calling for a collapse of the union.*
MIKHAIL GORBACHEV to RSFSR Congress of People's Deputies, May 23, 1990[1]

*I believe we have to take leave of the previous formula: everything for a strong center.
Our country and our union will be strong only if the republics are strong, and the
stronger and more self-reliant they are the stronger the Center and our union will be.*
BORIS YELTSIN, May 31, 1990[2]

Saturday, June 2, 1990, was the third full day of Gorbachev's second summit meeting in Washington. The formal negotiations had been completed the day before, and the two presidents spent a relaxed day at President Bush's Camp David retreat in Maryland. In the evening, senior members of both delegations joined them for dinner.

Yeltsin's election as chairman of the Russian parliament had occurred only four days before, just before Gorbachev had left Moscow for the United States and a day after I had left to participate in the Washington briefings before Gorbachev's arrival. I had not had an opportunity to sound Gorbachev out about Yeltsin's election, which must have been a heavy blow to him, particularly given his public attempts to block it. I hoped the dinner would be informal enough to take him aside for a chat.

It was. Guests were already mingling in the lodge over a choice of white wine or orange juice (nothing stronger, to the dismay of some Soviet officials), gossiping about how Gorbachev had thrown a ringer in his first try at horseshoes and had almost driven into a tree when he took his turn at the wheel of a golf cart, when the Gorbachevs came in.

I was the only American participant able to talk to him without an interpreter, which gave us a sense of privacy. As soon as we got through the initial small talk, I asked him whether he thought he could work with Yeltsin in the future.

"You tell me," Gorbachev said with a shrug. "You've seen him more than I have of late."

His comment, half jibe, half flattery, embodied a typical Gorbachev technique when he wanted to parry a difficult question and make a few points himself. His words suggested that I was a factor in Soviet internal political maneuvering, which could have been both a compliment and a warning, since it is risky for ambassadors to involve themselves in internal politics. Innuendo aside, I knew that what he said was true: I had seen more of Yeltsin over the past few months than he had. It seemed to me that this was a result more of political misjudgment on Gorbachev's part than an excess of zeal on my own. He should have been dealing with Yeltsin, no matter how distasteful that might have been personally. Nevertheless, I decided to take his statement at face value but not to let him evade my question.

"Well, he tells me he wants to cooperate," I said, "and he strikes me as sincere. But my opinion doesn't count. Yours is the important one."

"It all depends on whether Yeltsin is willing to take a constructive role or not. He has a tendency to play political games. But if he settles down and acts responsibly, we can work together." Gorbachev added that recent statements by Yeltsin had given him some hope that this would happen. However, Yeltsin's penchant for "demagogic appeals" that would encourage "leveling" had made it more difficult to create the sort of economic incentives perestroika required.

I did not argue with Gorbachev, but I thought his last comment was unfair. Yeltsin's attacks on Party privileges had been aimed at unjustified advantages, not at income differentiation based on merit. It seemed ironic that the term Gorbachev used to describe the effect of Yeltsin's statements, "leveling" (*uravnilovka* in Russian) was precisely the word Yeltsin had used with me in our first meeting in 1987, when he had described attitudes that needed to change if perestroika was to succeed. He was not in fact opposed to economic incentives, but obviously someone had convinced Gorbachev that he was. Also, while Yeltsin was increasingly given to populist rhetoric in general, it seemed to me that he resorted to it because he had to fight his way back into the political arena by votes, not because he had an irresponsible attitude toward reform. If Gorbachev had made a greater effort to keep Yeltsin on his team and move the reform process forward more rapidly, Yeltsin would have been deprived of some of the issues he was exploiting.

The Russian Elections

YELTSIN HAD SECURED the chairmanship of the Russian Supreme Soviet with great difficulty and by a hairbreadth margin. The March elections to the Russian Congress of People's Deputies had produced a sharply divided body with Yeltsin's supporters in the minority.

Nevertheless, in Moscow, Leningrad, Sverdlovsk, and several other major cities, democratic reformers had done extremely well, winning a large majority of those cities' seats in the Russian Congress. Many of these winners had already left the Communist Party to run under a different banner or else had never been Party members at all. Some prominent dissidents of the 1970s, who had served long sentences for political offenses, gained seats. Sergei Kovalev, a biologist friend of Andrei Sakharov, who had been arrested in 1974 for editing the underground newsletter *Chronicle of Current Events,* for years the main source of information on human rights abuses by the Brezhnev regime, was elected in a Moscow district. Gleb Yakunin, a Russian Orthodox priest who had been imprisoned for defending freedom of religion, won in a suburban Moscow district. Dmitri Volkogonov, the general who had written a critical biography of Stalin and had been retired from active duty in the Soviet military because of his support for democratic reforms, won a seat from Orenburg, a province east of the Urals on the border of Kazakhstan. Vladislav Starkov, the editor of *Argumenty i Fakty* whom Gorbachev had tried to remove, won in the district of Moscow where I lived.

In vast areas of Russia, however, the picture was different. While most "democrats" were loosely associated in the Democratic Russia movement, they did not have an extensive national organization and did not even have candidates to run in many electoral districts. In those areas, the local Communist Party organization prevailed by default and sent apparatchiks and managers of state-run enterprises to the Congress. Though the Party no longer enjoyed a legal monopoly, it still had its hand on the levers of power in much of the country.

Until the Russian Congress met in May, I—like other observers—

could not guess what the relative strength of the various political tendencies would be. Parties, groups, and coalitions were in flux, and the alliances of one week would fall apart the next. Many of the newly elected deputies were unknown political quantities whose outlook we could not predict, but we knew enough about them to feel that reformers would be better represented than they had been in the USSR Congress "elected" the previous year. Adherents of Democratic Russia would form a minority, but a significant one. It seemed questionable that the Communist Party machine could control the assembly to the degree it had the USSR Congress.

Just after the Russian Congress opened, I invited two of the new deputies to lunch: Leonid Volkov, a political scientist who had helped found the Russian Social Democratic Party and represented a Moscow district, and Valery Kiselev, a former coal miner from the Kuznetsk Basin in Siberia. Both were members of the Democratic Russia coalition, but they differed in their approach to economic reform: Volkov understood that reform would entail painful restructuring, but Kiselev was adamantly opposed to any measures that might increase unemployment or cause rapid inflation. As for the political tendencies of the Congress, however, they were in agreement: Democratic Russia, they believed, would control not more than 40 percent of the votes. If its policies were to prevail, it would have to attract a substantial number of deputies from the more liberal wing of the Communist Party group.

I asked about Yeltsin's chances of being elected chairman of the Russian Supreme Soviet, and they replied that it was possible but far from certain. The Party's candidate, Alexander Vlasov, had even less chance than Yeltsin of being elected, however, because he was considered too passive to provide effective leadership. The lackluster speech he had delivered at the opening of the Congress had reinforced the impression of weakness. Although the democrats had learned from their earlier disarray and would give Yeltsin solid backing, my guests believed he could win only if he got the votes of 10 to 20 percent of the Communist delegates. Otherwise, the chairmanship was likely to go to a dark-horse candidate such as Vadim Bakatin, the USSR minister of internal affairs.

The votes for chairman, which were cast during the following week, bore out the first of these predictions. Despite Gorbachev's strong support, Vlasov was not elected on the first ballot, which included seven names. Yeltsin outpolled him but nevertheless was shy of a majority. Vlasov and three others removed their names from the ballot for the second round of voting, and Yeltsin's principal opponent was hard-line Party boss Ivan Polozkov, already outspoken in his opposition to reform. Yeltsin again came in at the top of the list but was still twenty-eight votes short. At the same time, the hard-liners showed their strength by giving Polozkov almost as many votes as Yeltsin got.

When I left Moscow for the summit in Washington, I felt that Yeltsin's vote might have peaked and that there might be an opening for a new candidate such as Bakatin. However, Polozkov pulled out on the third round and Vlasov put his hat back into the ring. Apprehension over Polozkov's strong showing and a conviction that Vlasov was not up to the job swayed enough centrist votes for Yeltsin to squeak through: his margin was only four votes out of more than a thousand cast.

It was a signal victory but a tenuous one. The deputies who had voted for him did not form a cohesive group, and Yeltsin immediately announced that he would not be affiliated with any Party or faction but would represent the people of the RSFSR as a whole. He therefore rejected any effort to take control of the Russian Communist Party, which was just being organized, or to form a party of his own. At the time this decision seemed tactically shrewd, but it set a precedent that would eventually undermine Yeltsin's ability to deal effectively with his legislature.

In particular, it seemed most doubtful that he could attract a two-thirds vote in the Russian Congress to amend the Constitution to provide for a presidential system and direct presidential elections. He and his supporters were already beginning to talk of the need for a presidential system in Russia, and it was obvious why they were doing so. Given the opportunity, it was likely that Yeltsin could win an overwhelming majority in a direct presidential election and thus embarrass Gorbachev, who had avoided going to the voters when the USSR presidency was established. But in the summer and fall of 1990, Yeltsin simply did not have the votes in the RSFSR Congress of People's Deputies to introduce a presidential system.

Nevertheless, he had confronted Gorbachev directly in the Russian Congress and had won. His authority was rising just as Gorbachev's had started to decline.

Sovereign Russia

SOME TWO WEEKS AFTER Yeltsin was elected chairman of the Russian Supreme Soviet, that body voted to declare the Russian Socialist Federated Soviet Republic (RSFSR) sovereign. It was not the first of the fifteen Soviet republics to do so—the three Baltic republics and Azerbaijan had taken the lead—but its declaration was politically the most significant. The Russian action led to a stampede of the other republics to do the same, and before the end of the year all fifteen had passed declarations of "sovereignty."

The earlier declarations by Baltic parliaments had obviously been a step in an effort to leave the Soviet Union. In the case of Russia and most of the other republics, however, the action was ambiguous. In a strictly legal sense, a declaration of sovereignty was redundant; the USSR Constitution already defined the union republics as "sovereign" in a provision that read: "A union republic is a sovereign soviet socialist state that has united with other soviet republics in the Union of Soviet Socialist Republics."[3]

As Soviet rule evolved, the sovereignty provided in the Constitution proved to be as illusory as the right to secede. In declaring sovereignty, or a restoration of sovereignty, the various republics were in effect asserting their right to renegotiate the Treaty of Union on their own terms rather than Moscow's. Gorbachev had promised a "real federation" formed on a voluntary basis, but by the summer of 1990 it was clear that he viewed the negotiation process as one between the Center and the various republics, with the Center having the last word as to the division of power. A growing number of republic leaders thought he had it backwards: they began to support Yeltsin's logic that the various republics as sovereign entities should decide among themselves what sort of union they wished and then impose their will on the Center.

Gorbachev, of course, could not argue against the principle of union republic sovereignty. When he addressed the RSFSR Congress of People's Deputies on May 23, 1990, he complimented them for raising the question and announced his full support for "your efforts to strengthen the sovereignty of the Russian Socialist Federated Soviet Republic."[4] He then listed the steps he considered desirable, such as increasing the power of elective assemblies (soviets) on all levels, placing economic resources at the republic's disposal, and improving the cultural life of the various national groups. None of Gorbachev's recommendations would have enhanced the autonomy of the republic.

He did not concede this, of course, but argued that the difference between his concept of sovereignty and Yeltsin's was in their attitudes toward socialism. Yeltsin, he charged, would have them discard socialism and even Soviet rule, and he pointed out that Yeltsin had proposed changing the name of the RSFSR to simply the "Russian Republic," omitting both "Socialist" and "Soviet" from the name.[5] This interpretation of sovereignty, he concluded, could only lead to the collapse of the union.

This remark, doubtless intended as an irrefutable argument against Yeltsin's proposal, was less prophetic than it may seem. Discarding "socialism" and the Soviet form of government did not automatically bring about the collapse of the Soviet Union. Within a year Gorbachev himself would propose renaming the USSR the Union of Sovereign States, dropping both of the adjectives he had argued were essential only a year before. In the meantime, his attempt to preserve a socialist system with centralized controls blocked the way to the voluntary union he had proclaimed as his goal.

There were, however, two aspects of Russia's sovereignty declaration that exerted a direct influence on subsequent developments even though they were not debated extensively at the time. The first, and more profound, was what it implied for the definition of Russia as a nation-state. The second, more immediately relevant to the politics of the day, was its impact on the political positions of Gorbachev and Yeltsin.

Throughout Soviet history Russia had been an anomaly among the union republics. By far the largest in both population and area, and itself formally a federation, it had the weakest institutions. In most respects it was administered directly by the USSR ministries. There was no formally separate Russian Communist Party, as there was in the other union republics. The USSR Academy of Sciences administered scientific research in the RSFSR while the other republics had their own academies. The USSR Ministry of Culture maintained the principal Russian theaters, opera houses, museums, and libraries, but not those in the other republics. In theory, the RSFSR was one of fifteen union republics, but in practice most of its institutions were merged with those of the union.

This led to confusion in the public mind about the very identity of

"Russia." Was it, in essence though not in name, the same as the Soviet Union, the direct heir of the Russian empire? Or was it something more limited, confined to the borders of the Russian Socialist Federated Soviet Republic? Soviet legal theory said one thing, but experience often pointed to the other. For those who held to the first interpretation, the idea of the RSFSR seceding from the Soviet Union was a logical absurdity. How could part of Russia leave the whole and still be Russia? For those who held to the second, however, secession could be a rational step if necessary to free Russia from the control of a centralized, Communist-ruled state or to relieve it of the obligation of supporting the less-developed nations in the USSR.

When the RSFSR Supreme Soviet enacted its Declaration of State Sovereignty, it implicitly endorsed the concept of the Russian state as a more limited entity than the Soviet Union in its entirety.[6] Logically, if the RSFSR could declare sovereignty, the other fourteen republics had the same right, and that meant that they were not properly part of Russia. Politically, the Russian action *required* the remaining republics to declare their own sovereignty if they were to be in a position to negotiate a new treaty of union as an equal.

Boris Yeltsin's election as chairman of the RSFSR parliament, combined with passage of the sovereignty declaration he favored, transformed his political duel with Gorbachev. He was no longer merely the chairman of a relatively unimportant legislative committee in the USSR Supreme Soviet or the putative leader of an opposition that was still weak and bereft of organization but the leader of the largest constituent republic of the USSR. Previously he had aimed to force Gorbachev to take him back into the Soviet leadership and heed his advice. Now he had a power base independent of Gorbachev. If he could control his own divided legislature and make common cause with other republic leaders, he could force Gorbachev to relinquish much of his power and, if unsuccessful, call the union itself into question. The political game between them took on much more of a "zero-sum" character than before—though Gorbachev seems to have viewed it that way since 1987.

The possibility of getting at Gorbachev by destroying the union was, in 1990, still implicit. In fact, Yeltsin argued repeatedly—and I believe sincerely—that Russia should not force the breakup of the union. Most of his supporters were of the same opinion. They viewed Yeltsin's victory and the Russian declaration of sovereignty as pressure on Gorbachev to get on with decentralizing economic decision making and economic reform in cooperation with Yeltsin.

Reformers who were members of the Interregional Group in the USSR Congress of People's Deputies and Democratic Russia in the newly elected RSFSR Congress believed above all that they needed to encourage cooperation between Gorbachev and Yeltsin. Their concern mounted when Gorbachev seemed to be turning against the reformers in the Party, as he did when he launched the *ad hominem* attacks on critics of his proposal for a presidency and approved the Central Committee circular letter inviting them to leave the Party. I was seeing some of the reformers almost every day, and hardly a conversation occurred without reference to the need for a political reconciliation between Gorbachev and Yeltsin.

In fact, social conversation in Moscow had become as preoccupied with politics as it has long been in Washington. This struck me with force when, in April, I attended a dinner to celebrate Viktor and Oksana Yaroshenko's wedding. A member of the Interregional Group of Deputies, Viktor held the seat in the USSR Congress of People's Deputies from the Moscow district where our embassy was located, and we jokingly called him "our congressman." Yeltsin had been best man at the wedding and was the life of the party as he danced with all the ladies present and offered frequent toasts to the newlyweds.

Between toasts, however, the conversation invariably turned serious. While Oksana's guests were curators from the Kremlin museums where she worked, Viktor's were politicians. Despite the fact that Democratic Russia, with which all were affiliated, had emerged from the March elections as a political force second only to the Communist Party, the underlying mood was grim. The country seemed to be falling apart, and the Gorbachev-Yeltsin rivalry, if not checked, could result in chaos or civil war. Guest after guest spoke to me of the necessity of finding a way to induce the two to cooperate.

Our host at the dinner, Genrikh Igitian, a USSR deputy who ran a contemporary art museum in Yerevan, was even more pointed. "We must save Gorbachev and save Lithuania," he shouted into my ear over the loud music. "Those who would force Lithuania to stay in the Soviet Union will throw out Gorbachev at the first opportunity. Only an alliance with Yeltsin can save him—and Lithuania." The tragedy, as he and the other politicians at the dinner saw it, was that Gorbachev did not yet understand this.

A Russian Communist Party

AS SEPARATIST TENDENCIES in the non-Russian republics intensified, demands grew among Communist Party members in the RSFSR to form a separate Russian Party. Since the formation of the Soviet Union in 1923, when the name of the Party had been changed from "Russian Communist Party (Bolsheviks)" to "Communist Party of the Soviet Union," there had been no separate Party organization for the RSFSR. As if intentionally to blur the distinction between the two meanings of "Russia," the Party leadership had steadfastly refused to set up a Party organization in the RSFSR analogous to those in the other union republics.

In earlier years, I had often asked RSFSR officials whether they considered a separate "Russian Party" desirable. Rank-and-file members often said they did and pointed out that the existing Party structure in effect discriminated against Russians and the RSFSR. Senior officials, however, took the current line and denied any need for such an organization. For example, I put the question to RSFSR Premier Alexander Vlasov during a call in 1989. In general, he was more frank than his predecessors in discussing his views, but on this occasion he supported the official position that a separate Party organization for Russia would be undesirable. As it was, he explained, he could go directly to the CPSU Politburo for decisions. If, however, there were a Russian Party organization, he would have to go through it first before the question went to the Politburo. It would simply add a bureaucratic layer to the decision-making process, he said, which would diminish the influence of the RSFSR government.

Well into the spring of 1990, Gorbachev also rejected the idea of a Russian Party organization. But sentiment in favor of one grew rapidly within the Party as more and more of the republic parties took to challenging the Center and as non-Communist parties began to be formed within the RSFSR. Ivan Antonovich, who at that time was deputy head of the Party's Academy of Social Sciences, an institution that carried out secret opinion surveys within the CPSU, told me subsequently that by the spring of 1990 more than 65 percent of Party members in the RSFSR favored a separate organization.[7] In late May, when he addressed the first session of the new RSFSR Congress of People's Deputies, Gorbachev finally endorsed the concept. Party officials began making frantic preparations to organize a Russian Party before the CPSU Party congress convened in July.

Whether because of this haste or because of his preoccupation with other matters (he spent nearly a week traveling in the United States during this period) or political miscalculation (such as the May message to the Central Committee excoriating the reformers), Gorbachev lost control of the process. When representatives of the Russian Party organizations convened in June in what became their founding congress,[8] it was obvious that pro-Gorbachev reformers were in a minority. In fact, it seemed that one of the most retrograde old-line regional bosses, Ivan Polozkov from Krasnodar, the region next to Gorbachev's native Stavropol, might emerge as first secretary. He was known as one of the most vigorous critics of perestroika.

Belatedly, Gorbachev tried to head off Polozkov's election. Ivan Antonovich has recounted how he received a call at home after midnight with the word that Gorbachev wanted to see him urgently and that a car was already on the way to pick him up. He arrived in Gorbachev's office around 2:00 A.M. and found him exhausted, apparently not having slept for days. "His face was all gray." Antonovich recalled. "When Gorbachev was very tired, the color would leave his face."

Gorbachev told Antonovich, a delegate to the founding congress, that everything possible had to be done to avoid Polozkov's election as first secretary of the Russian Communist Party. Antonovich agreed to try to prevent Polozkov's election but found that Polozkov's candidacy had gathered too much momentum to be stopped in the few hours left before the vote.[9] Later the same day, the Russian Party congress elected Polozkov first secretary. Thus, though Antonovich was among those selected for the Politburo, the new Party organization—by far the largest unit in the CPSU—came under the control of a Gorbachev critic.

At the time I was not aware of Gorbachev's last-minute effort to block Polozkov, but it was obvious to everyone that the new Russian Party organization was more likely to sabotage perestroika than to support the reforms Gorbachev had proposed. This was something Gorbachev would hardly have welcomed, but if his intent was to deprive Party officials of a direct role in running the government, the defeat of his candidate could have a salutary effect. He would have all the more incentive to build a power base outside the Party.

Reformers were outraged, however, and more and more began to follow Yuri Afanasiev's example, terminating their membership in the Communist Party.

Boris Yeltsin, however, professed to be unconcerned. When he and Naina accepted our invitation to a private dinner at Spaso House a few weeks after his election as chairman of the RSFSR Supreme Soviet, I asked whether the antireform leadership of the Russian Communist Party would be a problem for him. "Not at all," he said with a boyish grin. "They are not relevant any more. The Russian Supreme Soviet is going to run the Russian government."

I asked whether he planned to remain in the Party himself. He hesitated, then said he hadn't decided. He intended to go to the Party congress, just a few days off, and see what happened. It would be the last chance for the Party to reform itself.

Naina then commented, "When your whole life has been tied up with an institution, it's not easy just to walk away."

A few weeks later, when he stalked demonstratively out of the Party congress, Boris Nikolayevich made it look easy.

Stalemate in the Baltic

HAVING IMPOSED A PARTIAL economic boycott on Lithuania just after Easter, Gorbachev seemed not to know what to do next. The economic and military pressures not only had failed to sway the Lithuanians and deter the Estonians and Latvians but had increased their defiance. The Soviet military and conservative elements in the KGB and Party were urging Gorbachev to act decisively to bring the Balts into line, but he could not risk the use of force. He would be going to the United States toward the end of May and hoped to sign a trade agreement. The economy was weakening even faster than before, and the press and public were already talking of a crisis. He would soon need massive credits from the West to slow the fall. Violence in the Baltic would end any hope of getting them.

In May, when Secretary of State Baker visited Moscow to prepare for the Washington summit, Lithuania was a major topic. Baker continued to press for real negotiations between the parties and made a point of meeting Lithuanian Prime Minister Prunskienė in Moscow following his meetings with the Soviet leaders.

Initially, during private discussions, Shevardnadze gave us little encouragement that Gorbachev was prepared to negotiate Baltic independence. In fact, he treated Baker to a stern lecture, in a most uncharacteristic manner. When Baker suggested that a distinction could be made between the legal status of the three Baltic states and that of the other republics, Shevardnadze objected that people in the Caucasus felt just as strongly as the Balts did about their forcible incorporation into the Soviet Union, and so did many in Central Asia. He also pointed out that while he disliked avoiding discussion by calling an issue an "internal matter," the United States should understand that the Soviet Union was a great power and had its pride. As much as he and Gorbachev desired better relations with the United States, the integrity of the Soviet Union was more important to them. If they allowed any republic to leave the union, civil war would follow.

He went on to point out that Gorbachev was the target of intense criticism on this issue and that some were saying that Stalin and Brezhnev had been more effective leaders. If these emotions should gain the upper hand, all the achievements of the past five years could be lost.

Many of these arguments were familiar, but it was the first time Shevardnadze had warned us explicitly that, if forced to choose between good relations with the United States and the territorial integrity of the Soviet Union as they defined it, Gorbachev would opt for the latter. He was beginning to sound like Primakov in April.

The following day, Gorbachev struck a more conciliatory note. He had just met with the Lithuanian prime minister. We thought this might be a sign that he was trying to end the economic sanctions on Lithuania before going to the United States for his second Washington summit. Without promising to negotiate Lithuanian independence, he said that if the Lithuanians would "suspend" their declaration of independence, he would immediately set up a commission for talks and end the economic sanctions he had imposed. Knowing that the Lithuanians might find it easier to suspend implementation of their declaration rather than the declaration itself, Baker asked if that would suffice, but Gorbachev avoided a direct answer.

Following his meeting with Gorbachev, Baker came to Spaso House to meet Mrs. Prunskienė. She was accompanied by two of Landsbergis's deputies, Bronius Kuzmickas and Česlovas Stankevičius, and by the Lithuanian representative in Moscow, Egidijus Bičkauskas. Until then I had been unaware of the tension that had developed between Prunskienė and Landsbergis, but the composition of her party suggested that

Landsbergis had sent two of his deputies to keep an eye on her. It would have been more normal for her to bring her own deputies or assistants. When, months later, she was forced out of office, I was less surprised than I might have been without this tip-off.

No less devoted to Lithuanian independence than Landsbergis, Prunskienė was a more effective negotiator. She avoided merely repeating slogans and striking poses—a Landsbergis habit—and knew how to listen and to respond intelligently to the suggestions and observations of others. Her main concern that day was whether suspending action on Lithuania's declaration of independence would indicate that Lithuania had voluntarily agreed to Soviet jurisdiction. Baker assured her that, whatever the Lithuanians decided to do in this regard, the United States would hold firmly to its nonrecognition policy. Though he refrained from giving advice, the implication of his words was clear: Lithuania had nothing to lose if it suspended its declaration of independence while negotiating with Moscow.

As I walked Prunskienė to the door after her meeting with Baker, I asked when she would return to Vilnius. She replied that she would fly home immediately, by a Lithuanian government plane. This was an interesting detail. While Moscow was refusing to accept the Lithuanian declaration of independence and was applying various forms of pressure on the Lithuanian government, it was also allowing the Lithuanians to pursue an independent course in many respects. The Lithuanian "government plane" was doubtless an Aeroflot aircraft that had been assigned to Lithuania before the declaration of independence. The Lithuanian leaders were now using it to travel freely to and from Moscow and presumably to other destinations as well. It was another piece of evidence that Gorbachev, despite the hostile rhetoric, was not yet going all out to crush the elected Lithuanian leaders but was preserving some possibility of negotiation.

Discussions on Lithuania during the summit broke no new ground, but Gorbachev's desire for a trade agreement provided some leverage against a decision to authorize the use of force. I had earlier recommended that negotiations for a trade agreement be halted when Moscow applied economic sanctions in April, but these negotiations had been continued on the understanding that no treaty would be implemented if the sanctions against Lithuania were not ended.

This, however, was not the only relevant issue. We had informed the Soviet leaders repeatedly that the president would not be willing to sign a trade agreement until the Soviet government passed a law that ensured freedom of emigration. Draft legislation had been before the Supreme Soviet for months but had not yet been passed when Gorbachev arrived in Washington.

Bush discussed the issue with his advisers the day before Gorbachev arrived. Although he made no final decision, he seemed inclined not to sign the trade agreement until the Supreme Soviet had passed an acceptable emigration law and Gorbachev had dropped the sanctions on Lithuania. The following day, as the summit talks began, Secretary Baker informed Shevardnadze that President Bush would probably not be able to sign the agreement, given the circumstances. Shevardnadze was very upset by this news and argued that the agreement had already been announced and that if Bush refused to sign it, the spirit of confrontation would reemerge. He argued that a dialogue with the Lithuanians was already under way and that emigration was already free in practice.

Negotiations on the question were then taken up by Bush and Gorbachev personally and continued even after guests had assembled in the East Room of the White House on June 1 to witness the formal signing of agreements reached during the summit. One to reduce chemical weapons was ready for signature, and the text of a trade agreement had been negotiated, but Bush had not yet decided whether to sign it then or not.

Gorbachev finally persuaded Bush to sign the trade agreement, but he had to accept two conditions. The first condition, announced to the public, was that Bush would not send it to Congress until the Supreme Soviet passed the emigration bill. The second, which remained private, was that Gorbachev must also lift economic sanctions against Lithuania before the agreement could go to Congress.

Shortly after Gorbachev's return to Moscow from the summit, tensions with Lithuania began to ease. Landsbergis met with Gorbachev on June 12 and with Ryzhkov the following day and secured a promise of increased supplies of natural gas. After Landsbergis returned to Vilnius, Prunskienė recommended to the Lithuanian Supreme Council that the declaration of independence be subjected to a "moratorium" during negotiations with Moscow. Nevertheless, even though it had the support of both the prime minister and the parliament chairman, the proposal turned out to be more controversial in the Supreme Council than expected: an intense debate ensued, and the proposal was not approved until June 30.

The decision did bring a formal end to the sanctions and improved the tone of the dialogue between Vilnius and Moscow. Conceptually, however, the stalemate continued. Moscow continued to insist that negotiations be conducted either according to the law on secession or in the context of a new union treaty, while all three Baltic republics were now insisting that independence was a de jure fact and the only thing to discuss was how it could be implemented.

Germany—and Europe—United

By January 1990, Gorbachev and Shevardnadze had abandoned the illusion that German unity was a question for the future. They were forced to deal with a reality both had hoped would wait for their successors. Nevertheless, while they realized that they could not hold back the political tide that was sweeping the German Democratic Republic to the west, they hoped to shape the outcome of this process. Conservatives in the Party, including Yegor Ligachev, along with Soviet military leaders, wished to block German unity and preserve the East German state at all costs. Longtime specialists in Germany, such as former Soviet Ambassador Valentin Falin, now head of the Party's International Department, realized that it was impossible to block a merger of the two German states but argued that a unified German state should be required to leave the North Atlantic Treaty Organization (NATO) and take a vow of neutrality.

The Soviet leaders were also particular about how the unification would come about. They were reconciled to a gradual process negotiated by the governments of East and West Germany, which would remain separate and sovereign for several years. This would allow Soviet troops to continue in East Germany for a lengthy and perhaps indeterminate period and would give Soviet diplomacy an opportunity to influence the conditions of unification. The USSR would lose these advantages if unification occurred on the basis of Article XXIII of the West German Constitution, as Chancellor Helmut Kohl had suggested. Under this procedure the East German *Länder* (states) would adhere individually to the federal German constitution; the GDR would simply disappear, and its constituent parts would be absorbed into the FRG without any change in the latter's constitutional structure.

The Soviet leaders took strong positions on these issues. When GDR Prime Minister Hans Modrow visited Moscow on March 5–6, Gorbachev told reporters that any form of participation in NATO by a united Germany was "absolutely out of the question."[10] The GDR press spokesman announced that the Soviet government had agreed that German unification must not occur on the basis of Article XXIII of the West German Constitution, and a Berlin newspaper quoted Shevardnadze to the same effect.[11] However, some Soviet officials would soon drop hints that the Soviet attitude might not be as rigid as the official statements suggested. They were aware that the Soviet Union had much to gain from friendly relations with a united Germany and were eager not to be seen as the enemy of German national aspirations.

In April, Vladlen Martynov, who had taken over from Primakov as head of the prestigious Institute for the World Economy and International Relations (IMEMO), remarked to me during a Spaso House dinner that "certain Western countries" (read: Britain and France) were more dubious about the prospects for German unity than was the Soviet Union, but they seemed to assume that the Soviets would take the heat for blocking rapid unification. "They're in for a surprise," Martynov observed. "We're not going to bear the onus for blocking the natural German desire for unity."

In early 1990, most Western diplomats in Moscow, including myself, had little hope that Gorbachev could agree to the summary dissolution of the GDR and a united Germany in NATO and survive politically with enough authority to keep perestroika alive. It was not that a future NATO with a united Germany would be harmful to Soviet interests: in fact, there was much to commend it from the point of view of a peaceful Soviet Union. German membership in NATO would provide a guarantee against some future German government deciding to acquire nuclear weapons—the ultimate security nightmare for Soviet leaders. Gorbachev also understood that some American military presence in Europe, and specifically in Germany, was in the Soviet interest, and NATO was the only legal and political basis for this.[12] He wanted to have fewer American troops in Europe but did not want them all to leave.

The problem was not that Gorbachev could not understand that a united Germany in NATO would be no threat to Soviet security; it was, rather, the difficulty of selling this novel concept to his own people. With the Warsaw Pact already in the final stages of dissolution, the image of NATO expanding to include all of Germany while Soviet troops abandoned the area and the other Soviet "allies" became neutral and potentially hostile suggested to the public a Soviet defeat tantamount to losing a war.

Secretary of State Baker recognized the problems facing the various parties in early 1990 and took the initiative to create a negotiating framework that would permit Germany and its Western allies to achieve their goals while reducing the political problem Gorbachev faced.

When Baker visited Moscow in February, he suggested to Shevardnadze a negotiating formula that he dubbed "two plus four." That is, the two German states would negotiate the internal arrangements for unification, then would be joined by the four powers that had gotten occupation rights in Germany following World War II—the Soviet Union, France, the United Kingdom, and the United States—for a negotiation of the "external aspects."

Shevardnadze first asked with a grin, "How about 'four plus two'?" Baker replied that the order of the digits might not matter in mathematics, but they did in politics. The outside powers must not leave the impression that they were imposing a settlement on the Germans. The two German states must first deal with each other, and only then should the other four enter the negotiation. After some further discussion and a nod from Gorbachev, Shevardnadze accepted the formula.

The already rapid pace of German unification gained further momentum in March when West German Chancellor Kohl's party, the Christian Democratic Union (CDU) won a stunning election victory in the GDR, receiving more than double the votes of its closest rival, the Social Democratic Party. Lothar de Maizière, the head of the East German CDU, became prime minister and worked closely with Chancellor Kohl to bring about unification in accord with Kohl's proposals. Within two weeks of Modrow's early-March visit to Moscow it became clear that German unification would occur by the eastern *Länder* merging with West Germany and not by the gradual fusion of two sovereign states. The prospect of Moscow manipulating a pliant GDR government to represent Soviet interests in negotiations with Bonn turned out to have been a mirage, and this heightened Gorbachev's political problems at home. The GDR elections that eliminated the East German Communists from political influence occurred precisely one week after Lithuania's declaration of independence and just a few days after Gorbachev had become president of the Soviet Union.

With Chancellor Kohl's active cooperation and the acquiescence of the other NATO allies, Baker put together a large package of changes in

NATO's structure and doctrine to present to Gorbachev when they met in Moscow in May. It would, he explained, be a new Germany and a new NATO. Desperate to find a way to insulate his domestic politics from the explosive issues the German question was raising, Gorbachev helped make NATO look less threatening to the Soviet public. Shevardnadze paid an official visit to NATO headquarters in Brussels and had favorable things to say about NATO's contribution to European security. He also invited NATO Secretary-General Manfred Wörner to visit Moscow.

Events, however, were moving so rapidly that even a forced march of diplomacy had trouble keeping up. During his meeting with Baker on May 18, Gorbachev continued to insist that he could not agree to a unified Germany in NATO since it would represent a "fundamental shift" in the balance of power and would look like a defeat for the Soviet Union. When Baker enumerated the ways in which the United States, West Germany, and their NATO allies had tried to take Soviet interests into account, Gorbachev maintained that Europe needed an entirely new security structure built around German neutrality. Though he did not spell out precisely what he had in mind, he seemed to be groping for some action by the West that could be portrayed as balancing the collapse of the Warsaw Pact. When Baker offered no hope that NATO would dissolve itself to provide the appearance of symmetry, Gorbachev observed that he might be driven to apply for NATO membership himself. Though he assured a surprised Baker that he was utterly serious, he did not elaborate further on the idea of Soviet membership in NATO. In fact, the discussion of Germany ended on a conciliatory note, with Gorbachev conceding that Baker had offered some sound arguments that would be given serious consideration.

While stressing political factors with us, Gorbachev and other Soviet leaders talked money with the Germans. When Horst Teltschik, Kohl's adviser on national security, met secretly with the Soviet leaders in Moscow in May, Ryzhkov and others talked at length of Soviet economic difficulties and pressed for large loans. A cynic would have sniffed the odor of blackmail, but a realist would not have been surprised that Gorbachev was seeking some tangible benefits to balance the political price he would have to pay if he sanctioned a united Germany in NATO.

As soon as the Soviet Party congress ended, Gorbachev acted swiftly to wrap up a deal on Germany. NATO Secretary-General Wörner arrived in Moscow for an official visit in July, just as the Soviet Party con-

gress was ending. Waiting with other ambassadors to greet him at the
terminal used for arriving chiefs of state, I marveled as I surveyed the
array of NATO flags on display. Hardly five years had passed since
there had been an intense Soviet propaganda campaign to vilify NATO
as a vicious, aggressive alliance bent on unleashing a new world war
And now its secretary-general was being received with the honors of a
chief of state and the alliance pictured as an important component of the
international structure for peace and security.

In the final analysis it was the German concessions that gave Gorbachev what he needed for an agreement. While the United States and
NATO as a whole had cooperated in redefining NATO's mission—these
decisions were formalized at a NATO summit in London on July 5–6—
only the Germans were able to offer limits on their military forces and
various types of financial support to ease Gorbachev's political dilemma. Chancellor Kohl came to the Soviet Union on July 15 for meetings with Gorbachev, first in Kislovodsk, near Gorbachev's birthplace,
and then in Moscow, and the deal was struck. The German armed forces
would be limited to 370,000 troops, and Germany would pay 12 billion
marks (around $8 billion) to facilitate the withdrawal of Soviet troops
from Germany and sign a friendship treaty and provide other types of
economic and technical assistance.

Thus, within four months after the CDU victory in the elections in
East Germany, the essential elements of a settlement were in place.
Within weeks the final documents were negotiated and signed: the Ger-
man Unification Treaty on August 31, the "Two Plus Four" treaty on
September 12, a Soviet-German Friendship Treaty on September 13,
and an agreement to end four-power rights in Germany and Berlin on
October 1.

German unification, which as late as the summer of 1989 had seemed to
be a remote goal, was a reality before the leaves fell from the Central
European trees in 1990. It happened so quickly that many people in the
West, once their initial surprise and disbelief passed, began to think of it
as an inevitable, almost automatic process.

Doubtless, the artificial East German state could not have lasted for-
ever. It was destined for eventual collapse since it had never enjoyed a
sense of legitimacy: it was obviously a structure imposed by a foreign
power. Nevertheless, there was nothing inevitable about the timing,

shape, and form of the settlements that reunited Germany and ended the artificial division of the European continent. I am confident that history will regard the negotiations that occurred between March and July 1990 as a model of diplomacy and their outcome as one of the most notable achievements of statesmen—ever.

"But wasn't Gorbachev too weak to protest?" skeptics may ask. "His country was falling apart and his position at home was so weak that he could hardly have resisted the Western demands. The only thing the Western countries had to do was to decide what they wanted, and the rest was automatic!"

I would not agree. While it was true that the cold war had ended and the Soviet Union was no longer in a position to apply or threaten military force abroad, Gorbachev could have played a spoiler's role in the negotiations on German unity and actually improved his political position at home. While he could not close borders and reimpose a puppet regime on the GDR, he did not have to give official blessing to the unification. He had 370,000 troops in East Germany, and neither the Germans nor NATO as a whole could have used force to expel them. It was vitally important for the stability of the united German state that the Soviets agree to the arrangements and to the withdrawal of Soviet troops from the eastern *Länder*. It was vitally important to Germany and NATO for the Soviet Union to relinquish all claims of special rights on German soil and to recognize the German right to choose its alliances freely. Gorbachev could have sulked and refused to participate in the arrangements. If he had, the Germans would have confronted the dilemma that they could have either NATO membership or unity but not both—at least, not both at that time. In time, public pressures to make a deal by accepting neutrality would probably have grown.

Of the Western leaders, the two most responsible for the successful negotiations were FRG Chancellor Helmut Kohl and U.S. Secretary of State James Baker. Kohl saw the opportunity and understood that it should be seized while conditions were propitious for an agreement. Baker organized the diplomatic effort, recognizing that the Germans had to be allowed to determine their internal arrangements and protected from pressure to leave NATO but that Gorbachev had to be given political "cover" if he was to be induced to sign on.

Gorbachev was criticized at the time and has been attacked since the collapse of the Soviet Union for not adequately defending Soviet (and Russian) interests during the negotiations for German unification. Such charges are doubtless inevitable, particularly when a country goes through the multitude of shocks that have shaken Russia and the other Soviet successor states. But they are wrong. The settlements on Germany were manifestly in the interests of the Soviet Union at the time — and of Russia today. A united Germany could hardly threaten the Soviet Union with the modest army the treaties permitted, the more so as it would be under NATO command. A friendly, prosperous Germany could be a profitable trading partner and potential investor in the Soviet Union or Russia. Understanding these advantages required replacing the attitudes of World War II and the ideology of class struggle with "new thinking" and a recognition that neighbors are more likely to be friendly and helpful if one stops trying to dominate them by force.

Gorbachev was utterly faithful to his country's interests when he concluded the agreements he did. He deserves the credit of history for discarding past attitudes, recognizing where the country's real interests lay, and resisting the political pressures at home to follow a different course. These pressures were substantial and were much in evidence at the Party congress that convened in early July. It was no accident that he postponed his agreement with Kohl until after the Party congress had ended.

The CPSU Marginalized

GORBACHEV'S FAILURE to establish control over the leadership of the new Russian Communist Party raised the stakes at the CPSU Party congress that followed a few days later. Although the congress was marked by strident criticism of Gorbachev's policies, it followed his recommendations when it came to electing top officials.

The result, however, was not a Politburo and Secretariat filled with reformers. Rather, the new Party leaders were a colorless group. Erstwhile stalwarts in the Politburo, of both "left" and "right," stepped down or were forced out; Shevardnadze, Yakovlev, Ligachev, and Ryzhkov all left the Politburo and were replaced by persons little known to the public at large. Gorbachev clung to his position as general secretary (though nearly a quarter of the delegates voted against him)[13] and pushed through his nominee for the new position of deputy secretary general: Vladimir Ivashko, who had succeeded Vladimir Shcherbitsky as head of the Communist Party in Ukraine.

Ligachev did not leave the leadership quietly. After urging Gorbachev to resign his Party post, he ran against Ivashko for deputy secretary general and, though he lost, received a respectable number of votes.

Speeches at the congress made it clear that Gorbachev's *rapprochement* with the West was no longer an unalloyed political asset. In fact, foreign policy had become one of the more divisive public issues. More and more voices accused Gorbachev and Shevardnadze of losing Eastern Europe and throwing away the fruits of victory in World War II by permitting Germany to reunite. Many still shied away from attacking Gorbachev directly and concentrated their fire on Shevardnadze.

Shevardnadze did not hesitate to pick up the gauntlet and in replying to his critics delivered one of the most eloquent and moving speeches of his career. On the question of who had lost Eastern Europe, he stated:

> We lost our strategic allies, comrades, . . . when we used force in Hungary in 1956, when we invaded Czechoslovakia in 1968, when we went into Afghanistan. And when we fell out with China before the time of perestroika. The crisis in Poland began not with perestroika but long before it.

Regarding Germany, he denied any "deal" to give the GDR to Bonn. "The people of the GDR will decide their fate for themselves. That's all there is to it," he explained.[14]

Gorbachev showed less vigor in defending his foreign policy, but this seemed more a matter of political discretion than a harbinger of a foreign policy shift.

My feelings were mixed when I analyzed the outcome of the congress. The debates had shown that opposition to reform was growing rapidly within the Party, but this had not prevented Gorbachev from getting his way once again. The fact that secret balloting had been conducted in electing the leadership was an innovation, and it was the first Party congress since Stalin's rise to power to conduct real elections of officials.

Nevertheless, the new Politburo had no reformers of the stature of Alexander Yakovlev and Eduard Shevardnadze. The only advantage it seemed to have over its predecessor was its lack of stature: Gorbachev could more easily ignore it if he desired. That did seem to be his unstated goal. One of the frequent charges made by his opponents at the congress was that he had failed to consult the Politburo before making important foreign policy decisions. Nevertheless, despite strong criticism of his German policy at the congress, he made his deal with Chancellor Kohl just days after the congress ended. There is no indication that his new Politburo uttered so much as a whimper.

In sum, the outcome of the Party congress was consistent with my assumptions regarding Gorbachev's intentions. Though he had not obtained a ringing endorsement of the more radical aspects of perestroika, he had survived as Party leader and had, in effect, downgraded the central Party institutions. He was now in a position to forge an alliance with reform elements and, in time, could discard the Party machinery if it opposed him.

At least that was how it seemed to me in July 1990.

Stampedes to Sovereignty

RUSSIA'S DECLARATION of sovereignty unleashed a predictable reaction in the other republics. Uzbekistan and Moldavia[15] declared sovereignty in June, Ukraine and Belorussia in July, and Turkmenistan, Armenia, and Tajikistan in August. By the end of October, all fifteen union republics had declared either sovereignty or full independence. Kazakhstan and Kyrgyzstan, whose leaders were still trying to cooperate with Gorbachev in forming a federation, were the last.

During the spring and summer of 1990, I made trips to Moldavia, Uzbekistan, Turkmenistan, and Kazakhstan, as well as to some of the autonomous republics in Russia such as Udmurtia and Buryatia. The changes in attitudes as compared with a year earlier were striking.

Kishinev, previously a listless provincial city, was buzzing with excitement when we arrived in early May. The Moldavian parliament had passed a language law a few months earlier that had restored the Latin alphabet to the language that had officially been called Moldavian but was as close to Romanian as the language spoken in the United States is to English. The law also required officials dealing with the public (such as in post offices, savings banks, and hospitals) to learn Moldavian within five years. At the same time the traditional Romanian flag, with its three vertical stripes of blue, yellow and red, replaced the red banner derived from the Soviet flag.

Moldavians were flush with success. Plans were well advanced for a massive demonstration the coming weekend on the Prut River, the border with Romania, which had hitherto been closed to most movement. At that time the Moldavians would mingle and exchange flowers with their cousins from across the border. Even the local Communist Party had endorsed the demonstration—perhaps having learned something from the futile opposition to the Baltic Way the previous summer. Communist Party First Secretary Lucinschi told me he planned to participate personally.

The ethnic Russians in the republic, however, felt threatened by the wave of local nationalism. At dinner one evening in a private room of a local restaurant, Rebecca and I witnessed passionate presentations of both sides of the debate. Two leaders of the National Front, Ion Hadîrcă and Ion Ungureanu, announced when they arrived that they would have to leave early to appear on a television program. The local councils in two cities east of the Dniester River, Ternopol and Bendery, had refused to fly the new Moldavian flag. The urban population there was predominantly Russian and Ukrainian, so the action was a protest against the growing Moldavian assertiveness. The Moldavian Supreme Soviet had voted that day to rule the actions of the local councils unconstitutional. Our guests had been invited to explain this position on television that evening.

I asked them how serious they considered the east bank challenge, and they replied that it was a major issue since it seemed to presage an attempt to secede from the republic. They then spoke at length about the discrimination Moldavians had suffered from Russian immigrants and defended the new language law as a matter of elementary justice. Russians working in public service jobs would be given time to learn enough Moldavian to deal with the public in that language, but if they didn't try they would be fired. As for the parliament, either Moldavian or Russian could be used, with simultaneous translation provided for all speeches.

They, like others in Kishinev, asked whether the United States considered Moldavia legally part of the Soviet Union. They were aware that we did not recognize the incorporation of the Baltic states. Since Moldavia had also been booty from the secret protocol to the Nazi-Soviet pact, they thought they should get the same legal treatment.

To their dismay, I had to explain that their situation was legally different. Most of the current Moldavian republic had been part of Romania between the two world wars, not independent like the Baltic states. After World War II, Romania had officially ceded the territory to the Soviet Union. Though this had been done under duress, Romania being a defeated German ally and the area being under Soviet occupation, the transfer had been incorporated in the peace treaty with Romania, to which the United States had also been a party. Therefore, we had no legal ground to challenge the status of Moldavia as a part of the Soviet Union.

"Too bad," Hadîrcă commented. Then after a pause he added, "We'll go for independence anyway. Then we can think about whether we want to return to Romania, stay independent, or negotiate some sort of association with the Soviet Union." It was the first mention of independence as a realistic goal I had heard from a senior Moldavian official. At that time Hadîrcă was not only leader of the National Front but also the deputy chairman of the Moldavian parliament and a member of the USSR Congress of People's Deputies. Ungureanu, a stage designer and filmmaker, was the Moldavian minister of culture.

While our Moldavian guests discussed their political and cultural aspirations, our Russian guest observed the scene silently but with a scowl on her face. Trained to be an English teacher, Ludmila Lobzova was then director of the local Pushkin Museum (the Russian poet had spent two years in political exile in the city in the 1820s) and had given us a fascinating tour of her facilities earlier in the day. When there was a lull in the conversation she suddenly proposed to recite, in Russian and English translation, a poem by the Moldavian poet Mihail Eminescu. The other guests listened respectfully, then resumed the previous conversation, upon which Ludmila's scowl returned.

When Hadîrcă and Ungureanu left for the television station and the other Moldavian guests were engaged in a side conversation, Ludmila suddenly began to pour out to me her frustrations and fears as a Russian. She felt that the Moldavian "extremists" considered Russians "occupiers" and were intent on expelling them. Defensive about her failure to learn Moldavian during the many years she had lived in Kishinev, she claimed that she had spent her time learning English instead, "which is useful to everyone." She had worked hard and saved for thirteen years to buy a cooperative apartment and had no ties elsewhere in the Soviet Union.

The "nationalists," she complained, were trying to move Pushkin's statue from the center of the park bearing his name to a side alley. Granted, it had originally been there, but it had been moved to a more prominent place when the park was named for him. She also objected to the contention that Russia had been an aggressor when it had annexed Bessarabia (present-day Moldavia) in 1812. "We came to protect the Orthodox Moldavians from their Turkish oppressors," she maintained.

Interspersed with these comments, she recounted facts from her own biography: the daughter of a naval officer, she had lived in Khabarovsk, near the Pacific coast, as a girl. Her father had been transferred to Ismail, a port on Moldavia's Black Sea coast, when she was in her teens. She had come to college in Kishinev and had lived there since. Now, well into middle age, she was alone in a city increasingly hostile, frightened of losing her job and the only home she knew.

Had they been part of this conversation, our Moldavian guests would doubtless have dismissed her fears. Surely, over the next few years, they would have argued, she could learn enough Moldavian to deal with Moldavian visitors to her museum. This requirement was neither unreasonable nor difficult to attain and would assure her a continued place in Moldavian society.

Ludmila, however, felt instinctively that her problem could not be solved so simply, even if she had been willing to make the effort. The attitudes she found offensive appeared to be harbingers of a policy that would reserve Moldavia for ethnic Moldavians alone and perhaps even bring rule from Bucharest. Real communication between most Moldavians and Russians had ceased.

Ferment of the sort I observed in Moldavia seemed absent or suppressed in Uzbekistan and Turkmenistan, but the local Communist authorities were acting with greater independence from Moscow and were attempting to coopt local nationalism.

In Samarkand, Palat Abdurakhmanov, the regional Party secretary, spoke to me at length about plans to shift away from cotton monoculture and grow more fruit and vegetables. He was upset that so little had been done to develop industry to process local products: the textile and food-processing industries seemed particularly suitable for expansion. Nevertheless, his region was still feeling the diktat of the central economic ministries. He complained that the Uzbeks were still not permitted to trade freely in products produced above plan or to export such products for hard currency. Laws had been on the books for months to permit such transactions, but the relevant ministries still had not brought their regulations into conformity with them.

New mosques were being constructed in most of the major cities of

Central Asia, although the Islamic institutions were still kept under close control and the Communist authorities in both Uzbekistan and Turkmenistan had refused to register Islamic political parties. An offer by Saudi Arabia to send a million copies of the Koran for use in Central Asia had not yet been implemented because Moscow had not issued a permit for the import.[16] Republic authorities had, however, reversed a long-standing policy of forbidding the observance of traditional Islamic holidays. In 1990, for the first time in decades, communities all over Uzbekistan were celebrating the festival of Navruz, which marked the beginning of the agricultural year.

Nevertheless, in some ways Uzbekistan and Turkmenistan reminded me more of the Soviet Union of old than did most other regions, which had experienced major transformation. Many appointments I requested, particularly with students, young people, and unofficial organizations, did not materialize. The sessions with the top officials differed little from similar meetings in years past.

For example, First Secretary Islam Karimov of Uzbekistan received me in a sumptuous conference room in the Party's new Tashkent headquarters. (In many other republics, the Party was already seeking a lower profile by transferring new buildings, now deemed inappropriately pretentious, to the government or to other organizations; in Kishinev, for example, the new city Party headquarters had been converted into a children's hospital.) He fielded questions with the commanding self-assurance of an old-line Party boss. When I asked why the principal opposition coalition, Birlik, had not been "registered" in accord with the new Soviet laws, he simply said that it did not deserve registration because it had been taken over by irresponsible elements who organized demonstrations that could result in rioting. A few weeks after my visit, Karimov had himself elected president of Uzbekistan and thus set off a parade of Central Asian Party leaders anxious to assume more imposing titles. This particular fad did not stop at the borders of Central Asia.

Karimov at that time did tolerate one small opposition group that was led by some prominent Uzbek intellectuals who had withdrawn from Birlik. Rebecca and I invited three of them to join us for dinner.

Erkin Vakhidov, a prominent Uzbek poet in his early fifties, explained that the movement he headed, Erk, "Will" in Uzbek, had the goal of establishing political and economic autonomy for Uzbekistan. Its members intended, however, to utilize "parliamentary means" exclusively and to avoid large public demonstrations that might risk violence.

Both of his colleagues at dinner that evening were also writers: Nurali Kabul wrote novels and political essays—a recent one on the future of Uzbekistan had drawn wide attention—and also ran a publishing house; Amman Marchan edited a magazine for young people and, though still youthful himself, had more than twenty slender books of poetry to his credit.

Their attention to environmental degradation was no surprise to me; it is so obvious in Central Asia that it would have been suicidal for political movements dependent on votes to ignore it. But their suggestions went beyond the usual list of ending cotton monoculture, increasing the flow of water to the Aral Sea, adopting less profligate irrigation techniques, and building industry based on local raw materials. They also—unlike many Moscow intellectuals—saw that Uzbekistan's economic problems could not be solved unless the right to private property was recognized.

They hoped to persuade the Uzbek legislature to approve a new constitution. When I asked what materials they were using in their draft, they complained that the libraries in Tashkent had few resources to help them understand constitutions outside the Soviet Union. However, they had copies of Andrei Sakharov's draft constitution and a Russian translation of the U.S. Constitution, which one of their members had picked up during a reception at Spaso House. We often offered publications of interest to our guests, and it was encouraging to find that one of them was actually being used.[17]

Most of Erk's goals seemed aimed at securing autonomy within the USSR, so I was surprised when one of our guests confessed that his ambition was to be the ambassador of an independent Uzbekistan to the United States.

"Is that realistic?" I inquired.

"Not right now, but give me five years!" he said with a laugh. But he was not joking.

Kazakhstan, which I visited once again in June, offered a political contrast to its neighbors to the south. Nursultan Nazarbayev had replaced Kolbin as party secretary, and he discussed the republic's problems and aspirations with apparent candor. He said that Kazakhstan wanted to stay in the USSR and that Gorbachev had his full support, but that the union had to be redefined to give full sovereignty to the republics. He was prepared to cooperate with Yeltsin and other republic leaders to bring that about and was at that time cooperating with other republics to produce a draft of a union treaty to replace the one proposed by Moscow.

He was acutely conscious of Kazakhstan's colonial status and was determined to change it. He rejected the idea, prevalent in Moscow, that Kazakhstan had been the recipient of more investment funds than it generated. He pointed out that the republic's extensive resources would enable it to hold its own in trade with other republics if market prices were used instead of the artificially low prices dictated by Moscow. He also believed that Central Asia needed better structures for regional cooperation and despite Moscow's hostility had chaired a meeting of the Central Asian leaders the previous week.

Though not as open and freewheeling as in Moscow, local politics seemed less controlled and more spontaneous than in Tashkent. A few years earlier, Olzhas Suleimenov, a prominent poet, had organized the Nevada-Semipalatinsk Society to campaign against nuclear testing. (Most Soviet nuclear tests were conducted on the Semipalatinsk test grounds northeast of Alma Ata.) The group had been successful in postponing some planned tests and was becoming a broader political movement. Suleimenov himself was an active member of the USSR parliament. Though still a member of the Communist Party, he seemed to be carving out an independent niche for his movement.

A determination to break the control of the imperial center was growing in all the union republics. In some, such as the Baltic states and Moldavia, the motive force came from national movements, usually led by intellectuals. In others, such as Uzbekistan and Turkmenistan, it came from Communist Party officials eager to preserve control of the political system, which would be endangered if perestroika took root in their republics. Even leaders like Nazarbayev, who wanted both reform and union, were demanding an end to imperial controls.

The separatist sentiment that now dominated most of the union republics was seeping into the RSFSR itself. Leaders of several "autonomous" units in Russia also began to claim rights of sovereignty. In August, the Karelian ASSR, on the border with Finland, declared its sovereignty. Within weeks the soviets in nine other ASSRs, ranging from Udmurtia and Tatarstan in the Urals to Yakutia (renamed Sakha) and Buryatia in eastern Siberia, voted in favor of sovereignty. Many also changed their official name, removing the term "autonomous" so as to call themselves "Soviet Socialist Republics" just like the union republics. This was more than symbolism, for with the change of name came claims to the same rights as those the union republics were demanding: control over natural resources and economic activity, an exclusive right of tax collection, and—often—a right to secede.

The hatred of central controls was such that the sovereignty fever spread to smaller and smaller units, including "autonomous" oblasts and districts, some with tiny populations.[18]

Most of these autonomous entities were in Russia, but two were in the Georgian republic: The Abkhazian Supreme Soviet declared its sovereignty and status as a union republic (thus seceding from Georgia) on August 25, but the Georgian parliament immediately annulled the act. The following month the soviet in the South Ossetian Autonomous Oblast also declared itself a republic and met a similar rebuff from Tbilisi. These two declarations reflected much deeper fissures than did most of those in the RSFSR: the Abkhazians and South Ossetians were pressing to be transferred from Georgia to Russia—or to sovereign status in the USSR. In time, both areas would be engulfed in a war with Georgia—in fact, one had already started in South Ossetia.

Most of the declarations in the RSFSR, on the other hand, stated explicitly that the sovereign republic would remain a part of Russia. The demands for more control over their political systems, resources, and economies were in part a natural reaction by the republics to the weakening central controls and past injusticies. Sometimes, however, local leaders were merely taking advantage of the weakened Center to grab more political power for themselves. Some—especially those in Georgia—received encouragement from conservative officials in Moscow. By creating difficulties in Russia, some of Yeltsin's more short-sighted opponents thought they might undermine his effort to make common cause with other union republics against the central bureaucracy. As for Georgia, Soviet hard-liners, particularly in the military and KGB, were determined to punish Georgia for its election of ex-dissident Zviad Gamsakhurdia and its headlong dash to independence. Some observers were convinced that Gorbachev himself approved of these risky and disruptive tactics.

Yeltsin and Gamsakhurdia reacted differently to the pressures. Gamsakhurdia refused to negotiate and responded with arrests and threats of military force—which were implemented in South Ossetia. Yeltsin, in contrast, was determined not to be outdone as a proponent of decentralization. Shortly after he was elected chairman of the Russian legislature, he made a tour of several autonomous republics and regions of the Russian Federation. In Kazan, the capital of Tatarstan, one of the most assertive of the "autonomies," as these republics were called colloquially, he told his listeners to "take all the sovereignty you can swallow."

These words would haunt him later, but at the time they seemed smart politics. In the summer of 1990, few imagined that any part of the Soviet Union aside from the Baltic states and possibly Moldavia and Georgia had a serious intent to break away, let alone territories in Russia itself. In his battle for status and power, Yeltsin would do what was necessary to secure both his rear and his flanks.

XV

—•◆•—

The Curse of the Purloined Property

Transferring state property to new owners is the main task of perestroika in the economic area.
GAVRIIL POPOV[1]

The only thing we should prohibit during our reforms is use of the words "socialism" and "capitalism." Games with words will drive us into a blind alley.
LARISA PIYASHEVA, August 1990[2]

How do you reform something that isn't?
ALEXANDER IVANOV[3]

Debate intensified during 1990 over the content and timing of economic reform. One plan after another was offered, by the Ryzhkov government, by various commissions, both official and self-appointed, and by individual economists, both Soviet and foreign. Repeatedly, the Supreme Soviet rejected government proposals or, having approved some in principle, sent the details (which contained the real substance) back for further work.

During the winter I had already concluded that the greatest barrier to meaningful reform was not ideology, though the stereotypes and habits of the past still needed to be overcome, but the Soviet economic bureaucracy. Following the Bolshevik Revolution, all land and income-producing property had been confiscated and placed, theoretically in trust for the nation, into the hands of bureaucrats to administer. In practice, the bureaucrats began to act as the owners. Any attempt to move from a command economy to a market economy was viewed by the economic ministries as theft of property and privileges that were rightfully theirs.

The ministries in Moscow had, in practice, nullified the legislation to accord economic autonomy to the Baltic states and thus bolstered the forces demanding independence. Now, by blocking every attempt to decentralize economic decision making, they were stoking the nationalist fires in all the other republics. The "ideological" *nomenklatura*—the professional Party apparatchiks—were in retreat and disarray, but the "economic" *nomenklatura* still held the economy in a tight grip.[4]

The Bolshevik nationalization of property had, in a real sense, placed a curse on the Soviet regime. Unless it could find a way to divest itself of the exclusive property rights its founders had seized, it would be torn asunder. It could no longer return property to the individuals who once had owned it, most of whom were dead, and there were no legitimate claimants other than the nation as a whole to the assets that had been created during the Soviet period. Nevertheless, if it was to survive, the regime needed to find a way to empower its citizens to own and administer property directly. The state bureaucracy, theoretically a trustee for the people, had proven to be not merely inefficient but faithless and corrupt as well.

Legends of the curse carried by ill-gotten property are staples in many cultures. Whether it is a stolen gem or the gold of the Rhine immortalized in Richard Wagner's cycle of operas or one of the many other variants, one invariable feature is that the greed of the illegitimate owner blinds him to the danger of possession.

Throughout 1990 and 1991, as I witnessed repeated futile efforts to reform the economy, I was often reminded of these legends. Unless the state could find a way to divest itself of control over most income-producing property, reform could not take hold since no real market system of economic interchange would be possible. Unless Gorbachev could find a way to terminate the central government's possession of most property in the Soviet Union, his own position would crumble under the pressure of newly empowered republics that were no longer willing to have their economic fate decided by bureaucrats in Moscow. Yet, like the protagonists of countless legends, he seemed oblivious to the curse. He could not bear the thought of some of his authority passing to others. By clinging to the power over property, he doomed his own office and the state he headed.

Government Bungling

RYZHKOV AND HIS MINISTERS never understood what it would take to create a market system. The problem was not that they were ideologically dogmatic or personally greedy, though some were both. Most of them were willing to discard some old dogmas and redefine others. And while some members of the government were unquestionably greedy, their voracious appetites could have been better satisfied by a reformed economy than one that had collapsed. They failed, in the first instance, because they did not understand what was required to create a market system that works.

Even the terminology they used was confusing. Once it was permissible to speak favorably of a market system, they talked about a "socialist market" without ever explaining how a socialist market would differ from any other. By 1990, the official goal was a "regulated market," but this too was not defined. Did it mean that the entire economy would be run like the European Community's Common Agricultural Policy or like regulated utilities in the West or—perhaps—like sugar prices in the United States? If so, one could hardly class it as a market system, for whatever the function of market controls in the West for specific sectors or situations, they work—to the degree they do—only when they are exceptions and not the rule. There is no way to "regulate" an entire market except through the sort of administrative controls that had already proved dysfunctional in the USSR and that perestroika had pledged to end.

Ryzhkov and his colleagues failed not only to grasp the essence of market economics but also to understand that without a substantial degree of private ownership, market relations would be exceedingly difficult and perhaps impossible to create. In practice, state-owned enterprises could not be expected to compete with one another in a manner that would create a genuine market. Yet the hostility to private property, particularly in land, was pervasive in the political leadership, and even those who would concede that private entrepreneurs should be encouraged in local service industries still viewed "collective property" as a superior type of ownership and the only permissible form for enterprises of any size.

Without a clear understanding of what makes a market work, they could not envisage the sort of institutions a market requires. An efficient banking system, market-oriented accounting rules, a tax system that can extract necessary revenues from the population without stifling private initiative—one could compile a long list of institutions essential to a workable market system that the Soviet Union lacked. These institutions could not be created overnight, but one fatal flaw in all the government plans for reform was the absence of any strategy that would have created them or allowed them to develop.

Nikolai Ryzhkov, prime minister until the end of 1990, was personally one of the most appealing leaders of the Gorbachev period. More sensitive and less dominating and manipulative in his personal relationships than Gorbachev was, Ryzhkov meant well. He knew the system required reform, but he thought he could do it by stages. Have Gosplan order military equipment suppliers to convert x percent of production a year to civilian goods, and—presto!—in y years the shops will be full and everyone will be happy. But this could not work in the real world of the Soviet bureaucracy. The system was designed to strangle private initiative. Market institutions transplanted piecemeal into the existing economic system would simply be rejected, as surely as a human would reject a lung transplant from a chimpanzee.

That fact led to another of Ryzhkov's failures of comprehension. One of his favorite phrases, both when he was in office and since, is that he wanted to "create, not destroy"—unquestionably a noble emotion. But the new would never work if the old was left in place to smother it.

As a result of confused concepts and the bureaucratic procedures common in the Soviet government—in which each institution defended its parochial interests without regard to the national interest—government plans typically managed to make a bad situation worse. One of the most egregious errors was to declare that the prices of many consumer goods would be raised over the months to come. Parliament rejected the plan, but as soon as it was public knowledge store shelves were stripped bare. Everyone wanted to stock up before the prices rose. Factories and farms began to hold back production in the hope of getting higher prices for their goods later.

The prices of many Soviet products were far below world market prices, and some were even below the cost of making them. Unwise expansion of the money supply had created a "currency overhang" that inevitably exacerbated inflationary pressures. Any real move to a market system would have to be accompanied by higher prices. But there is a fundamental difference between creating market conditions that will result in higher prices (and wages) in response to market forces and simply decreeing higher prices, giving extensive advance notice to the public. Repeatedly attempting to do the latter, despite the disastrous results each time it was tried, was characteristic of the Ryzhkov government's approach to reform. In fact, the programs were designed to keep the economic *nomenklatura* in control of the economy under the cover of reform rhetoric.

Russian Separatism Spreads

WHILE YELTSIN WAS WILLING to move faster in eliminating the central economic ministries, his rhetoric did not help the public understand what was ahead. His political instincts led him to tell people what they wanted to hear, and he did so with abandon. Radical reform was necessary, he argued, but it had to be implemented so that the public would not suffer. Prosperity, he suggested, would be just around the corner if only economic decision making were left to the republics. In 1987 and 1988, he had rightly criticized Gorbachev for implying that perestroika could be implemented without sacrifice. Now that he was gaining authority, he seemed to be making the same mistake. But what politician would choose to run on a ticket calling for higher prices, fewer welfare benefits, and high unemployment?

One politician who ran on a private property platform was catapulted into prominence when he was elected Yeltsin's deputy by the Russian Supreme Soviet. Ruslan Khasbulatov, an economist at the Plekhanov Institute in Moscow, had been elected to the RSFSR Congress of People's Deputies in Grozny, the capital of his native Chechen-Ingush Republic, situated just north of the Caucasus Mountains. I had not met him before, so I requested a courtesy call shortly after he was elected.

A handsome man in his forties, Khasbulatov reminded me of my friend Fazil Izkander, a popular writer from Abkhazia, not far from Grozny, but located in the Georgian Republic rather than Russia. His words were even more impressive than his looks, however: he turned out to be far more radical than Yeltsin was at that time. He was the first senior Russian official to tell me that Russia would soon become the successor state to the Soviet Union. The union, he predicted, would be converted into a loose confederation, which would not need a constitution since it would not have the attributes of statehood. It would be defined in a brief treaty of union, negotiated among the union republics, with perhaps ten or a dozen general points. Only the republics would have authority to tax, and they would decide what contributions to make to the union budget, much as member states of the United Nations do.

He professed to be sympathetic to Gorbachev and to wish him well, but he felt that the Ryzhkov government was "a millstone around [Gorbachev's] neck." Authority for economic decision making, he said, should be delegated to the republics. This, he argued, would be in Gorbachev's interest: "We can help him by doing what he cannot do from the Center." Russia was eager, he said, to get on with privatization of the economy, but the bureaucracy was blocking all real progress; only a transfer of authority to the republics would bypass the central bureaucracy and bring results.

He was willing to leave foreign policy largely in Gorbachev's hands for the time being, but Russia would insist on placing its own representatives in Soviet embassies, since it intended to conduct its foreign economic relations independently. Eventually, it would also develop a distinctive political approach—for example, it favored more forceful opposition to the Iraqi aggression against Kuwait than Gorbachev apparently did—and eventually Soviet embassies abroad should become Russian embassies, since Russia would be the successor state.

In fact, Khasbulatov felt that whatever union was established would have few functions: control of nuclear weapons might be one of them, but conventional military forces would be transferred to the republics. It could be governed by a Senate of ten representatives from each of the founding republics, eliminating the present Supreme Soviet and Congress of People's Deputies. As the successor state, Russia would assume the bulk of the Soviet debt—as much as 75 percent, in Khasbulatov's estimate.

I left Khasbulatov's office almost as stunned as I had been in March when Shevardnadze spoke of resigning. Most Russian reformers assumed that a Soviet state would continue. If they had their way, it would have little control over economic activity but would retain authority to determine foreign policy, provide for the common defense, maintain a monetary system, and exercise some control over basic infrastructure such as telecommunications and long distance transportation. They assumed that a few small union republics on the periphery (such as the Baltic states, Moldavia, and Georgia) might insist on a greater degree of independence but considered it important to avoid fracturing the "economic space" the Soviet Union occupied. Thus they sought enhanced power for the republics without dissolution of the union. Some saw a federation similar to the United States as the ideal; others wanted something looser to accommodate ethnic differences and satisfy national pride, but still with a confederal authority with the attributes of statehood.

Yeltsin himself had repeatedly endorsed a federal or confederal goal. He denied Gorbachev's charges that his proposals would lead to a breakup of the Soviet Union, arguing instead that a strong union required strong republics.[5] But now his principal deputy was talking directly of a Russian *successor state,* which would have only loose ties with the other union republics in a regional copy of the United Nations.

Two months before my meeting with Khasbulatov, I had sent a message to Washington pointing out that we must take seriously and prepare for the possibility that the Soviet Union could break up. I did not favor actions by the United States to bring this about (aside from insisting on the right of the Baltic states to recover their independence) but considered it imperative to position ourselves to deal with the consequences. However, even as I saw forces developing that could tear the Soviet Union apart, I assumed that if it happened it would be because the other republics, preeminently Ukraine, would insist on independence and thus would force Russia to go it alone. I did not anticipate that—apart from a few visionaries—Russian politicians would see such an outcome as one that Russia should welcome and promote.

Khasbulatov, however, was not an eccentric visionary but a prominent economist who had won the number two post in the new Russian parliament. Others, increasingly frustrated at Gorbachev's inability to define the economic reforms the country needed, began to talk the same way. Mikhail Bocharov was one.

An industrial manager turned politician, Bocharov had been elected to both the USSR and RSFSR Congresses of People's Deputies and had recently been appointed chairman of the RSFSR parliament's Higher Economic Council. In June he had been a candidate for chairman of the RSFSR Council of Ministers (prime minister) but had failed to receive a majority of the votes cast.

I had seen Bocharov periodically since early 1989 and was familiar with his views. He was convinced that a market economy could be established only by radical and rapid moves to end central control of the economy and to break up state enterprises so as to create competition. However, until the summer of 1990, he was thinking of the USSR economy as a whole.

But when we chatted in August, I found that his focus had shifted. Even though he was hopeful that Gorbachev was finally prepared to start a real process of economic reform, he felt that Russia had the means to carry out the reforms itself, should that prove necessary. Hence, if Gorbachev should, once again, hesitate to proceed with fundamental reforms, he expected Russia to assume the lead and to proceed with direct negotiations with other republics that could produce new structures to replace the recalcitrant central management system.

The transition to market relations, he thought, would be very difficult, but it would have to occur rapidly if it was to happen at all. The end result, he predicted, would be a Soviet Union not unlike the European Community after the Maastricht Treaty was implemented in 1993: a group of sovereign states with a common "economic space" and currency and with institutions exercising regulatory or advisory functions, such as the European Commission in Brussels and the European Parliament in Strasbourg.[6]

Khasbulatov, therefore, was not alone in thinking of a Russian successor state to the Soviet Union. People like Bocharov came to that conclusion not because they had some abstract allegiance to Russian separatism but out of frustration over Gorbachev's inability to make a full commitment to economic reform. Their numbers were likely to grow unless Gorbachev made decisive moves to dismantle central economic controls.

500 Days That Never Came

FROM MID-JULY THROUGH AUGUST, it appeared that my hunch about Gorbachev's intentions was correct. Having marginalized the Communist Party leadership in setting policy, Gorbachev began to speak of radical economic reform once more, agreed to cooperate with Yeltsin to develop a new, crash program, and joined Yeltsin in naming a commission to draft the plan. He had moved quickly when the Party congress was over to come to the historic agreement with German Chancellor Helmut Kohl, thus showing a new independence from the

Party hard-liners, and he seemed poised to do the same in respect to the country's economic transformation.

Gorbachev and Yeltsin jointly selected the specialists who would draft a reform plan to replace the abortive ones concocted by the Ryzhkov government. They selected a member of the Presidential Council, Academician Stanislav Shatalin, to chair the group, and named to it a dozen or so economists from both teams: Nikolai Petrakov, for example, was, like Shatalin, a member of Gorbachev's Presidential Council, while Grigory Yavlinsky and Boris Fyodorov came from the RSFSR government. While Yeltsin's nominees were younger and reputedly more radical than those from Gorbachev's team, the group seemed united on the need to take rapid steps to dismantle the central economic controls that were strangling economic activity and stimulating secessionist passions throughout the empire.

When they assembled on August 6 at a resort on Moscow's outskirts to work without the distractions of their offices and families, they took as their initial draft a program Yavlinsky and some of his associates had been working on for months. It was already known in economic and political circles as the "500-Day Plan," since it set forth an ambitious timetable to introduce a market system over a 500-day period.

Although the timetable seemed wildly optimistic—creating a market system in a mere eighteen months was clearly not possible—the steps it prescribed seemed precisely those that were necessary to begin a self-sustaining movement toward the market—and, for that matter, a democratic political system, which ultimately requires a diffusion of economic power through society as a whole. It recognized the need for the state to relinquish its monopoly over economic decision making and provided a tight schedule for the divestiture.

The Shatalin commission had been instructed to produce a report in thirty days, but, in contrast to Soviet bureaucrats, who rarely came close to meeting a deadline, it did its work in fifteen days, completing a draft on August 21. The Shatalin draft retained the basic contours of the "500-Day Plan," though not the name. When the commission offered a summary of its recommendations in a lengthy article in *Izvestiya* on September 4, it stressed the need to return property to the people, explaining:

> Privatization . . . is a mechanism for distributing to all who wish to take it responsibility for the condition and level of development of society. . . .

Property in the hands of everyone is a guarantee of social stability and one of the most important conditions militating against social and ethnic upheaval.[7]

The group also prescribed freedom of economic activity for individuals, freedom of choice for consumers, and managerial autonomy for enterprises, whether private, corporate, or state owned. The economic ministries would be abolished and state subsidies to enterprises ended, and managers would be required to establish their own "horizontal ties" with suppliers and customers instead of simply following orders from a ministry in Moscow. This "freedom of management" would require painful adjustments but would have its rewards: managers could lease and sell property (hitherto forbidden), engage directly in foreign trade, and make their own deals for investment capital and loans rather than waiting for allocations from above.

The basic responsibility for economic rule setting would devolve upon the republic and local authorities, with the Soviet government retaining authority only over union property and those functions delegated to it by the republics.

It was easy to find flaws in the Shatalin plan: many details still had to be worked out, some timetables were unrealistic, and the authors couched many sound recommendations in irresponsible populist rhetoric—a failing that would continue to plague Russian reformers in the years ahead. For example, the authors claimed that "movement toward the market would be primarily at the expense of the state, not at the expense of ordinary people"[8] and even postulated a "right" for citizens "to live better right now, not in the distant future."[9]

Nevertheless, for all its flaws, it was the best and most workable approach that had yet emerged. It was designed to alter precisely those fundamentals that would have to change if reform was to prevail.

Even its unrealistic timetable had a point: it would deprive the economic bureaucrats of their most potent weapon, procrastination. In the Soviet Union as elsewhere, when a bureaucrat was faced with disagreeable orders, the usual reaction was to agree "in principle" but postpone implementation on the ground that the time was not quite ripe. The time, of course, would never ripen, but the boss would probably be transferred or lose interest or enthusiasm. For this reason, no plan to eliminate bureaucratic control of the economy could work if it was not rigid in its requirements, radical in scope, and rapid in execution.

The lack of detail on some points was in fact a virtue rather than a shortcoming. There was no way to plan every aspect of the transition to a market economy. Most of the institution building would have to be done outside the state structure, by individuals given the freedom to do so. The government could not create a market system; it could only make one possible by getting out of the way and permitting individuals, acting in their enlightened self-interest, to do it. Ryzhkov never understood this, but Shatalin did, and that is why he called his recommendations a "program" and not a "plan"—which, however, did not prevent others from referring to the "Shatalin plan."

Throughout the summer, Gorbachev made several enthusiastic comments about the Shatalin program, and it seemed likely that he would adopt it. The scenario I had imagined the preceding winter seemed to be the script for the drama we were witnessing. He had obtained the presidency, abolished the Communist monopoly on power, reorganized the Party to diminish its influence, and now seemed poised to exploit the freedom of action the new situation provided. He was now ready to push, after so much talk, for real changes in the economic system. And, at the same time, he was carving an epitaph on the gravestone of the cold war.

A Common Interest with the West

AGREEMENTS FOR THE UNIFICATION of Germany and for removing the last vestiges of the iron curtain through Central Europe had been made (though not all were yet formalized) when Shevardnadze and Baker met in Irkutsk on August 1. The two had developed a rapport like that which had existed between Shevardnadze and Shultz, and Shevardnadze wished to repay the hospitality Baker had extended the year before when he had arranged meetings in Jackson Hole, Wyoming.

The scenery in the immediate vicinity of Irkutsk cannot match the majesty of the Grand Tetons, but it is impressive, and nearby Lake Baikal, the largest body of fresh water in the world,[10] offers incomparable views of still relatively unspoiled nature. The setting was an inspired choice for one of the most harmonious meetings of the two foreign ministers.

It was not that they solved all the problems—we still had some differences in the negotiations on strategic arms as well as on Afghanistan—but the differences were exceptions rather than the rule, and even they were not of the magnitude that had been typical of U.S.-Soviet problems in the past. The ministers had so few serious differences that they could afford to take a half-day excursion by hydrofoil up the Angara River to Lake Baikal and enjoy a relaxed dinner in a rustic fishing lodge.

During the final meeting on the morning of August 1, we received disturbing news: a report came in that Iraqi troops had crossed the border into Kuwait. Initially it was not clear whether this was a minor intrusion or a full-scale invasion, and the meeting broke up before there was time to discuss the report in detail. Baker left for a planned visit to Mongolia, and Rebecca and I, with some of Baker's party, returned to Moscow with Shevardnadze.

When we arrived, the news was in that Iraq had occupied Kuwait and announced its annexation. Two of Baker's closest aides, Dennis Ross, the head of the State Department's Policy Planning Council and Baker's expert on the Middle East, and Robert Zoellick, the counselor of the State Department who had worked on German questions and economic issues, were with us in Moscow. It was obvious that Baker would have to return to Washington immediately and not continue on his planned fishing trip into the Mongolian interior. The question, however, was whether he should travel by way of Moscow, in the hope of obtaining Shevardnadze's agreement for joint action in the U.N. Security Council, or by way of Beijing or Tokyo. (Mongolia was about equidistant from Washington by either route.) If there was any hope of getting Soviet agreement to joint action in the Security Council, stopping in Moscow would be worth it.

Until then, Iraq had been a Soviet ally, the recipient of massive supplies of military equipment. Thousands of Soviet military advisers and trainers lived there. Though we knew that the Soviet government was not behind the invasion of Kuwait, we understood that it would be difficult for it to act in concert with us to end the aggression, since this would mean making an about-face in its entire Middle East policy and perhaps placing a number of its citizens in danger. Nevertheless, the stakes were high, and we decided that we should make every effort to persuade Gorbachev and Shevardnadze to join us in resisting Iraq's aggression. If "new thinking" and the "common interests of mankind" meant anything, it should mean that the Soviet Union would condemn the aggression and join us in bringing pressure on Iraq to withdraw.

The first Soviet reaction was encouraging: on August 2, the Foreign Ministry issued a statement calling for "swift and unconditional withdrawal of Iraqi forces from Kuwait," supported a U.N. Security Council resolution with the same appeal, and called in the Iraqi ambassador in Moscow to deliver the same message officially. This was a welcome change from the past, but it did not necessarily mean that Moscow would be willing to work in concert with the United States to force Iraq out of Kuwait.

Ross discussed the question with Sergei Tarasenko, his counterpart in the Soviet Foreign Ministry. Tarasenko reported that, although Shevardnadze had not made up his mind and was being pushed by his Middle East experts to refuse joint action with the United States, Baker could probably convince him to go along if he talked to him personally. It was not the absolute assurance we would have liked to have, but Baker decided to act on it and instructed his pilot to head west out of Ulaan Baatar rather than east.

Baker and Shevardnadze met for several hours in the terminal at Moscow's Vnukovo II Airport, which was never used for commercial traffic but only for arriving and departing foreign chiefs of state and top Soviet officials. Tarasenko's advice proved accurate: the two agreed on a statement that was the precursor of a series of joint votes in the U.N. Security Council. Finally it seemed possible for the United Nations to operate as it had originally been designed to do. Talk of a new world order began to supplant the competitive rhetoric of the cold war.

August 1990 did not provide the usual vacation time for many statesmen and diplomats. As Iraq's grip on Kuwait tightened and reports of atrocities mounted, President Bush began to organize a multilateral effort to apply military pressure. Shevardnadze's agreement with Baker was encouraging, but Bush had to be sure of Gorbachev's continued support if he was to be successful in building a coalition on the basis of Security Council resolutions. To solidify that support, he proposed a meeting in Helsinki, which Gorbachev immediately accepted.

The two met for most of the day on Sunday, September 9, and the Persian Gulf crisis dominated the talks. Gorbachev wanted assurance on two points: that military pressure would be used to induce Saddam Hussein to abandon Kuwait without a fight and that U.S. forces would be withdrawn from the area when Kuwait was freed. Bush pledged to make every effort to dislodge the Iraqi grip on Kuwait without war but avoided making any assurance that force would not be used if Saddam Hussein continued his intransigence. As for U.S. forces in the area, he promised that they would be cut back to normal levels after Kuwait had been liberated. For many years, the United States had maintained some naval forces in the Gulf, and Gorbachev did not press for a complete withdrawal, only for the departure of those forces sent to the area specifically to deal with the Iraqi invasion.

There was also extensive discussion of the Soviet economy and the need for external support. Bush pledged continued support for perestroika but avoided any commitment to large-scale financial assistance. Instead he offered verbal support and promised efforts to eliminate cold war barriers to trade, provision of some humanitarian aid and technical assistance, and encouragement to private investors.

Neither spoke of the two topics as being in any way related, but it must have been clear without discussion that American willingness to be supportive of reform in the Soviet Union might not survive Soviet opposition to Western policy in the Gulf. While Gorbachev was determined to avoid a U.S.-led war in the region if he could, he must have realized that if he could not force Iraq to back down without war, he would not be able to block a U.S.-led invasion. What he needed was at least a few months to try to find a political solution. This George Bush was willing to grant, particularly since preparations for successful military action would take some time.

The understandings reached at Helsinki held, though not without periodic tensions and occasional misunderstandings. Following on the unification of Germany, the U.S.-Soviet political cooperation during the Gulf crisis and war convinced many that a breathtaking new partnership of erstwhile rivals was in the making. In addition, the two statesmen's frequent contact over the months ahead that these understandings engendered—both direct (by telephone) and indirect (by correspondence and through representatives)—created a remarkably strong personal bond between them.

Bush Sends a Mission

EVEN BEFORE GORBACHEV had made a decision regarding the future course of economic reform, President Bush offered to send Secretary of Commerce Robert Mosbacher to Moscow in mid-September with a group of top corporate executives to discuss investment and trade possibilities. Gorbachev was delighted, of course, since it was becoming increasingly obvious that his stumbling economy needed an infusion of capital and managerial expertise from the West.

I, too, thought that a mission of this sort could be helpful if properly timed and organized. However, the date suggested was not propitious unless the intent was to press Gorbachev to accept the Shatalin program, which could be done more effectively by the president himself, in private. If the Shatalin program had been accepted and the mechanisms to implement it were already in place, the delegation would have something to talk about, but it was clear that these conditions would not prevail at the time the group planned to be in Moscow.

The proposal for a presidential business mission, like Bush's support for perestroika, was not linked to Security Council votes on Iraq. Nevertheless, it seemed to be a clever way to call to Gorbachev's attention some of the economic benefits that might accrue if the USSR cooperated with the United States.

At first there seemed no reason to object to this implicit sweetener, but I became uneasy as I thought through the probable outcome of the mission. First, I doubted that Gorbachev needed extra blandishments to stick with us in the Gulf. It was manifestly in the Soviet interest not to leave its position in the Middle East hostage to the likes of Saddam Hussein. One of the basic thrusts of "new thinking" had been to break out of the isolation brought on by traditional Soviet foreign policy. Only by opposing Iraqi aggression could Gorbachev position himself to be one of the sponsors of an eventual peace settlement in the area. Therefore, it seemed a misreading of Soviet interests to assume that the United States needed to do something to buy Soviet support.

Second, as important as it was to oppose Iraqi aggression against Kuwait, the fate of the Soviet economic and political system was at least of equal long-term importance to the United States. We had leverage to nudge Gorbachev in the right direction, but we were not using it. A presidential business mission in September would be, at best, a waste of potential and, at worst, a signal that American economic support was likely to be forthcoming whether or not an effective program of reform was adopted, as long as Soviet foreign policy was congenial to us. This would be a dangerous illusion that could eventually create bitterness.

My unease grew as I detected signs in late August that Gorbachev might be backing away from his endorsement of the Shatalin program.

It was an open secret that Prime Minister Ryzhkov, members of his government, and conservative Party apparatchiks were lobbying strongly against it, arguing that it would bring strikes, chaos—even civil war. Finally, at the end of August, Gorbachev said at a press conference that the Shatalin group's recommendations should be combined with the government plan.

This suggestion sounded like a proposal to combine opposites. To their respective authors, the plans were totally incompatible and could not be combined. Yeltsin denounced the idea the following day, as did both Ryzhkov and Shatalin.

At this point I sensed a potential disaster with the presidential business mission. The American executives would probably (and rightly) not wish to take a clear stand on the various Soviet reform proposals being considered. But if their presence and their discussions with government officials left the impression that they were willing to make major investments in an unreformed Soviet economy, serious misunderstanding would be created on both sides. Unless Gorbachev and Yeltsin continued to cooperate—and this would be impossible if Gorbachev rejected the Shatalin program—American business could be caught between two power centers in competition.

I understood that the White House was most unlikely to postpone the visit since it was doubtless viewed as part of our strategy to commit Gorbachev to support us in the Gulf. Furthermore, most of the members of the mission seemed to be major contributors to political campaigns who probably saw their inclusion in the mission as a consequence of that fact. They might well resent being asked to adjust their calendars for reasons of state.

Nevertheless, I considered it my duty to give Washington objective advice, even if it was unwelcome. Therefore, I sent a personal message to Secretary Baker pointing out the pitfalls in the way of the scheduled presidential mission. I realized that we might send the wrong signal if we abruptly postponed it but recommended that we ask Gorbachev whether it might be more useful to him if the mission were rescheduled to visit *after* the Soviet government had determined what course it would take. He would almost certainly say, "Come on as scheduled," but would be forewarned that we were aware of the present disarray and lacked confidence in the "reform" plans of the current government.

My message was never acknowledged, and the mission came on schedule, stopping in Helsinki for a short meeting with President Bush after he finished his September 9 meeting with Gorbachev. I had hoped that, since the group had been designated a "presidential mission," it would be given some advice about the need to encourage more rapid economic reform, but this did not happen. They were given thick briefing books with factual descriptions of many specific issues but no clear guidance on policy.

In fact, the presidential mission lived up to my worst fears. After complaining that he often received conflicting advice on economic policy from foreign leaders, Gorbachev turned the group over to the head of Gosplan, Yuri Maslyukov, who assured them that they would soon receive a list of enterprises in which foreign investment would be welcome and agreed with Mosbacher to name a liaison committee within two weeks to facilitate negotiations. He dismissed the Shatalin program as visionary and destructive. To my consternation, when the group met with Ryzhkov the following day, several commented that he had been right not to listen to "those radicals." Though I was well aware that not all captains of industry understand the nuances of politics abroad, I never expected to hear respected, prominent American businessmen endorse retention of a state-controlled, Communist system!

The delegation did not schedule a meeting with Yeltsin, despite the fact that the Russian parliament had officially endorsed the Shatalin approach and Yeltsin had given notice that his government intended to take control of trade and investment on Russian territory.

I saw the delegation off with a sinking feeling. The future of the Soviet economic system was being debated; the United States had, implicitly but unmistakably, been invited to send experts and give advice, and we had blown it. In fact, the Soviet leaders very likely received an impression precisely opposite to that we should have wished to give.

Even the limited promises Maslyukov gave Mosbacher were not kept. Despite repeated prodding from our embassy, Maslyukov never delivered the list of enterprises for sale or named a liaison group. Whenever we inquired, the reply was always "It will be ready in a few days."

Dual Power: A Specter Forms

RUSSIANS HAVE BEEN CONDITIONED by history and education to abhor conflicts of authority at the top of their government. When they have occurred in the past, they have usually brought civil war or foreign invasion or both. This is one of the reasons most Soviet citizens welcomed the apparent truce between Gorbachev and Yeltsin when they agreed to establish the Shatalin commission. If both of them endorsed the commission's recommendations and secured a favorable vote in their respective parliaments, they should be able to work in tandem to implement an agreed transition to a market economy.

When the commission delivered its report toward the end of August, Gorbachev surprised the public when he stated that it should be reconciled with the government plan. Yeltsin immediately made it clear that this was unacceptable to him and that his government would proceed to implement the Shatalin program. During a meeting on September 4, Yeltsin told a group of American senators and me that no merger between the two plans was possible and that he would not accept the result of an attempt to "reconcile" them. He thought the USSR Council of Ministers had outlived its usefulness and should be replaced by a smaller Presidential Council. He added that he was not seeking a confrontation with the USSR government but that the RSFSR and other republics would insist on assuming many of its current functions because they wished to move ahead more rapidly with economic reform and did not want to be held back by the standpat central bureaucracy. He was willing, however, to leave functions such as defense, communications, energy distribution, and rail and air transportation to the central government.

What he told us was consistent with what he was saying in public—and presumably in private to Gorbachev. Gorbachev, however seemed deaf both to Yeltsin's message and to the comments of economists on both sides of the debate. I could find no one apart from Gorbachev himself who believed the two plans could be combined or reconciled. Nevertheless, on September 7, Ryzhkov announced that Gorbachev had directed that his government's plan and the Shatalin program be merged and that Abel Aganbegyan had been picked to head the effort.

A tall, heavyset man, Aganbegyan was born in Tbilisi, Georgia, of

Armenian parents. He studied economics in Moscow but in 1961 moved to Novosibirsk as the Siberian branch of the USSR Academy of Sciences was being organized. The economics section of the academy's Siberian branch developed a more critical approach to the "socialist economy" of the day than was possible at the academy's institutes in Moscow, and in 1983 Aganbegyan published in the journal he edited Tatyana Zaslavskaya's critique of the centrally planned economy that came to be known as the Novosibirsk Study. It was representative of the ideas that gave the original impetus to perestroika, and it was not a coincidence that both Aganbegyan and Zaslavskaya were transferred to Moscow after Gorbachev came to power. In 1990, Aganbegyan was running the Academy of the National Economy in Moscow, which aspired to be a Soviet counterpart of the Harvard School of Business. While he was still considered an economic reformer, his positions were less radical than those espoused by the Shatalin group, and he also had personal rivals in the group.

Even as he announced that Aganbegyan would meld the two programs, Ryzhkov defended the government program as "realistic" and implicitly criticized the recommendations for decentralization in the Shatalin program by arguing that a "strong state" should be maintained and economic separatism should be prohibited.

Without mentioning Yeltsin's threat to implement the reforms in Russia alone if necessary and to make "horizontal arrangements" with other republics, but doubtless with it in mind, Ryzhkov added that his government would seek Gorbachev's approval for a decree requiring that the existing economic links be preserved throughout 1991 under pain of severe penalties. He also suggested that the USSR government should coordinate the actions of the various republics in concluding economic contracts for the next year.

Yeltsin did not delay his reply. On September 11, the Russian parliament endorsed his recommendation by voting 213 to 1, with 4 abstentions, to approve the Shatalin program in principle and requested that the USSR Supreme Soviet do the same. It directed the RSFSR Council of Ministers to draw up detailed proposals for implementation within a month. Given the sharp divisions that had riven the Russian parliament on earlier votes, the near unanimity on this issue was striking— and ominous for Gorbachev if he persisted in ignoring the sentiments of the Russian parliament.

The Ryzhkov government was plummeting in popularity, and tempers were rising. Two motions of no confidence were proposed in the RSFSR Supreme Soviet, but Yeltsin argued that they were "premature" and they did not pass. Even if a no-confidence motion had passed, it would have had no legal effect since only the USSR parliament could remove the prime minister. Nevertheless, it would have been a heavy political blow to Ryzhkov.

Even after Gorbachev instructed Aganbegyan to combine the two plans, many observers hoped that it would be only a cosmetic exercise and that the outcome would essentially incorporate the Shatalin "500-Day" approach. Public polls indicated that the majority of Soviet citizens now approved transition to a market system (which, of course many did not understand) and that the majority of those polled had lost confidence in the Ryzhkov government. At last Gorbachev was in a position to undertake the radical reforms he had talked about for years, and, given the danger of a prolonged struggle with Yeltsin and the Russian parliament if he failed to do so, many believed that he would see to it that the Shatalin program was changed little.

These hopes were shattered when the compromise document was finally released in mid-October. It omitted most of the key elements of the Shatalin approach—rapid privatization and decentralization—and retained many features of the government approach that had already proved unworkable, such as decreed price rises.

The day after it was released, I invited Aganbegyan and several other economists to have lunch with Defense Secretary Richard Cheney, who was visiting Moscow. The economists who did not work for the Ryzhkov government, including Oleg Bogomolov and Pavel Bunich, expressed their incomprehension as to how Aganbegyan could have lent his name to such a pastiche. Aganbegyan did not even try to defend the plan that now bore his name. He admitted that he had done the draft but insisted it had been written at Gorbachev's direction and contained much that he could not approve. Gorbachev, he said, had gone over it line by line several times and had actually spent more than forty hours working on it.

The result proved what many had already suspected: Gorbachev had a poor understanding of economics in general and of market economics in particular. One also had to wonder if he had not lost his keen political touch, for the plan he approved was certain to increase internal tension in the country.

Yeltsin, who had been out of circulation for three weeks following an automobile accident, returned to the public eye to denounce the plan and to observe that it left the RSFSR with three choices: to reject it outright, to go its own way with its own program, or to wait six months until the inevitable economic collapse would force another approach.

The USSR parliament was not swayed by the Russian objections, and Gorbachev managed to secure its formal approval of his plan. Immediately, his own economic team began to disintegrate. On November 3, the reformist newspaper *Komsomolskaya Pravda* carried a stinging statement signed by the key people who had worked with Shatalin, including two members of the Presidential Council. It pointed out that the compromise program was too little, too late and would not work and that Gorbachev had squandered the support of the republics, all of which except Estonia had endorsed the Shatalin approach in August, and predicted that the inflation that had begun would spiral out of control. "The transition to market relations will now occur not through the stability of the ruble but through inflation and belated measures to control it," they concluded gloomily—and prophetically.[11]

Meanwhile, Yeltsin's government had been busy signing economic agreements with other republics and asserting claim to function after function, including the right to collect taxes in Russia and to decide what proportion of them to convey to the central government. The specter of dual power was beginning to take on substance.

By October, I realized that my assumptions in the spring and summer about Gorbachev's game plan were not being confirmed. While Gorbachev had managed to weaken the Communist Party to the degree that it could no longer automatically block reform, he had failed to follow through and take advantage of his victory. Shatalin's program had flaws and would not have worked as smoothly as its authors had predicted, but it would have moved the economic system in the right direction. Rejecting it was one of Gorbachev's fateful errors.

Why did he back away from radical reform as soon as he had a real opportunity to undertake it? Probably because he feared losing his power. Government bureaucrats, conservative Party officials, and the KGB joined forces in arguing that a rapid shift to private property and dissolution of central economic direction would lead to public disorder, including uncontrollable strikes and demonstrations. His enthusiasm for a plan that might have worked was replaced by fear, and the fear produced an incoherent approach that could not work. Meanwhile, Gorbachev's vacillation reinforced all the centrifugal forces that were tugging at the empire, just as its reinforcing rods were being severed.

XVI

——— ◆ ———

Gorbachev Swings to the Right

A dictatorship is coming; I declare this with all responsibility.
EDUARD SHEVARDNADZE, December 20, 1990[1]

*Even when he [Gorbachev] speaks for the right wing, the country
all the same moves to the left.*
ANDREI SAKHAROV, December 1989[2]

Though the economy was deteriorating, ethnic tensions rising, and violent crime a growing problem, many Soviet intellectuals experienced a rare and uncharacteristic optimistic mood in late summer 1990. Gorbachev, it seemed, had resisted the attacks of Party hard-liners and had completed the groundwork for a grand bargain with the union republics, including Yeltsin's Russia.

The time of sanguine expectations was, however, short. Gorbachev's order to combine the Shatalin and Ryzhkov plans came as a jolt. Those few observers who continued to hope that the "reconciliation" of the two plans would be a charade that would avoid altering the key features of Shatalin's approach lost their illusions when the Gorbachev-Aganbegyan redaction was issued in October. Nobody believed it could work, and the decline in Gorbachev's prestige, authority, and real power accelerated.

Simultaneously, and perhaps not coincidentally, rumors that Gorbachev would soon be overthrown by a coup d'état multiplied. Never specific about just who was planning to remove the president, the gossips believed that a cabal of conservative Communist Party officials and military and police officers was likely to exploit the country's political disarray and Gorbachev's growing unpopularity. Some cynics suspected that Gorbachev himself was encouraging the rumors in order to justify additional powers for the presidency.

Gorbachev Beleaguered

GORBACHEV FIRST ATTEMPTED to shore up his authority by obtaining special powers from the Supreme Soviet to issue decrees on economic questions and to establish institutions to "accelerate the formation of an all-union market." The proposal provoked a heated debate in the Supreme Soviet, which nevertheless approved it.[3] Some reformers, such as Moscow Mayor Gavriil Popov, supported the proposal on grounds that increased executive authority would be required to force reform on a reluctant bureaucracy and Communist Party establishment. But even as his formal powers increased, Gorbachev seemed increasingly incapable of acting decisively.

During the fall, nothing seemed to work. Even the November 7 Revolution Day parade on Red Square, traditionally an occasion for flaunting Soviet military power, was marred by an attempt to assassinate Gorbachev as he stood on the reviewing stand. Security guards wrestled to the ground a man from Leningrad just as he was aiming a shotgun at the president. Two shots meant for Gorbachev were deflected and went harmlessly into the air. Though no one was injured and the parade continued as if nothing had happened, the incident put the city on edge. It seemed to confirm the public impression of violence surging out of control, and it may have encouraged Gorbachev to take some of the actions he announced subsequently.

A few days after the Red Square incident, Gorbachev held a meeting with more than a thousand military officers who had been elected to public office.[4] The meeting was a disaster for Gorbachev. The officers did not hide their fury over what they considered Gorbachev's responsibility for the country's ills and spoke openly of their disenchantment with his leadership.[5] This meeting doubtless intensified his fear that the military would back a plot to remove him.

Just three days later, still shaken by his confrontation with the officers, Gorbachev delivered a lengthy report to the Congress of People's Deputies that was met with skepticism and hostility.[6] This was the culmination of a string of disappointments that finally convinced him to embrace a harder line. He returned to his office and called an immediate meeting of the Politburo and other advisers, mainly from the Party. With them, he decided to proceed with plans that had been developed as a contingency to strengthen the office of president and subordinate the government directly to it.[7]

Gorbachev returned to the parliamentary chamber the following day to propose a thoroughgoing reorganization of his presidency. The proposal had been assembled in such haste that many high-placed officials had not seen it. Ryzhkov first heard of it when Gorbachev telephoned him from his car while on his way to the Supreme Soviet.[8] If the Congress of People's Deputies agreed, the Presidential Council, less than a year old, would be dissolved in favor of a National Security Council. The post of vice president would be established. The Council of Ministers would be replaced by a Cabinet of Ministers—presumably a smaller body, comparable to the president's Cabinet in the United States, although this was not specified. The Council of Federation would become a consultative body for Center-republic relations.[9]

Deputies received this proposal with more interest than they had the lackadaisical "state of the union" message the day before. Though the changes smacked more of redrawing organization charts than of radical new policies, Gorbachev had recognized the need to do *something*. The legislators were tantalized, but as they debated the proposal they realized that its vague formulations would permit Gorbachev to configure the new institutions without consulting them.

Even so, most of the reformers were prepared to support greater powers for the president if he would use them to push through changes they favored. A group of prominent "democrats" signed an open letter calling on Gorbachev to make some hard decisions or resign. They demanded a grant of real sovereignty to the republics, distribution of land to farmers, isolation of the army and local governments from direct Communist Party control, a new, reform-minded cabinet, and a working partnership between Gorbachev and Yeltsin.[10]

Rather than endorsing what seemed to many of us sound ideas, Gorbachev took the appeal as an act of betrayal and set his mind even more firmly against the reform intellectuals he once had cultivated.[11] In fact, he would have had great difficulty gaining Supreme Soviet approval for such policies, but the politicians had become so desperate to be seen doing *something* that a firm push by Gorbachev might have convinced them.

As it was, the Supreme Soviet initially rejected Gorbachev's proposal as too vague and relented only when he agreed to a point-by-point debate. With these assurances the chamber voted to approve the plan "in principle," provided Gorbachev offered more details within two weeks. Prime Minister Ryzhkov did not campaign publicly against the proposals, but he let it be known that he had not been consulted in advance and was dismayed at the idea of transforming the Council of Ministers into a presidential Cabinet.

In December, Gorbachev finally got most of what he wanted from the legislature, when constitutional amendments were passed to establish a vice presidency and the other bodies Gorbachev had proposed.

Legislative maneuvering, however, failed to attract the public attention it had a year earlier. Shortages of food and goods in the shops preoccupied most citizens, who were spending more and more of their waking hours standing in line to obtain essentials. They also noticed a new tendency for Moscow officials to talk tough. Law and order became the new watchwords, and from November on hardly a day passed without a new harsh decree, a threatening speech or replacement of a key official by a hard-line politician.

In mid-November Gorbachev replaced Mikhail Nenashev, who had brought a degree of independence to radio and television and was planning to establish four independent channels, with propaganda hack Leonid Kravchenko—an obvious move to tighten control over the electronic media.

Threats aimed at Lithuania and the other Baltic states multiplied. As the three Baltic governments continued to assert their sovereignty, pass implementing legislation, and expand their administrative apparatus, Gorbachev stepped up his indirect threats to use force. After issuing a decree to "protect the property of public and collective organizations," he authorized the movement of additional troops into Lithuania, Latvia, and Estonia.

On November 27, Minister of Defense Yazov appeared on television with the warning that force would be used to prevent harassment of military installations and personnel. The following day, there was an unusual public announcement that the Politburo had urged Gorbachev to "combat violations of human rights against Soviet citizens" in Lithuania. On December 1, Gorbachev issued a decree nullifying all defense legislation in the union republics. The Baltic governments had begun to set up their own defense structures, but this decree could be used to block their efforts by force. The same day Gorbachev stunned the public by appointing hard-liner Boris Pugo to replace Vadim Bakatin as minister of internal affairs.

Since his appointment to head the Ministry of Internal Affairs in 1988, Bakatin had developed a reputation as the first police chief in Soviet (and probably Russian) history who had some understanding of what the rule of law means. A handsome man who always appeared in well-tailored suits, he could have been cast by Hollywood to play James Bond, but in reality he was more reflective than reflexive. When I called on him to discuss law enforcement, he was remarkably candid in describing the weaknesses in the Soviet "militia": poor training, low pay, corruption—all problems that had no easy solutions. Nevertheless, he understood that the militia had to be reoriented if it was to be effective in an open society. As he stated in his memoirs, he tried to adapt the police to serve "not ideology, not the CPSU, but the law and the state."[12] He began refusing to sanction police action on Communist Party instructions alone, which had been a normal practice until he became minister, and repeatedly infuriated hard-liners in the Party by insisting on scrupulous adherence to legal norms.

During 1989 and 1990, he often clashed with KGB Chairman Kryuchkov on policy regarding public demonstrations: Bakatin argued that they should be permitted as long as they were peaceful, while Kryuchkov insisted that most should be banned. Bakatin opposed calls to impose direct presidential rule in republics with active nationalist movements. He worked out agreements with the Baltic governments for more local control over police forces, despite Kryuchkov's opposition. He also angered his boss, Prime Minister Ryzhkov, by reproaching him during a formal meeting of the Presidential Council for opposing the Shatalin program. By fall, a broad coalition of "conservatives" was pressing Gorbachev to replace him: the prime minister, the head of the KGB, the rump Communist parties in the Baltic, and the Party leaders in Ukraine and Belorussia, as well as a vocal faction in the USSR Supreme Soviet that supported preservation of the union by whatever means were required.[13]

Although Bakatin would remain a member of the Presidential Council and subsequently be named to the new Security Council, his removal from the Ministry of Internal Affairs halted all practical efforts to establish the rule of law among the law enforcement agencies. He had been the only senior official who commanded one of the three "institutions of compulsion" (the others being the KGB and the army) who wholeheartedly supported development of a civil society and respect for the rule of law. His replacement by a man known to be more comfortable with the traditional way of doing things was ominous.

For his part, Boris Pugo wasted no time in confirming the public's suspicions of his stance. On December 5, he delivered a tough speech warning that he had instructions from Gorbachev "to ensure the full application of the USSR Constitution" throughout the country. The following day, Gorbachev addressed a conference of industrial managers and predicted that "tough, unpopular measures" were in store. On December 11, Kryuchkov delivered a speech warning that the country was threatened by dissolution and charging that "foreign intelligence organizations" were working to "destabilize" the Soviet Union.

The next session of the Congress of People's Deputies was scheduled to open on December 17 to consider the constitutional amendments that would formally strengthen Gorbachev's power. But it no longer appeared that Gorbachev would use his authority to implement reform as the November 18 open letter had urged. All signals were pointing in the opposite direction.

Redefining the Union

DURING THE PREVIOUS WINTER, Gorbachev had urged separatists in the Baltic states and elsewhere to try a "real federation" before attempting to leave the Soviet Union. A new treaty, he suggested, could be worked out in months and would provide a totally new and voluntary framework for the union. Negotiations proceeded in fits and starts throughout 1990, but it was November 24 before a draft treaty of union appeared in the press. It was not clear just how many republics were prepared to endorse it, but I read it carefully to determine just how much change Gorbachev was willing to tolerate.

In fact, the draft text embodied basic alterations in the relations of the "Center" and the republics. It stipulated that republics would control their own land and resources "except for those parts required to implement the union's authority" and set forth general principles for dividing federal and republic authority. Nevertheless, there were vast areas of ambiguity. Many functions, from economic development strategy to the use of gold and diamond reserves to social policy, were designated as "areas of joint control." It was not clear who would decide how authority over these important functions would be divided or what would happen if union and republic authorities disagreed. The role and rights of "autonomous" entities were not defined, nor were there provisions for enforcing the human rights guarantees in the text. The process by which republics might secede was also unclear.

Senior officials close to Gorbachev had been predicting that an agreement would soon be concluded among the majority of the fifteen union republics. Deputy CPSU Secretary General Vladimir Ivashko, for example, told me the day before the text was published that he thought there was a good chance that as many as twelve republics would adhere.[14] As soon as I read the text, I realized that such predictions were unrealistic.

It would be difficult to conceive of any sort of union without Russia and Ukraine, but the leaders of both republics had expressed reservations about some aspects of the text, and both were engaged in a parallel process to negotiate agreements with other republics that might eventually serve as the basis for a union treaty negotiated without Gorbachev.

When I visited Kiev a few days before the draft treaty was published, Ukrainian parliament Chairman Leonid Kravchuk told me that although he would participate in the meetings to draft a union treaty, Ukraine would not adhere to any new treaty until it had adopted a new constitution and conducted a referendum in accord with that constitution. When I asked how soon the new constitution might be approved, he replied, "Not before the second half of next year." That same day, Yeltsin also visited Kiev to sign a bilateral agreement between Russia and Ukraine.

During my visit to Kiev I not only called on Kravchuk, then chairman of the Supreme Soviet, and Stanislav Gurenko,[15] the Communist Party leader, but made a point of inviting several leaders from Rukh to dinner. Communist officials had stepped up pressure on their activities, and I considered it important to give them official attention. Their attitude toward the proposed union treaty was not totally negative, provided the conditions Kravchuk had mentioned were met, but they anticipated that any union treaty would be valid only during a transitional stage to full independence.

I asked whether they thought Ukrainian independence was a practical alternative, and Larysa Skoryk, who had a seat in the Ukrainian Supreme Soviet from an industrial district in Kiev, replied, "Not immediately, but within a few years, definitely. We are planning for full independence in a three- to five-year time frame." They were not even close to a majority in the Ukrainian parliament, but I did not dismiss this comment as merely a dream. If Moscow continued to try to exercise imperial control, might not many Communists swing over to their side?

As for Russia, Yeltsin and the Russian democrats attacked the draft treaty as soon as it was published. Meeting on December 8 and 9, representatives of Democratic Russia—which had evolved into an opposition coalition—declared that it was "unacceptable" because it "infringes on the sovereignty of the RSFSR and other republics." Furthermore, they demanded that the treaty be concluded only after a new RSFSR constitution was adopted and that it be the result of direct negotiations among the republics. Their position coincided with the Ukrainian approach, which Kravchuk had described to me in November.

As I surveyed the reaction of the various republics to the draft union treaty, I concluded that only the Central Asian republics and Belorussia were likely to support something like the published draft, and even they would insist on alterations that would give them more control over foreign policy, foreign economic ties, and natural resources. Russia, Ukraine, and Azerbaijan favored a loose confederation, and the first two would enter into that only after adopting new constitutions. The sort of thinking I had heard from Ruslan Khasbulatov during the summer seemed to be spreading rapidly. Armenia and Georgia were now seeking complete independence, after which they might consider establishing some loose federal ties, and Moldavia was also tending in that direction, though it had to cope with growing internal opposition. The three Baltic states were not willing even to pretend to negotiate a new union treaty.

For many of the republics, the Gorbachev-Yeltsin dispute was crucial. Until it was resolved, most of them would play for time and avoid any final commitments. The tension between the two spilled over into the substance of negotiations. Gorbachev's negotiators tried to bring pressure to bear on Yeltsin by offering the autonomous republics, most of which were in Russia, status as "subjects" of the new union, whereby in many respects they would have the same rights as Russia and the other union republics. This idea, however, was totally unacceptable to the union republics, and the use of it turned out to be shortsighted. Gorbachev was already losing his race with time to conclude a federal union on a voluntary basis. By attempting to apply divide-and-rule tactics to Russia, he lost time he could not afford.

Shevardnadze Sounds the Tocsin

DECEMBER 20, 1990, had been the date scheduled for a report by the Soviet foreign minister to the Fourth Congress of People's Deputies. When Shevardnadze mounted the podium, however, he announced solemnly that it would be "perhaps the shortest and most difficult speech" of his life. He briefly addressed some questions that had been raised— and that he considered insulting and provocative—regarding Soviet policy toward Iraq and alleged "plans" to send Soviet troops to the Persian Gulf. He complained of lack of support in high places, implying that Parliament Chairman Lukyanov, in particular, had tried to undermine him. With that, he dropped his bombshell:

> Democrats, I will put it bluntly. Comrade democrats, . . . you have run away. Reformers have gone to the bushes. A dictatorship is coming; I declare this with total responsibility. No one knows what kind of dictatorship it will be and who will come or what the regime will be like.
> I want to make the following statement: I am resigning. . . . Let this be my contribution, if you like, my protest against the onset of dictatorship.[16]

That morning I was in the "science town" of Dubna, some two hours' drive from Moscow, and when I arrived back at Spaso House to host a lunch, my new deputy, James Collins, met me at the door with the news.

Despite Shevardnadze's hint in March, I was stunned. "Did he say he *had* resigned, or that he *would*?" I asked.

"It sounded final. 'Я хочу в отставку' [I am resigning] were his exact words."

One of Shevardnadze's deputies, Alexander Belonogov, arrived for lunch, and we assaulted him with questions. He claimed to have had no inkling of the resignation until he heard the speech itself. I asked him if he thought Shevardnadze might be persuaded to reconsider. "Not if I know the man," he replied. "He will not want it to look like a stunt. His honor is at stake."

Of course. To anyone who really knew Shevardnadze, it was a silly question.

Many, however, did not know Shevardnadze well. When the Congress reconvened that afternoon, I was on hand to hear several highly respected speakers, including historian Dmitri Likhachev and editor Sergei Zalygin, suggest that his resignation not be accepted and that he be requested to continue in office. Others attacked him. Viktor Alksnis, one of Shevardnadze's most outspoken critics—who had said a few days earlier that now that they had gotten Bakatin, their next target would be Shevardnadze—sputtered a series of non sequiturs bordering on incoherence. Roy Medvedev, who in the 1960s and 1970s had posed as a dissident but now had gravitated to the Communist Party's conservative wing, spoke condescendingly of a hypersensitive Georgian unable to bear criticism. The audience, however, was waiting for Gorbachev. During the morning session, his face had betrayed both surprise and, it seemed, anger. It was now hours later, and he had had time to consider and compose his comments.

When he mounted the rostrum, he looked like a person who had just recovered from a blow to his midsection. What hurt him most, Gorbachev began, was the fact that Shevardnadze had not notified him in advance of his intent to resign. Although he had spoken to Shevardnadze twice on the telephone since his speech, he was still not sure just what had prompted the resignation, but he gathered that Shevardnadze thought he was protesting attempts to "exploit the difficulties and cast doubt on the policy of perestroika." Yet he should not have given up. He should have known that the going would be tough and persisted. Gorbachev could only condemn his action and the way he had gone about it.

Gorbachev then went on to ridicule the idea that a dictatorship might be coming. He himself was not looking for dictatorial power, only the authority necessary to lead society through its transformations. As for others,

I, as president, today do not possess any information—and I have rather broad information—that would confirm that someone somewhere has prepared a junta for us or some other dictatorship. . . . No, I do not have such information.[17]

Gloom, punctuated and accentuated by the ostentatious jubilation of small groups of superpatriots, hung over the corridors of the Palace of Congresses as the deputies emerged from the session. I caught up with Alexander Yakovlev as he strode scowling toward the coatroom. I asked him how he saw the future.

"Nothing good will come of this witch-hunt," he replied. "Remember McCarthyism in your country? It only did damage. It's the same with us here today."

That evening, both speeches were televised in full. I watched them with fascination. It would have taken a Shakespeare to capture the repressed emotional force of the interchange between the two statesmen. They had started a difficult task together five and a half years earlier. Shevardnadze had achieved brilliant success in meeting perestroika's foreign policy goals, but Gorbachev was now in evident retreat on the domestic front. I thought I knew Shevardnadze well enough to understand that he was not a quitter. He was obviously sensitive to criticism, but he would certainly have fought back if there was hope of winning. He must have sensed that Gorbachev was prepared to sacrifice him to the hard-liners who were gathering for a crackdown.

Curiously, in his reaction to Shevardnadze's resignation, Gorbachev had confirmed this. He said he had intended to nominate Shevardnadze for vice president. But this was a new job with no apparent duties. It would have been a kick upstairs—assuming Congress approved the nomination, and even this might not occur without an unpleasant fight.[18]

There had been speculation for more than a year that Shevardnadze might be moved to another job. He would have been ideally suited for prime minister, where his sensitivity to the attitudes of the non-Russian nationalities could, to a degree, have compensated for Gorbachev's blindness. But once Gorbachev opted for a right-wing government, Shevardnadze would have been an impossible choice to head it.

I wondered if there were other factors as well. Shevardnadze clearly hoped that his appeal to the "democrats" to get back into play before it was too late would rally them. But did he have information about plans for a coup? Or plans on Gorbachev's part to assume dictatorial powers himself? I had no way of knowing.

Although Shevardnadze agreed to stay on at the Ministry of Foreign

Affairs "for a few days," until a successor was named, he was not immediately available for an appointment. Seeking further explanation of his action, I called on Sergei Tarasenko, one of his most intimate associates. Tarasenko told me that Shevardnadze had thought seriously of resigning off and on for about a year. What precipitated his decision was a sequence of events that had convinced him that the Soviet government was headed for wider use of force, which he wanted no part of. He was particularly resentful that Gorbachev had given him little support when the military had reneged on some arms control agreements that he had negotiated and Gorbachev had personally approved.[19] Lukyanov had maneuvered in the Supreme Soviet to put Shevardnadze in a bad light by holding treaties submitted for ratification and then conveying them to the deputies at the last minute with the false accusation that the Ministry of Foreign Affairs had failed to submit them on time. He had also scheduled hearings when Shevardnadze was out of the country and unable to respond to questions. He did not believe Lukyanov would have behaved in this fashion if Gorbachev's support for Shevardnadze had been solid.

Tarasenko confirmed that Shevardnadze had consulted nobody in advance except his wife, his children, and his assistants, Teymuraz Stepanov and Tarasenko himself. They had unanimously agreed that he should resign.

I asked Tarasenko if Shevardnadze had specific information about an impending coup. He answered that he did not know of any specific plot, but he felt that there were groups determined to hold the country together by force and that Gorbachev was playing into their hands with his current policies. Gorbachev might think he was buying time, but he would eventually be cast aside by those he depended on. Given these circumstances, Shevardnadze could not remain in the government. He felt he could better serve the country by rallying democratic forces from the outside.

All parties assured us that there would be no change in Soviet policies toward the United States. Gorbachev sent a personal letter to President Bush on Christmas Day to reassure him that the policies Shevardnadze had followed would not be changed.[20] Shevardnadze himself told us that he would not have resigned if he had not been certain that the positive course of U.S.-Soviet relations was fixed. Three weeks later, when Gorbachev named a successor to Shevardnadze, he picked career diplomat

Alexander Bessmertnykh, reportedly not only because he respected Bessmertnykh's abilities but also because he wanted to reassure the United States.

We knew Bessmertnykh well and held him in the highest regard. He had served lengthy tours of duty in Washington, then had been director of U.S. affairs at the Ministry of Foreign Affairs in Moscow. When Shevardnadze had become foreign minister, he promoted Bessmertnykh rapidly to first deputy and in early 1990 had sent him to Washington as ambassador.

His knowledge of American ways, combined with intelligence, candor, and a constructive attitude made him a very effective representative of Soviet interests and a popular colleague. I had worked with him since the early 1970s, when I was director of the Office of Soviet Union Affairs in the State Department and Bessmertnykh was political counselor at the Soviet Embassy. Even in those cold war days, it was apparent that Sasha—as we all called him—was not a run-of-the-mill Soviet diplomat. He never exhibited any disloyalty to Soviet policy, but he could discuss issues rationally and without rancor. We had the feeling that, even when he could not agree with us, he understood what we were saying and would report it accurately.

Once I was outraged when Gromyko sent a personal message to Secretary of State William Rogers demanding that he forbid movie theaters in the United States to show a European-made film about Lenin that Moscow considered disrespectful. When I attended a reception at the Soviet Embassy that evening, I took Bessmertnykh aside and berated him for not explaining to Moscow how ridiculous this message made them all look. He made no effort to defend the message but remarked that the issue was a very emotional one in the Kremlin. Then he observed that it would probably be ten years or more before Lenin could be assessed dispassionately.

This was a remarkable statement for a senior Soviet diplomat when the Brezhnev regime was conducting an ideological counteroffensive against freethinking. Here was a man who could think for himself and was trying to be as honest as his job permitted.

It was mid-January before I learned that Bessmertnykh was Gorbachev's choice to succeed Shevardnadze. In the few weeks between Shevardnadze's resignation and Bessmertnykh's appointment, the strains on our relations intensified, but for reasons unrelated to either of the Soviet foreign ministers.

A New Vice President

THE FOURTH CONGRESS of People's Deputies limped to a close following the shock of Shevardnadze's resignation. The Congress passed most
of the constitutional amendments Gorbachev had recommended, and it
reluctantly approved his nominee for vice president, Gennady Yanayev.[21]

In his early fifties, Yanayev had made a career as a Komsomol leader
and then as head of the official trade union. I had met him several times
in the 1970s, when groups sponsored by the American Council of Young
Political Leaders had come to Moscow for meetings with young Soviet
"politicians," and he had been one of the Soviet officials who had organized the 1986 Chautauqua meeting in Jurmala, Latvia. I had not seen
him recently because we did not maintain ties with the captive Soviet
labor unions. Although he had not made a strong impression on me earlier, I asked to call on him shortly after he took office as vice president.

He received me in an office at Party headquarters. He would eventually move to the Kremlin, but the vice president's office there was not yet
ready for occupancy. We had a pleasant, relaxed discussion, and he assured me that Gorbachev was determined to stay on the reform course
and was aware that he needed a close relationship with the United
States. Nevertheless, Yanayev did not strike me as a strong leader. He
seemed to have no particular opinions of his own, and I sensed a tinge of
nervousness on his part. He chain-smoked cigarettes during our conversation, and at times his hand trembled as he lit them. I could not imagine
why the vice president of the Soviet Union would be nervous about
meeting a foreign ambassador and concluded that he must simply be ill
at ease with strangers, though this would have been a most unusual
characteristic for a politician, even one from a Communist country.

At first I had difficulty understanding why Gorbachev had selected
Yanayev as vice president, but then I recalled that his break with Yeltsin
had been motivated by his jealousy of Yeltsin's popularity. He obviously could not tolerate senior officials who might be his rivals for public
affection. Obviously, Gennady Yanayev would never siphon public support from Gorbachev. Nevertheless, Gorbachev needed someone to
strengthen the prestige of the presidency, and I could not understand
why he had gone to the trouble to have the Constitution amended if the
vice president was to be a nonentity.

The Economic Crisis Deepens

As 1990 DREW TO A CLOSE, the economic decline seemed to accelerate. It had been a difficult year, but despite all the talk of reform plans and "anticrisis" programs, conditions continued to deteriorate.

When Gorbachev rejected the Shatalin program, Yeltsin announced that the RSFSR would implement it alone, but this turned out to be impossible, since control of most economic enterprises remained in the hands of central ministries. Nevertheless, a battle of laws between the USSR and the RSFSR ensued, producing growing confusion. The Russian parliament approved legislation that declared that Russian laws would prevail over union laws when they were in conflict, and that new union laws would come into force only following ratification by the Russian parliament. Gorbachev countered with a decree that USSR laws were supreme until a union treaty that specified how authority would be divided came into force.

A dispute over tax collection and distribution proved particularly debilitating. The RSFSR asserted a right to retain all taxes collected on its territory and offered to transfer to the union treasury less than a fifth of the normal sum. On the final day of the Fourth Congress of People's Deputies, December 27, Minister of Finance Valentin Pavlov told the assembly that negotiations on the budget between the union and Russia had broken down.

Gorbachev then joined the debate to explain that the Russian Supreme Soviet had approved only 23.4 billion rubles for the 1991 USSR budget, 119 billion less than the RSFSR had paid in 1990! Unless the normal distribution of revenue was approved, he warned, the USSR would disintegrate.[22] Most thought that Yeltsin was trying to demonstrate that Gorbachev had no alternative but to deal with him and would yield before forcing financial collapse on the union, but one could not be sure. Instead of staying in Moscow to debate the issue while the Congress was in session, Yeltsin flew off to Yakutsk in eastern Siberia.

Just before the year ended, Gorbachev attempted to bring some order into the situation by using his new powers to issue sweeping decrees. One decree instructed all enterprises and ministries to continue 1990 contracts in 1991. This was intended to halt the growing tendency of republics and enterprises to alter arrangements made by central planners. The effect of the decree was directly counter to the goal of a market economy since it retained most features of the central planning system.

Other decrees introduced major new taxes: a 5 percent sales tax and new taxes on enterprises that would establish a "stabilization fund." The sales tax came into effect January 1 and was quickly dubbed "Gorbachev's New Year's Gift" by a public not accustomed to taxes added at the point of sale. Though traditionally taxes had been high, they had been extracted from the system in a manner that shielded the public from the knowledge of how much it was paying. Gorbachev's sales tax violated the traditional covert practice and exacerbated public discontent with his leadership.

It was the second week in January before a budget agreement was reached with Russia and the funding crisis that had loomed in December eased.

Grigory Yavlinsky and two associates, Mikhail Zadornov and Alexei Mikhailov, summed up the frustration most observers felt in a January 2 article in *Izvestiya* that lambasted the government's handling of the economic crisis. They ridiculed the idea advanced by Kryuchkov and others that external "destructive forces" were the root of the problem, placing the blame on the system itself and the way it had been mismanaged. They predicted that the government's attempt to heal the economy by raising taxes and freezing economic relations would fail and lead to a further fall in production, galloping inflation, a larger budget deficit, and even more serious structural imbalances.

Yavlinsky and his associates then urged the government to follow a set of policies similar to those they had previously prescribed in the "500-Day Plan": start denationalizing and privatizing industry and agriculture, establish commodity exchanges, stock exchanges, and real corporations, break up production monopolies, control the budget deficit, gradually free prices, and develop employment agencies and social welfare programs. Most of all, they pointed out, economic power had to be "redistributed" from the Center to the republics.

Hat in Hand

TRADITIONALLY, SINCE STALIN'S TIME, the Soviet Union had refused offers of economic assistance, considering them a potential source
of foreign influence. Even after the Chernobyl disaster in 1986, Gorbachev had rejected offers of assistance from foreign governments. His attitude changed when an earthquake struck Armenia in December 1988.
For the first time in many years, the Soviet government gratefully accepted the many offers of outside assistance and cooperated fully with
the delivery of equipment, supplies, and specialists to Armenia.

As the country's economic conditions worsened, the official stance
continued to change, and by the fall of 1990 Gorbachev was making direct appeals not only for foreign credits and credit guarantees but also
for gifts of food and medical supplies.

Our economists at the embassy were not as gloomy as the Soviet government was. They felt there would be sufficient food in the country to
avoid famine, though diets in some areas might be limited. The problem
was not so much a shortage of food overall but the wasteful and erratic
distribution system. Privatization of food processing and distribution
could solve most of the problems, they felt, but this was simply not happening.

The shortage of medical supplies was more serious. The Soviet medical care system had always been underfunded and its pharmaceutical industry was not only primitive but one of the country's most flagrant
polluters. Furthermore, within Comecon, the Soviet bloc's economic cooperation organization, East Germany had specialized in producing
medicines and a large proportion of those used in the Soviet Union were
imported from the GDR. With German unification, such imports began
costing real money and therefore were cut back sharply. At the same
time many of the Soviet chemical plants were closed to limit environmental pollution. As a consequence, the Soviet health care system faced
a crisis; even aspirin was unavailable in many areas, and modern drugs
were available only to the elite and those with relatives and friends
abroad who could fill prescriptions for them.

We in the embassy advised Washington that we did not foresee famine conditions, although food aid to some localities in which there were
spot shortages and to vulnerable groups, such as orphans and the el-

derly, would be helpful and appreciated. However, to be effective, it would have to be delivered directly to the recipients, not just introduced into the Soviet centralized distribution system. The latter was so inefficient and corrupt that most supplies would either be diverted to the black market or spoil.

The same principle applied to medical supplies, except here it was possible to deliver significant amounts by air. Since the European Community had embarked on a major program to supply food and could do so by truck, we suggested that U.S. aid efforts concentrate on medical supplies.

Eventually, Washington devised a presidential initiative to supply medicine and medical equipment. Despite its elevated title, it involved very little government funding: $5 million was allocated initially to pay for delivery of supplies donated by private firms. Project Hope, a nonprofit organization, took on the responsibility for soliciting donations and for organizing an airlift to key cities where the need seemed most acute. Their commitment and efficiency impressed me, and patients at a number of Soviet hospitals benefited. Nevertheless, medicines costing a few score millions of dollars did not go far in a country with such acute shortages.

In their panic over what might happen during the coming winter, Soviet officials were unusually cooperative in supporting the foreign aid efforts. Gorbachev assigned a first deputy prime minister, Vitaly Doguzhiev, to coordinate the foreign efforts to deliver humanitarian assistance. In what was probably the easiest negotiation of my career, we quickly agreed on the ground rules for humanitarian assistance, with the Soviet government giving the donors the right to deliver supplies directly to recipients, even to areas that had hitherto been closed to foreigners. The official cooperativeness was not only a measure of desperation over deteriorating conditions but also a sign of a deeper change of attitude. Previously, Soviet officials (and before them Russian imperial bureaucrats) had often preferred to let people suffer rather than give foreigners access to them.

I was heartened to observe how many governments and private organizations in the West began to supply humanitarian aid to the needy in the Soviet Union. It proved that the enemy image on both sides of what had been the iron curtain had faded—indeed virtually disappeared. It gave Soviet citizens a sense that they were not forgotten or shunned by the rest of the world. This was valuable, important, and encouraging.

Nevertheless, I recognized that there were dangers in even a well-planned humanitarian aid program. First, it does nothing to help a country solve systemic problems, which require internal reforms. Second, the reality rarely matches the rhetoric. Most feasible aid programs are necessarily small when measured against the needs of a country as large, varied, and abused as the Soviet Union was. Inevitably, many people would see none of the much-ballyhooed assistance and would feel betrayed. Third, such programs often leave the wrong impression in donor countries. Many people have the impression that the volume of aid is greater than it is in fact, and when it fails to transform the other country, support for any sort of assistance dwindles.

These dangers, I felt, were not arguments against humanitarian aid but cautions against exaggerated expectations. Governments and the public alike needed to understand that a humanitarian aid program is no substitute for a well-organized, well-planned, cooperative effort to assist a country that requires fundamental change in its political and economic system. While the problems facing the Soviet Union were not the moral responsibility of the outside world, which had not created them, the outside world had a deep interest in their successful resolution. If the Soviet Union and its constituent parts failed to create open, democratic political systems and to enter the larger world economy as full participants, they would once again become a security problem for their neighbors and for the United States.

This seemed crystal clear to me. But Washington had never done a serious study of the transition options available to the Soviet Union, and the president was preoccupied with maintaining a coalition to force Iraq out of Kuwait. Our Western European allies were divided on many issues and distracted by problems at home. The Japanese government had made its Soviet policy hostage to return of the southern Kurile Islands, north of Hokkaido—a just claim but not one that could be attained by direct pressure.

Even when Gorbachev solicited advice from his Western partners, they either failed to understand or were unwilling to make it clear that Western help could be relevant only if he chose to dismantle the central economic controls and began to put market mechanisms into place. Instead they indulged in emotional statements of general support for Gorbachev as an individual. For example, according to Chernyayev,

Chancellor Kohl gave Gorbachev the following pledge when they met in Bonn on November 9:

> I tell you entirely officially that as the federal chancellor of Germany and as citizen Helmut Kohl I am counting on you, Mr. Gorbachev. I am counting on you and not on anyone else in your surroundings. . . . Therefore, I feel called upon and duty bound to work with you as you carry out your fine goals. You can be sure I will be on your side on this difficult stretch of the way.[23]

Ten days later, when they met in Paris at the CSCE Conference, President Bush—again, according to Chernyayev's notes—assured Gorbachev, "We will try to do everything we can to help you in your difficult situation."[24]

In both conversations, Gorbachev had been asked about his relations with Yeltsin. He professed to be attempting cooperation but claimed it was difficult to do so in the face of Yeltsin's policy of "declamation, demagoguery, and confrontation."[25] Neither Kohl nor Bush seems to have thought it tactful to hint that welshing on the Shatalin reforms might have caused some to question his commitment to reform nor necessary to warn that outside aid would achieve nothing if a resort to repression tore the country apart.

Of course, they had every reason to be grateful to Gorbachev for the changes he had made in Soviet foreign policy and they should not have adopted a reproachful or didactic tone when his domestic problems came up for discussion. But to pledge unqualified support for him *as a person* just after he had precipitated a break with a political rival whose domestic program was superior to his and without whose cooperation he was certain to fail was not merely rash and misleading but downright irresponsible. It encouraged Gorbachev to think that Western support would be forthcoming whatever he did and failed to help him understand that no outside support could save him if his own policy took a wrong turn.

It would have been a far more effective gesture of friendship if the Western leaders had expressed their appreciation for his foreign policy but exhibited concern over the trend of his domestic policy. Their pledges of aid should have been not to him as a person (though that is doubtless what he wanted) but for policies that would move the country toward democracy and the market. The implicit message should have been "We want to help, but if you continue the way you seem to be headed, there will be no way we can help." And they should have had substantial help in mind if they were going to talk about it at all.

Could it have been that they were ill informed about the political and economic crisis that had developed in the Soviet Union or about the implications of Gorbachev's rejection of the Shatalin program? No, this is quite impossible. Embassies of all the Western countries were reporting in detail on the events I have recounted, and there was general agreement by those of us on the spot about their meaning. There was no "intelligence failure." In fact, there was no need to resort to secret agents or communication intercepts to understand the situation. All the information needed for informed political judgments was there for the taking by competent diplomats and journalists.

If there was a failure of comprehension, it was in the minds and emotions of the Western leaders. Preoccupied with other matters and infatuated with their new friend the Soviet leader, they did not want to hear that Gorbachev's position was increasingly desperate and instinctively rejected the thought that he himself could be at least partially responsible for his plight. Like juveniles in a secret club, his enemies were their enemies and loyalty was measured by commitment to one another as persons.

When Gorbachev most needed consistent advice and an international framework of support for a politically viable reform policy, the West was out to lunch. And by the end of 1990 he was lurching in a dangerous direction, emboldened by naïve assurances by his foreign friends that they would help him all the way.

The "Outside Agitator" Dodge

OFTEN WHEN A SOCIETY is struggling with fundamental problems, demagogues take refuge in accusations that the problems are not real but have been created by malicious outsiders. Following that pattern, Chebrikov had from time to time complained publicly that the United States was undertaking covert action to destabilize the Soviet Union. After he was replaced by Vladimir Kryuchkov, however, such public charges became rare. After all, it was in Gorbachev's interest to convince the country that his foreign policy was succeeding in eliminating tensions with the United States.

In 1990, some of the noisy jingoists in the Congress of People's Deputies, particularly Colonels Viktor Alksnis and Nikolai Petrushenko, began to charge that the CIA had spent "billions" to subvert Eastern Europe and pull it out of the Soviet orbit. Alksnis also claimed to have seen evidence of a CIA plot to break up the Soviet Union. Few people paid much attention, understanding that such accusations made no sense, although fringe groups of Stalinists and extreme chauvinists began to repeat them and even to charge that Gorbachev, Yakovlev, and Shevardnadze were in the pay of the CIA.

With Gorbachev's "turn to the right," the KGB reverted to public charges that Western secret services were trying to dismember the Soviet Union. In December, Kryuchkov delivered two speeches in which he referred to U.S. subversive activity. These charges were outrageously out of place: they were not only false but inconsistent with Soviet foreign policy. Such statements could only undermine confidence in Gorbachev's ability to live up to the agreements he had made.

Toward the end of December, I asked for appointments with KGB Chairman Kryuchkov and Gorbachev's foreign policy assistant, Anatoly Chernyayev, to discuss the matter. I had no illusion that I could convince Kryuchkov to stop telling lies, but I knew that Soviet officials would assume that even the most outrageous charge had substance if it was not immediately refuted. Furthermore, I knew that Chernyayev, at least, was capable of understanding the damage this sort of talk could do to U.S.-Soviet relations, and I hoped he would advise Gorbachev to order Kryuchkov to stand down.

The appointment with Kryuchkov came through just after New Year's Day, and on the afternoon of January 3 I sat down across from him at the end of a long conference table in his spacious office in the new KGB building on Kuznetsky Most, just across the street from the infamous Lubyanka.

After the initial small talk, I told him that we were disturbed by some of his charges and therefore I had requested the appointment. I then went over the text of one of his speeches as published in *Pravda,* quoting portions before I commented.

As for his accusation that U.S. intelligence services were working covertly to destabilize the USSR, I told him that if his people were making such claims, he should fire them because there could be no real evidence that this is the case. Such activity would be counter to our current policy of trying to assist an orderly transition to democracy and a healthy market economy.

He had also mentioned collection of economic information as dangerous espionage. I explained to him that data on hard currency reserves and
inventories of raw materials, fuel, and food were available to the public in
most countries of the world and indeed were published regularly by governments and private organizations. The information is essential for normal economic decision making. If the Soviet Union wished to take part in
the world economic system as a full partner, it must learn to divulge information of this sort and not consider its collection a hostile act.

Since he had cited Radio Liberty as an example of a CIA operation, I
pointed out that it had not been connected with the CIA for decades and
that it operated without secrecy and was openly funded by Congress. Its
policies prohibited inflammatory comments. If mistakes were made in
broadcasts, the Radio Liberty management was willing to take corrective action if specific violations of these principles were called to its attention.

His charge that the Soviet Union was being victimized by unscrupu-
lous foreign businessmen was not only inaccurate, I told him, but would
make it more difficult for the Soviet Union to implement its avowed policy of attracting foreign investment. In any country a certain portion of
business deals are unsuccessful and performance is not always perfect,
but there are commercial mechanisms to deal with this. There was simply no basis for claiming that an occasional unfortunate contract was
evidence of an international conspiracy against the Soviet Union. Foreign businesses could probably find at least an equivalent number of
poorly executed contracts on the part of Soviet enterprises, but nobody
was making absurd charges that these were deliberate efforts to undermine Western governments.

As for his claim that the United States maintained covert links to
workers' organizations, I pointed out that what links we had were completely open and proper. We neither maintained clandestine relations
nor tried to manipulate these movements; we in the government tried
only to understand them and our unions to cooperate with them.

I concluded my comments on his speeches by observing that the attempt to attribute the Soviet Union's problems to foreign influences of
various types not only missed the point (since the roots of the problems
were indigenous) but also made it harder to solve them.

Kryuchkov listened attentively to my presentation. When I had finished,
he paused, looked directly at me, and said that his speech at the Con-

gress of People's Deputies had been carefully drafted and had actually been toned down. He had evidence for all his assertions. Nevertheless, he was aware that it was not the policy of the United States to destabilize the Soviet Union. That would not be in the U.S. interest. However, when it came to the activities of intelligence organizations, it was likely that ambassadors were not informed of everything. "There are things that we don't burden our ambassadors with, and I am sure it is the same with the CIA," he said.

I was aware that Soviet ambassadors often claimed to be ill informed about KGB operations in their countries, and I found it interesting that Kryuchkov was willing to confirm this in such an offhand manner, as if it were common knowledge. It was even more revealing that he would assume that the CIA would systematically conduct operations at variance with U.S. policy: this said more about the KGB than the CIA. As for keeping ambassadors informed, though he should have been aware of U.S. operating procedures, I decided not to let his assertion pass without comment.

"Mr. Chairman, I don't know what your procedures are," I commented. "But I am confident that I am informed of *all* U.S. government operations in your country. In fact, none are directed at destabilizing the Soviet Union."

He dropped that topic and—almost apologetically—observed that at that time the Soviet Union was "easily wounded" and (by implication) hypersensitive. He said he personally welcomed the improvement in relations with the United States and was prepared for various types of direct cooperation: combating narcotics and terrorism, for example. Nevertheless, he was aware that espionage would continue.

I told him I had not been talking about collecting information but about covert political action such as that he described and implied in his speeches.

Before I left, Kryuchkov asked me what I thought of their situation. I told him I would be frank: I thought it was very tense. While many complained about the economy and the picture there was not good, I believed the most explosive issues were those connected with ethnic relations. Efforts by various elements to resort to force were especially worrisome, since violence would only breed more violence and could eventually produce an explosion that would engulf everyone. Therefore, we Americans hoped these problems would be solved without resort to force. In the long run, I was convinced that the Soviet Union could survive as a healthy state only if it could demonstrate to its major nationalities that they have a stake in being part of the Soviet Union. The task would be to convince them of this. If they were forced, they would not believe it. On the other hand, if they were given more authority and allowed to make up their minds without pressure from the Center, the economic and security advantages of remaining in the Soviet Union would begin to assert themselves, and an association might be structured on a voluntary basis.

He thanked me and did not try to respond to my arguments. I asked him directly if he thought it would be necessary to institute presidential rule in some republics. He replied that, in his opinion, it would be necessary but added that presidential rule did not mean arrests or suppression by military means.

The following day I called on Anatoly Chernyayev. I had requested an appointment the week before but had been told that he was busy (as he undoubtedly was). Nevertheless, I suspect the real reason was that he had not been prepared at that point to talk about Shevardnadze's resignation. He received me cordially, as usual. Always calm and collected, even when discussing contentious issues, Chernyayev seemed remarkably relaxed given the excitement and tension of the past two weeks. He must have gotten some rest over the holidays, I mused.

I first asked how Gorbachev was taking Shevardnadze's resignation. Chernyayev said that Gorbachev had not wanted Shevardnadze to leave and had tried to persuade him to stay on or take another job, but he had realized that Shevardnadze was determined not to continue in office—given his sense of honor he could not, in fact—and therefore Gorbachev had reconciled himself to Shevardnadze's departure. When Shevardnadze had unexpectedly announced his resignation, Gorbachev had been very upset that he had failed to consult him in advance. Later, he had begun to understand that Shevardnadze had avoided talking to him because he really wanted to leave and had feared that Gorbachev would dissuade him.

One thing, he stressed, we could be sure of: there would be no change in Soviet foreign policy. Relations with the United States were central, and Gorbachev understood that very well.

When I asked about the situation in the country as a whole, Chernyayev replied that Gorbachev was feeling much better about it than he had even two weeks ago. It seemed to be stabilizing, and the budget crisis seemed to have been worked out. (The agreement with Russia was in fact concluded the following week.)

Regarding the recent seizure of the State Printing House in Riga by Interior Ministry troops, Chernyayev called it a "provocation" and said he was certain that Gorbachev would not be taken in by it. I wondered how there could be any doubt as to who had authorized the action: Interior Minister Pugo had control over the troops and must have been following the developments in Latvia closely, being a Latvian himself and having been party secretary and KGB chief there.

Remembering Kryuchkov's comment the day before that presidential rule would probably be required in some areas, I asked if Chernyayev agreed. He said that it would be imposed only in specific jurisdictions where there was a life-threatening situation. Even so, it would not mean suppression by police or military means but would be more like sending Arkady Volsky to Nagorny Karabakh in 1988. It would not involve arrests, martial law, or dissolution of legislatures, although the last might be suspended temporarily.

This explanation gave me scant comfort. Any attempt to "suspend" parliaments in the Baltic states would doubtless lead to massive demonstrations, and if they persisted, arrests, martial law, and bloody encounters would almost certainly follow. It was disturbing enough to have Kryuchkov confirm that he considered presidential rule necessary "in some areas," although he made no secret of his attitude. To hear Chernyayev concede that it might be required suggested to me that Gorbachev must be giving it very serious consideration.

Before I left Chernyayev's office, I told him I hoped President Gorbachev was putting no stock in the unfounded accusations of people like Alksnis regarding CIA plots. (I actually wondered if Gorbachev was getting the same reports directly from the KGB but considered it indelicate to ask directly.) Chernyayev replied that we should not worry. Some rightists were rational, he said, but Alksnis was totally irrational, and Gorbachev paid no attention to his ravings. Gorbachev knew well that President Bush was supportive and not trying to bring him down. He also warned me not to think that Alksnis was typical either of the army or even of colonels. Most think quite differently, he claimed.

I was aware that Alksnis was an atypical extremist but suspected that more members of the Soviet officer corps shared his mind-set than we, or Gorbachev, would like to believe.

I told Chernyayev that I was relieved to get his assurances that there would be no change in foreign policy and to note his feeling that the domestic situation was stabilizing. Even so, the tone of domestic policy had changed since mid-November. Had Gorbachev really not changed course?

Chernyayev vehemently denied that any fundamental change had occurred. Those who talked about the "defeat" of the "democrats" were mistaken, he said. They were not defeated, he believed, but were simply becoming more practical, learning from experience. Popov and Sobchak, for example, were cooperating much more productively than they had previously.

As Tamara Alexandrova, Chernyayev's cheerful assistant, escorted me out of the Central Committee building, I had the feeling that, while what he had said about Soviet foreign policy was accurate, his claim that things were improving domestically had less basis. I didn't see how he could deny that Gorbachev's policy had shifted to a harder line, and his observation about the role of the "democrats" seemed no more than wishful thinking.

What I did not know, and learned only from the memoirs he published in 1993, was that he was trying to convince Gorbachev to name Anatoly Sobchak prime minister.[26] If Gorbachev had been willing to do so and to support Sobchak's leadership, this could have brought reformers back onto his team for constructive work.

Man of a Past Year

FROM THE TIME he became president, Gorbachev's popularity began to plummet. Polls by Yuri Levada's All-Union Public Opinion Center documented the steady decline. In December 1989, 52 percent of those polled said they completely approved of Gorbachev's activity. By January 1990, the proportion dropped to 44 percent, by May to 39 percent, by July to 28 percent, and by October to 21 percent.[27] A poll at the end of 1990 to select the "Man of the Year" revealed that 32 percent backed Yeltsin and only 19 percent Gorbachev. The year before, 46 percent had supported Gorbachev and only 6 percent Yeltsin.[28]

As for Yeltsin, some thought that his stature had begun to decline toward the end of the year. Unable to control his own Congress of People's Deputies—which was not yet ready to amend the RSFSR Constitution to establish a presidency—he was also ineffectual in opposing Gorbachev's proposals.

Some sections of the public, at least, had begun to note that he tended to promise more than he could deliver, changed his mind under pressure, failed to follow through on commitments, and was given to erratic behavior, sometimes dropping out of sight for weeks at a time.

Even so, he had shown that if he chose he could block whatever limited initiatives Gorbachev took. He espoused the sort of changes that the reformers considered essential—and that were anathema to the hard-line Communists. He was now the most popular politician in the country and arguably the most influential, since he had good, if superficial, working relations with most of the elected republic leaders.

Gorbachev's only hope for political survival and for preservation of some sort of union seemed to depend on his willingness and ability to make common cause with Yeltsin and the democrats. Yet, as I thought about the situation at the start of 1991, it was obvious to me that Gorbachev not only failed to see what seemed clear to me but was actually doing the opposite of what I had predicted.

Was it his blindness or mine? Had I misjudged the man, had he changed—or would he, once more, in the nick of time, switch tactics, abandon the Communist Party *apparat,* and put together an anti-Communist reform coalition? With tempers so high it would be much more difficult than in August 1990.

I had to admit I did not know the answer. It was a painful thought for one who, just four months earlier, had been confident he understood what Gorbachev was doing.

XVII

Rehearsal

What do you have to do to please the president these days? . . . Teach others to lie,
and you become the head of Central Television. Ruin the economy,
and he'll make you prime minister.
YURI CHERNICHENKO, January 20, 1991[1]

A regime in its death throes has made a last-ditch stand: economic reform has been
blocked, censorship of the media reinstated, brazen demagogy revived,
and an open war on the republics declared.
NIKOLAI PETRAKOV, explaining his resignation as Gorbachev's adviser,
January 1991[2]

Ronald Reagan was right. This is an evil empire.
VALENTIN OSKOTSKY at Moscow demonstration in support of Lithuania,
January 20, 1991[3]

D uring the week of January 7, 1991, Gorbachev began to tighten
the vise on Lithuania again, and this time his moves seemed
more threatening than they had been the previous spring. The Ministry
of Defense announced that it was sending a detachment of paratroops to
Lithuania, ostensibly to round up Lithuanians who had not responded
to the military draft. Demonstrations, organized by the Moscow-backed
Interfront, broke out in Vilnius to protest plans by the Lithuanian government to raise retail prices. When Parliament Chairman Landsbergis
announced that the price increases would be delayed, Prime Minister
Prunskienė offered her resignation and the Lithuanian Supreme Council
accepted it. Gorbachev then took advantage of the political disarray in
Vilnius to send an ultimatum to the Lithuanians. Putting all the blame
on them for the rising tension and accusing them of violating the Constitution, infringing human rights, and attempting to revive a "bourgeois"
system, Gorbachev's January 10 decree instructed the Lithuanian Supreme Council "immediately to restore the USSR and Lithuanian SSR

Constitutions in their entirety and to rescind the unconstitutional acts adopted previously."[4]

Even though I was well aware of Gorbachev's hardening stance, this decree shocked me. I noted in my journal that day:

> This decree will do nothing but exacerbate an already tense situation. If Gorbachev knows what he is doing, he is preparing the ground for a tragedy—and one that will engulf him as well. Why is he doing it? Does he really not understand, or is he already a hostage to the forces Shevardnadze described?

There was not the slightest possibility that any Lithuanian government could accept the harsh and sweeping demand Gorbachev had made; its only purpose seemed to be to provide a pretext for the use of force. And in fact, without waiting for a reply, Soviet troops began occupying buildings in Vilnius on January 11, the day after the decree was issued. The buildings were being used by Lithuanian security officials and as a press center and had previously been owned by the Communist Party and a Party-controlled paramilitary "public" organization.

Even before the buildings were occupied, Landsbergis issued an anguished plea to Western governments to take "determined action" to prevent Soviet military aggression against Lithuania. Specifically, Landsbergis appealed for formal diplomatic recognition and for a statement that the Soviet Constitution did not apply to Lithuania. He particularly feared that the international community's preoccupation with Iraq would deflect attention from the Soviet suppression of Lithuania.

Washington, however, did manage to see beyond the Gulf crisis. Even before officials saw Landsbergis's appeal, White House press spokesman Marlin Fitzwater condemned the threat to use paratroopers as "provocative and counterproductive," and urged the Soviet government "to cease attempts at intimidation and to turn back to negotiations." Acting Secretary of State Lawrence Eagleburger called in the Soviet ambassador, and I was instructed to deliver even more direct and pointed messages to senior Soviet officials in Moscow. On Friday, President Bush telephoned Gorbachev to warn him personally of our concern.

Bloodshed in Vilnius

AS THE TENSION ESCALATED, I received word from Yeltsin's office that he would like to see me on Saturday morning, January 12. I was eager to find out just what the Russian government was prepared to do to head off the growing threats against the Balts and would probably have sought the meeting myself if he had not asked me to come. I was not aware that the White House staff in Washington had considered instructing me to call on Yeltsin but, concerned that it might offend Gorbachev, had decided against it. Fortunately, they neglected to inform me of their decision.

Normally Yeltsin was punctual for his appointments, but on that Saturday morning he kept me waiting for ten minutes. As he joined me in his reception room, he explained that he had been working out a public statement on Lithuania with his Presidium. He called it a "strong statement" and said that it condemned the use of troops in Lithuania and demanded that no draftees from the RSFSR be used at trouble spots there or in other republics.

I asked him why he was doing this, although I was confident I knew the answer. He looked at me as if I had inquired whether it gets cold in Moscow in winter but explained patiently, "If they can use force against an elected assembly in Lithuania, they can do so against the Russian parliament. In fact, if they are successful against the Balts, we will be next on the list!"

Yeltsin was scheduled to attend a meeting of the Council of Federation that afternoon, and he said he believed several other republic leaders would take the same position he had. He also made it clear that the threats of force in the Baltic had set back Gorbachev's efforts to reach agreement on a new union treaty. He saw little hope that it would be completed in the near future.

When I returned from Yeltsin's office, I was informed that a letter had come in from Secretary Baker to Shevardnadze. Shevardnadze was still serving as foreign minister pending appointment of a successor, but we were told that he was not available that day, so I delivered the letter to Deputy Minister Alexei Obukhov, who was responsible for relations with the United States. The secretary's letter was a strong appeal to cool it in Lithuania, making it clear that our relations could be seriously damaged if force was used. I asked Obukhov to deliver it to the minister sealed (but with an interpreter, since it was in English) as soon as possible and to inform the minister that I was at his disposal over the weekend if he should have anything to communicate to Secretary Baker. Obukhov assured me that Shevardnadze would get the letter promptly, but even though his successor had not yet been named, I wondered if he was still actually working as foreign minister. Things were so tense in the Baltic that he risked being a member of a government "with blood on its hands" if he continued in office even that weekend.

In fact, Shevardnadze ceased to act as foreign minister that weekend, even though his replacement was not named until the following Tuesday.

During my call, Obukhov asked when the advance party would arrive to plan President Bush's visit to Moscow, which had been scheduled for February. Normally, a group would come five or six weeks before a summit meeting to prepare the schedule of meetings and events, but this time the White House had been uncharacteristically silent on the subject. I told Obukhov that I would inquire, but I frankly doubted that the trip could proceed with the atmosphere in the Baltic so tense.

Obukhov bridled, expressing mock surprise that we would let "an internal matter" interfere with something so important as a summit meeting. I told him that he knew very well that we did not consider the status of the Baltic states an "internal matter" and furthermore that if, as a result of Moscow's actions, blood should be spilled there, it would be inconceivable that a summit meeting could take place in that atmosphere. I reminded him of the U.S. reaction to the Soviet invasion of Afghanistan and asked him to make sure that Gorbachev and other top leaders fully understood the strength of our feelings on the issue.

That evening I watched the television news with particular attention since I wanted to hear just what the Russian legislature had said in the press release Yeltsin had reviewed for me. There was not a word about the Russian statement. The new chairman of the state television committee had obviously ordered that it be ignored. It had been several years since Soviet television had routinely ignored major news stories, and the reversion to an old habit proved to me that Gorbachev's replacement of Nenashev with Kravchenko was already having its effect.

The way recent events were treated in the newscast was ominous. The anchor read reports that suggested that order was breaking down in Lithuania because the Lithuanian Supreme Council was incapable of governing effectively.

Although it had been a long day, the evening was to stretch on longer still. I had been invited to a celebration of the "Old New Year"—New Year on the calendar used before the Revolution—in honor of the sixtieth anniversary of the crusading weekly *Moscow News*. The invitation was for 11:00 P.M., and the program would last well past midnight.

I did not like late evenings, and the political atmosphere was such that I knew the birthday celebration would be more like a wake than a party, but I had to attend. The leaders of Democratic Russia would be out in force, and the celebration would give me a chance to hear the latest political gossip and—much more important—would symbolize American support for reform and demonstrate solidarity with those who supported Baltic independence.

Yeltsin, accompanied by a single bodyguard, arrived a little later than most of the other guests—he enjoyed making a grand entrance—and, followed by cameramen, was ushered to the row in the auditorium where I was sitting. He greeted me profusely and insisted I move next to him so we could chat. His bodyguard, Alexander Korzhakov, shifted seats to make room for me. The lights of several television cameras turned on us as we made small talk.

He was using me to send a political message, and I might have been annoyed except that on that particular evening I was using him as much as he was using me. His message to the public was that he was dealing with a representative of the other superpower; mine was that we endorsed the call he had made that afternoon to leave Lithuania alone.

I had heard just that evening that Valentin Pavlov, the erratic minister of finance, would be named to replace Ryzhkov as prime minister. It would be a strange appointment; Pavlov had neither the stature nor the ability to be an effective head of government, particularly at such troubled times. I asked Yeltsin if he had been consulted. He replied that he had heard that Pavlov was one of the candidates and that he had told Gorbachev two days earlier that he considered him unsuitable for the post. However, he understood that Gorbachev intended to name him anyway, and if Gorbachev did, he, Yeltsin, would not fight the appointment. He had more important things to do, and besides, without clearer direction from Gorbachev, no USSR prime minister would be able to implement the reforms needed.

I asked him if he had noticed that the television news had ignored his statement on Lithuania. He replied, with a grin on his face and a snarl in his voice, "They don't know what to do with it!"[5]

As I had anticipated, the evening's program continued well past 2:00 A.M. Skit after skit was offered, and the script was often funny but the performers were not in a comic mood. There was frequent laughter, but it was brittle and forced. Everyone was worried and it showed.

It was a relief when the master of ceremonies declared the program at an end. I returned to Spaso House just after three. As my head hit the pillow, the KGB's elite Alpha Detachment was beginning an attack on the television tower in Vilnius. It was the same unit that, on December 24, 1979, had stormed the presidential palace in Kabul and assassinated President Hafizullah Amin, who had refused to request Soviet "fraternal assistance."

Who Gave the Order?

WHEN THE RINGING TELEPHONE penetrated my sleep, it was still pitch dark. Only half awake, I took the receiver off the hook. It was my deputy, James Collins, with the news that the television complex in Vilnius had been taken during the night with extensive loss of life. Though reports were still fragmentary, it was obvious that many civilians had been killed and hundreds injured. Furthermore, there were signs that an attack on the parliament building might be imminent. Most of the Lithuanian deputies had barricaded themselves inside, and thousands of persons had gathered outside to form a human shield. If the building should be attacked, it would result in a bloodbath.

Reports continued to filter in during the morning. Besides the accounts of foreign journalists, we had our own eyewitnesses there from our consulate general in Leningrad (the ban on foreign diplomats had been lifted a few weeks after it was imposed in March 1990).

At noon, I jotted down the following questions for myself:

Why this way? Gorbachev could not have had solid support in the Council of Federation for such action. To start such military action before the commission of that body arrives[6] smacks either of serious duplicity, or (is it conceivable?) that Gorbachev did not make the decision and that events are moving out of his control. Or was much of this pre-planned? Could Shevardnadze have known of these plans when he resigned? But if so, why did he stay on in office while it was happening? As I write this I do not know in fact whether the Supreme Council building in Vilnius is being stormed. I will be better able to grasp things when I know exactly what happens next—and something of the reaction of various forces in Russia and in other republics. I cannot imagine that all will sit still, but I doubt that there will be concerted action.

That afternoon, I received an invitation from the Soviet Ministry of Foreign Affairs to attend a meeting with First Deputy Minister Anatoly Kovalev. My British, French, German, and Finnish colleagues were also invited, along with a few others. The summons to us as a group, particularly on a Sunday afternoon, was a signal that the subject was both important and urgent.

We gathered in one of the medium-sized conference rooms where Shevardnadze had often received groups of senators or congressmen. One of the few remaining senior officials from the Gromyko era, the lanky, mild-mannered Kovalev was known as a Western European specialist and a serious poet. Now he was apparently acting foreign minister, since he made no reference to calling us on Shevardnadze's instructions. I wondered whether Shevardnadze had refused to conduct the meeting since he would have to make excuses on Gorbachev's behalf.

Kovalev told us that he had just come from the president's office and wished to convey a message from him to our chiefs of state and government. His hands shook as he read from his notes, and there was an uncharacteristic quaver in his voice. The president, he continued, wished to assure his foreign colleagues that he had not been responsible for the attack on the television tower. He did not himself know who had given the order. The situation throughout the country was extraordinarily tense, and he was doing his utmost to prevent civil strife from spreading. He wanted to assure his friends abroad that he was still determined to continue the reform course he had set and to avoid bloodshed.

I was stunned, but not by the denial that Gorbachev was responsible: that was to be expected. It was the statement that *Gorbachev did not know who had given the order* that caught my attention. If true, it meant that he no longer had full control over the Soviet security forces.

Although I had no instructions other than a telephone call alerting me that President Bush would issue a strong condemnation of the violence in Vilnius (it was still early Sunday morning in Washington), I thought it would be irresponsible to let Kovalev's presentation pass without a comment. Therefore, I told him that the American president and public had been shocked by the violence in Vilnius and that the president would likely issue a statement soon. But, speaking for myself, I would say that I was relieved to hear that President Gorbachev had not authorized the violence. Since that was the case, I assumed that President Gorbachev would immediately make a public statement condemning the attack and see to it that those who were guilty would be punished in accord with the law.

Kovalev assured us that my comments would be conveyed to President Gorbachev. Another ambassador asked whether he had correctly understood that the president did not know who the perpetrators of the violence were. Kovalev looked at his notes and repeated, word for word, the statement he had made earlier.

As we left the building, one of my colleagues asked if I believed the denial of Gorbachev's complicity. I told him I didn't know what to believe: it was most difficult to accept that he had not known what was going on, but at the same time I could not understand why he would send us the message he had if it was not true. He would hardly wish to encourage the suspicion that he was no longer in control of his own government.

"Then what's worse," my colleague inquired, "the possibility that Gorbachev planned this or that he has lost control of the armed forces?"

"I'm not sure," I told him. "I don't like either possibility."

Neither Gorbachev nor any other senior Soviet official made a public statement on the tragedy that day. However, when the head of the press office at the Ministry of Defense, Major General Gennady Kashubin, gave an interview to Moscow Radio, he placed all the blame on the Lithuanians. According to his account, the Committee of National Salvation had repeatedly asked the Lithuanian authorities to discontinue making inflammatory statements on the radio and television station they controlled. When these requests had been disregarded, he alleged, it had been decided that some volunteer militiamen should take control of the station. When they had approached the building, however, Lithuanian irregulars had fired upon them, at which time they had appealed to the army garrison in Vilnius to help. He then launched into a tirade against the elected Lithuanian government, asserting that it was violating the Constitution and trampling on the rights of servicemen in particular.

This turned out to be one of the most inept cover stories since the one in 1983 denying that the Soviet air force had shot down a Korean airliner. Every eyewitness agreed that the attackers—who were not from the army garrison in Vilnius but from the KGB—had fired first on the crowd and on people in the studios and control rooms of the broadcasting complex. But the question of who had fired first was not the most important one; the more important one was who had tried to use heavily armed troops to seize a facility that belonged to the Lithuanian government.

While Gorbachev was silent, Yeltsin swung into action. He immediately flew to Tallinn, Estonia, and signed a statement jointly with the three leaders of the Baltic republics. In it, each "recognized the others' state sovereignty" and forbade its citizens to participate in "armed action infringing on one another's sovereignty." Furthermore, they announced that they would develop relations "on the basis of international law"—that is, as independent countries, not as constituent parts of the Soviet Union. To stress the latter point, they announced that the statement would be submitted to the United Nations, other international organizations, and parliaments and governments throughout the world.

Yeltsin went even further. He issued a direct appeal to servicemen from the RSFSR not to obey orders to attack civilians in the Baltic states. Echoing more eloquently what he had told me the day before, he appealed to Russians in the armed forces to "remember your own homes, the present and the future of your own republic, and your own people. Violence against legal institutions and the Baltic people will bring about crises in Russia itself and harm Russians living in other republics."[7]

Yeltsin had already challenged Gorbachev on economic policy and taxes; now he was challenging his right to control the armed forces against the wishes of union republic governments. Since the military command hated Yeltsin because of his sharp criticism and his program of slashing military budgets, the officers would certainly not heed his call. But with his statements on January 12 and 13, 1991, he began to make the case that the ultimate loyalty of servicemen from Russia was to him as Russia's leader, not to Gorbachev, the president of the Soviet Union. Elements of dual power were growing.

Simultaneously, more citizens were taking to the streets to protest. The crowds around the parliament building in Vilnius swelled as people came out to reinforce the human shield around their elected leaders. They defied the tank crews surrounding the area, who used megaphones to order them to disperse by 5:00 P.M. or face attack. Rallies also occurred in most other Lithuanian cities, as well as in Latvia and Estonia. Riga was almost as tense as Vilnius, and demonstrators began building barricades around the parliament building there. Demonstrations in support of Lithuania also swept Moscow, Leningrad, Kishinev, Lviv, and many other cities across the empire.

Gorbachev said nothing in public about the Vilnius tragedy until he addressed the USSR Supreme Soviet the following day, January 14. To my dismay, his comments seemed to exculpate the attackers. Interior Minister Boris Pugo and Defense Minister Dmitri Yazov also reported to the Supreme Soviet on the recent events in Lithuania. The only problem any of them saw was that of a recalcitrant Lithuanian leadership given to lawless acts. Military units reacting to provocations should not be blamed, they claimed.

I watched their speeches on television with disgust and made the following note to myself:

> The explanations offered by Pugo, Yazov, and even Gorbachev of the events yesterday were not at all convincing. It seems that the order to attack the Vilnius television tower was given by a local commander in response to a request for assistance from the so-called Committee of National Salvation. Gorbachev said he first heard of it when he was awakened at 3:00 A.M. Conceivable, so far. But—who created the conditions which made this possible? Who issued what was in effect a blank check to the local military commander? And why is there no effort to discipline him?
>
> After all, the Committee of National Salvation has no legal status whatever. Its membership has not been disclosed, and Gorbachev sent word yesterday that he himself did not know who its members are. If all that is true, how can the action of a military commander who "responds to the request" of an unknown, illegal body, to attack a civil objective be tolerated? Yet, it is not only being tolerated; to judge

from the words of the speakers today, the action was understandable and justified.

Let's compare this to what happened in Azerbaijan when the Azerbaijan National Front assumed control. The army put it down on grounds that it was an illegal seizure of power. Yet the attempts of this shadowy group to seize power from the elected government seem to be justified by the highest authorities of the union government! The only question is who is giving orders to whom. . . .

Gorbachev simply cannot escape responsibility for the current situation. Either he planned it, or he irresponsibly prepared the ground for it, or he was forced into it. Whatever alternative may be most accurate, the implications for our policy are the same: continue to make very clear the serious consequences for Soviet interests which further conflict there will bring.

The attack on the Lithuanian parliament, which many feared would follow the capture of the television complex, did not occur Sunday night or Monday night. Someone, it appeared, had given orders to freeze the situation and not provoke further violence—at least for the time being. However, the television complex was not returned to the Lithuanian government and political pressure was intensified in Latvia. A spokesman for the just-formed Latvian Committee of National Salvation (headed by the Communist Party leader, Alfreds Rubiks) demanded that the elected legislature be dissolved and power transferred to it.[8] Others demanded that direct presidential rule be applied to all three Baltic states. I recalled Kryuchkov's comment to me just ten days back. The whole scenario seemed designed to prepare for "suspending" the elected governments on grounds that they had lost control of the situation. What I did not know was whether Gorbachev was behind the plan or whether it was a plot to force him to act.

On Tuesday he made another speech on the situation in Lithuania but showed no inclination to criticize the forces that had carried out the violence in Vilnius. On the contrary, he continued to place all the blame on the Lithuanians. Calls continued to come in from Communist Party and military sources in the Baltic for him to impose direct rule on the area.

I was not the only person to be dismayed by Gorbachev's failure to condemn the criminal acts that had occurred in Vilnius on Sunday morning. Vadim Bakatin, who had been removed as minister of internal affairs six weeks earlier, was the first senior Gorbachev associate to speak out clearly on the question. In an interview with *Komsomolskaya Pravda,* he stated:

> First, I cannot understand why the country's president has not distanced himself clearly and unambiguously from what happened in Vilnius. His actions as president and demands that the processes connected with Lithuanian independence be returned to a normal channel and that human rights be observed have no connection with attempts to seize power in the night. . . .
>
> Second, I cannot understand all the bustle in parliament about the lack of information. . . . They know who has that information and who should be asked for it. Indeed, in the final analysis it is immaterial who opened fire first. . . . What is important is the absolutely illegal and unconstitutional action which took human lives. It is obviously unconstitutional for any general to follow the orders of a street crowd, or a self-styled committee, no matter how loud it may shout.[9]

This was the only accurate legal judgment by a member of Gorbachev's entourage I had seen in public print. I was impressed with Bakatin's courage and pained to realize that Gorbachev, for all his avowed attachment to creating a state based on the rule of law, was either unwilling or unable to acknowledge the obvious.

Journalists began to draw even broader conclusions. Writing in a newly founded newspaper called *Nezavisimaya gazeta* ("The Independent") on Tuesday, January 15, Vitaly Portnikov declared that the confusion over who had ordered the use of force in Vilnius showed that "the paralysis of power in the Soviet Union has entered its final phase, the power of paralysis" and then compared the Soviet system to a dying octopus, still thrashing about, not realizing that its tentacles were being severed, one by one.[10]

Portnikov's image was striking, but I was not certain that many tentacles had really been severed. Some might be just stunned and able to lash out again.

Nevertheless, there was no doubt that Gorbachev's authority was shrinking rapidly. He was exhibiting a tendency to bluster and threaten, then stop short of carrying out his threats. Usually, he was wise not to carry them out, but then he should not have issued the threats in the first place.

A case in point was his reaction to the growing violence in South Ossetia, an autonomous district in Georgia. When some of the Ossetian political leaders began to talk of secession from Georgia and union with their ethnic brethren in North Ossetia, a part of the Russian Federation, Zviad Gamsakhurdia, the newly elected Georgian leader, arrested them and held them without trial. Irregular armed bands from both groups began skirmishing in South Ossetia, but when the Ossetians began to drive ethnic Georgians out of the province, Gamsakhurdia sent in regular Georgian troops. They blockaded the Ossetian capital of Tskhinvali in the middle of winter, causing acute distress in the city. In Georgian eyes, the Ossetian political leaders were tools of Moscow, which was trying to force Georgia to stay in the Soviet Union by threatening dismemberment.

Instead of trying to defuse the crisis by pressuring both parties to come to terms, Gorbachev chose to issue decrees he could not enforce. On January 7, he ordered the Georgian government to withdraw its troops from South Ossetia, but the Georgian parliament voted overwhelmingly not to and Gamsakhurdia announced that any attempt to implement the decree would result in a state of war between Georgia and the Soviet Union.

I did not condone the outrageous treatment the Georgians meted out to the Ossetians. While resisting Soviet attempts to treat Georgia as a colony, they were demanding that minorities in their midst accept a subordinate status or leave. Nevertheless, Gorbachev's threat of military intervention only made the situation worse: if he failed to enforce it, his credibility would plummet, but if he tried to enforce it, he would have a bloodbath and a probable civil war throughout Georgia.

Since mid-November, Gorbachev had set a consistent pattern of issuing futile, self-defeating orders. Two days before the attack on the Vilnius television complex, I recorded the following comment on Gorbachev's threat to send troops to South Ossetia:

> Unlike the Balts, who will make every effort not to fall into the trap of resisting Soviet troops, the Georgians are very likely to back up their threats. While I can understand the frustration in Moscow with the centrifugal tendencies and do not feel that the Georgians have behaved properly in regard to the Ossetes, I cannot understand why Gorbachev is pushing things this way. . . . The current course is idiotic—it is as if Gorbachev is too stupid to see that those who are pushing him to "exercise his authority" in this manner really wish to remove him! Since he is certainly not stupid, then he himself must entertain illusions that force—or the threat of it—is likely to work. Sad, sad, sad, if true.

As I typed this on my personal computer in Spaso House, I hoped that the KGB listening devices could read what I was typing and that Gorbachev would get a copy of my comment. I was far from certain that he would, however, since my message was one the chairman of the KGB would not have wanted him to see.

Throughout the week of January 15, tension was at fever pitch in Lithuania and Latvia and only slightly lower in Estonia. Delegations sponsored by the USSR Supreme Soviet went back and forth to the Baltic capitals on "fact-finding" missions, but few real negotiations were evident. In Vilnius, members of the Supreme Council continued to expect a military attack at any time. When Richard Miles, our consul general in Leningrad, visited the parliament building in midweek he found the deputies grimly determined to stay in the building no matter what might happen and to die there if necessary.

Landsbergis was one of the determined ones, but he did emerge to attend the funeral of the persons who had died Sunday. So many people wanted to attend that the service was held in a football stadium. The Russian Orthodox metropolitan delivered a remarkable oration in which he expressed shame as a Russian that Russians had done the killing, said that the central media had distorted the events, and concluded with the statement "Lithuania will be free!" Not all Russians in Lithuania were marching to the tune of the Committee of National Salvation.

On Sunday evening, January 20, a serious incident occurred in Riga that at first seemed to reflect a decision to apply force there. A detachment of special riot troops (known by their acronym, OMON) attacked the building of the Latvian Ministry of Internal Affairs, killing five or six people in the process. After taking the building, they withdrew a couple of hours after midnight. Latvian Prime Minister Ivars Godmanis immediately telephoned Boris Pugo, the Soviet minister of internal affairs (who had jurisdiction over the OMON "black berets") when the fighting started, and Pugo claimed that he knew nothing about it. He offered to send his deputy to Riga to investigate.

It turned out that, in fact, this attack was the result of an aberrant act by an OMON officer and had not been authorized by a higher authority. Nevertheless, it added to the tension felt by all.

Though he seemed to have given orders to avoid further attacks on the Baltic government buildings, Gorbachev waited a full nine days before he labeled—even indirectly—the attack on the Vilnius television complex as illegal. Finally, however, on the evening of January 22, he made a statement that continued to criticize the Baltic governments and insist they rescind their "unconstitutional laws" but then added that groups could come to power only by constitutional means, not by force, and that any attempt to appeal to the armed forces in a political struggle was impermissible.[11]

It was a mild rebuke given the gravity of the violation that had occurred, but it was something.

Another Inept Appointment

AT THE HEIGHT OF DEBATES during the Fourth Congress of People's Deputies, Prime Minister Ryzhkov suffered a heart attack and was hospitalized December 25. He had been under constant attack during the year, and demands for his resignation had become ever more shrill. I was saddened by the news. I liked Nikolai Ivanovich and admired his courage and integrity. Yet I also knew that he had failed to understand the country's most pressing needs and had as a consequence become a barrier to the structural changes that were required. If the Soviet Union was to retain a prime minister as well as a president, it needed someone who would view the principal task as redistributing economic power from the Center to enterprises, localities, and republics. Ryzhkov had demonstrated that he was not that person.

Ryzhkov's illness freed Gorbachev's hand. Although tensions had grown between the two, Gorbachev had been reluctant to seek his resignation and break definitively with yet another member of his original team. Now he could name a prime minister of his own choosing. Many expected him to use the opportunity to restructure the Council of Ministers, turning it into something resembling the American presidential Cabinet, with twenty or so ministries rather than sixty-odd. Transferring the functions of the economic ministries to the republics would meet the republic leaders' principal demand and thus facilitate agreement on the Treaty of Union.

Gorbachev took three weeks to choose a successor to Ryzhkov, and when he announced his selection of Valentin Pavlov on January 14, the day after the bloodshed in Vilnius, it was scarcely noticed in the agitation over the violence that had occurred. In fact, Pavlov seemed an improbable choice for prime minister. Gorbachev's intent to name him had leaked a few days earlier, but many had had trouble believing the report. Even Gorbachev's close associates had difficulty explaining Pavlov's qualifications for the job.

A chubby man with a round, porcine face, Pavlov had been finance minister since 1989, a period marked by an expansion of the money supply well beyond the availability of goods for purchase. Since prices were still controlled, the "ruble overhang" had exacerbated shortages in the shops and threatened sudden inflation if prices were liberalized. Observers outside the government held the minister of finance at least partly responsible for this situation and therefore had difficulty understanding why he should be selected for a promotion, particularly at a time of growing economic disarray.

I had met him the year before, when I had called on him to arrange a visit to the United States. He struck me at the time as erratic and not totally serious. Furthermore, there seemed to be a touch of arrogance in his behavior. We were trying to set a date for him to travel to the United States with Viktor Gerashchenko, the chairman of the USSR State Bank. I had discussed dates with Gerashchenko, who told me he would not be able to come on one of those suggested. When I mentioned this to Pavlov, he picked up the telephone, called Gerashchenko, and in my presence ordered him to alter his schedule to travel on the date he had tried to avoid. His only reason seemed to be to demonstrate to me his authority over the State Bank chairman.

Sometimes his observations seemed so bizarre that I wondered if he was joking—but subsequent developments proved he had been serious. For example, during lunch at Spaso House on January 11, just three days before he was named prime minister, he scoffed at the idea that the "ruble overhang" was a problem and estimated it at a "mere" 25 billion rubles. Most economists I knew put it at 100 billion or more. Since the excessive use of the printing press had occurred when he was minister of finance, his defensive attitude was understandable, but his attempt to deny the problem by citing an obviously false figure could not have convinced even modestly well informed people. It only made him look silly.

When someone mentioned the ruble exchange rate on the black market, he turned to me and said, "This may surprise you, but I set that price." His statement surprised me so much that I was not sure I had heard him correctly and asked him to repeat it. It would not have shocked me to learn that the Finance Ministry was dabbling in the black market—in fact, I heard rumors to that effect—but I did not expect the minister to brag about indulging in such transactions. He gleefully repeated his statement and went on to explain that selling dollars on the black market was a good way to soak up rubles from speculators since he could get about 40 rubles to the dollar. The official rate at that time was 5.6.

Though there was general skepticism that Pavlov could deal effectively with the growing crisis, there was no organized opposition to his appointment. The Supreme Soviet confirmed the nomination by an overwhelming vote.

Most observers—myself included—were also surprised a few weeks later when the new "presidential Cabinet" was announced. We had expected Gorbachev to slash the size of the central bureaucracy by reducing the number of economic ministries now that he had the power to do so and had no need to spare Ryzhkov's feelings. It seemed a propitious time to transfer much economic decision making to the republics.

But this did not happen. When the list of ministries and "state committees" (ministries in all but name) in the new Cabinet was published, it seemed that the number of ministries had been increased rather than decreased. This could only infuriate the republic leaders, who were clamoring for more economic autonomy, which Gorbachev had repeatedly promised.

In March, Gorbachev finally named a Security Council to replace the now defunct Presidential Council. Some of the names on it were, in effect, *ex officio:* the vice president, prime minister, ministers of defense, interior, and foreign affairs, and KGB chairman. To these obvious choices Gorbachev added three other names to round out the list: Yevgeny Primakov, Vadim Bakatin, and Valery Boldin, his chief of staff.

When it voted on the list, the Supreme Soviet approved all but Boldin and Primakov. Gorbachev insisted on a second vote, and Primakov squeaked through. It took a third try to obtain a majority vote for Boldin, however. I asked several Supreme Soviet deputies why the legislature had twice rejected Boldin, who was reputedly very close to Gorbachev. All of them said he was mistrusted because he had a reputation for sending slanted information to Gorbachev. As one put it, "He's a troublemaker, always feeding Gorbachev rubbish to arouse his suspicions. We can't understand why Gorbachev keeps him around."

Opposition Sharpens Criticism

AS CONFIDENCE IN GORBACHEV'S commitment to reform ebbed, the reformers adopted an increasingly anti-Gorbachev stance. The thought, in August and September, that Gorbachev might use his new powers to implement economic reforms had vanished when he had allied himself with the forces of repression. It seemed to many that the "dictatorship" of which Shevardnadze had spoken might be that of Gorbachev himself.

During the weekend in January when blood flowed around the Vilnius television complex, the Council of Representatives of Democratic Russia met in Moscow under the chairmanship of Yuri Afanasiev and Gavriil Popov. It was the second stage of a meeting held on December 8–9, and it illustrated the growing disenchantment with Gorbachev and the rapid development of organized opposition.

The organization claimed to have 300,000–400,000 active members. Its local organs were said to publish about five hundred newspapers in forty cities, with a combined circulation of half a million. (If these figures were correct, many of these newspapers must have had only a tiny circulation, since the average would have been only a thousand.) However, its unofficial national newspaper, *Demokraticheskaya Rossiya,* claimed a circulation of a million and a half.

During the meeting, Popov announced that hopes of forming a "center/left coalition"[12] with Gorbachev were now dead and therefore the democrats were required to oppose the current government and develop a mass party organization. As recently as October, Popov had been optimistic that there could be what he called a "center/left" coalition— meaning an alliance between Gorbachev and Yeltsin.

The meeting approved a number of resolutions that called for a shift of power from the central government Gorbachev controlled to the RSFSR government and the other union republics. Within the RSFSR it endorsed rapid and radical reform, including transfer of land to private owners, distribution of state property to citizens, and a new RSFSR constitution with provision for an elected president. The assembly also approved negotiating treaties between republics and called for a structure for political cooperation with democratic groups in other union republics.

In addition, the conference condemned the use of force in the Baltic states and warned of an impending dictatorship by the most reactionary forces, which it identified as the Communist Party *nomenklatura,* the military and KGB elite, and the leaders of the military-industrial complex under the direction of "the initiator of perestroika acting as dictator."

The reference to Gorbachev was the most sweeping condemnation yet by a group that, only six months earlier, had considered him an ally.

During the following week, the two most prominent economists on Gorbachev's previous Presidential Council publicly parted company with him. Stanislav Shatalin announced that he no longer considered himself a member of Gorbachev's team. Nikolai Petrakov, the other economist on the council, excoriated Gorbachev mercilessly in an open letter. Some samples:

> A regime in its death throes has made a last-ditch stand: economic reform has been blocked, censorship of the media reinstated, brazen demagogy revived, and an open war on the republics declared. . . .
>
> The events in Lithuania can be classified unambiguously as criminal, . . . [and Gorbachev] justified or approved the tactics . . .
>
> While opposing the onslaught of dictatorship and totalitarianism, we are pinning our hopes on the leadership of the union republics.[13]

With this manifesto, most of the signers signaled their defection to the Yeltsin team.

On January 19 I noted in my journal:

> These public statements, coming on top of the Bakatin interview in Wednesday's *Komsomolskaya Pravda,* are building a crescendo of sharp criticism by many of Gorbachev's closest former associates. Will he begin to take it to heart, or (more likely) will he simply consider them as evidence of personal disloyalty and stubbornly pursue the course he seems to have taken? If the latter turns out to be the case, then I must quickly modify my previous assessments of his staying power.

The next day, January 20, Moscow saw one of its largest demonstrations so far. Democratic Russia organized it to protest the violence in Lithuania and Latvia, as well as Gorbachev's alliance with the reactionaries, and more than 300,000 persons turned up. While some anti-Gorbachev slogans had appeared at previous demonstrations, this was the first large

one in Moscow that was solidly anti-Gorbachev. A resolution read out
to the crowd to loud cheers called for:

- The resignation of Gorbachev and Yazov
- The withdrawal of Soviet troops from Lithuania
- Dismissal of the USSR Supreme Soviet and Congress of
  People's Deputies
- Trials of those responsible for the use of force in Lithuania
- Foreign aid only to the republics, not to the union government

Yeltsin did not attend but was treated by many as the hero of the day
and, as one said, "Russia's last great hope." The crowd chanted his
name whenever it was mentioned. Gennady Burbulis read a message
from him that said that the dictatorship of which Shevardnadze and others had warned had now come to pass. Gorbachev was blocking democratic reforms and had taken the dangerous step of defending the use of
force in the name of a self-appointed Committee of National Salvation
against the lawfully elected representatives of the people. Opposition,
however, must be through peaceful, parliamentary means. "We cannot
give the central government any excuse to use force against us," he
stated.

Gorbachev on "Zigzags"

WHILE THE TURMOIL in the Baltic states and Georgia continued and
the polemics between Gorbachev and the reform intellectuals mounted,
military action by the U.S.-led coalition in the Persian Gulf began with
air strikes against Iraqi positions. Gorbachev had consistently tried to
avoid war in the area, but Saddam Hussein's intransigence had brought
the Soviet-sponsored peace efforts to naught. When the fighting started,
Gorbachev continued reluctantly to cooperate with the United States in
the Security Council, even though he was meeting increased domestic
opposition to his turnabout in Middle Eastern policy. Harmony with
the United States had become a linchpin of his domestic authority.

Many observers continued to suspect that there was an agreement—
perhaps tacit—between Bush and Gorbachev: as long as Gorbachev
backed Bush's policies in the Gulf, Bush would give Gorbachev a free
hand at home, specifically in Lithuania. These suspicions had no basis.

Bush continued to pay close attention to events in Lithuania even at the height of the crisis in the Gulf. He immediately condemned the seizure of the Vilnius television complex. For several weeks from January 13, hardly a day passed without a message, warning, or public statement by President Bush, Secretary of State Baker, or their press representatives.

When Gorbachev failed to move against the forces that had instigated violence, President Bush sent him a detailed letter outlining the steps he would be required to take if force continued to be used in the Baltic states. The text of the letter came to the embassy by telegram just before midnight on January 23. First thing the next morning, I asked for an appointment with Gorbachev to deliver it, and Anatoly Chernyayev telephoned me at midmorning to say Gorbachev could see me at one o'clock.

When I went to my car at 12:45 for the drive to the Kremlin, I found that a large group of Iraqi and Palestinian demonstrators had gathered in front of the embassy to protest the U.S. role in the liberation of Kuwait. The gates leading into the embassy had been closed, but I ordered the marine guards to open them long enough for my car to pass through, and as we drove out the Soviet guards pushed the demonstrators aside to make a path for the car. It was perhaps foolhardy to drive through a throng of hostile demonstrators, but ambassadors are not late for appointments with presidents, and I felt I had no choice. It was the only time during my entire tour in Moscow that the armored Cadillac the State Department had provided was a comfort.

Gorbachev, looking tired but calm and smiling, met me in the building in the Kremlin that previously had housed the Council of Ministers but now had been converted to the office of the president. I came alone because the contents of the letter were sensitive and I felt I could have a more candid conversation if a colleague was not present taking notes. We sat across from each other at a conference table, and Chernyayev sat down to his left.

After we exchanged greetings, I explained that I had been asked to deliver a letter from President Bush. I handed him a copy in English, then translated the text into Russian line by line. Bush pointed out that he had acted with great restraint following the turmoil in Lithuania and the other Baltic states, but that he was coming under increasing pressure to do something. He had accepted Gorbachev's assurances in 1990 that force would not be used and on this basis had authorized a number of programs to support economic reform in the Soviet Union. However, it would be impossible to continue these programs in the face of intimidation, pressure, and the use of armed force in the Baltic states. Unless the situation there changed, he would have no alternative to suspending the steps he had initiated. He would do this not as a punishment but because the basis of reform would have been removed. He urged Gorbachev to halt the growing wave of violence and return to earlier policies of conciliation.

When I finished reading the letter, Gorbachev asked, "Did he say he *has* taken these steps or that he *will* take them?"

"He said he would, if . . . ," I answered.

Gorbachev paused for a moment and, without commenting on the letter, said, "Tell me, Jack. How do you read the situation here?"

His question took me by surprise. I had hoped that I could find a way to convey some of my doubts about his recent decisions, but I had not anticipated that he would invite me to do so. I didn't have a presentation prepared and no instructions other than the letter itself, but I had thought often about the various things that seemed to be going wrong. The opportunity to explain them directly was too tempting to pass up.

I made no notes as I spoke, but I jotted down the main points as soon as I left the meeting, and these provide a jog to my memory as I write. First, I said I was having great difficulty explaining the rationale of his policies over the past few months. I had long been convinced that he was genuinely seeking fundamental reform in his country, and I had consistently reported this to my government. However, of late, I was finding that I could not make the case I once had. I knew that he still insisted that perestroika was going forward, and I knew also that this was in his and his country's interest, but what I saw happening did not fit these assumptions. The facts seemed to show that his policy had changed, but I could not figure out why he would have changed his policy and therefore was reluctant to conclude that he had. But I could not square his repeated verbal attacks on the democrats and on Yeltsin with the professed goal of perestroika.

Regarding Lithuania and its neighbors, I noted that military pressure polarized the situation, undermined negotiation, and created a potential for violence. The events there had placed President Bush under great pressure—from Congress, the press, and the public in general. While I did not believe that he had ordered troops to fire on the television tower in Vilnius, I could not understand many things he had done or allowed others to do: sending in military forces, seizing buildings, issuing uncompromising ultimatums. None of this seemed to make sense if his aim was peace. I added that I understood very well the pressure he was under to use force, but it seemed to me that those exerting that pressure were no friends of his or of reform, and therefore I could not explain why he had succumbed to it, particularly since the steps he had taken could be exploited by those bent on violence.

I noted that he often stressed that a solution had to be found within the Constitution. Of course no one could object to this in the abstract, but he should try to understand the point of view of those who held that if they had been forced into the union, they were not bound by its Constitution. Even so, the interests of both parties could be met if legislation made a referendum the controlling event for secession. The current law in effect denied the right of secession rather than implementing it.

Finally, I pointed out that it seemed to outsiders like myself that the elected leaders in the Baltic states were not the ones threatening violence. They seemed to understand that they could achieve their goals only by nonviolent means and had exhibited remarkable restraint. The violence we had seen had been perpetrated by Soviet forces under Moscow's command—and under his ultimate authority. While I did not doubt his attachment to a peaceful, negotiated solution to these problems, I was finding it impossible to explain to my government how his recent actions were consistent with his aims.

When I had talked for maybe fifteen minutes, I rested my case. Gorbachev, who had listened intently throughout my monologue, thanked me for my candor without a trace of irony.

As for my difficulty in understanding recent events in the Soviet Union, he appealed to me to take account of "the full seriousness" of what was going on. "Try to help your president understand," he continued, "that we are on the brink of a civil war. As president, my main task is to prevent it." At times, he would have to do things that might seem inexplicable. We should expect a period of "zigs and zags."

We are living under high tension and high emotions, he observed. Many issues are explosive and the forces are very hard to control. We suffer from a low political culture; there is no tradition of compromising on the issues. But he had to insist that the political process follow a constitutional path. He himself was not hostage to anyone.

He was willing to conduct a dialogue with the Baltic leaders, he claimed, and there had been some success with the Latvians. He had worked out an agreement with Gorbunovs, the Supreme Council chairman, and Communist Party leader Rubiks had agreed. However, things were different in Lithuania. He doubted that an agreement there would be possible as long as Landsbergis was in charge. Prunskienė had been reasonable and they had been able to make some progress, but the government's attempt to raise prices had given Landsbergis the opportunity to dump her. As for Yeltsin, he was difficult to deal with. He would make agreements, then renege, and he often promised more than he could deliver. But he, Gorbachev, would keep trying.

As he concluded, he asked me to tell "my friend George" that however much pressure he might be under in respect to the Gulf War, the German question, and the ratification of the conventional arms agreement, he would continue to act as he had promised. At home, his principal desire was to ensure that basic changes were not accompanied by acts of violence, and he would not abandon the goals he had set for himself.[14]

As I later thought about this conversation, I was struck by the contrast in Gorbachev's public and private manner. Many political leaders who are irascible in private project a different public image: calm, thoughtful, empathetic. Gorbachev seemed to exhibit an opposite tendency. In public, he had become exceedingly irritable of late and his presentations less and less cogent. But in private I found him collected, even judicious. I doubted that he was that way with everyone but had to concede that he had reacted to President Bush's message with great skill.

Instead of protesting that we were interfering and undermining perestroika by threatening to end economic cooperation, he had taken the news calmly, given us a chance to make our case, and made two telling points. By sending his assurance that he would keep his promises regarding the Gulf War, Germany, and the CFE agreement, he was reminding Bush of the importance of his cooperation but avoiding any threat to change these policies if the United States withdrew its cooperation in response to the repression in Lithuania. In fact, he was giving assurance that these policies would be followed *no matter what.* If Bush proceeded to impose sanctions in the face of such assurances, it would seem churlish and mean-spirited. Second, he justified his recent actions as a tactic to avoid a coup d'état rather than as a fundamental change of policy.

I did not buy the second argument, though I had no reason to doubt that Gorbachev was rationalizing his "turn to the right" that way in his own mind. I concluded that he was all but blind to the dangers of encouraging and cooperating with the hard-liners. They were openly pressing him to declare "presidential rule," which would give them the upper hand as enforcers. Once he did, or if he continued to refuse, he would be swept aside.

Nevertheless, I saw no reason to slap him with sanctions unless and until it became clear that he was systematically using force to suppress the Baltic independence movements. Washington agreed, and since massive military force was not used in the Baltic, the sanctions Bush threatened were never implemented.

By the time I delivered the president's letter, it was obvious that it would be impossible to arrange a Moscow summit in February. Until it was clear that no further major bloodshed would occur in the Baltic states, it would be politically difficult for Bush to come to Moscow. Furthermore, the war in the Gulf had just started, and it would not seem proper for him to leave the United States while it was in progress. When we discussed Bush's letter, Gorbachev remarked that if there should be a postponement of the planned summit, he hoped President Bush would coordinate the announcement with him in advance. Obviously, he did not want a postponement attributed to the situation in Lithuania.

Subsequently, when the postponement was officially announced, we explained that the president had to stay in Washington and give his full attention to the Gulf War.

Pavlov's Fog

SHORTLY AFTER HE TOOK office as prime minister, Valentin Pavlov announced the most unpopular and ill-considered action since the antialcohol campaign in 1985: the government declared invalid all 50- and 100-ruble banknotes—the two largest denominations in circulation at that time. The public had to exchange all such banknotes within a few days, and limits were imposed on the amount any individual could exchange. This seemed to be a strategem to reduce the "ruble overhang"— although Pavlov had told me he was not worried about it. But this was not the explanation given. Pavlov explained the exchange of banknotes as directed at "speculators and swindlers" who were hoarding ill-gotten profits from illegal trade. In fact, it hit ordinary people hardest, particularly those who had stashed their savings in mattresses—a common practice, since the official savings banks paid only 2.5 percent interest and were not trusted since large withdrawals were often difficult to make.

As people spent long hours in lines at the few bank branches, their tempers rose. Nobody believed the official explanation, since they knew that "speculators and swindlers" would have no difficulty finding a way to exchange their banknotes. The government employees who administered the exchange could easily be bribed.

Apparently recognizing that public opinion was turning against him, Pavlov came up with an even more improbable explanation, but one he obviously hoped the Soviet public, conditioned to believe in conspiracy theories and to distrust foreigners, would be more inclined to accept. During an interview with the newspaper *Trud,* he stated that the action had been taken to thwart a plot by "foreign banks," which were holding 8 billion rubles and planned to use them to bring down the Soviet government by suddenly flooding the country with currency.[15]

The public, in the Soviet Union and abroad, concentrated most of its attention on this silly charge, but I found his comments on future economic policy equally disturbing. He rejected private property in land, claiming that it would just be bought up by criminal elements and black marketeers. He implied that the RSFSR legislation would let that happen, ignoring the fact that the law allowed the transfer of land only to those farming it or putting houses on it and sales back only to the local authorities, not to third parties. He called for a shift from concentration on consumer goods to more capital goods, which could only be done by preserving the command economy. At the same time, he pictured the Soviet economy as one moving rapidly to the brink of collapse. In fact, he predicted that if something was not done, in six months the economic devastation would compare with that during the civil war of 1918–20.

When I read this interview, I noted in my journal:

The most disturbing aspect of this hodge-podge of comment is the strong streak of xenophobia, not only in the absurd accusations regarding foreign banks, but also in other passages. A second troublesome aspect is his habit of distorting facts to bolster his arguments. The one on the RSFSR land law, for example, is totally misleading. Finally, when he attributes virtually all problems to criminal elements, greedy foreigners, and assertive nationalist radicals, one is left wondering why the government would let these forces weaken a presumably healthy economy to the point that it faces utter ruin within months. In other words, if the only problem is law enforcement, why was there perestroika to begin with? Also, conspicuously absent from this farrago of contradictory statements is any reference to the need to become part of the world economy. In fact, if Pavlov's logic is followed, one should stay away from the world economy like the plague, since those scheming furriners are out there panting to rape Mother Russia.

Bottom line: either this fellow doesn't have a clue as to how a market system works, or else he is too devious to have any hope of moving toward one. The combination of ignorance and opportunism will drive off serious investors and leave him with what he claims to despise: the crooks and con men. We haven't heard the last of this, and if Gorbachev doesn't find another prime minister *tout de suite,* business interest in other than the quick, sure sales deal is likely to plummet.

Pavlov's charge that Western banks were plotting to bring Gorbachev down elicited only derision from both the Soviet and foreign press and an indignant statement from the State Department pointing out that, as finance minister, Pavlov had printed far more money than that held by Western banks.[16]

Gorbachev tried to repair the damage by having his press spokesman, Vitaly Ignatenko, comment that "Our money is not capable of changing a political system" and Viktor Grushko, Kryuchkov's principal deputy, announce that the KGB knew absolutely nothing about such a plot. *The New York Times* captured the typical foreign reaction when it noted editorially,

> Prime Minister Pavlov's policies have been decisive—decisive and wrong. He's drawn back from pushing the Soviet economy toward markets. Instead, he's fallen back on a confused mishmash of sclerotic bureaucracy, socialist slogans and xenophobic attacks that alienate the one external source of help.
>
> Eventually, the Soviet Union will be forced to come knocking on Western doors for investment, expertise and help. When no one answers, Soviets should remember this week, and Pavlov's fog.[17]

This would not be the last time Gorbachev's new prime minister would embarrass him.

The Referendum Boomerang

WHEN, IN DECEMBER, Gorbachev persuaded the USSR Congress of People's Deputies to approve a referendum on preservation of the union, he seems to have thought he was playing an ace. Using the Communist Party to mobilize a vote, he could expect to win widespread endorsement of the union, and this would create pressure on Yeltsin, Kravchuk, and other recalcitrant republic leaders to agree to his union treaty.

Gorbachev proposed the referendum in his December 17 report to the Congress, but it was received skeptically by the republic leaders, and not only by those who were increasingly at odds with Gorbachev. Nursultan Nazarbayev of Kazakhstan was one of the most vigorous proponents of preserving a union but, after reviewing Gorbachev's proposal, advised against the referendum unless a republic wished to secede or its parliament refused to adhere to the union treaty. To require a referendum in all republics at the same time would, he warned, simply cause further confrontation with the republics.[18]

Gorbachev, however, refused to heed Nazarbayev's advice. He complained to the Congress that his suggestion had been ignored and insisted on a separate vote. As they usually did when he pressed, a majority of deputies voted in favor. In this way Gorbachev got his referendum, but it did not bring the result he sought.

The proposition itself was confusing since the USSR Supreme Soviet had ornamented it so that it contained not one but several questions. As it eventually emerged, it read:

> Do you consider necessary the preservation of the Union of Soviet Socialist Republics as a renewed federation of equal sovereign republics, in which the rights and freedoms of an individual of any nationality will be fully guaranteed?

While the campaign in favor of the referendum presented it as a simple vote in favor of retaining a voluntary federation, a "yes" vote could be considered a vote for socialism, for the current name of the country, for a renegotiated federation, and for individual rights. However, the terms of the "renewed federation" had not been worked out, nor had the mechanism for protecting individual rights been designed. This made it impossible to relate any particular proposed text to the referendum, since the disputes centered precisely on the meaning of a "renewed federation" and on whether various formulations in fact respected the "sovereignty" of republics.

Furthermore, although the referendum was supposed to be held throughout the Soviet Union, the governments of many republics refused to conduct it, and some that did reworded the proposition or added their own. What had been conceived of as a demonstration of unity turned into an example of disunity even before it occurred.

The three Baltic states refused to conduct the all-union referendum and, after some debate, decided to hold referenda of their own before March 17. Georgia, Armenia, and Moldavia also refused to conduct Gorbachev's referendum, and the first two scheduled later votes for independence.

Nursultan Nazarbayev, who had opposed the idea of a referendum when Gorbachev suggested it in December, insisted that a different question be asked in Kazakhstan. The question posed there was:

> Do you consider it necessary to preserve the Union of Soviet Socialist Republics as a union of equal sovereign states?

Nothing here about a "renewed federation" or of individual rights, but of a "union of equal sovereign states" rather than "sovereign republics." Nazarbayev's wording implied a union created by juridically independent states, while Gorbachev's implied a restructuring of the existing USSR.

In Ukraine also, a supplementary question asked whether Ukraine should be a member of "a union of sovereign states" (no mention of the USSR) in accord with Ukraine's Declaration of State Sovereignty. In the Western regions voters were given the opportunity to vote for or against Ukrainian independence.

It was Yeltsin, however, who turned the referendum to the greatest political advantage. In December, he had argued against holding it at all in Russia but had then agreed to conduct it provided the RSFSR conducted its own referendum simultaneously. Voters in Russia would be asked whether they favored establishing the post of president, to be elected by direct vote.[19]

Up to then, the RSFSR legislative organs had refused to amend the

Constitution to provide for a presidency. A strong vote in favor of the presidency, however, would give Yeltsin's ambitions a boost. Since he was still by far the most popular politician in Russia, a landslide vote in favor of the presidency could be expected.

Nevertheless, Gorbachev pulled out all stops in an effort to obtain an overwhelming vote on *his* referendum, mobilizing the Communist Party apparatus to concentrate on getting out a positive vote. I was perplexed as I observed his tactics, since I could not imagine what he would gain from even a massive vote in favor of his proposition. It was too amorphous to serve as a clear mandate. The question of the Russian presidency, on the other hand, was one that could make a difference. If it led to a constitutional amendment and a vote for a Russian president, Boris Yeltsin would win the post hands down. His authority would rise dramatically as compared to that of Mikhail Gorbachev, the unelected president of a faltering state machine. If, in addition, Ukraine should vote against the union—or even show a lukewarm attitude—it would make it much more difficult for Gorbachev to come to terms with Kravchuk and the Ukrainian Rada on a union treaty.

With his ill-advised referendum proposal, Gorbachev had unwittingly set a trap for himself. On February 7, Yeltsin sprang it when his Supreme Soviet approved holding the RSFSR referendum on the same day as the all-union vote.

Yeltsin's Direct Challenge

CALLS FOR GORBACHEV'S RESIGNATION had marked the demonstrations in Moscow and Leningrad following the violence in Lithuania, but Yeltsin waited a month before he voiced the demand himself. He made sure, in particular, that he had the approval of the RSFSR Supreme Soviet to pose a referendum question on the Russian presidency. He also formed a new Advisory Council, recruiting many of the reformers who had been on Gorbachev's team the year before.[20]

Having thus won both a legislative and public relations victory at a time when Gorbachev was being criticized for allowing violence to erupt in the Baltics, failing to choose strong lieutenants and to adopt a plausible reform plan, and doing nothing to stop the precipitous decline in the economy, Yeltsin went on a nationwide television program on the evening of February 19. After responding to questions for a half hour, he pulled out a prepared statement and read it.

In it he said that Gorbachev was conducting a policy of retaining power for the central authorities. His policies were now directed against the public's best interest, as witness the "manipulation" of monetary and price reform. His policies had led to interethnic bloodshed and economic breakdown, and perestroika had become an attempt to strengthen the old command administrative system. Furthermore, Yeltsin said, the Center had not allowed the republics to take steps toward autonomy.

Yeltsin claimed he had made sincere efforts to cooperate with Gorbachev, but this had turned out to have been a mistake. Gorbachev, he charged, was leading the country toward dictatorship. Before this happened, he should resign as president and transfer power to the Council of Federation. "I have made my choice, and I won't go back on it," he concluded.

Previously, Yeltsin had said that Gorbachev should get on with reform or resign and let someone else do it, but now he had thrown down the gauntlet. In a mature democracy, occasional demands by the opposition that the head of government resign are taken in stride as part of the political process. But the Soviet Union was not yet a democracy, let alone a mature one, and the president supposedly had a fixed term and was not dependent on votes of confidence in the legislature. Under these circumstances, Yeltsin's demand was interpreted—as it was doubtless intended—as a declaration of political war. I noted that evening that whatever slim hope might have remained that Gorbachev and Yeltsin could cooperate had disappeared. A fight with no holds barred seemed inevitable.

The showdown was not delayed. Immediately after Yeltsin's demand that Gorbachev resign, Communists in the Russian parliament opened a noisy campaign to impeach and remove Yeltsin. In a planned maneuver that Gorbachev had personally orchestrated, Communist Party stalwarts rose in the Russian legislature, one after another, to demand Yeltsin's removal. The tactic was the same as the one that had been used in 1987 when Yeltsin was expelled from the Politburo: having a procession of speakers condemn his behavior and demand his ouster.

Svetlana Goryacheva, who represented the region around Vladivostok and was one of the Supreme Soviet's deputy chairmen, led the attack by reading a statement that she and five other deputy chairmen had signed. It accused Yeltsin of avoiding necessary but unpopular measures to improve the economy, undermining the union treaty by negotiating directly with other republics, acting without authority in signing agreements with the Baltic governments, subverting the legislature by relying on a closed circle of personal advisers, weakening the unity of the USSR and Russia itself, and appealing for Gorbachev's resignation when this was not the view of the Supreme Soviet.[21]

The Russian parliament, however, was not the Party Central Committee of 1987. For one thing, the campaign to remove Yeltsin was conducted in full view of television cameras, and his opponents came across as vicious Communist apparatchiks reverting to the despised habits of the past. Rather than turning their backs on Yeltsin, most citizens criticized Gorbachev for attempting once more to remove their hero and thus flout public opinion.

Yeltsin's opponents proposed convening the Russian Congress of People's Deputies (which had the power to remove Yeltsin) on March 4—that is, before the March 17 referendum was held. Yeltsin's supporters fought back, and after a second day of bruising debate the legislature agreed to convene the Congress on March 28—well after the vote on the referendum would be in.

After watching these debates on television, I made the following note:

> Neither side is playing very effective politics, but if I had to bet I would put my money on Yeltsin. Gorbachev's most effective tactic would be to "kill him with kindness," keeping the door open to negotiation and making sure Party hacks do not go after him. However, his pride will not permit that, and his attempts to exact vengeance will simply put a shine on Yeltsin's martyr image. If Yeltsin can get himself on the ballot in Russia as a candidate for president, he will turn the tables on the whole lot.

These debates in the Russian Supreme Soviet coincided with the final preparations for the ground assault to remove Iraqi troops from Kuwait. Though he had consistently (sometimes after considerable persuasion) voted with us in the United Nations on Gulf issues, Gorbachev had throughout tried to avoid a ground war and had kept making increasingly frantic peace proposals right up to the beginning of the assault. While he had repeatedly assured President Bush that he would not waver in condemning Iraqi aggression, he had hoped he could persuade Saddam Hussein to withdraw without a fight. The victory of a U.S.-led coalition against a country armed largely with Soviet weapons would inevitably be a blow to Soviet prestige and military pride. Criticism of Gorbachev's support for the United States had intensified at the plenary session of the Party Central Committee at the end of January.

Saddam Hussein's behavior proved a point we had been making to Gorbachev ever since he came to power: that it was a mistake to grant irresponsible leaders such as Hussein and Moammar Qaddhafi leverage over Soviet policy. With considerable help from Shevardnadze, he had come to understand this, but it was nonetheless politically difficult to bless a military campaign conducted by former adversaries against a country that for years had been considered a Soviet client.

Even before the ground assault began, Soviet officials began to question whether the air strikes were not excessive. For example, on February 12, when I called on Deputy Foreign Minister Alexander Belonogov to urge Soviet support for a vote in the U.N. Security Council, he began to complain that the U.S. air strikes were producing numerous civilian casualties. When I assured him that our military command would take every reasonable precaution to minimize civilian casualties, he responded that there was a line that must not be crossed between the liberation of Kuwait and the destruction of Iraq. While the United States had not yet crossed that line, if it should, the USSR would have to raise the matter in the Security Council.

Comments of this sort had to be squelched or they would have become more frequent and perhaps led to attempts to debate tactical military decisions in the Security Council. Therefore, I responded sharply. I told him that I could not understand the comment he had made. The United States had taken on the brunt of enforcing the Security Council resolutions, though it was properly the responsibility of the whole world community. We were staking the lives of our young people in this effort, and we stood to get absolutely nothing out of it other than respect for international law and for Security Council resolutions. Our public would never understand carping by nonparticipants that implied that we were acting improperly by trying to minimize our own casualties. While I felt that the U.S. and Soviet attitudes toward Iraq's aggression were basically consistent, most Americans would consider the threat he had uttered as inexcusable.

Belonogov hastily retreated, assuring me that he did not mean to say that we should not try to limit our casualties and was not making any accusations of improper activities on the part of the United States. I told him I was pleased to hear his clarification, and in light of his explanation I assumed we would hear less from Soviet officials about concern that we might be exceeding the Security Council mandate.

In general, the Ministry of Foreign Affairs did refrain from undermining our diplomatic position in the United Nations. But military spokesmen and some journalists continued to raise questions as to the degree of force being applied, with the implication that the United States was seeking a permanent strategic position in the area rather than just the liberation of Kuwait. Therefore, when I was invited to take part in a television roundtable on the Gulf War, I accepted, realizing that it would be an effective way to take our case to the broader public.

Most of the discussion was amicable until one of the Soviet participants opined that the United States might be using excessive force against Iraq. It was just what I was waiting for, and I came in with a rebuke designed for our Soviet audience. "I cannot understand this tenderness for aggressors," I replied. "When your country was invaded, you did not worry about damage to Germany. In fact, you had a very popular slogan, 'Annihilate the fascist beast in his own lair!' We don't go so far as attempting to 'annihilate the aggressor,' but we don't think we should limit the fighting solely to Kuwaiti soil. Are you prepared to argue that we should not have bombed Germany in World War II and that Allied troops should have stopped at German borders?"

Immediately, there was a chorus of protests that this was not what they meant at all. As I was leaving the studio, Valentin Zorin, our moderator, remarked that he did not believe that anyone would have the temerity to raise this question with me again. "There's not a person in this country who won't understand your point," he said.

In fact, the Soviet public as a whole was not deeply moved by the events in the Middle East. While Gorbachev doubtless received some criticism from the more reactionary Soviet military officers and conservative Party types, who still viewed the United States as a competitor if not an adversary and who were not happy to see an alliance in which so much had been invested simply discarded overnight, most of the country was preoccupied with problems closer at home: shortages in the shops, growing crime, social dislocation, and political uncertainty.

Once the ground war began, it was over in hours. And with it went most of Gorbachev's potential leverage on Bush. We still needed Soviet support at the United Nations, but once the fighting in the Gulf ended, it was not vital.

Gorbachev's rift with the Soviet intellectuals who had been the darlings of perestroika's first phase was almost complete by January 1991. A year before, most of them had still considered Gorbachev the best hope for reform and Yeltsin too much of an unreliable crowd pleaser to steer an intelligent course. The alliances they had made with Yeltsin at that time had been more tactical than strategic. But in 1991, disillusioned with Gorbachev's move toward repression and challenged by Shevardnadze to come out of the bushes, they began to leave Gorbachev in droves and join Yeltsin's team.

Gorbachev seemed incapable of understanding the reasons, though they were clear enough to most. Instead, he nurtured a sense of betrayal and had fits of anger. I received a strong though indirect dose of Gorbachev's bile when I called on Chernyayev February 11 to deliver a letter from President Bush concerning the problems that had arisen in implementing the agreement to reduce conventional weapons in Europe.

When I remarked that the Soviet Union's position regarding some of the reductions was not consistent with the treaty text, Chernyayev said with a smile, "Not the Soviet Union's position but that of some of its generals," and assured me that the matter would be taken care of since Gorbachev had appointed a commission, including civilian advisers such as himself, to deal with it.

When I turned to the domestic situation, however, his good humor vanished. He said that Gorbachev was deeply offended at the criticism from abroad (presumably of the crackdown in Lithuania and the "turn to the right," though he was not specific). Gorbachev, he continued, had thought he had built up a basis of trust with the Western leaders, but it seemed suddenly to have disappeared. Since he, Gorbachev, had not changed his policies, the hostile Western attitude was not deserved.

"He seems to tolerate Soviet generals who violate formal agreements he has signed, while taking offense when his negotiating partners point this out," I thought to myself, but I held my tongue. Instead of harping on the obvious, I told Chernyayev that he was exaggerating. There was still good U.S.-USSR understanding and cooperation in many areas, including in the Gulf. But we did have anxieties, particularly as regards Soviet actions in the Baltic states. We had been assured that force would

not be used, but Soviet troops had killed people in Vilnius and the condemnation by Moscow had been neither swift nor categorical. Nearly a
month had passed since the bloody and illegal seizure of the television
complex, yet nobody had been arrested and the building had not been
returned to Lithuanian control. Doesn't Gorbachev understand the sort
of impression this leaves abroad? I asked rhetorically.

The treatment of Lithuania, though, was only a part of a trend away
from the reform policies Gorbachev had previously defended, I continued. We noted that he seemed to have a different team now.

"What do you mean, different? Besides Shevardnadze, who? Most,
including Chernyayev, are still with him," he objected, referring to himself in the third person.

I conceded that his continued presence was reassuring but pointed
out that the departures, in addition to Shevardnadze, included Vadim
Bakatin, Alexander Yakovlev, Nikolai Petrakov, Stanislav Shatalin,
and many others. In fact, few of the intellectuals who had traveled with
Gorbachev to the United States in 1987 and 1988 seemed to be working
with him still.

Bakatin and Yakovlev had not left the team, he replied—they were in
regular touch with Gorbachev and would get influential positions. As
for the others I had named, they were no real loss. Petrakov had proved
to be an unprincipled renegade, Shatalin mentally unbalanced, and Arbatov (whom I had not mentioned) simply an ambitious schemer who
had gone over to Yeltsin when he had not gotten one of the senior positions he had sought. "How can Gorbachev base his administration on
people who have betrayed him?" he asked, adding that Gorbachev
could not understand why President Bush was determined to punish
him.

Chernyayev did not normally indulge in such tirades, which suggested to me that he was playing out Gorbachev's feelings more than his
own. I could not believe that he was incapable of understanding why
Gorbachev was being criticized from abroad—and by reformers at
home. There was no point in arguing with him, except that I thought it
important to set the record straight regarding President Bush's attitude.

Therefore, I told him that he was misreading the president's policy.
President Bush had no desire to punish the Soviet Union. But he, too,
was operating in a political environment and knew that he could not
offer assistance to the Soviet Union if violence continued in the Baltics
or if there was a move toward repression within the Soviet Union rather

than reform. In pointing out these constraints, he was simply trying to be frank with Gorbachev, whose achievements he admired and whom he still considered a friend and partner.

As for our perceptions, I noted that we simply could not escape the conclusion that we were witnessing a change in policy since the previous fall. We were seeing more reliance on instruments of repression and more concessions to those who controlled the instruments. We were seeing backtracking in arms control negotiations, even when agreements had been formally signed. We were seeing a harsher treatment of domestic critics and a pattern of government appointments that suggested a harder line. In our bilateral relations some promised improvements had not materialized. For example, we had been assured that legislation guaranteeing freedom of emigration would be passed in 1989, but it was still stuck in the Supreme Soviet and Gorbachev didn't seem to care. President Bush had made it clear in Washington the previous June that the trade agreement they signed could not be implemented until the emigration law was in force. We couldn't understand why Gorbachev had not been more active in persuading the Supreme Soviet to pass it.

Chernyayev let most of the items in my catalog pass but picked up on the last one, commenting testily that we should know why they had not yet enacted emigration legislation: the United States obviously could not cope with the numbers already allowed to leave.

In fact, our embassy then had a waiting list of more than 300,000 applicants for immigration and we were able to issue documentation for few more than 50,000 a year. But this, of course, was not the point, which was that Soviet citizens should have the right to depart the country if they chose.

Before leaving, I asked Chernyayev to reassure President Gorbachev that his efforts to build confidence had not been in vain. He should not think that the criticism he was hearing wiped out his achievements. But it should be taken as a friendly warning. The fact was that we in the West *were* worried about the direction his policy seemed to be taking, and we hoped he would soon get back on the course he had previously set. If he did that, the criticism that had irritated him would surely cease.

Chernyayev's reaction was much more emotional than Gorbachev's had been when I had delivered President Bush's letter less than three weeks before. Nevertheless, I felt that Chernyayev understood and possibly sympathized with the points we were making. A feeling of frustration at having, out of loyalty, to defend a proposition he knew to be false had probably honed his emotions to a sharp edge. In the memoirs he wrote subsequently, he indirectly confirmed this supposition. He had seriously considered resigning after the attack on the television tower and had written a letter to Gorbachev containing more pungent accusations than any leveled by President Bush, Secretary Baker, or myself. But he had decided not to send the letter and to stay on the "team."[22] My comments about the change of team, when he himself was still tempted to resign, must have cut to the quick.

Some two weeks later, Gorbachev embarked on a long-delayed trip to Belorussia. Though Minsk is only an hour's flight from Moscow, Gorbachev had not visited the republic since the Chernobyl catastrophe. The Belorussian public had noted his apparent indifference—he never seemed to have trouble finding time for visits abroad—but assumed that, at long last, he would have something to say about the cleanup task and would announce financial support for the effort. Belorussia, after all, had suffered more than any other republic from the accident, even though the nuclear plant was located in Ukraine. The union government, which operated the plant, bore both a legal and a moral responsibility to finance corrective measures.

Gorbachev, however, preoccupied with his struggle with Yeltsin and his estrangement from the reform intellectuals, seemed to forget where he was. He made only perfunctory reference to Chernobyl, concentrating instead on attacking the reform intellectuals, whom he excoriated not only for trying to undermine socialism and restore capitalism, but for serving as the front for hostile foreign forces. Echoing the unfounded accusations Kryuchkov had made in December, he charged that the reformers were using false slogans "to cover up far-reaching intrigues, which in a number of cases have been born in foreign think tanks and in alien heads."[23] He then attacked Gavriil Popov by name for advocating the breakup of the Soviet Union into forty or fifty states. (Actually, Popov had only pointed to this as one possible outcome of the nationalist fervor then sweeping the Soviet Union; he had not described it as a desirable outcome.)

But even this was not enough. As he warmed to his subject, his language became more vituperative. The "democrats" were accused of "neo-Bolshevist" tactics—using demonstrations and strikes—to destabilize the organs of government and prepare for a forcible seizure of power. (Nothing made Communists more nervous than the thought that others might be using their own tactics against them.)

Gorbachev stopped just short of accusing the democrats of plotting a coup d'état, but his implication was unmistakable:

> So I ask the question: Who then is preparing a coup? Who is calling for unconstitutional forms of political struggle? We categorically reject any attempts to repeat a violent seizure of power, which would almost inevitably be followed by civil war. I declare this decisively, and I hope you understand what we are talking about. We have the experience, we have the lessons, both our own and those of other peoples, in order to draw such conclusions.[24]

This was language that easily fitted the actions of the so-called Committees of National Salvation in the Baltic, and of the shadowy cabals of apparatchiks and military and police officers in other areas, but it was not these groups Gorbachev chose to condemn. He seemed unable to make a distinction between legal forms of political struggle and illegal ones. His only criterion seemed to be whether a group criticized him openly or not. His words made one wonder if he was at the point of abandoning his habitual opposition to using force against the political opposition.

Since December, I had been hearing with growing frequency a worry, expressed *sotto voce* in private conversations—usually by reformers but also by uncommitted observers—that Gorbachev might be losing touch with reality. When I read the text of this Minsk speech, I could only wonder if they were right. His misinterpretation of events seemed either willfully perverse or tragically misinformed.

The speech damaged more than his ties with the reform intellectuals. Belorussians, preoccupied with the mammoth health and environmental problems created by Chernobyl, saw his use of their podiums to conduct his political vendettas as downright insulting. His visit to Minsk accelerated the estrangement of what had been one of the most loyal republics in the Soviet Union—an estrangement that culminated in December in a hunting lodge on its territory, at a meeting to which Gorbachev was not invited.

When Secretary of State Baker came to Moscow in mid-March, we tried to find a way for him to meet with Yeltsin without offending Gorbachev and to recognize the growing importance of the union republics. In deference to Gorbachev's sensitivity to contacts with Yeltsin, the White House staff in Washington (and presumably President Bush himself) felt that Baker should not call on Yeltsin in his office. To finesse this problem and yet provide for a meeting, we decided to invite all of the twelve non-Baltic republic leaders to a dinner at Spaso House (the Baltic leaders had been invited to a separate meeting). In addition, we invited a few reform intellectuals and several officials who were close to Gorbachev such as Foreign Minister Bessmertnykh, Ivan Laptev, Vadim Bakatin, and Yevgeny Primakov. We realized that many republic leaders would not be able to come to Moscow for the dinner but assumed some would. We also realized that Yeltsin might decline to come unless he could be assured of a private meeting with Secretary Baker. Baker was willing to see him privately after the dinner, and we hoped this would satisfy him.

Initially, we received an acceptance from Yeltsin's staff, but then difficulties arose. His foreign minister, Andrei Kozyrev, a professional diplomat who had left a middle-level position in the USSR Foreign Ministry to become RSFSR foreign minister, contacted us with the demand that Baker call on Yeltsin in his office before the dinner. We explained that Baker's schedule would not permit that. Then he asked whether Baker could see Yeltsin briefly at the Russian Foreign Ministry's "guest house" in the Lenin Hills. Baker's schedule also made this impossible, and as a result Yeltsin refused to come to the dinner and sent Vladimir Lukin, the chairman of the RSFSR Supreme Soviet Committee on Foreign Relations, in his stead.

I was annoyed by these maneuvers, since I thought it was clearly in Yeltsin's interest to see Baker, and his jockeying to extort treatment on a par with that due a chief of state was petty and self-defeating. Nevertheless, his tactics did not surprise me. In fighting to extricate himself from the political exile Gorbachev had decreed in 1987, he had become accustomed to using every lever at his command to gain status, and there was no reason to think he would refrain from using his contacts with us to the same ends.

Yeltsin, however, was not the only politician involved who was guilty of childish behavior. When the group finally gathered for dinner, we had representatives from only a few union republics—Georgia, Armenia, and Kyrgyzstan, in addition to Russia, but Kazakh leader Nazarbayev, who was hosting a foreign visitor in Alma Ata during the day, arranged to come for a meeting with Baker after dinner. Reform intellectuals, in-

cluding economist Shatalin, *Literaturnaya gazeta* editor Fyodor Burlatsky, Gavriil Popov, and Anatoly Sobchak also came, as did Archbishop Kirill of the Russian Orthodox Church. However, to my
surprise, not a single member of Gorbachev's team came. Some had sent
regrets, but others just did not show. Obviously they had received instructions from Gorbachev to boycott the function.

The dinner was successful despite the various absences. Zviad Gamsakhurdia, who had sent regrets but turned up anyway with his prime
minister in tow, made it clear that Georgia would leave the union and
would not even participate in Gorbachev's referendum. The Armenian
prime minister, Vazgen Manukian, also described Armenia's plans for
secession, which would be initiated by a referendum in September.
Shatalin ridiculed the draft Treaty of Union, observing sarcastically that
the Council of Federation could not even agree on a name for the country, and predicted that the Pavlov government's policies would lead the
country to disaster. The other guests were divided as to whether any sort
of union could be salvaged. Sentiment was so critical of the current Soviet leadership that Baker rose to Gorbachev's defense: he reminded his
guests that the dinner would not be taking place had it not been for the
reforms Gorbachev had initiated.

I could not understand why Gorbachev thought he had anything to
gain by forbidding his associates to go to social functions with Yeltsin.
He often complained in private about the "low political culture" in the
Soviet Union, but his own actions demonstrated that this condition prevailed at the top of the government as well as among the population at
large. Neither Gorbachev nor Yeltsin showed himself in a favorable
light in mid-March 1991.

One clue to the reason for Gorbachev's sensitivity emerged when Baker
met with him during the same trip to Moscow. Following a private
meeting, Baker told me that Gorbachev had mentioned getting a report
from one of Yeltsin's associates that Yeltsin had asked me what the U.S.
reaction would be if he came to power by unconstitutional means. Baker
had suggested that I join them immediately to comment, but Gorbachev
had said it was unnecessary—he had full confidence in my integrity and
did not want to suggest that I had acted improperly.

I explained to Baker that the alleged report was a canard. Yeltsin had
never suggested in any way that he might consider committing unconsti-

tutional or illegal acts to come to power. If he had, I would immediately
have severed all contact with him. Besides, the whole idea was absurd:
how could Yeltsin stage a coup with the army, the KGB, and the Party
apparat opposed to him? Baker suggested that I find a way to set Gorbachev straight.

First, I called on Chernyayev to explain the situation. Chernyayev
confirmed that, indeed, Gorbachev had received the report he had mentioned to Baker. When I explained that it was a fabrication, Chernyayev
said that this was very important. He promised to tell Gorbachev the
report was false but suggested that I mention it to him directly at the
next opportunity.

As luck would have it, two days later I received a letter from President Bush for delivery to Gorbachev. It contained some suggestions for
settling the remaining misunderstandings on implementing the treaty to
reduce conventional weapons in Europe. Normally, I would have delivered the letter through Foreign Minister Bessmertnykh, since I felt he
was trying to solve the problems mentioned and it would be useful to
have the letter go to Gorbachev with his comments. This time, however,
it seemed more important to have a chance to talk to Gorbachev directly
in order to refute the false report on Yeltsin.

Chernyayev arranged the appointment promptly, and Gorbachev received me in his office at Communist Party headquarters rather than in
the Kremlin, explaining that he was there to meet with a Japanese visitor
who had come as the leader of a political party rather than as a government official. I reviewed for him the proposals President Bush had made
in his letter, and Gorbachev promised a prompt reply. I then referred to
the report he had mentioned to Baker and told him it was false: Yeltsin
had never even hinted at the possibility of taking power by unconstitutional means. Gorbachev said the report had come from one of Yeltsin's
people. I told him I did not know why someone would make such a report, but I did know that it had not happened. Therefore, his source was
either misinformed or lying.

Gorbachev did not question my statement but launched into a rambling lecture for fifteen minutes or so to the effect that Rebecca and I
had a very high public profile, that people paid a lot of attention to us,
and that this was good, but it did mean we needed to be very alert to the
political significance of our contacts.

Though he did not say so directly, the thrust seemed to be that we
should not be too chummy with people close to Yeltsin but instead

spend most of our time with people Gorbachev trusted—as if that were easy to determine, since an intimate counselor one day might be considered a traitor the next. I had been careful to balance my social invitations and office calls across the responsible political spectrum and felt that the implication that we might be playing favorites was not just, though I had to admit that we saw more reformers than hard-liners and rarely dealt with the extreme reactionaries. Intellectuals, who tended to be on the reform side, were more likely to respond to invitations and were more accessible than apparatchiks were. Many Communist Party officials still seemed reluctant to maintain frequent social contact.

I told Gorbachev that I recognized the danger of seeming to play favorites but that we genuinely tried to have contact with persons covering a range of professions and politics. These contacts were not for the purpose of interfering or instigating but for understanding the political forces at work. I could not refuse or minimize contact with important groups, as that would indeed be sending undesirable political signals.

Somewhat to my surprise, he did not object but rather complimented Rebecca and me on our success in "becoming part of our society."

Chernyayev walked out of Gorbachev's office with me, and as we went down the corridor he said that the meeting had been most important, and—indeed—"necessary." His comment was echoed that afternoon in a laconic TASS dispatch that read as follows:

> On March 25 M. S. Gorbachev received J. Matlock, the ambassador of the United States. He conveyed a letter from George Bush, in which the U.S. president, in his usual friendly spirit, continued a discussion of certain urgent aspects of Soviet-American interaction. There followed a short, important conversation.[25]

I presumed that Chernyayev's comment and the last sentence in the TASS announcement meant that my message had been accepted, but the more I thought about the exchange the stranger some aspects seemed. First, the fact that Gorbachev would seize on a fabricated report of a conversation to conclude that Yeltsin was plotting a coup seemed downright irrational. There was no way Yeltsin could seize power without the support of groups that detested him. Furthermore, if there had been a plot, surely the KGB would have uncovered more evidence than an informer's claim about a conversation with me. Nevertheless, it seemed clear that Gorbachev had drawn dramatic conclusions from this report alone. If he, however illogically, had been convinced that Yeltsin was trying to remove him by force, this would explain the vitriol in his February speech in Minsk.

The second strange aspect was that Gorbachev, having believed the initial report, seemed to accept my refutation without question. Why else would Chernyayev have called the conversation "important" and "necessary," and TASS—doubtless with Gorbachev's personal approval—have added the line about the "short, important conversation"?

Finally, the incident proved what I already had reason to assume: the KGB was actively spreading false information about Yeltsin and probably other reform intellectuals.[26] If there was a calculated KGB campaign of disinformation, it would at least partially explain why Gorbachev seemed at times to lose his grip on political reality. If he still believed that Landsbergis represented a minority view in Lithuania, he was capable of believing anything!

An Elusive Goal

SINCE THE SPRING OF 1990, it had been apparent that Gorbachev was in a race with time to conclude a new union treaty on a voluntary basis. Nevertheless, Gorbachev was holding out for maximum powers for the Center, which he in theory controlled, and this was causing continued delay. The draft treaty that had been published in November 1990 had proved to be unacceptable to almost all the republic leaders and may have made Gorbachev's task more difficult, since it gave impetus to the thought that the treaty, if there was to be one, should be imposed on Gorbachev, not negotiated with him.

As the March 17 referendum on preservation of the union approached, pressure to produce a more acceptable draft mounted. It was illogical to ask people to vote on a "renewed federation" without any indication of what that meant, and while there were many other illogical elements in the referendum exercise, there is a limit to permissible confusion in every society.

The rejection of the November draft had taught Gorbachev that he could not simply impose a treaty on the republics. Therefore, he invited the republic governments to send representatives to hammer out an agreed text in Moscow. A majority—but only a bare majority—

responded. The three Baltic states, Moldova (as Moldavia now preferred to be called), Georgia, and Armenia refused to participate at all, and Azerbaijan sent a representative only as an observer. Even though Yeltsin, Kravchuk, and Nazarbayev continued to talk about a treaty negotiated without the Center, they named representatives. Therefore, the meetings included what eventually came to be called the "core" republics—Russia, Ukraine, Belorussia, and Kazakhstan—and all the Central Asians.

The revised text appeared in the central press just a week before the scheduled referendum.[27] As expected, it gave the republics considerably more power than the previous draft had. Whereas federal laws were to be supreme in matters under federal jurisdiction, this draft substantially trimmed the authorities delegated to the Center. The republics, for example, would set the rules for admission to and secession from the union. They would have broader property rights and the right to establish direct diplomatic and other ties to foreign countries.

Like its predecessor, this draft provided that many functions would be decided jointly by the federal authorities and the republics but did not make clear how this joint authority would be exercised. It also failed to resolve a basic dispute over how the autonomous republics would be represented. One variant would give only union republics equal representation in the upper house. The other would make the former autonomous republics (all had now declared themselves simply "republics") equal subjects of the federation and thus entitled to the same representation in the Council of Republics—a body designed as a counterpart of the U.S. Senate.

The second variant resulted from Gorbachev's decision to invite the former autonomous republics to participate directly in drafting the union treaty. It was a tactic to undercut Yeltsin's authority, since most of these units were located in Russia, but the result pleased nobody except the autonomous republics, which would gain enhanced status. Union republics other than Russia were adamantly opposed to granting the "autonomies" equal representation since this would dilute their influence in the parliament and give Russia an automatic majority of votes. The Russian government was skeptical since it would tend to fragment Russia.

The Council of Federation discussed the text on March 6 and, according to Gorbachev, resolved all disputed issues except the one dealing with the representation of former autonomous republics.[28] Other participants, however, were less optimistic, and Yeltsin immediately rejected the draft as having serious flaws.

Gorbachev interpreted the results of the March 17 referendum as a victory, but in fact the referendum laid bare the degree to which support for any sort of union had eroded. True, in Russia a strong majority voted "yes," and in Belorussia and Central Asia the votes were overwhelmingly in favor. Nevertheless, six republics did not participate at all, and—even more ominous—the vote in Ukraine was extremely close: the proposition was defeated in Kiev as well as in the western provinces, which voted heavily for Ukrainian independence. Most portentous of all, however, was the fact that more people in Russia voted for a presidency than for the union.

Another Futile Show of Force

THROUGHOUT THE PROCESS OF DEMOCRATIZATION, public demonstrations had been used by proponents of change as a potent weapon against entrenched authority. In 1990, as the old system came under relentless attack, hard-liners in the Party, KGB, and military began to yearn for the days when only officially organized processions had been permitted. Vadim Bakatin's persistent refusal to ban peaceful demonstrations had led to his removal as minister of internal affairs in December 1990. Soviet law, however, gave local and municipal authorities the right to authorize demonstrations, and in Moscow, Leningrad, and many of the western republics these were under the control of popularly elected officials who were not only proponents of democratic processes in principle but also the organizers and beneficiaries of most of the demonstrations. As Gorbachev's rift with the reform intellectuals grew and his alliance with the forces of repression deepened, the stage was set for confrontation on this, as on other issues.

Just before the New Year, the reformers were shocked by a joint announcement by Minister of Defense Yazov and Minister of Internal Affairs Pugo that joint patrols of army and militia (i.e., police) personnel would be organized from February 1, 1991, to ensure order in major cities. Since neither the union republic authorities nor the municipal authorities had requested such assistance in law enforcement, there was no legal basis for the order, and in fact several republics, including Russia, protested. Nevertheless, Gorbachev ignored advice from his civilian staff to countermand the order and issued a decree on January 29, 1991, to legitimate it.[29] In fact, the decree had scant effect; little joint patrolling was actually done since local authorities everywhere opposed it. Subsequently, the Committee for Constitutional Oversight criticized it as legally defective.[30]

Although this particular decree came to naught, it illustrated disputes over the division of authority that persisted. Could the central authorities override municipal and republic authorities to ban peaceful demonstrations? If so, how could this be reconciled with the right of assembly guaranteed in the Constitution as amended? Gorbachev's signature on the decree of January 29 was a clear indication that he was no longer a scrupulous adherent of the rule of law he had earlier espoused—and to which he still paid lip service.[31]

In March, these issues came to a head again and this time brought Moscow to the brink of bloodshed. Reacting to the Communist effort to remove Yeltsin from the chairmanship of the RSFSR Supreme Soviet, Democratic Russia called for mass demonstrations in Moscow on March 28, to coincide with the opening of the session of the RSFSR Congress of People's Deputies called to consider Yeltsin's fitness to stay in office.

Gorbachev reacted as if panicked. When the Moscow city authorities refused to ban the demonstration, Gorbachev issued a decree subordinating the police in Moscow and the surrounding oblast to the USSR Ministry of Internal Affairs and also ordered military units into Moscow to reinforce police protection of the central portion of the city. Apparently the KGB was once again fabricating reports that demonstrators were planning to "storm the Kremlin."

Both the RSFSR government and the Moscow city authorities vigorously protested: there was no threat to the peace, they argued, and furthermore bringing troops into the city would not only set a precedent inconsistent with the democratic procedures perestroika was pledged to defend but would create an atmosphere that risked violence. Nevertheless, Gorbachev persisted.

As tensions rose, concern in Washington grew. Images of Tiananmen Square arose in many minds. An urgent message came to the embassy the morning of the twenty-eighth for me to seek out the most senior available official and warn that any bloodshed would create a serious impediment to improved relations. Although I thought this message was unnecessary—Gorbachev had more powerful reasons than relations with us to avoid bloodshed—I dutifully contacted Chernyayev and asked him to convey it to Gorbachev. He assured me that every effort would be made to make sure there were no casualties.

In the event, our warning was superfluous. Yeltsin was capable of taking care of himself and his supporters. The majority of the deputies to the RSFSR Congress were outraged by Gorbachev's attempt to usurp the republic's authority and voted overwhelmingly to suspend Gorbachev's decree and to demand removal of the troops. When Gorbachev insisted that they would remain until the next day, the Congress adjourned and resumed work only after the troops were withdrawn.

More than 100,000 people came out to demonstrate in the face of a drumbeat of official warnings not to do so. But they were peaceful, and the soldiers were largely passive. Many chatted amiably with demonstrators. When the authorities wanted to clear an area, they used the police, not the army.

When the troops were withdrawn on March 29, it was evident that, once more, Gorbachev had damaged his own position. He had violated the strict bounds of legality to prevent a legitimate expression of opinion, primarily to remove a rival rather than to preserve order, but his action made it more difficult to achieve his objective. Whatever remote chance might have remained that the Russian Congress would vote against Yeltsin following the overwhelming referendum mandate for a Russian presidency (which all saw as a vote for Yeltsin) vanished when the Congress had to assemble surrounded by Soviet troops it had not requested. Still, there were those who had not given up all hope of a reconciliation.

The day troops were brought into Moscow to face the demonstrators, Adam Michnik, one of the intellectual fathers of the Solidarity movement in Poland, interviewed Eduard Shevardnadze in Moscow. Shevardnadze expressed his deep concern that Gorbachev seemed to be going in the opposite direction of democracy and foresaw only disaster if he continued. But Gorbachev did not have to continue on the current course, he argued; if he had been able to come to terms with Ronald Reagan, why should it be impossible to deal with Yeltsin?

Our society is torn apart by serious contradictions that complicate social and political processes. However, the real tragedy is the fact that dialogue has vanished. Without dialogue, it will be impossible to solve the contradictions.

. . . This situation of confrontation can lead only to chaos and anarchy. If that happens, we will not have long to wait for a dictator to appear on the scene.

. . . It is not too late for a dialogue between Yeltsin and Gorbachev. We managed to reach an understanding with the Americans. We began the dialogue with Reagan. . . . Why cannot two people who come from the same nation reach some kind of understanding?[32]

Shevardnadze was not the only one who wondered.

XVIII

—•◆•—

Gorbachev Looks for Compromise

Our statehood and federation are endangered. . . . The economy is coming apart.
The institutions of power are paralyzed. . . . We must put aside our feuds and
prevent the country from sliding into catastrophe.
MIKHAIL GORBACHEV to Council of Federation, April 9, 1991[1]

The only real way out I can see is this: the president must give the republics more
freedom, and we will undertake greater responsibility in return.
LEONID KRAVCHUK, April 1991[2]

Winter had been more brutal politically than climatically, and spring brought no respite. Retail prices of food and many essential consumer goods rose sharply on April 2, 1991—not because of market forces but by presidential decree. The price of bread, milk, and eggs doubled; meat went up by a factor of three or more. Clothing now cost about twice what it had. The government offered some income supplements, but they did not match the hefty price increases, and some seemed more sleight of hand than real. For example, people with savings accounts were credited with an additional 40 percent of their balances, but for two years they were prohibited from withdrawing more than 200 rubles (roughly $7.25 at the new "tourist" exchange rate) of the compensatory credit.

If the shops had filled with goods, the public might have accepted the price increases. Most urban dwellers had more money than they were able to spend. But the shortages were as severe as ever, and lines continued to stretch around blocks.

If Gorbachev had approved the Shatalin program the year before, he could have blamed the price rises on the republic leaders, who would have assumed the responsibility for most economic policy. But his insistence on ruling by decree (the Supreme Soviet having repeatedly rejected mandated price increases) made him the principal culprit in the public's eye.

The Economy: How Bad Can It Get?

IN MARCH, a wave of strikes had begun—this year, as before, with the coal miners. Those in the Donets Basin in Ukraine went out on March 1, and they were soon followed by miners in the Kuznetsk Basin, in Vorkuta on the Arctic Ocean, and in Kazakhstan. Unlike the year before, when the demands had been largely economic, now the miners wanted political change: they endorsed Yeltsin's call for Gorbachev's resignation and insisted on new national elections. When the strike continued for nearly a month, the Supreme Soviet passed a law ordering the miners back to work and providing criminal penalties for the strike leaders. The strikers ignored it.

To his credit, Gorbachev refused to arrest the strike leaders or send troops to force them back into the mines. Instead, he negotiated. On April 3, he and Prime Minister Pavlov met with representatives of the miners and offered extensive economic concessions but no political ones. They offered to double wages in stages over the next twelve months. However, the strikers refused to agree. Negotiations continued with the independent union leaders granted a status alongside the Party-sponsored "official" union. The miners' free trade union thus received de facto recognition as a collective bargaining representative.

Following the price hikes in April, factory workers in Minsk and other cities also walked out. The Communist Party, official trade unions, and enterprise managers had clearly lost control of the workforce in many places. Negotiations with the miners dragged on with political demands blocking agreement. As the weeks passed, it became obvious that only Yeltsin could end the miners' strike, since he was the only political leader who had the workers' confidence.

Throughout the winter it had seemed that Alexander Yakovlev was as much on the sidelines as Shevardnadze was. He had left the Party Politburo the previous summer, and his position on the Presidential Council

had lapsed when that institution was abolished in January. Nevertheless, as Chernyayev had predicted in January, he was eventually named
senior adviser to Gorbachev. When I heard that he had moved from the
Central Committee office on Staraya Square into a new Kremlin office
near Gorbachev's, I requested an appointment.

He asked me to come by on April 2, the day the price rises went into
effect. I noted that he had a spacious office—one of those previously
used by a deputy prime minister—and in the Soviet bureaucratic world,
this was significant. I wondered whether Gorbachev might be thinking
of reassembling the old team or was just trying to protect an old friend
from the steady onslaught of the chauvinists, who were as determined to
root out "new thinking" as Joseph McCarthy had been to rid American
society of "pinkos." In any event, Yakovlev could only be as influential
as Gorbachev desired, since he no longer had a political base aside from
his tie to Gorbachev.

His mood was philosophical, and I found him more upbeat than he
had been in recent conversations. Not that he minimized the problems
the country faced: perestroika, he said, was going through a period of
organized opposition. On the land, it came from what he called "our
new latifundians," the directors of state and collective farms. In industry, the opposition crystallized around "superpatriots" in the military-
industrial complex.

Furthermore, he explained, the army was suffering from extreme
frustration as the result of sharply lowered standards of living. Sovereignty "euphoria" had many republics in its grip, not only outside the
RSFSR but also inside it. And if that were not enough, the financial errors of the Ryzhkov government, particularly its excessive printing of
money, had landed them in an economic jam from which it would be
difficult to escape.

He thought the country was facing three major tests: gaining public
acceptance of the price increases, adopting a viable economic reform
package, and concluding, finally, a new union treaty. Achieving each of
these would be difficult but not impossible. In fact, he thought that nine
republics might soon sign the Treaty of Union.

All of the tests Yakovlev mentioned were real, and the economic figures
for the first quarter of the year, released in mid-April, made clear that
those who spoke of an economic crisis were not indulging in hyperbole.

The data showed that the gross national product had been down 8 percent in the quarter and foreign trade down a whopping 33.8 percent. Imports had fallen by 45.1 percent and exports by 18.4 percent. Oil output, on which most of the foreign currency earnings depended, had decreased by 9 percent, and coal production had gone down by 11 percent.

The budget deficit was expected to reach 31.1 billion rubles in the first quarter, although only a 16.7-billion-ruble deficit had been projected for the entire year. This would inevitably fuel inflation, which had already shifted from a trot to a gallop: it had reached 22 percent in the twelve months ending in March, and that, of course, had been before the April 2 price increases.[3]

Gorbachev's initial reaction was to continue the sort of threats that had marked his policy since the previous fall. Addressing a truncated Council of Federation on April 9,[4] he demanded more financial discipline from the republics and threatened reprisals against those that failed to meet contractual obligations to the Center or refused to sign the union treaty. He also called for a strike moratorium and a ban on political demonstrations during working hours. The only concessions he made to reform were to urge that "land reform" be implemented by the following year's agricultural season and to suggest that plans be developed to privatize some services and retail trade.[5]

In this speech, which was carried in full on national television, Gorbachev promised that the Council of Ministers would, within a week, offer the Supreme Soviet a program for dealing with the crisis. It took Prime Minister Pavlov a few days longer than that to get it ready, but by April 20 he had a draft to discuss with prominent economists outside the government. If his aim was to gain endorsements, the meeting was a failure. For example, Grigory Yavlinsky commented that Pavlov's program failed to address inflation, falling production, worker unrest, or the budget and balance of payments deficits.

Undaunted, on Monday, April 22, Pavlov presented his "anticrisis program" to the Supreme Soviet. After shocking the deputies with a worst-case prediction that the Soviet GNP could fall by 25 percent that year, he lambasted the miners, who were still on strike, and restated his policy of prohibiting wage increases in excess of productivity gains. While he promised to privatize small business rapidly, his program would actually intensify the central controls on most of the economy. A new central bureaucracy, for example, would be established to see that agricultural products were delivered and distributed in accord with the central plan. Such reforms as were mentioned were vaguely worded and projected for the future; the immediate steps reimposed central administrative controls.

The deputies received his message in stony silence, refusing even perfunctory applause, but after a short debate they voted overwhelmingly for it. Few liked it, but no alternative was available and it was obvious that *something* had to be done.

Nursultan Nazarbayev was the only republic leader to attend the session. After stating that he would support the measure since he did not want to embarrass the new government as it made its first formal proposal, he urged that the plan be amended to eliminate its centralizing provisions. Some, he asserted, would "drag us back to the diktat of the Center" and violate agreed-upon provisions in the draft union treaty. He then uttered a pointed warning:

> I am profoundly convinced that the implementation of the anticrisis program and the transition to a market should, in our situation, be based on two foundations: on an economic sphere that is unified for the whole country and on the recognition of the state sovereignty of the republics. No matter how many attack this concept in this or the other chamber, there is no going back on it.[6]

In other words, a unified economic sphere for even the core republics could be preserved only if most economic decision making was delegated to the republics—one of the basic provisions of the Shatalin program, which government spokesmen still vilified as hopelessly impractical. In truth, the "conservatives" in the Party were totally disillusioned with the reform process and argued that central planning must be revived. Yegor Ligachev, still a member of the Supreme Soviet, put it more bluntly than most dared when he argued for "a substantial strengthening of the planning element in the country's economic and social development," but many in fact shared this view.

For most of the public, however, the plunging economy discredited the institutions and shibboleths of the past. A poll conducted in April revealed that only 20 percent of those questioned thought that "socialism should be our goal," while nearly twice as many (38 percent) thought that "socialism has shown that it is bankrupt." In 1990, the polls had consistently shown that most people still favored some form of social-ism.[7]

Another poll, conducted on March 31 in fifteen major cities of the USSR, revealed that the government's prestige had reached a new low: less than 8 percent expressed confidence in Pavlov's Council of Ministers. While 25 percent backed the Russian government, 15.7 percent wanted to see a coalition government and 11.8 percent a government by Democratic Russia. The same survey revealed that Yeltsin's popularity then stood at 61 percent while only 15 percent supported the Communist Party.

Gorbachev's attempt to shore up the power of the presidency had not worked; matters had clearly gone from bad to worse over the past six months, and only a congenital optimist with tunnel vision could believe that Pavlov's despised government could summon either the loyalty or the fear necessary to reverse the centrifugal forces that were shattering the Soviet Union.

Nor had Gorbachev's "swing to the right" neutralized the opposition from that quarter. In fact, just when Gorbachev had embittered the reform intellectuals by his equivocal reaction to the use of military force in Lithuania and his vicious verbal attacks on the "democrats," conservative forces also began to call for Gorbachev to step down.

Throughout 1990, conservatives in the USSR Congress of People's Deputies and Supreme Soviet had begun to coalesce to defend the union against what they saw as destructive nationalistic forces. They had pressed most insistently for the March referendum, and the more outspoken members of the group had spearheaded the campaign against Bakatin, Shevardnadze, and Alexander Yakovlev. We in the American Embassy had observed the group with some concern since the more extreme adherents combined their support for preserving the union with a rabid anti-Americanism.

Not all members of Soyuz (Union) were openly hostile to the West, however. The group was a very loose coalition of representatives of the military-industrial complex, ethnic Russians from the non-Russian republics, and some non-Russians who were either Russified, and thus divorced from their ethnic roots, or from minorities in other republics who feared discrimination if power shifted from Moscow to the republic capitals.

We had maintained contacts with members of the group and included some in social invitations, but I had not personally had an opportunity for a serious discussion with the group's leaders. Since they had become a significant force in Soviet politics, I thought a meeting might be useful: it would help us judge what methods the group might use to preserve the union and would provide an opportunity to rebut the charges voiced by the extremists that the United States was conspiring to dismember the Soviet Union. Therefore, I invited Yuri Blokhin, the group's chairman, to come to a working lunch along with several other leaders of his choosing. He agreed, and we set the date for April 11.

The day before our lunch, the press was filled with reports that Soyuz was pressuring Gorbachev to declare presidential rule over the entire country or resign. Blokhin and others had met with Gorbachev on April 8 and were reported to have been dissatisfied with that meeting. Their spokesman had told the press that they opposed the current draft of the union treaty for giving too much autonomy to the republics; criticized Gorbachev for not bringing order to South Ossetia (where Georgian forces were still blockading the capital) and for considering return of the southern Kuriles to Japan; attacked Shevardnadze, Bakatin, and Yakovlev as having "compromised themselves"; and were debating whether to demand an extraordinary Congress of People's Deputies to impeach the president.[8] The lunch we planned promised to be an interesting one.

Blokhin arrived as scheduled with two colleagues who were known as Soyuz moderates:[9] Georgy Tikhonov, an ethnic Russian from Tajikistan with an economics degree and a job in the Council of Ministers dealing with fuel and energy questions, and Anatoly Chekhoyev, an Ossetian who had made a career in the Georgian Communist Party apparatus. Blokhin himself was an ethnic Russian economist from Moldova.

During our discussion, they denied that they had called for Gorbachev's resignation. Rather, they said, they were insisting that he use his powers to bring order to the country and to stabilize the economy by restoring "vertical integration"—meaning, of course, control by Moscow. They denied that they thought the United States was trying to dismember the Soviet Union but hoped we would give more active support to preservation of the union.[10]

Throughout our conversation Blokhin stressed that his group would insist that all attempts to preserve the union be in accord with the law. Since they felt that Gorbachev had the right to declare presidential rule over troubled localities, this was their principal demand.

The Soyuz leaders who came to lunch doubtless tried to put the most moderate, democratic face on their movement. In fact, the group sheltered those who were in favor of preserving the union by force, and by summer it had become one of the strongest critics of Gorbachev's restraint and his willingness to compromise with the republic leaders in negotiating a union treaty.

Yeltsin on the Rise

BY THE TIME the RSFSR Congress of People's Deputies met on March 28, most of the steam had gone out of the Communist Party effort to oust Yeltsin as parliament chairman. The referendum had clearly shown that Yeltsin's popularity was still intact and Gorbachev's action in bringing troops into Moscow to head off public demonstrations had offended many deputies who were not Yeltsin supporters.

Nevertheless, Yeltsin faced an uphill battle to secure his goal of a Russian presidency. Initially, the Congress refused to put the question on its agenda, but as the days went by, public pressures began to affect votes at the Congress. The turning point occurred on April 4, with three nearly simultaneous events: Russian Communist Party leader Ivan Polozkov announced that there should be "no changes in the RSFSR leadership at the present time," which signaled an end to the effort to unseat Yeltsin; a hitherto obscure military pilot and veteran of the war in Afghanistan, Alexander Rutskoy, announced formation of a "Communists for Democracy" faction, which took an important bloc of votes into the Yeltsin camp; and—in a masterstroke of timing—Yeltsin requested approval of emergency powers analogous to those previously granted Gorbachev in respect to the USSR as a whole.

Yeltsin had managed—as I had anticipated some weeks earlier in a journal entry—to turn the tables on his accusers. He had transformed the session they had called to remove him into a political catapult. Some of his opponents continued to struggle. Shortly before a vote was taken that approved Yeltsin's request in principle, Svetlana Goryacheva, the person who had led the attack on Yeltsin in the Supreme Soviet in February, mounted the rostrum to deliver a rebuke:

> Boris Nikolayevich, . . . It has become clear . . . that for you the presidency is the main goal. For it you have engaged in deceit and misrepresentation and are prepared to go to any length, not even stopping

at plunging the country into crisis, for the sake of power. You will do anything.

. . . I am horrified and shudder to think of the possibility of your occupying that post. You ask for additional powers, yet you have not been able to make proper use of the ones you already have.[11]

At one point, her words were almost drowned out by catcalls and boos, but Yeltsin, who was chairing the session, sternly brought the hall to order and let her finish.

Despite Goryacheva's impassioned appeal, the deputies proceeded to vote overwhelmingly for Yeltsin's proposal[12] and the following day approved a motion that not only granted him temporary authority to rule by decree but also gave him what he had been seeking for months: a date certain for a presidential election. Although the RSFSR Constitution had not yet been amended to provide for a presidency, the resolution called for the election of a Russian president and vice president on June 12. The next session of the RSFSR Congress would meet on May 21 and—presumably—approve the necessary constitutional amendments. Nevertheless, the Congress did not give Yeltsin all he asked for: it voted down resolutions demanding a coalition government for the USSR and roundtable negotiations with the central government on a new economic plan.[13]

Yeltsin won the vote in the Russian Congress of People's Deputies on the Thursday before Orthodox Easter. On the following Saturday evening, he appeared in Moscow's Yelokhovsky Cathedral for the Easter service conducted by Patriarch Alexii II. Television cameras caught his entrance, and images of him standing respectfully, candles in hand, alternated with those of the service itself in the national television coverage. For believers, it was a powerful symbol: the leader of Russia had come to terms with the traditional Russian national church, which had been vilified by the militantly atheist Bolsheviks and suppressed, at times to the verge of extinction, by the Communist regime.

Once again, Yeltsin had upstaged Gorbachev. While Gorbachev had loosened official controls on religious bodies, had included clergymen in the USSR Congress of People's Deputies, and at times had consulted them, he made no pretense of any religious belief and, as far as the public was aware, had never attended a church service as an adult.[14] Yeltsin still had not declared himself a believer, but his gesture suggested that he would treat the Orthodox Church as an authentic and valued part of Russian tradition.[15]

A week later, Yeltsin made a trip to France that was viewed at the time by the foreign press as a public relations disaster but quite differently by the Russian public. Initially, when he visited the European Parliament in Strasbourg, he was publicly insulted by Jean-Pierre Cot, the chairman of the European socialist legislative group, who labeled him a "demagogue" and "irresponsible" in his opposition to Gorbachev, "with whom we feel more secure."[16]

This incident, and what seemed to be a cool reception overall by senior French officials, were covered at length in the Soviet press—but only belatedly by Central Television[17]—and most Russians reacted in outrage. They resented the presumption of foreigners who would insult their elected leader. Additionally, they suspected that Gorbachev and the KGB had encouraged the insults: a report appeared in the press that Soviet Ambassador to France Yuri Dubinin had officially requested that Yeltsin be given no special treatment.

Yeltsin reacted by denying any desire to replace Gorbachev—preferring instead a "roundtable" that might produce a coalition—and by pledging to support a union treaty.[18] When he returned to Paris from Strasbourg, he was belatedly granted interviews with President Mitterrand and other senior French officials.

Yeltsin's trip to France unexpectedly produced a positive impact on his relations with Gorbachev. Mitterrand's decision to receive Yeltsin in the face of Gorbachev's clearly expressed displeasure indicated that, no matter how enamored Western leaders might be of Gorbachev personally, they would not be willing indefinitely to ignore a popular Yeltsin just to please their friend. At the same time, Yeltsin's public announcement of his desire to work with Gorbachev to conclude a union treaty and put perestroika back on track was, in effect, a withdrawal of his February demand that Gorbachev resign. As Yeltsin told his French interviewer:

> Gorbachev is not resigning; he is the country's president. . . . We must cooperate, we must work in such a way that Russia and the whole country do not suffer. And we must do this despite the fact that Gorbachev and I disagree on several matters of principle.[19]

In February and March, any reconciliation between Yeltsin and Gorbachev had seemed out of the question. Now, suddenly, an opening appeared. Neither was oblivious to the growing strength of the right-wing forces that were determined to sweep them both from power.

While Yeltsin was still in France, I traveled to Washington, where I hoped to get more satisfactory instructions for our contacts with Yeltsin. I had maintained close contact with him from the time he had been elected to the USSR Supreme Soviet in 1989 but had done so without encouragement from my superiors. Washington had never instructed me not to see him, and my colleagues in the State Department obviously recognized the value of staying in touch with him, but White House staffers were skeptical about his political staying power and the president was nervous about offending Gorbachev. I suspected that they had refrained from ordering me to give Yeltsin a cold shoulder only because they feared that a press leak would create political problems at home.

Nevertheless, Yeltsin was steadily growing in political importance and his policies were in harmony with U.S. objectives: he sought deep cuts in the Soviet military budget, a cutoff of aid to irresponsible regimes like Saddam Hussein's in Iraq, and freedom for the Baltic states, as well as other republics if they chose. Internally, he backed real economic reform, including full rights for private property and the privatization of state enterprises. Whatever doubts one might have of his executive ability or of his willingness to follow democratic principles should they not serve his political interests, it was important for the United States government to maintain contact with him: one could not fully understand the changes that were convulsing the Soviet Union without doing so. Furthermore, as Yeltsin gained power and authority, it was important to establish a pattern of communication in case he should at some point come to power through a democratic process.

It was not a matter of choosing Yeltsin over Gorbachev or of trying to weaken the Soviet Union, though some apologists for the White House attitude talked as if that were the case. Of course we should not have treated Yeltsin as if he were president of the USSR or tried to undermine Gorbachev's position. But dealing with Yeltsin as we would the leader of the opposition in a democratic country would not have violated diplomatic norms.

In fact, the Soviet Constitution explicitly gave the union republics the right to maintain diplomatic relations with other countries, and each had its own ministry of foreign affairs. Thus, heads of union republics theoretically had greater authority than American state governors to deal with foreign governments—and our governors never hesitate to travel around the world and to meet with foreign leaders in pursuit of trade and investment, the very topics Yeltsin was most interested in talking to us about.

For these reasons, I could not understand why the White House staff felt we had to make a choice between Gorbachev and Yeltsin. I thought we should deal with both, each in his own sphere, and reject the notion that this was playing favorites. By mid-April, I had also concluded that Gorbachev might soon be willing to make another attempt at cooperation with Yeltsin. If so, our having good relations with both would encourage the effort. As I noted in my journal on April 5:

> The events of the last seven to eight days seem to be producing a swing toward the reformers. If Yeltsin cannot be removed, and if he continues to consolidate his position, Gorbachev may be constrained to deal with him once again, despite his personal animosity. The miners' strike may turn out to be something of a touchstone event. Now it would seem that only Yeltsin has the authority to stop it. He made it clear at the Congress of People's Deputies that he would not attempt to end it if he did not receive the enhanced authority he sought.
>
> As for Gorbachev, he cannot have missed the spectacle of some of the "right" speaking in favor of his resignation, just as Yeltsin has done. With friends like that, he may as well see what kind of deal Boris Nikolayevich would consider.

The following day, Andrei Kozyrev, the RSFSR foreign minister, came by Spaso House for a chat. Frank Carlucci, our just-retired secretary of defense, was making a private visit, and the three of us reviewed recent developments. Kozyrev volunteered that he felt events were forcing both Gorbachev and Yeltsin to seek accommodation. The confrontation of March 28, when Gorbachev had brought troops into Moscow to prevent demonstrations that took place anyway, had frightened both sides. Suddenly, there seemed to be the potential for civil war, and this was acting as a deterrent. "It's like nuclear weapons in U.S.-Soviet relations," Kozyrev explained. "Once we understand the danger, we realize we have to cooperate to prevent their use." The prospect of Yeltsin's election, Kozyrev continued, would force Gorbachev to compromise, whatever his personal likes and dislikes. "You can deal with Communists only from a position of strength," he observed, grinning in tacit acknowledgment of the source of his observation.

The specific issue before us was whether I could assure Yeltsin that he would be received by President Bush if he should travel to Washington. He had received invitations from Congress and had several from private groups as well. While he would have preferred to come at the invitation of the executive branch, I had explained to him that this was impossible, and he seemed to accept it. But he did not want to travel to the United States at all unless he could be sure of a meeting with President Bush. Until I went to Washington in April 1991, I had been explicitly warned not to promise Yeltsin the meeting he wanted.

I met President Bush in the Oval Office on the afternoon of April 18 and spent most of my time describing the Gorbachev-Yeltsin relationship. I argued that their political interests were linked, no matter how stubbornly they resisted recognizing the fact. I noted that Gorbachev had gotten off the reform track the previous fall and had simultaneously reneged on his commitment to Yeltsin. The policies he had followed since then were not working. Gorbachev, I pointed out, was responding to the military-industrial complex, since the republics would sharply curtail the resources available to the military if they controlled the purse strings. I mentioned Kozyrev's observations that both sides were deterred by the threat of civil war and that advisers to both were urging a compromise. Whether one would be possible remained to be seen, but I saw little prospect of ending the strikes that were raging unless Yeltsin was given the authority to grant the mines managerial autonomy. That would require the liberation of management from the central ministries, which to the workers represented the oppressive and exploitative Communist system.

As far as dealing with the situation was concerned, I advised that we should talk to all parties and not be drawn into the internal political struggle. (In encouraging us to boycott Yeltsin, Gorbachev was doing just that.) As far as aid and technical assistance were concerned, I felt we should finesse the Center-republic issue and deal with localities—municipalities and regions—that favored development of a private sector. I also thought that aid should be directed at the private sector, rather than being funneled through the central government, as Gorbachev was urging.

The president asked about the request Gorbachev had just made for an additional $1.5 billion of credit guarantees to buy U.S. agricultural products. I told him I would consider this primarily a domestic issue. Congress had approved the program to support U.S. agricultural exports. If he thought it would serve that purpose, he should approve it, provided we were convinced that the USSR could repay the loan. He should not approve the request, however, as assistance to economic reform in the Soviet Union because the loan would not have that effect. The Soviet Union might in fact face food shortages the following winter, but Gorbachev's policies were making matters worse. I thought that any large loans should be in support of specific reform measures.

The day after I spoke with President Bush, Edward Hewett, who had joined the NSC staff as the principal specialist on Soviet affairs, contacted me to say that when I returned to Moscow I could notify Yeltsin that the president would see him if he came to Washington. Before doing so, however, I was to call on Foreign Minister Bessmertnykh and explain to him that President Bush would make sure that Yeltsin did not use the visit to drive a wedge between Gorbachev and Bush.

Nine Plus One

ON APRIL 23, 1991, shortly after I returned to Moscow, Gorbachev met nine republic leaders, including Yeltsin and Kravchuk, in a marathon nine-and-a-half-hour session at a government dacha in the suburban village of Novo-Ogaryovo. The next morning, *Pravda* carried the text of a statement signed by all ten calling for a new union treaty of sovereign states and steps to stabilize the collapsing economy.[20] The declaration put the brake on what had been an accelerating trend toward disintegration. Finally it looked as if Gorbachev might be prepared to meet the republic leaders halfway.

Gorbachev's position in the negotiations on the union treaty had become increasingly desperate. The previous drafts had proven unacceptable to virtually all the republics, and independence fever was spreading. After repeated delays, formal negotiations with the Baltic governments on the terms of independence had begun in early April.[21] On April 9, the Georgian Supreme Soviet had unanimously voted for the restoration of the state sovereignty and independence of Georgia. Moldova, Armenia, and Azerbaijan had also dropped out of the negotiating process.

As these centrifugal tendencies intensified, representatives of five "core republics" (Russia, Ukraine, Belorussia, Kazakhstan, and Uzbekistan) met in Kiev on April 18—while Gorbachev was on a state visit to Japan—to coordinate their positions on the proposed union treaty. The gathering endorsed the demands by Yeltsin and Kravchuk that the treaty create a "union of sovereign states," not a union state—in other words, a loose confederation much like the one Ruslan Khasbulatov had described to me the preceding August. In addition, they opposed the proposal to give former "autonomous republics" the same status as union republics, which had grown out of Gorbachev's attempt to weaken Yeltsin by catering to Russia's "autonomies."[22]

The April 23 agreement represented a sharp shift by Gorbachev toward the demands of the republics. Though many details still had to be negotiated, the agreement seemed to form a basis for a grand bargain between Gorbachev and the majority of the republics—including the largest ones.

Gorbachev's spokesmen hailed the agreement as a major victory for unity and initially called it the "One Plus Nine" agreement. But—as was the case with negotiations over German unification—the order of the digits was significant, and within days, at the insistence of the republic leaders, the formula was changed to "Nine Plus One."

The declaration was published in the central press on April 24, 1991. Echoing the resolution by the "core republics" in Kiev the previous week, it specified that the new union treaty would be of "sovereign states" and would require a new constitution, to be presented to parliament within six months after the treaty was signed. New elections would then be held in accord with the new constitution.

The agreement seemed to finesse the secession issue: it stated that those republics that signed the union treaty would be given most-favored-nation treatment. What would happen to the others was not specified, but the declaration implied that they would be outside the new union and, as sovereign political entities, would be required to negotiate the terms of any relationship with it. When I asked some of Gorbachev's advisers whether this was in fact the case, some conceded that it would provide an easy and automatic way to secede, while others claimed that failure to adhere to the new union would leave republics in their existing status as parts of the USSR. The latter, however, were unable to explain how this could be if the existing USSR was replaced by a new union; the institutions of the old Soviet Union would simply disappear and there would be no state structure to preserve the existing Center-republic relationship.

Gorbachev was forced not only to accept the republic leaders' concept of the new union but also to relent on several tax and price initiatives he had earlier decreed. For example, he agreed to drop the 5 percent sales tax levied since January 1, to increase scholarship payments to students, and to reduce the prices of air and rail tickets.

For the first time, Gorbachev seemed on the verge of meeting the demands of the republic leaders for the sort of loose federation they were willing to accept. If he could resist the counteroffensive by the hard-liners, who were certain to be infuriated by the concessions he had made, he might yet succeed in preserving some sort of union structure for the "core republics" and preside over the orderly separation of the others. But for this, he would have to reverse the political alliances he had made in November and December and at the same time ensure that the people determined to maintain the old empire would not be able to remove him.

Conservatives Turn on Gorbachev

GORBACHEV'S NEXT TEST came the day after the Nine Plus One declaration was signed, at the plenary session of the Communist Party Central Committee. For weeks, rumors had been rife that hard-liners in the Party would utilize the session to lambaste perestroika and Gorbachev personally; some provincial first secretaries were bragging openly that Gorbachev would be forced out of his Party post as the first step to removing him from the presidency.[23] Nevertheless, the Supreme Soviet approval of Pavlov's "anticrisis program," and particularly the signing of the Nine Plus One declaration, strengthened Gorbachev's position. The declaration was published the very morning the Central Committee convened, and at first glance it seemed a political breakthrough to unity. Only gradually did some of its implications sink in.

Furthermore, Gorbachev took another step designed to appease Party conservatives when he issued a decree declaring illegal the Armenian government's nationalization of Communist Party property in the republic.[24] I wondered at the time how he could possibly enforce the decree, but that was not the point: he wanted to pose as a bulwark against further dissolution of the Party in order to undermine the growing conviction that he was, at heart, not a Communist but a social democrat.

Rumors had circulated for some time that there would be a serious

effort to remove Gorbachev from his Party position at this plenum, and
senior Soviet officials behaved as if they believed them. When we were
trying to schedule a meeting between Foreign Minister Bessmertnykh
and Secretary of State Baker at a resort near the Caucasus during one of
Baker's trips to the Middle East, Bessmertnykh asked me to explain that
he could not come on the day Baker preferred. "Tell Jim I absolutely
have to be in Moscow on April 24," he said. "I can't miss this plenum
because Gorbachev will need every single vote he can get!"

Initially, it appeared that Gorbachev had managed once again to outmaneuver his critics. In his opening speech he warned that if he was
forced to resign, a power vacuum would be created that could lead to a
dictatorship. He blamed "radicals of the left and the right," thus implying that he was solidly in the center. Votes were then cast on discussing
his resignation and also on demanding that he give an accounting of his
stewardship, and both motions were defeated. A motion to discuss the
separation of the posts of Party general secretary and president was also
defeated.

Despite these votes, the criticism of Gorbachev continued, and much
of it was vicious. In contrast to speeches at legislative assemblies, which
were usually broadcast live or with only a few hours' delay, those at the
Central Committee plenum were in a closed session. Reports of them
filtered out piecemeal, and it was difficult for anyone outside the hall to
be sure what was really going on inside. But after the April 24 session,
most of the reports indicated that Gorbachev had beaten back the challenges to his position.

The plenum continued on April 25, however, and just after noon rumors swept through Moscow that Gorbachev had resigned. I was occupied that afternoon addressing a large public meeting and answering
questions, after which I rushed off to a concert at Finnish Ambassador
Heikki Talvitie's spacious residence. The music was pleasant, but it was
difficult to keep my mind on it, since I had not heard what had really
happened at the plenum. During an intermission in the concert, editor
Vladislav Starkov told me that he had heard that Gorbachev had resigned, and he almost made this the lead story in *Argumenty i Fakty*
when his printing deadline arrived that afternoon. However, he decided
not to take the chance and to wait until there was an official announcement.

After the concert was over, I learned bit by bit what had happened.
Following a morning of heavy criticism, Gorbachev had angrily pro-

claimed that the general secretary could do his job only if he had the support of the membership. Therefore, "If this is the way you feel, I will go!"[25]

His statement struck the hall like a thunderbolt, and Deputy General Secretary Ivashko immediately called an intermission in the proceedings. During the break, seventy-two members of the Central Committee signed a petition stating that if Gorbachev resigned, they would too. The Politburo met in emergency session. It suddenly became apparent that if Gorbachev was allowed to resign it could be the end of the Party itself. Not only would a substantial number of members leave with him, but he would be in a position to use the power of the state bureaucracy to wreck the Party structures. Yeltsin was already showing how dangerous an apostate could be; if Gorbachev joined him in his efforts to eradicate the Party, the future of most of the delegates in the hall would be bleak.

When the plenum reconvened, Ivashko announced that the Politburo had recommended that the last proposal be stricken from the record. It carried by an overwhelming margin.

Before turning in that evening, I jotted the following comment in my journal:

> Actually, it might not have been damaging to Gorbachev if he had in fact resigned. Starkov, for example, thought it would increase his popularity, since it would give him a chance to run against the *apparat.* Maybe so, but it also could have given the impression of a mortally wounded leader, and the opposition could have become even more active in seeking his removal as president. As it is, it would seem that he has bought some time, maybe quite a lot, depending on how solid his deal is with the nine republic leaders.

Later, I wondered if the danger to Gorbachev's position had been as great as many thought. All votes had been overwhelmingly in his favor, which might suggest that sentiment had not become as negative as many supposed. Nevertheless, I realized that it was probably a much closer affair than the votes indicated. After all, few Central Committee members would want to be caught on the losing side of a vote (though the actual penalties had greatly diminished). Therefore, many who were opposed to him would probably vote for him until convinced that his opponents had a majority. At that point, there could be a massive shift against him.

In fact, though I did not know it at the time, there had been a conspiracy to remove Gorbachev at the April plenum, organized by some of the same people who would later participate in the August coup attempt. Following the arrest of the coup leaders, investigators found evidence that Alexander Tizyakov, a Sverdlovsk factory director who headed the Association of State Enterprises, had organized a campaign of telegrams to the Central Committee before the April plenum with demands to bring order into the economy. His goal was to convince the plenum to remove Gorbachev and to establish an emergency committee similar to the one formed in August. The plan involved controlling the podium at the session so that the case against Gorbachev could be made most forcefully and excluding the independent press. With Gorbachev out of the way, the emergency committee would set about the task of "restoring the CPSU's authority" as it had existed before Gorbachev had come to power in 1985.[26]

Gorbachev's maneuver on April 25 saved the day, but his opponents did not concede defeat. They simply waited for a better opportunity.

On Saturday, April 26, I tried to sum up the rapid-fire events of the past few days:

> It *has* been an important week. Gorbachev made significant moves, and so did Yeltsin and several other key players. As I noted above, it is not certain that Gorbachev was ever in any real danger of losing his party position (though I suspect he was), and it is not certain that losing it would have cost him his real job. Nevertheless, if he is going to resign, it is better that he not be forced out. The timing would be better when the pressure has eased.
>
> At present, I would say that Gorbachev has strengthened his position. However, he may only have bought some time, and the question is whether he will use it well. In my view, he has showed the extreme right that they cannot remove him, even from the Communist Party, by legal means, and has forced the reformers to recognize that they really do not want him to go. So now is an ideal time to swing to the "left" once again. He seems to have set the stage for it, but I cannot be sure that he intends to proceed with the performance.
>
> Just how much Yeltsin meant by his signature on the [Novo-Ogaryovo] declaration is not clear. It is hard to believe that he will really back some of the points in it. However, he must have realized (even before his trip to France) that it is not in his interest for Gorba-

chev to be forced out when he is in no position to replace him. Therefore, he, too, has signaled readiness for at least a degree of cooperation. The decisive questions are likely to be whether Gorbachev will yield further on the powers of the republics, and whether Yeltsin will try to settle the strikes. It seems to me that Gorbachev could accept a round table, maybe even a coalition government, if push comes to shove. And it may have.

The litmus test: what will happen to the economic branch ministries? So long as Gorbachev hangs on to them, he will be in trouble because nothing will really change in the perceptions of the republics, although the system itself will continue to disintegrate.

Поживем, увидим (Loosely: "We shall see what we shall see.")

Not all of the reformers were pleased with Gorbachev's efforts to keep his Party position. When I called on Shevardnadze the following week to discuss his forthcoming visit to the United States, he remarked that Gorbachev should have resigned his Party post voluntarily after resisting the effort to remove him. If he had left the Communist Party voluntarily, Shevardnadze thought, Gorbachev could have freed himself from the *apparat,* taken reformers out of the Party with him, and regained much of his popularity with the public. This would have split the Communist Party, but that would be healthy since it would strengthen the multiparty system they were trying to develop. "Let the 'conservatives' and 'democrats' [in the Communist Party] have their own parties—and others, too," he remarked. As it was, he feared that Gorbachev would remain a captive of the hard-liners and would be pushed to adopt policies that could be implemented only by force. Recent threatening statements by Prime Minister Pavlov seemed to him to be pointing in this direction.[27]

But others felt that it would have been reckless for Gorbachev to attempt to split the Party without careful preparation. As Foreign Minister Bessmertnykh commented to me on the same day I met with Shevardnadze, Gorbachev's resignation as Party general secretary would have been interpreted by many as a political defeat and could have led to the rapid disintegration of his presidency as well.

Yeltsin, the Elected President

YELTSIN CROSSED ANOTHER HURDLE on his race for the Russian presidency when, on April 24, 1991—the same day Gorbachev was fending off critics at the Central Committee—the RSFSR Supreme Soviet passed a law authorizing the election of a president and vice president. Any candidate who could collect at least 100,000 signatures of Russian citizens could run in the election set for June 12. Voting would be by secret ballot, and the winner would have to obtain a majority of the votes cast—a change from the requirement in parliamentary elections that deputies receive a majority of all those registered to vote. The law specified further that the president would have a term of five years and would be required to suspend membership in political parties and public associations while holding office. The law also stipulated, in a provision that would become a subject of strife two years later, that the president could be removed for violating the Constitution, laws, or oath of office by a two-thirds vote of the Russian Congress of People's Deputies if the Constitutional Court—the first to be established in Russia's history—so recommended.[28]

The legislature approved the law on the presidency contingent upon appropriate amendments to the RSFSR Constitution that would be considered by the Congress of People's Deputies, which was scheduled to meet on May 21. Both Yeltsin and his opponents, however, expected the Congress to pass the amendments, and Yeltsin's rivals stopped opposing the concept and began organizing their own election campaigns.

I could only marvel at the mercurial quality Russian politics was taking on: for months, the Russian Supreme Soviet and Congress of People's Deputies had refused to establish a presidency, and a mere six weeks earlier Yeltsin had seemed in grave danger of being removed as chairman of parliament. But now opinion was moving in his direction so unmistakably that even those skeptical of his leadership were being forced by their constituents to support him.

A few days after the Nine Plus One agreement and the Russian parliament's approval of the law on the presidency, Yeltsin demonstrated his political strength by brokering an end to the miners' strike, which had dragged on for nearly two months. As grounds for returning to work, the miners accepted Yeltsin's promise to see that they were freed from the control of the central Ministry of the Coal Industry. In facilitating an end to the strike, Yeltsin relieved some of the immediate pressure on Pavlov and Gorbachev but showed that they could no longer rule without his cooperation and, furthermore, that the relief would be temporary if the central ministerial structure of economic management was not rapidly dismantled. Pavlov never got the point, but Gorbachev, for a time anyway, seemed to.

Yeltsin's choice of a running mate surprised many, for he bypassed all the prominent leaders of Democratic Russia, the organization that had given him most consistent support, and selected instead Alexander Rutskoy, the veteran of the war in Afghanistan who had led the Communists for Democracy faction to Yeltsin's side when he was threatened with impeachment in March.

At the time it seemed to be a shrewd move. Most military officers had been opposed to Yeltsin, but with Rutskoy on the ticket Yeltsin could expect to attract some of the military and even more of the moderate reformers still in the Communist Party. Since the duties of the Russian vice president were as ill defined as those of the American vice president, it seemed of little substantive consequence who might be selected. Therefore, like many American candidates for the presidency, Yeltsin based his choice on short-term political calculation.

When the scramble to nominate candidates for the Russian presidency was over, five candidacies in addition to Yeltsin's were registered. Nikolai Ryzhkov, now recovered from his heart attack and bitter over what he considered Gorbachev's betrayal, was the most formidable.[29] He seemed to have the backing of the great majority of the Communist Party *apparat*, but he suffered from the image of failure. Vadim Bakatin, urged on by Gorbachev, who was eager to prevent Yeltsin from receiving a large majority, also entered the race—and it seemed to many that he had the best chance of taking votes away from Yeltsin, since he was respected by moderate reformers and seemed to have a more democratic style than Yeltsin, who continued to vacillate between populist rhetoric and the autocratic habits of a provincial Communist secretary.

The other candidates seemed out of the mainstream of Russian politics—if such a body can have a mainstream. Albert Makashov, a mustachioed three-star general, ran on a platform that was fascist in all but name. Amangeldy Tuleyev, an ethnic Kazakh from Kemerovo, barely on the Russian side of the border with Kazakhstan, was more a regional favorite son than a genuine national candidate.[30] Vladimir Zhirinovsky was the most enigmatic of these lesser-known candidates. He seemed well organized and financed, but the source of both his organization and his money was obscure, and—at least until the campaign unfolded—his political program was also vague.

Zhirinovsky had first appeared on the national political stage some weeks before the Russian parliamentary elections in June 1990. His Liberal Democratic Party had actually been the first to be officially registered for those elections, in advance even of the Communist Party, and he had been given several minutes on prime-time television news to announce his party's campaign. It was, as he explained it, anti-Communist and pro–liberal democracy.

I was skeptical. In December 1989, during Andrei Sakharov's funeral, a man whose calling card carried the name of Voronin had introduced himself to me, claimed to be a close friend of Sakharov's, and helped us make our way through the crowd. He seemed to be assisting those who had organized the funeral. When Yelena Bonner invited us to the cemetery, he offered to show my driver the way. As we chatted in the car, I determined that he had no discernible occupation: he was in his early fifties, but said that he was retired on a disability—the nature of which, however, was neither specified nor apparent. He professed to be an organizer of a political party that would "carry out Sakharov's ideals." Subsequently, however, when I asked Yelena Bonner if she knew him, she stated flatly that he had never been a Sakharov associate and in fact was an "imposter."

I had made no further attempt to contact him, but a few weeks later Voronin had accosted me at a reception at the Hungarian Embassy and guided me over to some of his "political associates." They were organizing, they said, a truly anti-Communist political party, following Sakharov's ideals. Each gave me a calling card, one of which bore the name of Vladimir Zhirinovsky.

When I returned to our embassy, I asked my staff to find out about the group. We were already in contact with most of the politicians in Moscow who were pursuing democratic policies, and I wondered how we had missed this group—if it was in fact genuine. While their approach seemed suspect for several reasons, I realized that we did not know everyone in the political arena and that new leadership might come from hitherto obscure elements of society.

A few days later I got my answer: when our people inquired about the group, they were told that, while nobody seemed to be sure, most responsible Russian politicians suspected that it was sponsored by the KGB, or perhaps elements within it, to divert votes from the real democratic forces. I instructed our diplomats to avoid further contact with the group; our contacts were followed closely by politically active Soviet citizens, and there seemed no reason to lend legitimacy to Zhirinovsky's group by our attention.

The coverage the Soviet media gave Zhirinovsky's party in the spring of 1990 seemed to confirm the report I had received earlier. Obviously, this "party" had powerful friends in the Soviet bureaucracy, since the other parties were registered only with difficulty and delay and were allowed television time grudgingly if at all.

Yeltsin's success in establishing the office of an elective president in Russia emboldened other politicians from the democratic movement to create elective positions on lower political levels. The chairmen of the city councils in both Moscow and Leningrad, Gavriil Popov and Anatoly Sobchak, had encountered great difficulty in retaining consistent support in their fragmented assemblies. Therefore, both proposed amending the city charters to provide for a mayor elected by popular vote, rather than by vote of the council. The proposal carried in both cities, and voters were given the opportunity to select a mayor at the same time as they voted for a Russian president. Just as Yeltsin was using a direct election to outflank his opponents in the Russian parliament, Popov and Sobchak attempted the same in their cities.

The election campaigns were vigorous, freer than any had been up to then, and mercifully short. The democratic parties, groups, and coalitions held together in their support of Yeltsin but otherwise continued to splinter. For example, the Democratic Party of Russia, led by Nikolai Travkin, held its second congress in Moscow on April 25–27 and, though it called for a broad coalition to support Yeltsin's candidacy, suffered a split itself as chess grand master Gary Kasparov and physicist Arkady Murashev, one of the most proficient organizers of public demonstrations, parted company with Travkin to form their own party.

In contrast to his behavior in May 1990, when Yeltsin had been running for the chairmanship of the Russian parliament, Gorbachev did not campaign openly against Yeltsin. Nevertheless, few doubted that Vadim Bakatin was his surrogate. Although most observers expected Yeltsin to win, some thought he might be forced into a runoff against Ryzhkov if Bakatin succeeded in taking 10 percent or more of the vote that would otherwise have gone to Yeltsin.

This, however, did not happen. Yeltsin won handily on the first ballot, with more than 57 percent of the vote. Ryzhkov came in second, as expected, but weaker than most anticipated: instead of the 20 to 25 percent predicted, he got less than 17 percent. The real surprise, however, came with the third place: it was not, as most anticipated, Vadim Bakatin, but the mysterious Vladimir Zhirinovsky, who received more than 6 million votes, almost eight percent of the total cast. The others received 6 percent or less, and, surprisingly, Bakatin came in at the bottom of the list with slightly more than 3 percent of the vote. The rebuke by the voters was, however, directed not so much at him as at Gorbachev.

Though it was a severe political blow, Gorbachev accepted Yeltsin's election with good grace. When Yeltsin took the oath of office in the Palace of Congresses on July 10, 1991, Gorbachev was present. Yeltsin took his oath on the RSFSR Constitution and the Declaration of State Sovereignty of the RSFSR. In his inaugural address, he made it clear that the existence of an elected president marked the beginning of a new period in Russian history, quite apart from what might happen to the Soviet Union:

> Citizens of Russia have not only selected a personality, not only a president . . . but they have first of all selected the road our Motherland is to take.
> Great Russia is rising from its knees. . . . Having passed through so many trials, with clear goals in mind, we can be absolutely certain of one thing: Russia will rise again![31]

His Holiness Alexii II, Patriarch of Moscow and All Russia, bestowed his blessing on the new Russian president.

For the first time in its history, Russia had a leader elected by the people. And for the first time since Tsar Nicholas II had succeeded to the throne in 1894, a Russian leader had sought the blessing of the Church.

XIX

Blindman's Bluff

Our Fatherland is on the brink of catastrophe. . . . Circumstances are such that
it is simply impossible to avoid emergency measures.
VLADIMIR KRYUCHKOV, June 17, 1991[1]

There is no crisis in my relations with V. S. Pavlov . . . Somebody would like
to drive a wedge between the president and the prime minister.
MIKHAIL GORBACHEV to USSR Supreme Soviet, June 21, 1991[2]

We [democrats] have managed to disorganize the country but not to reorganize it.
GAVRIIL POPOV, July 1991[3]

Soviet-American contacts took on an unprecedented intensity in
the spring and summer of 1991. With the end of the Gulf War,
Washington's attention shifted to resolving the remaining major issues
with the Soviet Union. Our foreign ministers met several times every
month, and our presidents talked on the telephone almost every week.
Every day I was in Moscow, I saw one or more senior Soviet officials—if
not the president, prime minister, or foreign minister than at least their
senior aides.

Despite his efforts to prevent a U.S.-led war in the Gulf, Gorbachev
had kept the promise he had given Bush in Helsinki to cooperate in ending Iraqi aggression. Though at times he had seemed on the brink of
ordering or permitting the use of force in the Baltic states, Gorbachev
had drawn back from a policy of force when we made clear that cooperative relations with us were at stake. There was a feeling of gratitude in
Washington, coupled with increasing concern for Gorbachev's domestic
position.

Nevertheless, nagging problems remained. The attempts by the Soviet military to fudge on the commitments made in the agreement to reduce conventional weapons in Europe had not ended. Negotiators continued to haggle over the terms of a strategic arms agreement; although there had been general agreement on the key issues for over a year, various technical and verification issues continued to crop up. The latest was a dispute over "downloading"—whether to allow, and under what terms, modification of missiles with multiple warheads to carry fewer than the maximum number of warheads for which they had been tested. The USSR Supreme Soviet had still not passed a law ensuring the right to free emigration (although in practice hardly anybody was barred from leaving the country if he or she desired), and as a consequence the trade agreement signed by Bush and Gorbachev in Washington in 1990 had still not been sent to Congress for approval.

Bush's visit to Moscow, originally planned for February 1991 and postponed ostensibly because of the Gulf War, had still not been rescheduled. The president wanted to sign the START agreement when he came to Moscow, but he knew that—even if the strategic arms issues were resolved—it would be impolitic to do so before the Soviet Union was in full compliance with the conventional forces agreement of the previous year.

Meanwhile, Gorbachev chafed. He had been uncomfortable with the postponement of Bush's visit from the beginning, had not expected to have to wait for Bush to approve his April request for $1.5 billion of credit guarantees to buy grain, and was not yet sure he would be invited to join the Group of Seven industrialized nations during their meeting in July. At home, his political enemies were accusing him of naïvely supporting Western interests without securing commensurate benefits for the Soviet Union.

George Doesn't Love Me Anymore!

THE TREATY TO REDUCE conventional forces in Europe, known to specialists by the acronym CFE, which was signed in Paris on November 19, 1990, was one of the events that formalized the end of the cold war. It provided for substantial reductions of forces and arms on the European continent and ceilings on forces in various regions. With much the larger force to begin with, the Soviet Union accepted a disproportionate share of the reductions so that a balance would result in the end.

However, soon after the treaty had been signed, it was discovered that the Soviet high command was attempting to violate some of the provisions. Some of these (involving unannounced movement of forces east of the Urals) violated the spirit of the agreement. Others (such as a claim that units of naval infantry—the Soviet version of the U.S. marines—should not be counted) contravened both the letter and the spirit of the agreement. Gorbachev's failure to force the Soviet military to comply fully with the agreement was one of the factors that had led to Shevardnadze's resignation.

Given Soviet noncompliance, the United States and its allies refused to ratify the treaty, and negotiations to correct the Soviet violations dragged on throughout the winter and into the spring. Gradually, after resisting on every point, the Soviet Union began to give way, but only a small step at a time. It was Gromyko tactics all over again.

By May, however, only a few issues were left, and I received instructions to call on Gorbachev to urge a prompt settlement. I was given an appointment for Tuesday, May 7, 1991.

Gorbachev met me with only Chernyayev present. He listened carefully to the points I had been instructed to convey. Since the Soviet Ministry of Foreign Affairs had been unable to bring the Soviet military into line, we proposed that Gorbachev send General Mikhail Moiseyev, chief of the General Staff, to Washington to deal with the issue directly. Gorbachev replied that he appreciated the importance of reaching a prompt settlement on the remaining CFE issues so that the treaty could go into effect. While he thought he had already made a reasonable proposal for settling the naval infantry issue, he agreed that it would be useful for Moiseyev to go to Washington.

He then pushed aside the paper that had been prepared for the meeting, looked intently at me across the table, and launched into one of the plaintive monologues in which he, from time to time, indulged—usually with the effect he intended. It would have been impolite to glance at my watch, but I am sure he went on for at least fifteen minutes; more likely it was twenty.

What concerned him, he said, were the mounting signs that President Bush was "reassessing" their relationship. Public statements in Washington had taken a more critical tone on a range of topics. Furthermore, he understood that the credits he had requested for grain purchases had been turned down, and he was getting reports of other trade barriers. For example, the United States was refusing to deliver computers that would improve safety at Soviet nuclear power stations, even though he had been assured by both Reagan and Bush that there were no export restrictions and he had personally signed the contract when he had visited Minneapolis the year before. He could not understand why we did not consider the safety of power stations a mutual interest. Also, he had been informed that there were licensing problems with a proposed joint project to build a commercial airliner.

As he rambled on, he mentioned my planned departure, which had just been announced. "Why should you leave now?" he asked rhetorically, adding that we had "worked together productively" for several years and he couldn't understand why I had decided to end my tour as ambassador. "Maybe you think this ship will sink?" he said as he glared at me, then broke the tension with a sudden smile.

When I managed to break in, I explained that President Bush had not altered his support for perestroika, and if critical voices were occasionally heard in Washington, they were reactions to specific Soviet actions, such as violations of the CFE agreement. As for economic relations, as far as I knew, no final decision had been made regarding the credits to buy grain. I asked him to understand that President Bush faced numerous legal and technical difficulties in making a positive decision; in particular we did not yet have adequate data to support a ruling on creditworthiness, which our law required.

My mention of "creditworthiness" set him off again. He complained that Bush had called attention to the problem in a public statement and said that his critics were using that statement and others like it against him.

I told him that he was seeing connections where there were none. My departure was purely for personal reasons—I simply felt that it was time for me to do something else, after eight years of concentration on Soviet affairs, and knew that our embassy would benefit from fresh leadership. I knew that President Bush continued his strong support for perestroika and Gorbachev personally, but he, Gorbachev, should recognize that we had great difficulty finding a way to assist him as long as he persisted in retaining a command administrative system. For example, we had expected to see the monopolistic central ministries broken up, but in fact they had been preserved in the new Cabinet. "It is, of course, your business how you organize your government," I said. "But we are simply unable to help you make your current system work. We know of no way that can be done, and besides, we have no experience running a system like yours."

As far as the grain credits were concerned, I told him that we would like to be helpful, but at the same time we believed it would make more sense to improve the distribution of food products within the Soviet Union. I reminded him of his comments as far back as 1985, during our first meeting, on the problem of wastage and noted that the situation really had not changed since then. I personally questioned the wisdom of borrowing more money in order to funnel more grain into the profligate state sector. The loans in question must be paid off in three years, and that could place an increased burden on the Soviet economy just when the money would be needed to support economic reform.

Somewhere along the line, I also put in a plug for passage of the emigration bill. (I had been informed by its supporters in the Supreme Soviet, such as Fyodor Burlatsky, that it would be blocked unless Gorbachev gave it a strong personal push.)

Though Gorbachev often spoke at length, he was usually a good listener, except when his own people were involved. I probably talked as long as he had, yet he heard me out patiently, jotting down a note from time to time. Then he addressed many of my points.

As for the central economic ministries, he remarked that of course they must be abolished, but he could not do it overnight or chaos would result. The present state, therefore, was only a temporary expedient, to permit a rational transition to a market system. Already, the new minister of the chemical industry was working out a plan for his ministry's abolition, he asserted.

Regarding the emigration bill, he claimed that there was concern over how much it would cost and how to implement it but seemed optimistic that it would pass. I pointed out that the current text of the law provided adequate time for administrative authorities to implement it and I hoped this would not be used as a pretext for further delay.

We agreed that I would convey his views to President Bush, and I assured him that the latter still remained very much committed to work in partnership.

Nevertheless, Gorbachev was still in a truculent mood when he met newspaper magnate Rupert Murdoch the following day. In fact, he indulged in even more cutting comments in public than he had with me the day before. Speaking in the presence of reporters, he went so far as to suggest that the Bush administration was risking a new cold war.

Gorbachev's *cri de cœur* galvanized President Bush. Just as he had after a similar, but vaguer, message two years before, he reacted rapidly with assurances of his continued commitment to the relationship. It happened that Bush was scheduled to meet with three Baltic leaders— Parliament Chairman Vytautas Landsbergis of Lithuania and Prime Ministers Edgar Savisaar and Ivars Godmanis of Estonia and Latvia— on May 8. The report of my conversation with Gorbachev had arrived the day before, and news of Gorbachev's public comments during his meeting with Murdoch came in that morning. They made such a deep impression on the president that he seemed to forget who his visitors were. Implausibly, indeed incredibly, he used their visit to heap public praise on Gorbachev.

Even before he met the Baltic leaders, Bush told reporters that he would tell them about his "strong and, I think, good relationship" with Gorbachev, whose accomplishments had been "enormous." Since the Balts had come seeking U.S. support for their independence and viewed Gorbachev as totally unsympathetic, Bush's words, in the context of their meeting, seemed almost an insult. They concluded, incorrectly, that Bush had probably entered into the sort of deal they had feared and suspected from Malta on: that the United States would turn a blind eye to their plight if Gorbachev let the Eastern Europeans go their own way. The strong statements from Washington in January had put most of these suspicions to rest, but now they were aroused again, to no good purpose.

It was not that Bush should have used his meeting with the Balts to criticize Gorbachev. That would have been neither appropriate nor useful. And it would not have hurt to tell them in private that he was convinced Gorbachev was trying to prevent the hard-liners from using violence against them. But the focus of attention during their visit should have been on the United States' commitment to their freedom. A different, unrelated occasion could have been found to reassure Gorbachev, whose suspicions were unfounded and self-serving.

Gorbachev ignored the fact that most of the criticism emanating from Washington was his own fault. Given the crackdown Gorbachev had permitted at home, the violence he was unable to control in the Baltic states and elsewhere, his passivity when his generals backtracked on solemn agreements, and his tolerance of senior officials who baited the West with unfounded accusations, President Bush could have compiled a much more impressive list of gripes than Gorbachev had managed.

There was no need for Bush to go overboard with "assurances" or react as if he had been the negligent party. Nevertheless, he obviously had empathy for his colleague in distress and reacted in a manner that suggested to Gorbachev that, whenever he needed something from Bush, all he had to do was complain that George's affections had cooled.

Bush did not confine his reaction to public statements during the Baltic visit, however. He also—and much more appropriately—immediately sent Gorbachev a letter designed to calm the anxieties he had expressed. On Saturday, May 11, he called him directly on the telephone. He assured him that he had not rejected the request for credit guarantees but was still working through some of the legal technicalities. Meanwhile, he offered to send a high-level delegation headed by Under Secretary of Agriculture Richard Crowder to study ways in which the United States might help with pilot projects to improve food distribution. It wasn't much, but it was well meant, and Gorbachev agreed to see the delegation when they came.

When I delivered the president's letter to Chernyayev at the end of the week, I also tried to clarify some of the other complaints Gorbachev had made. Jim May, our commercial counselor, had been unable to discover any recent refusals of export licenses for the computers he had mentioned, but he did learn that delivery of some of the computers ordered for the nuclear power stations had been delayed since payment had not been made as agreed. I gave Chernyayev a paper describing the situation and told him, "Somebody has convinced your president that we are blocking shipment of these computers, but that is nonsense. Your bureaucrats simply didn't pay the invoice on time and are trying to shift the blame to someone else."

Chernyayev chuckled in response, muttering something like "They're the same the world over," and assured me that he would set Gorbachev straight. He also noted that he must make sure that Gorbachev gave Moiseyev his instructions before the latter left for Washington.

The main questions still at issue regarding the CFE treaty were relatively small in substance but important in principle. The Soviets had assigned equipment to naval infantry units in Murmansk and the Crimea that they wanted to exclude from the ceilings the agreement imposed. They also argued that equipment in units guarding strategic missile sites should not be counted. The agreement, however, did not provide for these exceptions.

Moiseyev came to Washington on May 20 with some new proposals and discussed them directly with President Bush as well as with senior officials in the State Department and the Department of Defense. During these discussions he argued that these units had a mission related to internal rather than external security; in effect, they were to be used in case of domestic disturbances, not a conflict with the West. The Americans were sympathetic when it was a matter of defending missile sites but felt they had to be strict in applying the negotiated limits to the naval infantry units, which were, after all, clearly covered by the language in the treaty.

Moiseyev's visit cleared the air somewhat, but his proposal was not acceptable to the United States. However, shortly after he returned to Moscow he notified us that he thought he had found a solution, and in fact agreement was reached when Baker and Bessmertnykh met in Lisbon on June 1. On June 14, all the ambassadors to the CFE negotiations gathered in Vienna to confirm agreement on the disputed interpretations. Finally, President Bush could send the CFE treaty to the Senate for ratification.

As for the credit guarantees, several weeks passed before President Bush made a final decision. In the meantime, the Crowder delegation came to Moscow as proposed and discussed several pilot projects with Soviet agriculture officials. Gorbachev offered the group a lengthy meeting, enthusiastically endorsed the idea of projects, but bridled when Crowder explained that they needed more information on the Soviet Union's creditworthiness.

"We have always paid off these credits punctually," he said with heat. "I have given you my word. To ask for more is an insult!" When Crowder explained that our legislation required us to obtain data to support a determination of creditworthiness, which was in no sense an insult, Gorbachev rejected the explanation.

Whenever Gorbachev vented his frustration, he rarely confined himself to the issue in question but lashed out in whatever direction happened to come to mind. In this meeting, he asserted that President Bush had surrounded himself with "anti-Soviet advisers" who were feeding him false information. He even named Robert Gates, the career CIA official who was deputy to National Security Adviser Scowcroft and had been nominated by Bush to be director of central intelligence.

As I listened to this complaint, I became outraged. If anyone had a valid complaint about being given false information, we did. Kryuchkov and the KGB were obviously reporting fabrications to him—as I had

had occasion, more than once, to point out. U.S. intelligence and Gates personally had never, to my knowledge, lied to the president. Our interpretations of events might differ, but they were always honestly presented as opinion and not camouflaged as pseudofact. I was not about to let Gorbachev's comment pass unchallenged.

Without waiting for his accusations to be translated into English for the benefit of our visitors, I broke in in Russian, "What you say is not correct and is unfair. Gates is much less anti-Soviet than Kryuchkov is anti-American!"

Gorbachev muttered that he had his opinion of Gates just as we had ours of Kryuchkov and returned to his request for credit guarantees. "I have personally asked President Bush for the credits," he stated. "If he wants to grant them, fine. If not, that's his business."

On June 11, I delivered a letter to Gorbachev notifying him that the request for $1.5 billion in credit guarantees for grain purchases had been approved.

Searching for Support

GORBACHEV'S PROFESSED WORRIES about Bush's continued commitment to the relationship were in part stimulated by distorted reports from the KGB, but he nevertheless had reasons for concern, though not about the U.S. president's personal loyalty. By the spring of 1991, the Soviet economy was obviously headed for collapse. All the prescriptions for a cure contained possibly lethal doses of political poison, and Gorbachev began to dream of a *deus ex machina.* If only his friends in the advanced industrial countries could get together and mobilize a massive international rescue effort! After all, they had poured scores of billions into saving tiny Kuwait and risked lives to boot. Surely it would be worth that and more to transform a deadly threat into a cooperative partnership. And, besides, they were all buddies, who by now—in private, at least—had pledged their undying support. The mere $20 billion or $30 billion a year that might keep him in office would be only a fraction of what they had already saved via the reductions in defense budgets his policies had made possible.

And thus Gorbachev began to dream of joining the heads of the world's leading economic powers at their next G-7 meeting, scheduled for London in July. In fact, he was hoping for an invitation to become the eighth member of that exclusive club.[4] In April and May, Gorbachev started sounding out members of the "Seven"—usually during private telephone calls—about the possibility of an invitation to London.

When I learned of these—still private—probes in early May, they worried me. It was not that I doubted that he would get an invitation: none of the G-7 leaders would want to offend him or to increase his problems at home by a public rejection. But there was no realistic possibility that he would come home from the meeting with large commitments of aid or full membership in the organization.

All the countries in the Group of Seven were facing fiscal and political problems that would make aid to the Soviet Union a hard sell: the United States had a growing budget deficit, it had recently adopted a controversial tax increase, and the president was facing an election campaign the following year during which any support for additional foreign aid would likely be considered suicidal; Germany was just beginning to realize the magnitude of the resources required to bring the eastern *Länder* to the level of the West; Japan still insisted on return of the southern Kuriles before substantial aid could be made available, and it was obvious that Gorbachev was not strong enough politically to cede the territory—certainly not so soon after the "loss" of Eastern Europe. And so on: each member would have cogent reasons for opting out of giving all but modest assistance.

Furthermore, the Soviet Union did not yet have an approach to reform that would permit the constructive use of foreign aid. The sorts of things Gorbachev wanted—large loans, support for currency stabilization, debt restructuring—would merely provide life support for a brain-dead system. Some of these things would make reform more difficult rather than ease the way. For foreign aid to be relevant, Gorbachev needed a credible program that would have some chance of success.

I also feared that, unless Gorbachev's involvement with the Group of Seven was presented to the Soviet public with unusual delicacy, it could backfire in public opinion. Unless the public received the impression that Gorbachev was attending the meeting because he was invited, not because he had invited himself, and also that he was going to discuss world economic issues, not assistance to the Soviet Union, he would be accused of begging for aid and—when the results turned out to be meager—of having been rejected. Gorbachev's team had proved to be extraordinarily inept in presenting economic policy to the public.

I discussed these concerns with my Soviet contacts in May, suggesting that they wait for an invitation without going public and in the meantime work on a program that would carry greater conviction than Pavlov's retrograde "anticrisis program." I also encouraged them to stress that Gorbachev was going to London because the Soviet Union was entering the world economy and wished its views to be heard by the other principal powers. If, in fact, new measures of cooperation emerged, this would be good news, but the public should be encouraged to think that the trip was not one primarily in pursuit of foreign aid.

My advice regarding presentation to the public fell on deaf ears—by mid-May reports began to appear in the media that Gorbachev was fishing for an invitation,[5] and then, when Italian Prime Minister Giulio Andreotti visited Moscow on May 22, Gorbachev himself made his request public when he stated to journalists, "It is vital that the Soviet Union have the possibility of making its views known at the meetings of the Group of Seven," making it clear that what he had in mind was massive economic assistance to the Soviet Union.[6]

Regarding the substance of Gorbachev's presentation, on the other hand, I soon had reason to be more optimistic. The first hint I received that there might be a serious effort to develop a realistic reform program came when I called on Yevgeny Primakov on May 7—the same day Gorbachev complained to me about Bush's cooling affection. I had requested the appointment as a courtesy call on Primakov in his new capacity as a member of Gorbachev's Security Council and was expecting to discuss outstanding arms control issues with him.

Primakov's office was spacious and in the same Kremlin building as Gorbachev's, indicating that Gorbachev intended to grant the Security Council at least the trappings of power. In Washington terms, it was like getting a window office in the West Wing of the White House. When I mentioned some current security issues, Primakov told me that he would not be dealing primarily with security but with international economics. He then said that his initial task would be to develop a strategy for bringing the Soviet Union into contact with the principal international economic institutions: the General Agreement on Tariffs and Trade (GATT), the World Bank, the International Monetary Fund (IMF)—and the Group of Seven. He also repeated some of the complaints Gorbachev had made that morning about U.S. policy, and I gave him the same answers.

I told him that I had yet to find a foreign economist who thought that the "anticrisis program" would work and asked whether Gorbachev was giving any thought to modifying it before he went to London—assuming, as seemed likely, that an invitation would be forthcoming. Primakov replied that, indeed, more work was being done. He said that he himself had coauthored an article with Grigory Yavlinsky for presentation to an international economic forum and that further work would continue along the same lines.

Four days later, on May 11, Gorbachev told Bush during a telephone conversation that he had asked Yavlinsky to work on a new program of economic reform and would send him to Washington with Primakov to brief Bush and others on it. Bush readily agreed to receive them.

A Window of Opportunity?

YAVLINSKY'S RENEWED INVOLVEMENT in planning for reform was good news. After Gorbachev had rejected the "500-Day Plan" and Yavlinsky had learned that the RSFSR was not able to pursue reform on its own, he had, in late 1990, resigned his position as deputy prime minister of the RSFSR. Since then he had headed an economic institute in Moscow. To my mind, his ideas were the most practical, among the welter of competing plans and programs, for creating market conditions in the Soviet economy.

Early the next week I went by to see Yavlinsky. He told me he was convinced that Gorbachev was now finally committed to undertaking more radical reform measures. Yavlinsky had attended a recent Cabinet meeting during which Gorbachev had made stinging comments about Pavlov's "anticrisis program" on five different occasions. Gorbachev had told the group that every foreign leader he had spoken to, including President Bush, President Mitterrand, and Chancellor Kohl, had told him the program wouldn't work and had added at one point, "Even the American ambassador tells me it's no good, and he knows the country pretty well." (So much for my relations with Pavlov, I thought to myself—but that didn't matter, since I didn't expect anything from him anyway. I did wonder, though, how Gorbachev could depend on the loyalty of his senior officials if he bullied them this way, even when they deserved it.)

In sum, Yavlinsky was sure that Gorbachev now recognized the shortcomings of Pavlov's plan. He said Gorbachev had personally assured him of his support; for his part, Yavlinsky had made it clear that he would withdraw from the effort if his ideas were not eventually accepted.

Yavlinsky also explained that he considered some parts of the "500-Day Plan" no longer workable. Furthermore, he recognized that the earlier plan had not been sufficiently realistic politically. He intended to go to Harvard the following week to work on these problems with Professor Graham Allison. He would then join Primakov in Washington for calls on U.S. officials, as Gorbachev and Bush had agreed on the telephone.

I explained to him my concern about the possibility of public misunderstanding if Gorbachev's meeting in London was viewed as primarily a quest for aid. Yavlinsky seemed to understand my point but felt that the prospect of the London meeting was Gorbachev's main incentive for considering an effective reform program, and therefore he wanted to use it as a spur.

Yavlinsky seemed to understand that it was important to have a program that could inspire Western confidence that the USSR was cutting back on the military-industrial complex, moving seriously to a market system, and at the same time reducing tensions with the republics. He hoped that a realistic program would attract Western support in whatever forms were appropriate. Unlike Gorbachev, he was skeptical about credits unless they were tied to specific reforms. I could only agree with him when he observed that credits were not the primary issue. "Money will play a role, of course," he said, "but whether the priority is in third place, fifteenth place, or twenty fifth, remains to be seen." The point was that any material assistance should be part of a properly sequenced, synergistic program of action undertaken by the Soviet Union itself.

Graham Allison, Yavlinsky's Harvard partner, was also in Moscow that week and I took the opportunity to discuss the project with him. We had met a few years back when I participated in a seminar at Harvard on U.S.-Soviet relations and had maintained sporadic contact since then. He consistently impressed me with his insights into Soviet reality and his balanced assessment of future possibilities.

Allison explained that Yavlinsky would prepare the economic recommendations in their joint report, while he and his colleagues at Harvard would work on the political problems. The goal would be to blend the two so that the program would take into account political factors better than the "500-Day Plan" did. In particular, Allison felt that there had to be a real and substantial transfer of authority to the republics, along with efforts to develop democratic institutions and enhance openness in economic and financial management.

His thoughts on these points were identical to mine, but I pointed out that it would be essential to find some realistic mechanism to deal with the social problems created by rapid contraction of the defense industry. Current plans for gradual "conversion" to civilian industry were not working, yet the country could not risk simply closing defense plants and throwing millions of workers out on the street. I suggested that the group consider something like a G.I. Bill for the defense industry: unemployment benefits and a program of retraining, to ease the transition. While expensive, it would cost less than keeping unneeded defense plants open.

On May 19, Yavlinsky and Allison went to Massachusetts to immerse themselves in work on a program that Yavlinsky called "Window of Opportunity"[7] and Allison "The Grand Bargain." While I understood and agreed with the logic behind the "Grand Bargain" (the West would support economic reform in the Soviet Union if the Soviet Union would commit itself to democracy and partnership), I preferred the Russian label. "Window of Opportunity" implied that it was an opportunity for all parties to act in their own interest. This seemed to me to be a sounder way to think of the issue than as a negotiation of conflicting interests, which the word "bargain" implied. Nevertheless, the substance was more important than the label, and all parties seemed to understand that they faced an uphill fight if they were to obtain Western assistance on the scale needed. They were convinced, however, that Gorbachev would support the program within the Soviet Union.

While Gorbachev obviously hoped his Western friends could bail him out, his public statements began to show flashes of realism. The evening of my meeting with Yavlinsky, I watched televised excerpts from a speech Gorbachev had made to the Cabinet that day. After citing some dismal economic statistics, he said that outsiders could not save the situation for them; the Soviet Union had to "rescue itself." "With this kind of economy, not even a hundred billion dollars can put it right," he added. Nevertheless, in private he kept using the $100 billion figure with his foreign friends. He also intensified his lobbying for a massive program of foreign aid. One of his significant converts was Margaret Thatcher.

Lady Thatcher came to Moscow toward the end of May as the personal guest of the Gorbachevs. Though I had met her in Washington some years back, when I had served as note taker during her private meetings with President Reagan, I did not anticipate that she would either remember me or have any desire to see me while she was in Moscow. Therefore, it was a surprise when my British colleague, Sir Rodric Braithwaite, telephoned to say that Mrs. Thatcher wished to discuss her meetings with Gorbachev with me. Since she would be dining with the Gorbachevs, the Braithwaites suggested that I have dinner with them so that I would be on hand when Thatcher returned from the Gorbachev dacha. I was delighted at the opportunity, not least because I knew that the Braithwaites were among the keenest observers of the Soviet scene; the evening would be well worthwhile quite apart from the chance to hear the former prime minister's views.

Lady Thatcher returned to the British residence, just across the Moscow River from the Kremlin, shortly before 10:00 P.M. and joined us in Sir Rodric's study. From its windows we had a magnificent view of the Kremlin walls and the buildings within, all resplendent under powerful searchlights. The imposing yet serene sight belied the political maelstrom that was raging within those meticulously preserved ancient walls.

Settling down with an after-dinner drink in hand, she came right to the point: "Please get a message to my friend George," she requested. "We've got to help Mikhail. Of course, you Americans can't and shouldn't have to do it all yourselves, but George will have to lead the effort, just as he did with Kuwait."

She paused, then began to explain why she felt so strongly. "Just a few years back, Ron and I would have given the world to get what has already happened here." Now that Gorbachev had helped end the cold war and set a course of real reform, "history will not forgive us," if we fail to rally to his support, she continued. The evening's conversation with both Gorbachevs had convinced her that he was now ready to restore full private property rights, even though he might not yet consider it timely to say so publicly. But she also had the impression that his political position had become desperate.

She urged that Gorbachev be invited to attend the G-7 summit in

London and that he not be sent home empty-handed. She felt that all the allies should pitch in and help but that it would take the pressure of the United States to force them to "do their duty." She was aware that Germany had already promised substantial aid but felt that the Germans should do more, since up to then they had just been paying a price for their unification. And the Japanese should be encouraged to put their territorial claims on hold until the Soviet Union was more stable. If Gorbachev granted their demands now, it could bring him down, and this was a risk that neither they nor the rest of the free world should run.

I assured her that I would send her message to President Bush and that I agreed with her on the stake we all had in Soviet reform. I was confident that President Bush wanted to help in any way he could. However, we had to face the practical difficulties in formulating an effective assistance program. The unfortunate fact was that Gorbachev had not yet adopted policies that made foreign assistance relevant: the budget deficit was out of control, there were as yet no effective plans to separate social services from state industry, private enterprise was not yet protected, most of the economy was still in the grip of monopolies, and there was still no strategy for building the institutions necessary for a market system. To pour money into the country at this time would do no good and might do a lot of harm.

"You're talking like a diplomat!" She glared at me. "Just finding excuses for doing nothing. Why can't you think like a statesman? We need a political decision to support this process, which is so much in everyone's interest."

Then, shifting to a less strident tone, she mused that Gorbachev was quite right to point out that the same sort of energy that President Bush had applied to defending Kuwait was needed to assist the Soviet Union through its transition. "Only American leadership can do it," she concluded, "and make sure my friend George gets my message."

When I returned to Spaso House, I drafted a telegram to the president informing him of Lady Thatcher's views. I then made the following entry in my journal:

> I think that Mrs. Thatcher is right. One can find many excuses, indeed reasons, for doing nothing, but there is no question that the further evolution of the Soviet Union toward openness and democracy is

in the West's vital interest. Our leaders will simply be bereft of wisdom or courage, or both, if they fail to respond to the challenge. Aid, of course, should be contingent, and should be tied to specific projects or objectives. But we should organize a very substantial program to support and help guide the reform effort here.

There were of course sound reasons for refusing to throw money indiscriminately at the problem—some of which I had mentioned to Lady Thatcher—but basically she was right. These were excuses for not trying to devise a rescue effort that could succeed. For that we would have to work with Gorbachev (and Yeltsin) to build an international structure that would encourage effective steps to transform the Soviet economy, one that would help Gorbachev make the right decisions and sell them to his public. Yavlinsky was right. Money was not the main point, though a time would come when some money would be required.

The opportunity was clear, but I was not optimistic that it would be seized. Although President Bush was sympathetic to Gorbachev's problems and committed to support him politically, he did not seem willing to organize an international structure to help bring the Soviet Union into the world economy as a constructive partner. He lacked the vision of how his leadership might shape the future and thus chose a reactive stance: waiting for Gorbachev to find the keys to reform for himself, he would from time to time mumble words of either encouragement or reproach, carefully avoiding commitments to specific action.

Yet maybe the Yavlinsky-Allison study would provide a stimulus for a more imaginative policy. Maybe lobbying by old friends like Margaret Thatcher would galvanize Bush.

In May and June 1991, I was grasping for evidence that Gorbachev's policies might change and that something might happen to convince my own government that we had enough at stake to try to help Gorbachev find constructive answers to his problems.

A Warning to the Deaf

GORBACHEV WAS CONCENTRATING on how he would approach the Group of Seven in London when he was confronted by a very strange legislative maneuver. On June 17, Prime Minister Valentin Pavlov, constitutionally the head of the president's Cabinet, asked the USSR Supreme Soviet to grant him certain extraordinary powers that up to then had been granted to the president alone.[8] When questioned, he stated that he had not discussed the proposal with Gorbachev. In effect, he was asking for his boss's power without even checking with the boss.

Pavlov's speech was to an open session of the Supreme Soviet, but the assembly went into executive session to discuss it. KGB Chairman Kryuchkov, Minister of Defense Yazov, and Minister of Internal Affairs Pugo supported it vigorously. Summaries of their speeches immediately leaked to the press,[9] and most political observers were aghast: how could four senior Cabinet officials maneuver to undermine the president's authority? they wondered. And having thus challenged the president, how could they be left in their jobs? After all, it was as if the secretaries of state and defense, along with the director of central intelligence and the head of the FBI, had gone to the U.S. Congress without the knowledge of the president and asked that they be allowed to overrule the president.

Gorbachev had the power to appoint and dismiss all these officials, yet his immediate reaction to Pavlov's proposal was confined to a statement that he had not endorsed it. Some Soviet observers thought he must have secretly encouraged the maneuver, for reasons none could explain. Knowing how jealous he was of his power, I doubted he had been behind the maneuver, yet I found his inaction inexplicable. I discussed the matter with Soviet politicians, journalists, and diplomatic colleagues, and nobody seemed to have a likely explanation for what was going on. Still searching for answers, I invited several political leaders, including Moscow's Mayor Popov (who, like Yeltsin, had just won election), to lunch on June 20.

Yeltsin was in Washington that week. He had just been elected president of the RSFSR, though he had not yet been inaugurated into that office, and he had an appointment to see President Bush in the Oval Office at 10:00 A.M. on Thursday, June 20.

Midmorning on Thursday, a staffer in the mayor's office telephoned to say that Popov would be unable to attend the luncheon but would like to call on me beforehand to say farewell, since he might not have another opportunity before my scheduled departure from Moscow in early August. I sent word that I could see him at noon, lunch being scheduled for one o'clock.

Popov arrived promptly and joined me in the Spaso House library. The butler brought a tray of drinks, but we both asked for coffee. I congratulated Popov on his election, and he asked about my plans after leaving Moscow. Then, when the butler had closed the door, he took out a sheet of paper and, as we talked, scribbled a note, then handed it to me. There, in a large, uneven Russian scrawl was the message:

A COUP IS BEING ORGANIZED TO REMOVE GORBACHEV. WE MUST GET WORD TO BORIS NIKOLAYEVICH.

Careful to keep the conversation flowing as naturally as I could manage, I scribbled in Russian on the same sheet:

I'LL SEND A MESSAGE. BUT WHO IS BEHIND THIS?[10]

Popov glanced at my note, wrote a few more words, and shoved the paper back to me. On it I saw the following names:

PAVLOV, KRYUCHKOV, YAZOV, LUKYANOV

When I had read the note, Popov retrieved it, tore it into small bits, and thrust them into his pocket.

Our conversation continued for another ten or fifteen minutes. There was no need to raise suspicions by ending the meeting abruptly. We talked about the election campaign, Popov's plans for the further development of Moscow, and his assessment of the prospects for a private sector. It was probably an adequate cover for the KGB microphones, though neither of us paid much attention to what we were saying.

Popov left around 12:30 and I hurriedly scribbled a message, placed it in a sealed envelope, and sent it by a U.S. Embassy officer to my deputy, Jim Collins, with instructions to convey it to Washington by the most rapid and secure method available. It was to go to Secretary of State Baker (who was then in Berlin), Brent Scowcroft, the president's assistant for national security, and the president, with no further distribution unless they directed.[11] Because of the time difference, a few hours remained before President Bush was to meet Yeltsin.

Later in the afternoon, I received a call by secure telephone from Under Secretary of State Robert Kimmitt, who told me that President Bush would pass the message to Yeltsin but that I should go to Gorbachev and warn him. I agreed but told him that while President Bush should of course tell Yeltsin that the message was from Popov, it was important not to reveal my source to anyone else. Also, I thought it not proper to name any individuals. We had no independent confirmation that Kryuchkov or the others were in fact plotting against Gorbachev. Therefore, I proposed to tell Gorbachev simply that we had a report that we could not confirm but of which he should be aware, namely that there was an effort under way to remove him. Kimmitt agreed that this was a reasonable approach and assured me that all understood the importance of not citing Popov, except directly to Yeltsin.

Even if our information had been more precise, I would have hesitated to give Gorbachev the names of the reported conspirators. How could the American ambassador credibly tell the chief of state of a power that until very recently had been an adversary that his prime minister, intelligence chief, minister of defense, and speaker of parliament were conspiring against him? Would it not smack of self-serving meddling, a flagrant attempt to sow suspicion and discord? No, if there was anything to this, Gorbachev would have to be shrewd enough to figure it out for himself. Considering what was happening at the Supreme Soviet, he should not require much prompting.

I telephoned Chernyayev and requested an urgent appointment with Gorbachev. A few minutes later he called to say I should come right over. It was early evening in Moscow, but still broad daylight, since it was the day before the summer solstice. Gorbachev was getting ready to leave the office when I entered, accompanied only by Chernyayev, since I brought no note taker. He was in a mellow mood and seemed to be in no hurry to hear what I had come to say.

Greeting me as "Comrade Ambassador," he asked me not to take offense—he was not implying that I was serving any interests other than those of my country—but they had come to think of me as a member of a joint team to harmonize U.S. and Soviet policies. I had become, he continued, an influential member of their society and a strong supporter not only of better understanding between our countries but also of reform within the Soviet Union. As he had remarked in a previous meeting, he could not understand why I would choose to leave at such a crucial time, just when both countries needed me to help keep things on track. He hoped that we could meet for a more lengthy farewell when he returned from the G-7 meeting in London the following month.

Gorbachev's praise made me uncomfortable, and it must have showed. At least Chernyayev noticed, as he reported in his account of the conversation.[12] I was preoccupied with the message I had been instructed to deliver, and as one compliment followed another from Gorbachev's lips, I could only think to myself, "How will I ever put this into a report?" Normally I would report any conversation with Gorbachev as near verbatim as memory and scanty notes permitted, but if I repeated, even in paraphrase, Gorbachev's compliments, it would reek of self-promotion, and some officials, always quick to discern any hint of arrogance on the part of colleagues, might even suspect that I had deliberately exaggerated his words. I decided to ignore the whole exchange in my report, covering it with a brief reference to his rhetorical query as to why I was leaving so soon.

We sat down at the long table in his office, by then quite familiar to me, I facing the window and Gorbachev and Chernyayev on the opposite side. Gorbachev asked why President Bush had sent me. Using words I had prepared carefully, I said, "Mr. President, President Bush has asked me to notify you of a report we have received which we find greatly disturbing, although we cannot confirm it. It is based on more than rumor but less than hard information. It is that there is an effort under way to remove you, and it could happen at any time, even this week."

Gorbachev shook his head and chuckled, then grew serious. "Tell President Bush I am touched. I have felt for some time that we are partners, and now he has proved it. Thank him for his concern. He has done just what a friend should do. But tell him not to worry. I have everything well in hand. You'll see tomorrow."

I told him that I was pleased to learn that the report had no foundation. As I had said, we could not confirm it, although it seemed serious enough to warrant attention, and President Bush felt an obligation to let Gorbachev know.

Gorbachev then lapsed into the sort of soliloquy of which he was fond. He conceded that there could be talk, here and there, of overthrowing the government. Times were unsettled. Pavlov, while a competent economist, was not an experienced politician and was still learning. He had already recognized the mistake he had made Monday. But there had been of late a distinct movement toward political conciliation. Habits of cooperation were even being developed with Yeltsin. The union treaty would soon be signed, and his visit to London for the G-7 meeting would represent a further step into the world economy. The public supported economic reform and had showed it when they had voted for Yeltsin, but they also wanted an end to political confrontation.

Nevertheless, Gorbachev continued, there were forces that were trying to block reform. Some of them were even in parliament. This was the attitude of many in Soyuz, though not all its members felt that way. The discontented were against the healing process that was under way. He didn't exclude the possibility that some of them had been talking about overthrowing the government, and maybe that was the basis of our report.[13]

I told Gorbachev that I was relieved to hear that things were moving in the right direction and that in particular it was encouraging to see his developing cooperation with Yeltsin. If that should break down, it would be difficult to view the future with optimism.

As he saw me out, he repeated that I would see tomorrow that he had matters under control. And, in fact, the next day he went before the Supreme Soviet and obtained an overwhelming vote to reject Pavlov's request for additional power. In doing so, however, he inexplicably went out of his way to attack those who were trying to "drive a wedge" between the two of them. I was glad I had decided not to name Pavlov and the others, since this would probably have heightened Gorbachev's suspicion of the report. It was only later that I realized that Gorbachev may have thought that our report had come from grumbling by the likes of Colonel Alksnis rather than from the machinations of those who were trying to persuade the Supreme Soviet to curb his power.

Was Popov's report a false alarm (as it may have seemed on the weekend of June 22–23), or was it an accurate report of plans that were postponed to a more propitious time, when Gorbachev would be out of Moscow but under KGB control in the Soviet Union? Only the persons named know for sure, but circumstantial evidence supports the latter interpretation.

However that may be, the way the report was handled by both presidents, and by the American secretary of state, revealed amateurish flaws in their modes of operation. What I did not know on June 20 but learned later was that, even before Popov's message was given to Yeltsin, Secretary of State Baker had insisted on an urgent meeting with Soviet Foreign Minister Bessmertnykh in Berlin and had conveyed to him the substance (though not the source) of the report.

It should have been clear to anyone with even an elementary knowledge of Soviet procedures that, however good his intentions, there was nothing Bessmertnykh could do to alert Gorbachev. All Soviet official communications were controlled by the KGB, and one of the prime conspirators was reported to be the KGB chief. To his credit, Bessmertnykh told Baker that, given the persons allegedly involved, he could not get a private message to Gorbachev and if we wished to alert him, I would have to do it. That should have been obvious from the start, and apprising Bessmertnykh of a sensitive report when he could not possibly do anything about it was the height of folly. Even if he had a means of secure communication, he might well have hesitated to pass on an unsubstantiated report from a foreign source about his Cabinet colleagues.

While Baker's reaction was thoughtless, President Bush's was reckless. When he telephoned Gorbachev to assure him that Yeltsin had done nothing disloyal while in Washington, he told Gorbachev that Popov had been the source of the report. This on a telephone line monitored by the KGB! I was informed after the conversation that, despite our earlier agreement, the president had "let slip the identity of the source" during his conversation with Gorbachev. I would not have expected this from a former head of the CIA, who prided himself on professionalism and was quick to condemn any leak of the most trivial information, but it was a measure of how deep his infatuation with Gorbachev had gone.

Popov later told me that the next time Gorbachev saw him—ironically during the state dinner when President Bush visited Moscow in July—he shook his finger at him and said, "Why are you telling tales to the Americans?" And when the group he had fingered tried to take power from Gorbachev a scant three weeks later, Popov's name was near the top of the list of persons scheduled for arrest. One shudders at the possible consequences of George Bush's indiscretion if the coup had succeeded.

And what about Gorbachev? He was the one with the most to lose, and yet he was acting like a somnambulist, wandering around oblivious to his surroundings. He had dismissed and resented Shevardnadze's warnings of December, sacrificed loyal aides like Bakatin, ignored the advice of Alexander Yakovlev and others who had helped him craft perestroika to begin with, and continued to trust the duplicitous Kryuchkov and an impudent clown like Pavlov.

According to Chernyayev, the report I brought on June 20 did lead to some momentary concern, even though Gorbachev joked about American credulity. But then he recalled that Yevgeny Primakov had warned him just the day before that he should not place too much trust in the KGB and his personal security guard. Gorbachev had been inclined to dismiss Primakov's suspicions as a reflection of bureaucratic jealousy, but Chernyayev advised him to pay attention. For his part, he recalled that he had heard reports of suspicious military movements in Moscow.

Nevertheless, despite a firm speech in the Supreme Soviet on June 21, Gorbachev took no concrete steps to make it difficult for his security chief to cooperate in a coup attempt.[14]

Bessmertnykh returned to Moscow on June 21 and accompanied Gorbachev to a wreath laying the following day. During a few moments in private he mentioned his conversation with Baker in Berlin and inquired whether Gorbachev had gotten the message from me. Gorbachev assured him that he had and added that he had given "those officials" a good talking to. He then asked whether Baker had mentioned any particular time when the coup was supposed to take place, and Bessmertnykh replied that no specific date had been mentioned but that Baker had said something like "it could happen any day now."[15] Bessmertnykh inferred that Gorbachev had deduced the identity of the persons named in the report, but in retrospect it seems that Gorbachev actually had in mind the Soyuz leaders he had criticized in his speech to the Supreme Soviet.

When I asked Popov, in March 1992, for permission to write about this incident, he readily agreed, then commented that at first he had been furious when he learned that Gorbachev had been told that he was the source of the report. After all, his message had not been for us, to use as we pleased, but for Yeltsin, and he had staked much on our reliability in delivering it. Nevertheless, in retrospect, he felt that the leak might have turned out to be beneficial.

"When the plotters learned that I was getting information about their conspiracy, they had to limit their plans to so few people that they could no longer plan the coup properly. That may well have contributed to their failure," he surmised.[16]

Well, maybe. But that is an event still ahead of us.

Bureaucrats Win Another Round

EVEN AS YAVLINSKY AND ALLISON were working on their "Window
of Opportunity" (or "Grand Bargain") at Cambridge, bureaucrats in
Moscow started a campaign to nullify their effort. Although both Yavlinsky and Allison had been assured by Gorbachev that their project
would have his full backing, and although Anatoly Chernyayev had also
given them strong encouragement when they had briefed him in mid-
May, we learned a few days later that the Soviets were making an official
request for appointments for Vladimir Shcherbakov, Pavlov's principal
deputy, and Primakov with President Bush and Secretary Baker for the
end of the month. Gorbachev had told Bush on the telephone that he
would send Yavlinsky and Primakov to discuss new ideas, but now it
seemed that Shcherbakov and Primakov would be going to Washington
to defend Pavlov's "anticrisis program" and Yavlinsky would simply be
pushed aside.

I immediately called on Primakov to discuss the situation. I told him
that the president had welcomed Gorbachev's suggestion that he and
Yavlinsky come to Washington to discuss the project Yavlinsky was
working on at Harvard. Bush had understood that Yavlinsky's ideas
would be the focus of discussion and that Primakov's participation reflected Gorbachev's commitment to them. However, although Gorbachev certainly had the right to send anyone he wished to represent him in
Washington, he should be aware that an official delegation headed by a
representative of the prime minister was not what President Bush was
expecting.

Primakov said that Yavlinsky would be part of their group—the two
of them were working together—but there should be no mistake that
Shcherbakov would be the head of the delegation. I then asked what the
purpose of the group was. (We had understood from Gorbachev's proposal to Bush in their telephone conversation of May 11 that it was to
discuss Yavlinsky's ideas, but if that was the case, there was no reason to
make Shcherbakov head of the delegation.) Primakov replied that it was
to help Gorbachev prepare for his hoped-for meeting with the Group of
Seven in London; Gorbachev wanted to consult Bush in advance and
get his reaction.

"Fine," I observed. (I paraphrase from notes.) "I am sure the president will appreciate the consultation. However, you and your president should be aware of one thing—I am going to be blunt, to avoid any possible misunderstanding—President Bush and Secretary Baker are mainly interested in hearing Yavlinsky's ideas. If Shcherbakov's presence is meant to give these ideas official blessing, you will make a good impression. However, if this is a maneuver to upstage Yavlinsky and sell something like the 'anticrisis program' to our government, you're making a big mistake."

Primakov countered that Gorbachev would not approve any program that his government could not stomach. If there was going to be economic reform, it would have to be conducted in cooperation with the Pavlov government, not in opposition to it.

My heart sank. The issue had become one of bureaucratic politics, which was only to be expected, but Primakov's apparent backing for the Pavlov approach was a disappointment. Presumably, he had been given the economic portfolio on Gorbachev's new Security Council specifically to look for new approaches. There was abundant evidence, even aside from Yavlinsky's comments, that Gorbachev was dissatisfied with the "anticrisis program" and was ready to look for alternatives. However, his point man, Primakov, seemed to have thrown in his lot with the bureaucrats.

I replied, doubtless with some astringency in my voice, that of course any reform plan had to have the support of the government to be successful, but if he, Primakov, was advising his president to go to London with anything resembling the "anticrisis program," he was preparing the way for disaster. It would be better for Gorbachev not to go to London at all unless he had something better in his briefcase. I strongly advised Primakov to make sure that Yavlinsky had the opportunity to present his ideas to President Bush and other officials in Washington and to listen carefully to their reaction. Then he would be in a better position to advise Gorbachev on the most fruitful approach to take in London.

In order to head off a useless meeting, President Bush telephoned Gorbachev once again and stressed that he was looking forward to hearing what Yavlinsky had to say. Nevertheless, this did not prevent persistent efforts by Primakov to minimize Yavlinsky's participation in the Washington meetings. Consequently, they left a bad taste all around and undermined what faint hope remained in Washington that Gorbachev might be willing, finally, to adopt economic reforms with some prospect of success.[17]

The effect of the May 31 meeting on President Bush was just what I had predicted to Primakov: it convinced him that Gorbachev did not have a program that would justify committing large financial resources, and he began to doubt that it was in Gorbachev's interest to come to the G-7 meeting in London at all.[18] Unfortunately, he did not convey this directly or indirectly to Gorbachev (which might have served as a powerful wake-up call), and Gorbachev interpreted his hesitation over setting a date for a meeting in London simply as jockeying for advantage.[19] In the end, Kohl and Mitterrand, both of whom had promised Gorbachev to support an invitation, convinced Bush that it would be too damaging to Gorbachev's position if it appeared that he had been snubbed by the Group of Seven. By mid-June, Gorbachev had received an official invitation from British Prime Minister John Major to meet with the Seven—as a guest, following the formal meetings, not as a member of the group.

Despite the attempts to push him aside during the meetings in Washington at the end of May, Yavlinsky continued to work with Allison. In fact, they had been encouraged by positive remarks that both Bush and Baker had made during their meetings and were unaware of the damage Primakov's private comments had done.[20] By mid-June their draft was complete, and the authors sent a copy to Washington for the information of Bush and Baker and took one to Moscow for presentation to Gorbachev. Then, in Yavlinsky's words,

> In the middle of June, the program was presented to Bush, and his assistants told me they were sure he would find it of great interest. They also said that I should watch for a speech by Baker in Berlin later in June. . . . If it included a specific phrase, it would mean that the document had American support.
>
> I returned to Moscow and had one collision after another. I had a most difficult meeting with Burbulis,[21] but I told both Yeltsin, who had just been elected president, and Gorbachev about my understanding with the Americans: I was waiting to see if Baker would use the agreed phrase in his speech. They looked at me like—like a being from another planet. But Baker did use that phrase, and just at that time Yeltsin left for the United States. When he was asked about the program there, he said he had not read it yet. As for Gorbachev, his reaction was even more interesting: he turned the program over to Vadim

Medvedev to use in preparing his trip for London. . . . He assured me
that he always did it that way and that they would use all the good
parts of my program. When he did that, I understood very well what
"all the good parts" meant.[22]

On July 6, the Saturday before Gorbachev was scheduled to leave for
London, I received an urgent letter from Bush to Gorbachev. When I
called for an appointment to deliver it, I was told that Gorbachev was
working at a dacha outside Moscow but would receive me that afternoon. The Soviet chief of protocol came by in an official car to lead my
driver to the dacha complex at Volynskoye, to the west of the city. Gorbachev was working in one of the Stalin-era rest houses, which, according to my escorts, had often been used by Stalin himself.

When our cars pulled up to the main building, I noted that a number
of men were milling about, some in open shirts (it was a hot weekend
day), others with loosened ties and a jacket slung over the shoulder.
Gorbachev had apparently called a break in their meeting so he could
receive me privately.

The chief of protocol escorted me upstairs, and Gorbachev invited
me into a pleasant room that resembled a screened-in balcony. He was
wearing a crisp, short-sleeved white shirt and no tie. He thanked me for
bringing the letter out to him and remarked that he was meeting with his
advisers to prepare himself for London. I told him President Bush had
been favorably impressed by Yavlinsky's work, and he said he knew that
and that they were "making good use" of the ideas. We then discussed
the president's letter—it had to do with finishing off the remaining issues
in the negotiations on strategic nuclear weapons and setting a date for
Bush's trip to Moscow—but before leaving I asked Gorbachev how he
felt about his upcoming meetings in London.

He replied that he was feeling very good about them: the program he
was taking was shaping up very well, and he was looking forward to
"some very important discussions, some critical decisions." The pleasure of his anticipation seemed genuine; finally he was playing in the international big league, even on economic issues. He seemed remarkably
relaxed and confident, given all he had gone through during the past
weeks—and months.

As I left, I shook hands with the officials who were lounging about
waiting for their meeting to resume: Prime Minister Pavlov (who
smirked as I greeted him); his deputy, Vladimir Shcherbakov; Yevgeny

Primakov; Presidential Adviser Stepan Sitaryan; Ryzhkov's deputy for economic reform, Leonid Abalkin; and several others. Grigory Yavlinsky and those associated with him were not there. Nor was Stanislav Shatalin, Oleg Bogomolov, Nikolai Petrakov, or Vladlen Martynov—or anyone else associated with genuine movement to a market economy.

As I drove back into town, I felt optimistic that we would soon settle the issues that had delayed an agreement to reduce strategic nuclear weapons and that we would arrange a summit meeting by the end of the month. But I also knew for certain that Gorbachev would not be able to take advantage of whatever opportunity the London meeting might offer. The bureaucrats who had piloted the economy into its tailspin were still sitting in the cockpit.

Friends in Spirit, but in Need?

GORBACHEV'S MEETINGS IN LONDON did not bring public humiliation, yet they produced nothing that would not have materialized without the meetings. The "Seven" agreed to grant the Soviet Union associate membership in the International Monetary Fund and its sister institution, the World Bank, and to instruct those organizations to work out programs to assist the Soviet transition to a market economy.[23]

As for the United States, President Bush had informed Gorbachev by letter a few days before both left for London of the sort of assistance the United States would undertake: a pilot project to privatize wholesale food distribution in one area, a mission to survey the possibilities of defense conversion and one to look at the energy sector. The letter warned that if he chose to retain administrative controls, as the "anticrisis program" prescribed, it would make assistance more difficult. It also advised Gorbachev to privatize his food distribution system and to clarify the ownership of energy resources in order to attract foreign investment. Bush also discouraged any appeal for restructuring or rescheduling the Soviet debt, despite the fact that little of this debt was owed the United States.

What Bush offered was minimal and did not include an effort to advise on the overall policy that would be required to make reform in individual sectors workable. Furthermore, the advice against debt rescheduling seemed to remove one of the principal ways in which the Western world could have assisted a reform program. It would have been more helpful to have pointed out that, should debt rescheduling become necessary, the terms might be easier if the Soviet Union had adopted a realistic approach to reform. As it turned out, the debts had to be rescheduled anyway, but without any reform quid pro quo.

The Group of Seven would have made the decisions it did even if Gorbachev had not gone to London. They fell far short of what would be needed to support a transition of the Soviet economy. Also, by relying entirely on existing mechanisms, the Group of Seven failed to recognize that these organizations were not up to the unprecedented task they were being given. The IMF had extensive experience assisting countries with market economies, especially developing countries, to stabilize their currencies, but little experience with the problems faced in the transition from a command economy to a market economy and none at all with the unique problems the Soviet Union was facing. The World Bank, also, had worked mainly with developing countries, not countries like the Soviet Union with distorted, though developed, economies. Both of these organizations might have played useful subsidiary roles in a more comprehensive effort, but it was a mistake to think that they were equipped to manage Western participation in the effort to transform the Soviet economy.

The meager result was, however, primarily Gorbachev's fault. It would have been better for him if he had stayed away from London, for he damaged his personal credibility by pressing for assistance without presenting a convincing program. His approach to Bush, in particular, could serve as a classic example of how not to be persuasive.

They met at a working lunch on July 17. The final touches had been put on our strategic arms negotiations just minutes before Gorbachev's armored ZIL drove up to Winfield House, the American ambassador's residence in London. With the START agreement now in hand, both presidents knew they would meet again in Moscow in less than two weeks and have an opportunity for much more extended discussions. The mood should have been festive and conducive to a sympathetic hearing for Gorbachev's plans for economic reform—if he had any. But Gorbachev missed the moment.

Inexplicably, he adopted a querulous, challenging stance. Anatoly

Chernyayev, his most loyal aide, could not understand what had gotten into him. Chernyayev quoted his notes of the meeting in his book, and they make it clear how unsuitable Gorbachev's arguments were. As soon as the talk at lunch turned serious, Gorbachev launched into one of his rambling soliloquies, such as the one he had delivered to me in May. Chernyayev summarized it as follows:

> I know that the president of the United States is a serious man. He thinks through the political implications of his decisions thoroughly and is not given to improvisation. As regards security policy, we have already accomplished a lot as a result of these decisions. But at the same time I have the impression that my friend, the president of the United States, has not yet reached a final answer to one fundamental question: What does the United States want the Soviet Union to be like? Until we get an answer to this question, many issues in our relations cannot be clarified. And time is running out.

Chernyayev noted at this point that Bush grimaced and his face flushed, but he mastered his emotions and continued to eat. Gorbachev went on:

> So I ask: What does George Bush want from me? If my colleagues among the "Seven" tell me, when we meet later, that they like what I am doing and they want to support me but first I have to stew in my own soup for a while, I must tell them that we are all in that soup. Isn't it strange: a hundred billion dollars were scraped up to solve a regional conflict. Money can be found for other programs. But what we have here is a project to transform the Soviet Union, to give it a totally new quality, to bring it into the world economy so that it will not be a disruptive force and the source of threats. There has never been a task so great and so important!

It seemed to Chernyayev that Bush was uncharacteristically cold and detached when he replied that he apparently had not adequately explained his view. He thought he had made it clear that he wanted to see the Soviet Union become a democratic state with a market economy, integrated with the Western economies, with a successful federation agreed between the Center and the republics. He pointed out that not everyone in the United States agreed with his attitude toward the Soviet Union and that had created some practical problems, but nobody wanted to see an economic catastrophe there, and he considered the collapse of the Soviet Union to be contrary to American interests.

Chernyayev observed that this relieved the tension a bit, but it did not erase the bad impression Gorbachev's tirade had left on Bush and the other Americans present. It had been the wail of a desperate man whose control over his country was visibly slipping away, and—even more disturbing—of one who no longer understood what he was trying to achieve.[24] According to Michael Beschloss and Strobe Talbott, Bush commented upon his return to Washington, "It's funny. He's always been his own best salesman, but not this time. I wonder if he isn't kind of out of touch."[25]

Chernyayev speculated in his memoirs on the reasons for Gorbachev's self-defeating behavior in London and advanced two theories: one, that some of Kryuchkov's many reports of alleged U.S. treachery had rubbed off, despite Gorbachev's skepticism about them; the other, that Gorbachev genuinely felt wounded by what he read as Bush's inadequate response to his efforts to move toward a real partnership with the United States.[26] I believe that both these factors affected his mood, along with a third one: his frustration that he had failed to bring a more convincing economic reform package with him to London. He must have recognized, if only subconsciously, that he had lacked the courage to take advantage of the opening Yavlinsky's proposals offered.

I wondered at the time, as I have repeatedly since, whether things could have turned out differently. On one level, Bush and Gorbachev had developed an unprecedented intimacy. Since their summit in Malta they had communicated in direct, human terms, not as distant chiefs of state. The personal trust that had developed, while not unbounded, was remarkably deep. And yet, on the most important issue before them, communication failed. They seemed to talk past each other.

Gorbachev could not bring himself to say straight out what had been on his mind, at least since 1989. He was not psychologically capable of uttering his deep, perhaps only semiconscious, longings, and had he been, he would have signed his political death warrant by doing so. But what would he have said, if it had been feasible? Nobody can know for sure, probably not even Gorbachev himself, but as one who observed him at close hand for several years, my guess is that, translated into colloquial American, it would have been something like the following—95 percent of which I have heard him say at one time or another, while the remaining 5 percent is based on a hunch:

My country has never known real freedom and never experienced democracy. It has always been ruled from the top down. That is its tragedy and the root of its current plight, both economic and political. Looking at the rest of the world, I can see that successful societies are free societies, societies with the rule of law that protect their citizens' rights and both stimulate and harvest their creativity. That's what I want for my country, because if it does not change, it will be left behind by the rest of the world. Not only the United States, Western Europe, and Japan will put us further in the shade, we won't even be able to keep up with the South Koreas, Taiwans, and Singapores if we stay the way we are. I can never say this in public, but what I really want is to remake my country in your image.

Now this may sound simple, but, believe me, it isn't. The entire history of Russia runs in a different direction, so I have to turn Russian history upside down. Peter the Great could knock heads and chop heads, but you don't create democracy that way. I have to do it the hard way. Our people have not been allowed to make decisions for themselves, so they haven't learned how to do it. You've had more than two hundred years to develop your institutions. We don't have any free institutions at all, and we won't have the time you have had to build them. Even so, I can't just pick up your institutions and plant them here and expect them to work. We have to do away with our old system and give people time to adapt. I have to work with the material I have been given; I can't invent a different population or a different history.

Although I have a general idea of where we have to go, nobody has been able to show me a road map of how to get there. There is going to be a lot of trial and error. And don't assume that I have a lot of support here for what I want to do. Most of the country either does not understand or is opposed, particularly those with a stake in the old system. I'm going to have to manipulate and outwit the latter and educate the former, and that will make some of my actions look strange. I hope I can bring enough of the Communist Party with me to make the task easier, but if this doesn't work the Party will have to go. I just have to make sure it doesn't get me before I take care of it. It's going to be nip and tuck, but don't think the worst if sometimes I have to talk out of both sides of my mouth.

So what do I need from you? Well, first, understanding. Understanding and respect. I'm trying to do what you have prayed for ever since World War II: eliminate the Soviet military threat to other countries, open up my society, establish the rule of law, start building democratic institutions, and move to a market system—what your ideologues like to call capitalism, but I trust you understand that I can't use language like that—not yet, at least. This is exactly what you folks have dreamed of for decades, but without any expectation it could happen.

I am determined to make it happen, but not because *you* want it. It is my goal because my country needs it. It will be a cripple in the twenty-first century—if it survives at all—if it doesn't modernize. If this century has taught us anything, it is that only a free society can be competitive in a high-tech world. So I'm not doing this to do you a favor, but you must admit that it does, objectively, do you a favor. How much have you spent over the past forty-five years to counter the Soviet threat? (And, by the way, it was a real threat, even if you sometimes exaggerated it.)

When I say understanding and respect, what I mean is, don't treat me like a defeated enemy. Knock off the talk about winning the cold war. If you make me look like a loser, how do you expect me to lead the country down the next difficult steps on the road? And besides, don't I deserve a little bit of the credit? I'm the one who took on the Soviet military leaders and forced them—sometimes tricked them—to do the necessary. I refused to let them threaten force in Eastern Europe. I developed a philosophy to explain why ending the cold war was in our interest, and I didn't notice you giving me much help there. Let's face it, George, you and Ron and I ended the cold war together. No need to get uppity about who won; didn't we all?

Where I really need help, though, is with the economic side of things. On the political side, I have a pretty clear idea of where I want to go. I studied law, after all, and even though it was a funny kind of law, they also taught us about the principles of "bourgeois law." I may not always show it, but I do know where we're going in this area. Economics, on the other hand, is something else. To be frank, I know we have to change the system we have, but—much as I hate to admit it—I really don't have a clue how to do it. Your system seems to work, but it won't work in my country unless people change a lot.

Now for the crunch: when I say I need your support, I don't just mean money. I need help figuring out what it is I have to do. My people are hopeless. They don't know any more about a market system than I do. Five years ago they were explaining to all and sundry why we had the best system in the world, and now they say everything was wrong, but just do what they say and that will fix everything. And if I get twenty-five of them in a room, I hear thirty-nine opinions.

You want to sit back, kibitz when you feel like it, and wait until we have a market system up and running. Then you'll see what you can do. You should have been a banker; I hear yours are never interested in lending money unless the borrower can prove he doesn't need it. But I thought statesmen were different. They're supposed to lead, not just play the sure bets. Aren't you willing to risk anything to change the world for the better?

All right, you tell me our current program won't work. I know you're right, and that's one reason I'm snappy today. But, damn it, I've been hinting for over two years that we could use some advice. And I don't mean bromides like 'If it's going to cause pain, do it fast.' I learned that from Machiavelli long before I met Jim Baker. You sent a bunch of businessmen to see me last year, and they agreed we were right to reject the Shatalin plan, but now everybody is saying I should have accepted it. If you thought that then, why the devil didn't you say so? I would probably have told you to mind your own business, but if you had let me know that you'd be there to help if things got tough— well, that would have made a lot of difference.

Don't misunderstand me. I know you can't tell me exactly what to do. And I certainly don't want you to start trying to teach us lessons. Your institutions probably won't work here without a lot of adaptation, and we'll have to do that for ourselves. We're also mighty proud and don't take kindly to foreigners trying to tend our business. I wouldn't claim we are the easiest people in the world to work with. But I do think our problem is to a great extent yours as well. If we fail it will be a tragedy for us, but it will also be pretty hard on you. Where are you going to find an extra forty or fifty billion a year for your defense budget if our would-be totalitarians take over? There are still over thirty thousand nuclear warheads in my country, you know, and that's just for starters.

You have a lot of experience running a market system. We have none, but we understand our own society better than you can. Why can't we approach this thing cooperatively? Equals, working on a common problem. Truman and Marshall found a way to do it with Western Europe in 1947, and my people tell me that the most important thing was not the money but the institutions, the habits of cooperation, the pooling of expertise. Our situation is different, but isn't the principle the same? Can't you suggest some way that we can put our best brains together, and those from the other G-7 countries, and work together for some solutions? I'll take all the sound advice you can give if you offer it in the right way, but I want your assurance that if I do take it and get into a jam, you and your friends are going to be there to help! Don't just sit back and look for excuses—even good ones. If we blow this opportunity, we won't look very good in the history books. And I mean both of us.

Fanciful? Of course. Accurate? I'll bet on it.

Was there anything Bush should have said that he didn't? Maybe, though it was probably too late to make any real difference. Given their relationship, however, I believe that Bush, in private, could have demonstrated his friendship more effectively by giving some blunt advice—and I believe Gorbachev would have taken it very seriously.

In my fantasy world, I could imagine that, when dessert was served, Bush would have invited Gorbachev to a side room for a private chat, with just interpreters and no note taking. I think he could have been quite direct, particularly since he could be reasonably confident that there were no KGB listening devices in the room. His comment might have gone something like this:

Mikhail, I can understand your frustration. The fact is, we haven't done what we should to help, and you're right to point that out. But it's not because we don't want to help. We do, but—quite frankly—you don't make it easy. It's not going to do you any good for me to throw money down that rathole of a state sector you've got, even if I could get the money, which I can't. It would not work and would quickly turn off people on the whole idea of helping you so that I couldn't do it even if you later came up with a reasonable program.

Now I know you can't do everything overnight, but you've got to find a way to unleash forces that will, willy-nilly, take you to a market economy. You can't do it from above, but you've got to take control of the economy out of the hands of the bureaucrats. Make room for a private sector and turn people loose. Yes, it will look like chaos for a while, but my guess is that your people will react more responsibly and creatively than you think. If you make a decision that holds a reasonable prospect of success, I'll do my best with our colleagues to organize some very substantial support. But it will have to be contingent on a viable program, and it must be tied to specific projects. There is no way I'm going to raise money to prop up collapsing state enterprises.

I don't profess to know precisely what you should do to get to a market economy, but what worries me is the feeling that right now you are moving in the wrong direction. Maybe we ought to think about some joint effort with our European and Japanese friends to seek answers. If the idea appeals to you, let me know and I'll try to get things rolling as fast as possible.

Another thing: I don't want to get personal or presume to advise you on appointments, but I wouldn't be your friend if I didn't let you know that your prime minister is a disaster. Unless you can find a more credible person for that job—or maybe run your Cabinet yourself (I manage without a prime minister)—you are going to have trouble convincing anyone that you're serious about economic reform.

I'm glad things worked out with your parliament in June, but I'm still a little nervous. I hope you're giving that report I sent you serious attention. I know you feel it's unfounded, and I hope you're right, but I still have an uneasy feeling. I can't tell you what to do, but I will say one thing: I make sure my personal security is not in the hands of either the CIA or the FBI, and it's not that I don't trust them. It just isn't prudent to concentrate too much of that kind of power in the hands of one organization. And, by the way: somebody seems to be feeding you a lot of nonsense about us. If I were you, I'd call them on the carpet. We're not trying to undermine you or harm your country in any way. If anybody claims we are, he's lying. You should try to find out why such people are doing it, because it's no service to you.

So much for my fantasy. It never happened, and it might have made no difference if it had. But, remarkably, the personal rapport of the two presidents had developed to the point that the sort of bluntness I have described could have had an impact on Gorbachev's subsequent actions.

To work, though, it would have required a commitment on Bush's part that he was unwilling to make. In 1991, despite all his sympathy for Gorbachev the politician, he seemed to be looking for reasons not to assist the Soviet Union rather than ways to do so. Gorbachev's accurate sense of his reluctance lay behind the outburst in London that left such a bad impression.

Socialism? What's That?

NORWAY'S PARLIAMENT HAD AWARDED Gorbachev the Nobel Peace Prize in 1990, but he had delayed traveling to Oslo to deliver his acceptance speech, citing pressing business at home. When he finally went to Oslo on June 11, 1991, he took with him a speech that, in effect, discarded the last elements of Marxism-Leninism that were still officially the ideological foundation of the Party he headed.

Gorbachev's attitude toward "socialism" was frequently misunderstood by foreign observers, including the Western statesmen who considered him their friend. They noted that he still professed allegiance to the principle and also that he had little understanding of market economics. What they missed was that, while Gorbachev doggedly continued to use the term—he feared alienating potential supporters if he dropped it—from 1988 and 1989 he systematically emptied it of the meaning it had carried for more than seventy years of Soviet history. By mid-1991 he was in fact a cryptocapitalist, even though he himself still did not understand all the implications.

The evolution of his thinking is apparent from a close reading of his Nobel Prize address, from which the classical concepts of Marxism-Leninism were conspicuously absent. But the most telling evidence of Gorbachev's ideological evolution—and of his thoughts for the future—came in July, a few weeks after Oslo, when a new draft program for the Communist Party was published. Not only were Marxist-Leninist concepts absent, there was no longer even lip service paid to "socialism."[27] The daily newspaper *Nezavisimaya gazeta* ran its story on the new Party program under the apt headline GORBACHEV TRIUMPHS OVER MARXISM-LENINISM.

Gorbachev forced the new draft program through a reluctant Central Committee plenum on July 25, 1991, and obtained approval to hold another Party congress in November or December. It seemed to many that Gorbachev was finally upon a track that would lead to a split in the Communist Party, with Gorbachev supporters backing a social democratic orientation and the hard-liners forced to leave or to expel the reformers.

On July 20, just before the July plenum was to convene, Boris Yeltsin escalated his battle against the Communist establishment with a potentially devastating decree that prohibited organized activity by any political party in state institutions on RSFSR territory.[28] If enforced, the decree would deliver a fatal blow to the Communist Party in Russia, since it had been organized on the basis of cells in workplaces. Every office, every factory, every school, every farm, every military unit had its Party organization, and the Communist Party exercised its control of society through these organizations. Even when the Party had relinquished its legal monopoly of power, these structures had been left intact, usually continuing to operate as they had before. Without workplace Party organizations and the privileges they provided, most members would simply let their Party membership lapse.

Communist Party organizations had campaigned actively against Yeltsin, and this decree was his revenge. But it was not merely a personal vendetta. A truly democratic, multiparty system of government could not develop in the country if one party continued to enjoy the benefits of a national organization, indirectly supported by the country's monopolistic state structures.

Communist Party officials lobbied furiously with Gorbachev to issue a decree countermanding Yeltsin's order, but he refused.[79] It was another signal that he was at the point of breaking his alignment with the hard-liners. The apparatchiks had to content themselves with a resolution at the plenum condemning Yeltsin's decree, but this, of course, had no legal effect.

Meanwhile, several of the original founders of perestroika began to organize a political movement outside the Communist Party. Some, like Eduard Shevardnadze and Alexander Yakovlev, were still formally Party members. Others, like Moscow's Mayor Gavriil Popov and Leningrad's Mayor Anatoly Sobchak, had just recently left the Party. They formed what was initially named the Movement for Democratic Reforms (often known by its Russian initials, DDR), and several prominent politicians gravitated to the group: Arkady Volsky, an erstwhile Gorbachev confidant who had taken on the thankless task of governing Nagorny Karabakh in 1989 and now headed the League of Industrialists; Alexander Rutskoy, Yeltsin's vice president; and Ivan Laptev, speaker of the lower house of parliament and former editor of *Izvestiya,* joined what briefly became a parade of political figures entering the movement.

Many suspected that the movement was being formed to provide Gorbachev with a political alternative if he lost his position in the Communist Party. Though he refrained from endorsing the group, he was careful not to vilify it as he had the Democratic Russia movement—many of whose leaders were aligning themselves with the new movement. Certainly, some of its founders wanted to demonstrate that it was possible to organize support for reform outside the Communist Party. If they succeeded, their movement could provide a refuge for reform-minded Communists if the upcoming Party congress should result in a split—which by the summer of 1991 seemed all but inevitable.

This is precisely what the Party conservatives feared, and they reacted vigorously against the leaders of the DDR who were still Communist Party members. When Shevardnadze gave an interview to an Austrian newspaper in early June and spoke of the need for a "democratic party" to parallel the CPSU, the Central Control Commission, the Party's highest disciplinary body, was asked to investigate. Shevardnadze refused to wait for the outcome and resigned his Party membership forthwith. Alexander Yakovlev, on the other hand, waited until the Central Control Commission recommended his expulsion. Before his primary Party organization, which formally had the authority to expel a member, could act, Yakovlev resigned, complaining publicly that "a powerful Stalinist group" had formed in the Party leadership.[30]

In late July, shortly before I left Moscow, I discussed the future of the democratic movement with Mayor Gavriil Popov, one of the organizers of the Movement for Democratic Reforms. He was dubious that the "democrats" would be in a position to govern the country for another three to five years. Their lack of discipline and divisiveness were factors, but he also felt that the Soviet organs of coercion were still intact and were still dominated by Communist Party apparatchiks. He considered the most urgent task to be that of eliminating Communist Party control of the army, law enforcement agencies, and the media. This, of course, was one of the goals of the Yeltsin decree, but until an analogous one was issued by Gorbachev, it would be unlikely to affect the army and the KGB.

Popov saw the Movement for Democratic Reforms as a possible framework for rallying the democratic forces but was annoyed that the leaders could not decide whether to become a political party or not. He himself felt that it should organize itself as a party or disband. He did feel, however, that the "democrats," despite their divisions, had the advantage of momentum. His greatest worry, he said, was not the activities of conservatives in the Communist Party but the potential threat of reactionary zealots like Vladimir Zhirinovsky. If living standards should continue to deteriorate, opportunistic parties like his might not only do better at the ballot box but would be able to enlist the direct support of military and police groups.

Whatever Popov's limitations as a political leader, he turned out to be a first-rate political analyst.

Bush's Moscow-Kiev Summit

GEORGE BUSH ARRIVED IN MOSCOW on the evening of July 29, 1991, for his first visit to Moscow as president of the United States. I was pleased to note that visits to each other's capitals were now taking place on an annual basis, as I had recommended at the start of the Bush administration. Other meetings, in third countries, were held from time to time when there was a need or a convenient opportunity, as in Helsinki in September 1990 or London just two weeks earlier, but there now was a tacit understanding by both parties that they would hold "full-scale summit meetings" alternately in each other's country once a year.

Most of the bilateral issues that hung over Gorbachev's visit to Washington the year before had now been settled. A treaty that would reduce strategic nuclear weapons forces was finally ready for signature—after nearly ten years of negotiation. The Soviet Union had moved into compliance with the treaty to reduce conventional weapons in Europe, and the president had sent it to the Senate for ratification. The Soviet parliament had finally passed a law guaranteeing the right to emigrate, and the president had sent the trade agreement signed the year before to the Congress. U.S.-Soviet trade would now be on a most-favored-nation basis, with no discriminatory tariffs.

There were few contentious bilateral issues left to discuss. When the START treaty was signed, the four-part agenda originally set by President Reagan in 1984 and 1985 had been fully implemented. In fact, by 1991 we had moved beyond it into areas of cooperation that only a visionary could have glimpsed in the 1980s and that President Bush had refused even to study as recently as 1989. Nevertheless, there was much to talk about. The state Gorbachev headed was visibly crumbling; these problems haunted both presidents and dominated most of their private conversation.

Both presidents made an effort to take note of the growing prominence of the republic leaders, Bush by visiting Kiev following his talks in Moscow, calling officially on Yeltsin, and inviting several republic leaders to his state dinner, Gorbachev by inviting both Yeltsin and Nursultan Nazarbayev to take part in a working lunch with Bush and to form part of the Soviet delegation for some discussions.

Nazarbayev came to Moscow from Alma Ata for the occasion, with the result that investment in Kazakhstan became one of the principal topics of discussion. Yeltsin, however, rebuffed Gorbachev's invitation, remarking that he preferred to receive Bush in his own office rather than to participate in a group meeting with others.

Inaugurated president of Russia just a few weeks earlier, Yeltsin had been allocated the same office in the Kremlin that Gorbachev had occupied when he was chairman of the USSR Supreme Soviet, and he chose to receive Bush there rather than in his office in the Russian White House. I hoped that his recent political victories had made it possible for him to mute his way of acting like a scrappy underdog. This did not happen, however. He continued his penchant for petty one-upmanship and grandstanding: he kept Bush waiting almost ten minutes, prolonged their meeting well beyond the appointed time—even though there was little substance to his presentation—and arranged for a press conference without telling his guest. At the state dinner hosted by the Gorbachevs, he sent his wife through the reception line alone, waited until all the other guests had gone in, and then tried to escort Barbara Bush to the table as if he were the host.[31]

Yeltsin's behavior was both boorish and childish, designed to draw attention to himself and make both Gorbachev and Bush uncomfortable. It pained me to note that he continued to use such tactics even after he had achieved his immediate political goal and no longer had the excuse that they were necessary to prevent his opponents from blocking his contact with the public. Still, these social frictions were trivial and deserve mention only because they pointed to deeper problems.

A much more serious incident intruded upon the meeting Bush and Gorbachev held at the Novo-Ogaryovo dacha on July 31. Our embassy received a report that unknown assailants had attacked a Lithuanian customs post during the night and brutally murdered all six customs officers. A U.S. Embassy officer notified staffers at the dacha, who sent in a note to President Bush. Confronted with the news, Gorbachev was embarrassed not only that the atrocity had occurred but that his visitor had been informed of it first. It seemed that the outrage had been organized specifically to embarrass Gorbachev during his meetings with Bush. And, indeed, it was a reminder of his declining authority and less-than-efficient staff.[32]

The idea of Bush's visit to Kiev arose naturally. During his trip to the United States the previous year, Gorbachev had made stops in Minneapolis–St. Paul and in San Francisco and the bay area. With all the republics becoming more assertive, Bush thought it would be appropriate not only to call on Yeltsin in Moscow but also to stop in at least one of the republic capitals. This would give him a chance to make a speech directed at the non-Russian republics in which he could call attention to their cultural and national distinctiveness and welcome the movement toward democracy that was sweeping many, but unfortunately not all, of them.

Kiev seemed the obvious choice. It was the capital of the second-largest republic, was moving more rapidly toward democracy than many republics in Central Asia, and was free of the strife that had convulsed the Transcaucasus. Furthermore, it was convenient. Bush could stop there for a few hours on August 1 and still get back to Washington the same day.

I checked the idea of visiting Kiev with the Soviet Ministry of Foreign Affairs and encountered no objections, so we began discussing the trip with Ukrainian officials, who were enthusiastic. We had several American diplomats stationed in Kiev, preparing to open a consulate general. Plans were well advanced when, to my astonishment, Ed Hewett telephoned me on Sunday afternoon, July 21, from Washington to say that the Soviet chargé d'affaires had come to the White House with a message from the Soviet president's office saying that, in view of the tensions then existing, it would be inadvisable for Bush to visit Kiev. Instead, he could spend the day with Gorbachev at one of the resorts in the Stavropol region.

Obviously, the president couldn't go to Kiev if Gorbachev asked him not to, but calling off his trip at that point would create a public relations disaster. Since we were already in contact with the Ukrainians about the visit, we would have to tell them why we were canceling it, and word that Gorbachev had forbidden Bush to visit Ukraine would become *the* story of the summit. It would overshadow everything else and defeat the purpose of the meeting, as far as public relations were concerned.

We discussed on the open telephone line, for the benefit of the KGB monitors and the officials they reported to, the likely result if we were to cancel the visit, and I sent word to the Ministry of Foreign Affairs that I needed to see Bessmertnykh the following morning. When he received me, he professed to know nothing of the message that had been sent to Washington but promised to check into it. A few hours later he called to say we should proceed with planning the visit to Kiev if that was what President Bush wanted. Subsequently, he explained that he had checked with Gorbachev and, although Gorbachev had seemed annoyed, he had agreed that Bush should go wherever he wanted.[33]

This exchange made Bush and his staff hypercautious to avoid anything that might embarrass Gorbachev during the Kiev trip. In fact they began to think of ways it could be used to "help Gorbachev." Speechwriters scoured their drafts with orders to remove anything Gorbachev might find offensive. As often happens in such exercises, they overdid it. To compound the error, they failed to consult either our embassy in Moscow or our diplomats in Kiev about how the speech might be interpreted.

I saw the text for the first time as we were flying from Moscow to Kiev on the new Air Force One, a luxurious and roomy Boeing 747 that provided a sharp contrast to the cramped staff section of the Boeing 707 that had served presidents for decades. The flight lasted slightly more than an hour, and the text of the speech Bush would deliver to the Ukrainian parliament had already been reproduced for distribution to the press. I read it hurriedly and thought it had many strong points, particularly its warning that independence and democracy are not identical.

Nevertheless, several sentences heaping praise on Gorbachev seemed unnecessary and out of place. It would be better to endorse the goals of creating democratic institutions and entering the world economy, I believed. As long as Gorbachev was perceived as promoting these goals, that would be an indirect endorsement. Naming him might delight him personally but would do him no good politically, since his critics were already attacking him as Bush's lackey; lavish personal praise would simply give them more ammunition to use against him.

I also doubted that it was a good idea to endorse specifically the new union treaty as the speech text did. Inevitably, the treaty was the result of many politically charged compromises, some tenuous and some still ambiguous. For a foreign statesman, injecting himself into the process was both presumptuous and also fraught with the risk that it might produce an effect opposite to that intended. (Imagine what the American reaction would have been if a British or French chief of state had tried to advise American states how to vote on the Constitution during the debate in 1789 and 1790!) President Bush could have avoided this misstep and still defended the important principles involved by speaking of the importance of replacing ties among the republics based on compulsion with ones based on agreement. What form the agreement might take was a matter for them to decide, not for outsiders.

I called one of the speechwriters over to my seat and told him I liked most of the text but felt that some of the phrases could be misunderstood. In particular, I singled out the praise for Gorbachev and the endorsement of the union treaty. "He really shouldn't personalize things by referring to 'Gorbachev's Soviet Union,'" I said, adding, "and he shouldn't imply that we are against independence if that is their free choice."

"I see your point," he replied, "but I don't think I can get them out. We've already printed copies for the press. Besides, the president put those references in himself. That's the way he wants to say it."

We were due to land in just a few minutes, and it seemed pointless to persist, but I did make one more suggestion. "I see you have 'the Ukraine' several times in the text. Make sure the president leaves out the article. He should just say 'Ukraine.' Ukrainian Americans think the article makes it sound like a geographic area rather than a country."

"But we say *the* United States, don't we?" he protested.

"Never mind," I told him. "I didn't say it was logical, I only said that a lot of people feel strongly about this. If the president says 'the Ukraine,' the White House will be getting thousands of letters and telegrams in protest next week."

He agreed to slash out the definite article when Ukraine was mentioned, and when the president came by our section in the plane to say hello I made sure he understood.

The text would have bothered me more if I had not known that we had gone to great lengths to cater to Ukrainian sensibilities in our arrangements for the visit. For example, we were aware that the Ukrainians had been furious when Chancellor Kohl had visited Kiev in early July and Gorbachev had excluded the Ukrainian leaders from some of his meetings. Therefore, we agreed that the president would meet privately with Parliament Chairman Kravchuk and that Soviet Vice President Yanayev—or other representatives from Moscow—would not be present. All speeches and toasts were to be given in Ukrainian and English only, and the president would use a Ukrainian interpreter (even though Kravchuk was perfectly bilingual in Russian). In short, we had gone out of the way, as no other foreign visitor had ever done, to treat Ukraine as distinct and sovereign. Given these arrangements, I thought it was unlikely that an ill-chosen phrase or two in the president's speech would do much damage.

I should not have been complacent. Even before we arrived in Kiev, some of the nationalist Ukrainian leaders, apparently oblivious to the efforts we had made to arrange the trip at all and to keep it concentrated exclusively on U.S.-Ukrainian relations, criticized President Bush to American correspondents. Speaking at a press conference, Ivan Drach, the chairman of Rukh, observed that "President Bush seems to have been hypnotized by Gorbachev," and Lev Lukyanenko made the incomprehensible allegation that the American president "has consistently snubbed the democratic movements in the republics." This, after he had met with the three Baltic leaders more than once, with Yeltsin three times, and with Nazarbayev several times—and had refused, the year before, to give the Communist prime minister of Ukraine an appointment in Washington precisely because he did not consider him representative of Ukrainian opinion. These charges were also made despite three years of growing contacts between official U.S. representatives and the Rukh leaders. In fact, the Rukh leaders had received invitations to visit the United States at U.S. government expense far more often than representatives of all other Ukrainian political movements put together had. Yet they had received less than a quarter of the votes in Ukraine. If accusations of U.S. favoritism were in order, it would have been that we had given Rukh disproportionate attention.

The Rukh attitude toward Gorbachev was also distorted. When one is engaged in what seems a desperate political struggle, memories can be short. Without Gorbachev's pressure on the Ukrainian Communist leadership, most of the Rukh leaders would still have been in jail, not running for office, holding press conferences in Kiev, and going to formal dinners with the president of the United States. Ukrainian Communist leaders like Shcherbitsky were totally opposed to the liberalization Moscow had forced upon them. If Rukh had been left by Moscow—and Washington—to fend for itself against the Ukrainian Communist leadership of the late 1980s, it could never have made the gains it had.

The visit itself combined a few elements of the old with many more of the new.

The reception ceremony at Kiev's Borispol Airport inspired visions of the old. A highly select group had been admitted to the reviewing stand near the terminal to greet the president upon arrival. They were waving American flags, along with the official flag of Soviet Ukraine: a slight adaptation of the flag of the USSR, it was mostly red with a thin blue stripe near the bottom. Parliament Chairman Leonid Kravchuk made a formal speech of greeting in Ukrainian; President Bush replied in English, followed, paragraph by paragraph, by a Ukrainian translation on the loudspeakers. I recalled that in 1972, when President Nixon had visited Kiev, the scene had been similar, but only Russian and English had been used.

Once our motorcade left the airfield, the scene was entirely new. Large numbers of people were gathered in the square in front of the terminal with the yellow-and-blue flags of the Ukrainian independence movement. Signs calling for independence and condemning the current Communist government and communism in general were waved for President Bush to observe. Similar demonstrations occurred on the way into town and were particularly numerous in the city itself. The contrast to the atmosphere when Nixon had visited and when Secretary of State Shultz had come, as recently as 1988, was astounding. In 1988, not only had the streets used by the motorcade been cleared of traffic, people had even been barred from standing on the sidewalks!

President Bush met privately with Kravchuk for an extended period. I waited in a side room with Soviet Vice President Yanayev and Ukrainian Prime Minister Vitold Fokin, chatting. Fokin was particularly worried that there might be a food shortage during the coming winter. Though Ukraine had long been known as the "breadbasket" of the Soviet Union, Stalin had caused a devastating, genocidal famine in the 1930s with his program of forced collectivization. Now the growing economic dislocation threatened even the unsatisfactory level of agricultural production that had been sustained since then. The Communist regime was still unwilling to break up Stalin's collective farms and restore private agriculture, even with the system breaking down. Fokin talked about the future like a desperate man; he seemed to see no feasible way, given the political forces at work, to avert economic catastrophe. The Ukrainian nationalists were no help against the entrenched Communist bureaucracy; they wanted independence first, and then they would think about what to do with it.

Following the meeting with Kravchuk, President Bush addressed the Ukrainian parliament. His delivery was not punctuated by applause, but the legislators gave him a prolonged standing ovation at the end. Then there was a formal dinner in the meticulously restored baroque Mariinsky Palace, attended by representatives of all the political factions, including five leaders from Rukh. Toasts were delivered in Ukrainian and English, with no Russian translation. Viktor Komplektov, the Soviet ambassador to Washington, who was seated next to Rebecca, observed that it was good that he understood English; otherwise he would have been unable to follow what was going on.

From the palace, the president made a pilgrimage to Babyi Yar, the site of one of Nazi Germany's most frightful atrocities, where both he and Kravchuk delivered moving speeches. Then they went back to the airport, where they held a brief departure ceremony, and Air Force One took off for a direct flight from Kiev to Washington.

The entire visit lasted only five hours, but for the observer with a knowledge of the past, it was precedent shattering. For the first time since the early seventeenth century, the leader of a major power had come to Ukraine, had treated its leaders as sovereign, and had dealt with them exclusively in their own language. Furthermore, he had insisted that all significant political factions have a part in his visit and that nobody be muzzled. The fact that Bush had also praised Gorbachev and endorsed the union treaty (which Ukrainians had participated in drafting) was secondary to the more fundamental message the Bush visit carried. After all, he had also stressed that the future was theirs to choose—and that should have been the most important issue for friends of Ukraine, and of the other Soviet republics.

The politically inept Ukrainian nationalist leaders failed to grasp the larger issue. By ignoring the substantive elements of the visit and focusing on a few unfortunate phrases in one of the president's speeches, they missed an opportunity to bolster their fundamental goal: to have Ukraine regarded as a political entity distinct from Russia with a sovereign right to define its relationship with its neighbors, including Russia. This was much more important than differences of opinion on Gorbachev's policies or on the merits of the union treaty, for it implied that Ukraine had the right to make these decisions for itself.

The American press, of course, picked up the complaints of the Rukh leaders. They made better news than philosophical discussions of a historic turn in official attitudes. Columnist William Safire, always eager to embarrass President Bush, seized upon the unfortunate phrases in the speech to the Ukrainian parliament and dubbed it his "Chicken Kiev" speech. The fundamental inaccuracy of this joke made it no less memorable.[34]

Safire's phrase might, and did, entertain Americans, but it had little effect on the developments in Ukraine. The lack of perspective on the part of the Rukh leaders, however, was more ominous. Would they put the trappings of statehood ahead of democracy and reform? If they did, they would inherit a weak and divided state that would have difficulty retaining the independence they wanted. Would they look to outsiders to hand them the future they desired, or would they work for a consensus and a healthy society within Ukraine?

One part of President Bush's message was unquestionably correct: independence is not the same thing as freedom and democracy. An independent state that is oppressive is as bad for its citizens as an empire is. The first goal should be democracy, because if that is introduced and independence also seems desirable, that choice would be available. The union treaty the Ukrainian nationalists were rejecting preserved the right to secede and had safeguards against an autocratic center's denying that right.

An alliance of the nationalists with the economic *nomenklatura,* motivated by a desire to retain bureaucratic control of the economy and to insulate itself from the reform tendencies emanating from Moscow,[35] struck me as a dubious proposition. It might bring statehood and independence more rapidly, but the result would be a country without the domestic cohesion necessary to sustain the fundamental reforms that would be required, which in turn could threaten the unity of the country. The promise of independence would turn to ashes.

I was disturbed to see so many of my Ukrainian friends oblivious to what I thought was self-evident.

Rebecca and I said farewell to the Bushes as they reboarded Air Force One at Kiev's Borispol Airport. We then walked over to the Aeroflot plane that was waiting to return Vice President Yanayev to Moscow. He had invited us to join him, along with Viktor Komplektov and his wife, Alla.

The five of us settled into the VIP compartment of the medium-sized jet. Caviar, smoked salmon, champagne, and cognac appeared. We toasted what had seemed to be a very successful visit by the American president. Yanayev showed no resentment over his treatment in Kiev, but rather pleasure that the Ukrainians had seemed to be satisfied.

It was Rebecca who turned the subject from small talk. "Tell me, Mr. Vice President," she said, "what is going to happen to your country?"

Yanayev grew pensive, and his expression sobered. "People are upset," he said. "Their life is getting worse, and they don't understand why. Next fall or winter somebody is going to turn up and promise them stability, vodka, and sausage—and we'll be swept away."

An Ever-looser Union

THROUGHOUT MAY, June, and July, negotiators from the nine republics that had signed the Novo-Ogaryovo (Nine Plus One) declaration
(often the presidents themselves) worked with Gorbachev and his assistants to flesh out the text of an acceptable union treaty. For a time, Gorbachev hoped that the text would be agreed upon before he went to
London to meet with members of the Group of Seven, but this proved to
be impractical.

On June 7, *Izvestiya* carried an interview with Grigory Revenko,
whom Gorbachev had entrusted to manage the negotiation process, that
indicated a more modest schedule than had been assumed in May. He
said that the current draft would be sent to the Supreme Soviets of the
republics for discussion in June and that the final stage of negotiations
would begin in July. These, he indicated, might last several months, but
he thought the treaty could be signed before the end of the year.

Meanwhile, the republics were not waiting for a union treaty before
taking unilateral action. As *Izvestiya* reported in the same issue that carried the Revenko interview, the Ukrainian Supreme Soviet passed a resolution calling for the republic to take over control of all firms and
organizations on Ukrainian territory that hitherto had been controlled
by Moscow. There would be no compensation to the Center.

The Ukrainian parliament based its action on the Declaration of
State Sovereignty of the previous year and explained that it was acting
now because the central ministries had started turning the enterprises
into joint-stock companies without first transferring the property to the
republics. Gorbachev and the Center were now paying the price for their
failure either to break up the monopolies and privatize or to transfer
control of the process to the republics. Demands by the republics for
control over state-owned property on their territories were growing as
the central authority weakened. This issue, more than any other, united
the local Communist economic *nomenklatura* with the hitherto antagonistic independence movements driven by national-minded intellectuals.
Just a year back, these forces in Ukraine had been opposed to each
other. Now they were uniting to oppose the imperial Center. What was
happening in Ukraine was likely to happen in many other republics.

On June 18, Revenko announced that the draft was being submitted
to the republic Supreme Soviets even though some issues remained in

dispute. They included some of the thorniest ones: the tax system, control of military forces, ownership of natural resources, and the status of former autonomous republics, Tatarstan in particular. Tatarstan was the largest of the former autonomous republics that had declared sovereignty and was demanding equal status with the union republics and threatening secession if this should be denied.

The Ukrainian parliament discussed the draft on Wednesday, June 26. Of the thirty-five deputies who spoke, twenty-four had objections of one sort or another. Parliament Chairman Kravchuk listened but did not express a view. The body then voted overwhelmingly to accept the draft as a basis of discussion, to form a permanent commission to examine it and report back on September 1, to obtain reports from the government and from scholars on the legal implications of the powers delegated to the Center, and to instruct the assembly's Presidium to evaluate these various reports and convey its opinion to the entire Supreme Soviet on September 15, 1991. Many advocates of independence apparently voted in favor of this procedure, since they assumed that the various reports would divulge flaws sufficient to delay the union treaty indefinitely.[36]

Since April, at least, Gorbachev had been acutely aware that delays in concluding the union treaty were holding up everything else: economic reform, foreign assistance, and reorganization of the central government, to name just a few. The extended schedule Revenko mentioned in early June was not acceptable to him. He pushed hard throughout July to complete a key stage of the process before the end of summer. The USSR Supreme Soviet approved the text in principle on July 12 but recommended certain changes that the republic leaders rejected. Gorbachev compromised with the republics—Russia in particular—and by the end of the month—as he told President Bush—he thought he had an acceptable arrangement in hand.

On August 2, the day after Bush departed, Gorbachev announced that the treaty would be "open for signing" on August 20 and that the Russian Federation, Kazakhstan, and Uzbekistan would sign on that date.[37] Others would presumably adhere later, when they had met their internal legislative requirements.

When he made his announcement, Gorbachev described the new treaty as reflecting "a judicious balance of interests" that would permit it to be the basis of "a new, genuinely voluntary association[38] of sovereign states."

Aside from Gorbachev, however, the text had few enthusiasts. It conceded unprecedented authority to the republics and dropped both "socialist" and "soviet" from the name of the country, which was bound to infuriate the Party conservatives and the partisans of empire. Even before Gorbachev made additional concessions to the republics toward the end of July, a number of vocal supporters of the existing empire published an open letter appealing to Gorbachev not to accept the treaty as drafted since it would lead to a collapse of the Soviet state.[39]

Others, however, opposed it because it would preserve too much of the Soviet state. Even though the draft embodied virtually all their recommendations of a few months back, the more radical reformers began to argue against it. On August 8, Yuri Afanasiev, Sakharov's widow, Yelena Bonner, and other prominent democrats published an open letter to Yeltsin, appealing to him not to sign.[40] The following week Democratic Russia issued an analogous appeal, which set the following conditions for an acceptable treaty, all of which were absent from the current draft:

1. Signature by Belorussia, Kazakhstan, Ukraine, and the RSFSR as a minimum (in other words, no signature until Ukraine was ready to join)

2. Prior discussion of the final text by the RSFSR Supreme Soviet and by the public as a whole

3. Removal of any provision that would permit the USSR Congress of People's Deputies or Supreme Soviet to approve a new constitution

4. Inclusion of explicit procedures for secession

5. Provisions that would preclude membership in the new union by republics that permitted gross violations of human rights or genocide

Given this pressure from his most organized supporters, some wondered subsequently if Yeltsin would in fact have signed the treaty on August 20, even if Gorbachev had returned for the ceremony.[41] Nevertheless, when they met in Alma Ata on August 18, both Yeltsin and Nazarbayev seemed to be prepared to go through with the signing.

Rebecca and I had postponed our departure from Moscow by ten days in order to host President and Mrs. Bush at Spaso House during their trip to Moscow. We began packing our belongings when we returned from Kiev on August 1, aiming to leave on Sunday, August 11. Our last ten days on official duty in Moscow became a blur of activity: besides packing, there were farewell luncheons and dinners, several media interviews a day, and concluding press conferences, one in Russian for the Soviet media and one in English for American journalists.

Normally I gave a press briefing every week, alternating sessions in Russian and in English. Most briefings were conducted on "background," meaning that the journalists were enjoined not to attribute quotations to me by name. If they wished to use something I said, they could attribute it only to "a senior Western diplomat."

We received requests, however, for a final press conference on the record, so that comments on my experiences over the past four and a half years could be quoted.

At first I was dubious. I knew that if I spoke on the record I would be forced to deal with delicate questions about Gorbachev's political viability. If I had thought he faced removal by the people I believed were conspiring against him, I would not have agreed to speak on the record, for I could not have dealt with the question honestly.[42] The American ambassador simply could not be quoted as predicting that President Gorbachev would be removed. This would be interpreted everywhere as a signal that the American government had given up on Gorbachev, and it could actually precipitate an attempt against him, since it would imply that the United States would acquiesce to whatever happened.

However, I did not believe that those who were plotting against him could remove him, even though they might try. Since so many rumors about his imminent ouster were in the air, I decided it might be useful if I could find some way to warn that there could be a coup attempt but, if so, it was likely to fail. Therefore, I agreed to do the press conference on the record.

It was scheduled for August 5 and was attended by several dozen journalists. As I had anticipated, one journalist asked about Gorbachev's future in the context of a union treaty. I replied that, as long as he maintained his cooperation with Yeltsin, I thought his prospects were excellent until the next elections, which presumably would be held in a year or two. What would happen then, I thought, was unpredictable.

Another correspondent asked whether I thought that democratic changes had penetrated society sufficiently to be irreversible. This gave me my opening, and I answered as follows:[43]

> I think that the momentum of change and the degree of change now makes it impossible to successfully return either to a command econ-

omy or to a totalitarian system of rule. Now, that does not exclude efforts to do so in one area or another, and I suspect that there are forces working underneath the surface with this in mind . . . but things have gone too far to permit that. So if one means "Can they go back to a command administrative economy à la Brezhnev?" I would say, "No." That is simply impossible. And even if attempts were made to clamp down here or there, that could slow things down a bit, . . . but that particular system has been shattered and I don't see any way to put it back together.

Even more so, with totalitarian methods of rule. I know that there are forces here who are asking for, who are calling for some other leadership response . . . , and yet I think there are real inhibitions to using force in a widespread way. If there should be attempts, heaven forbid, if there should be, I think they will fall apart. So I am not saying that there can't be attempts to seize power, conceivably there could be, but I think these attempts are likely to fail.

Few of the journalists present reported on the press conference, and those who did quoted me as saying that Gorbachev's prospects were "excellent" without mentioning the qualifications I had carefully, though clumsily, added. Nobody reported that I had said that an attempt to overthrow Gorbachev was unlikely to succeed.

It was difficult to explain in sound bites the complexity of what was happening. And yet, if one went beyond sound bites, the response was usually a yawn. Critics, of course, did not hesistate to charge later that we did not understand what was going on.

Our last evening in Moscow was perhaps the most memorable of all those we had spent in that city. The Shevardnadzes invited us to a private dinner—we were the only four adults present—and we thought there could be no better way to end our eleven years of official duty in that country.

Of course we talked politics. Shevardnadze was still worried about a right-wing seizure of power; he felt the dangers he had warned of the previous December had not receded. But if he knew who and what and how, he was as discreet as he had been when he had offered his resignation as foreign minister. I think he had a general foreboding rather than precise knowledge of a specific plot.

Despite the talk of politics, it was a family evening, and that is what made it memorable. The Shevardnadze household was not the typical abode of most senior Communist Party officials I had visited, filled with pretentious kitsch. It was, rather, a typical upper-class *Georgian* household. Shevardnadze's soft speech and courteous habits were simply the outward manifestations of a sensitive human being with deep cultural roots.

Just before we went to the table, a small girl about five years old came in. They introduced her to us as their grandniece, visiting from Tbilisi. She was just beginning to learn Russian and spoke mainly in Georgian. She went with us to the table, and Nanuli Shevardnadze asked if we minded waiting for the child to offer a prayer. Of course we agreed, and we stood with bowed heads while she chanted an invocation in Georgian; it was not the simple "God is great, God is good, thank Him for our food, Amen" many American children are taught to recite but one that went on for minutes, complete with the rising and falling intonations one hears in Georgian churches. When she finished, our hosts crossed themselves, we all murmured "Amen," and we took our seats.

For thirty years Rebecca and I had watched and dealt with a country whose traditional cultures had been subjected to an unrelenting assault. The Communist regime had used every instrument it could devise to force a metamorphosis from the varied cultures of old to the homogeneous norms of the "new Soviet man." That Saturday evening, August 10, 1991, we saw proof that traditional values had survived. The preschool child who recited the Georgian prayer demonstrated that the values of the past would also have a place in the future.

This was encouraging, indeed exhilarating. But before euphoria overcame me I could not help wondering if, along with the good traditions, there might also be a revival of those unsavory, destructive practices that the police state had both exploited and restrained.

XX

Coup Perdu

*In connection with Mikhail Sergeyevich Gorbachev's inability to fulfill the duties
of the office of president of the USSR, . . . I have assumed the duties of
president of the USSR as of August 19, 1991.*
DECREE BY GENNADY I. YANAYEV[1]

*In connection with the acts of a group of people who have declared themselves
the State Committee on the State of Emergency, I hereby decree: 1. That the
committee's announcement violates the Constitution and the actions of its
organizers constitute a coup d'état and a state crime.*
DECREE BY BORIS YELTSIN, August 19, 1991[2]

*If he [Gorbachev] had signed the union treaty and then gone on vacation,
everything would have worked out for him.*
MARSHAL DMITRI YAZOV, August 17, 1991[3]

*I believe that history will record the twentieth century essentially ended
August 19 through 21, 1991.*
BORIS YELTSIN, 1994[4]

O n July 29, 1991, the day before President Bush arrived in Moscow, Gorbachev spent the day with Yeltsin and Nazarbayev
at the Novo-Ogaryovo dacha. They agreed to set August 20 for the signing of the union treaty but both Yeltsin and Nazarbayev insisted on major changes in the Soviet government. According to Yeltsin, Gorbachev agreed to replace Kryuchkov, Pugo, and Pavlov soon after the signing.[5] Though the meeting was held in what the three thought was strict privacy, a KGB transcript of the conversation was later discovered in a safe in the office of Gorbachev's chief of staff, Valery Boldin.[6]

On August 4, Gorbachev left Moscow for his annual vacation in the Crimea. Immediately, Kryuchkov sent a small team to the KGB safe house in the suburban village of Mashkino to work out plans for introducing a state of emergency (the Soviet equivalent of martial law).[7] When, however, the team reported to Kryuchkov on August 8 that there was no critical need to do so, the KGB chairman objected that there could be no delay since a state of emergency could not be introduced after the union treaty was signed.

The following week Kryuchkov sent a team back to Mashkino to do further work on contingency plans. As he did so, he told Alexei Yegorov, one of the KGB officers on the team, that since Gorbachev was psychologically incapable of dealing with the current situation, a state of emergency would be introduced without him.[8]

On Friday morning, August 16, drafts of announcements that would be made to establish a "State Committee on the State of Emergency" and to introduce martial law were on Kryuchkov's desk. He immediately gave his deputy orders to send to the Crimea technicians who could sever Gorbachev's communications.[9] Nevertheless, the plot still consisted of little more than contingency plans. Several key figures had not yet signed on.

The Bathhouse Deal

THERE WAS A TIME in American politics when key political decisions were made in smoke-filled rooms—or so the legend goes. In Russia, the equivalent is the steam-filled room of a Russian bath—a place not only to relax, drink, and chat but also to do serious business, particularly confidential business. On August 17, Kryuchkov invited several colleagues to steam themselves at a secret KGB facility in Moscow known by the code name "ABC Complex." With all the amenities of a luxury hotel, the ABC Complex offered far more comfort than the hotel rooms normally used by American politicians.

Valentin Pavlov, the prime minister, and Dmitri Yazov, the minister of defense, responded to the invitation. Their names, along with Kryuchkov's, had been on the shortlist of alleged plotters Popov had given me in June. In addition, Valery Boldin, Gorbachev's chief of staff; Oleg Baklanov, the Central Committee secretary responsible for the defense industry; and Oleg Shenin, the Central Committee secretary responsible for personnel, were in attendance.

According to testimony taken by the Russian state prosecutor following the coup, the group took a steam bath and then repaired to a cooling room where drinks and snacks had been laid out. Yazov, Shenin, and Pavlov chose vodka, while the rest joined Kryuchkov with a Scotch whiskey. Kryuchkov broached the subject by telling Pavlov he was about to be fired. "I'm ready to resign right now!" Pavlov exclaimed with bravado. Then he began to grumble about conditions in the country: they were close to catastrophe, he muttered, with outright famine just ahead. All discipline had disappeared, and no one was willing to follow instructions any more. He beleived that only a state of emergency could save the country.

Pavlov's complaints were predictable since they had become his constant refrain. Kryuchkov agreed with him and added that he had sent Gorbachev regular reports about the difficult conditions in the country but that Gorbachev's reaction had always been "inadequate." Kryuchkov felt that Gorbachev simply did not want to hear the truth, since he would break off the conversation and change the subject whenever Kryuchkov tried to enlighten him.

At this point, Kryuchkov made his proposal: to form a committee to impose a state of emergency, then send a delegation to Gorbachev to seek his support, and, if he refused, leave him incommunicado in the Crimea, announcing that he was incapacitated. Yanayev would become acting president, after which the Supreme Soviet, with Lukyanov's assistance, would meet and legalize the whole procedure.

The vodka ran out, and Yegorov, the KGB official who had worked on the contingency plans—and seems to have been the prosecutor's source for the conversation—was sent out for more. By the time he returned, discussion centered on who should confront Gorbachev.

Some key figures were not present: when Yazov proposed that actions by the army, KGB, and militia be coordinated, Kryuchkov informed the group that as yet Pugo knew nothing about the plan. And Yanayev? He, too, was out of the loop, but Shenin was sure he would cooperate. As for Lukyanov, they were not certain since, as Shenin put it, he continued to vacillate.[10]

When the group broke up a little past 6:00 P.M., the main lines of the conspiracy were set. But even then—less than forty-eight hours before the group confronted Gorbachev in the Crimea—they did not have the consent of the one person whose participation was essential if it was to have any semblance of legitimacy. What if Gennady Yanayev refused to go along and play the role of acting president? This question apparently did not worry the plotters; they were confident their man could be had.

A Junta Is Formed

JUST BEFORE FIVE O'CLOCK on Sunday afternoon, August 18, 1991, Gorbachev was informed that a group had come to see him at the presidential vacation house at Foros, on the Crimean shore. Since he had made no appointments, he was surprised that they had been allowed to enter without his permission. He was told that they had been admitted to the house because "Plekhanov is with them." Yuri Plekhanov was in charge of the KGB's Ninth Directorate, the unit responsible for the personal security of the president and other government leaders. His American counterpart would be—roughly—the head of the U.S. Secret Service.

In order to find out what was going on, Gorbachev picked up a telephone to inquire. It was dead. He hastily, and in rising panic, tried the other telephones on his desk—each special line terminated in a different instrument. None worked. He summoned other family members from their rooms nearby to alert them that they had been isolated and that an attempt might be made on their lives.[11]

Only then did Gorbachev confront his visitors, who had already unceremoniously barged into his upstairs study. Besides security chief Plekhanov, the group was made up of Chief of Staff Valery Boldin, two Central Committee secretaries, Oleg Baklanov and Oleg Shenin, and General Valentin Varennikov, commander of the Soviet ground forces, well known as one of the most strident and pugnacious hard-liners in the Soviet military establishment. When Boldin had been selected for the mission during the bathhouse meeting, Yazov had joked that Gorbachev would mutter *"Et tu, Brute"* when he saw him; Boldin had in fact been one of Gorbachev's most trusted subordinates.

At first the group tried to persuade Gorbachev to endorse the introduction of a state of emergency and the temporary transfer of his powers to Yanayev. When he refused, Varennikov angrily demanded his resignation. Gorbachev reports that he tried to reason with them, predicting that their efforts would fail and could lead to a bloody civil war, but when it was clear that the die had been cast, he dismissed them with choice imprecations.[12]

As the members of the "delegation" flew back to Moscow, their fellow conspirators began to gather in the Kremlin. According to evidence collected subsequently by the prosecutor, Pavlov, already tipsy early Sunday evening, came late, and Yanayev bounced in later, even more drunk. Lukyanov followed Yanayev, and as he entered, Kryuchkov yielded his place at the head of the table and took a seat on the side.

Despite his gesture of subordination, Kryuchkov conducted the meeting, first reporting to the group that Gorbachev had refused to follow the recommendation of the "group of comrades" who had gone to the Crimea. He then added that the president could no longer carry out his duties because he was ill.

"If he is sick, there should be a medical certificate or the president's own declaration," Lukyanov observed with some anxiety.

"We will get a medical statement later," Kryuchkov replied. "And when the comrades get back, they can share their impressions with us."

Lukyanov then demanded that his name be struck from the list of emergency committee members. As a representative of the legislative branch, he considered it improper for him to serve on it. The group argued with him until, at 10:15, Shenin, Baklanov, Boldin, and Plekhanov came in (Varennikov had gone to Kiev to keep the Ukrainian authorities in line). All had been drinking. Shenin and Baklanov in turn described their encounter with Gorbachev and his categorical refusal to endorse the emergency committee or declaration of a state of emergency.

The focus then shifted to Yanayev, who had taken little part in the conversation earlier. He had not yet signed the document assuming power as acting president and seemed to be hesitating. Kryuchkov reportedly told him, "Can't you see? If we don't save the harvest, there will be famine, and in a few months the people will take to the streets and we'll have a civil war."

Yanayev was not persuaded. He knew very well that Gorbachev was not incapacitated because he had talked with him on the telephone the same day (before Gorbachev's communications were cut) regarding his planned return to Moscow the following day. He continued to chain-smoke cigarettes and read the document that had been prepared for his signature.

"I will not sign that decree," he announced suddenly. The room fell silent. Yanayev continued, "I believe the president should come back after his vacation, get well, and come to himself. Besides, I don't feel I have the moral right or experience necessary to carry out his duties."

The prosecutors who published this account commented that it was difficult in retrospect to know whether Yanayev was expressing sincere doubts or putting on a show of resistance to avoid later charges that he was lusting for power. In any event, he soon broke down. The other conspirators assured him that they would take the responsibility upon themselves and that of course the president would take charge again as soon as he got well.

It was after eleven o'clock when Yanayev, hand shaking, picked up the pen and affixed a jagged, upward-slanting signature to the document declaring his assumption of power as acting president. Immediately, Yazov, Pugo, Kryuchkov, Pavlov, and Baklanov signed State Committee on the State of Emergency Order No. 1, which proclaimed a six-month state of emergency.

Foreign Minister Alexander Bessmertnykh, who had been summoned to the meeting from a vacation home in Belorussia, entered the room just after the documents were signed. He was wearing jeans and a denim jacket.

As soon as he heard what had happened, Bessmertnykh grabbed a blue marker and struck his name off the list of members of the emergency committee, protesting that it was ridiculous to put his name on the list and that no foreign leaders would deal with him if it were there.

When all the documents were signed, Kryuchkov observed that there were plans to "intern" some of the democratic leaders and mentioned a list with "more than ten names" that had been prepared. "You should pick up a thousand!" Pavlov advised in a loud, mocking voice.

Shortly after midnight, some of the plotters went home. Yazov later testified that as he left the Kremlin's Spassky Gate, facing on Red Square, he looked at the clock in the tower and noted that it showed the time to be 12:16 A.M.[13]

The Junta Takes Over

THE TASS NEWS AGENCY made the first announcement of the takeover some five hours later, just before 5:30 A.M. Moscow time on August 19.[14] The salient points of the various announcements were that Yanayev had assumed the duties of the president, that a State Committee on the State of Emergency had been established, and that all governing bodies in the USSR would be subordinated to it—and suspended if they did not obey. Furthermore, Order No. 1 by the emergency committee suspended all political parties and public organizations, banned strikes and street demonstrations, reintroduced censorship of the media, and threatened to impose a curfew whenever and wherever necessary. Later in the day, a subsequent order forbade publication of most independent newspapers.

Although Bessmertnykh had refused to be a member of the emergency committee, he allowed the Ministry of Foreign Affairs to send out an instruction to all Soviet ambassadors abroad to deliver a message from the emergency committee to the governments to which they were accredited. This message, signed by Yanayev as acting president of the USSR, was also issued by TASS. It assured foreign governments that the measures taken were temporary and that they would not affect the Soviet Union's international commitments.

Lukyanov gave even stronger implicit support to the emergency committee when he issued a highly critical statement on the union treaty draft, which had been scheduled for signature the following day. He pointed out that it did not embody some of the provisions demanded earlier by the USSR Supreme Soviet (they had been rejected by the republic leaders) and insisted that the draft would have to be discussed further by the USSR Supreme Soviet "and probably the Congress of People's Deputies" before it could be considered ready for signature.[15] While Lukyanov did not directly associate this statement with the formation of the emergency committee, it was issued by TASS just after the first emergency committee announcement, as part of a package of announcements. It was doubtless intended as a justification for blocking signature of the union treaty on August 20.[16]

Two additional persons joined the emergency committee during the day on August 19: Alexander Tizyakov, the factory manager who had been intriguing for months to replace Gorbachev with a junta, and Vasily Starodubtsev, a collective farm chairman who headed the USSR Peasant Union, a lobbying group that represented not peasant interests but those of the state and collective farm managers. Neither was politically prominent, but they could be presented to the public as representatives of large segments of the public.

A few organizations and political leaders immediately endorsed the junta. These included Vladimir Zhirinovsky's misleadingly named Liberal Democratic Party,[17] Communist leaders in the Baltic states who had remained loyal to Moscow when their parties had split (and who had been involved earlier in the year in the Committees of National Salvation),[18] and Marshal Sergei Akhromeyev, who rushed to Moscow from his vacation in the Crimea to offer his services to the emergency committee.

During the day, military equipment moved into Moscow from several directions. However, aside from clearing demonstrators from Red Square and Manezh Square, both just outside the Kremlin walls, the law enforcement units simply stood guard. A number of political leaders from the democratic movement were placed under surveillance and two were picked up, but there were no large-scale arrests.

But the emergency committee and its supporters were not the only forces active that day.

Yeltsin Reacts

ON AUGUST 18, Yeltsin was in Alma Ata, conferring with Nursultan Nazarbayev. He was scheduled to depart on his Russian government aircraft at 5:00 P.M., but Nazarbayev pressed him to stay for dinner, and he delayed his departure until 8:00 P.M. The government officials in Kazakhstan who were handling the logistics were not familiar with the notification procedures for government aircraft, and the Soviet Air Defense Forces did not receive a revised flight plan.[19] This subsequently led to rumors that the sudden change in flight time had thwarted orders from the coup plotters to shoot the plane down.[20] No credible evidence of such an order has been made public, but at one point orders had in fact been given to divert Yeltsin's plane to a military airport near Moscow, to arrest him when it arrived, and to incarcerate him at a government hunting lodge at Zavidovo, north of Moscow. The orders were changed—presumably by Kryuchkov—before his plane arrived, however. It landed at the civilian airport as usual, and he was driven directly to his dacha in Arkhangelskoye, a Moscow suburb.

Instead of arranging for an immediate arrest, Kryuchkov ordered KGB units to place Yeltsin under surveillance. He seems to have decided that he would wait until Yeltsin violated some order issued by the emergency committee so that he would have a pretext for picking him up.

Yeltsin was awakened the next morning by his daughter Tanya, who told him to watch a television announcement. He says that it was immediately apparent to him that there had been a coup, and he began to telephone other republic leaders as members of the Russian government began to arrive at his dacha. He tried to call Yanayev just after seven o'clock, but was told that Yanayev was resting since he had worked all night. He then tried to call Gorbachev but after some delay was told that officials in the Crimea had refused to put him through. He did manage to talk to Kravchuk, Nazarbayev, and the Belorussian leader Nikolai Dementei and was shocked that they were unwilling to commit themselves without further information.[21]

Ruslan Khasbulatov, then acting chairman of the Russian parliament—he had not yet been confirmed as Yeltsin's successor in that office—soon arrived at the dacha, as did other Russian officials: Sergei Shakhrai, Gennady Burbulis, Ivan Silayev, Mikhail Poltoranin, and Viktor Yaroshenko.[22] The group collectively composed an appeal to the Russian people, which they took down in longhand and then made photocopies of so that each would have several to distribute. As they worked, Leningrad's Mayor Anatoly Sobchak looked in briefly, then hurriedly returned to his city.

Once the group drafted the appeal, they decided to make a dash for the Russian White House, the large building facing the Moscow River that housed the Russian government. They were aware that the dacha complex had been placed under KGB surveillance and that they could be arrested at any time, but they were not sure what orders the security forces had. The squad of the KGB's Alpha Detachment that had been dispatched in the wee hours of the morning to Yeltsin's dacha apparently had no instructions other than to keep the premises under observation. Therefore, they simply watched as Yeltsin and the other Russian officials left the dacha compound for the city.[23]

At about ten o'clock they reached the White House, issued the appeal they had composed, and began a round of furious activity. Khasbulatov convened a meeting of the RSFSR Supreme Soviet Presidium, while Yeltsin met with foreign diplomats who had been summoned. Shortly after noon, when he learned that the tanks from the elite Taman Division that had arrived at the White House were friendly (they had been ordered simply to take up positions there), Yeltsin went down, talked to the tank crews, then climbed on one of the tanks, thereby creating one of the best photo opportunities of the decade.

Most of the Soviet media were closed to the Russian leaders, but this turned out to be only a minor inconvenience, since there were many alternatives. The independent news agency Interfax reported promptly on all of their statements, as did foreign correspondents. Telephone lines to the outside remained open, as did television circuits. If TASS and the Ostankino channel controlled by Kravchenko refused to report on statements by the Russian leaders (and other critics of the coup), citizens could turn to foreign radio broadcasts to get them in full detail. Even Gorbachev, under close guard in the Crimea, got the news from BBC, the Voice of America, and Radio Liberty.

The Russian government appealed for a general strike, but at first their appeal seemed to be ignored. However, more and more people began to turn up at the White House. A crowd that numbered only a few thousand at noon had swelled to tens of thousands by evening. By mid-afternoon reports reached the Kremlin that the coal miners in the Kuznetsk Basin were going out on strike. Pavlov telephoned Yazov to demand that the army arrest them, but Yazov did nothing. He later told investigators that he had thought Pavlov was drunk.[24] And, in fact, following a midafternoon Cabinet meeting on August 19 that he chaired, Pavlov went to his dacha and was not heard from again during the coup attempt.

While the elected governments in the three Baltic states and Moldova immediately condemned the coup, a few leaders, such as Karimov in Uzbekistan and Dementei in Belorussia, endorsed the emergency committee. Others seemed to hesitate at first, but by Tuesday morning, August 20, both Kazakhstan's Nazarbayev and Ukraine's Kravchuk had declared the attempted takeover illegal. The Ukrainian Communist Party, however, endorsed the emergency committee's decree.

Muffled Response

PRESIDENT BUSH was at his vacation home in Kennebunkport, Maine, when the reports arrived that Gorbachev had apparently been deposed. According to Michael Beschloss and Strobe Talbott, whose account seems reliable, National Security Adviser Brent Scowcroft notified the president just before midnight of the initial TASS announcements. Realizing that Bush would have to make some statement by early morning, they discussed what he should say. Scowcroft said that, based on historical experience, the coup would probably be successful. Since we might have to do business with the coup leaders, he said, we should not "burn our bridges with them." Therefore, he advised against using words such as "illegal," "illegitimate" or "unconstitutional." Bush agreed, and they finally decided that "extraconstitutional" might do.[25]

The next morning, Bush talked on the telephone with James Collins, to whom I had turned over the embassy just a week before, and learned that he had already called on Yeltsin, who was determined to resist the attempted takeover. He was also given a CIA analysis that indicated that the coup had been poorly planned, but Scowcroft is supposed to have said, "That's all just speculation at this point, no doubt with some wishful thinking mixed in." Therefore, when the president made his first statement to the press, he sounded as if he thought the coup had been successful and he intended to deal with the emergency committee. He spoke of Gorbachev's contributions in the past tense, expressed the expectation that the coup leaders would carry out the Soviet Union's international obligations, and described their obviously illegal action as merely "extraconstitutional."

Though he was to issue a much sterner statement that evening, the initial statement was damaging, particularly within the Soviet Union. The junta used it repeatedly in the controlled media on August 19 and 20, ignoring Bush's subsequent correction. Throughout the crucial day of August 19, Bush also avoided telephoning Yeltsin directly, even though Yeltsin had invited him to do so in a message conveyed by Chargé Collins.[26] The rationale seems to have been that this would look as if Bush had given up on Gorbachev, but that ignored the fact that Yeltsin was publicly insisting on the return of the Soviet government to Gorbachev's control. To contact Yeltsin directly would have been seen by all as support for Gorbachev.

Although Bush's error on the morning of August 19 was corrected later and, given the way events turned out, did not have a lasting negative effect, it did illustrate some of the flaws in the White House's judgment of events in the Soviet Union that plagued Bush's team throughout Bush's term.

In the first place, given the profound changes that were under way in the USSR, the least valuable touchstone for interpreting events was "historical experience." The Soviet Union had in many ways become a different country and was most unlikely to duplicate historical paradigms. Yet, initially, this was the principal reason Scowcroft gave for guessing that the coup would succeed and suspecting that the CIA was indulging in wishful thinking when its analysts pointed out that the coup leaders were not well organized.

But this was not the only mistake, and not the most important one. The more profound errors that lay behind Bush's statement had to do with the assessment of the people who had led the coup and the judgment of what tactics should be used with them. There should have been no doubt as to what sort of people Kryuchkov, Yazov, and Pavlov were. They were all in favor of using the iron fist to stop what they saw as the disintegration of the Soviet Union, and they had obviously moved to block the new union treaty. To hope that they would continue the reform process was fatuous.

Furthermore, they were strongly opposed to the compromises on foreign and military policy that Gorbachev had made with the United States and the West in general. Kryuchkov had concocted a whole series of cock-and-bull stories about the efforts of U.S. intelligence to undermine the Soviet Union. Yazov had done his best to use sleight of hand to violate the CFE treaty and had delayed the conclusion of the START agreement for years by his intransigent stance. As for Pavlov, from his very first week in office he had been blaming Western bankers or Western businessmen or Western governments for the problems of the Soviet economy and had made it abundantly clear that he opposed forging closer economic ties with the West. Was this a group the U.S. president should try to cultivate, even if it should turn out to hold power for a while? Would saving the coup leaders' feelings gain anything for the United States?

Finally, the attempt to avoid burning bridges that had never existed ignored the influence that American statements and policies can have on developments in the Soviet Union. This is a tricky area, since words are not always understood as they would be in the United States, but there is no question that American statements can bolster favorable trends and undermine unfavorable ones. An obvious example is Ronald Reagan's use of the term "evil empire." While this offended the Soviet rulers at the time, it did much to undermine the claim to legitimacy of the Soviet empire—particularly since Reagan had readily recognized favorable changes there as they occurred.

As should have been apparent from the junta's initial announcements and the fact that there was no evidence of extensive military or police preparation for a takeover by force, the conspirators were banking heavily on the appearance of legitimacy. If they could make their action look legitimate, people could be expected to fall in line and those few who did not could be neutralized by arresting them as lawbreakers. The greatest danger to their enterprise was the rejection of their claim to legitimacy. They needed the acquiescence of the outside world, of the United States in particular, much more than the outside world needed "bridges" to them.

What, then, should the president have said? If I had been asked, I would have advised him to make three simple points: (1) The attempt to seize power is illegal; (2) We continue to recognize Gorbachev as president of the Soviet Union; and (3) If the president of the USSR is incommunicado, we will make a special effort to deal directly with the elected governments of the republics, which, under the Soviet Constitution, have the right to enter into relations with foreign countries.

Such a statement, particularly if other Western leaders were willing to make comparable ones, would have sent shock waves through the junta. It would have removed any hope that the West would simply acquiesce in their seizure of power, and—more important—would signal that, unless Gorbachev was restored, we would start dealing with the republics as if the Soviet government did not exist. This was the ultimate political weapon we had against an anti-Western junta in Moscow. To have invoked it would have meant dealing with the junta from strength, not supplication.

From the evening of August 19, President Bush began to get it right. His second statement condemned the coup as illegal and unconstitutional, which was an important step forward. The next morning he telephoned Yeltsin and stayed in close contact with him until he was able to talk to Gorbachev. The junta continued to play his first statement on the controlled Soviet media throughout Tuesday and ignored the second one.

Although the administration's understanding of the scene in Moscow gradually came into better focus, Bush still seemed to view the political maneuvers there more in personal terms than in the perspective of interests and policies. He never completely freed himself from the instincts that had led to his unfortunate statement on the morning of August 19.

Those instincts provide an example of the difference between Bush's approach and Reagan's, differences that have nothing to do with the overworked and often-distorted labels of "conservative" versus "liberal" or the even more superficial and misleading contrast of "right" and "left." It has to do with fundamental assumptions.

Reagan, who assumed that there could be changes for the better and that he could influence them, would most likely not have made the mistake Bush did on the morning of August 19, 1991. He would have had instinctive confidence that his statement would make a difference and that he should design it not to curry favor with a hateful regime but to bring it down. And he would have had confidence that he could deal with whatever unexpected developments a fluid situation might bring.

Bush, on the other hand, was uncomfortable with change. Even when it was for the better, he had difficulty recognizing the improvement at first. He always seemed just a step behind—not so much that he endangered anything vital but enough to miss opportunities Reagan would probably have seized. Not having confidence that he could mold the future, he concentrated on managing the present and avoiding the mistakes of the past. And while Reagan was confident of his political base at home and was therefore willing to take chances, Bush was always looking over his shoulder.

This time President Bush was lucky. The self-styled emergency committee in Moscow began to disintegrate on the second day of its existence, not because of foreign pressure but because of its own fragility and incompetence.

The Coup Collapses

YELTSIN AND HIS COLLEAGUES went through two agonizing nights in the Russian White House, not sure whether they would survive or not. But in retrospect the fate of the effort to overthrow Gorbachev was settled during the fourteen or fifteen hours following the cabal's first public announcement by its failure to take Yeltsin into custody immediately, Yeltsin's public defiance, the unwillingness of many military units to use force against their own people, the growing bodies of demonstrators in major cities, and finally—in the evening—a press conference held by the coup leaders.

Yanayev, Pugo, Baklanov, Starodubtsev, and Tizyakov appeared together. Apparently, Kryuchkov and Yazov stayed away because they wanted to stress the junta's civilian character. Nevertheless, the press conference was a disaster. All the coup leaders seemed frightened, and Yanayev's hands shook. Yanayev seemed apologetic and repeatedly promised that their rule was temporary, that they hoped Gorbachev would be back soon. When asked what specific illness Gorbachev was suffering from, Yanayev gave only evasive answers, such as "He is now resting and under treatment."

As the press conference went on, the questions became less and less respectful, impudent even. Tatyana Malkina of *Nezavisimaya gazeta* asked whether they realized that they had carried out a coup d'état. The *Corriere della Sera* correspondent asked whether they had consulted General Pinochet. Finally, using the intimate *ty,* Alexander Bovin, whose silhouette might pass for Alfred Hitchcock's, asked Starodubtsev, whom he had known since school, "How did you fall in with this lot?"[27]

Our son David was traveling in Yakutia with his wife, gathering material for a book on nature in Siberia, when the coup attempt occurred. They told us how their Soviet acquaintances, at first fearful over the implications of Gorbachev's ouster, had laughed in relieved amazement as they had watched the telecast of the emergency committee's press conference. What they had seen were neither confident leaders nor bullies who could terrify a nation into submission but frightened, defensive bureaucrats who were themselves terrified by what they had done.

Russians will tolerate many vices in their leaders, but weakness and cowardice, never. When the members of the emergency committee appeared before the country as objects of contempt, their defeat was inevitable. The country would not follow, and they had neither the will nor the means to force it to. Most of the country seemed to sense this already on Tuesday morning, August 20, though many still feared that some desperate act—most likely, a military assault on the Russian White House—could produce a massacre of the thousands of people who had assembled to defend it.

The emergency committee itself began to unravel that day: Pavlov stayed out "sick" and Yanayev himself soon vanished. The USSR Committee for Constitutional Oversight raised serious questions about the legality of the emergency committee. Lukyanov reported to the coup leaders Tuesday morning that his Monday consultations with Supreme Soviet deputies had convinced him that he could not muster the two-thirds vote necessary to legitimate the committee's formation. No report by physicians on Gorbachev's health was published, as had been promised.

Outright opposition mounted. Vadim Bakatin and Yevgeny Primakov, both members of Gorbachev's Security Council, which the emergency committee had ordered abolished, issued a statement branding the coup illegal, and they were joined by Arkady Volsky, the president of the Scientific-Industrial Union.[28] The leadership of the Komsomol, the Communist Party's youth auxiliary, condemned the coup, demanded to see Gorbachev, and appealed to soldiers "not to stain your military honor and consciences with the blood of fellow citizens."

Crowds had gathered not only around the White House in Moscow and in the Baltic states but in Leningrad, Kiev, Sverdlovsk, and other cities. Foreign leaders increasingly made their hostility clear.

Nevertheless, fears mounted that there would be an assault on the White House the night of August 20–21. The reports of an assault on August 19 had proven false,[29] but troops still surrounded the building and could easily have taken it—though not without much loss of life, given the large number of people massed around the building.

There was reason to worry. Overcoming his vacillation of the day before, Kryuchkov ordered the arrest of Yeltsin and his associates. Yazov tried to persuade one military commander after another to take the White House. Some, like General Yevgeny Shaposhnikov, the air force commander, and General Pavel Grachev, commander of airborne troops, refused point-blank. Shaposhnikov even threatened to bomb the Kremlin if an attack on the White House occurred. Others went through the motions only partway. Major General Alexander Lebed brought troops from Tula, south of Moscow, as ordered, but immediately informed Yeltsin that he would not attack. Some of his soldiers actually joined Yeltsin's defenders of the White House for a time.

Nor were the KGB elite troops prepared to fire on their compatriots. The famed and much-feared Alpha Detachment—the one that had seized the television complex in Vilnius in January—opted out when two of the commander's three deputies voted against following orders to take Yeltsin by force. They were dissatisfied with the treatment they had received since their action in January, particularly with the lack of support for the family of one man in the unit who had been killed. Besides, fighting Lithuanian "rebels" was one thing; attacking an elected Russian government was something else again. Even the KGB's elite wanted no part of a civil war.

Librarian of Congress James Billington, one of the most perceptive historians of Russian culture, was in Moscow at the time and has described the mood graphically.[30] Rumors swept the city of an impending attack on the White House at 4:00 P.M., and when it did not occur many were convinced that it was sure to come that night. A strict curfew, announced that evening, did not prevent tens of thousands from rallying at the White House to challenge the leaders of the coup to kill them if they dared. The crowds that gathered in Saint Petersburg to denounce the coup were even larger, but the tension in Moscow was greater since all understood that the focal point of resistance was Yeltsin and the Russian government.

It was remarkable that the crowds supporting the Russian government included not only many young people but an unusual number of middle-aged and elderly. Women were as numerous as men. As one elderly librarian told Billington as she set off for the White House on the evening of August 20, it was particularly important for persons of her generation to participate, "since we are the ones who for so long remained silent."[31] The sentiments expressed in the notes left on Andrei Sakharov's bier in December 1989, "Forgive us" and "Never again!," were very much alive.

Yelena Bonner, Sakharov's widow, was of course among those who shielded the Russian government with their bodies, as were Eduard Shevardnadze, Alexander Yakovlev, and Mstislav Rostropovich, who flew in from Paris with his cello. Many of the defenders had severely criticized Gorbachev, and he had lambasted them while making excuses for those who were trying to remove him. These differences were not forgotten, but a question more important than personalities was at stake: Could Russia be a state based on law, or would it revert to the arbitrary rule that had characterized most of its history?

As Yelena Bonner put it in a speech to her fellow "defenders":

> Gorbachev is our President. We are the ones to judge him, not they. They think they can rule us and order us about. . . . But we will show them, we will prove to them that we are people, people and not just livestock.[32]

The anticipated attack on the White House never came, but the night did not pass without casualties. Three young men, Dmitri Komar, Ilya Krichevsky, and Vladimir Usov, were killed in an encounter with a tank crew on the Garden Ring just in front of the U.S. Embassy's old office building. Although the deaths were not the result of a military attack, they brought home to the demonstrators the dangers they faced and to the military commanders proof that the mere presence of heavy military equipment manned by soldiers untrained in crowd control risked further loss of life, even if the soldiers were not ordered to take action against the demonstrators.

By 3:00 A.M. Wednesday morning, barely fifty-one hours after the decisive meeting of the conspirators in the Kremlin had ended, Kryuchkov and Yazov saw that the game was up. Yazov ordered the military units to leave Moscow and go back to their bases, and Kryuchkov telephoned Yeltsin to say that there would be no attack on the White House.

A few hours later, those members of the emergency committee who were still ambulatory (Pavlov and Yanayev were arrested later in the day, dead drunk) flew to the Crimea, apparently to make amends to Gorbachev. Gorbachev refused to see them and returned to Moscow late in the evening with a group of officials from the Russian government and members of his own entourage who had stayed loyal, such as Bakatin and Primakov.

The members of the emergency committee and their active collaborators were arrested—those who were members of the Supreme Soviet only after that body had voted to lift their parliamentary immunity. A few escaped by committing suicide: when officials went to arrest Minister of Internal Affairs Pugo, they found him and his wife dead of self-inflicted gunshot wounds. Two days later, Sergei Akhromeyev hanged himself in his Kremlin office after writing a detailed report to Gorbachev of his activities on behalf of the emergency committee and a farewell note to his family. Characteristically, he also left 50 rubles to pay his bill at the staff cafeteria.[33]

Gorbachev's Double Take

SHAKEN BY HIS seventy-two-hour ordeal in the Crimea, Gorbachev had nothing to say publicly when he and his family returned to Moscow late Wednesday evening, August 21, with an escort organized by the Russian government and directed by Russian Vice President Alexander Rutskoy. As he walked down the ramp in view of television cameras, he looked stunned, and Raisa had to be assisted down the steps.

The following day he conducted a lengthy press conference in the same hall in which he had appeared with President Bush three weeks before.[34] He recounted, in some detail, his experience at Foros and then responded to questions. The pressure to which he had been subjected had left its mark: his answers were more rambling and disjointed than usual, and he would sometimes change his thought in midsentence. Yet, for anyone who knew him, there could be no doubt about his sincerity.

This made his reply to a question from Vladislav Terekhov of the Interfax News Agency all the more striking and troubling. Noting that the Communist Party had kept silent for three days while its leader was illegally incarcerated, Terekhov asked, "Don't you think that it is time to pay serious attention to our Communist Party of the Soviet Union as a tool and a political organism that is not in keeping with the present day?"

One would have thought that, at the very least, Gorbachev would have replied that the Party's activities over the recent days would have to be examined carefully to determine if its composition, organization, and structure were compatible with a democratic, law-based state.

Instead, he chose to defend the Communist Party as a whole and to reiterate his long-cherished intention to transform it into an instrument of change:

> I see my duty—I will do it to the end, as long as I have the strength—as being to hold in check, to hamper in every possible way, more than that, to get rid of reactionary forces and drive them out of the CPSU. On the basis of this new program we have put forward, I consider that there is the possibility of uniting all that is progressive, all that is the best thinking. . . .
> We must therefore do everything to ensure that the Party is reformed and becomes a living force of perestroika.[35]

Subsequently, when a Mexican journalist asked him if he might lead "the forces which espoused a new line" out of the CPSU, he retorted, "I am a convinced adherent of the socialist idea,"[36] and though he went on to argue that the "Stalinist model of social organization" was the antithesis of socialism and must be rooted out, the reformers—like many in the West—concluded that he had learned nothing from his recent experience.

The impressions left by this press conference ruined whatever faint prospects he might have had to regain some of his power after his return from Foros.

During Gorbachev's address to the nation, carried on television at 9:00 P.M. the same day, he did not speak of the Communist Party or "socialism" at all. He thanked Yeltsin and the Russian government for their support, praised those who had come out in his defense, and admitted some of his own errors, particularly in his appointments. The Congress of People's Deputies, he said, had been correct to reject his candidate for vice president, and it was his fault that he had insisted on a second vote. As for the future, he proposed to continue on the course he had already set: conclusion of a union treaty, to be followed by adoption of a new constitution and new elections for president and parliament. The only hint of change from his earlier plans (as opposed to changing personnel) came in his comment that the state security system had proven "insufficiently reliable" and would require "the most painstaking study."[37]

On the very next day Yeltsin forced Gorbachev to confront, in public and in the most humiliating way, the treachery of his entire government and the majority of the Communist Party leadership.

When Gorbachev appeared at the RSFSR Supreme Soviet on August 23, Yeltsin forced him to read from the podium minutes of meetings at which his closest associates had supported the coup attempt. The only member of the Cabinet to have opposed it directly was Nikolai Vorontsov, the minister of the environment, who—not coincidentally—was the only member of the Cabinet who did not belong to the Communist Party.[38]

Yeltsin moved rapidly against the Communist Party. He banned the publication of *Pravda* and other Party newspapers, ordered the headquarters of the CPSU Central Committee (where most sensitive records were kept) sealed, and suspended all activities of the Russian Communist Party. Gorbachev, however, continued to resist supporting a ban on the Party itself. Under intensive questioning by Russian legislators, he doggedly insisted that prohibiting the Communist Party would be a mistake.

Nevertheless, on the following day, Saturday, August 25, Gorbachev had no alternative but to resign his position as general secretary of the CPSU. At the same time, as president of the USSR, he issued two decrees. The first instructed local soviets to take Communist Party property into custody and to dispose of it in accordance with USSR and republic law. The second ordered a cessation of all activity by political parties in the armed forces, the militia, the KGB, and all other law enforcement bodies, as well as throughout the civil service.[39]

Gorbachev also fired the entire USSR Council of Ministers and appointed Russian Premier Ivan Silayev to head a committee that would take charge of the Soviet economy. Reform economist Grigory Yavlinsky, whose advice he had spurned a month earlier, became Silayev's deputy. Thus the RSFSR government was now in control of what was left of the Soviet state economic structure.

The day before, on August 24, Gorbachev had placed Vadim Bakatin in charge of the KGB, with orders to conduct a fundamental reorganization. Simultaneously, furious crowds filled Dzerzhinsky Square, where KGB headquarters were located, and tore down the statue of Felix Dzerzhinsky, the founder of Lenin's Cheka, a forerunner of the KGB. Inside KGB headquarters, officials frantically destroyed incriminating documents until Bakatin took charge.[40]

Thus, by the end of the week that had begun with an effort to topple Gorbachev and restore total Communist control of the country, the Communist Party of the Soviet Union ceased to exist as an organized force. Even though all but a few of its officers and members were free to pursue political activity as they chose, including organizing new parties, things would never be the same for them.

The Communist Party of the Soviet Union had not been a political party as the term is normally used; it had been an instrument of government, or rather an instrument to control government, that had the entire apparatus of the state at its disposal. Even if some sort of Communist Party, with or without the name, should be organized from the remnants of the CPSU, it would no longer have tentacles in all state and public organizations or be able to appropriate to itself the state's instruments of compulsion. In other words, it would be forced to become a political party in the normal sense.

Why They Failed

CONVENTIONAL WISDOM could not allow the possibility that, in a country that had always been ruled by authoritarian, and often totalitarian, regimes, a conspiracy including the vice president, the head of government, and the chiefs of the armed forces, the secret police, and the normal police could fail. Such a proposition would seem even more dubious if one added that the country was in dire economic straits, the president was unpopular, and the conspiracy had either the connivance or, at least, tolerance of the chairman of parliament. The fact is that those who belonged to and sympathized with the emergency committee *were* the government of the USSR, except for the president himself. How could they fail in a country in which legal niceties had never determined political developments?

Many would say that they failed because of their own incompetence. They had organized their coup haphazardly, refrained from taking such necessary steps as arresting Yeltsin at the beginning, and eventually lacked the ruthlessness required for such an enterprise.

Obviously, the emergency committee was neither efficient nor decisive, but most Soviet organizations were not efficient. Its opponents were also not well organized; their enthusiasm and determination were not matched by organizational structures that would have helped them survive a concerted assault. They had been squabbling among themselves right up to the day the emergency committee announced its takeover—and began again within days after it collapsed.

The coup was poorly organized, but that is not the reason it failed. It failed because changes that had taken place in the country made it impossible to organize a successful illegal takeover. The organizers' greatest mistake was their failure to recognize that these changes had occurred. They thought they were dealing with the Soviet Union of the 1960s: announce a takeover, put a few tanks into the street, and that would be it. People would go about their daily business, some happy, some unhappy, most not really caring. Just promise them that life would get better. It wouldn't matter whether they believed it since they would know there was nothing they could do to influence the situation.

The coup leaders were the victims of their own prejudices. Kryuchkov had been arguing that only an iron hand could restore order and keep the USSR intact so long that he had begun to believe it. Or—perhaps—he had fabricated and distorted "evidence" to "prove" this point because it was what he wanted to believe. Either way, it was self-deception. The country was no longer what he and his fellow conspirators imagined it to be.

Yet they were not entirely wrong. Most people would probably have accepted the coup without overt resistance. But this was not the point, for enough people in Moscow were determined to resist a return to the past to ensure that the conspirators would not win without a fight. The elective organs that had arisen as the result of Gorbachev's political decisions blocked easy acquiescence in many of the republics. Yeltsin was only the most prominent and most strategically located of many regional leaders around whom resistance to the takeover crystallized. Not everyone had to take to the streets in opposition; only enough to show the plotters they would have to shed a lot of blood to stay in power.

"When have Communists ever worried about spilling blood?" cynics might ask. The answer is: when it is their blood that might be shed. The events in Moscow on August 19 and 20, 1991, demonstrated what should have been obvious earlier: the Soviet army was not a reliable instrument for use against a civilian population in Russia. (Conceivably, under certain circumstances, the troops might have attacked non-Russian republics, a threat that hung over the Baltics for a year and a half.) The army was filled with conscripts trained to defend against enemy troops, not to shoot civilians. No wonder commander after commander found excuses for not attacking the White House. The astounding thing is that Yazov and Kryuchkov thought their orders would be obeyed.

Obviously, if they had persisted, the coup leaders might have found a unit willing to take on that fairly simple military task. But what then? Suppose mobs had gathered in other cities? They already had throughout the Baltic, in Leningrad, in Sverdlovsk, in Kiev, Lviv, and Kishinev. How many military or KGB units could be trusted? How many would join the other side? And what would the rest of the world do while this went on? In 1918 the Germans came as far as Kiev, though under quite different circumstances.

Civil war was not an option any of the coup leaders ever dreamed they had, and when the prospect confronted them they knew they had failed.

A Surprise?

WHENEVER BOTH THE GOVERNMENT and the public are taken by surprise, there are accusations of "intelligence failure"—"intelligence" not in the sense of gray matter but in the sense of espionage reports. However, when political surprises occur, they result more often from a failure to think than from a failure to spy.

Now that we know what happened and can be reasonably sure of why and how, we may judge what might have been predicted and what could not have been foreseen. For months before the emergency committee tried to take power, various elements in the Communist Party, army, and KGB had worked on contingency plans to apply "emergency rule" or "presidential rule" to parts of the country experiencing political unrest. The new elective assemblies in the Baltic states were a particular concern to them, but they knew that the democratic movement in general was dangerous to them personally and had to be curbed. As the Party's power eroded, the army lost resources, prestige, and bases in Central and Eastern Europe and the police faced pressure to end the abuses of the past and comply with the rule of law. These groups, once part of a machine that could "decide everything," were facing the loss of their jobs if the trends they abhorred continued.

At first, they concentrated on persuading Gorbachev to declare presidential rule, "suspend" elected bodies, and give them a mandate to bring society into line, using whatever coercion was necessary. At first he gave them hope that he would cooperate—that was the implication they drew from his "turn to the right" in the fall of 1990. The attack on the Vilnius television tower in January 1991 was not only a rehearsal for seizure of power by an emergency committee but a ploy to force Gorbachev to legitimate the use of force to remove the Lithuanian government.

Whether from conviction or for fear of losing Western support—or, probably, both—Gorbachev refused to go along. But he did not totally exclude applying presidential rule if circumstances, in his opinion, required it. Therefore, those closest to him—Kryuchkov, Boldin, Pavlov once he became prime minister—concentrated their efforts on convincing him that it was necessary. Gorbachev bowed to their wishes again in March, when he ordered troops into Moscow—but, again, learned quickly that he had made a mistake.

Meanwhile, many of the regional Party bosses grew ever more restive. Each time they came to Moscow for Party plenums or congresses—certainly from the summer of 1990—they vowed to force Gorbachev to authorize the iron fist or abdicate. Each time he outmaneuvered them, in part by dropping hints that he was seriously considering applying presidential rule but more importantly by convincing them that they would lose a direct vote to remove him. In July 1991 Yeltsin saved the day for Gorbachev by banning the Party from state institutions in Russia, thus presenting the apparatchiks with a more imminent threat than their general secretary posed.

Doubtless, wish lists of desired actions and contingency plans of the sort found in Tizyakov's papers abounded. The regional Party secretaries and subordinate military or KGB commanders, however, could not by themselves organize a successful coup. That would require the leaders of these key organizations, plus enough support in the Central Committee Secretariat to prevent any significant challenge from the Party apparatus.

By June 1991, when Pavlov made his bid to the Supreme Soviet for additional authority, a cabal of the most important players had jelled, but their plan still seems to have been to force Gorbachev to turn over power to them rather than eliminate him entirely. The intention to confront him with a choice of transferring power voluntarily or facing isolation and de facto imprisonment seems to have hardened only when some of the key players learned that they would soon be dismissed as a consequence of Gorbachev's deal with Yeltsin and Nazarbayev for a union treaty.

The dynamics of this situation were well understood by the better-informed embassies in Moscow. Western policy responded accordingly. The West brought great pressure to bear on Gorbachev throughout the year *not* to introduce presidential rule. This was considered necessary to counterbalance the pressure he was feeling from the KGB, the army, and many in the Party Secretariat. In general we knew who was likely to be on what side—and our hunches turned out to be better than Gorbachev's.

Fine. But did we know there would be a coup the night of August 18–19? No, certainly not—we could hardly know more than the conspirators themselves knew, and they made their final plans at the last minute. But we did know enough to permit well-informed policy making.

First, we knew that powerful forces were determined to apply martial law to key parts of the country, one way or another, and that their frustration was growing because Gorbachev continued to refuse to authorize it. We understood that this might well lead to a desperate act to force his hand, but it was impossible to predict exactly what form this might take. The new openness of society made planning for a conspiracy impossible on the scale necessary to be confident of success. Any extensive advance planning would be certain to leak, and Popov's knowledge of the machinations in June would have brought that point home. Without advance consultation with the commanders, the reliability of KGB and army units could not be assumed. Conspirators might, therefore, never find the right combination of circumstances to activate their plans before it became too late.

As it was, the idea of confronting Gorbachev at Foros and isolating him if he refused seems to have been agreed only on Friday, August 16, and the precise contours of the emergency committee took shape only *after* the confrontation in Foros. In fact, until Yanayev signed the fateful document at about 11:00 P.M. Moscow time on August 18, no one could be absolutely certain that the plot would go forward.

Besides knowing that a coup might be attempted, it was important to know whether it was likely to succeed. Secret information does not help much in forming such a judgment; close knowledge of a country and its society does.

In the summer of 1991, our embassy commented repeatedly that, while an attempt to remove Gorbachev was possible, it was very unlikely that an *illegal* putsch could succeed. That is also what I tried to explain to American journalists in Moscow on August 5, 1991.

If the White House seemed surprised and unprepared the morning of August 19, the American and other foreign media did no better. Virtually all the headlines screamed the news of Gorbachev's "ouster" as if it were final (even the coup leaders claimed it was only temporary), and this attitude persisted also in the Tuesday newspapers, which had closed hours after the disastrous press conference in Moscow and the initial signs that the coup was beginning to unravel.

For example, *The New York Times,* which presented more detailed and nuanced coverage than most did, proclaimed in a banner headline on August 19:

GORBACHEV IS OUSTED IN AN APPARENT COUP
BY SOVIET ARMED FORCES AND HARD-LINERS;
ACCUSED OF STEERING INTO A 'BLIND ALLEY'

Two of the phrases used in the headline distorted the facts: Gorbachev had not been "ousted" (though that might eventually be the effect of the emergency committee's action), and the coup was not the work of the

"Soviet armed forces"—the minister of defense is not synonymous with the "armed forces" as a whole. In *The New York Times,* at least, a careful reader might have spotted these distortions—in fact, a second headline in the same issue used the words "Gorbachev Apparently Ousted"—but newspapers in most parts of the country did not print such qualifications.

On the second day, August 20, *The New York Times* proclaimed across its front page:

K.G.B.-MILITARY RULERS TIGHTEN GRIP

But by then it was apparent that the emergency committee's grip was not as tight as people had assumed the day before. News was flowing out in profusion despite efforts to control the media.

Despite these lapses, the coverage in *The New York Times* was not as misleading as that in most of the country's newspapers. The *St. Louis Post Dispatch* used the word "ouster" without qualification not only on August 19 but in at least four different stories on August 20. Its analysts without exception assumed that the coup had been successful; one even stated that it had "thrown some of the U.S. government's highest hopes into Limbo." Its readers must have been amazed when two days later they read that the coup had been "foiled."

Television coverage was, on the whole, no better informed. When I was interviewed on ABC's *Nightline* on August 19 and said that the coup could not succeed, every other commentator seemed skeptical: they not only dismissed the possibility of reversal but implied that it was foolish to think that the KGB and army could not maintain control if they wished. None seemed to appreciate that neither the KGB nor army was monolithic and that both could be unreliable in dealing with civilian resistance.

Very few observers appreciated the profound changes that had occurred in the Soviet Union, even though in many cases they had observed and written about them. In fact, they tended to make the same mistake the coup leaders had.

XXI

Fatal Blows

*Our good intentions . . . were not fulfilled largely because we failed to change the old
mechanism of power. I have in mind the state bureaucracy. . . . We . . . have not
yet really started decisive democratic changes in the economy.*
MIKHAIL GORBACHEV to USSR Supreme Soviet, August 26, 1991[1]

*Today I have much more faith in Mikhail Sergeyevich Gorbachev than I had
even three weeks ago, before the putsch.*
BORIS YELTSIN, September 4, 1991[2]

*It is difficult to say how many states will join the union, but I am firmly convinced
that there will be a union.*
BORIS YELTSIN, November 14, 1991[3]

*Yes, now they say: we are going to create a confederation. And after a comma
they add: but we are for a unified state. How can that be?*
LEONID KRAVCHUK, November 26, 1991[4]

B y Sunday evening, August 25, 1991—just one week after Gennady Yanayev agreed to assume presidential authority—he and
all his coconspirators were either in jail or dead, the activities of the
Communist Party of the Soviet Union had been suspended, and most of
the republics had begun to follow the three Baltic states in a rush for the
exits. To make matters even more difficult for Gorbachev, the central
Soviet government was in total disarray. The Council of Ministers had
been dismissed, the KGB, shocked and afraid, placed under a reformist
director, and the military command thoroughly shaken up.

Yeltsin had used the coup attempt to extend his authority into areas
that were normally under central or federal jurisdiction, and—since this
had been necessary to save Gorbachev—Gorbachev could only endorse
what Yeltsin had done in his absence. But as a result, the political initiative was now totally with Yeltsin, the more so since Gorbachev had hesitated, upon his return to Moscow, to move against the Communist
Party and to disavow his attachment to "socialism."

Just as Gorbachev had been unable to save his presidency without Yeltsin's help, he could now no longer preserve any sort of union without Yeltsin's active cooperation. Fortunately for Gorbachev's state of mind at the time, Yeltsin reaffirmed his earlier statements that he believed a union treaty could be signed and implemented.

But by no means was all the action in Moscow. Events elsewhere would narrow the choices both Gorbachev and Yeltsin could make.

Independence Fever

ONE OF THE PRINCIPAL AIMS of the coup plotters had been to establish martial law in the three Baltic states, suspend their legislatures, and end the agitation for independence. The first steps came immediately after the announcement that the emergency committee had been formed in Moscow, when General Fyodor Kuzmin, commander of the Baltic Military District, declared the Baltic governments subordinate to him and Alfreds Rubiks, the hard-line Latvian Communist, announced formation of a local emergency committee. Although military and police forces occupied a number of communications facilities and other strategic points in the Baltic, there was little violence, and the coup collapsed before action was taken against the republic governments and their legislatures.

The Baltic parliaments and governments were not cowed by the show of force on August 19 and 20. They immediately denounced the emergency committee, and the two countries that had not yet definitively declared independence did so immediately, Estonia on August 20 and Latvia on August 21.[5] Lithuania, of course, had made its declaration the year before, and just before the coup attempt, the RSFSR had concluded a treaty with Lithuania that recognized its independence.[6] When Estonia and Latvia issued their declarations, Russia immediately extended recognition.

Gorbachev still hesitated to endorse the independence of the Baltic states, insisting that only the Congress of People's Deputies could make that decision. However, he approved steps to free them from the threat of military intervention by Soviet forces. General Kuzmin was replaced, Baltic citizens serving in the Soviet armed forces were released, and KGB properties in all three countries were turned over to the elected governments. Latvian authorities arrested Rubiks on August 24 on charges resulting from his participation in the coup attempt.

On September 6, the newly formed State Council of the USSR voted unanimously to recognize the independence of Estonia, Latvia, and Lithuania. The divorce became official and final, though many matters were left to negotiate, including a schedule for withdrawal of Soviet armed forces from the area. Many foreign countries had already extended recognition, and after the Soviet action virtually all did.[7] The three became members of the United Nations at the next session of the General Assembly.

The formal exit of the Baltic states from the Soviet Union set an important precedent. For the first time, the Soviet Union had allowed republics to exercise the right of secession Stalin's Constitution had hypocritically granted them. Gorbachev might have diminished the force of the precedent if, in 1989, he had been willing to declare that the Baltic states had become part of the Soviet Union by an illegal process and therefore could leave in a manner not required of the other union republics. At that time, he could probably also have negotiated rights to maintain military bases and protect other Soviet interests in the Baltic. Having made a different choice, Gorbachev was forced to concede the exit of the Baltic states under the most damaging circumstances for the Soviet Union as a whole: besides the encouragement it provided to other republics, it demonstrated that the Center no longer had the power to hold a republic against its will.

For a while, Gorbachev, Yeltsin, and the rest of the world treated the non-Baltic republics differently. Though many proceeded to declare independence, it was not clear that all of these declarations represented a serious desire to be completely independent. The reasons differed from republic to republic. In some cases the declarations were made in response to popular pressure, but in others they represented a desperate effort by local Communist rulers to insulate themselves from reforms that Moscow might decide to undertake.

Whatever the reason, republic declarations of independence became almost a daily occurrence as soon as the coup attempt failed. Ukraine declared independence on August 24, subject to a referendum to be held December 1. The Belorussian Supreme Soviet declared the "political and economic independence of Belorussia" on August 25. The Moldovan parliament approved its declaration on August 27, Azerbaijan on August 30, and Uzbekistan and Kyrgyzstan on August 31. Georgia, which had declared independence back in April, on the second anniversary of the Tbilisi massacre, announced on September 6 that it was breaking all ties with the USSR because the latter had failed to accept the declaration as legally binding. Tajikistan, preoccupied with an internal shift of power, waited until September 9. Armenia held off until it conducted a long-scheduled referendum on September 21. When nearly 95 percent of the people voted for independence,[8] the Armenian parliament issued its formal declaration.

Thus, by the end of September 1991, *all* of the union republics except Russia, Kazakhstan, and Turkmenistan had declared independence, and Turkmenistan did so in October. Nevertheless, most continued to participate in the remaining USSR institutions and to negotiate with Gorbachev on a new union treaty.

Republics in Turmoil

WHILE THE FAILED COUP strengthened all of the republic leaderships relative to the central authorities in Moscow, it triggered shock waves that transformed the internal politics of many of the republics. Some republic leaders—usually those who had opposed the coup—gained; others lost.

Belorussia is a case in point. Nikolai Dementei,[9] the chairman of the republic's Supreme Soviet, failed to condemn the coup attempt on August 19 and 20, and the Central Committee of the Belorussian Communist Party issued a statement on August 21, just before the emergency committee collapsed, supporting it. Moderates in the parliament, led by Stanislav Shushkevich, joined the National Front opposition in calling for a special session of the Supreme Soviet, which convened on Saturday, August 24.

Dementei came under heavy attack at the session for his behavior on August 19–22, and although he defended himself vigorously, arguing that his actions had been misinterpreted, an overwhelming majority of deputies voted against him at the end of the day. However, a quorum was not present and the vote was therefore not legally valid. The session resumed the next day.

By then the atmosphere had changed radically. After the Saturday session adjourned, the deputies learned that Gorbachev had resigned as general secretary and suspended the activities of the CPSU. There would be an investigation into the activities of Party organizations during the coup. Suddenly, the Belorussian Communist leaders realized that the only way they could head off a hostile probe into their activities by Moscow was to declare independence. They came back to the session Sunday and voted with their normal opponents, the National Front, in favor of independence. Dementei was forced to resign and yield the chair to Shushkevich, his first deputy.[10]

A subsequent session of the Belorussian Supreme Soviet, on September 18, renamed the country "Belarus" and elected Shushkevich parliament chairman (and chief of state). A physicist who had spent most of his professional career at the Belorussian State University in Minsk, he entered politics only in 1989 when, already in his mid-fifties, he won election for a seat in the USSR Supreme Soviet. He told me in an interview in 1992 that his outrage over the Communist Party's mishandling of the Chernobyl disaster had propelled him into politics as soon as contested elections made it possible.[11]

The Communist deputies who voted for him as chairman probably thought his reputation as a moderate reformer would provide some cover for them to continue life as usual. If so, they misjudged him. Despite his gentle, soft-spoken demeanor, he pushed hard, though fruitlessly, for market-oriented reforms and played a key role in destroying the Soviet Union.

Ukraine and Moldova, whose leaders had opposed the coup,[12] experienced a shift of power of a different sort. Both Leonid Kravchuk and Mircea Snegur, the Moldovan leader, gained authority as a result, since the Communist Party elements in both countries that had opposed the movement toward sovereignty and then independence, were routed.

Kravchuk had positioned himself well to benefit from such a turn of events—though there is no reason to think he had any means of predicting just when and how it would occur. As recently as the spring of 1990 he had held the number two position in the Ukrainian Communist Party, but after he was elected chairman of parliament in June he began to distance himself from the Party by taking a more aggressive line in negotiating for Ukrainian sovereignty. He called public attention to his independent stance in February 1991 by debating Party First Secretary Stanislav Gurenko (Hurenko) at a meeting of the Ukrainian Central Committee. Even before the coup attempt occurred in Moscow, he was well on the way to leading a large faction of national Communists into an alliance with Rukh and other nationalist leaders. The failed coup sealed the deal, and the national Communists were able to survive the dissolution of the Communist Party because of their support for a break with Moscow.

In Moldova, where the local Communist Party had been banned even before Gorbachev broke with the CPSU, there was a comparable tendency—those Communists who backed independence survived politically (though they had to assume different titles for their parties), while those who had been skeptical and had supported CPSU policies were swept from the scene—at least in Kishinev, now officially called by its Romanian name, Chişinău.

There was, however, one big difference in Moldova. Unlike Ukraine, it was faced with a rebellion on its territory, in the region east of the Dniester, where the urban population was mostly Slavic and many retired military personnel lived. With the connivance of local military authorities, a group of apparatchiks in the area had proclaimed it a separate "Dniester Soviet Socialist Republic." There had been similar efforts to set up an autonomous region in an area west of the Dniester where the Gagauz, a Turkic-speaking people, lived, but they presented a smaller threat.

Repercussions of the August putsch were less direct in Georgia, Azerbaijan, and Armenia. The Transcaucasus had too many troubles of its own to allow events in Moscow to dominate its attention.

Georgia was in the midst of a domestic political crisis the weekend the emergency committee tried to take power in Moscow. President Zviad Gamsakhurdia, who had won election with an overwhelming majority in May, was showing an increasingly despotic streak that had estranged the major figures in his coalition. On August 17, 1991, he precipitated a confrontation by forcing moderates out of his government, abruptly dismissing Prime Minister Tengiz Sigua plus a deputy prime minister, the foreign minister,[13] and the KGB chairman. On August 19, he continued his purge by sacking Tengiz Kitovani, the commander of the Georgian National Guard. Members of the National Guard, however, reacted by turning against Gamsakhurdia. Moscow, whether in the form of Gorbachev's Soviet government or of Yeltsin's Russian government, had lost its influence on developments in Georgia.

The Nagorny Karabakh issue still dominated political life in both Armenia and Azerbaijan. Presumably hoping for more support from Moscow in this struggle, Azerbaijan President Ayaz Mutalibov initially endorsed the coup attempt but, when it failed, supported a declaration of independence to insulate himself from Moscow's retribution. His switch, along with his failure to resolve the dispute over Nagorny Karabakh on Azerbaijan's terms, weakened his position and left him vulnerable to the Azerbaijan National Front, which had been suppressed by the Soviet army in January but was regathering its strength. Furthermore, Mutalibov rival Heidar Aliev, a member of the Brezhnev Politburo who had been expelled shortly after Gorbachev had come to power, had reestablished his position in his home base of Nakhichevan, the Azerbaijani enclave between Armenia and Turkey.

Armenia, in contrast, maintained political stability at home. Levon Ter-Petrosian, the Supreme Soviet chairman elected in 1990, was leading the country in an orderly fashion to secession from the Soviet Union, and he had spoken out against the coup attempt from the very beginning. The country, however, which had been subjected to lengthy transportation boycotts and the dual strain of rebuilding from the 1989 earthquake and pursuing the undeclared war against Azerbaijan, was an economic shambles. Its future would continue to be hostage to the conflict over Nagorny Karabakh.

Central Asia offered the greatest variety of reactions to the dramatic events in Moscow. Both Nursultan Nazarbayev of Kazakhstan and Askar Akayev of Kyrgyzstan had condemned the coup from the outset, and Akayev subsequently supported a declaration of independence. Nazarbayev, in contrast, remained loyal to Gorbachev and became practically the last republic leader to campaign for a union treaty and a restructured federation or confederation.

The three republics to the south—still in the grip of the old Communist Party machine—either welcomed or acquiesced in the coup attempt. When it failed, they declared independence to escape the liberalizing winds then blowing from Moscow. Uzbekistan President Islam Karimov and his counterpart in Turkmenistan, Saparmurad Niyazov, thereby tightened their grip on power and began to move against the democratic opposition that had grown up during perestroika—to a significant degree in Uzbekistan, though it had always been under pressure there, but only slightly in Turkmenistan, which had never conformed to the more liberal standards Moscow had tried to set.

Tajikistan, the poorest of all the union republics by conventional economic indices, was plunged into political conflict. The democratic opposition in that country, led by national-minded intellectuals, forced the local Communist Party leader, Kakhar Makhkamov, to resign for having supported the coup attempt. Their victory over the Communist political machine was short lived, however. Makhkamov's successor, Kadriddin Aslonov, immediately banned the Communist Party, but it changed its name to the Socialist Party and the legislature it dominated reversed the ban and brought back to power Makhkamov's predecessor, Rakhman Nabiev, who had been removed by Gorbachev in 1985. The presidential elections that followed resulted in a Nabiev victory, but foreign observers found evidence of extensive fraud.

As a result the "democrats" began to make common cause with two Islamic-oriented opposition parties, and the stage was set for a civil war, all the more devastating since the Islamic groups were supported by *mujaheddin* in Afghanistan, who, following their victory over the Soviet-backed regime in Kabul, had a surplus of weapons to pass on to their friends across the border.

The USSR Transformed

MOSCOW HAD LITTLE WILL to involve itself in these local struggles, though Yeltsin did join Nazarbayev in a brief trip to Nagorny Karabakh in an attempt to mediate the conflict there. Attention in the capital focused on the attempts to shore up the crumbling Soviet government, the steady expansion of the Russian government's effective jurisdiction, and the frantic negotiations for a new union treaty.

The Soviet Congress of People's Deputies was convoked in a special session the first week in September to deal with the issues resulting from the attempted coup d'état. After a sharp debate, it voted overwhelmingly in favor of creating a "Union of Sovereign States," as requested by the leaders of ten republics who participated in the first meeting of the new State Council. It was understood that this would mean the end of the Congress as an institution.

Although some thought that a confederal treaty could be signed within weeks, since the opponents to a loose association had now been routed, the Congress also created a new governmental structure for the Soviet Union, which was to last until the new treaty or constitution came into effect. The principal institutions were to be a State Council, made up of the presidents of those republics that wished to sign the union treaty and chaired by the president of the USSR; a restructured Supreme Soviet; and an Interrepublic Economic Committee to coordinate economic policy. Most management of enterprises would, however, devolve upon the republics—which were already, in fact, asserting control over the state property on their territory.

The debate was acrimonious since most of the deputies were not pleased with voting their institution out of existence. They were finally bought off with a guarantee of salary and privileges until the end of 1994, when their original term of office would expire.

Although the new state structure was devised hurriedly to cover what most thought would be a brief period of transition, it embodied some compromises that could have, under more auspicious circumstances, settled some of the disputes that had stalled the union treaty negotiations before August. For example, the upper house of the legislature— which was to have veto power over laws passed by the lower house—was made up of twenty representatives from each participating union republic, plus one from each former autonomous republic. Since most of the former autonomous republics were in Russia, this gave Russia more seats than any other republic had. However, each republic had only one vote in that assembly, so the extra representation gave Russia additional voices but not additional votes.

Another innovation was the provision that even those republics that did not choose to adhere to the union treaty would be eligible to participate in the Interrepublic Economic Committee. If the union treaty had been signed, this institution could have provided a mechanism for coordinating the economic policy of independent successor states. A year earlier it would have been considered a radical concession to the various independence movements. Gorbachev and others were arguing at that time that independence and economic cooperation were incompatible. But the political atmosphere in autumn 1991 was transformed to the degree that the innovative aspects of the proposed institution attracted little attention.

Gorbachev also replaced his Security Council with a new Political Consultative Council. This was the third form his principal advisory council had taken in less than two years. The Presidential Council had been in existence for barely a year when it was replaced by the Security Council, and it was just getting organized when its leading members tried to usurp power from Gorbachev. This time, Gorbachev made no pretense of including the Party conservatives and the Russian chauvinists. He named some of his original advisers, such as Vadim Bakatin, the economist Nikolai Petrakov, Alexander Yakovlev, and physicist Yevgeny Velikhov, to the council but also reached out to the more radical reformers by including Moscow's Mayor Gavriil Popov, longtime Yeltsin supporter Yuri Ryzhov, Saint Petersburg's Mayor Anatoly Sobchak, and Yegor Yakovlev, the editor of *Moscow News* who had just been appointed to run Central Television. Gorbachev also nominated Eduard Shevardnadze, but he refused to serve.

If, in 1990, Gorbachev had relied on the advice of a council similar to this one, he might have avoided some of his most serious errors. In reality, however, his councils were more window dressing than effective institutions. Gorbachev rarely consulted the members as a group but simply dealt with individual advisers, accepting or rejecting advice according to his whim. In this respect, the Political Consultative Council fared no better than its predecessors, but by the time it was named none of the institutions of the Soviet government was able to influence the course of events anyway.

Most people paid less attention to the new institutions of government than to two of the old ones, the KGB and the armed forces. The fact that the heads of both institutions had participated in the coup attempt made both organizations vulnerable to a purge, even though the institutions as a whole (particularly the armed forces) had not united in support of the plotters.

Initially, the KGB was subjected to more radical structural change than the army and navy were. As soon as the coup attempt collapsed, the protection unit, the presidential communications unit, and the Alpha Detachment were removed from KGB jurisdiction and placed under the direct control of the president. Then, on October 11, the State Council decided to abolish the USSR KGB and split it into three separate agencies: border guards, a foreign intelligence service, and an interrepublic internal security service. Yevgeny Primakov was appointed to head the Foreign Intelligence Service, while Vadim Bakatin supervised the reorganization of what remained. The successor Interrepublic Security Service, known by its Russian initials MSB, was formally organized just a few weeks before the Soviet Union collapsed, and it was merged with the Russian security service.

Although some senior KGB officials were arrested for direct participation in the attempt to remove Gorbachev, most KGB employees were retained by the remnant agencies. While Bakatin insisted that the organization he headed limit its activities to those appropriate for a law enforcement organization, he opposed demands to make a general purge or to open the KGB files to determine who had worked as informers. He felt that the latter would result in unfair and often unfounded accusations against innocent people.

Bakatin cooperated fully with the republics to sever central control over the internal security forces on their soil, signing a series of agreements that turned over KGB assets on their territory to them. He also worked with the Russian authorities to set up an RSFSR Federal Security Agency.[14]

The armed forces were not dismantled as the KGB was, but the high command was thoroughly shaken up: by October over half the members of the Defense Ministry's collegium[15] had been replaced. General Yevgeny Shaposhnikov, the air force commander who had refused to cooperate with the coup leaders, was appointed minister of defense, and Pavel Grachev, the airborne commander who had refused to attack Yeltsin in the Moscow White House, was made his deputy.

Despite the loyalty Shaposhnikov, Grachev, and other key military officers had shown to the constitutional order, nobody doubted that the cutbacks in the armed forces that had been under way since 1990 would be accelerated. The previous military command had resisted the cutbacks and, in order to block them or at least to slow them, had made no effective preparation for large-scale demobilization of the officer corps. The new defense leadership would be required to deal with the problems their predecessors had created by their inaction.

In early October, Grachev stated in an interview that he personally considered a cut of at least 1,200,000 troops essential. Since the Soviet armed forces then had about 3,500,000 men, this would be a cut of about 35 percent, and no realistic plans had been made to absorb the officers who would be forced into the civilian economy by early retirement. This would have been a problem even without the troop withdrawals from Eastern and Central Europe, which made the situation much worse. And the withdrawals from Germany would continue for another three years.

Even so, manpower cuts were not the most troubling problem facing the Soviet military. Given the political uncertainty, young men had begun resisting the draft. It was not clear that the Soviet army could maintain even the reduced troop level Grachev had recommended. Additionally, more and more of the republics were making plans to form their own armies, and some were insisting that their nationals serving in the Soviet armed forces be released to serve in independent forces at home. Since the Soviet forces had not been organized along national lines—officers and conscripts alike had often been assigned to units far from home, and personnel had deliberately been mixed to prevent units taking on national characteristics—such moves could affect the efficiency and readiness of Soviet units everywhere.

Ukraine's aspirations seemed particularly ominous to the Soviet military. On October 23, the Ukrainian Supreme Soviet approved enabling legislation for a Ukrainian army of 450,000 men and a national guard of 30,000, to be taken out of Soviet forces stationed in the republic.

The Ukrainian position made it clear that, unless a union treaty could be signed, the Soviet armed forces would have no future at all in their existing organizational structure. The unified Soviet military command would be split into smaller military organizations that might or might not cooperate with one another. Even though the largest numbers would doubtless remain with Russia, their doctrine and, indeed, the very rationale for their existence would have to change.

Russia Takes Center Stage

BORIS YELTSIN FORMALLY RETURNED his jurisdiction over the armed forces, the KGB, and the Ministry of Internal Affairs—which he had asserted by decree during the coup attempt—to Gorbachev's Soviet government on September 9 and soon after suddenly took a three-week vacation. Meanwhile, his associates in Moscow squabbled over what to do next. The fundamental issue was whether Russia should support a meaningful union of those republics willing to join or declare independence and simply deal with the other republics on a bilateral basis or through limited multilateral organizations such as the Interrepublic Economic Committee.

When he had organized his presidency, Yeltsin had drawn personnel from three broad categories: (1) former colleagues in the Sverdlovsk Communist Party apparatus, such as Yuri Petrov, the provincial first secretary, who was made chief of staff; (2) officials from the state managerial bureaucracy, many of whom had come out of the military-industrial complex; and (3) politicians from the democratic movement, most of whom were in their thirties and early forties and because of their age and their comparative radicalism were often dubbed "Young Turks" by outsiders.[16]

Initially, Yeltsin had placed the Russian government under control of the first two groups and relegated most of the "Young Turks" to an advisory body, the State Council, where they had no direct managerial control over the Russian government. Those who ran the Russian government, including Ivan Silayev, the prime minister, were in favor of preserving the union, while the "Young Turks" believed that Russia would be better off with full independence. They felt that a union with other republics, most still dominated by the old Communist *nomenklatura,* could block the economic reforms Russia required and furthermore would drain the resources Russia needed for its own reform and development. An independent Russia would also provide more important jobs for them. Andrei Kozyrev, the Russian foreign minister, for example, would no longer be junior to the Soviet foreign minister.

To many in this group, practical considerations were reinforced by (or perhaps gave birth to) the conviction that Russia had taken the wrong road historically when it had assembled an empire and now must join other twentieth-century metropoles in shedding its imperial appendages. Otherwise, they thought, it would be impossible to create a modern, democratic state.

Those who opposed the "Young Turks'" desire for an independent Russia were not all old or Communist or imperialist minded. A number of democratic reformers, including Anatoly Sobchak and Grigory Yavlinsky, campaigned for a voluntary union, arguing that Russia would be discarding part of itself if it left the union, particularly given its existing borders.

Alexander Tsipko, a philosopher who, in an early test of glasnost, had been the first to publish an article in the Soviet media directly attacking Marxism-Leninism, advanced vigorous arguments against any Russian attempt to destroy the union. As he put it in an article in *Izvestiya* on October 1, 1991:

> A union without union property, without respect for its president and constitution on the part of union institutions, and without a common union army is of no use to anyone. The union could exist only so

long as Russia existed as a unifying principle. But a Russia that has pulled itself out of the core of the union inevitably becomes a factor making for disunion. . . .

The disintegration of the USSR along the lines of its present internal borders is leading not only to the death of the Soviet empire but to the disintegration of the state's historical core. Many areas that were settled by Russians over the centuries are now outside the bounds of the new Russian state.[17]

Tsipko attributed the centrifugal tendency to the personal political ambitions of republic leaders. The desire to seize local political and economic power was certainly strong, but this was not the only factor at work. As the union structures became less and less effective, it began to seem that the only way to get on with reform would be to ignore the union and implement reform on the republic or local level.

Meanwhile, pressures were building in Russia for a change of government. During Yeltsin's absence from Moscow, Russian Premier Ivan Silayev resigned amid intense criticism of the Russian government's ineffectiveness in implementing reform. Following the coup attempt, Silayev had also taken on the chairmanship of the USSR interim Committee for the Management of the Economy. In resigning his Russian post, Silayev in effect chose to cast his lot with the union. His departure from the Russian premiership, however, left a vacuum at the top of the Russian government that the "Young Turks" soon exploited.

When Yeltsin returned from his vacation in mid-October, political discontent was rising. The euphoria of late August had evaporated, and the country was again embroiled in political intrigue. The media were filled with comments that the opportunities created by the blocking of the putsch had been dissipated by bickering and indecision. While the activities of the Communist Party had been suspended, in many localities Party officials had simply taken over the local and provincial governments, which gave much of the country an antireform cast.

The gray, chilly October days announced that winter was just ahead, but the economy was disintegrating to the point that famine and freezing were distinct possibilities. Finally, the radical reformers were able to get Yeltsin's ear.

In late October, following their advice, Yeltsin took a series of actions that created a basis for Russia to chart a course independent from that of the union government and the other republics. On October 28, he presented a plan for radical economic reform to the Russian Congress of

People's Deputies and requested a year's power to introduce economic reforms by decree and to appoint provincial governors. Many of the deputies objected to the request and the reform plan, but the Congress eventually approved it. It also formed a constitutional court—the first in Russia's history—and elected Ruslan Khasbulatov chairman of the Supreme Soviet. Before August, Khasbulatov had failed on several ballots to win a majority, but Yeltsin's strong support put him over in the post-coup atmosphere.

On November 4, the republic leaders meeting in the USSR State Council agreed to abolish all USSR ministries except those for defense, foreign affairs, railways, electric power, and nuclear power.

On November 6, Yeltsin issued a decree appointing himself chairman of the RSFSR Council of Ministers. He also named, as his principal deputy, Gennady Burbulis, the former teacher of Marxism-Leninism in Sverdlovsk who had managed Yeltsin's campaign to be elected chairman of the Russian parliament and who was considered the leader of the "Young Turks." Other deputy chairmen included Yegor Gaidar, the head of an economics institute who had been deeply influenced by the Chicago School of monetarist economics, and Alexander Shokhin, who had been minister of labor.

Each of the deputies would supervise a particular group of ministries: Burbulis was assigned the oversight of foreign affairs, justice, and the media, Gaidar the economic ministries, and Shokhin those dealing with social welfare. Yeltsin himself retained oversight responsibility for defense, security, and law enforcement.

These appointments finally put radical reformers in charge of the RSFSR's governmental apparatus. They would no longer be mere advisers, whose advice could be ignored. But they had to confront the fact that the country's key financial levers were still under the control of the union government. Yeltsin quickly remedied that problem for them with a package of ten decrees issued on November 15 that asserted control of virtually all Soviet financial institutions as well as export licenses for oil, gold, and diamonds produced on RSFSR territory.

When it met a week later, the RSFSR Supreme Soviet assumed control of the USSR State Bank. The fact that the parliament took control of the bank, rather than leaving it subordinate to the executive branch (as it had been in the Soviet period) or independent (like the Federal Reserve Bank in the United States or the German Bundesbank), was to have serious repercussions in the future.

To inhibit organized opposition to the reforms he planned, Yeltsin also issued a decree banning the Communist Party of the Soviet Union and the Russian Communist Party. (Gorbachev's earlier suspension of Party activity had not constituted a legal ban.[18]) It was probably no coincidence that Yeltsin proclaimed the ban on November 6, the day when traditionally a Politburo member delivered a speech to mark the Bolshevik Revolution and exactly four years after Gorbachev had delivered the Revolution Day speech whose text had been under discussion in the Central Committee when Gorbachev led the attack on Yeltsin and demanded his expulsion from the Politburo. On that day in 1987, Yeltsin had sat nervously with the other Communist Party leaders on the podium in the Palace of Congresses, fully aware that the hall was filled with whispers about his impending ouster. He now had his revenge, and it was total. The Party that had tried to ban him from political life had now suffered the same fate with a stroke of his own pen.[19]

By the end of November, there was little left of the union government other than an army and navy in disarray, security forces in the throes of dismemberment, courts and prosecutors without clear jurisdictions, an office of the president, and a foreign ministry that had just been renamed the Ministry of External Affairs.

Common Cause with the West

GORBACHEV'S FOREIGN POLICY was attacked in 1991, and has been even more since, as involving too many concessions to the West and to the United States in particular. Some of his opponents even accuse him of conspiring with the United States to break up the Soviet Union.

To anyone with a respect for facts, such accusations are absurd. It should be obvious that Gorbachev's foreign policy was a brilliant success. Its aim, from the onset of perestroika, was to reduce tensions with the rest of the world so that Soviet attention and resources could focus on internal reform. Gorbachev achieved this goal by forging a policy that served the mutual interests of the Soviet Union and its erstwhile Western adversaries.

It was not Western policy that caused the breakup of the Soviet Union but the failure of the political process within the Soviet Union. When the country was at its most helpless, the external environment was benign. In Asia, Europe, and North America alike there was a desire to assist the Soviet leadership in the difficult transition it had chosen, not to exploit the difficulty and make it worse.

The benefit to the Soviet Union of Gorbachev's foreign policy was at no time more apparent than in the fall of 1991, when the country was falling apart. The West was as supportive as it knew how to be, not hostile, which gave the peoples of the Soviet Union the opportunity to make their own decisions about the future without interference from abroad. The fact that the Western sympathy and support could not compensate for the flaws in the country's political process does not alter the truth that the Soviet Union, during its time of decline, was much better off in the friendly international environment that existed than it would have been in a hostile one.

During the months after the coup attempt, the Soviet Foreign Ministry was subjected to radical change. Charged with having been "too passive" when the emergency committee tried to seize power, Foreign Minister Bessmertnykh resigned shortly after Gorbachev returned to Moscow from the Crimea, and Boris Pankin, the Soviet ambassador to Czechoslovakia, was awarded the post since he was one of the few Soviet ambassadors to have denounced the coup attempt publicly before it collapsed. A number of ambassadors who were thought to have carried out the junta's orders with unseemly enthusiasm were recalled, and the Ministry of Foreign Affairs was subjected to severe personnel cuts.

Although the USSR Ministry of Foreign Affairs was busy during this period—it hosted a major international conference on human rights in September, received many foreign visitors,[20] and prepared Gorbachev for his final international gathering as president of the USSR, the opening of the Conference on the Middle East in Madrid on October 30, at which Gorbachev and George Bush were cochairmen—the control of foreign policy was shifting to the republics. Several republic leaders traveled abroad and were invariably received by chiefs of government. Yeltsin visited Germany in October, and Nazarbayev went to the United Kingdon the same month. Akayev and Ter-Petrosian visited the United States in November. Yeltsin traveled abroad again in December, this time to Italy. Also, when foreign statesmen went to the Soviet Union, they usually met with Yeltsin and frequently made a stop or two in some of the republic capitals: when he visited in September, Secretary of State Baker went to Alma Ata as well as Moscow (and also to the three now-independent Baltic states). German Foreign Minister Hans-Dietrich Genscher visited Kiev in October—and these are only a few examples.

The republics were getting more attention than they had previously, but foreign ministries were still focusing on the Soviet government. At the urging of the Group of Seven, international institutions hastened to make offers of assistance. The World Bank, the International Monetary Fund, and the European Bank for Reconstruction and Development all announced significant programs. The Soviet public, however, did not grasp that these programs were contingent on successful reform measures and that in any case their effects would not be felt for years.

With the military hard-liners now out of favor, Gorbachev quickly solved the few remaining problems in U.S.-Soviet relations: when Baker visited Moscow in September, he was able, finally, to reach agreement on ending arms supplies to all parties in Afghanistan. Gorbachev also agreed to withdraw the remaining Soviet forces from Cuba. A few weeks later, in a gesture intended to build confidence, Vadim Bakatin furnished my successor, Robert Strauss, with diagrams showing where the KGB had installed listening devices in the new U.S. Embassy building. We had, of course, discovered them on our own, but Bakatin's gesture was nevertheless appreciated as an indication that we could now deal more openly with each other.[21]

In mid-November, Eduard Shevardnadze was finally persuaded to come back to the renamed Ministry of External Affairs and take charge, in what turned out to be its final weeks. By then, Yeltsin was pushing for an 80 percent cut in the ministry's staff, but before this happened, the USSR ministry was merged with the Russian ministry under the command of Andrei Kozyrev, who not long before had been one of Shevardnadze's junior lieutenants.

A Union of Independent States?

UNTIL THE MIDDLE OF NOVEMBER, it seemed likely that some sort of state, if only a transitional one, would be fashioned by a majority of the twelve republics that had remained in the Soviet Union when the Baltics seceded. In early September, the leaders of ten of the republics[22] endorsed the concept. However, instead of the federation envisioned in the treaty scheduled for signature on August 20, Gorbachev and the republic leaders now agreed that the union would be confederal. Before the coup attempt Gorbachev had consistently argued that a confederation would not work; now his position was so weak that the looser union was the best he could hope for. Yeltsin also indicated that he now opposed the idea of a new union constitution. The union treaty would be a sufficient legal basis for the new association, he argued.

Negotiations, however, did not begin immediately. Given the accelerating economic dislocation, the State Council first turned its attention to an agreement that would govern interrepublic economic relations. These showed, from the very beginning, that the republics were intent upon stripping most of the power from the Center.

The original draft agreement, prepared under Grigory Yavlinsky's supervision in September, provided for several common institutions, such as a central bank and a bank for foreign trade, along with commitments to promote private property, maintain a common currency and open borders, share Soviet debt obligations, and coordinate fiscal policy. When representatives of the various republic governments reviewed the draft, however, they removed or weakened many of the essential provisions for economic unity.

For example, the Russian representative vetoed a provision that would extend the ruble zone to all full members of the proposed economic community while Ukraine blocked a proposal for coordination of the budget and tax policies of the associate members. The republics also rejected a provision for a concrete mechanism to ensure payment of the Soviet debt (by levying a tax on hard-currency receipts from exports) and replaced it with a general obligation to share in the debt payments, leaving it up to the republics to decide how the money would be raised. There was also strong opposition by a number of republics to endorsing private property, but this provision, which was removed after one round of negotiations, was readopted later.[23]

Yavlinsky was so distressed by the surgery performed by the republics that he wondered publicly if "the patient" he had "set out to cure," the union, was still alive.

Despite these setbacks, the Treaty on an Economic Community of Sovereign States was signed by the leaders of eight republics on October 19. Ukraine and Moldova refused to sign at that time but did so a few weeks later. Georgia and Azerbaijan, however, never adhered to it.

Signed with fanfare and hailed as a major step forward, the economic treaty was in fact little more than a promise to continue negotiating. Though it purported to establish an economic community, it required two dozen additional agreements before a real economic community could come into existence. Some open questions were basic: the status and powers of the Economic Community's institutions, the charter for a bank union, ownership rights, movement of people across borders, and external debt service. All were likely to be contentious.[24]

The experience with the economic treaty demonstrated that political union—an even more sensitive issue than economic cooperation—would have to assume a very loose form if it was to be possible at all. When Yeltsin announced his reform plan at the end of October without consulting Gorbachev, many concluded that it was a signal that he would try to destroy the union, but Yeltsin continued to insist that he was in favor of it. In fact, he surprised everyone at the November 4 meeting of the State Council by announcing that Russia had no intention of establishing its own armed forces.

His statement followed a report by Defense Minister Shaposhnikov that predicted that, if the current trends continued, the Soviet Union would be transformed into "a conglomeration of principalities fighting with one another."[25]

Yeltsin was the first to comment on Shaposhnikov's presentation. Russia had no intention, he said, of creating its own army, no matter what some other republics might do. Adopting the stentorian tone he always used for emphasis, he declaimed: "We will not be the first, or the second, or the third, or the fourth, and that is Russia's answer to those who are concerned that it may threaten someone." Then, borrowing words used frequently by Gorbachev, he added, "Since we are trying, despite all difficulties, to create a new state, the Union of Sovereign States, it unquestionably should have a unified army, unified armed forces."[26]

In his statement, Yeltsin had not only endorsed Gorbachev's position regarding the armed forces, he had also used another key term of Gorbachev's when he spoke of creating a "new state." This implied that the union would be a subject of international law with real powers, not just an association for discussion and coordination.

Yeltsin tended to be mercurial, and one could not be certain how long he would stick with his views. And, in fact, he opened the question of whether the new union should be a "state" or not when the State Council gathered again on November 14 at the Novo-Ogaryovo villa where the Nine Plus One agreement had been concluded in April.

With Shushkevich's support but to the surprise of the other participants, who thought the question had been decided, Yeltsin spoke against creating a "unified state." He preferred to call it simply a confederation. Gorbachev and Nazarbayev objected that while they had agreed on a confederated *state,* a formless, amorphous structure would not do; Gorbachev tried to resurrect the word "union," but Yeltsin and others refused to accept it.

To those for whom the definitions learned in Poli Sci 101 are hazy, this debate might smack of hairsplitting. But it was not; the argument was over whether the union they were creating would be a state with a president and legislature, one that sent out and received ambassadors and belonged to international organizations, or an international organization, the mere instrument of its members, with—perhaps—a secretary-general to manage its bureaucracy, but not a president. Gorbachev could feel the ground crumbling under him, and he argued doggedly that any useful union would have to have the attributes of statehood. When Yeltsin and Shushkevich refused to yield, he uttered a fateful challenge:

> If there is not going to be any effective state structure, why do we need a president and a parliament? If you make that decision, I am prepared to go.[27]

According to Grachev's notes, Yeltsin shrugged off the statement as "emotion," whereupon Gorbachev stood up, insisted that he would not take responsibility for an amorphous organization, then turned abruptly to face Yeltsin directly and, obliquely referring to Burbulis and the "Young Turks," spat out a challenge:

> Boris Nikolayevich, think about where those people who want Russia to throw off everyone and go it alone are dragging us![28]

Yeltsin, surprisingly, backed down, muttering, "I do not support the extremists. Let's record it honestly as 'a confederative state.' "[29]

After further discussion, the group reached a decision that the new union would be called a confederative state but would have no constitution, being based solely on the treaty they would sign plus the Declaration of Rights that had been passed by the Congress of People's Deputies in September.

Just before the meeting ended, Shushkevich suggested that they meet again to initial the text as a commitment to support it when it was considered in their respective legislatures. There was general agreement that it could be signed before the end of the year, but Nazarbayev suggested, in a half-joking reference to August 20, "This time, let's not set a date in advance."

The participants filed out and were met by bright television lamps and impatient journalists, who had been waiting for hours in another room.

Gorbachev asked Yeltsin to speak first, and Yeltsin announced, "It is difficult to say how many states will join the union, but after today's discussion I am firmly convinced that there will be a union."[30]

Nazarbayev pointed out that Kazakhstan had always been for a union, not the one of old, to be sure, but "the union that really exists today, a union of sovereign states that are independent and equal." He added that only the future would tell whether that union would be "confederal or something else."

Shushkevich agreed that a union was likely, and three presidents from Central Asia echoed his judgment.

Responding to subsequent questions, Yeltsin was more specific about the day's understanding. They had agreed, he said, to "a union of sovereign states—a confederative state, fulfilling the functions delegated by state participants in the treaty."[31]

The republic presidents confirmed that all that was required before the document could be signed was discussion with their respective legislatures and perhaps a few minor amendments.

The document itself, however, raised a lot of questions. For example, it stated in one paragraph that "The Union of Sovereign States acts in international relations as a sovereign state, a subject of international law, and the successor to the Union of Soviet Socialist Republics." A subsequent provision, however, declared that "The states forming the Union are full-fledged subjects of international law." In other words, they would have foreign ministries, accredited diplomats, separate membership in international organizations—all means of conducting a separate foreign policy, even if it conflicted with the policy of the union. It was difficult to see how this was going to work in practice.[32]

The provisions relating to the armed forces also seemed more likely to lead to disputes rather than a clear delineation of authority. Republics were given the right to create military units, but their size and function were left to subsequent "interstate agreements." The Union of Sovereign States would keep "the unified armed forces and the centralized command of strategic forces, including nuclear missile forces." Given the strong movement in most republics to establish their own ministries of defense and uniformed services, it was obvious that no concrete understanding had been reached, with the important exception of responsibility for nuclear forces. There were bound to be further disputes over the size and subordination of the national military forces.

Gorbachev managed to preserve the office of the president, as well as a much-truncated government headed by a prime minister. The union would also have a Supreme Court, Court of Arbitration, and state prosecutor, but much of the central government's authority was being shifted to the republics, so that these institutions would have far more limited jurisdiction than their predecessors in the old USSR had had. There were precious few unchallengeable powers left to the central authorities.[33] Though little was left for him to do, Gorbachev had pried as much as he could from the republic presidents.

Gorbachev planned a high-profile ceremony when the State Council gathered again at Novo-Ogaryovo on November 25 to initial the treaty. His press secretary, Andrei Grachev, arranged for a large number of journalists and television crews to be on hand to record and report on the historic event.

The meeting, however, did not go as expected.

As soon as Gorbachev opened the meeting, Yeltsin announced that he could not initial the document that day because his consultations with the RSFSR Supreme Soviet had revealed that it would not be approved in its present form. He added that the Russian legislators did not like the conception of a unified state and would not accept even a confederative state. He suggested, therefore, that they use the term "confederation of democratic states."

Gorbachev was furious and accused Yeltsin of going back on his earlier agreement, but Shushkevich came to Yeltsin's support. Although it was he who had proposed initialing the text at the current session, he now argued that the initialing should be delayed since his parliamentary committees had not yet finished their work on the text. Uzbek President Karimov, to the surprise of all, also spoke in favor of delay.

The arguments became quite heated, and during them Yeltsin added that it would be unwise to initial the text before the elections in Ukraine, since that might provoke the Ukrainians to be even more negative toward the union. Gorbachev countered that, on the contrary, it was important to demonstrate to Ukraine that the union would be formed in any event. If it was a going proposition, Ukraine would have no alternative but to join, he argued.

Although Shushkevich tried to assure him that they would probably be ready for initialing within ten days and that he shouldn't worry, Gorbachev understood that the delay would likely be fatal. Yeltsin and Shushkevich seemed to have ulterior motives.

Finally, exasperated, Gorbachev told the group that they no longer needed a president, stood up, and berated them in the sort of off-color language he habitually used when he dealt with recalcitrant Communist Party subordinates. Grachev quotes him as saying, "I don't understand how you plan to get along. You know, when you have set up your shantytown instead of a united state you will put your people through torture. We are strangling in the shit as it is! . . . If you reject the confederated state version, then just go on without me!"[34]

With that he stalked out of the room, followed by his entire entourage.

The participants put different interpretations on Gorbachev's walkout. Gorbachev and his associates, such as Bakatin, Chernyayev, and Grachev, say that though he was angry, he called a break because he wanted to give the republic presidents an opportunity to sort out their views without his presence. Thus, Grachev explains that when he said "You don't need a president anymore," he had in mind in *that meeting* at *that moment.* He expected to return when invited to conclude the discussion. Gorbachev's associates also suggest that Yeltsin and Shushkevich must have planned their performances in advance; by raising artificial issues, they engineered the breakdown of the negotiations in order to justify their subsequent actions.[35]

Shushkevich and Yeltsin tell a different story. They claim that Gorbachev's outburst shocked them because they thought that their negotiations, although prolonged, were progressing. As Shushkevich described to me a year later, he and Yeltsin felt they were negotiating in good faith—having always made agreements conditional on consultation with their parliaments—but that Gorbachev heard only what he wished to hear and habitually pocketed a conditional agreement as if it were final. Both he and Yeltsin, he said, were committed to working out an agreement that would be acceptable to Ukraine, but Gorbachev always brushed off their concerns and demanded conditions Ukraine would not accept. As a result, when Gorbachev stormed out of the November 25 meeting, it was for them the last straw. While Gorbachev was out of the room, they decided they would meet soon in Belarus and invite Kravchuk to join them.[36]

While Gorbachev waited in a study upstairs, the republic presidents discussed what to do. Representatives of the media were waiting, still expecting the treaty to be initialed in their presence. The presidents decided to propose to Gorbachev that the treaty be submitted to the republic legislatures for approval, with a target of signing and ratification before the end of the year. Yeltsin and Shushkevich were delegated to break the news to Gorbachev.

When they entered Gorbachev's study upstairs, Yeltsin joked that they had been sent to "kowtow to the tsar," and Gorbachev countered by addressing Yeltsin as "Tsar Boris." The comments of both had a cutting edge: Yeltsin's called attention to Gorbachev's regal habits, while Gorbachev's "Tsar Boris" had specific historical overtones: Boris Godunov, the only real Tsar Boris in Russian history, had been considered by many a usurper of the throne and had met a tragic end.[37]

Nevertheless, Gorbachev seemed pleased that Yeltsin had been willing to help break the stalemate, and they went downstairs, resumed the meeting, and quickly agreed on the announcement the republic presidents had suggested. The members of the State Council refused, however, to meet the press as a group, as they had done at the previous meeting. This time Gorbachev had to face the cameras and steno pads alone.

He did not attempt to conceal his disappointment, remarking that the republic leaders had made a step backward from the union treaty.

It was a giant step backward. The State Council never met again.

XXII

Coup de Grâce

Russia will never be the initiator of the union's collapse.
BORIS YELTSIN, October 18, 1991[1]

Three republics that were the founders of the USSR have halted the spontaneous process of disintegration. . . . We found the only possible formula for life together under new conditions—a commonwealth of independent states. . . . [T]he existence of the USSR is coming to an end.
BORIS YELTSIN, December 12, 1991[2]

I don't know why they decided, behind the president's back, to ignore the union treaty . . . We could have found a way out of the stalemate in negotiations with Ukraine—for example, with an associated membership. The Russian leaders . . . exploited the Ukrainian position.
MIKHAIL GORBACHEV, December 12, 1991[3]

Although it had been announced on November 25 that the draft union treaty would be sent to the various republic parliaments for discussion, this was merely a cover to avoid having to announce that the meeting had ended in a stalemate. While Gorbachev was pushing for the most rapid possible conclusion of the process, he was still unwilling to agree to a solution that would deprive the Center of substantial authority and himself of a meaningful job. The republic leaders—Yeltsin in particular—were not in the same hurry; until they knew for sure what Ukraine would do, it was hard to determine what sort of association would be suitable.

In fact, putting together a state structure to accommodate one huge component and several much smaller ones presented problems significantly greater than those faced by other working federations and confederations. While there is a wide discrepancy between the area of Rhode Island and that of Alaska and between the population of Alaska and that of California, these differences in magnitude pale when compared to the differences of size among the Soviet republics. Russia, after all, occupied more than three quarters of the area of the entire Soviet Union and had half its population.

One can only imagine the difficulties we would have making the U.S. federal system work if everything in the United States west of the Mississippi comprised a single state and all states to the east were in their present borders. And yet the situation in the Soviet Union was even less stable: there, the units were populated, in the majority, by different nations, and the largest unit had a long history of imperial dominion over the others.

To some, it seemed that the effort to create a single state was tantamount to getting a large shark, a couple of tuna, and a half-dozen minnows to swim in a single school. No matter how it might be structured and how many assurances the shark might give, the others could only be skittish.

So long as Ukraine was part of the picture, a union seemed more feasible. With a population a third the size of Russia's and a comparable level of economic development, Ukraine, in combination with the others, could offer substantial assurance against Russian domination. But without Ukraine, no combination of non-Russian republics could come close to balancing Russia's size and power.

From the Russian point of view, a Ukraine-less union also had much less appeal. Rightly or wrongly, most Russians assumed that the resource flow tended to be from Russia to the Central Asian republics and—to a lesser degree—to Belarus. A "union" with just those republics would be viewed as an impermissible drain on Russian resources, and many people would oppose it.

Ukraine Makes a Choice

DECEMBER 1, 1991, had been set for a referendum on the Ukrainian Supreme Soviet's declaration of independence; subsequently, the election of Ukraine's first president was scheduled for the same day. Until the August coup attempt, support for Ukrainian independence was not overwhelming except in the western provinces. When I visited Kiev in the spring, most political observers thought that a popular vote would go against independence if the choice was a union treaty that respected Ukraine's sovereignty. After all, in March, a majority had voted in favor of preserving the union.

In late spring and summer, however, sentiment in favor of full independence made rapid headway. The deteriorating economy, combined with Moscow's unwillingness to part with control over economic matters and its inability to carry out a coherent economic policy, persuaded a growing number of residents in Ukraine that the only way to avoid economic collapse would be to leave the union. By August 1, when I visited Kiev with President Bush, senior officials—not all of whom favored independence—told me they thought any future vote on independence might be too close to call.

The attempted coup in Moscow accelerated the trend. The Ukrainian Communist Party, which had provided most of the support for preserving the union, collapsed and was banned when the coup failed. The great majority of people, including much of the Russian-speaking population, were unwilling to tie their future to the chances of political stability in Moscow. If a group of fewer than a dozen officials could make a serious attempt to seize control of the entire USSR, the only safe place to be was out of the USSR altogether.

When the independence referendum and vote for president were held in Ukraine on December 1, 1991, it was no surprise that a majority voted for independence and for Leonid Kravchuk. The proportions and distribution of the vote, however, astonished observers. Eighty-four percent of eligible voters went to the polls, and more than 90 percent of those voted for independence. Even in the oblasts in east Ukraine and in the Crimea and Odessa, which had large Russian populations, comfortable majorities voted for independence.

Kravchuk's victory was not quite so one-sided, but in receiving nearly 62 percent of the vote in a field of seven candidates, it was nearly as impressive. Vyacheslav Chornovil, the erstwhile imprisoned dissident, came in second with 23 percent of the vote—and with a majority in his native west Ukraine. Both were strong proponents of independence.

As soon as the results of the referendum were in—on December 3, 1991—the RSFSR officially recognized Ukraine as independent. The three Baltic states, the Eastern European countries, and Canada, which has a large Ukrainian population, also extended prompt recognition, but the Russian government's recognition was the most important one. Russia, for the first time in more than three centuries, gave up its claim that Ukraine was properly part of Russia.

The Russian recognition was not without a political cost. Many Russians were emotionally unprepared to accept the separation of Ukraine from Russia, and Yeltsin was bound to be charged with betraying the 10 million ethnic Russians living in Ukraine—even though a majority of them had voted for Ukrainian independence.

I recalled a conversation I had with Russian Foreign Minister Andrei Kozyrev just a few days after the Ukrainian parliament's declaration of independence in August. We were both attending a conference in Budapest, and during dinner he took me aside and expressed concern about the declaration. "This is a big political issue at home," he observed. "What can we do?"

I told him I thought Russia had no choice. If Ukraine voted for independence, Russia would have to recognize it or enter into a long political struggle that it couldn't win and that could do Russia great damage. "If that is their decision, there is no way to stop them," I pointed out, urging, "Be as gracious as you can. Don't treat them like Gorbachev did the Baltics. You both need to cooperate in many areas, but that will be possible only if Russia genuinely accepts an independent Ukraine."

"I know you're right," he replied. "We really have no choice." And then he added, grimacing as if in pain, "But don't think it isn't hard—or that a lot of people won't be upset."

The Russian action was more than generosity forced by necessity, however. It also fitted the game plan Yeltsin seems to have been following, at least since the middle of November: to use Ukraine's refusal to enter the union as an excuse for breaking his long-standing promise not to be the initiator of the union's collapse. Now, he could argue that Ukraine, not Russia, had brought the Soviet Union to an end.

The Ukrainian political leaders were pleased to play their part. On December 5, the Ukrainian legislature voted to annul Ukraine's accession to the 1922 treaty that had created the USSR, and the following day it voted not to sign any union treaty and to create its own armed forces.

Buoyed by these actions and his own election victory, Kravchuk accepted an invitation from Shushkevich and Yeltsin to meet them the following weekend in Belarus. Before he left Kiev, he made his position toward the draft union treaty crystal clear. During his first press conference after taking the oath of office, Kravchuk stated that Ukraine would "conclude political ties with republic-states" but would not enter into any union that had a central governing organ.[4] This, of course, meant that Ukraine would not be part of any union acceptable to Gorbachev, if Gorbachev meant what he had said repeatedly in State Council meetings in November.

Meeting in a Hunting Lodge

A FEW MILES NORTH OF BREST, along the border of Belarus with Poland, there is a forest preserve maintained as a habitat for the last descendants of the European bison. In Russian it is called Belovezhskaya Pushcha, or Bison Forest. It is a spot where Nikita Khrushchev liked to hunt (presumably his targets were animals other than the protected bison), and an elaborate lodge was built in the preserve while he was first secretary of the CPSU. Since his time, it had been used most often by senior Belorussian Party officials.

Given its seclusion and its rustic comfort, Shushkevich thought it would be an ideal setting for the meeting he had discussed with Yeltsin when Gorbachev had stormed out of the State Council meeting on November 25. To ensure privacy, however, advance announcements of the meeting indicated that it would be held in Minsk.

Though the meeting was held in secret, the fact that the three leaders were meeting was not. During the week before, the press had reported that Yeltsin would come to Minsk for a meeting with Shushkevich and that Kravchuk might join them. At first, journalists assumed that the main topic of conversation would be coordination of economic policy, since both Belarus and Ukraine were deeply troubled by Russia's announced intention to free many retail prices as of December 16.[5] By Saturday morning, December 7, however, the word was out: the three leaders would discuss the future of the union. *Izvestiya*'s banner headline that day proclaimed, ON THE EVE OF THE MEETING IN MINSK: WILL THEY CONCLUDE A TRIPLE ALLIANCE?[6]

Yeltsin discussed the situation with Gorbachev the day before he left Moscow for Belarus, and both agreed they could not imagine a union without Ukraine. Apparently they had not yet heard what Kravchuk was saying in Kiev that day, for Gorbachev continued to insist that Ukraine would eventually adhere to the union treaty. Revealing the extent of his self-deception, Gorbachev said that Ukraine's vote for independence had been intended as nothing more than a way of establishing a basis of equality with the other republics in a future union. "I am sure," he continued, "that in Ukraine today people are thinking about the union just as people in other corners of our vast country do."[7]

Both Yeltsin and Kravchuk were whisked off to Bison Forest with a small group of assistants after their planes landed in Minsk on Saturday, December 7. Each leader was accompanied by his prime minister—or, in Russia's case, the newly appointed first deputy prime minister, Gennady Burbulis—and just a few others. The lodge would not accommodate large delegations. Journalists were not invited at all.

All three leaders deny that they knew in advance how the meeting would come out.[8] Shushkevich and Yeltsin say they were not sure Kravchuk could be persuaded to accept any sort of association, given the overwhelming vote in Ukraine for independence and the statement Kravchuk had made when he was inaugurated as president. It seemed vital, to Belarus in particular, to make sure that there would be an open border with Ukraine. This could no longer be guaranteed in a union treaty to which Ukraine was not a party; only a separate deal with independent Ukraine would do.

Since the fall of 1990, there had been desultory discussions between Russia and Ukraine about what a commonwealth negotiated by the republics might look like. Politicians in both countries who opposed the union treaty as an inevitable infringement on Ukrainian or Russian sovereignty had worked on drafts of a commonwealth agreement. In Russia, Gennady Burbulis and his associates had also tried their hand at drafting a loose agreement that would give Russia a pretext for absorbing USSR institutions and becoming the successor to the USSR in international law. Burbulis brought these drafts with him when he accompanied Yeltsin to the meeting.

Yeltsin later recounted that he had initially asked Kravchuk whether anything could be done to the union treaty negotiated with Gorbachev to induce Ukraine to adhere. When Kravchuk had answered with a flat "no," they had turned their attention to crafting an agreement that Ukraine could accept. That meant that the union could not be a state or a "subject" of international law or have any attributes of a government that might limit the sovereignty of its members.

Staffs worked all night, and when the document seemed ready for signing on Sunday morning, the three principals contacted Nazarbayev, whose plane had just landed in Moscow and could have flown on to Brest in little more than an hour, and invited him to join them. At first he agreed, but then, after talking to Gorbachev on the telephone, he did not go. He said later that he felt he could no longer influence the negotiations and did not wish to be part of what many would see as a conspiracy.

Yeltsin and Shushkevich, however, did not get word that Nazarbayev was not coming. They had a big table set up for a ceremonial signing, brought journalists in to witness it, and went off to the airport to meet him. When Nazarbayev did not arrive, they went ahead and signed a joint declaration and the Agreement on Creating a Commonwealth of Independent States. Although some commentators referred to it as a "Slavic commonwealth," this was apparently not intended. The joint declaration stipulated that it was open to all former members of the USSR, as well as other states that "share the goals and principles" of the agreement.[9]

As host of the conference, Shushkevich was delegated to contact Gorbachev and inform him of what had happened. Yeltsin volunteered to call President Bush and put through his call first. Shushkevich later denied to me that it had been planned that way; he said he had not wanted to give the news to Gorbachev on an open line and had not had a secure government telephone at the lodge, so he had waited until he returned to Minsk to call Gorbachev. Yeltsin, however, called Bush immediately. Whether this was preplanned or not (and many find Shushkevich's explanation not convincing since government lodges normally have secure telephone facilities), Gorbachev was understandably outraged when he learned that Bush had been informed first.

Shushkevich told me that when he telephoned Gorbachev and explained what had happened, Gorbachev's first question was "What happens to me?"[10]

A "Commonwealth," Not a Country

THE COMMONWEALTH FOUNDED at the lodge in Bison Forest had no president, prime minister, or even secretary-general. The agreement in fact specified no permanent organ, only that any "coordinating bodies" that might be established would have their seat in Minsk, the Belarusian capital.[11]

The commitments it contained were to general principles or to an obligation to coordinate; the Commonwealth itself would have no power and no authority apart from the collective will of its members. If its members chose to neglect the obligations they had undertaken, it would have no mechanism for enforcement. It would also have no authority to levy taxes.

Some of the commitments were significant, however. One of the most concrete ones was to "preserve and maintain under united command a common military-strategic space, including unified command over nuclear weapons." The procedures for doing so, however, were still to be worked out.

A commitment to "recognize and respect one another's territorial integrity and the inviolability of borders within the Commonwealth" was also important, because as recently as August and September, some Russian spokesmen had talked of the need to revise borders to bring areas with a large Russian-speaking population into Russia. The eastern and southern provinces of Ukraine and northern Kazakhstan were most vulnerable in this respect, and this provision was the price the Russian leadership paid the other republics for their adherence to the Commonwealth. Though it would remain controversial in Russia for years to come, it was potentially of historic significance, since it represented a renunciation of territory that Russia had claimed for centuries.

The commitment to protect human rights, "in accordance with generally recognized international norms," borrowed from the September declaration of the USSR Congress of People's Deputies, was also noteworthy. Though it could not be enforced by the Commonwealth, it recognized international standards as appropriate for domestic law and provided a yardstick by which to judge the status of human rights in the member states. The human rights provisions in the Commonwealth agreement were, however, far less specific than those in the Soviet Congress's declaration.

The agreement also stipulated that the member states would "guarantee the fulfillment of the international obligations binding upon them from the treaties and agreements of the former USSR," but the wording implied that individual member states would assume these obligations, not the Commonwealth as a whole, and that the member states would be the judge of which obligations were binding on them. Therefore, the provision added little if anything to the obligations they had already assumed with the various declarations of independence.

Most of the other provisions seemed more like pious aspirations than obligations: the parties were to cooperate in foreign policy, economic strategy, transportation and communications, environmental protection, migration policy, and crime prevention. Disputes would be solved by negotiation, and any member could withdraw by simply giving the others twelve months' notice.

The three prime ministers also signed a brief economic cooperation agreement that was replete with high-sounding commitments to coordination and cooperation but lacked any mechanism to ensure that policies would in fact be harmonized.

For example, the government heads agreed to "conduct coordinated radical economic reforms to establish effective market mechanisms, to transform property relations, and to ensure free enterprise," but the agreement failed to mention the reforms that Yeltsin had already announced and that Shushkevich and Kravchuk had rejected.

Likewise, the commitment to conclude an "interbank agreement" that would control money emission and establish ceilings for budget deficits was devoid of any agreed policy guidelines.

In short, the meeting in Bison Forest left much more undecided than decided. Whether the Commonwealth of Independent States would actually amount to anything would depend on negotiations still to come. Lacking any enforcement mechanism, the agreements could not guarantee that any commitments would be met. On one point, however, the agreement was unequivocal: the Union of Soviet Socialist Republics would cease to exist. The three who signed had sufficient strength to guarantee that, and that alone.

Futile Resistance

YELTSIN WAS DELEGATED by his two colleagues to explain the agreement to Gorbachev when he returned to Moscow on December 9. He did so in a meeting that Nazarbayev also attended. Meanwhile, Gennady Burbulis and Andrei Kozyrev answered questions about the Commonwealth agreement at an international press conference. They argued that the agreement was "the only way to save what could still be saved" of the Soviet Union and therefore was not the cause of the Soviet Union's collapse but rather a step that would arrest further disintegration of authority on its territory.[12]

Gorbachev could not be expected to accept this interpretation, but his initial public comment was not as negative as his private reaction was. He went on Moscow television just after the newscast on Monday evening, December 9, to say that the agreement had positive aspects, but its declaration that the USSR was ceasing to exist was out of order. He conceded that every republic had an unquestioned right to leave the union but asserted that nevertheless "the fate of a multinational state cannot be determined by the will of the leaders of three republics." He suggested that the Commonwealth agreement and the draft union treaty be discussed by the republic legislatures as well as the USSR Supreme Soviet and that perhaps a referendum should be conducted.[13]

Nazarbayev's reaction, however, was more important. He had been the principal champion among the republic leaders for the union treaty and had consistently opposed depriving the new union of the attributes of statehood. He was also the last who still vigorously supported Gorbachev as a political leader. Would he demand a debate on the Commonwealth?

His initial statements, at a press conference in Moscow that same Monday, were circumspect but critical. He stated that he had had no idea beforehand that the Slavic leaders would make the agreement they had and that he felt it should be discussed by all the republics and by the USSR Congress of People's Deputies. Without totally closing the door to Kazakhstan's participation in the Commonwealth, he made it clear that he still favored the union treaty and believed that the Commonwealth agreement should simply be considered a proposal by the three signatories that could be discussed along with the union treaty.[14]

Many other people opposed the Commonwealth agreement, not only the unreconstructed imperialists such as the members of Soyuz, Vladimir Zhirinovsky, and former Communist apparatchiks, but also respected democrats like Saint Petersburg's Mayor Anatoly Sobchak, Moscow's Mayor Gavriil Popov, Nikolai Travkin of the Democratic Party, and most of the leaders of the Movement for Democratic Reforms.

Nevertheless, the Russian, Belarusian, and Ukrainian Supreme Soviets quickly ratified the Commonwealth agreement, and the three governments ordered their representatives not to take part in the USSR Supreme Soviet or Congress of People's Deputies. This deprived these institutions of a quorum and left the opponents of the Commonwealth without legal recourse. Nazarbayev quickly saw that the suggestions he had made in Moscow on December 9 were impractical and began to encourage the Central Asians to accept the Commonwealth agreement with the sole condition that they be treated as founding members. The Kazakhstan parliament finally declared independence on December 16 so that its republic would have the same status as the others in the final negotiations.

Daily headlines in *Izvestiya* tell the story:

December 11:
AGREEMENT ON COMMONWEALTH OF INDEPENDENT
STATES RATIFIED
[by Ukraine and Belarus]

M. GORBACHEV AND B. YELTSIN SEEK COMMON LANGUAGE WITH
MILITARY: PRESIDENT OF RUSSIA GUARANTEES THE ARMY
SOCIAL SECURITY

December 12:
SUPPORTERS OF COMMONWEALTH GROW;
RUSSIAN PARLIAMENT RATIFIES AGREEMENT ON CIS

CENTRAL ASIAN REPUBLICS AND KAZAKHSTAN INTEND
TO SUPPORT CIS

BELARUSIAN DELEGATION LEAVES UNION PARLIAMENT

December 13:
PARTICIPANTS IN ASHKHABAD MEETING PREPARED TO BE
MEMBERS OF COMMONWEALTH—BUT—WITH EQUAL RIGHTS

UNION PARLIAMENT SHRINKS FROM CONFRONTATION

WASHINGTON RECOGNIZES THAT SOVIET UNION
NO LONGER EXISTS

December 14:
RESULTS OF ASHKHABAD MEETING EVOKE SIGH OF RELIEF
IN COUNTRY AND WORLD

ARMED FORCES SUBORDINATED TO SUPREME COMMANDER
AND MINISTER OF DEFENSE

December 16:
JAMES BAKER BEGINS A JOURNEY FROM THE USSR TO THE CIS

STRUGGLE FOR NATIONAL SELF-DETERMINATION MAY THREATEN
INTEGRITY OF RUSSIA

December 17:
RUSSIA'S PARLIAMENT DECLARES ITS RIGHTS TO PROPERTY
OF USSR SUPREME SOVIET

December 18:
RUSSIAN PARLIAMENT TAKES OVER IN KREMLIN

UNION PARLIAMENT PASSES INTO HISTORY

December 19:

ROAD TO COMMONWEALTH: MINSK—ASHKHABAD ALMA ATA

UNABLE TO MUSTER QUORUM, USSR SUPREME SOVIET ACCEPTS
INEVITABILITY OF ITS DEMISE

GORBACHEV PROPOSES NAME: COMMONWEALTH OF
EUROPEAN AND ASIAN STATES

COUNCIL OF FIVE CENTRAL ASIAN REPUBLICS
AND KAZAKHSTAN CONFIRMED

December 20:

HISTORY OF SOVIET UNION TO END IN CAPITAL OF KAZAKHSTAN

December 23:

ELEVEN REPUBLIC LEADERS SIGN DECLARATION ON
COMMONWEALTH

HEADS OF STATE ENTRUST COMMAND OF ARMED FORCES TO
SHAPOSHNIKOV UNTIL MILITARY REFORM DECIDED

The Declaration of Adherence to the Commonwealth of Independent
States was signed in Alma Ata on December 21, 1991, by the leaders of
all the former Soviet republics except the three Baltic states and
Georgia.

Throughout November and December, Russia had systematically absorbed the remaining union institutions on Russian soil, and the other
republics had done the same on their own territory, with the exception
of military bases and forces. By Monday, December 23, there was little
left to do but to decide when Gorbachev would vacate his office.

Was It Legal?

GORBACHEV SOON DROPPED his initial moderation in commenting on
the Commonwealth agreement. As it became clear that he would get neither a debate in the USSR Supreme Soviet nor a session of the USSR
Congress of People's Deputies, let alone a referendum, he became more
vituperative. He began to characterize the Bison Forest meeting as just
as much an illegal coup d'état as the formation of the emergency committee in August had been. The only difference he would concede was
that the first had failed and the second had succeeded.

Politicians and legal experts are still arguing that issue, and historians will doubtless continue for generations to come. Those who mourn the Soviet Union are naturally inclined to look at the impotent Commonwealth of Independent States as the illegitimate offspring of a conspiracy, while those who wanted to avoid any effective limit on their republic's sovereignty will argue that all proceeded with strict regard to legality.

Whatever the verdict of experts in constitutional law may be, it is clear that—unlike the organizers of the August putsch, who had to make the fraudulent claim that Gorbachev was ill to create an illusion of legality—Yeltsin, Kravchuk, and Shushkevich have an arguable case. They were the leaders of their respective republics, chosen by the constitutional process in each republic, and two of them had been elected by popular vote. All three republics had declared sovereignty, two of them full independence. Their republics had been the founders of the Union of Soviet Socialist Republics,[15] the Constitution of which provided a right of secession. Presumably the original parties to the treaty had the right to terminate it, particularly if the treaty preserved the principle of republic sovereignty, which it did.

Fine, some will concede. The republics may indeed have had an inherent right to withdraw from the USSR, but the leaders who attended the meeting in Bison Forest were not empowered to make that decision. After all, the citizens of all three republics had voted in favor of preserving the union during the referendum in March.

The referendum in March, however, had been worded so confusingly that it could hardly have had legal effect. And in the case of Ukraine an overwhelming majority had more recently voted in favor of a legally binding proposition to establish full independence and its parliament had forbidden the current government to adhere to the union treaty. In the case of Belarus, the parliament had voted a declaration of independence by a huge majority. In Russia, Yeltsin's mandate was less specific, but, like Shushkevich and Kravchuk, he subsequently had the Commonwealth agreement ratified by his legislature. Most Russian citizens might well have preferred a union that included Ukraine to independence, but it is unlikely the majority would have backed a union without Ukraine.

Nevertheless, whatever can be said to justify the secret meeting that put an end to the USSR, the founders of the Commonwealth were obviously not meticulous in satisfying Soviet legal procedure. The secrecy of the meeting in Bison Forest, the lack of a referendum in any republic on the specific question of dissolving the USSR, and the refusal to enter into a debate of the respective merits of the union treaty and the Commonwealth agreement, as well as the machinations to prevent a final session of the USSR Congress of People's Deputies to dissolve itself and nullify the USSR Constitution, have given critics ammunition with which to attack the legitimacy of the agreement reached on December 8, 1991.

Konstantin Lubenchenko, the last speaker of the Soviet parliament, who initially branded the Commonwealth agreement as illegal, told me in March 1992 that he had no doubt that the USSR Congress of People's Deputies would have agreed to liquidate the Soviet Union in an irreproachably legal fashion if the republic presidents had made a direct request. The deputies would have realized that they could not have continued to function in the face of opposition from the republics and, however regretfully, would have granted the request. As Lubenchenko, a law professor by profession, saw it, the tragedy of the forced dissolution of Soviet state structures was that it undermined respect for the rule of law, still a fragile shoot in Russia and the other former Soviet republics. Furthermore, he thought that it clouded the legitimacy of the new Russian state and provided both arguments and incentives for malcontents to resort to unconstitutional methods.[16]

Russia on Its Own

LEGALITY ASIDE—for there will never be total agreement on the propriety of the methods used by Yeltsin, Kravchuk, Shushkevich, and the other republic leaders to end the Soviet Union—supporters of the commonwealth concept point to practical factors that, they argue, gave the republic leaders no real choice but to act as they did.

The Soviet legislature and its government had repeatedly demonstrated their incapacity to chart an effective course of reform. Yet, as long as the union institutions persisted, they had tended to block reform efforts by Russia and other republics. Meanwhile, the economy was no longer merely declining; it had begun to disintegrate. If Russia wished to preserve any semblance of coherence in its reform policies, it would have to eliminate the union institutions. Otherwise there would have been endless haggling over jurisdiction, and the Soviet bureaucracy would have blocked any real change. Besides, as negotiations for the economic community in September and October had shown, most of the republic governments aside from Russia were opposed to radical economic reform. A union government would provide levers with which they could distort and even derail the Russian efforts.

This line of argument, associated with Gennady Burbulis and the "Young Turks" he led at the time, is difficult to refute. Even if the union treaty had been signed in November, it is doubtful that it could have lasted even six months under the economic and political pressures that were to come, and it could have fallen apart with more ill will and fewer commitments to cooperation than the Commonwealth provided.

If the new Russian government had been able to carry through an effective program of reform in Russia, it would in the eyes of many have confirmed the pragmatic justification for ending the Soviet Union. When its reform efforts proved more disruptive than anyone had imagined, however, old grievances would take on new life.

Even as Yeltsin was successfully maneuvering to liquidate the Soviet Union, the Russian political leadership was beginning to show fissures that would have profound implications for the future. Opposition in the RSFSR Supreme Soviet to the reform program espoused by the government Yeltsin installed in November turned out to be surprisingly strong. Yeltsin finally obtained the power he sought to rule by decree for a year, but if his government's program did not produce quick results, serious friction would be inevitable.

In early December, just as Yeltsin was preparing for his trip to Bison Forest, Vice President Alexander Rutskoy, who had stood firmly with Yeltsin and the defenders of the Russian White House in August, announced his opposition to the Russian government Yeltsin had just named and that Yeltsin formally headed. He jeered at Burbulis, Gaidar, and Shakhrai as inexperienced "theoreticians" whose policies would have unpredictable and probably ruinous results. In particular, he condemned the decision to free retail prices, first scheduled for December 16 and then postponed, but only until January 2, 1992.

Rutskoy's verbal attacks on the new Russian government were savage, but when he was asked if he intended to resign, he said he was determined to stay on and fight against policies he considered harmful to Russia. Gossips began to speculate that if there should be a putsch against Yeltsin and the Russian government, it might well be led by Rutskoy.[17]

Russia, therefore, approached the dawn of independence from Soviet power mired in a political crisis of its own. It was still operating under the old Soviet Constitution, which had originally been designed for a different cog in a totally different machine. To be sure, the Constitution had been amended a hundred times or so, but the result was a patchwork with enough contradictions and ambiguities to turn every political debate into a constitutional struggle.

Yeltsin had decided not to write and campaign for a new Russian constitution in the fall of 1991, when the postcoup shock might have encouraged quick agreement. Instead, he had chosen to use his energy to dismantle the union government. Though he achieved his goal, he inherited a state infested with political booby traps. And in the future, when policies failed, there would be no Gorbachev to blame.

Finale

GORBACHEV ACCEPTED HIS FATE with dignity but not without complaint. Virtually every day until he resigned, he issued a statement or conducted an interview, warning of the dangers ahead if the union state should be abandoned. He foresaw ethnic strife, economic chaos, the disintegration of Russia and other republics, and a high probability of civil war.

Few were listening anymore, but Gorbachev either did not know or did not care. Even when his own resignation was certain, he continued to hector the republic presidents. Except for his occasional meetings with Yeltsin, however, the harangues were from afar: interviews with journalists, messages circulated by TASS, community to visiting groups. The republic presidents pointedly refused to invite him to their gatherings.

On December 17, I called on Gorbachev with other participants in a conference in Moscow on ethnic hatred organized by Elie Wiesel and Vitaly Korotich. As he greeted us one by one, he called me "Mr. Ambassador" and added, "We have a custom, once an ambassador, always an ambassador."

"We have the same one," I countered. "Only it is 'Once a president, always a president.' "

He was calm and apparently reconciled to his fate but told us he had not yet set the date for his resignation. First he wanted to see what would emerge from the meeting of republic leaders in Alma Ata, scheduled for December 21. He obviously hoped to address the meeting but seemed to realize that he would not be invited, since he said that whatever happened, he would send them a message.

At the beginning of our meeting, Gorbachev talked at length about the popularity of his books abroad. He knew how many millions of copies had been printed and was proud of the fact that they were still bringing in substantial royalties. Not that he got the money personally, he added hastily, since he gave it all to charitable organizations, but he was pleased to see that people were interested in his writings and paid attention to his opinions. His influence in the world was obviously an important consolation as he contemplated his bleak political future.

His message to the Alma Ata meeting offered some moderate and potentially useful suggestions, including the desirability of strengthening the protection of civil rights, the advantages of a common citizenship, and the need to keep a centralized command over nuclear arms. In his conclusion, he made a special plea to allow the USSR Supreme Soviet to meet and formally dissolve the Soviet Union, explaining the advice in this fashion:

> We should begin a new era in the history of the country with dignity and in conformity with standards of legitimacy. One of the reasons for the historical misfortunes of our peoples has been the gross discontinuities, destructive revolutions, and preemptive methods inflicted upon society. We have both the prerequisites and the experience needed to act in the framework of democratic rules.[18]

As far as the Alma Ata conference was concerned, his advice was ignored. The substance of the original Commonwealth agreement signed in Belarus was not changed.

The only practical negotiation Gorbachev had left was over his own future. This he conducted in private with Yeltsin, and the meeting went on for more than ten hours. Yeltsin has portrayed Gorbachev's demands as exorbitant, but few in the West would consider the settlement he received inappropriate for a retired chief of state. Gorbachev was given control of a building that had housed one of the Communist Party institutes to use for a public affairs foundation. The precedent was important: for the first time Russia was allowing a leader to continue to participate in public life following retirement.

Although at one time Yeltsin had agreed that the Soviet Union would formally end at midnight, December 31, and that Gorbachev could occupy his office until the middle of January, his impatience subsequently prevailed, and he pressed for an earlier transfer of power. Gorbachev delivered his resignation speech before television cameras on December 25 in the room where he had often held important meetings. As soon as he came back to his office, he directed that the codes necessary for releasing nuclear weapons be transferred to General Shaposhnikov, who had come at Yeltsin's request.

When Gorbachev approached his office the next day for a scheduled meeting with foreign visitors, he was intercepted on the way and told that Yeltsin's staff had already occupied the premises. The Russian tricolor now fluttered over the dome of the Kremlin's Senate Building, which housed the offices of the country's president.

XXIII

Reflections on Some Answers

*What has occurred, of course, had reason to occur, but this by no means signifies
that all other combinations were impossible . . .*
ALEXANDER HERZEN, 1850[1]

*In the final analysis, I think that what they called my "indecisiveness," my
"slowness"—that is, my tactics and my approach—permitted forces to grow
in society that . . . form a basis for preserving and developing
democratic transformations.*
MIKHAIL GORBACHEV, March 1992[2]

*[In 1991] Gorbachev represented the union, the empire, the old power,
and I represented Russia, an independent republic, a new and as yet nonexistent
country. . . . The Soviet Union could not exist without the image of the empire.
The image of the empire could not exist without the image of force.*
BORIS YELTSIN, 1994[3]

The events we have reviewed brought three profound changes to the world: the end of the cold war, the end of communism as a system of rule in the USSR, and the end of the Soviet Union itself. These three events were intimately connected but are separable, both in time and in logic.

"Socialism," as defined by Lenin, was doomed from the start because it was based on mistaken assumptions about human nature. Only a police state capable of isolating a society from the rest of the world permitted this form of government to survive for decades. The Marxist theory of the class struggle provided an apparent justification for rule by force, just as it offered the Communist regime both internal and external enemies. Societies or elements in societies not under Communist control were, by their very existence, threats to the system of rule in the Soviet Union.

The cold war that followed World War II was, therefore, inevitable as long as there were major countries that were not under direct Soviet control. The cold war could not end, truly and definitively, until the Soviet Union abandoned its system's ideological linchpin, the class struggle concept. And once it did, the system itself had no arguable rationale.

Since Communist rule and the cold war rested on a common ideological foundation, removal of that foundation undermined both. The Soviet state, in contrast, rested on a different theoretical foundation: though an empire in reality, it was formally a voluntary federation of sovereign republics. Gorbachev's challenge was to inject content into the empty form by converting the imperial state into one based on the consent of the governed. When this effort failed, the state itself collapsed.

When Gorbachev came to power in 1985, the Soviet economy was showing definite strains, though the political system seemed thoroughly entrenched. Perceptive observers could predict with confidence that the Soviet economy would not be able to compete with the more dynamic economies in the world, and—barring fundamental reform—would fall further and further behind. Under these conditions, social and political tensions were certain to rise with potentially explosive force. Nobody, however, could be sure whether this was something that could happen in a decade or might take the better part of a century.

Historical experience with entrenched political systems, even those with much less efficient instruments of compulsion than the Soviet Union, was not encouraging. The Ottoman Empire was known as the "sick man of Europe" for more than a century before Mustafa Kemal Atatürk and his "Young Turks" brought it down. The patchwork Hapsburg Empire persisted for eight decades after it was severely shaken by the revolutions of 1848 and fifty years after it achieved the grand compromise with Hungary and established the dual monarchy. Chinese dynasties tended to linger for well over a century after they passed their prime.

To understand why the cold war ended in 1989 rather than 2089 and the Soviet Union collapsed in 1991 rather than 2091—and why the latter occurred with little violence in the empire's heartland—we must think about the decisions actual people made. Impersonal social and economic trends may have molded the environment in which decisions were made, but it was the decisions made by political leaders that determined the timing and character of events.

Who and When?

THREE MONTHS AFTER the Soviet Union passed from the scene, I traveled to Moscow and Saint Petersburg and met individually with more than a dozen Russian political leaders. I had drawn up a list of specific questions about events of the past, but I wanted better insight into their perceptions of how the Soviet collapse had occurred. Therefore, I started each interview with two questions: "Who was the key figure in the collapse of the union?" and "What was the decisive event?" Afterward, I supplemented these interviews with others and with statements in memoirs.

Of course, I did not expect unanimous views of so complex an event, particularly from participants caught up in it. But the range of opinion was striking.

Several made the point that the Soviet system had always been genetically doomed to oblivion since it had been designed to block just the sort of change that could have made it viable. Although in their view no political leader could ultimately have saved it, most were willing to name political leaders who had, by their decisions, hastened its dissolution. Others thought that an opportunity to transform the Soviet Union into a modern democracy had been missed and had their candidates for the person most responsible.

Regarding the key figure, opinion was split at least five ways: some said it had been Ukrainian President Leonid Kravchuk; others, Russian President Boris Yeltsin; still others, Soviet President Mikhail Gorbachev or KGB Chairman Vladimir Kryuchkov. Finally, one or two passed the credit (or guilt) back to Leonid Brezhnev.

Each had a cogent reason for his answer. Moscow's Mayor Gavriil Popov and Alexander Yakovlev fingered Kravchuk because his action in leading Ukraine to complete independence had removed an essential component of any possible union. Without Ukraine, their argument went, a union would be unworkable, since the discrepancy in size between Russia and each of the other republics was so great. At least one unit of intermediate size was needed to create the sort of balance a federation, or even confederation, would require.

Others, such as Anatoly Sobchak and Konstantin Lubenchenko, the last speaker of the USSR Supreme Soviet, did not agree with this logic.

Russia, Belarus, the countries of Central Asia, and perhaps one or two from the Transcaucasus could have formed a viable union even without Ukraine, they argued. Only one republic was irreplaceable, and that was Russia. Ergo, Yeltsin had been the key figure. If he had not conspired with the leaders of Ukraine and Belarus to form the Commonwealth of Independent States, some form of confederation could have been cobbled together to the benefit of all.

"No," said others, including Vladislav Starkov and Sergei Stankevich, who felt that Gorbachev's stubbornness, his failure to understand the force of nationalism, his devotion to a discredited socialism, and the authoritarian streak in his personality had prevented him from voluntarily transferring the sort of power to the republics that their leaders demanded. His failures in leadership, in short, had determined the collapse of the state he headed, and no other political figure could have saved it.

Anatoly Chernyayev, ever loyal to his boss, would have none of that. He felt that a union treaty would have been signed if the attempted coup had not occurred in August. This implied that Vladimir Kryuchkov had been the key figure. He, after all, had organized the coup, and nobody else could have done it without his cooperation.

Starkov, who named Gorbachev as the principal culprit, also pointed out that Leonid Brezhnev had shared much of the responsibility, for he was the Soviet leader who had set the stage for collapse by neglecting the country's economic, social, and ethnic problems and by permitting local "mafias" under the guise of the Communist Party to obtain a hammerlock on power in many of the union republics.

Opinions were also split when I asked about the decisive event in the Soviet collapse.

Russian President Yeltsin cited the breach of the Berlin Wall in November 1989. As he put it in his subsequent memoirs, employing characteristic hyperbole, "The USSR ended the moment the first hammer pounded the Berlin Wall."[4] This, however, had not been his judgment in 1990 or early 1991 but seems to have been formed retroactively.

Former Soviet Prime Minister Ryzhkov felt that the declaration of sovereignty by the Russian parliament in June 1990 had been the crucial event. Thereafter nothing could prevent the slide to dissolution. Once Russia had been defined as a sovereign state smaller than the Soviet

Union as a whole, dispersal of the union was inevitable because the other republics had no alternative but to become sovereign themselves. A position of formal subordination to Russia would have been politically indefensible.

Ivan Laptev cited the Central Committee's approval of a separate Russian Communist Party in the summer of 1990. When the new Russian Party had come under the control of Party conservatives, it had so polarized the Party that it had become impossible to move forward with necessary reforms.

Others, including former Soviet Foreign Minister Eduard Shevard-nadze (to judge from his resignation speech), considered Gorbachev's "turn to the right" in the fall of 1990 the determining event. By reneging on the agreement with Yeltsin to implement the Shatalin program and forming a government with those forces that subsequently betrayed him, Gorbachev had set the stage in the fall of 1990 for the drama that was played out the following year.

Armenian President Levon Ter-Petrosian felt that the crucial turning point had occurred on January 1, 1991, when the republics had taken control of tax collection and begun to limit transfers to the central budget.[5]

"No, those were serious problems, but in early 1991 there were still possibilities to retrieve the situation," ran another school of thought. Some identified the use of force in Lithuania in January 1991 as the point of no return. Its "halfhearted" application had left everyone dissatisfied: those who had been for a democratic solution blamed Gorbachev for the use of force and the loss of life, while those who had favored holding the USSR together at any cost felt he had betrayed them when he belatedly condemned the use of force.

Vitaly Tretyakov, editor of the influential *Nezavisimaya gazeta,* felt that the turning point had been Yeltsin's election as president of Russia. "As the day of June 12, 1991, drew to a close," he wrote a year later, "the collapse of the USSR became a foregone conclusion."[6]

Others felt that time had still not run out. If Gorbachev had learned from the January violence in Lithuania and mistake in March of bringing troops into Moscow and had promptly proceeded to change course, it would not have been too late to create a different sort of union. If he had concluded a union treaty with the nine republics in the early summer of 1991, replaced Pavlov with someone like Sobchak—or even, conceivably, Yavlinsky—and forced the Communist apparatchiks into opposition, he might have recovered some momentum for reform and headed off the attempted coup.

For those who reasoned this way, the August putsch had doomed the Soviet Union. Until then anything except a return to the past had been possible; afterwards there was no way at all to preserve the union.

A few, however, refused to agree that total dissolution had been inevitable even in the last week of August 1991. Some sort of union—perhaps part confederation, part association—could still have been salvaged, they felt, had it not been for the political ambitions of national-Communist leaders in many republics and the Gorbachev-Yeltsin rivalry. For these few there had still been hope that a loose but democratic confederation could be formed—until the successful "conspiracy" by Yeltsin, Kravchuk, and Shushkevich at the Belarusian hunting lodge. This would not have happened, they felt, had it not been for Yeltsin's personal feud with Gorbachev.

The Personal Side of History

BY DECEMBER 1991, there were powerful arguments, quite apart from the personal antagonism between Yeltsin and Gorbachev, for Russia to destroy the Soviet state. Not having inherited the full panoply of institutions required by a sovereign state—since the RSFSR had essentially been ruled directly by the central ministries—Russia had either to appropriate the union institutions or to destroy them and create its own from scratch. Otherwise, the competition to exercise authority could result only in political gridlock on a grand scale.

This consideration, along with the others that were adduced, were hardly conclusive, however. There were also valid arguments in favor of Russia's remaining part of a larger federation or confederation, even one without Ukraine. First, a larger state would find it easier to deal with a number of security and foreign policy issues: if nuclear weapons were controlled by a federation, years of negotiation and uncertainty could be avoided. A federation would also have the right to defend its borders without triggering charges that Russia had set upon an imperialist course. Furthermore, a federation could ease the transition to a market system by keeping internal borders open and maintaining a uniform monetary and financial system. A federal system might also provide a better mechanism for dealing with ethnic conflicts within the republics than would be available if all were totally independent.

Had the personal relations between Gorbachev and Yeltsin been better, Yeltsin might well have opted to preserve some sort of union government. As it was, the chance to remove Gorbachev from the political scene was very likely the factor that tipped the balance for Yeltsin.

Some of Gorbachev's friends argue that cooperation between Gorbachev and Yeltsin had never been possible, since Yeltsin had always wanted to replace Gorbachev and would never have been content with a subordinate role. Possibly they are right, but I am not convinced that Gorbachev could not have kept Yeltsin on his team and harnessed his energies and public appeal to bolster the reform effort.

As I pointed out earlier, Gorbachev's reaction in 1987 to Yeltsin's effort to speed up and broaden the reform effort was excessive—and counterproductive. If Gorbachev's aim was to push the Communist Party in the direction of political reform, he needed someone like Yeltsin in the leadership to spark the effort and to keep pressure on the conservatives. Personal factors, however, triumphed over political calculation: Gorbachev did not wish to share the limelight with an appealing colleague. He was comfortable only with silent or mediocre associates, and this is one of the keys to his failure, in regard not only to Yeltsin but to his selection of personnel in general.

It is hard to be sure just when Yeltsin's attitude toward Gorbachev congealed into unalloyed hate. As late as the spring of 1989, he was saying both in private and in public that he wanted nothing more than to go back onto Gorbachev's team. Perhaps he didn't mean it and would never have been satisfied with a junior partnership. We will never know for sure because he was not given a chance to work with Gorbachev in 1988, 1989, or 1990, when it might have been possible.

Even after Yeltsin had proven beyond a doubt his popularity with the public—and thus his potential for selling the program Gorbachev professed to want—Gorbachev continued to fight him every step of the way, not even shrinking from using the KGB's bag of dirty tricks. (He did, nevertheless—and significantly—stop short of authorizing moves that would have posed a physical danger to Yeltsin.)

After Yeltsin's election as chairman of the Russian parliament, when he could no longer be safely ignored, whenever there was an agreement between them, it was Gorbachev who reneged, all the time accusing Yeltsin of playing political games. Yeltsin's antics and penchant for grandstanding were doubtless annoying, but Yeltsin never walked away from major agreements the way Gorbachev did in October 1990, in regard to the Shatalin program, or in May 1991, in regard to Yavlinsky's reform efforts.

Looking at the public record of the relationship, it is easy to understand how an egotist like Yeltsin would develop a visceral hatred for Gorbachev.

Having said that, one must also recognize that Yeltsin frequently exacerbated the relationship with irresponsible appeals and was often inconsistent in his own approach. Despite his verbal disclaimers, his behavior—particularly in 1990 and 1991—was usually designed to show Gorbachev in the worst possible light. He knew what psychological buttons to push to get a rise out of Gorbachev, and he was crafty in his timing. His demand in February 1991 that Gorbachev resign is a case in point: Yeltsin could have had no doubt that Gorbachev would respond by trying to use Party hard-liners to unseat him. But such an attempt, played out before the television cameras, was just what he needed to give his campaign for the Russian presidency new life.

Gorbachev seemed never to grasp the obvious fact that it was his opposition to Yeltsin, more than any other factor, that made Yeltsin popular with the public. It was doubtless an unpleasant, even bitter, fact for a person as proud and—let's be frank—intellectually arrogant as Gorbachev. But any politician who is misguided enough to humiliate and embitter a potential rival and then adopt tactics that enhance his rival's popularity is unlikely to possess the keen judgment required to lead a country through a difficult crisis.

The only real hope that the Soviet Union could transform itself peacefully (or relatively peacefully) into a democratic state was that, before it was too late, Gorbachev and Yeltsin would realize they must cooperate. Until July 29, 1991 (the day he agreed to dismiss Pavlov, Pugo, and Kryuchkov), Gorbachev was more to blame than Yeltsin for the fact that this did not happen; after August 21, 1991, it was Yeltsin's behavior that ultimately made it impossible to convert the empire into a federated or confederated state. In human terms, the attitude of both was understandable, but in political terms history will regard both as statesmen *manqué* because they let their personal animosity blind them to the political consequences of their rivalry.

The Gorbachev Legacy

GORBACHEV'S RIVALRY WITH YELTSIN, though possibly decisive in December 1991, is by no means the only salient aspect of Gorbachev's political stewardship. Yeltsin was, from 1985 until mid-1990, a peripheral issue. Any appraisal of Gorbachev the statesman must look beyond his personal relationships.

Current Russian judgments of Gorbachev are deeply split, often influenced by the observer's personal relationship to Gorbachev. If we ignore the hysterical and totally irresponsible accusations that he acted as a paid or unpaid "agent" of the West, we can discern three distinct schools of thought:

1. Gorbachev was merely "a pimple on the skin of Russian history,"[7] not a genuine reformer. He initiated certain changes to enhance his own power, and if these led to reforms, that was the result of others' efforts, not Gorbachev's.

2. Gorbachev initially began reforms but then lost his way. The changes in society outpaced his ability to comprehend or control them. Therefore, in the end he became a victim of the reforms he had set into motion.[8]

3. Gorbachev was a genuine reformer, who, however, had to deal with a Communist Party leadership that opposed the innovations he favored and that could have removed him from power if he had pressed for reforms in a straightforward manner. This led him to make tactical compromises while he maneuvered to free himself from Communist Party control. His own understanding of the reforms that would be required evolved and gradually became more radical, and if he had been given even a few months more time, he might have succeeded in destroying the Communist Party, founding a state based on the rule of law, and preserving a confederal union of the core Soviet republics.[9]

Gorbachev himself insists that he was a genuine and radical reformer. Speaking in Munich in March 1992, he pointed out that every previous Russian leader who had attempted reform early in his rule became reactionary toward the end. Tsar Alexander I was a case in point: initially Alexander had backed the constitutional reforms devised by Mikhail Speransky, his secretary of state, but in the face of conservative opposition and what he interpreted as revolutionary activity, he had become a reactionary and instituted a police state. "That is how reformers are changed by the pressure of circumstances! The opposite of what they wanted at first, of what they strove for," Gorbachev exclaimed.[10] Then he denied that he had followed that pattern.

> It is extremely difficult to preserve to the end one's moral position. But I was determined not to retreat from my most important political choice. A moral choice. In the final analysis, I think that what they called my "indecisiveness," my "slowness" (I place these words in quotes)—that is, my tactics and my approach—permitted forces to grow in society that, as they say now, form a basis for preserving and developing democratic transformations.[11]

In my view, Gorbachev's claim in his Munich address is justified. Those who would deny him any causative role in the liberation of his country from the Communist system are blind to the obvious fact that *Gorbachev's initiatives in 1988, 1989, and early 1990 made it possible for independent political forces to undermine and eventually destroy the Communist Party's monopoly on political power.* His support for political openness and democratic changes was not always unqualified and was at times self-serving, but the fact remains that no fundamental change would have been possible as long as the Communist Party's grip on power remained. Unlike most of his colleagues in the Politburo, from 1988 Gorbachev usually backed democratic change rather than the Communist Party's narrow interests. When he failed to do so, it was to avoid being swept from power before he could implement his programs.

His judgment, of course, was not always above reproach, and many of his errors—recounted in detail in my narrative—were probably avoidable. But the fact remains that, despite his temporary alliance with the enemies of reform in the winter of 1990–91, *he consistently refused to authorize the use of force to keep himself in power.* He was, in fact, the first Russian leader in history who used force not as a first but a last resort. As he pointed out in his Munich speech, all his predecessors who had come to power with visions of reform had abandoned the effort when they perceived threats to their own position. Gorbachev could have declared presidential rule at any one of several points in 1990 or 1991 and rallied the repressive forces in Soviet society to his side, but even though he may have come perilously close to doing so at times, in the end he refused to crush the embryonic democratic institutions and practices. For that service and for that precedent, Russia owes him a homage he has yet to receive.

Gorbachev also left an important heritage in foreign policy. Within just a few years, he evolved from a dogmatic defender of traditional nationalistic, exclusive, and intolerant Soviet attitudes to a champion of universal human values. His rejection of the class struggle ideology was essential if the country was to overcome the isolation, hostility, and permanent tension with the outside world that the Bolshevik Revolution had engendered.

He did not originate the specific program that eventually ended the cold war and eliminated the East-West divide. But he came to understand that the Soviet Union could benefit from joining the rest of the world, and he made an essential contribution when he found and adopted an ideological justification for making peace with the world.

Ideological pronouncements would have been of slight importance if they signified only a shift in rhetoric. But they meant more, for Gorbachev reoriented Soviet foreign policy in conformity with them. In agreeing to reduce armaments on the basis of equality at the end (rather than proportional reductions, which would have preserved Soviet superiority), to end Soviet military involvement in conflicts elsewhere, to allow Eastern Europe to leave the Soviet sphere, to cooperate in the unification of Germany, and to oppose aggression by an erstwhile protégé in the Middle East, Gorbachev acted in accord with the new principle he had proclaimed. Every decision he made was consistent with Soviet interests, but each one also met the interests of the other states involved.

Basing foreign policy on "universal human values" or "the common interests of mankind" may smack of fuzzy sentimentalism to self-styled "realists," but they are wrong. Any foreign policy that seeks to beggar neighbors or to derive a one-sided advantage at the expense of others is going to fail in the long run and, before it does, risk destructive conflict costing far more in lives and property than any attainable advantage could justify. In an interdependent world, a successful foreign policy must be crafted so that it is consistent with the interests of other countries.

That is the clear implication of the proposition that foreign policy should be based on common interests. It does not imply that a country should ignore its own interests, rather that its interests should not be perceived as exclusively those of a single class, or group, or ideology, or nationality. The world community will fail to benefit from the opportunities the end of the cold war has created unless it finds a way to instill this philosophical principle into normal international practice. There can be no New World Order without it.

Gorbachev's achievements are impressive, but they do not negate the fact that he conspicuously failed in his larger goal to transform the Soviet Union into a voluntary federation of states governed by the rule of law and with a market economy performing on the level of the world's advanced industrialized countries. Perhaps this was an impossible dream for a single political generation to accomplish. The distance to be traveled was so great, the obstacles so severe, and the terrain so obscure that we should not assume that any political leader could have completed the course.

Many of Gorbachev's associates feel he could have preserved the Soviet Union, at least in truncated form, without the Baltic states but with most of the others, if, in 1989 or early 1990, he had offered a confederation of the sort he was willing to accept in the summer of 1991. The republic leaders and nationalist movements, they argue, would have been so grateful that they would not have haggled over the "gift"—and as they wrestled with the problems of managing economic activity in their republics, they would quickly have learned that they needed some central institutions.

When I interviewed Gorbachev in September 1992, I put the question to him. I asked if he felt he had made a mistake by not moving more quickly to grant the republics real autonomy.

"Jack, I can see you are a professor now, because your question is academic," he replied. "In some abstract sense, it is probably right that I moved too slowly, but I did not have the luxury of living in the abstract. I lived in a harsh world of political reality. Let me ask you: What would have happened to me if I had proposed a confederation in 1989?"

"I suppose the Central Committee would have removed you at its next plenum," I replied.

"Yes, and they would have advanced the meeting to get rid of me without delay. Even as it was, when I began to talk of a federation in early 1990, most of the Central Committee was in opposition. I had to fight them all the way. I simply did not have a free hand and should not be judged as if I had."[12]

Gorbachev had a point, and it is a point that his reformist critics failed to appreciate either then or now. He could not openly espouse policies that were strongly opposed by the Party bosses. He had to introduce changes with careful preparation and occasional deceit. He had to maneuver to stay in power while he forced or tricked the Party to do what it had always opposed. Sometimes even his illusions had functional utility—for a time, at least.

The illusion that the Communist Party of the Soviet Union could be turned into an instrument of fundamental change muddled Gorbachev's political judgment until Yeltsin forced him to confront, in public, proof of the Party's treachery. Objectively speaking, however, the illusion had one important side effect: it provided a rationale for steps that diminished the Party's authority and eventually brought its total collapse. These steps, which required the formal endorsement of the very bodies whose power was being undermined, could hardly have been taken if Gorbachev had not convinced many Party officials that the Party could stay in power even if the reforms were adopted.

Illusions aside, Gorbachev's tactics were often not based on a clear strategic vision. He should not have used his need to placate the Party *apparat* as an excuse for the treatment he gave Yeltsin in 1987. If he was unable to pack the Politburo and Central Committee with reformers and therefore needed to free himself from their control, it was clearly a mistake not to seek popular election as president as early as possible— say, sometime in 1989. It was utterly self-defeating to encourage reformers to leave the Communist Party before the 1990 Party congress and to allow his opponents to dominate the Russian Party when it was organized. While he might not have been able openly to endorse reformers like Andrei Sakharov, Yuri Afanasiev, and Gavriil Popov, he could have avoided insulting them and could have offered tacit protection rather than vicious public criticism. Their influence on the public was critical to the success of perestroika, but from 1990 Gorbachev forgot this and let spats over tactics destroy what should have been an implicit strategic alliance.

Gorbachev also underestimated the rapid change in public attitudes that occurred from 1989 on. In private, he would complain that he could not move faster than public opinion, but in fact public opinion was ahead of him. It was the Party *apparat,* not society as a whole, that failed to keep up, and when Gorbachev deferred to it, he alienated much of society. He was still defending "socialism" when polls showed that more than 60 percent of the public considered it bankrupt. By failing (one is tempted to say refusing) to understand the mounting anti-Communist sentiment in the country, Gorbachev handed Yeltsin issue after issue to exploit.

How can we explain what appears to have been willful blindness on Gorbachev's part? If he was genuinely in favor of reform, how could he have made so many errors in judging people, and, with all the sources of information at his command, how could he have been ignorant of the changes in society and attitudes within his own country?

I believe that elements of his personal character contributed to these failings.

Gorbachev is by nature a private person, and this made it difficult for him to develop effective consultative and advisory bodies. He had neither a Cabinet nor a kitchen Cabinet in the real sense. There were, of course, councils of various types, members of which came and went, meeting with him from time to time. But they never coalesced into effective advisory bodies for two reasons. First, Gorbachev often chose people for them who were unable to work together, and, second, he never used them as genuine advisory bodies, to be consulted regularly and taken seriously. Furthermore, he normally talked to them rather than listened.

Gorbachev's social life seemed to be either official and public or exclusively in his own family. He had no circle of cronies or intimates who might have provided a link, however tenuous, to the broader public. Raisa was his only close friend, and valuable as she was in offering the psychological support that sustained him under intense pressure, she was unable to provide the breadth and depth of advice that a wider circle of intimates might have contributed. Furthermore, if it is true that duplicitous aides like Valery Boldin maintained their position by currying favor with her, her judgment of individuals was as faulty as her husband's.[13]

People noticed that he had no personal friends, aside from his foreign colleagues. In 1991 several senior Soviet officials commented to me, quite independently, that Gorbachev felt more comfortable with foreigners than with his own people. "He is closer to President Bush, Secretary Baker, and you than he is to any of us," one remarked. "You can have a franker conversation with him than we can. He really has no close friends here."

Another factor that inhibited the flow of sound information and advice to Gorbachev was his penchant for naming second- and third-raters to key positions. Particularly as his power waned and his unpopularity grew, he developed an intense allergy to anyone who might shine brighter in the public eye than his own fading image. His placement of weaklings like Yanayev and Pavlov in key positions was the result. Even apart from their treachery in August 1991, their ineffectiveness contributed to his downfall.

Finally, his trust in Vladimir Kryuchkov and his gullibility to KGB disinformation turned out to be a fatal weakness. Not only did he fail to separate his own security from KGB control—which he should have been able to do when Kryuchkov replaced Chebrikov in 1988—he allowed himself to be misled by reports that misrepresented the real situation in the country. Any chief of government can be fooled occasionally by a false report, but a statesman who is unable to detect and correct a long-standing and consistent pattern of false reporting is not doing his job properly.

Enumerating Gorbachev's failings is easy. What is hard, maybe impossible, is to determine just how far he could have gone at various times without being removed. We cannot say for sure that his judgment was faulty in that respect. It is possible that a cabal similar to the one formed in August 1991 might have made an earlier attempt—say, in the fall of 1990—if he had moved more rapidly on the reform course. A coup at that time might have had a better chance of success than the one in August 1991. Yeltsin had not yet been elected president of Russia; Muscovites had not yet learned from the Lithuanians how to protect their parliament with their bodies; there was less apprehension about the possibility of a civil war; and the "democrats" were less numerous, more poorly organized, and less self-confident than they would be nine months later.

But without a vice president and a cooperative prime minister, no putsch in 1990 could have pretended to the legality sought by the coup leaders in 1991. If Gorbachev had taken the precaution of rotating his minister of defense, splitting some key functions out of the KGB, and naming a competent and loyal prime minister, it would have been exceedingly difficult for anyone to organize a coup. Therefore, if Gorbachev faced a serious risk of removal before 1991, he was in part to blame for not taking reasonable precautionary steps.

Nevertheless, these mistakes and misjudgments should not blind us to

Gorbachev's courage in attempting to change the system he inherited. If, as some of his critics allege, his only goal was to accumulate more power, the whole reform effort he initiated makes no sense. He could have retained personal power by keeping the country under the control of the Communist Party. His efforts to reform it and to establish a representative government of limited powers cannot be explained as merely an exercise in self-aggrandizement. His reforms were genuine, and though they had consequences he did not anticipate, he is correct when he says that if Russia has a chance to build democratic institutions today, it is because of the changes that occurred in the country on his initiative.

I am convinced that Russia will eventually regard Mikhail Gorbachev as the person who led it out of bondage. The fact that he was unable to reach the Promised Land is secondary.

The Yeltsin Record

AT THIS WRITING, Boris Yeltsin is still president of the Russian Federation. His record as a politician and statesman is still being written. But what can we say about his role in the collapse of the Soviet Union?

Contemporaries are as divided on his record as a *Soviet* politician as they are on Gorbachev's. Some view him as a mere opportunist whose only consistent trait has been a thirst for power and who never outgrew the operating style of a provincial Communist Party first secretary. Others consider him an irresponsible populist, a politician who shifts with the wind. His admirers reject both characterizations, pointing out that, from 1987, he consistently supported first liberalization and then democratization. He was the first erstwhile Politburo member to break completely with the Communist Party and go into outright opposition to it. And they would add that, despite his Communist background, he had at least some instincts of a democrat: he never shied away from the test of a direct election.[14]

Certainly, Yeltsin and Gorbachev had contrasting personalities: Gorbachev was the more thoughtful, the more calculating, Yeltsin the more instinctive and impulsive. Gorbachev's formal education was superior: the country's premier university offered many advantages over the provincial construction institute Yeltsin attended. But both shared the professional experience of long and successful service in the Communist

Party apparatus; both had made their names initially as provincial first secretaries. Even here, however, there was a contrast.

Though Gorbachev's family background was modest—his father was a tractor driver—he had the luck to be selected for study at Moscow University. His solid record there—both academic and as an active Komsomol leader—allowed him to return home on the fast track for Party leadership. Responsible positions, first in the Komsomol and then in the Party itself, followed in quick and seemingly automatic succession.

Yeltsin did not benefit from such an initial advantage: he had to claw his way into the *nomenklatura* by wit and will—and liberal use of his elbows. As a consequence, the two viewed power differently: to Gorbachev it was his due, while to Yeltsin it was something to fight for and win.

And fight he did. But he fought by the rules. His election campaigns and his tactics in parliament, up through his election as president of Russia in June 1991, would be considered normal in any democracy. Of course he attacked his opponents' vulnerabilities, took advantage of their mistakes, and sometimes made campaign promises that he could not fulfill, but only people still wedded to the idea of a one-party dictatorship would find such practices abnormal.

In the winter of 1990–91, when Gorbachev was teetering on the brink of authorizing the use of force in the Baltic states, Yeltsin's firm position, along with warnings from the West, probably caused Gorbachev to draw back from what would have been a tragic and bloody mistake. Though it was in his political self-interest to defend elected assemblies against forcible dissolution, Yeltsin's support for Baltic independence required both political and physical courage, as did his immediate and unequivocal condemnation of the coup attempt in August.

If it had not been for Yeltsin, the hard-liners who tried to remove Gorbachev in August 1991 would probably have gained control of the Soviet Union that year, possibly with Gorbachev's reluctant acquiescence. They might not have stayed in power for long, but their policies would have shattered the new democratic institutions, demolished the economy, and run the risk of extensive bloodshed.

While it might be going too far to say that Boris Yeltsin saved democracy in Russia (since democracy was still in an early stage of development there), it is no exaggeration to say that his actions during the first eight months of 1991 preserved the possibility of developing democracy in Russia when that cause was under mortal threat.

After the August coup, it is a different story. Instead of concentrating on institution building now that he had the chance—getting a new constitution written and adopted, for example, reforming and replacing the old bureaucracy, helping to build national political parties and the institutions essential to a market economy—Yeltsin devoted his energies to a struggle with the Center, simply seizing without modification the bureaucratic structures of the Soviet Union. In doing so, he not only undermined respect for the rule of law but saddled his Russian government with many of the liabilities of the past. Furthermore, he brought Russia into the international arena as a new, independent state without an unequivocal mandate from its citizens and with an unworkable constitution. These were serious handicaps that could have been mitigated had he been willing to tolerate a more deliberate transitional process.

Boris Yeltsin's performance in 1991 will doubtless be assessed in the context of his subsequent record as president of Russia. If the country can find its way as a democratic state with a viable market economy, few will be inclined to dwell on his shortcomings. He will be considered the founder of a new Russia, one fit for the twenty-first century and beyond. But if the country disintegrates further, drifts into a morass of crime and corruption, and is riven by demagogic appeals to revive the empire, he could be put down as a tragic Tsar Boris II, whose reign of questionable legitimacy brought on a Time of Troubles and of national shame.

Kryuchkov the Wrecker

IF I WERE TO REPLY to the question I posed to Russian politicians regarding the person most responsible for the collapse of the Soviet Union, my answer would be Vladimir Kryuchkov.

He was the organizer of the August 1991 attempt to seize power that accelerated the disintegration and thus made it much more difficult to create a voluntary federation of at least part of the empire. No credible attempt to overthrow Gorbachev could have been mounted without the support of the KGB chief—which is one of the reasons Gorbachev failed to anticipate the move against him. His trust in Kryuchkov's loyalty was as complete as it was misplaced.

Kryuchkov's betrayal of his president would itself justify considering him the most immediate wrecker of the Soviet Union, but his claim to the title rests on more than that act alone.

He consistently failed in his primary duty to supply Gorbachev with accurate intelligence. His reports were deliberately skewed to promote the particular policies he favored. Furthermore, he resorted to outright lies to undermine Gorbachev's trust in colleagues who did not support his views. He bears a heavy responsibility for Gorbachev's failure to recognize the strength of nationalist sentiment and the rapid growth of public hatred for the Communist Party. His shrill alarums over nonexistent foreign interference, while perhaps useful in maintaining a bloated intelligence budget, deflected attention from the real problems the Soviet Union faced, while the "solutions" he favored were certain to exacerbate them.

It would be, of course, naïve—even utopian—to suppose that an organization like the USSR Committee on State Security could be converted into a law enforcement agency compatible with a democratic state. Its habits of operating outside the law and of shielding its operatives from any external accountability, even to the country's political authorities, were too deep seated to be totally overcome, even by a determined chairman.

In this regard, Vladimir Kryuchkov was anything but a determined chairman. While he did not share the truly bestial habits of predecessors like Lavrenty Beria and Nikolai Yezhov—his KGB did not commit mass murders of innocent persons—he kept the organization beyond the reach of law, subservient to his own policy preferences rather than to those of constituted authority. Furthermore, he continued activities that had formally been discontinued (such as spying on "dissidents") and that—in some cases—were clearly not approved by Gorbachev.

In this matter, however, Gorbachev shares responsibility. There was supposed to be no surveillance, for example, of members of the Central Committee, but Yeltsin was placed under what seems to have been continuous observation, including listening devices in his residence. Gorbachev received the reports and could not have been deceived about their origin. For example, the report that Yeltsin had asked me what the United States would do if there was an unconstitutional seizure of power could have come only from a KGB informer or a listening device. As long as the rules were broken to keep Gorbachev informed about his rivals, Gorbachev accepted, even encouraged, the activity. Inexplicably, it seems not to have occurred to him that a KGB chairman who would bend the rules was also capable of placing Gorbachev himself under surveillance and even recruiting agents from among his personal staff.[15]

Vadim Bakatin has commented that, throughout his tenure, Gorba-

chev retained something of a provincial Party chief's awe of the KGB.[16]
It thrilled him to get a folder every morning marked EYES ONLY GENERAL
SECRETARY, and he was convinced that he was getting inside information
available to no one else. The gullibility he had shown during Nicholas
Daniloff's arrest in 1986 persisted. He continued to do the KGB's bid-
ding even when it was damaging to other, more important issues. For
example, when Oleg Kalugin broke with the KGB in 1990 and denounced it for continuing illegal practices, Gorbachev illegally deprived
Kalugin of his pension and previous awards rather than using Kalugin's
accusations to pressure Kryuchkov to clean up his act.[17] Gorbachev
never questioned the KGB's good faith until it was too late.

While it would be fantasy to imagine that any KGB chairman could
have reformed the organization totally in the late 1980s and early 1990s,
we can speculate how that organization might have differed if it had
been under different leadership. For example, if Vadim Bakatin rather
than Vladimir Kryuchkov had been in charge of the KGB in 1990 and
1991, we can be certain that there would have been no conspiracy
against Gorbachev, and also reasonably confident that the practice of
keeping opposition leaders under surveillance would have ended. The
Alpha Detachment could not have been used to storm the television
complex in Vilnius, and reporting of conditions in the country would
very likely have been much more objective. Bakatin states that the professional intelligence officers in the KGB did not like Kryuchkov's penchant for "cooking" the evidence; they would have preferred more
accurate reporting.

People do make a difference, and Vladimir Kryuchkov made a big
difference. The Soviet Union might exist in some modified form today if
another person had been running the KGB in 1990 and 1991.

The Role of the West

OPINIONS ON THE ROLE of the West, and of the United States in particular, in the end of the cold war and the collapse of the Soviet Union vary
as much as evaluations of Gorbachev and Yeltsin do. Here, too, the
opinion often seems to be based more on a person's political attitude
toward the statesmen in question than on a dispassionate examination
of the facts. Those favorably disposed toward Reagan or Bush or
Thatcher or Kohl will attribute much of what happened to their policies.

Those who opposed them politically tend to deny *any* contribution on their part. For them, Gorbachev alone transformed the international political map in the late 1980s and early 1990s. This, for example, seems to have been the opinion of the Norwegian parliament when it awarded the Nobel Peace Prize to Gorbachev alone in 1990.

To think clearly about the question of responsibility, we must distinguish among three transformations: the end of the cold war, the end of Communist rule in the Soviet Union, and the end of the Soviet Union itself. Despite the obvious connections and the fact that the end of the cold war set into motion developments that led to the other two events, the United States and its allies approached them separately.

The cold war ended on the terms set by the United States, implicitly from its onset and explicitly by the Reagan administration from January 1984. These terms were not to the detriment of the real interests of a peaceful, reforming Soviet Union, though they did include fundamental changes in the way the country was ruled—changes that were certain to alter the nature of the Soviet regime.

Gorbachev knew from the outset of his term as Soviet leader that he could not have successful internal reform as long as East-West tensions remained high. At first he tried to lower the tension by dealing with arms control alone. When this did not work (the turning point was probably the Reykjavik summit in October 1986), he began to respond across the full breadth of the four-point U.S. agenda. This was, however, not primarily a concession to the United States: events at home had convinced him that he would have to open Soviet society to the rest of the world and begin a process of democratization if the reforms he envisaged were to be feasible. Thus, the American (and Western) agenda began to coincide with his own.

As there was progress across the four themes on the agenda, concrete issues were solved with accelerating rapidity—just what American policy had been designed to encourage. Emigration became freer; the media opened up to a variety of influences; real elections began to be held; and—at the same time—we were agreeing to abolish intermediate-range nuclear missiles, to facilitate Soviet troop withdrawal from Afghanistan, and to help the parties settle local wars in Angola, Namibia, Nicaragua, and Cambodia. Improvements in one area gave impetus to solutions in others.

Could this have happened with the rapidity it did and in the form it did if U.S. policy had been different? If one looks carefully at the conditions under which decisions were made in Moscow, it would be hard to argue that everything would have been the same.

Those who argued for a weaker policy on arms—for nuclear freezes, unilateral reductions, or a refusal to meet the SS-20 threat with deployments in Europe—would have eliminated much of the Soviet incentive to reduce armaments. Even if Gorbachev had been wise enough to understand the need, these policies would have undermined the only argument likely to convince the Soviet military to go along with the reductions. The obvious fact that the Soviet Union could not win the arms race and therefore would have to find a way to end it was Gorbachev's most powerful weapon in dealing with his hard-line critics. Our "doves" would have deprived him of it, most likely prolonging the cold war and increasing the risk that those Soviet generals who believed they could win a nuclear war would engage in reckless activity that might have brought one on.

If those Western politicians who wished to make arms control the center of the relationship and everything else subordinate to it had set policy, it is also unlikely that the cold war would have ended with the speed it did. Arms control agreements might have been signed more rapidly (though even this is not certain), but internal Soviet reforms would probably have been delayed, perhaps for years, until the Soviet leaders were convinced that reducing their military burden would not alone solve their deeper problems. Meanwhile, if there had been no clear ideological shift, if the class struggle had still remained the basis of Soviet foreign policy, the agreements reached would probably have become sources of further dispute and argument rather than the basis of building confidence.

A policy in the hands of skeptics who doubted that the Soviet leaders would ever be capable of reaching a fair agreement and observing it would also have prevented a rapid end to the cold war. If the United States and its Western allies had not been prepared to move rapidly to conclude agreements on a reasonable basis, Gorbachev's effort to come to terms with the West could have stalled, and he might have been forced to curtail reform earlier and more forcefully than he eventually did.

In sum, I believe the cold war ended because, in the mid-1980s, we had the coincidence of (1) a Western policy that combined strength and firmness with a willingness to negotiate fairly and (2) a Soviet leadership that finally realized that the country could not go on as it had, that it had to change internally, but that it could do this only in cooperation with the outside world. Gorbachev, Reagan, and America's allies all deserve full credit for the essential roles they played in this process. No one person could have pulled it off, and no one person did. But the scenario was written in Washington, and it is doubtful that it could have been written in Moscow, even by a leader as ingenious as Mikhail Gorbachev.

While the Reagan administration articulated a strategy for ending the cold war, it did not have a plan to end Communist rule in the Soviet Union. Not that it would have considered that an undesirable goal, but the key members of the administration understood that the United States could not, from the outside, bring down the Soviet regime, and that direct attempts to do so would only strengthen it. President Reagan wanted the Soviet Union to stop threatening others and believed that its aggressive tendencies could best be held in check by the influence of an informed Soviet public on its government. He supported policies that encouraged democratization, human rights, and the free flow of information but stopped short of attempts to prescribe a political structure for the Soviet people. That was a matter for them to decide for themselves.

If the Communist regime had been able to evolve into a government based on people's consent, the United States would have had no reason to complain.

Some may immediately object that, if this was the case, the United States government was implausibly naïve. How could a Communist regime evolve into its opposite? Surely the Americans must have known that democracy, freedom of movement, and access to information were totally incompatible with continued Communist rule. Either the new freedoms would be a sham, or Communist rule would not survive.

Yes, in the abstract, we knew that. But Gorbachev was not living in an abstract world, and neither were we. No one could tell *how much* freedom (if freedom can be measured) would be sufficient to bring the system down or whether—over time—the system might not show an unexpected capacity to modify itself. The leaders who started the reforms, after all, were Communists, and though they were encouraged by Western policy, they adopted a reform course for their own reasons, in what they considered their own interests. Cynics had long doubted that any leader conditioned by the Soviet system would be capable of understanding, much less insisting on, genuine reform. Many of the same cynics refused to recognize the changes as they took place. But, despite the cynics, Gorbachev happened—and Shevardnadze and Yakovlev and Yeltsin. And many others. Hardly Jeffersonian democrats, but a lot closer to Thomas Jefferson than to Josef Stalin.

Adapting, if this was possible, was their business, not ours, and if they had done so successfully, it would not have hurt the United States or Western Europe, even if they had wished to continue to call themselves Communists and their system socialist.

While the end of Communist rule in the Soviet Union was not an explicit objective of U.S. policy, we should recognize that the United States and other democratic countries were major factors in bringing it about. But this was not so much a result of their policies as of their *existence*. The prosperity and freedom enjoyed by the citizens of the democratic countries stood in stark contrast with the blighted lives of most Soviet citizens. Once increased contacts and information made the contrast clear, support for the existing system melted away.

The Soviet system turned out to be incapable of reforming rapidly enough to meet the outside competition for the hearts and minds of its people. Never mind that the people in the Soviet Union often saw foreign pastures in a greener hue than closer inspection would have revealed. One consequence of decades of lies is that people are conditioned to believe the opposite of what they have been told.

Nevertheless, if we are to credit any one individual for the collapse of Communist rule in the Soviet Union, it has to be Mikhail Gorbachev. It was, after all, he who insisted upon the changes that ultimately threw the Communist Party from its dominant position, and it was he who refused to sanction the use of force to preserve the old system. Through a succession of crises, he placed the interests of the country above those of the Party.

And is it not fitting that the first Communist leader of the Soviet Union who put country before party was also the last Communist leader of the Soviet Union?

Once it was clear that Communist rule had come to an end in the Soviet Union, the United States and most (perhaps all) other Western countries hoped that Gorbachev would succeed in establishing a voluntary union—without the Baltic states, of course, and perhaps without a few others like Moldova and Georgia. For one thing, they had confidence in Gorbachev, and though they were beginning to give Yeltsin some of the attention they had previously withheld from him, they still considered him more erratic and less reliable than the familiar Gorbachev.

Personal relations mattered, but they were not the whole story. Obviously, it would be simpler to reach agreements on issues such as nuclear weapons with one country than with a dozen. Many policy makers also feared that the collapse of the Soviet Union could lead to the sort of ethnic conflict that had begun in Yugoslavia.

If it had been in the power of the United States and Western Europe to create a democratic union of the Soviet republics, they would have been delighted to do so. But, of course, it was not in their power. So they could only watch with dismay as the empire fell apart and then scramble to establish ties with the bolting republics as best they could.

The United States and the West had little to do with the final collapse of the Soviet Union, except to the degree that the policies they had espoused had helped create the conditions that had made it possible. Political forces within the country, not hostile forces from without, were responsible for the failure to forge an acceptable union. As I have noted, it is ironic but perhaps appropriate that the former chairman of the KGB, Vladimir Kryuchkov, probably bears a heavier personal responsibility for this failure than any other single individual.

An End and a Beginning

WHEN THE SOVIET UNION finally collapsed, I did not mourn its passing, but it surprised me at the time that I also felt no urge to celebrate. Fifteen countries held in the shackles of empire finally liberated—was this not cause for jubilation by all friends of freedom? One corner of my mind thought so, but another said, "No, wait. National independence is no more absolute than personal freedom, and the two are not the same. How do we know people are going to be better off now?"

It was not a preference for the familiar over the new and unknown that made me hesitate. Most of the familiar aspects of the Soviet system were crying out for change—and by September 1991 they *had* changed. The question was how best to create a new political and economic system, one that, in Gorbachev's words, would "turn Russian history upside down" by creating a society where decisions flowed from the bottom up rather than from the top down.

No national leadership could do that directly. Political leaders would have to stop pretending that they had all the answers and be willing to stand aside and allow people to create a civil society and the habits of a market economy in their own communities. If the politicians could find ways to encourage the change, it would be even better, but their main task was to prevent those who had run the old, coercive machinery from blocking the new. However, most of the political leaders in the republics were representatives of the old machinery and could not be expected willingly to hand over power to others. In fact, they had supported independence precisely because it would give them a firmer grip on power.

Except for Russia, Armenia, and the Baltic states—the latter already independent—not a single Soviet republic had a political leadership in place that was inclined to implement real economic reforms. Even Russia and the Baltics faced formidable obstacles, particularly since nothing had been done, despite years of discussion, to establish a social safety net to protect the average person during the transition from a state-run to a private economy.

If there had been a realistic possibility in 1991 of a transitional arrangement—such as the union treaty—that would permit a consistent approach to political and economic reform and time to adapt institutions suitable for democracy and market economics, it would have been preferable to the sudden collapse of the Soviet Union that actually occurred. By late 1991, however, gradual changes—so long delayed—were no longer possible. Only radical measures were feasible, and these were certain to bring widespread distress and political turmoil. Unless the "democrats" then in charge in Russia were remarkably skillful and lucky, much of the population would lose its enthusiasm for democracy and develop a new affection for the old empire, prettied up by the distorting lens of selective memory.

Gradualism, however, was by the end of 1991 no longer feasible, even though sudden independence meant that the unsuitable central institutions were simply inherited by most of the successor states. They were bound to work even less effectively in the individual republics than they had when the Soviet Union was whole, because none of the republics had a government or an economy designed to stand alone.

I kept the champagne corked.

Each country formed from a fragment of the Soviet empire would, in the future, be responsible for its own fate. But what happened to Russia would be crucial for all. If Russia could evolve into a democratic state content to live within its current borders and concentrate on developing its vast human and physical resources, it would help all the other successor states to find their way. Conversely, if Russia should sink into dictatorship or revert to imperialism, it would make it exceedingly difficult for any of the other heirs of the Soviet Union to develop a workable democracy and a healthy economy.

Russia, like the other former Soviet republics, faced the trauma of decolonization. For Russia, however, the process was more complicated than for the others, since Russia had to redefine itself. Was the Soviet empire a Russian empire? If so, Russia had lost half its people and much of its territory. Or had Russia been a colony of a Communist empire? If that was the case, it had escaped an imperial ruler and was now free to be itself.

The truth was that Russia was some of both, part metropole and part colony. In December 1991, Yeltsin acted on the assumption that Russia had been a colony and forswore efforts to force other republics into a new empire. He and his government recognized the independence and the borders of all the other erstwhile Soviet republics.

To understand how important that was, we must consider both Russian tradition and what would have happened if the Russian leadership in 1991 had perpetuated that tradition. The historical record of the Russian state is that of an imperial power. From the early fourteenth century, when the ancient chroniclers first began to record the actions of the tiny principality of Moscow, the rulers of the country seemed to possess a relentless drive to expand. First, Moscow absorbed most of the other Russian principalities; then it moved to absorb territories in which non-Russian peoples lived, to the east, south, west and north. At its largest extent in the nineteenth century, it stretched from the borders of Sweden, Prussia, and Austria-Hungary in the west to the Pacific Ocean. For a time, it also had a foothold in the Western Hemisphere, owning Alaska and having settlements in California.

Almost without exception, Russian historians praised the growth of the empire. Those who might criticize some autocratic practices would nevertheless praise territorial expansion and any strengthening of state power. Even a tyrant as bloody as Ivan the Terrible was generally credited with, and praised for, strengthening the Russian state. For most ethnic Russians, the nation's dignity, honor, security, and even well-being required a strong imperial state.

The Soviet Union claimed not to be a Russian empire, but its leaders cleverly exploited the penchant for empire that had become a normal component of the Russian political psyche. Following a few years of tsar bashing just after the Bolshevik Revolution, the Soviet leaders adopted the imperial tradition as their own. The territorial acquisitions of the tsars became glorious chapters in the history of the Soviet Union.

This was the tradition Yeltsin and his political associates rejected in 1990, when they pressed for a declaration of RSFSR sovereignty, and in December 1991, when they formally obligated their country to respect the boundaries of the other newly independent states.

Suppose the Russian leadership had taken a different course. Would it have made any difference? For that answer, we have only to look at Yugoslavia. Suppose all the former republics of Yugoslavia had decided, in 1990 or 1991, to dissolve the federation and go their separate political ways. If Serbia had been willing to recognize existing boundaries and Croatia and the others had reciprocated, there might have been some economic dislocation as a result, but there would have been no war. There would have been political struggles but little bloodshed.

Many people, including Mikhail Gorbachev, feared that the Soviet Union would descend into an inferno of civil war if the republics became independent. But this did not happen. The ethnic struggles that went on after independence had already started while the Soviet Union existed, and they were on the periphery, not in the heartland. Why was the Soviet collapse relatively peaceful? Because the Russian leaders did not follow the Serbian example, did not try to redraw borders or gather all ethnic Russians into a Great Russia and expel non-Russians from the country. If they had, the Soviet Union could have become a Yugoslavia writ large—*very* large, for, unlike Yugoslavia, the Soviet Union possessed tens of thousands of nuclear warheads that could have escaped responsible control.

Yeltsin's redefinition of the meaning of Russia was a historic decision, on a par with Gorbachev's refusal to use force to perpetuate his rule. If it can be maintained, and if the bulk of the Russian people come to accept it in their minds and their emotions, it will be a true turning point in Russian history and as important for the future of peace and justice in the world as the end of the cold war and the end of Communist dictatorship in the Soviet Union.

In December 1991, however, it was by no means clear that the Russian nation had defined its new identity. The wiser Russian leaders understood that empires were no longer sources of prestige and power but rather costly burdens. This insight was not widely shared. Most Russians had been trained to believe otherwise. In the hard times sure to follow, how many would associate economic distress with loss of empire? There would certainly be no shortage of unreconstructed imperialists and political opportunists to stimulate and exploit the feelings of loss and betrayal, just as, earlier in this century, German fascists had ridden to power by accusing their adversaries of having stabbed the country in the back.

Emotionally and spiritually, Russia still had to redefine itself if democracy was to have a chance. Democracy could develop and flourish only if the Russian nation remained content to live within its current borders and cultivate a relationship of equality with its neighbors. Attempts to reassemble the old Russia, the empire, would inevitably lead to dictatorship in Russia itself and misery for everyone in the neighborhood.

The recognition that these crucial struggles still lay ahead was what kept me from celebrating the end of the Soviet Union on Christmas Day 1991.

Autopsy Report

HAVING TRACED THE PROCESS by which the Union of Soviet Socialist Republics collapsed and passed into history, we can now summarize our findings in a final report.

THE DEMISE OF THE USSR

The deceased was a being of vicious habits that his physicians set out to cure. They managed to alleviate the patient's paranoia and curb his aggressive behavior, but the drugs administered undermined his immune system, and he eventually died from the spread of infections that would not be life threatening to a healthy body.

Since the patient's vicious habits had caused the death of tens of millions of people and continued to blight the lives of hundreds of millions, it was manifestly more important to cure the habits than to save the patient. Furthermore, the patient's chronic resort to power abuse had created a sclerotic system that was minimally responsive to therapeutic intervention. The responsible physicians, therefore, should be credited with fulfilling their most important objective. The fact that the patient failed to survive the treatment should be regarded as a consequence of the patient's self-induced morbidity rather than the treatment administered.

Fifteen offspring, three illegitimate, survive the deceased. All have expressed a determination to avoid the behavior patterns that undermined the health of the deceased and from which, indeed, all suffered. However, it should be noted that the offspring may carry some of the genetic material that contributed to the deceased's depravity. Malignancies are in fact already evident in some. Therefore, community medical authorities should keep the surviving generation under attentive, though sympathetic, observation.

XXIV

Epilogue

The USSR is not quite dead in Russia. It has just shrunk to the size of Russia proper.
VITALY TRETYAKOV, July 1992[1]

Not a single reform effort in Russia has ever been completed.
BORIS YELTSIN[2]

An unreformed Russia will not have the strength for empire. A reformed Russia will not have the will.
JACK F. MATLOCK, JR., 1995

As Gorbachev predicted, the Commonwealth of Independent States turned out—at least in its first four years—to be ineffective as a unifying or even coordinating institution. The questions left open for subsequent negotiation either remained without agreement or were settled in such general terms that disputes continued. Even when agreements were reached, there was no enforcement mechanism, so that the Commonwealth remained little more than an arrangement for periodic meetings by chiefs of member states and governments. They did hold meetings, but when they went home they usually continued to do just what they would have done anyway.

Except for Estonia, Latvia, and Lithuania, which had experienced national independence in living memory, the successor states immediately faced a need to define themselves, to decide what their nation was and what sort of state they would build. For Russia, the task was to redefine its place in the world and its place in history. It, and all the others, had to determine whether a single group would have an advantage or whether the country would give its ethnic and religious minorities equal protection and privileges under the law.

These would have been difficult, divisive questions even if the economic transition had gone smoothly. But it didn't. The definition—in Russia's case, redefinition—of national identity coincided with mounting economic distress that provided fuel for demagoguery and pretexts for avoiding the hard decisions transition to a market economy required. In Central Asia, Belarus, and Ukraine, the economy remained in the hands of the Communist Party *nomenklatura,* even though the Party was formally abolished or renamed. Bureaucratic corruption, never absent, spread rapidly, as did organized crime, which used the bureaucrats and often made common cause with them.

The original Commonwealth (CIS) agreement had stipulated that the members would "preserve and support a common military-strategic space under a common command,"[3] but the unified command was destined to last only a few months. Just a week after the CIS treaties were signed in Alma Ata, Ukraine and Russia disagreed about how the command would operate, and by early January 1992, Ukraine was staking its claim to all general-purpose forces on its territory and to the Black Sea Fleet as well.[4] By summer, virtually all CIS members were moving to create independent armed forces, and Russia assumed what was left of the CIS command structure after it created its own defense force in May 1992.[5] From then on, military relations among the CIS member states were determined by bilateral negotiations, even though a few members adhered to a CIS collective security agreement promoted by Russia to give its military activities in other ex–Soviet states a multilateral "cover." The Commonwealth of Independent States, as such, was not a factor.

The CIS was no more successful in preserving a single "economic space" than it was in retaining a unified military establishment. Every Soviet successor state claimed jurisdiction over all property within its borders, and few agreed with the program of radical reform that Russia implemented from January 1992. Economic policies diverged substantially and encouraged protectionist measures and barriers to what had now become international trade. The ruble came under Russian control, which in time forced all but one of the other ex–Soviet states to replace it with national currencies.

All the successor states rejected Gorbachev's suggestion, in his final message to the republic leaders, to retain a common citizenship, and questions of who would qualify for citizenship where became one of the emotion-charged issues between Russia and several of the other former Soviet republics.

The history of the territory once occupied by the Soviet Union became, from 1991, the history not of one successor organization but of fifteen separate countries, struggling with enormous stresses internally while trying to manage their relationships with one another. In 1995, four years after the Soviet collapse, the Commonwealth of Independent States was still just a concept. It seemed that it still might, at some time in the future, be granted greater substance by its members, but, if this happened, it would probably take years of gradual steps, for the real action was elsewhere.

Russia's Travail

THE YOUNG REFORM INTELLECTUALS to whom Yeltsin initially entrusted his government were optimistic that they could force Russia to create a market system rapidly by freeing prices, ending subsidies to state enterprises, and exercising budget restraint. Their initial policies came to be called "shock therapy," particularly by critics. In fact, many elements of the "shock therapy" applied earlier in Poland and before that in developing countries with serious financial trouble were absent in Russia. "Shock therapy" is, therefore, a misnomer for the Russian government's initial economic reform policy.

Whatever the proper name for the policy, the shock was real. When most consumer prices were freed with the New Year in 1992, they shot up overnight, and within weeks many goods cost ten times or more what they had before. Salaries did not keep pace, and the value of savings evaporated.

Uncontrolled prices, however, did not produce competition since most production was still monopolized. Privatization of all but the smallest retail establishments was delayed for over a year, and new businesses were handicapped by ruinous tax rates and a hostile bureaucracy. With no reform or reduction of the bureaucracy, still structured as a barrier to private endeavor, the Communist-era regulations became licenses for corruption.

The Russian parliament, which had never been sympathetic to the reform program, quickly moved into active opposition. Exercising its con-

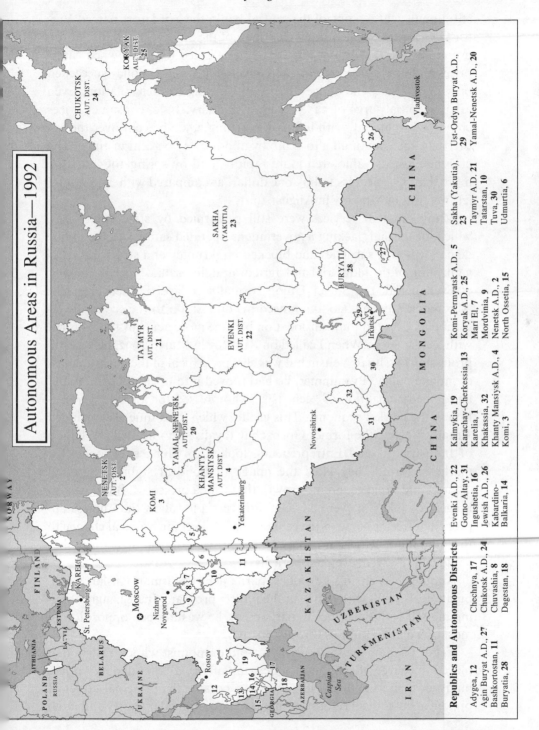

Autonomous Areas in Russia—1992

Republics and Autonomous Districts

Adygea, 12	Chechnya, 17	Komi-Permyatsk A.D., 5	Sakha (Yakutia), 23
Agin Buryat A.D., 27	Chukotsk A.D., 24	Koryak A.D., 25	Taymyr A.D. 21
Bashkortostan, 11	Chuvashia, 8	Mari El 7	Tatarstan, 10
Buryatia, 28	Dagestan, 18	Mordvinia, 9	Tuva, 30
	Evenki A.D., 22	Nenets A.D., 2	Udmurtia, 6
	Gorno-Altay, 31	North Ossetia, 15	Ust-Ordyn Buryat A.D., 29
	Ingushetia, 16		Yamal-Nenetsk A.D., 20
	Jewish A.D., 26	Kalmykia, 19	
	Kabardino-	Karachay-Cherkessia, 13	
	Balkaria, 14	Karelia, 1	
		Khakassia, 32	
		Khanty Mansiysk A.D., 4	
		Komi, 3	

stitutional right to control the central bank, the legislators named Viktor Gerashchenko, the former chairman of the Soviet State Bank, to run it and insisted that heavy subsidies be continued to state-owned enterprises and farms. Tax receipts were declining, and this policy succeeded only in enlarging the budget deficit and fueling further inflation. Even after an initial surge of 245 percent in January, 1992, consumer prices continued to mount, with inflation reaching 2,500 percent over the entire year, then continuing to climb by another 847 percent in 1993.[6] The currency lost its value even more rapidly, and by spring 1995, it took more than 5,000 rubles to buy one dollar, as compared with 27.6 when I left my post in Moscow in August 1991.

Many essential services were still performed by state enterprises, which meant that, lacking a government-operated safety net, the public demanded large subsidies and blocked bankruptcy and structural reorganization of the industrial and agricultural dinosaurs.

Even before the Soviet Union formally collapsed, Vice President Alexander Rutskoy had announced his opposition to the economic reform plans. As economic dislocation became more acute in 1992, his rift with Yeltsin grew. When I called on Rutskoy in March 1992, he was still professing loyalty to Yeltsin but was sharply critical of the government's economic policy. By summer, he had moved into open opposition and had joined a coalition of "centrists" who pressed for a gradual transition to the market economy. This group, which for a time also included Arkady Volsky, the former Gorbachev loyalist who headed the Union of Industrialists and Entrepreneurs, looked to China as a model for market reform. They liked the image of political stability, gradual change, and rapid economic growth that China projected. But it was no longer possible, if it ever had been, for Russia to follow the Chinese approach of freeing some of the economy while keeping political change to the minimum. Russia no longer had strong political structures that could be preserved, even temporarily.

Another of Yeltsin's key allies, parliament Chairman Ruslan Khasbulatov, also split with him over the reform program. Increasingly aligning himself with the critics in parliament, he was in open opposition to most of Yeltsin's policies throughout 1992.[7]

Yegor Gaidar, the thirty-five-year-old economist whom Yeltsin had placed in charge of economic policy, initially as a "first deputy" prime minister, then as acting prime minister, became the principal target of opponents of radical reform. A man of unquestioned integrity and intellectual brilliance, the pudgy, baby-faced Gaidar lacked the charisma so useful in elective politics and he had difficulty explaining his policies in terms the broader public, unversed in market economics, could understand. He was a disciple of the "Chicago School" of monetary economics associated with Milton Friedman but had no experience managing bureaucracies or operating the institutions that make a market work.

As a result, while the Gaidar government could claim some notable achievements, such as price liberalization, legalization of most private economic activity, free convertibility of the ruble, and new laws appropriate to a market economy, the public grew increasingly restive as inflation soared, production plummeted, and the monopolies gouged. Furthermore, the parliament-controlled State Bank undermined the government's monetary policy, the keystone of its reforms, by printing money with abandon. Private investment had few protections and taxes were raised to the point that an entrepreneur who paid them could not break even. Inevitably, tax collections decreased as people concealed income, and potential investment funds fled the country. By the fall of 1992, informed observers estimated the capital flight at $18 billion or more.[8]

Yeltsin stuck with Gaidar and his team through most of 1992, in the face of mounting criticism. In September Yeltsin told me in a private interview that he considered Gaidar a "brilliant economist" and would absolutely refuse to "give him up."[9] But in December Yeltsin bowed to demands in parliament and replaced Gaidar with seasoned executive Viktor Chernomyrdin, who had been running the mammoth state-owned natural gas monopoly.

This concession to the majority in the Russian Supreme Soviet failed to relieve tension between it and President Yeltsin. The parliament refused to extend his authority to rule by decree and began attempts to reverse some of the reform moves already taken. When pressed, Yeltsin would negotiate, but each agreement he reached with Khasbulatov and other Supreme Soviet leaders fell apart before it could be implemented. Yeltsin wanted a referendum to endorse a "presidential" republic rather than one in which the legislature would be the final authority, adopt a new constitution, and approve early elections for a new parliament. The Russian Congress of People's Deputies consistently rebuffed his proposals, and the conflict degenerated into all-out political warfare, with the Congress threatening to impeach Yeltsin and Yeltsin threatening a suspension of parliament pending new elections.

In April 1993, a nationwide poll was conducted on four questions that Yeltsin and the parliamentary leaders had laboriously negotiated, and the results showed that Yeltsin still had majority support in the country, that more people approved than disapproved of the reform policies, and that most people wanted new elections, particularly for parliament.[10]

Yeltsin tried to use the referendum to force the Supreme Soviet to call early elections and grant a constitutional assembly the right to adopt a new constitution. At one point he offered to hold a presidential election at the same time the vote was taken on a new parliament. Nevertheless, the Russian parliament continued to resist, refusing not only to hold early elections but also to allow the constitutional assembly to do more than prepare a draft constitution. It completed its draft in July 1993, but the new Constitution could not come into effect until approved by the provinces and republics, a process that would have taken many months at best and might never have been adopted by the requisite number.

Much as Gorbachev had staked his political future on the March 1991 referendum on the union, Yeltsin had hoped that the April 1993 referendum would give him a mandate to pursue his reform policies and override the reluctant legislators. But this was not to be. During the summer, Yeltsin's rift with the leaders of the Supreme Soviet, who now could command a majority on most votes, widened. In fact, the struggle became total, with each trying to undermine the other and thus become the ultimate power in Russia. Russia's patchwork Constitution was not adequate to resolve the struggle for power and arguments continued on how the new Constitution should divide power between the executive and legislature.

Both sides of the executive-legislative dispute began to violate the existing Constitution. The Russian Constitutional Court, not even two years old, proved incapable of dealing with the crisis, not least because Valery Zorkin, its first chairman, went beyond his authority as a jurist and attempted to play an active political role. Zorkin unwisely involved himself in mediating the political issues between the president and parliament and, when this did not work, threw in his lot with the parliamentary extremists, thereby discarding any attempt at judicial dispassion and proper procedure. His partisanship reached the point of declaring an announced Yeltsin decree unconstitutional before the text was signed and its precise terms were known. By involving his institution in a political battle that was beyond the ability of a fledgling court to solve, Zorkin effectively destroyed the institution and set back efforts to build a judiciary that could enforce the rule of law in Russia.

Meanwhile, the extremists in the Russian Supreme Soviet, now led jointly by Vice President Rutskoy and Speaker Khasbulatov, shifted from violent language to violent action. Disregarding procedures set forth in the Constitution, Khasbulatov repeatedly ruled that a quorum was present when this was obviously not the case. He also ignored flagrant violations when votes were taken; at times even the television cameras caught deputies manipulating the electronic voting devices at the desks of absent colleagues. This allowed a minority of deputies to pose as the majority and to win votes that the real majority was unlikely to have approved.

Finally, it came to outright war, when Yeltsin dissolved the Supreme Soviet on September 21, 1993, and the rump parliament (with far fewer members than a quorum required) barricaded itself in the Russian "White House," voted to replace Yeltsin with Rutskoy, named a new "minister of defense," and—using these irregular acts as a pretext—assembled a private army, made up largely of roughnecks and freebooters who opposed the dissolution of the Soviet Union. On Sunday, October 3, Rutskoy sent his ragtag "army" to seize key buildings in Moscow. They quickly took the Moscow mayor's office, located across the street from the parliamentary complex, and almost succeeded in seizing the television broadcasting complex in the Ostankino district of Moscow, several miles away. They were stopped by forces loyal to the Yeltsin government before they gained control of the tower, but scores of people were killed in the process.

The extremists in the Russian parliament had turned a political battle into an armed rebellion, and for a few hours it looked as if they might succeed in taking control of Moscow. The police either had orders not to resist or else were too cowed to do so; they had put up no effective resistance to Sunday's attacks. Shortly before midnight, Yegor Gaidar went on television to appeal to the citizens of Moscow to come out to protect their legal government, as they had done two years before.

Yeltsin, who had inexplicably been resting at his dacha out of town, returned to the Kremlin late in the day and—reportedly—after a few hours of persuasion convinced Defense Minister Pavel Grachev to use military force against those deputies who had barricaded themselves in the parliament building. By early morning, October 4, 1993, troops and tanks had surrounded the Russian White House—just as they had in

August 1991—but this time they attacked the building and forced the remnant parliamentarians out. Cameras from the Cable News Network observed the entire operation and showed the world tanks firing into the upper floors of the building and bedraggled deputies filing out of it under military guard. Khasbulatov, Rutskoy, and their closest associates were placed under arrest.

Russian citizens were given the opportunity to elect a new parliament on December 12, 1993, but under new rules, not those of the Soviet period. After Yeltsin defeated the leaders of the old Supreme Soviet, he offered a new constitution for approval by referendum. It was basically the draft that had been worked out by the Constitutional Assembly, but without some of the special privileges the assembly had granted the former "autonomous" republics. The new legislature had a different structure: the Congress of People's Deputies and its subordinate Supreme Soviet were replaced by a bicameral legislature with a lower house named, like its predecessors in tsarist times, the Russian State Duma, and an upper house, the Federation Council, modeled to a degree on the U.S. Senate but with fewer powers.

Voters approved the new Constitution by a comfortable majority of nearly 60 percent, but the elections to the State Duma shocked Russia and the rest of the world. Half the deputies were selected proportionately, by party lists, and the other half by election districts. To the astonishment of most observers, the election list put forward by Vladimir Zhirinovsky's Liberal Democratic Party, the platform of which seemed more fascist than democratic, attracted more votes than any other list. Although Gaidar's "Russia's Choice" party in the end won more seats than Zhirinovsky's LDP since it was more successful in individual districts, the combined vote of the LDP, the Communist Party, and others opposing rapid reform—the Agrarian Party and Women of Russia— was sufficient to deprive the various reform parties of a majority.[11]

Several factors contributed to the failure of the "democratic" parties to win a clear majority in the State Duma. The "democrats" were divided among themselves and conducted an inept campaign;[12] Yeltsin stood aloof from the election campaign and refused to endorse any candidates; the nationalist and neo-Communist parties were able to exploit the economic distress, now attributed by many to the reformers rather than the old Communist system.

The Constitution approved in December 1993 granted the Russian parliament less power than its predecessor, and some of Yeltsin's critics condemned it as dictatorial. Their charge seemed exaggerated to me: while the 1993 Constitution established a strong executive presidency, it also had numerous safeguards to curb executive excesses. In fact, it had few features that cannot be found in one or more constitutions of Western democracies. For example, the powers of the Russian president—on paper, at least—do not significantly exceed those of the French president.

In one of its first acts, the Russian State Duma in effect declared its independence of the chief executive by voting to pardon all those involved in the attempted coup d'état of August 1991, and the parliamentary rebellion in October 1993. Yeltsin tried to persuade the prosecutor's office to defy the parliament's amnesty and refuse to release Khasbulatov, Rutskoy, and their close associates, but to no avail. Prosecutor General Alexei Kazannik ordered them released and then tendered his own resignation. Kazannik was not only a Yeltsin appointee but happened to be the deputy in the old USSR Congress who in 1989 had yielded his seat in the Supreme Soviet to Yeltsin.

The State Duma's action in ending legal prosecution of earlier plotters had ambiguous implications for the rule of law in Russia. Freeing violators of previous constitutions hardly enhanced respect for the law, but at the same time the Duma had the constitutional right to grant amnesties and pardons, and Yeltsin's inability to overrule the Duma underscored the separation of powers the new Constitution provided. In addition, Kazannik's refusal to bend to executive pressure and ignore the Duma vote gave substance to judicial independence, although his subsequent resignation made clear that such independence could not be assumed in the future. Nevertheless, the new Constitution passed its first serious test unscathed.

A constitution, however, must be more than a formal document if it is to be effective, and the 1993 Russian Constitution has not been in force long enough to provide a test of its viability. During 1994, Yeltsin's relations with the State Duma were not as stormy as they had been with its predecessor the year before, but this was largely because he ignored the Duma most of the time. The Constitution allowed him to rule by decree, so long as the decrees were not revoked by the legislature, and he used that power more and more.

Rule by decree, however, did not strengthen Yeltsin's control of the country, since the decrees were rarely enforced. In fact, most of the country slipped increasingly out of Moscow's direct control. Although

Yeltsin had appointed most of the regional governors, they generally went their own way and opposed Moscow whenever it seemed to be in their personal interest or that of their region. Russia was rapidly becoming a federation not only in theory but also in practice.

By the end of 1994, the majority of Russia's state enterprises had been formally privatized,[13] but—to the consternation of many and the surprise of few—the new owners were, for the most part, the old "socialist" managers. Some learned with great rapidity how to operate profitably under the new quasi-market conditions, often by simply converting state-owned property to their own use. Others, particularly managers of state and collective farms and managers of defense plants, remained trapped by the old system of state controls and subsidies and continued to demand handouts from the budget.

Official statistics showed a fall in production of catastrophic proportions: if they were to be believed, at the end of September 1994, industrial production was little more than half of what it had been in January 1990. The figures, however, were suspect, since much production was hidden from the tax inspectors and thus the statisticians as well. Other data, such as those on the consumption of electric power, which usually moves in tandem with production, showed less severe declines.[14]

Post-Soviet statistics seemed as least as deflated as Soviet production data had been inflated. Furthermore, declines in some types of industrial production did not diminish the supply of consumer goods: if the country made fewer tanks, missiles, and submarines, the income of the workers in these industries might be affected, but the population as a whole would not be deprived of essential commodities.

In fact, despite many hardships, most Russians coped, and some coped very well. Official statistics for the first quarter of 1994—which may have understated personal income—showed that 1,127,000 people were making more than $25,000 a month! This was only .7 percent of the population, but the statistical office considered 10 percent of the population "rich" and about 30 percent to be "middle class." But that left about 27 percent classified as "poor"—that is, able to buy food but not much else—and around 33 percent in poverty, with hardly enough income to live.[15]

Everyone seemed to be complaining, but when pollsters asked people in 1994 how their own families were doing, more than 50 percent said fair or better. Nearly 70 percent of the same sample group said, however, that conditions in the country were bad or very bad.[16] Analysts noted that most of those who considered their own condition and that of the country bad or very bad had voted for Zhirinovsky's LDP or the Communist Party in December 1993.

By early 1995, even the official statistics indicated that the drop in industrial production was slowing: in January 1995, industrial production was only 0.7 percent lower than that of the previous January.[17]

Unfortunately, the halting steps toward a market economy and the rule of law were marred not only by falling production, intense inflation, and ideological uncertainty but also by two social cancers, which not only grew rapidly but began to interact with each other in a symbiotic fashion: organized crime and a bureaucracy that perversely expanded even as its legitimate duties contracted.

Criminal activity had deep roots in the Soviet system, particularly as it had developed under Brezhnev's leadership, but as long as the police state endured it had been kept largely out of the public view, and, despite periodic scandals—usually brought to light as the result of political infighting in the leadership—had been limited in its ability to influence government policy or to extend its operations from crevices on the margins of society.

With the breakdown of the old system, these restraints disappeared. Equally important, the population as a whole had little understanding of the attitudes, practices, and ethics that make a free economy work. For decades Soviet citizens had been told that buying low and selling high was not only illegal but immoral; now Russians were told that this was an integral part of market economics. Many concluded that all constraints had disappeared, that anything went.

State property had never been considered the same as individual property, since everybody's property was, in a sense, nobody's. Petty theft had been common throughout the Soviet period. But large-scale thievery and embezzlement had been punished severely, at times by death, and as a consequence were not common. Even before the Soviet Union collapsed, in 1989 and 1990, this had begun to change, with executives in state enterprises and military officers beginning to divert state property to their own use—to start businesses and to build protective networks in the law enforcement and tax agencies.

When the Soviet Union finally collapsed, this malign process accelerated, and the government seemed helpless to control it. Neither the Soviet Union nor Russia had adopted laws controlling conflicts of interest as it set course toward a market economy;[18] as a result, nobody could be certain what was proper and what not. They knew only that if they maintained ties with the right people they were unlikely to be called to account. Certainly, by no means all officials indulged in outright theft, but it was a common practice for executives in state enterprises to organize parallel private firms, then use their official position to obtain "sweetheart" deals. Not only civil servants, but also elected officials, and military and police officers often held private jobs while continuing in their official duties.

Official agencies seemed increasingly incapable of carrying out even the most basic tasks. In particular, they did little to enforce commercial contracts or even to protect entrepreneurs from extortion. As a consequence, provision of armed guards and other security services became one of the growth industries of the early 1990s. Those who could not bear the expense of a security service were prey to extortion gangs, often tied into larger criminal organizations, that initially demanded a percentage of the profit and, if the firm grew, escalated their demands to part ownership—and eventually outright control—of the firm.

As is the case in other societies, rival criminal organizations often fought one another for market control. The number of assassinations increased and, when prominent persons were involved, attracted media attention. It was often not clear whether the victim had been killed because he was involved with a criminal organization or because he had resisted involvement. Official information was sparse and unreliable; what was obvious was that the violent crimes were rarely solved.

The government seemed helpless in dealing with growing crime, in part because the Duma delayed approving legislation to make racketeering a crime but more fundamentally because the criminal gangs had penetrated the bureaucracy, including the law enforcement agencies. Although the government had stopped planning and managing all economic activity, the number of civil servants grew. Russia not only took over the Soviet bureaucracy, which had run a country with twice its population, but added to it. The Office of the President became a prime example of bureaucratic bloat: by the spring of 1994, Yeltsin's office had 20,000 employees, many with duties that duplicated those in other government agencies.

In most government agencies, salaries did not keep up with inflation, and sometimes, during spasms of budget austerity, civil servants were not paid for several months on end. Often given poor direction and unclear instructions, even normally honest bureaucrats could be tempted to make the most of whatever authority they had by selling their influence.

Corruption, furthermore, was not confined to the lower and middle reaches of the government. Evidence is necessarily anecdotal, but most Western businessmen looking for investment opportunities found that key ministries would usually demand that large fees be paid shadowy "consultants" before necessary approvals and licenses were issued. One Russian friend who managed a medium-sized state firm in the provinces told me he had been offered a ministerial portfolio in Moscow in 1992 but had turned it down since he was taking his firm private and wanted to finish the job. Six months later the person who had been appointed to the Cabinet position approached him with a request to invest a million dollars in his firm.

"I have known 'Sasha' [the minister in question—not his real name] for years," my friend commented. "Before he took that job in Moscow, he didn't have a kopek to invest. But in six months he had a million of hard American cash to throw around. And most are like that, though not, probably, Chernomyrdin and Yeltsin himself."

Pervasive corruption and underfunding also led to a sharp deterioration in government services. Health care, never very good, became even worse, with outbreaks of epidemics of diseases that had almost been eliminated, a rise in infant mortality, and an accelerating decline in life expectancy. Government funding of education, science, and culture was cut sharply, which disoriented many intellectuals who saw their compensation fall and their job security vanish. Few were able to adapt quickly to the commercial valuation of services that the state had traditionally subsidized.

The flaws in Russia's democratic development and economic system were so glaring and well publicized that many observers failed to notice some of the good things that were happening. The political scene was fragmented and anything but orderly, but citizens could form political parties and associations without serious interference from the authorities. The press kept its freedom despite pressures from the government and meager financing. Travel abroad was finally free of government restriction, though not within every citizen's financial means. There was a political opposition, and, despite the bloody clashes that occurred in October 1993, elections were held and a parliament dominated by the president's political opponents was seated. Even those who had tried to overthrow the government by force were released from detention and allowed to resume political careers. A new constitution guaranteed the basic human and civil rights, and, though the system of justice was inadequate to enforce the guarantees fully, a vigilant press and dedicated human rights advocates ensured that systematic violations could no longer be cloaked in secrecy.

Even the much-maligned economy had some bright spots. Within months of the time prices were freed, shortages disappeared, and, as if by magic, one could find virtually any consumer product for sale in urban centers without waiting in line. Prices were high by traditional standards and many persons could not afford the new luxuries, but most of those who were active in the market economy could. When we visited Moscow in September 1992, one of Rebecca's Russian friends complained about the price of fresh pineapple. Rebecca remarked that she had lived in Moscow for eleven years and up to our departure the year before had never seen a pineapple for sale. Her friend laughed and observed, "See how much we've changed! We didn't worry about price when we couldn't get something, and now the price is the only problem!"

Despite the anxieties aroused by widespread economic dislocation, the loss of job security, and the shock of runaway inflation, many Russians, particularly the young, adapted to the new circumstances. While only a few—at most a third of the population—lived better than before, even fewer, according to the polls, favored a return to the past. The real debate was over the pace, manner, and fairness of reform, not its direction.

When the Russian Federation approached its third anniversary as an independent sovereign state in the fall of 1994, it seemed to many that the worst, in both an economic and a political sense, was behind them. Plenty of problems remained, but most seemed on the way to gradual solution—or, at least, amelioration. The relations of the president and the parliament, though neither close nor warm, were not explosive as they had been just a year before. The flight of capital out of the country seemed to have eased, and some was returning. The spring and summer of 1994 had also witnessed a growth in foreign investment, and the International Monetary Fund was expected to provide substantial support to stabilize the ruble, provided the Russian government reduced its budgetary deficit in 1995.

The guarded optimism of summer 1994 did not last long. During the fall, the ruble took a sudden tumble and capital flight resumed.[19] And then, in December, the country was plunged into a political and moral crisis when President Yeltsin ordered the Russian army to invade Chechnya, where a breakaway regime had declared independence, armed its people, and for three years had resisted Moscow's writ. But before we look at the roots and impact of that conflict, we should review the events in the other fourteen countries that had been ruled by the Soviet Union.

The Baltic States Cope

OF ALL THE STATES that spun out of the Soviet Union, Estonia, Latvia, and Lithuania were by far the best prepared for independence. They had been independent before, and once they had decided, in 1989, to insist that their independence be restored, they had begun systematically refurbishing or developing the institutions an independent country requires.

The economic transition, however, was not easy, particularly in Lithuania, the economy of which was not as developed as those of Estonia and Latvia. After a year of mounting economic problems, the former Communist Party, now renamed the Lithuanian Democratic Labor Party, won control of the Seimas, the Lithuanian parliament. Then, in February 1993, the man who had defied Gorbachev to take most of Lithuania's Communists out of Moscow's control, Algirdas Brazauskas, won the presidency of Lithuania in a direct election.[20] Vytautas Landsbergis, who had led the country to independence, became leader of a conservative opposition party, the Homeland Union, formed out of the non-Communist remnants of Sąjūdis. Though some newspapers proclaimed Brazauskas's election as the "return of Communists," this was unfair. The Lithuanian Democratic Labor Party had much more in common with the social democratic parties of Western Europe than with the Communist Party of its Soviet past.

An economic upturn began sooner in Estonia and Latvia than in Lithuania, but not in time to prevent political shifts there also. Free elections held after independence produced younger, more radical legisla-

The Baltic States

Gulf of Finland

St. Petersburg

Tallinn

Narva

Baltic Sea

ESTONIA

Lake Peipus

RUSSIA

Pärnu

Tartu

Gulf of Riga

Pskov

Ventspils

Riga   LATVIA

Liepāja

Klaipeda   Daugavpils

LITHUANIA

RUSSIA

Kaunas

BELARUS

Vilnius

POLAND

Minsk

0   40 mile

0   40 kilometer

tures, and many of the leaders who had pushed for independence were nudged aside. The Estonian parliament replaced Prime Minister Edgar Savisaar in January 1992, but his successor, Tiit Vähi, the former minister of transportation, held office for only nine months, until he in turn was replaced by the thirty two-year-old Mart Laar, a historian who headed the Christian Democratic Party. By the fall of 1992, Estonia had adopted a new constitution, and the parliamentary elections conducted under its rules led to the replacement of Chief of State Arnold Rüütel by the younger and more radical Lennart Meri, who became the new Estonia's first president.[21] The former Communist Party won no seats at all in the new parliament.

Prime Minister Laar managed to stay in office for two years, during which time he stabilized the currency, removed most customs barriers, and accelerated transition to a market economy by reducing subsidies. Nevertheless, in October 1994, several months after Laar's party lost heavily in municipal elections and two of his coalition partners abandoned him, the Estonian parliament forced his resignation and replaced him with a caretaker government until new parliamentary elections were held in March 1995.[22] Those elections gave control of the Estonian parliament to parties that advocated greater attention to social protection than to the speed of reform and brought Tiit Vähi back as prime minister.[23]

Despite the fluctuations in the popularity of individual parties, the fundamental lines of Estonian policy were set and shifts in political coalitions were unlikely to change them much.

Latvia waited until 1993 to hold its first postindependence elections, and these brought changes in its government as well. Since only citizens of the prewar Latvian Republic and their descendents were eligible to vote, 34 percent of Latvia's residents were unable to participate. Even so, the vote was fragmented among many small parties, and a coalition formed by two of the largest controlled only the barest majority in the Saeima, Latvia's parliament 51 seats out of 100. As a consequence, the new prime minister, Valdis Birkavs, held the position for barely a year and was forced to step down the following summer in favor of Maris Gailis, who had been one of his deputies.

Estonia moved most rapidly and successfully to enter the world economy, working closely with Finland and the Nordic countries to do so. The Estonians were the first to establish their own currency, the kroon (pronounced like "crone"), and they successfully pegged it to the German mark. Though there was a spurt of inflation in 1992, it soon was reduced to a monthly rate of 4 to 5 percent, which would be very high in Western Europe but was moderate in comparison with the double-digit monthly price rises in the other former Soviet republics.

Latvia followed a course similar to Estonia's, except that it lacked the special relationship with Finland and moved more slowly in privatizing its large industrial establishments. It tied its currency, the lat, to the American dollar but experienced higher inflation rates than Estonia. Nevertheless, by 1994, the worst effects of economic adjustment seemed to be over in both countries. Estonia's trade with Finland that year actually exceeded trade with Russia. Russia was still Latvia's largest single trading partner, but trade with the West and the Nordic countries was growing. Even Lithuania, whose problems were greater, was showing some signs of greater economic stability.

When the Soviet Union collapsed, Soviet troops were still stationed at bases in all three Baltic republics. Persuading Russia to remove them became the most important goal of Baltic diplomacy. Lithuania reached a quick agreement with Moscow, and the Russian troops left in 1993. Estonia and Latvia had to negotiate longer, however, because Russia objected to their refusal to grant automatic citizenship to ethnic Russians who had immigrated during the Soviet occupation. Ultimately, agreements were reached, and the last Russian military forces left Estonia and Latvia on September 30, 1994.

The citizenship issue continued to burden relations between Russia and the two northernmost Baltic countries. Lithuania, with only 20 percent of its population non-Lithuanian, had granted citizenship to all residents, but many Estonians and Latvians felt that their nations were so small that they could not absorb large numbers of ethnic Russians and retain their national character. Therefore, while they did not expel Russians or others who were not Estonian or Latvian, they disenfranchised most and made naturalization exceedingly difficult.

The citizenship issue was particularly acute in Latvia, since ethnic Latvians made up only slightly more than a majority of the population. Laws proposed in 1992 made citizenship practically unattainable for non-Latvians who had settled in the republic since 1940, and even for their descendants born in Latvia. This legal barrier infuriated many Russian democrats who had defended Latvia's right to seek independence. It also disturbed human rights advocates in the West, and the Council of Europe delayed accepting Latvia until it liberalized the citizenship law. The Saeima amended the law in late 1994 to permit most current residents to qualify for Latvian citizenship by the end of 2003, and Latvia entered the Council of Europe a few months later.

By 1995, all three Baltic states seemed to have the worst of the transitional problems behind them. Nevertheless, they were by no means carefree. All three continued to have unfavorable trade balances, exacerbated by Russia's refusal, in 1994, to extend most-favored-nation tariff treatment to their exports. Inflation was still a problem, although their currencies were relatively stable on foreign exchange markets. Living standards of much of the population continued to fall or to stagnate at an unsatisfactory level. Though crime and corruption were not as serious as in Russia, both were present to a troubling degree. Tax evasion was common, and the attempt to reduce budget deficits while tax receipts were declining squeezed pensioners and persons on government salaries.

Nevertheless, these problems were more manageable than those facing the other Soviet successor states, including Russia. Despite their internal political jockeying, all three Baltic states seemed to know who they were and where they were heading. The general direction was west and—in the case of Estonia—north. The odds were that they would reach that destination before long.

Ukraine: A New East-West Struggle

THE ALLIANCE OF UKRAINIAN NATIONALISTS, mainly from west Ukraine, with the national-minded Communists, mainly from the east and south, which produced the overwhelming vote for independence in the fall of 1991 was unnatural, and it quickly disintegrated. As a consequence, Ukraine was unable to agree on a reform strategy for the first three years of its independence. The economy showed all the ills that emerged in Russia, but in exaggerated form. Inflation was even worse than in Russia. The Ukrainian karbovanets, or "coupon"—intended as a temporary currency before the new hryvna was introduced fell in value from a premium over the ruble in 1991 to less than a twentieth of the ruble's value three years later, when it took more than 100,000 coupons to buy one American dollar.

Ukraine's economy suffered from its dependence on imported oil and gas. Russia, its principal supplier, quickly began demanding world mar-

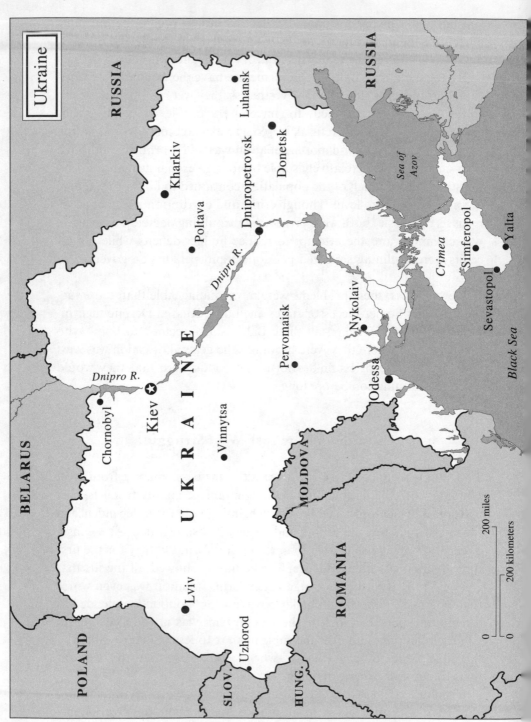

ket prices for energy products. Periodically, Ukraine's unpaid bills mounted so high that the oil and gas were cut off—always to be restored after some negotiation and part payment, but not before the shortfalls disrupted industrial production and created severe consumer shortages.

Simultaneously, political and military disputes with Russia escalated. When the Soviet military forces were broken up, Ukraine demanded not only the ground and air forces located on its territory—which Russia conceded immediately, although it required a complicated process of swapping officers and men—but also the Black Sea Fleet. Russians had always considered the Black Sea Fleet Russian and most of its officers considered themselves Russian, but since Khrushchev had transferred the Crimea to Ukrainian jurisdiction in 1954, its home base, Sevastopol, was on Ukrainian territory. Russia initially rejected Ukraine's demand for the Black Sea Fleet but subsequently agreed to divide it. Negotiations continued for nearly two years before a settlement was reached. Ukraine agreed to settle for considerably fewer than half the vessels when Russia offered to purchase part of Ukraine's share. Nevertheless, negotiations on the use of the base at Sevastopol continued into 1995.[24]

Soviet nuclear forces located in Ukraine became another bone of contention, not only with Russia but with the United States. When the Soviet Union collapsed, these forces were formally under the command of the Commonwealth of Independent States, but Yeltsin controlled the "black box" and assumed formal operational control on behalf of Russia in 1992. Despite the Ukrainian government's earlier agreement to relinquish the weapons and become a nonnuclear state, the Ukrainian parliament refused to authorize transfer of the weapons to Russia.

The Ukrainian parliament's attempt to gain control of nuclear weapons[25] created a major rift with the United States, which had recognized Ukrainian independence with the understanding that Ukraine would abide by the strategic arms agreements signed with the Soviet Union and would also adhere to the Nuclear Non-Proliferation Treaty. Eventually, in January 1994, the issue was settled by an agreement brokered by the United States whereby Ukraine agreed to return the missiles to Russia for destruction and Russia agreed to supply Ukraine with fuel for its nuclear power plants.[26] Subsequently, the Ukrainian parliament ratified this agreement and, at the end of 1994, became a party to the Nuclear Non-Proliferation Treaty as a nonnuclear state.

In 1992 and 1993, the Russian Supreme Soviet frequently exacerbated tensions with Ukraine by indulging in imperialistic rhetoric—

many Russian "patriots" continued to deny Ukraine's right to be independent at all—and by clamoring for total control of the Black Sea Fleet and the return of the Crimea to Russia. In July 1993, the Russian parliament went to the length of approving a resolution that declared that Sevastopol "was and remains part of the territory of the Russian Federation." This directly contradicted its own vote in December 1991, when it had approved the Commonwealth Treaty, which recognized the existing borders of all CIS states.[27]

Such shenanigans, which Ukrainians believed had widespread popular support in Russia, made cooperation between Ukraine and Russia difficult, even when it was in the best interest of both countries. Ukraine not only refused to adhere to the CIS Collective Security Treaty but initially also resisted all attempts to coordinate economic policy. In September 1992, Ukrainian Prime Minister Vitold Fokin told me that he opposed Ukrainian participation even in an unofficial council to advise on economic policy if Russia was represented on it. A year later, one of his successors, Leonid Kuchma, who had been director of a missile factory in eastern Ukraine, showed more interest in repairing frayed economic ties with Moscow and hosted a conference in Kiev to organize an unofficial coordinating body. Kuchma, however, resigned as prime minister before much was done.

Meanwhile, the Ukrainian economy continued to slide and public discontent rose. It was particularly dangerous because it followed regional lines: the provinces in the east and south, where many Russians lived and many of the original Ukrainians were culturally Russified, were strikingly more discontented than those in the west. Except in the Crimea, however, ethnic tensions were a secondary factor: the eastern half of Ukraine was where most of the heavy industry was located. The mammoth state enterprises there were unable to compete in a market economy. They were not only overstaffed and poorly organized but also based on obsolete technology. Many were heavy polluters. Inevitably, the sort of reforms necessary to give Ukraine a viable market economy would place an exceptionally heavy burden on the people in its eastern regions. Some observers began to wonder if Ukraine could retain its unity if the process of regional estrangement continued.

In June 1994, I went to Kiev for a joint Ukrainian-U.S. seminar on national security decision making and found that Ukrainian officials and scholars used the term differently from Americans. We think of national security primarily as security against threats from the outside; the Ukrainians were focusing on threats from within. They described for us public opinion surveys that showed a dangerous polarization of political attitudes. They felt that the growing disaffection of Ukraine's eastern and southern regions was a greater immediate threat to Ukraine's independence than Russia, though they also complained of the Russian tendency to look at Ukrainians as wayward relatives rather than as neighbors of equal status.

The most acute regional problem developed in the Crimea. Russians made up over two thirds of its population, and it had been considered part of Russia for most of the past two hundred years. Furthermore, it was economically dependent on Russian tourism and the Black Sea Fleet. Although the majority of the population had voted in favor of Ukrainian independence in December 1991, that vote was in the context of independence from the Soviet Union more than a direct endorsement of Crimea's inclusion in a Ukrainian state. When the Ukrainian economy deteriorated more rapidly than the Russian, the Ukrainian claim to the Black Sea Fleet estranged many active and retired naval families, and Russian tourists stopped vacationing in Crimean resorts, Crimeans elected a legislature that demanded autonomy and a president who ran on an independence ticket—which many considered a transitional step to reunification with Russia.

The government in Kiev managed separatist tendencies in the Crimean more successfully than it did economic reform. It granted the Crimea autonomy in the otherwise unitary Ukrainian state but rejected all Crimean attempts to escape Kiev's ultimate authority. A "battle of decrees" took place between Kiev and Simferopol, the Crimean capital, through much of 1994, but the Ukrainian authorities were careful not to use force. And, in fact, separatist tendencies seemed to dissipate as Russian nationalist Yuri Meshkov, who was elected president of the Crimea in January 1994, became embroiled in a protracted political struggle with the Crimean parliament. By the end of 1994 the local parliament had stripped most authority from Meshkov, which took much of the force out of the push for Crimean secession. Furthermore, the Russian government, recognizing the incendiary potential of the Crimean question, acted to cool Russian nationalist hotheads on the peninsula. Both Yeltsin and Chernomyrdin refused to deal with Meshkov and reiterated that Russia respected Ukraine's territorial integrity. When the city council of Sevastopol declared the city part of Russia in July 1994, Russian authorities rejected the move—as did the Crimean government in Simferopol.

In fact, the population of Crimea was not united behind the drive to leave Ukrainian jurisdiction. Non-Russian minorities, which make up more than 30 percent of the population, including the Crimean Tatars exiled to Central Asia by Stalin who have been returning in large num bers, prefer Ukrainian to Russian control of the province.

In March 1995, President Kuchma took advantage of the political divisions in Crimea to abolish the office of Crimean president, dissolve the local legislature, and order new elections. He made it clear that the Crimean constitution must be amended to eliminate provisions that conflict with the Ukrainian constitution. His action stimulated indignant speeches in the Russian State Duma—one right-wing deputy even burned a Ukrainian flag during the debate—but Yeltsin's government conspicuously refused to support the Crimean separatists. Given its problem with Chechnya, it had no stomach for challenging recognized state boundaries.

Despite the spring crisis between Kiev and Simferopol, there was less fear in 1995 than there had been in 1992 and 1993 that Ukraine and Russia would come to blows over the Crimea. If Ukraine can settle the dispute over the Black Sea Fleet, pull out of its economic slump, and bring Russian tourists back to the peninsula, the Crimean desire to go it alone or join Russia is likely to fade.

Regional tensions within Ukraine became obvious to all during the elections of 1994. In 1993 labor unrest in the eastern regions—in particular a long strike by Donbas coal miners—had forced the government to arrange for elections of both parliament and president in March 1994, a year earlier than the Constitution required. The eastern provinces elected mostly Communists and pro-Communists to parliament, while nationalists and democrats won almost all contests in the western provinces.

Seven candidates entered the presidential race in June. President Kravchuk was the favorite, but observers doubted that he could win on the first ballot. They were right. When the votes were counted, Kravchuk had a plurality but not a majority. He was forced into a runoff election with former Prime Minister Leonid Kuchma, who had also polled more than 30 percent. The campaign was heated, with Kravchuk partisans accusing Kuchma of wishing to return Ukraine to Russia, while Kuchma's supporters blamed Kravchuk for Ukraine's economic problems. By the time citizens went to the polls for the second round, on

July 11, Kuchma had pulled ahead. He won with 52 percent of the total vote and replaced Kravchuk as president of Ukraine. Support for the two, however, was heavily regional: Kuchma received more than 80 percent of the vote in the east, while Kravchuk was favored by 87 percent of the voters in the three western provinces, only 4 percent of whom voted for Kuchma.

Despite the regional and political polarization that occurred during the election campaigns, the transition from Kravchuk to Kuchma proceeded smoothly. Kravchuk and his supporters were good losers and proved their respect for democratic procedure. For his part, Kuchma moved quickly to unite the country, pledging accelerated economic reform and promising to cooperate with Russia when this benefitted Ukraine but also to defend Ukraine's sovereignty and independence. Accordingly, he opposed creating any supranational CIS coordinating structure, fearing that Russia would dominate it, but insisted that Ukrainian-Russian relations be governed by bilateral agreements.

Kuchma also moved quickly to improve relations with the West. He paid an official visit to the United States in November 1994, stressing his commitment to reform and determination to carry out Ukraine's obligations to become nuclear free. When he returned to Kiev, he persuaded the Ukrainian parliament to ratify the Nuclear Non-Proliferation Treaty and to grant him extensive powers to implement a reform program. He also managed to raise substantial loans and promises of economic assistance from the United States, the European Union, and international financial institutions—all of which had tended earlier to hold back from assisting Ukraine because of its nuclear policy and the absence of a credible reform program.

Ukraine began 1995 still seriously burdened by its dependence on energy imports. It owed Russia $2.5 billion and Turkmenistan more than $700 million for natural gas deliveries and had not yet found the means to pay for them by exports. Nevertheless, the prospects for real reform in the Ukrainian economy were brighter than they had been at any time since independence, and if Ukraine proceeded on the reform path, foreign assistance would be available to ease the way.

Though the elections in 1994 had been divisive, the results in fact enhanced the prospects for Ukrainian unity. The most disaffected area in Ukraine elected the new president, but this put him in a position to press for economic reform, which forces in the east had up to then blocked. At the same time, the regional polarization taught the Ukrainian nationalists in the west that, if they wished to keep Ukraine's territory intact, they had to avoid policies of Ukrainianization and build a Ukrainian state on an interethnic basis. Thus, in 1995, an objective observer could say that, with all its problems, Ukraine had weathered its first three years of independence and had passed the first tests of democracy. If it continues to develop among its people a sense of loyalty to the Ukrainian state that transcends ethnic affiliation, it should have no trouble preserving its independence and eventually taking its proper place as one of the significant European powers.

Belarus: Don't You Want to Take Us Back?

BELARUSIAN INDEPENDENCE seemed almost accidental, despite the determination of the small band of Belarusian intellectuals who had demanded it as a prerequisite for national rejuvenation. Most officials in the Belorussian[28] Communist Party and, in particular, the managers of industry and agriculture, had never given any real thought to independence until the failure of the August 1991 coup attempt suddenly deprived them of their patrons in Moscow. That shock impelled Belorussia's Supreme Soviet to declare independence and bow to the nationalist intellectuals' desire to have the country known by its name in their own language, Belarus, rather than by the Russian form of the name, which had been used up to then.

Most in the Belarusian Supreme Soviet, however, did not have their heart in independence. In fact, they continued to rule the country as it had been ruled in the past, keeping an anxious eye on Moscow for any change that might convince Big Brother to take them back in the family. Stanislav Shushkevich, the chairman of parliament and chief of state (until a president was elected in 1994) believed in Belarusian independence—after all, he was one of the three founders of the CIS—but was unable to control either the Supreme Soviet or Prime Minister Vyacheslav Kebich, a political rival who also loyally represented the interests of the old *nomenklatura*.

During a lengthy interview in September 1992, Shushkevich complained to me that he had been unable to force the economic bureaucracy to take even the first steps toward economic reform. An attempt by the nationalist opposition to force new elections by petition—as the Constitution provided—was rebuffed by a parliament that simply ruled

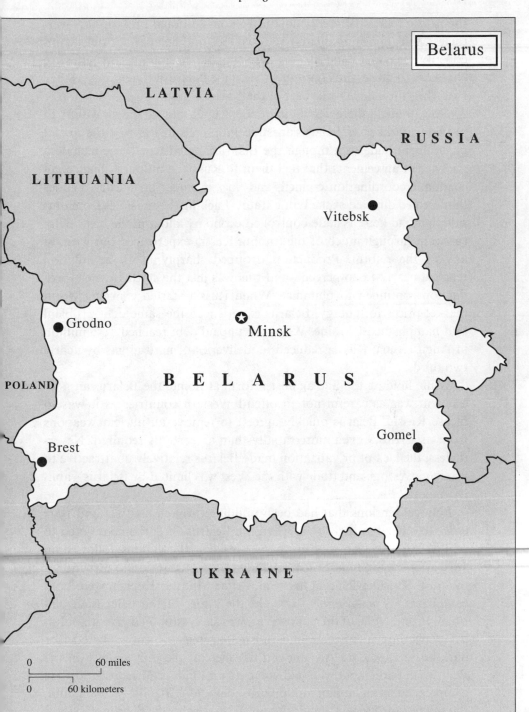

Belarus

LATVIA

RUSSIA

LITHUANIA

Vitebsk

Grodno

Minsk

POLAND

BELARUS

Gomel

Brest

UKRAINE

0   60 miles

0   60 kilometers

the petition illegal, directly violating a constitutional provision. Nevertheless, the opposition offered no resistance to the Supreme Soviet's unconstitutional act, and it was also unable to mount any effective challenge to those who continued to run the Belarusian economy as they had when the country was part of the Soviet Union.

Now, though, there was a difference. Russia was no longer willing to provide subsidies to Belarusian state industries in the way the Soviet government had, even though the Belarusians hastened to conclude a package of agreements that tied them to Russia: a military alliance, an economic coordination council, and an agreement on border regimes that seemed directed at the Baltic states. Lacking the subsidies from outside that had kept its state-controlled economy afloat in the past, Belarus went through much of the trauma Russia experienced but without any of the reform. Production dropped sharply in 1992, inflation reached nearly 1,000 percent, and this was just the start. In 1993, production continued to plummet. When Russia started charging world market prices for energy, Belarus experienced the same debt problem that had plagued Ukraine. When the unpaid debt reached $350 million in August 1993, Russia reduced its deliveries of natural gas by nearly two thirds.

While holding the line against reform at home, the Belarusian government was as careful not to offend Western countries as it was to please Russia. Belarus quickly agreed to remove all nuclear weapons from its territory even more rapidly than agreements required. Nevertheless, the lack of privatization made Belarus relatively unattractive to foreign investors, and trade with the West was limited by Belarus's ability to pay.

Political tensions that had been building throughout 1992 and 1993 came to a head in early 1994 when the Belarusian parliament voted to remove Shushkevich as chairman. Presidential elections followed in June after the Supreme Soviet amended the Constitution to provide for the post. Shushkevich and his rival, Prime Minister Kebich, were both candidates, as was Zenon Paznyak, the leader of the Belarusian National Front. None of them, however, was successful. Fed up with political bickering and economic mismanagement, people voted for dark-horse candidate Alexander Lukashenka, the only deputy in the Belarusian parliament who had voted against independence in 1991. He campaigned as an anticorruption crusader and a friend of Russia, and, though he failed to win a majority on the first ballot, in the runoff balloting against Kebich he received more than 80 percent of the vote.

Though he had skillfully exploited popular emotions and fears, Luka
shenka had no real program, and as soon as this became apparent and
his appointees were criticized, he moved to muzzle the press. Several reform-minded members of his government who had supported him in the
election campaign resigned, and Belarus entered 1995 once again in political turmoil.

Many Belarusians had thought that closer ties with Russia could save
them. Shortly before the presidential elections, Prime Minister Kebich
signed an agreement with Russian Prime Minister Chernomyrdin for
Belarus to enter the ruble zone; Russia would control monetary policy
and would have the use of military bases in Belarus without compensation, but Belarusians could exchange some of their local rubles for Russian rubles at a one-for-one rate. Since the Belarusian ruble was then
worth only a tenth of the Russian ruble, this appeared very advanta-
geous. However, the understanding quickly unraveled because of opposition in both countries: most Russian economists and finance officials
thought it would be too costly and would make it impossible to keep
Russia's money supply under control. Many Belarusians were reluctant
to see control of their monetary policy pass to Russia in return for a
limited, onetime gain. The agreement had not been implemented a year
after it was reached, and it seemed most unlikely that it would be.

The hard fact was that Russia was no longer willing to pay the price
of economic union with a country still burdened by a Soviet-style economic system. Even Belarus's strategic position astride historic invasion
routes from the West was not enough to make it worthwhile to pour
resources into an uncompetitive economy. Of course, the eagerness of
the Belarusian *nomenklatura* to accept subordination to Russia stoked
the pride of the Russian "patriots." But as soon as Russians read the
price tag on unity, the joy abated.

The Belarusian National Front, which had forlornly campaigned for
independence in 1990 and 1991 and, without winning a battle, had seen
its dream suddenly and unexpectedly fulfilled, continued to demonstrate
its political ineptitude. Though not a member of the National Front and
a moderate rather than radical reformer, Stanislav Shushkevich was
dedicated to preserving Belarusian independence and was the Front's
best hope for exerting political influence. Nevertheless, it never made
common cause with him, and in the presidential elections it split the reformers' vote by running against him. Like its democratic counterparts
in Russia, it seemed always to make the theoretical best the enemy of an
attainable good.

Ultimately, Belarus will be required to find its own way. Even if those now in political control of the country yearn for a closer association with Russia, they will have to make it worthwhile for Russia. They will not be able to preserve a Soviet-style economic system on subsidies from Moscow, for Moscow can no longer afford them. But if Belarus makes partnership worthwhile, by reforming its economy and making it attractive for investment, it will no longer need Russia—except as a good neighbor.

Moldova: Fifth Column with a Big Brother

MOLDOVA'S PREOCCUPATION since independence has been with a revolt in its territory to the east of the Dniester River, which runs from its northern border with Ukraine roughly parallel to its eastern frontier. Even before independence, a breakaway regime led by ethnic Russians had taken effective control of "left-bank" Moldova and declared its independence.[29] Neither Russia nor any other country recognized this "Dniester Republic,"[30] not least because it seemed to represent only a minority of the population in the area, where Russians were outnumbered by both Moldovans and Ukrainians. But the leaders of the Soviet Fourteenth Army stationed there supported the breakaway regime and effectively prevented the Moldovan government from establishing its control of the area.

The Russian government never officially endorsed the Dniester Republic but at the same time not only did nothing to control the freewheeling Fourteenth Army but even provided economic support to the regime in Tiraspol. Moldovan President Snegur entered into long negotiations with Moscow on the issue, and by early 1995 had obtained an agreement for withdrawal of the Russian army from Moldovan territory within three years. Nevertheless, even if this schedule were kept, the breakaway regime had by then secured arms for a substantial military force of its own that seemed strong enough to resist any attempt by the weak Moldovan forces to occupy the area.

Although the "Dniester Republic" leaders professed to be acting on behalf of Russian speakers in Moldova, they in fact had little support among Russians in "right-bank" Moldova, who preferred to deal with the Moldovan government in Chişinău. Their principal goal seemed to be to establish a Soviet-style regime in the area, and they ruthlessly sup-

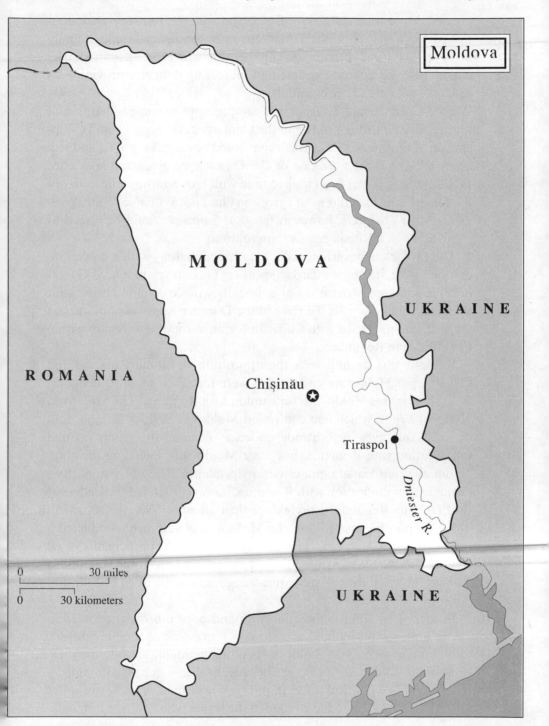

pressed Moldovan and Ukrainian culture in the territory they controlled. However, economic conditions in the enclave worsened rapidly in 1994. The local currency quickly became worthless, many factories closed, and the Dniester regime had increasing difficulty providing its residents with even bare essentials.

Both Chişinău and Tiraspol had good reasons to come to terms, and they received a strong prod from the Conference on Security and Cooperation in Europe (CSCE), which sponsored peace talks in 1994 and recommended that the area east of the Dniester be given special status. President Snegur met from time to time with Igor Smirnov, the leader of the Dniester regime, but as of early 1995 had not yet come to an agreement. Most observers, however, felt that Smirnov would be forced to come to terms if Russia pressed him to do so.

The Moldovan government dealt more successfully with a smaller secession threat, that by the Turkic-speaking Gagauz (pronounced Ga-ga-ooze) in southern Moldova. For a time, they made common cause with the Slavic regime across the river in the Dniester Republic, but in 1994 Gagauz leaders settled with Chişinău for an autonomous region within the Moldovan Republic.

While it was dealing with the opposition of ethnic Russians and Gagauz, the Moldovan leaders also were forced to fend off demands from some ethnic Moldovans for a union with Romania. The Moldovan National Front, which had controlled Moldovan politics in 1990, split on this issue even before independence. A minority group favored reunification with Romania, but most Moldovans, including the older National Front leaders, preferred independence. The noisy minority's campaign for unification with Romania, however, handed the leaders of the "Dniester Republic" a pretext for their attempt to secede from Moldova. To put the issue to rest, the Moldovan government conducted a referendum in March 1994, in which 95 percent of the participants voted against merging with Romania.[31] The referendum cooled emotions and set the stage for the subsequent negotiations between Snegur and Smirnov.

Burdened by secessionist minorities and poor crop years, the Moldovan government initially was slow to implement economic reforms, though there seemed no doubt of its ultimate intent. Despite the pressures on its statehood—or maybe because of them—it has maintained a relatively stable political leadership. It is one of the few ex-Soviet states outside Central Asia to have retained the leader who brought it to independence: President Mircea Snegur's position seems practically unassailable, but he has maintained it by political leadership, not repression.

Moldova's current prime minister, Andrei Sangheli, who heads a multiethnic coalition, has been in office since mid-1992. Parliament Speaker Petru Lucinschi was Communist Party first secretary in 1989 and 1990. He was serving in Moscow in the Central Committee Secretariat in 1991 and returned to Moldova when the CPSU was dissolved. His Democratic Agrarian Party won a plurality in the 1994 parliamentary elections. Despite his Communist past—and he was, in any case, a Gorbachev-style reformer—he has proved to be a solid supporter of market reforms, which accelerated following the 1994 elections.

The World Bank and the International Monetary Fund responded to Moldova's reform steps with substantial loans in 1994 and 1995. The Moldovan currency, introduced in late 1993, proved surprisingly stable, and during 1994 inflation dropped from a 45 percent monthly rate in January to less than 5 percent in December.

The most remarkable thing about Moldova's political leadership since 1991 is that it has managed to keep an open society on the territory it controlled in the face of hostile military provocations, including atrocities against ethnic Moldovans. Consequently, Moldova is building statehood on a multiethnic basis. This was, of course, a rational course to take, since the Moldovan government could not hope to defeat the secessionists across the Dniester by military means. However, less tolerant and skilled leaders might have reacted by fanning ethnic hatred in the areas they controlled and expelling minorities—witness Transcaucasia and the former Yugoslavia. President Snegur and his associates deserve credit for maintaining a policy of conciliation and nondiscrimination. If the Moldovan economy picks up, they may be able to bring the Dniester separatists under control by peaceful means—or, if not, to seal them off and let them wallow in their misery.

Georgia: The Price of Disunity

GEORGIA'S FRAGMENTED, quarreling political factions, its restive national minorities, and misjudgments by its increasingly autocratic and irrational president plunged it into a civil war as the Soviet Union collapsed.

Following his overwhelming election as president of Georgia in May

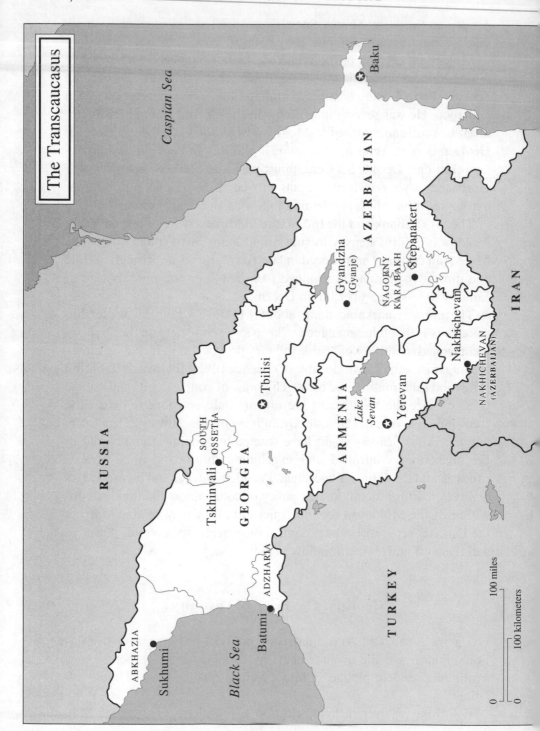

The Transcaucasus

1991, Zviad Gamsakhurdia began to have his political opponents arrested and continued his attempt to subdue the South Ossetians by force. This led to a political crisis in August 1991, and a break with some of his principal supporters, including Prime Minister Sigua and Minister of Defense Kitovani. By December 1991, most of the country except for Gamsakhurdia's native region of Mingrelia was in revolt. Crowds gathered in Tbilisi demanding his resignation, and they were supported by armed formations under the control of Gamsakhurdia opponents, who formed a military council and surrounded the Georgian parliament building, where Gamsakhurdia had taken refuge. On January 4, 1992, the Military Council announced that it had taken power in "a national democratic uprising against a criminal regime," and Gamsakhurdia fled the country two days later—first to Armenia, then to the breakaway Russian province of Chechen-Ingushetia, just across the Caucasus range from Georgia.[32]

Although the Military Council managed to resist an attempt by Gamsakhurdia to return and formed a coordinating council to rule the country until there could be new elections, it was plagued by dissention and by questionable legitimacy. Although the United States and members of the European Community had recognized Georgia's independence when the USSR collapsed, they delayed establishing diplomatic relations because of the political turmoil. Following several weeks of uncertainty and fruitless negotiations among themselves, leaders of the anti-Gamsakhurdia forces invited Eduard Shevardnadze, who was living in Moscow, to come home and form a new government. Shevardnadze arrived in Tbilisi in early March 1992 and encouraged formation of a new state council with representatives of most of the political parties and ethnic minorities. Elections to the Georgian parliament were held, as promised, in October, and Shevardnadze, running unopposed, was elected chairman of parliament with close to 96 percent of the votes cast.

Shevardnadze did his best to unite the Georgian factions and to negotiate settlements with the minorities. However, he did not control the two principal anti-Gamsakhurdia military formations, and undisciplined actions by these groups undermined his efforts to bring peace to the country. In fact, Defense Minister Kitovani's unauthorized attack on the Abkhazian parliament in Sukhumi in the summer of 1992 ignited a war that the Georgian troops were unable to sustain. Russian military commanders with a personal grudge against Shevardnadze for his support of arms reduction when he was Soviet foreign minister gave support to the Abkhazian rebels, as did some of the north Caucasian leaders, and, by September 1993, Georgian forces had been driven out of Abkhazia, along with more than 200,000 ethnic Georgian refugees.[33] The final Georgian defeat occurred when Shevardnadze, trying to end the conflict, agreed to remove Georgian troops and heavy artillery from Sukhumi in return for a cease-fire and negotiations. When the artillery and most of the troops had left, the Abkhazians violated the cease-fire and overran what was left of the Georgian forces.

As Georgian forces were fleeing Abkhazia, Gamsakhurdia launched another attack, forcing Shevardnadze to seek Russian support. After requiring Georgia to enter the Commonwealth of Independent States and grant Russia military base rights, which up to then it had refused to do, Russia helped the Georgian forces defeat Gamsakhurdia and hold the line at the Abkhazian border.

Gamsakhurdia's threat to Shevardnadze's leadership ended with 1993; his widow announced in January 1994 that he had committed suicide. Other reports alleged that he had been killed by some in his entourage or had died in other ways, but it soon became clear to all but a few of his most fanatical supporters that he was, in fact, dead. The Abkhazian challenge persisted, however; Abkhazian nationalists controlled the entire territory and continued to block the return of Georgian refugees to their homes.

The war and internecine political struggles ruined the Georgian economy. Under the chaotic conditions of the early 1990s, real reform was impossible. In 1992 industrial production virtually collapsed, reaching barely a third of its level two years earlier.[34] Disintegration continued in 1993, and though the decline was less noticeable the following year—Georgia having reached virtually a level of bare subsistence—there was little real improvement.

Politics remained turbulent even after Gamsakhurdia's death. Shevardnadze managed to rebuff periodic efforts to force his resignation and gradually reduced the influence of the hitherto autonomous military formations. Tengiz Kitovani and Dzhaba Ioseliani, both of whom had private armies, were eased out of the Defense Council in 1993, and Kitovani was replaced as minister of defense. Subsequently Kitovani was arrested, in January 1995, when he tried to lead an unauthorized attack on Abkhazia. Gradually, banditry by forces technically but not actually under government control diminished. When Rebecca visited Georgia in August 1994, she found the people exhausted by the fighting and economic chaos but hopeful that the worst was over and the country could get on with putting itself back together again.

In fact, in early 1995, prospects seemed somewhat brighter than they had at any time since the Soviet Union had collapsed, though the problems remained daunting. Abkhazia was acting as a de facto independent entity and as yet had prevented any substantial return of Georgian refugees, but Russian peacekeepers enforced a cease-fire and talks sponsored by U.N. mediators preserved some hope for a settlement. The Georgian currency was almost as worthless as the German mark had become in the hyperinflation of the early 1920s: at the end of 1994 one dollar could buy more than a million Georgian "coupons." Criminal bands and corrupt officials still preyed on what little was left of the economy. Politics continued to be a fractious, highly personal affair. Nevertheless, the fighting had stopped and the opportunity existed to begin a process of reconstruction—provided further outbreaks of serious fratricidal conflict could be avoided.

In many ways, Eduard Shevardnadze faced a more difficult task than he did when he took on the Soviet military to come to terms with the West so that Gorbachev's reforms would have a chance. But if he could succeed in bringing to his country the tolerance and civility he personally exemplified, he would go down in history not only as one of the statesmen who ended the cold war but as the father of the modern Georgian state.

Armenia and Azerbaijan: The Price of Ethnic Hatred

NAGORNY KARABAKH DOMINATED not only the relations between Armenia and Azerbaijan but also the internal politics of both countries. Increasingly, actions by Armenian forces in the enclave controlled events. The Armenian government supported the Armenians in Nagorny Karabakh but found its policy, and its economy, increasingly hostage to events there. In particular, the Armenian government was unable to force the militants in Nagorny Karabakh to make peace with Azerbaijan, in the absence of which neither country could put its economy into order.

Military success emboldened Armenian leaders in Nagorny Karabakh to resist appeals to compromise. When the Soviet Union collapsed, fighting in the enclave intensified, and within months the

Armenians there had defeated all Azerbaijani forces sent against them and forced the Azeri population to flee. They also pushed a corridor through Azerbaijani territory to provide a ground link to Armenia. These actions displaced hundreds of thousands of Azeris, in addition to those expelled earlier from Armenia.[35]

Azerbaijani defeats in Nagorny Karabakh led to the fall of more than one government in Baku. Shortly after independence, in February 1992, President Ayaz Mutalibov was forced to resign following the massacre of an Azeri village in Nagorny Karabakh. A few months of political turmoil followed until new presidential elections were held in June. The leader of the Azerbaijani Popular Front, bearded Orientologist Abulfaz Elchibey, received 60 percent of the vote, and the Popular Front, which had been deposed by the Soviet army in January 1991, regained control of the Azerbaijani government.

Elchibey, however, managed to serve only a year of his term before he was forced to flee Baku to avoid an impending military attack by his political opponents. Following a series of complex machinations, Heidar Aliev, who had been Communist boss in Azerbaijan during Brezhnev's time and had been removed from the Soviet leadership in the 1980s, wrested control of the government in Baku in June 1993, when Elchibey left. A few months later he arranged another round of presidential elections and claimed to have received more than 98 percent of the vote.[36]

Aliev maintained his position by a combination of repression and adroit maneuver. He attempted to mobilize support from most factions but muzzled political opponents and the media. He turned his back on his Communist past and proclaimed a policy of market reforms—which, however, were slow to materialize. Most of all, he staked Azerbaijan's economic future on a multibillion-dollar contract with a consortium of foreign oil companies for the exploitation of petroleum reserves under the Caspian Sea. Russia, however, challenged the legality of Azerbaijan's claim to that portion of the Caspian seabed and also demanded that any pipeline to export the oil pass through Russian territory. These issues were still under dispute and negotiation in 1995.

While the oil deal provided some hope for the future, the Azerbaijani economy has been in rapid decline since independence and as yet shows no clear signs of picking up.

Armenia is experiencing even more disastrous economic chaos. Largely cut off from ground transportation routes by an Azerbaijani boycott and the disarray in Georgia and not yet recovered from the devastating earthquake of 1988, the entire population has been living in extreme distress. Nevertheless, privatization and other economic reforms have moved more rapidly in Armenia than in either Georgia or Azerbaijan, and, in 1994, official data indicated that its economy was beginning to recover. Industrial production was said to have risen 1.8 percent over the previous year, national income 2.6 percent. But the people had yet to sense an improvement in their dismal living standards.[37]

Nevertheless, in contrast to Azerbaijan and Georgia, Armenia enjoyed a large degree of political stability during its first three years of independence. President Levon Ter-Petrosian, elected in 1991, stayed in office, though by 1994 Armenian opposition parties were becoming more active and had begun demanding his resignation. He, in turn, began to use strong-arm tactics against some of his opponents. During a political crisis in October 1994, for example, he issued a temporary ban on the opposition Dashnak Party on grounds that it had harbored a terrorist organization that was conducting political assassinations—a charge the Dashnak leaders denied.

It is difficult to see how either Armenia or Azerbaijan will be able to stabilize their economies or their political life until a settlement is reached over Nagorny Karabakh. In early 1995 a tenuous cease-fire was in effect, but up to then all attempts at mediation had failed. Earlier, when a proposal had been accepted by both Armenia and Azerbaijan, it had been rejected by the Armenian leaders in Stepanakert, the capital of Nagorny Karabakh. So the confrontation continues, and life is unlikely to improve for millions in the Transcaucasus until it abates.

Central Asia: The Reform States

ETHNIC PROBLEMS BURDENED all the former Soviet republics, but potentially Kazakhstan's problem was the most serious of all. Kazakhs, who with independence controlled the levers of power, were in a minority in their own republic. Ethnic Russians were almost as numerous as Kazakhs, and the country was also home to many other nationalities, such as Volga Germans, Uighurs, Ukrainians, and Koreans. After all, Kazakhstan had been one of the major dumping grounds of deported people in Stalin's time, and Khrushchev had moved millions of settlers into northern Kazakhstan to farm what had up to then been grazing land. As a consequence, the various nationalities were unevenly spread through the country, with Russians predominating in the north and Kazakhs in the south and east. Ethnic hostility between Kazakhs and Russians could literally split the country.

In 1992, I asked Kazakhstan President Nursultan Nazarbayev what had caused him, despite his strong support for Gorbachev's union treaty, to lead the Central Asians into the Commonwealth of Independent States. He replied that, as soon as it had become apparent that the three Slavic republics were determined to leave the Soviet Union, he had realized that if the Soviet Union should break up with the Slavs in one group and the Turkic peoples in another, it would be a disaster for all. Though he had hoped for a stronger union, he had urged the Central Asian republics to join the CIS to prevent the formation of exclusive Slavic-Christian and Turkic-Islamic groupings.

What he did not say, but what was obvious, was that such a polarization would have made it exceedingly difficult to keep Kazakhstan together as one state. Indeed, some Russians were already agitating for the annexation of northern Kazakhstan: it was part of the Slavic Commonwealth Alexander Solzhenitsyn had proposed in a widely noted 1990 article.[38] Nazarbayev continued to be one of the strongest voices in favor of strengthening the CIS and, though he was never subservient to Russia, made it clear that he wanted good and close relations.

At home, although he saw himself as the leader of the Kazakh people, Nazarbayev repeatedly assured non-Kazakhs, and Russians in particular, that they had a place in Kazakhstan. Nevertheless, some began to leave Kazakhstan after independence, since in practice the government tended to favor Kazakhs over others for key positions. Furthermore, Nazarbayev was eager to encourage the Kazakh diaspora to return home. There were not only many Kazakhs in neighboring ex–Soviet republics, but also in western China, particularly Xinjiang province, to which many Kazakhs had fled during the famine brought on by collectivization in the 1930s. In 1992, Nazarbayev sponsored a World Congress of Kazakhs in the capital of Kazakhstan, which was now officially known as Almaty, as the Kazakhs spell it, rather than by the Russian form of the name, Alma Ata. The Kurultai, as the Congress was known in Kazakh, was an obvious effort to encourage Kazakh immigration.

In fact, the Kazakh population continued to grow as Russians left. At

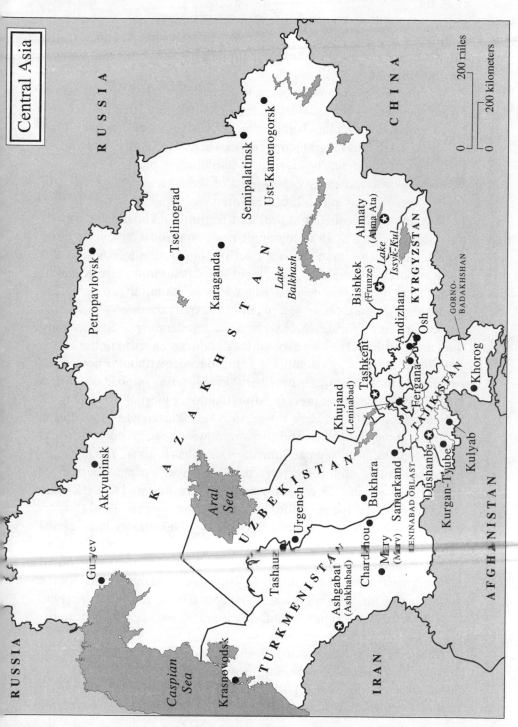

Central Asia

independence, Kazakhs made up only a slightly higher proportion of the population than did Russians, but three years later official statistics indicated that around 44 percent of the population was Kazakh and only 40 percent Russian.

Although Kazakhstan occupies a vast territory and has more natural resources than any other Soviet successor state except Russia, it experienced economic difficulties comparable to those in other republics: high inflation, sharp falls in production, dislocation in general. Economic reform moved more slowly in Kazakhstan than it did in Russia, but Nazarbayev was more active than most of the other republic leaders in seeking foreign investment. It came more slowly than he hoped, in part because of an inadequate physical and institutional infrastructure but also because Kazakhstan's geographic position made it difficult to build export industries without Russia's active cooperation and Russia did not invariably cooperate. Development of oil fields in western Kazakhstan, for example, was delayed when Russia made unreasonable demands for the construction of a pipeline to export the oil.

Despite these difficulties, Kazakhstan enjoyed more political stability than most of the other successor states did. Nazarbayev maintained his position as the country's dominant political leader without serious challenge, even though he was more liberal in registering opposition parties and allowing a degree of press freedom than were most of his colleagues in Central Asia. Nevertheless, the press in Kazakhstan was by no means as free as it was in Russia, and there were widespread reports of fraud and manipulation during parliamentary elections in 1994. The new parliament proved even less receptive to Nazarbayev's proposals than its predecessor, and in March 1995, when the Constitutional Court of Kazakhstan ruled the 1994 elections invalid, Nazarbayev dissolved the parliament and called new elections. Up to 1995, Nazarbayev had seemed to maintain his control more by his skill at political maneuver and consensus leadership than by repression, but his actions in 1995 caused many to wonder whether he might be drifting toward frequent use of the authoritarian methods common in the countries to the south, particularly when he used a "referendum" to extend his term as president to the year 2000.

Although Nazarbayev was diligent in expanding Kazakhstan's ties outside the former Soviet Union, improving relations with China, promoting direct air links with Turkey and Germany, and cultivating warm personal ties with American political and business leaders, he recognized that his country's relations with Russia were the decisive ones, and not only because of geography and the ethnic Russians in his country. The fact was that no other country, or combination of countries, could replace Russia as Kazakhstan's principal economic partner in the foreseeable future.[39] This, in addition to ethnic considerations, prompted Nazarbayev's repeated attempts to put more substance into the Commonwealth. It was obviously preferable to deal with Russia as part of a larger organization rather than exclusively on a bilateral basis, where Kazakhstan would always be at a disadvantage.

Nazarbayev's proposals for a more effective Commonwealth were rejected or ignored by the other countries. But, by 1995, it seemed that, step by step, Kazakhstan and Russia were defining their relationship in ways that both could live with. In January 1995, Kazakhstan signed sixteen bilateral agreements with Russia, ranging from military relations to economic cooperation.[40] They provided that Russia could continue to use military test ranges in Kazakhstan for a rent and that a system of joint planning and training would be developed for their armed forces. In principle this bordered on a merger of the armed forces of the two countries, which caused concern in Kazakhstan, but Nazarbayev defended the military agreement by pointing out that Kazakhstan could not operate the test facilities itself and was better off with the income from them. Furthermore, he knew that the fledgling military establishment in Kazakhstan could not survive hostility to Russia. After all, most of its officers were ethnic Russians, whose loyalty was, at best, divided.

The agreements also provided for a customs union (something that had been in the original CIS agreement but never implemented), but it was not clear when it would go into effect since it specified that controls would be eliminated on their common border "if there are unconditional mutual guarantees that the external borders of the 'single customs space' will be effectively and reliably protected." Skeptics noted that the proviso could be used by Russia to justify its control of the external borders of associated states.

The January 1995 agreements were a step toward reintegration of Kazakhstan with Russia, but Nazarbayev doubtless intended them to permit consolidation of Kazakhstan's sovereignty. If implemented, they would diminish discontent in Kazakhstan's northern provinces, where ethnic Russians predominated. And on one key issue Nazarbayev stood fast: he refused to allow dual citizenship, which had been one of Russia's principal demands. Instead, he offered a streamlined process of registering citizens in both countries, as well as protection for citizens of each country resident in the other. But each would have to make a choice, and residents of Kazakhstan who chose to be Russian citizens would be treated as aliens.

When he signed the agreements in Moscow, Nazarbayev observed that they proved that the idea of building a "Eurasian union" on the territory of the former Soviet Union was viable.[41] I was not so confident. To me, it seemed that they (and other agreements under negotiation between Russia and Belarus, Ukraine, and others) demonstrated that relations among the states formerly part of the Soviet Union were more likely to be regulated by bilateral agreements than by a supranational organization.

Kazakhstan's small neighbor to the east, Kyrgyzstan—previously known by the Russian form of its name, Kirgizia—has been in many ways the most reformist of the ex-Soviet states, though it faced greater handicaps than most. It had been one of the poorest of the Soviet republics, and its infrastructure had not been developed to the level reached in the Soviet republics in Europe. Its economy was tied more closely to Russia than those of its Central Asian neighbors were, and few of its managers and administrators were ethnic Kyrgyz. But it also was the only Central Asian republic led by a person who had not been a Communist Party official: Askar Akayev, elected president in 1990 during a political crisis, was a physicist whose career had been in the Academy of Sciences.

Akayev outlined for Kyrgyzstan an ambitious reform program that rivaled those in the Baltic states and Russia, but his task was more difficult. His legislature was more interested in preserving the old system than reforming it, and most of Kyrgyzstan's economy remained in the hands of the former Communist *nomenklatura,* which was unsympathetic to Kyrgyz national aspirations. Furthermore, Kyrgyzstan's geographic position was even more constraining than Kazakhstan's: wedged in a scenic but inaccessible mountain area between China, Kazakhstan, Tajikistan, and Uzbekistan, it is about as far from maritime trade routes as one can get. The old "Silk Route" from Europe to China, which Marco Polo traveled, passes through a corner of Kyrgyzstan but has limited relevance for present-day trade.

Kyrgyzstan was the first of the Central Asian republics to establish its own currency, but it did not have the strength of the Baltic currencies and was devalued even faster than the Russian ruble. It has put out the welcome mat for foreign investment, and gold mining and tourism have some promise—Kyrgyzstan is often called the Switzerland of Central Asia—but its distance from the most promising markets militates against export development.

Kyrgyzstan had experienced ethnic violence before independence, with bloody riots between Kyrgyz and Uzbeks in its southern province, but since independence has kept the ethnic peace. In fact, Akayev disappointed some Kyrgyz intellectuals who favored an ethnic-based state by insisting on giving citizenship to all residents and treating them alike. Tensions remain, however, and some ethnic Russians have begun to leave. But most have not, and a mass exodus seems unlikely provided they are offered reasonable economic opportunity. During a 1992 visit to Bishkek, the capital (formerly Frunze), I spoke at length with a young Russian man who ran a car rental service. He observed that relatives in Russia were advising him to leave Kyrgyzstan, but he had decided against it. "I grew up here and this is my country," he explained. "Why should I leave? Things are not great here—the Communists still have too much power—but they are no better in Russia. And business is picking up."

He had a five-year-old Mercedes-Benz that he had bought in Germany a few months earlier and driven all the way to Bishkek. "Can you get spare parts?" I asked, aware that as recently as 1991, parts even for Soviet cars had been hard to find in Moscow and for foreign cars quite impossible.

"No problem," he replied. "If I need a part, I call a friend in Germany and he has it on the next plane." Apparently, finding the deutsche marks to pay for it was also no big problem, since the Kyrgyz currency, though declining in value, was convertible.

That was in 1992, and the Russian entrepreneur may have been prematurely optimistic, for economic troubles mounted in Kyrgyzstan and by 1994 had reached catastrophic proportions. The foreign aid granted as a reward for Akayev's democratic aspirations was not adequate to compensate for the general disruption of production. Akayev blamed the parliament for blocking necessary reforms and scheduled new elections in early 1995 but, as difficulties mounted, both the executive and legislative branches of government assaulted Kyrgyzstan's fragile press freedom. A new state secrets law even prohibited reporting on such topics as price increases, livestock deaths, and the condition of roads.[42]

Kyrgyzstan citizens elected a new parliament in February and March 1995, but there seemed little prospect that the new assembly would do much better than the old. The road to true democracy in a country like Kyrgyzstan may simply be too steep for representative institutions to climb.

Central Asia: The Autocracies

LEADERS OF THE OTHER THREE Central Asian countries refrained from any attempt to establish democracy. Uzbekistan and Turkmenistan were taken into the grip of autocrats more repressive than the Soviet rulers had been in their latter years. Tajikistan was devastated by civil war, which brought on a brutal dictatorship there also.

Uzbekistan, the largest of the three, was ruled by Islam Karimov, who initially established his authority in the republic when he was first secretary of the Communist Party. When I last met with him, in 1990, he assured me that he welcomed a "responsible opposition" in Uzbekistan and singled out the Erk (Will) party as a case in point. After Uzbekistan's independence, however, he suppressed all competition to the Communist Party, since 1991 renamed, ironically, the People's Democratic Party. Not only were leaders of Erk and other opposition parties harassed and imprisoned inside Uzbekistan, but, in 1994, Uzbek agents began to kidnap Uzbek human rights activists and opposition party leaders in other countries and bring them to Tashkent for trial.

Although elections were conducted in 1994 for a new parliament—now named the Olii Majlis (Supreme Assembly) instead of Supreme Soviet—the only "opposition party" allowed was one under Karimov's control. The new assembly seemed most unlikely to challenge his authority.

Karimov did announce that Uzbekistan would move toward a market economy and in 1994 began some privatization of small shops, but the country continued to be run as before. In foreign affairs it cultivated ties outside the former Soviet Union so long as they did not affect Karimov's one-man rule, and it joined Kazakhstan and other Central Asian states in forming various economic associations, most of which had little effect.

Economic statistics suggested that Uzbekistan's economy suffered less from the post-Soviet slump than those of most of the neighboring states, but they were highly suspect. The bureaucracy that had traditionally fabricated cotton production data was not likely to be constrained by facts in compiling the statistics. Pragmatic observers could find no convincing evidence that the Uzbek economy was faring better than its neighbors.

Meanwhile, nothing significant was done to repair the ecological damage of the Soviet era. The Aral Sea continued to dry up and the chemical industry and cotton growing to pollute. Although the leaders of all five Central Asian countries met in January 1994 and again in February 1995 to consider the future of the Aral Sea, neither Uzbekistan nor Turkmenistan, which drained off most of the water required to maintain it, was willing to curtail its consumption.[43] The cotton monoculture—against which nationalists had long campaigned—continued to be the mainstay of the economy.

Turkmenistan maintained an autocracy as rigid as Uzbekistan's—even when Moscow proclaimed perestroika, the local Communist leaders had prevented any opposition from developing—and added to it a cult of personality that rivaled Stalin's and Mao Zedong's. President Suparmurad Niyazov's picture was everywhere, and people were encouraged to wear Mao-style buttons with his portrait. Any incipient opposition was immediately suppressed by police action. In 1994, Niyazov arranged for a "referendum" in which 99.9 percent of the population was reported to have voted to exempt him from the reelection scheduled in 1997, giving him tenure until 2002.

Turkmenistan's economy fared better than those of most of its neighbors, but not because it was better managed. Extensive gas deposits gave Turkmenistan a ready export product, and Niyazov used proceeds from gas sales to prop up the economy. He announced a program of small-enterprise privatization in 1994, but it moved slowly, and it seemed unlikely that a true private economy would be allowed to develop, since that would diminish Niyazov's control of the country.

For the same reason, Niyazov resisted most Russian attempts to gain special privileges in Turkmenistan. Instead, he cultivated ties with Iran and also with the West. Turkmenistan was, for example, the first Central Asian state to enter NATO's Partnership for Peace. Nevertheless, these ties were not likely to translate into more freedom or better living conditions for the average citizen. Although the country can earn foreign exchange much more easily than any other ex-Soviet republic except Russia, the Niyazov regime is not likely to use it efficiently for the country's development. But there will be enough to avoid the extremes of privation that can lead to revolt.

Tajikistan, the poorest of the Soviet republics, has also been the most unlucky. Plunged into civil war shortly after the Soviet Union disintegrated, it has suffered tens of thousands of casualties, hundreds of thousands of refugees, and a shambles instead of an economy.

The civil war started in 1992 between Communist officials who had traditionally ruled the country and a coalition of Islamic, nationalist, and democratic parties. The Communist forces finally won with some help from Russian troops, who had been requested by the government, but their opponents continued political opposition abroad and armed incursions from Afghanistan, where many of the supporters of the Islamic Renaissance Party had taken refuge.

At present, Russian border troops continue to guard the border with Afghanistan. Fighting has been sporadic and in small groups, but it continues. In 1994, the United Nations sponsored efforts to bring Tajik government representatives and exiled opposition politicians together for talks. Although a temporary cease-fire was agreed, the opposition parties, which had been outlawed, were not able to field candidates in the presidential election in November 1994 and refused to concede the validity of President Imomali Rakhmonov's election. Thus the country entered 1995 with an uneasy truce that could break down at any time.

Meanwhile, Tajikistan had become totally dependent on Russia for its continued existence as an organized state. Not only did Russian troops guard the border with Afghanistan, but Russia was the only source of economic assistance, albeit meager. Alone among the other non-Russian ex-Soviet republics, Tajikistan continued to use the Russian ruble, and some officials spoke of merging the Russian and Tajik economies. Moscow, however, was skeptical about assuming more of the burden of keeping Tajikistan afloat and encouraged attempts to find a political solution to its internal problems.

The civil war in Tajikistan had repercussions outside the immediate region since it was often cited by the Russian government, as well as some of the governments in Central Asia, as an example of the threat

"Islamic fundamentalism" poses to stability in the area. Persons closer to the scene were dubious: the Islamic parties in Tajikistan and elsewhere in Central Asia did not conform to the pattern of radical religious fundamentalism that had come to the fore in Iran. They were Sunni Muslims, unlike the Iranian Shi'ites, and though the Tajiks had a linguistic affinity with Iran, they were skeptical of the rule of mullahs there. The charge that they represented an offensive of "Islamic fundamentalism" in the area, therefore, seemed primarily an excuse for Communist officials to cling to power and exclude Muslim believers from the political process. It was instructive that in Tajikistan the Islamic resistance allied itself with Western-oriented democratic parties in the struggle against Communist rule.

As for Tajikistan, there seems little hope that the fighting will stop and give the country a chance to rise from its ashes unless the current rulers can be induced to share power with other political forces in the country. Russian forces may be able to prevent the return to a full-scale civil war but are not capable of pacifying the country. Russia would best serve its own interests, and those of the region, by threatening to withdraw its troops and its economic support unless the current regime comes to terms with its rivals.

Russia's Minorities

LIKE THE OTHER SOVIET successor states, Russia faced a serious problem dealing with its ethnic minorities when it threw off Soviet rule. Utilizing momentum gained when Gorbachev encouraged Russia's "autonomous republics" to demand more freedom as a means of reducing Yeltsin's authority, many regions within the Russian Federation had started claiming sovereign rights. In most instances, the region's leaders concentrated on ownership rights to natural resources, authority to collect taxes, and the form of the region's representation in the Russian parliament's upper house, but some made a bid for independence.

Tatarstan, the former "autonomous" republic on the Volga River, was the largest in population and one of the richest, with extensive oil reserves and a well-developed industrial base. Russia itself had once been ruled from Kazan, its capital, but after Ivan the Terrible's troops had taken it in 1552 it had been absorbed into the Russian empire. The Turkic-speaking Muslim Tatars, however, had tended to keep both their language, and—until the Soviet period—their religion as well, despite periodic Russification and anti-Islamic campaigns sponsored by Moscow. In 1989 the Soviet census indicated that 48 percent of Tatarstan's 3.6 million people were ethnic Tatars, but the republic had almost as many Russians, who made up 44 percent of its population. Tatarstan was larger, in both area and population, than some of the union republics that in 1991 had become independent.

When the Soviet Union collapsed, Tatarstan initially refused to sign the treaty of federation and opted instead for the status of a "sovereign state and subject of international law associated with the Russian Federation"—in other words, an independent country with special ties to Russia but not a constituent part. To emphasize its special status, the republic's leaders took control over assets in Tatarstan and even refused to remit tax payments to the Russian Federation.

Yeltsin's government dealt with Tatarstan with alternating threats and bouts of negotiation. Finally, in 1994, Yeltsin signed a treaty with the president of Tatarstan that granted almost complete autonomy to Tatarstan but required it to pay some federal taxes and to drop its claim to be a subject of international law.[44] The treaty was controversial both in Russia, where superpatriots rejected the idea of a treaty with a part of the country, and in Tatarstan, where the more extreme nationalists were still campaigning for total secession. But it stuck, and it seemed to provide a model for settling disputes with other Russian territories that were still dissatisfied with their status.

Unfortunately, the approach Moscow used in dealing with Kazan did not work everywhere. Its most conspicuous failure occurred with Chechnya, a small republic in the Caucasus, where Moscow's attempt, in December 1994, to regain control by military force turned the area into a bloody battlefield and shook the entire Russian political system, with consequences still to be witnessed and assessed. One of the crucial turning points in post-Soviet Russian history, the conflict in Chechnya deserves more than perfunctory analysis.

Chechnya: Political Blunder or Resurgence of Autocracy?

EVENTS IN 1991, just before the Soviet Union collapsed, started a sequence of action and counteraction that culminated in the carnage of December 1994 and early 1995, when thousands of persons were killed and hundreds of thousands turned into homeless refugees.

Chechen-Ingushetia, an "autonomous republic" of the RSFSR with about 1,300,000 people in 1989, was one of the political units in Russia that pressed for union republic status in the negotiations on a union treaty. It also had a nationalist movement that, in its early stages, was similar to the ones in the Baltic states. The National Congress of the Chechen People was formed in 1990 from several "informal" organizations, and at its founding congress elected Dzhokar Dudayev its chairman. Dudayev was a Chechen who had risen to the rank of lieutenant general in the Soviet Air Force and at that time was in command of an air base in Estonia. The organization became more active in 1991, and Dudayev began organizing and arming a "national guard." When the leaders of the Chechen-Ingush Supreme Soviet briefly supported the attempted coup against Gorbachev in August, Dudayev moved to replace them.

The Russian government agreed that the precoup government in Chechen-Ingushetia should be replaced but insisted that this be done on the basis of elections. Dudayev and his supporters, however, defied the provisional government set up to conduct the elections, took over the government buildings in Grozny by force, and then, with little advance notice and no real campaign, held "elections" that were obviously rigged.[45] Controlling the government buildings in Grozny, Dudayev then declared independence.

Yeltsin reacted by declaring a state of emergency in Chechen-Ingushetia and sending several hundred Interior Ministry troops to Grozny, who were quickly captured by Chechens and expelled. Meanwhile, Gorbachev, still president of the USSR, injected himself into the dispute, ordering the Russian Interior Ministry of Internal Affairs to cease activities in the area and persuading the Russian parliament to annul Yeltsin's decree.[46] Although the Russian parliament also rejected Dudayev's attempt to secede, insisting that the territorial integrity of the RSFSR be preserved, and called for strict controls on the import of weapons into the area, it stipulated that only peaceful means should be used to deal with the situation.

For his part, Dudayev reiterated his demand for independence and refused any negotiation with Russian authorities unless they recognized the republic's independence. He also continued efforts to arm Chechnya, and the Russian government seemed powerless to enforce the arms ban stipulated by its parliament. Military bases in Chechnya were surrounded by armed Chechens who blockaded them. The soldiers drifted away, and in the spring of 1992, with only a handful of officers left in the garrisons, Russian authorities evacuated them and turned over the arms to Dudayev.[47]

Dudayev not only captured the Soviet weapons that had been deployed in Chechnya[48] but also began to acquire arms elsewhere. By the summer of 1992, Chechnya had become a major hub of both arms and narcotics trafficking. Every attempt by Moscow to embargo trade with Chechnya proved ineffective, and arms, drugs, and money moved freely across the ill-guarded borders. Meanwhile, Chechen gangs in other Russian cities intensified their activities, shaking down business establishments, funneling the proceeds of illicit trade and racketeering into ostensibly legitimate fronts, and dealing with their competitors and traitors in typical gangland fashion. The Russian police noted that Chechen criminal activity intensified and became better organized following Dudayev's seizure of Grozny and assumed that there was a connection between the two.[49]

Stymied by his own parliament and disarray in his bureaucracy and law enforcement agencies, Yeltsin tried to ignore the festering problem in Chechnya for more than two years. The Russian government never recognized Chechnya's proclamation of independence or accepted Dudayev's government as legitimate, but it did make sporadic attempts to negotiate. The answer from Grozny always seemed the same: "Only if you first recognize our independence," which of course made negotiations impossible.

Nevertheless, Dudayev was able to act as if he were head of an independent country. His influence spread well behind the borders of Chechnya: he was one of Georgian president Gamsakhurdia's main backers, gave him refuge when he was forced out of Georgia, and provided military assistance when Gamsakhurdia tried to return to power in Georgia. He also supplied arms, and probably fighters, to the Abkhazians when they revolted against Georgian control. He contrived to recruit allies and "business partners" throughout Russia, particularly in military units, and was usually more effective in buying and manipulating the Russian bureaucracy than Yeltsin was in controlling it.

Deprived for long of a military option and unable to bring economic pressure to bear, the Russian government in 1994 attempted to exploit divisions within Chechnya by covertly backing one of Dudayev's rivals, Umar Avturkhanov, who attempted to unseat Dudayev by force. Though they had the backing of the Federal Counterintelligence Service, the successor of the KGB, Avturkhanov's irregulars were stopped short of Grozny by forces loyal to Dudayev in October 1994. This reverse made it clear that Yeltsin had made no real headway in bringing the Chechen rebellion under control. In fact, he had lost ground, since his failures strengthened Dudayev and convinced him that there was no need to negotiate with Moscow.

On December 9, 1994, Yeltsin signed a decree to "restore order" in Chechnya, and two days later the Russian Army launched an all-out offensive against the breakaway region. But it was not the quick and easy victory that Russian Defense Minister Pavel Grachev predicted. The Chechens repulsed with seeming ease the untrained recruits the Russian commanders initially threw into battle and continued to defend Grozny for a good two months in the face of almost continuous air and artillery bombardment. Military casualties mounted to the thousands, and many more civilians died or were maimed. More than a hundred thousand residents fled Grozny alone, and the surge of refugees into the neighboring republics in the middle of winter added to and widened the misery.

As the war began to take its toll and the press and television gave Russia and the world heartrending pictures of the suffering, it became clear that Yeltsin's decision to authorize the use of force in Chechnya had brought Russia to the brink of crisis. It laid bare the weakness of Russia's army, the ineffectiveness of its civil administration, and the fragmentation of its body politic. And it called attention once again to Yeltsin's impulsiveness and weakness for authoritarian methods. In fact, his decision had been not merely a colossal political blunder but a license to commit atrocity.

Following the democrats' defeat in the December 1993 elections and the steady decline in his own popularity, Yeltsin had severed direct ties with many of his earlier supporters and retreated into a cocoon with a few cronies, most apparently advocates of solving problems by applying force. This group reportedly persuaded him to launch the campaign against Chechnya in the belief that a triumph there would lift his sagging authority. If this is what happened, his advisers were wrong not only in their expectation of an easy conquest but also in their assessment of the public effect of bloodshed in Russia itself. By February 1995, public opinion polls indicated that only 9 percent of respondents approved of the way Yeltsin was doing his job, and only 4 percent thought he had handled Chechnya well.[50]

Many observers saw an eerie parallel in Yeltsin's apparent alliance with his enforcers and Gorbachev's "turn to the right" in the winter of

1990 and 1991. Some predicted that Yeltsin's removal or even Russia's disintegration might follow. Others thought a dictatorship was on the way that would extinguish Russia's hard-won and still tenuous civil liberties. After all, if the Chechens should react by unleashing a campaign of terrorism in Moscow and other Russian cities, the authorities could—and probably would—use this as an excuse to arrest and deport suspects en masse. The few protections against arbitrary arrest Russian citizens had won could disappear overnight, and restrictions on freedom of speech, assembly, and political activity would probably follow, they reasoned. Even if these things did not happen, many feared that Yeltsin's associates might use the political confusion that followed the misadventure in Chechnya as an excuse to delay or cancel the scheduled elections for the State Duma in December 1995 and for president in June 1996.

As spring approached in 1995, such a turn for the worse in Russia seemed possible but by no means inevitable. For the country as a whole, the Chechen tragedy produced not only villains but heroes, most notably Sergei Kovalev, the chairman of the Russian human rights commission who went to Chechnya when the invasion began and stayed in Grozny to witness, and bear witness to, the savagery. Collectively, the Russian media, so long a captive of the Soviet regime, truly came of age in Chechnya by reporting the facts and refuting false government claims. The once meretricious propaganda organ *Izvestiya* ran banner headlines more tendentious than most Western papers would have dared, such as "Military Madness and Victims by Design," "In Such a War Even the Victors Will Be Judged."[51]

As long as Russia had a free press and political leaders who were able and willing to speak out in opposition, democracy would have a chance. But the emotions unleashed by the fighting in Chechnya brought new pressures to bear on the mass media and on Yeltsin's critics. Defense Minister Pavel Grachev condemned both the press and human rights spokesmen such as Sergei Kovalev, as did some of the right-wing deputies in the State Duma. However, a more shocking blow to the media came when Vladislav Listyev, one of the most popular television anchors, who had recently been placed in charge of one of Russia's major television networks, was shot down in March 1995 as he left his home for work. The killers were not immediately known, but the Listyev assassination dramatized the growing problem with crime and violence. During 1994 and early 1995, three members of the State Duma, several prominent businessmen, and at least one journalist had been murdered, and none of the persons ultimately responsible had been apprehended.

Yeltsin responded to Listyev's murder by dismissing Moscow's police chief and chief prosecutor and proposed draconian measures to deal with crime and corruption. Moscow's Mayor Luzhkov, however, objected to the dismissals as unjustified and accused Yeltsin of trying to make scapegoats of honest professionals while ignoring the real culprits. Many democrats also worried about the tendency to suspend civil liberties in the name of fighting crime. They wondered if authoritarian forces were not exploiting the public's genuine outrage over burgeoning crime to establish a police state. Some even hinted darkly that spectacular assassinations like that of Vladislav Listyev might not be the work of a criminal organization but a provocation designed to justify a crackdown, just as Stalin had used the murder of Sergei Kirov (which most believe he engineered, though it has not been proven) as a pretext to initiate the bloody purges of the 1930s.

Fears that the authorities would use crime as a pretext for a general crackdown had not materialized by the summer of 1995, but predictions that the invasion of Chechnya would result in terrorists acts came true in June, when a group of Chechen guerillas seized the Russian city of Budyonovsk, over a hundred miles north of the Chechnya border, and held two thousand persons hostage in the local hospital. Two assaults by the elite Alpha Detachment failed to free the hostages, and Prime Minister Chernomyrdin was forced to negotiate with the hostage-takers. He finally agreed to allow the terrorists to return to their mountain hideouts and to begin negotiations to end the war in Chechnya, but it was not immediately clear whether the susequent talks would lead to a settlement or merely a pause in the fighting.

The human cost of the invasion of Chechnya and the murders of prominent people underscored one of the failures of the post-Soviet Russian leadership. Russian democrats, though courageous in standing up against the use of force by the authorities, had generally proven inept at the essential but unglamorous tasks of institution building. When they had had power in late 1991 and 1992, they had failed to take effective steps to reform the bureaucracy—including the military and police—and to start the process of building an independent judiciary and more effective law enforcement. They had tried to reform the economy by applying macroeconomic formulae without creating the institutions necessary for a market economy or taking public opinion into account. In the December 1993 elections they had been so overconfident that they had spent their time debating esoteric propositions among themselves rather than talking directly and sensibly to the Russian people.

President Yeltsin shared responsibility for the failure to build effective institutions because of his habit of standing aloof from the day-to-day problems of governance and—from 1994—making ill-informed decisions prompted by a small circle of intimates. By 1995 people were asking whether he could still learn from his mistakes—as he had done at times in the past—or whether he would end his tenure in disgrace. Unfortunately, he had done nothing to develop a successor; in fact, he tended to distance himself from his supporters.

Reflecting on Yeltsin's position in 1995, I recalled a conversation with him in 1992 when he had volunteered that many people claimed to speak for him but none in fact did. "I keep them all at arm's length," he had explained, drawing a circle in the center of a piece of paper and then lines radiating from it like spokes in a wheel. "That way," he had continued, "I can use them when I wish, but they don't control me or speak for me."

This approach did prevent any one faction in his motley entourage of 1991 and 1992 to control him, but it also undermined his colleagues' efforts to build a broad-based political party to campaign for and support reforms. Then, having broken with many who were on his original team—he publicly belittled loyalists like Gennady Burbulis and Yegor Gaidar in a book published in 1994—he seemed to fall under the influence of a group dedicated to solving problems by force rather than persuasion and legal action. That influence not only worried democratic reformers in Russia but also raised questions abroad about Yeltsin's reliability as a negotiating partner. In particular, the war in Chechnya raised the possibility that Russia might, once again, be embarking on an imperialist course that would wreck the plans for partnership developed in 1992 and 1993.

A New Russian Empire?

RUSSIA'S HONEYMOON with the West lasted through 1992, when a second agreement to reduce strategic arms was negotiated with the United States, votes in the U.N. Security Council were in harmony with the Western powers, and international lending organizations made large, though conditional, commitments for financial and economic assistance to Russia. But in 1993, these good feelings began to fray as hard-liners in the Russian parliament began to accuse the West, and the United States in particular, of having caused the Soviet collapse and Russia's economic misery.

Some of these critics, such as former leaders of Soyuz, the parliamentary faction that tried to force Gorbachev to declare presidential rule, used the KGB disinformation Kryuchkov had been peddling in 1991 to "prove" America's malign intent. Some may even have been convinced that the KGB nonsense was true, but others knowingly employed false accusations in a cynical effort to get at their political rivals by reviving the old Soviet propaganda image of a hostile West. In 1992, Russia had no enemies abroad, so the opponents of reform had to invent them.

Ruslan Khasbulatov, the "speaker" of the Russian parliament in 1992, is a case in point. In 1990 and 1991 he was one of the driving forces to pull the RSFSR out of the Soviet Union. He had shocked me in 1990 when he predicted with relish that the Soviet Union would soon disappear, to be replaced by a loose organization not unlike the United Nations. But in 1992, when he saw it in his political interest to oppose the Yeltsin government, he began to accuse the United States of conspiring with Gorbachev to dismember the Union, even going so far on one occasion to charge that President Bush had promised Gorbachev $20 billion to break up the Soviet Union but had reneged on the promise.

In 1993, the anti-Western theme was pushed even more vigorously by the "right-wing" "patriots" and the "left-wing" Communists, whose programs differed only in their details. Their argument was that the current economic and political disorder in what had been the Soviet Union had been caused by a Western plot to buy or hoodwink Russian leaders to break up the Soviet Union and then keep a remnant Russia weak. Their prescription was to reject the link with the West, reassert Russian control over the territory that had been in the Soviet Union, and reestablish a strong, unitary state, using whatever means were required.

While rejecting the use of force or territorial expansion, some Russian democratic reformers also began to play on the nationalist sentiments the "patriots" were exploiting. Concentrating on the position of Russian minorities in other Soviet successor states, they demanded that the Russian government assume explicit responsibility for defending them, both to protect their human and civil rights and also to avoid the economic and social burden a mass return of expatriates would cause. They focused particularly on the status of Russians in Latvia, Estonia, and Kazakhstan, since most recognized that Ukraine and Moldova had not treated resident Russians unfairly, despite the claims of the extreme right.

Agitation by the superpatriots and in his own camp led Yeltsin to resort to political pressures on neighboring successor states that often smacked of imperialist practice. Particularly after the strong showing of nationalists in the December 1993 elections, Yeltsin's rhetoric became more strident, but even before that he had encouraged, or at least permitted, Russian bullying tactics in several countries.

During negotiations on the withdrawal of Russian military forces from Latvia and Estonia, Yeltsin repeatedly linked the issue to the status of ethnic Russians in those countries. He demanded that Kazakhstan and Ukraine allow their citizens also to be citizens of Russia if they wished. He did nothing to prevent the Fourteenth Army in Moldova from supporting the breakaway "Dniester Republic" and tolerated interference in Abkhazia by local Russian commanders, interference that initially was justified on grounds that it was to protect ethnic Russians from the fighting between Georgians and Abkhazians. He approved Russian military intervention in Tajikistan, which had the effect of keeping dictatorial regimes in power. Both the Ministry of Defense and the Ministry of Foreign Affairs developed doctrines that called, in effect, for Russian hegemony in what had been the Soviet Union. Speaking at the United Nations in the fall of 1994, Yeltsin seemed to stake a claim to a right of unilateral intervention in CIS states when he said that Russia's ties with them "exceed those of mere neighborliness," spoke of a "blood relationship," and asserted that the "main burden of peacemaking rests on the shoulders of the Russian Federation."

Despite the aggressive edge of some Russian practices, Yeltsin consistently refused to make territorial claims against Russia's neighbors, even when urged by his parliament to do so. Russian troops left Estonia and Latvia by the end of September 1994, despite Russia's continued dissatisfaction with the citizenship laws there. The Russian government negotiated an agreement to withdraw the Fourteenth Army from Moldova. Russia repeatedly reaffirmed the territorial integrity of Ukraine and Kazakhstan, not just bilaterally but jointly with third parties such as the United States.

Nevertheless, the attack on Chechnya seemed to represent a shift in Yeltsin's policy. Although Chechnya was legally part of Russia, which gave the Russian president rights he would not have had if Chechnya had been recognized as independent, his resort to force suggested that he might be willing to do the same outside his borders if disputes became acute.

These fears were understandable but probably misplaced. The difficulty in subduing Chechnya and the extreme unpopularity of that war throughout Russia made future aggression less likely, not more. If the Russian Army could not subdue a small, rebellious province without fearful losses and destruction, how could it be used effectively against an independent country that was determined to resist? In fact, it could not without threatening the integrity of Russia itself.

In 1995, Russia's future was still cloaked in uncertainty. The contradictory currents in its political institutions, in its economy, and throughout society did not permit confident prediction of short-term developments. There might well be further repressive moves by the authorities, which would undermine hard-won liberties. There might be another spasm of reform. Or there might continue to be elements of both as the authorities grappled with the dislocation and confusion that had followed the end of empire, the end of Communist authority, and the end of ideology.

Nevertheless, two things do seem as certain as anything in human affairs can be:

1. The Soviet system cannot be rebuilt. The circumstances that made it possible in the first place no longer prevail, and even at its height it was not competitive with free economies. Attempts to revert to the past, which may well occur, will fail and ultimately generate pressures to move ahead.

2. The Russian empire cannot be reassembled, even if the Russian people nurse an emotional attachment for an ill-understood past and are periodically victimized by demagogues. Only a healthy Russian economy could bear the cost, but the economy cannot be cured if Russia embarks on an imperialist course.

I can well imagine the objections to the second proposition since I have heard them from many friends whose judgment I respect. They usually go something like this: "You must be blind and deaf. Don't you hear what many Russian political and—even more ominously—military leaders are saying? They not only want the empire back but are planning to take it and are willing to use whatever means that requires. And they don't have to invade other countries. Russian chauvinists have meddled all around the former Soviet Union, keeping troops in Tajikistan, encouraging rebellions in Georgia and Moldova, making sure Armenians and Azerbaijanis continue fighting each other, demanding unacceptable concessions from the Balts. They seek a monopoly of 'peacekeeping' duties in the former Soviet republics and even have had the gall to ask others to pay them for it, when in fact what they want is free military bases abroad. Their economic policies are equally imperial, demanding, in effect, the tribute monopoles collect from colonies. Russia objected when Azerbaijan signed an agreement with foreign oil companies, even though a Russian company was part of the deal. It treats the Caspian Sea as if it were a Russian lake rather than a body of water surrounded by several sovereign states. All of which adds up to a consistent pattern of imperial reconquest."

Most of these allegations are true, but not the conclusion, for it ignores some basic facts. One of these is that Russia can no longer afford an empire, however acquired. If the twentieth century taught us anything, it is that empires are costly burdens. The British and French economies improved when they discarded their imperial dependencies. Though the Russian counterparts of Colonel Blimp may still use the language of imperial reconquest, they no longer have the means to achieve it. As the Belarusian political leaders are learning, Russia is unable to take on another dependency even if the country offers itself up.

Furthermore, most of Russia's attempts to bully its neighbors have not had the effect intended. They have simply made it more difficult to put substance into the Commonwealth of Independent States and have slowed the economic cooperation and integration that would benefit all of them. Even if some of Russia's neighbors are forced to grant military base rights or other specific concessions, they are likely to draw the line at direct Russian control over their internal policy or a Russian veto of their foreign contacts.

Zbigniew Brzezinski and others have pointed out that Russia can be an empire or a democracy but not both. That is true in theory, but in practice the long-term choice is between democracy and an autocracy that would threaten not its neighbors but Russia itself. Attempts to rebuild an empire would more likely trigger the fragmentation of Russia than the subjugation of neighbors.

As our earlier review suggests, internal nation building is the principal challenge in every one of the Soviet successor states. External factors can complicate or assist, but each country has the means of writing its own future. They will stay independent if that is their genuine desire, but they cannot flourish until they have decided who they are and where they are going, and until they have a state which attracts the loyalty of its people, rather than one that is the instrument of oppression by a single ethnic, political, or economic faction.

The cold war ended when American and Soviet policy—the latter driven by the need for internal reform—converged. The end of the cold war and the opening of Soviet society cleared the way for democratic institutions in the Soviet successor states: cleared the way but did not do the job. Some successors, notably the Baltic states, are on the road to democratic societies on a par with those in Western Europe and North America. Others, such as some in Central Asia, have regressed and fallen under rigid dictatorships. Still others have been riven by conflict and civil war. But the two largest, Russia and Ukraine, while denied the rapid transition evident in Estonia and Latvia, have, with all their problems, preserved the potential to enter the world economy and to build a civil society and democratic institutions. If they succeed, they can have a powerful and positive influence on all their neighbors.

As for Russia, it must, in the long run, reform or fall apart. True reform is going to take time—most likely measured in generations rather than years or even decades—and there will doubtless be setbacks, but Russia, like every other nation, can fulfill its potential only as a part of the wider world. Shutting out the world it does not control may have deep roots in Russian history, but they are not the only roots, and they must not be allowed to flourish if Russia is to develop a healthy society.

And what about the man who started it all? Since December 1991, Mikhail Gorbachev has been president of the Foundation for Social and Political Research in Moscow, usually called the Gorbachev Foundation. It was the golden parachute Yeltsin provided when he forced Gorbachev to resign. But even the disappearance of the Soviet Union and Gorbachev's retirement did not end the rivalry between the two men: Within months, Yeltsin reacted to the occasional criticism Gorbachev voiced in public by stripping the foundation of much of its property and withdrawing cars and security guards from the ex-president.

Nevertheless, Gorbachev has persisted in speaking his mind on public issues, though he vehemently refused a court subpoena in 1992 to testify in a case that challenged Yeltsin's order banning the Communist Party. At times he even hinted that he might run for president of the Russian Federation in the election scheduled for 1996. His friends, however, hoped he would not, for he seemed to have no chance at all. The hostility much of the public felt for him in 1991 had turned into indifference, and there seemed little hope that he could stage a political comeback. The Moscow newspaper *Nezavisimaya gazeta* conducts a monthly poll of political observers to rate the hundred most influential politicians in Russia. By 1994 and 1995, Gorbachev usually placed somewhere between sixtieth and eighty-sixth place.

Most Gorbachev associates found it easier to adapt to the turbulent new society than Gorbachev did. The young diplomat David Chikvaidze, who had brooded about his future under the shock of Gorbachev's farewell address, is now working on humanitarian issues in the U.N. Secretariat in New York, filling a position allocated to the Georgian quota.

Acknowledgments

Dr. David Hamburg, President of the Carnegie Corporation of New York, first suggested to me, over lunch in 1989, that I write a book about perestroika when I left my post as Ambassador to the USSR. The idea appealed to me, and I first thought of doing a commentary on Gorbachev's achievements and the problems that had arisen during his tenure as Soviet leader. By October 1991, when I had left Moscow, retired from the Foreign Service, and begun to plan the book in detail, it was immediately apparent that events were moving so rapidly that they could not be addressed usefully in a book; even daily newspapers had difficulty keeping up with the kaleidoscopic changes. When, several weeks later, the Soviet Union finally collapsed, what was initially conceived as an analysis of contemporary events became an inquest into the immediate past.

The book devotes more attention to my experiences than objectivity would require and I personally would prefer. Yet these experiences are precisely those that only I can record in detail, and I offer them not to "prove" that I was the center of events—of course I was not—but only to offer whatever insights my glimpses of the central events may provide.

The people to whom I am indebted for whatever understanding I may have of the events this book narrates are too numerous to name. My colleagues on the National Security Council staff and in the Department of State from 1983 to 1986, in particular, were a constant source of intellectual stimulation and practical support. It was my privilege, as U.S. Ambassador to the Soviet Union, to work with a group of the finest and most dedicated diplomats ever assembled in a single mission. They worked under the most trying circumstances and yet achieved more than even the most sanguine visionaries could have imagined. I have dedicated this book to them but would be remiss if I failed to single out a few whose support was irreplaceable. My deputies, Richard Combs, John "Mike" Joyce, Joseph Hulings, and James Collins, not only managed Embassy Moscow so that I could spend most of my time dealing with Soviet citizens and officials, but also consistently provided sage counsel. My executive secretaries, successively Ernestine Munsey, Kay Thomas, and Mary Frances Wilson, organized my days and evenings to make optimum use of the time available and saw to it that I was adequately prepared for the activities. As staff aides, Michael Klecheski, Bernadine Jocelyn, and Theodore Lyng were particularly adept at organizing trips, seeing that social functions were properly planned, and helping me make new contacts. If, as I intend, I write in greater detail about the U.S. Embassy in Moscow during this period, I shall be able to acknowledge more adequately the work of many other outstanding members of the staff.

I am also grateful for the confidence with which most senior Soviet officials dealt with me when I was on official duty in Moscow and subsequently, when I interviewed them specifically for this book. Presidents Gorbachev, Yeltsin,

Kravchuk, and Nazarbayev, former Prime Minister Ryzhkov, former Foreign Ministers Shevardnadze and Bessmertnykh, and many other senior officials, such as Belarusian Parliament Chairman Stanislav Shushkevich, Mayors Popov and Sobchak, Dr. Alexander Yakovlev, and Mr. Anatoly Chernyayev, not only granted interviews after I retired from the diplomatic service but were generous in giving me permission to describe earlier conversations with them.

A grant from the Carnegie Corporation of New York made it possible for me to concentrate on research for the book and to make several trips to Russia and other successor states of the Soviet Union in 1992 and 1993. The Harriman Institute of Columbia University not only is responsible for my earlier training in Soviet affairs but provided me a home, as Senior Research Scholar, during my research for the book. The Dickey Foundation of Dartmouth College, then headed by Dr. Leonard Rieser, offered me a Dickey Fellowship during the summer of 1992, which provided an idyllic environment as I was drafting the early chapters.

I was particularly fortunate to have Nancy Carney, who earlier had worked on our staff in Moscow, as a research assistant, and am also indebted to Amanda Leness, who ably replaced Nancy for a period in 1992.

As the book was written, many colleagues offered encouragement and suggestions: Ambassador Herbert S. Okun and Professors Herbert Ellison of the University of Washington, Richard Pipes of Harvard University, Marshall Shulman, Robert Legvold, Richard Ericson, and Alexander Motyl of Columbia University discussed the issues with me and several read all or parts of the manuscript. Their comments, and those of my eldest son, James G. Matlock, substantially improved the final text.

I took much longer to write the book than I initially planned, but the confidence and consistent support of my literary agent, Fifi Oscard, helped me through what, at times, seemed an almost endless task.

I owe a particular debt of gratitude to my editor, Jason Epstein, who taught me that my prose had more defects than I had imagined. His astute guidance improved the book's structure and his blue pencil its readability. If he allowed me at times to lapse into the convoluted bureaucratese that had permeated my professional environment, it was doubtless to prove that I had, indeed, once worked for the government.

Rebecca Matlock is an integral part of this story who also made valuable suggestions as the manuscript was prepared and supplied most of the photographs. Without her, much of it might not have happened and this book would certainly never have been written.

Names and Transliteration

Any account of events in the Soviet Union and its successors gives an author two headaches: (1) selecting and applying a reasonably consistent system of transliteration from languages not using the Latin alphabet, and (2) making sense of the frequent official changes of place-names and names of national groups.

Regarding transliteration from Russian, I have followed a pragmatic rather than pedantic approach, trying to suggest the actual sound of the word as closely as phonetic differences between the languages permit. This means, for example, that I have transliterated the Cyrillic letter "e" as "ye" when it occurs initially in a word or after a vowel, for that is how it is pronounced. Conversely, I have normally omitted the Cyrillic "soft sign" (ь), often rendered as an apostrophe in transliterations, since that symbol has a different significance in English, and the nonspecialist reader cannot be expected to know that it merely indicates that the preceding consonant is pronounced with the tongue raised toward the palate. People who know Russian know where the "soft signs" belong; those who don't find apostrophes confusing. An example of applying these two exceptions is the spelling of the name of the first Russian president: I refer to him as "Yeltsin," while a literal transliteration would be "El'tsin."

Other exceptions to literal rendition include use of "y" for the adjectival endings ий and ый, of "ovo" and "(y)evo" when ого and его are pronounced that way, of "yo" for "ë", and of "x" for кс in some personal names—though not in those that are widely known in the more literal spelling. Throughout, I have tried to minimize strangeness to the degree that was possible, even at the expense of literal consistency; for example spelling the familiar first name "Alexander," not "Aleksandr." I have, however, tried to be consistent throughout the book in my transliteration of particular words and names.

In footnotes and bibliographical citations, I have used a more literal system of transliteration, as is normal practice in that context.

Transliteration from Russian may seem complicated enough in itself but in fact is perhaps the simplest part of the task, for the book has many names that derive from languages other than Russian. Some writers simplify things for themselves by rendering them all as if they were written in Russian, but this can lead to major distortions and furthermore is offensive to many people who do not want their culture and language Russified. A different alphabet can be not only a selective filter (omitting sounds not in the target language), but also a distorting lens. For example, Russian has no exact equivalent to the aspirated "h" in English. By tradition, the letter is rendered as a "g." But this means that the English surnames Garrison and Harrison are identical in Cyrillic, and that "Harry Hopkins" becomes "Gary Gopkins."

When referring to persons and places in the three Baltic states and Moldova, which use the Latin alphabet, I have done my best to determine and use the original spelling, not a transliteration from Cyrillic. In cases where the name is also known by its transliteration from Cyrillic, I have indicated the alternate. I would note in this connection that some citizens of the Baltic states and Moldova have names that were originally Slavic and therefore have valid Cyrillic forms. However, if the individual considers himself or herself an Estonian, Latvian, Lithuanian, or Moldovan, I have tried to comply with the individual's preference and use the non-Cyrillic form. Thus, Igor Gräzin (Estonian), not Gryazin (transliterated Cyrillic); Anatolijs Gorbunovs (Latvian), not Anatoly Gorbunov; and Petru Lucinschi (Moldovan), not Pyotr Luchinsky.

For Ukrainian names, I have used the Ukrainian form of place-names (Lviv and Kharkiv instead of Lvov and Kharkov), since these have come into general use since Ukrainian independence. Kiev, however, is so familiar to the foreign reader that I thought it would be a foolish consistency to render it Kyyiv. As for personal names, I have tried to use the form the individual prefers but if in doubt have used the more familiar Russian form.

Belarusian (formerly Belorussian) presents a special problem because there is as yet no generally accepted standard transliteration into Latin characters: some authors use Polish orthography, others German, others personal systems. Furthermore, the phonetic shifts that distinguish Belarusian from Russian tend to look quite different to a reader not trained in East Slavic phonology. For example, the name of the Communist leader who was forced to resign after the August 1991 coup is Dementei (or Dementey) in Russian but Dziemyantsiei (or Dziemianciej, or—there could be a half dozen other variants) in Belarusian. For these reasons, I have reluctantly decided to keep most Belarusian names in their Russian form, and if this offends my friends there, I apologize.

Names from languages that use neither the Cyrillic nor Latin alphabet (Georgian and Armenian), or which have used more than one alphabet in recent times (the Turkic languages), present additional complications. In general, I have taken the following approaches:

- For Georgian, I have used transliteration from Cyrillic, since this normally does not differ greatly from transliteration from the Georgian alphabet, except that the Georgian alphabet would require the addition of diacritical marks not readily understood by the English-language reader.
- For Armenian, I have also basically used transliteration from Cyrillic, but with some alterations to align it with Armenian orthography in regard to persons active in Armenia. Since Armenian has an "h" sound and Russian does not, I have added the letter in personal names when it belongs there. Furthermore, a common Armenian ending for names, spelled "-ian" in Armenian, is rendered "yan" in Cyrillic. Thus, the Communist Party first secretary in Armenia in 1989 was called Harutiunian, not Arutyunyan. If the person is active not in Armenia but in Russia, I have used the translation from Cyrillic even if the name is of Armenian origin, since this is the way the name is normally transliterated. Abel Aganbegyan would be a case in point.
- For the Turkic languages the problem is even more complex since

during this century they have been written in three alphabets (Arabic, Latin, and Cyrillic) and many are now in the process of reverting from Cyrillic to Latin. I have considered it best not to try to anticipate the future but to use transliteration from Russian, except in those instances when I was aware that a given individual preferred a different form or it was a matter of correcting the Russian "g" to an original "h"—as in Heidar Aliev, not Geidar.

It is much simpler to describe my approach to changing geographical names. I tried to use the name that was current at the time of the event I was describing. Thus, Anatoly Sobchak was elected mayor of Leningrad but, without changing jobs, is now mayor of Saint Petersburg. Andrei Sakharov was in exile in Gorky, but, if his widow visits their apartment there, she will have to go to Nizhny Novgorod. The country to the west of Smolensk was Belorussia when it was part of the Soviet Union but is now Belarus. Moldavia became Moldova even before independence, but many persons continued to use Moldavia through 1991. If all this is confusing to the reader, I can only plead that it was no less so for me, but since the changes had political importance they could not be ignored without distorting the story.

I have used the terms "Baltic" and "Balts" in their geographic rather than ethnic or linguistic sense. Thus, "Baltic states" is shorthand for "Estonia, Latvia, and Lithuania." In a linguistic and ethnic sense, only Latvians and Lithuanians are Balts; Estonians are Finno-Ugrian. However, this distinction was not relevant to the political topics I discussed and I therefore allowed myself to use "Balts" as a collective term for all three nationalities rather than writing "Balts and Estonians," which would have been more precise.

Finally, I would note that in referring to official titles I have used "chairman of the Council of Ministers" and "prime minister" interchangeably. Both titles refer to the head of government in a Soviet republic or in a successor state. The chief of state, on the other hand, was usually the chairman of the Supreme Soviet (or the Supreme Soviet Presidium) until, beginning in 1990, the office of president began to be established, first in the USSR and then in many republics, though not in all. Even before the office of president was created in the USSR in 1990, many journalists referred to Gorbachev as "president," but this was not his official title. Since the creation of the office of president normally implied a change in the structure of government, I have tried to be meticulous in maintaining the distinction between "chairman" and "president" in regard to the title of the chief of state. In order to avoid confusion with the head of government, I usually called the latter "prime minister" rather than "chairman" unless I used the full title, chairman of the Council of Ministers.

Chronology

1985

March 11 Gorbachev elected general secretary of the Communist Party of the Soviet Union.

March 13 Vice President Bush meets Gorbachev in Moscow and delivers a letter from President Reagan proposing a summit meeting.

March 25 Gorbachev's reply to Reagan's letter is delivered in Washington. Its tone is conciliatory, but it contains few specifics.

April 23 The CPSU Central Committee approves a resolution to reform economic management and elects Chebrikov, Ryzhkov, and Ligachev to full membership in the Politburo.

April 26 Gorbachev and the leaders of the East European states agree in Warsaw to a formal extension of the Warsaw Pact for twenty years.

May 1 The United States announces an agreement with the USSR to conduct regular consultations on regional issues, including Afghanistan.

May 1 Reagan sends a letter to Gorbachev urging negotiations.

May 14 Secretary of State Shultz and Foreign Minister Gromyko meet in Vienna.

July 1 Romanov, a Gorbachev rival, removed from the Politburo; Shevardnadze promoted from candidate to full member and Yeltsin named to the Secretariat.

July 2 Shevardnadze replaces Gromyko as foreign minister; Gromyko named chairman of the Presidium of the USSR Supreme Soviet.

July 3 The United States and USSR announce that Reagan and Gorbachev will meet in Geneva in November.

July 29 Gorbachev announces a unilateral suspension of nuclear testing.

September 27 Shevardnadze meets with Reagan to discuss the Geneva summit. In Moscow, Ryzhkov replaces Gorbachev rival Tikhonov as chairman of the USSR Council of Ministers.

October 2–5 Gorbachev makes a state visit to France. He uses the term "reasonable sufficiency" for the first time, de-links INF, and rejects ideological differences as a basis for foreign policy.

November 19–21 Reagan and Gorbachev meet in Geneva and find a common language in talking about war and peace.

December 24 Yeltsin replaces Grishin as Moscow Party secretary.

1986

January 1 Gorbachev and Reagan exchange New Year's messages.

January 15 Gorbachev proposes the total elimination of nuclear weapons by 2000.

February 11 Anatoly Shcharansky, one of the most prominent political prisoners, is freed and expelled from the USSR in a prisoner exchange.

February 18 Yeltsin is made a candidate member of the Politburo.

February 25–March 6 Twenty-seventh CPSU Congress elects a new Central Committee, but its orientation is much like that of its predecessor. In his opening speech, Gorbachev calls the war in Afghanistan a "running sore."

April 26 A major accident at the nuclear power plant in Chernobyl, Ukraine, kills many people and spreads radioactive material over a wide area. A mass evacuation of the immediate area is carried out over the next few days.

April 29 Commercial air service between the United States and the USSR, which was interrupted after the Soviet invasion of Afghanistan, is restored.

May 23 Shevardnadze holds a conference in the Soviet Ministry of Foreign Affairs to discuss "new thinking."

July 31 A speech by Gorbachev in Khabarovsk refers to "perestroika of the political system."

August 23 U.S. correspondent Nicholas Daniloff is arrested in Moscow in retaliation for the arrest of a Soviet intelligence agent in the United States.

September 15–18 A "Chautauqua" meeting at Jurmala, Latvia, where U.S. spokesmen describe nonrecognition policy, is covered in the Soviet news media.

September 17 The United States expels twenty-five officials from the Soviet Mission to the United Nations in retaliation for Daniloff's arrest.

September 29 Daniloff leaves the Soviet Union; arrested agent Gennady Zakharov is allowed to leave the United States after pleading "no contest" to the espionage charge and after the Soviet government agrees to release political prisoner Yuri Orlov and allow him to leave the Soviet Union.

October 11–12 Reagan and Gorbachev meet in Reykjavik, Iceland. They settle most arms-reduction issues, but fail to reach a comprehensive agreement.

October 19 Five U.S. diplomats are expelled from the Soviet Union in retaliation for the expulsion of diplomats in the Soviet Mission to the United Nations.

October 21 The United States expels fifty-five Soviet diplomats from the Soviet Embassy in Washington and the Soviet Consulate General in San Francisco and establishes quotas for each.

October 22 The USSR expels five more U.S. diplomats and withdraws Soviet employees from the U.S. Embassy and Consulate General.

December 16–18 Riots break out in Alma Ata when Kunayev is replaced by a Russian as Party first secretary.

December 19 Gorbachev calls Sakharov in Gorky to tell him that he and his wife, Yelena Bonner, can return to Moscow.

1987

January 15 The United States lifts its embargo on the export of oil and gas drilling equipment to the Soviet Union.

January 20 Soviet jamming of the BBC ends.

January 27 A plenary meeting of the CPSU Central Committee, postponed three times, focuses on democratization and political reform. Gorbachev surprises all by his radicalism, replaces "developed socialism" with "developing socialism," and proposes real elections and secret ballots.

March 28–April 1 British Prime Minister Thatcher visits the USSR; stresses human rights and calls for Soviet withdrawal from Afghanistan.

April 14 U.S. Secretary of State Shultz visits Moscow to reactivate negotiations following the Reykjavik meeting.

April 16 Shultz is interviewed by Soviet television.

May 6 The United States and USSR conclude an agreement to establish Risk Reduction Centers in their capitals.

May 23 Soviet jamming of the Voice of America ends.

May 28 Mathias Rust lands a Cessna in Red Square.

May 30 USSR Minister of Defense Sokolov is replaced by Dmitri Yazov; the chief of the Soviet air defense forces and scores of generals are removed.

June 25–26 Gorbachev links democratization to economic reform at a plenum of the CPSU Central Committee; Yakovlev is elected to the Politburo.

July 6 Crimean Tatars begin to demonstrate in Red Square for the right to return to the Crimea from their exile in Central Asia.

August 23 Demonstrations are organized in the Baltic capitals on the anniversary of the Nazi-Soviet pact.

September 10 Chebrikov accuses Western intelligence agencies of stirring up national minorities.

September 10 Yeltsin and Ligachev clash in the Politburo.

September 12 Yeltsin sends letter to Gorbachev complaining of Ligachev and offering resignation.

October 21 Gorbachev clashes with Yeltsin at a plenum of the CPSU Central Committee.

November 1 Demonstration in Minsk to commemorate executions at Kuropaty during Stalin's time.

November 11 The Moscow City Party Committee removes Yeltsin at Gorbachev's request.

November 18 Yeltsin is appointed first deputy chairman of the State Committee on Construction.

November 23–24 Shultz and Shevardnadze meet in Geneva and complete negotiations for a treaty to eliminate intermediate-range nuclear missiles (INF).

December 7–10 Reagan-Gorbachev summit meeting in Washington; they sign the INF treaty.

1988

February 8 Gorbachev announces his intent to withdraw the Soviet military forces from Afghanistan.

February 13 Riots take place in Nagorny Karabakh.

February 18 Yeltsin is removed from the Politburo at a plenum of the CPSU Central Committee.

February 24 Four thousand people demonstrate in Tallinn to mark the seventieth anniversary of Estonian independence.

February 28 Pogroms take place against Armenians in Sumgait, Azerbaijan; several persons are killed, but rumors exaggerate the numbers.

March 13 A letter from Nina Andreyeva, a teacher in Leningrad, criticizing reforms from a Stalinist point of view is published in *Sovetskaya Rossiya.*

April 14 International accords on Afghanistan are signed in Geneva.

May 21 Leaders of the Communist parties in Armenia and Azerbaijan are replaced.

May 27 The "Theses" for the nineteenth CPSU Conference, calling for democratization and the rule of law, are published.

May 29–June 1 Reagan and Gorbachev meet in Moscow; Reagan also meets with dissidents and praises freedom in an address to students at Moscow State University.

June 5–12 With government support, the Russian Orthodox Church celebrates the millennium of the establishment of Christianity in Russia.

June 9 Foreign travel regulations for Soviet citizens are simplified.

June 13 The Azerbaijan Supreme Soviet rejects a petition from Nagorny Karabakh legislators to transfer the territory to Armenia.

June 14 Demonstrations are held in the Baltic capitals to mark the forty-seventh anniversary of mass deportations.

June 15 The Armenian Supreme Soviet gives consent to the annexation of Nagorny Karabakh.

June 28 In his address to the nineteenth CPSU Conference, Gorbachev proposes extensive political reform including contested elections and a new legislative body.

July 1 Yeltsin's request for "political rehabilitation" at the Party Conference is rejected.

July 4 The CPSU Conference issues resolutions favoring political reform.

July 7 A declaration of principles by the Ukrainian Helsinki Union calls for the restoration of Ukrainian statehood.

July 12 The Supreme Soviet in Nagorny Karabakh votes to secede from Azerbaijan and to change its name to Artsakh. The Presidium of the Azerbaijan Supreme Soviet declares the action null and void.

July 18 Gorbachev rejects the Armenian position on Nagorny Karabakh during a session of the Presidium of the USSR Supreme Soviet.

July 23 Mass demonstrations occur in Tallinn, Riga, and Vilnius to protest the Soviet annexation of the Baltic states.

July 25 Addressing a conference in the Soviet Ministry of Foreign Affairs, Shevardnadze rejects the class struggle as the basis of foreign policy.

August 5 Ligachev defends the class struggle concept in a speech in Gorky.

August 12 Yakovlev defends the "common interests of mankind" in a speech in Vilnius, Lithuania.

August 19 A draft program of the Estonian People's Front is published in an Estonian newspaper.

September 8 The program of the Latvian People's Front is published in a Latvian newspaper.

September 21 A state of emergency is declared in parts of Nagorny Karabakh following disorders.

September 30 Ligachev and Chebrikov are given new assignments while Yakovlev takes charge of the Party Central Committee International Department.

October 1 Gorbachev is elected chairman of the Presidium of the USSR Supreme Soviet, replacing Andrei Gromyko as titular chief of state.

October 12 The Sąjūdis Program is published in Lithuania.

November 16 The Estonian Supreme Soviet declares sovereignty and assumes control of state property.

November 22 Anti-Armenian riots take place in Baku.

November 26 The USSR Supreme Soviet Presidium annuls the Estonian action, taking control of state property in the republic.

December 1 The USSR Supreme Soviet approves a new election law providing for contested elections and secret ballots.

December 7 Gorbachev addresses the United Nations, announcing unilateral troop cuts and stressing that the "common interests of mankind" and "freedom of choice" are mandatory, universal principles.

December 7 Gorbachev meets with Reagan and President-elect Bush on Governors Island.

December 7 A major earthquake in Armenia causes Gorbachev to cut short his visit to New York.

1989

January 12 Nagorny Karabakh is placed under direct rule from Moscow by the USSR Supreme Soviet; Arkady Volsky is named temporary administrator.

January 17–19 The CSCE Review Conference closes in Vienna with an agreement to begin negotiations on the reduction of conventional forces in Europe (CFE).

January 18 The Estonian Supreme Soviet makes Estonian the state language.

February 1 Latvian is designated the state language in Latvia.

February 15 The last Soviet troops leave Afghanistan.

February 24 The flag of independent Estonia is raised in Tallinn on the prewar republic's independence day.

March 6 Negotiations between members of NATO and the Warsaw Pact on conventional forces in Europe (CFE) begin in Vienna.

March 12 A mass demonstration is held in Riga in support of the Latvian National Front.

March 26 Elections are held for the USSR Congress of People's Deputies; Yeltsin wins big in Moscow.

April 9 The Soviet army suppresses a peaceful demonstration in Tbilisi, killing at least twenty people and wounding hundreds.

April 14 The Communist Party leader in Georgia is replaced.

April 25 Seventy-four members of the CPSU Central Committee are removed.

April 25 Soviet troops begin leaving Hungary.

May 15–19 Gorbachev visits China and announces the "normalization" of relations.

May 18 The Lithuanian Supreme Soviet declares sovereignty.

May 25 The first session of the USSR Congress of People's Deputies convenes and elects Gorbachev chairman of the Supreme Soviet and chief of state.

May 29 Yeltsin receives a seat in the new USSR Supreme Soviet when Alexei Kazannik withdraws in his favor.

June 3–15 Scores are killed in ethnic rioting in Uzbekistan.

June 4–18 Elections in Poland result in an overwhelming victory by the anti-Communist Solidarity movement.

July 1 In a television address, Gorbachev warns of ethnic conflict.

July 6 Gorbachev addresses the Council of Europe in Strasbourg; says the USSR will not block reforms in Eastern Europe.

July 10 A wave of strikes begins in coal mining areas. They spread and continue for several weeks.

July 28 The Latvian Supreme Soviet declares sovereignty.

July 30 The "Interregional Group of Deputies" is formed in the USSR Supreme Soviet by Yeltsin, Sakharov, and other reformist deputies.

August 22 A Lithuanian Supreme Soviet commission declares the secret protocol to the 1939 Nazi-Soviet pact null and void *ab initio*.

August 23 Over two million participate in the "Baltic Way" demonstration.

August 24 A non-Communist government headed by Tadeusz Mazowiecki is formed in Poland.

August 26 The Central Committee issues a stiff warning to the Balts.

August 31 The Moldavian Supreme Soviet establishes Moldavian (Moldovan) as the state language and replaces the Cyrillic alphabet with the Latin.

September 4 A general strike starts in Azerbaijan to demand recognition of the National Front and reassertion of control over Nagorny Karabakh. The strike subsequently results in a blockade of the principal rail line from European Russia into Armenia.

September 8–10 Rukh holds its constituent congress in Kiev and displays the banned blue-and-yellow flag of independent Ukraine.

September 11 Hungary announces that it will no longer prevent East German citizens from crossing the border to Austria.

September 22–23 Baker and Shevardnadze meet in Jackson Hole, Wyoming. Shevardnadze drops the Soviet linkage of strategic missile reductions with limits on the Strategic Defense Initiative (SDI).

September 23 The Azerbaijan Supreme Soviet designates Azeri as the state language, reasserts sovereignty over Nagorny Karabakh, and reaffirms Azerbaijan's right of secession from the USSR.

September 24 Republic parliaments designate Kazakh and Kyrgyz as the official languages in Kazakhstan and Kyrgyzstan.

October 2 Large anti-Communist demonstrations begin in Leipzig.

October 6 Gorbachev meets Erich Honecker and urges reform in the GDR.

October 8 The Latvian Popular Front endorses the goal of independence.

October 10 Hungary's ruling party is reconstituted as a socialist party.

October 11 GDR Communist leader Honecker resigns; is replaced subsequently by Egon Krenz.

October 23 Hungary is declared a republic on the twenty-third anniversary of the 1956 uprising. Free elections are scheduled for 1990.

October 27 A meeting of Warsaw Pact foreign ministers renounces the Brezhnev Doctrine.

October 31 Krenz visits Moscow and endorses perestroika.

November 9 The GDR abolishes travel restrictions and the Berlin wall is breached by a rush of East Germans into West Berlin.

November 10–17 Party boss Todor Zhivkov and other hard-liners are removed from the Party leadership in Bulgaria.

November 12 The Estonian Supreme Soviet annuls the act of the Estonian parliament of 1940 requesting incorporation in the USSR.

November 16 Moldavian Party first secretary Semen Grossu is replaced by Petru Lucinschi (Pyotr Luchinsky) following rioting in Kishinev (Chişinău).

November 19 The Georgian Supreme Soviet declares sovereignty and resolves that the Soviet occupation of Georgia in 1921 was a violation of the 1920 treaty between Georgia and Russia.

November 27 The Politburo issues a statement condemning the attempt by the Lithuanian Communist Party to remove itself from Moscow's control.

November 28 West German Chancellor Helmut Kohl presents a plan for unifying the two German states.

November 28 The USSR Supreme Soviet votes to end direct rule over Nagorny Karabakh despite protests by deputies from Armenia and Nagorny Karabakh.

December 1 Gorbachev calls on Pope John Paul II in the Vatican; promises a law guaranteeing freedom of conscience and legalization of the Ukrainian Catholic Church.

December 2–3 Bush and Gorbachev meet on Malta; Gorbachev pledges that force will not be used to keep Communist regimes in Eastern Europe; Bush agrees to eliminate most controls on U.S.-Soviet trade.

December 3 Egon Krenz and all the leaders of the East German SED (Communist) Party resign.

December 9–10 President Gustav Husák resigns and a government dominated by non-Communists is formed in Czechoslovakia following several weeks of street demonstrations.

December 12 The second session of the USSR Congress of People's Deputies convenes; Gorbachev refuses to discuss the elimination of Article VI in the Constitution and hounds Sakharov from the podium.

December 14 Andrei Sakharov dies.

December 20 The Lithuanian Communist Party withdraws from the Communist Party of the Soviet Union.

December 22–25 Nicolae Ceauşescu is deposed, then executed during an anti-Communist revolution in Romania; the USSR refuses the invitation of the anti-Ceauşescu forces to intervene.

December 24 The USSR Supreme Soviet declares the secret protocol to the

Nazi-Soviet pact invalid, but does not rescind the incorporation of the Baltic states and other territory that was acquired as a result of that agreement.

December 25–26 The CPSU Central Committee meets and rejects the Lithuanian Communist Party's request for independent status.

December 28–29 Alexander Dubček is named chairman of the Czechoslovak parliament and Vaclav Havel is inaugurated president of Czechoslovakia.

1990

January 11–13 Gorbachev visits Lithuania but fails to persuade the majority of Lithuanian Communists to remain in the CPSU.

January 13 Anti-Armenian pogroms break out in Baku.

January 19 The Soviet army begins an assault on Baku and removes the Azerbaijan National Front from power.

January 22 The Azerbaijan Supreme Soviet threatens to hold a referendum on secession if Soviet troops are not withdrawn within forty-eight hours.

February 4 A mass demonstration in Moscow by reformers draws over 100,000 people.

February 5–7 The CPSU Central Committee approves a draft Party platform which would amend Article VI of the Constitution to eliminate the Party's monopoly on political power.

February 8 Secretary of State Baker visits Moscow and proposes the Two Plus Four approach to negotiations over German unity.

February 12 The foreign ministers of West Germany, the GDR, and of the "Four Powers" (U.S., U.K., France, USSR) agree at a meeting in Ottawa to begin formal talks on German unity.

February 24 Sąjūdis wins a majority of seats in the Lithuanian Supreme Soviet.

March 4 Reformers and nationalists do well in elections to republic legislatures in Russia, Ukraine, and Belorussia, but do not win majorities.

March 11 The Lithuanian Supreme Council declares a restoration of Lithuanian independence and elects Vytautas Landsbergis Supreme Council chairman and chief of state.

March 13 The USSR Congress of People's Deputies amends the Constitution to create the post of president and to revise Article VI to eliminate the Communist Party's monopoly on political power.

March 14 Gorbachev is elected president of the USSR by the USSR Congress of People's Deputies.

March 18 The conservative CDU wins elections in the GDR.

March 30 The Estonian Supreme Soviet resolves to begin the process of restoring Estonia's independence.

April 3 The USSR officially admits responsibility for the massacre of Polish officers in Katyn Forest in 1940.

April 18 Moscow sharply reduces the delivery of oil and natural gas to Lithuania following an ultimatum issued by Gorbachev.

May 1 The May Day parade in Red Square is marred by anti-Gorbachev protesters.

May 4 The Latvian parliament endorses the goal of independence.

May 29 Yeltsin is elected chairman of the RSFSR Supreme Soviet.

May 30–June 4 Gorbachev meets Bush in Washington, then visits Minneapolis–St. Paul and San Francisco.

June 8 The RSFSR Supreme Soviet declares sovereignty and gives its laws precedence over those of the USSR.

June 12 The USSR Supreme Soviet passes a law guaranteeing freedom of the press.

June 19–23 The Russian Communist Party holds its first congress and elects Ivan Polozkov, a critic of perestroika, first secretary.

June 30 Deliveries of oil and gas to Lithuania are resumed after the Lithuanian parliament votes a temporary suspension of implementation of its independence declaration.

July 2–13 The twenty-eighth CPSU Congress is held in Moscow. Gorbachev is reelected general secretary, but with significant opposition. The new Politburo is made up largely of mediocre figures.

July 12 Yeltsin resigns from the Communist Party in a dramatic speech at the Party Congress.

July 15–16 Gorbachev and Kohl meet near Stavropol and agree on the remaining questions of German unification.

July 16 Ukraine declares sovereignty.

July 23 The Ukrainian Supreme Soviet elects Leonid Kravchuk its chairman.

July 27 Belorussia declares sovereignty.

August 1 Gorbachev and Yeltsin agree to cooperate in developing an economic reform plan and jointly name a commission headed by Stanislav Shatalin to draft a program.

August 1–2 Shevardnadze meets Secretary of State Baker in Irkutsk.

August 2 Iraq invades Kuwait.

August 3 Baker and Shevardnadze sign a joint statement in Moscow condemning the Iraqi invasion.

August 4 The Armenian Supreme Soviet elects Levon Ter-Petrosian its chairman, rejecting the Communist Party candidate.

August 9 The USSR Council of Ministers legalizes the private ownership of businesses and the hiring of labor.

August 15 Gorbachev issues a decree restoring the citizenship of Alexander Solzhenitsyn and other prominent political exiles. Solzhenitsyn rejects the offer.

August 22 Turkmenistan declares sovereignty.

August 25 Tajikistan declares sovereignty.

August 25 The Supreme Soviet in the Abkhaz ASSR declares independence from Georgia and union republic status within the USSR.

August 31 Gorbachev orders that the Ryzhkov government plan and the Shatalin plan be combined.

September 2 Ethnic Russians in Tiraspol establish a "Dniester Soviet Republic" on territory east of the Dniester River and secede from Moldavia.

September 9 Bush and Gorbachev meet in Helsinki and agree to cooperate to end Iraqi aggression against Kuwait.

September 11 The RSFSR Supreme Soviet approves the Shatalin plan 213–1.

September 12 The Two Plus Four treaty is signed in Moscow, ending four-power rights in Germany.

September 20 The South Ossetian Supreme Soviet declares independence from Georgia. The Georgian parliament immediately invalidates the action.

September 24 The USSR Supreme Soviet votes to grant Gorbachev emergency powers for eighteen months to carry out economic reforms.

October 1 The USSR Supreme Soviet passes a law on freedom of worship.

October 3 The unification of the Federal Republic of Germany and the German Democratic Republic enters into legal force.

October 9 The USSR Supreme Soviet enacts legislation to establish a multi-party political system.

October 19 The USSR Supreme Soviet approves a plan for transition to a market economy but most economists doubt that it can work.

October 20–21 Democratic Russia holds its first congress in Moscow.

October 23 Ukrainian Premier Vitaly Masol resigns in the face of mass protests.

October 25 Kazakhstan declares sovereignty.

October 27 Saparmurad Niyazov, who ran unopposed, is elected president in Turkmenistan.

October 28 The Kyrgyzstan Supreme Soviet elects Askar Akayev, an opponent of the Communist leadership, president of the republic.

October 28 Pro-independence parties win parliamentary elections in Georgia.

October 28 The Rukh congress in Kiev adopts Ukrainian independence as an explicit goal.

October 30 Kyrgyzstan declares sovereignty.

November 7 An attempt to assassinate Gorbachev is made during the Revolution Day parade on Red Square.

November 13 Yeltsin announces that the RSFSR cannot implement the Shatalin plan without the cooperation of the central government.

November 16 Gorbachev's report to the USSR Supreme Soviet is poorly received.

November 17 Gorbachev proposes an extensive reorganization of the Soviet government.

November 19 The Treaty on Conventional Armed Forces in Europe (CFE) is signed in Paris.

November 24 The draft union treaty is published. Most republic leaders find fault with it.

November 29 The UN Security Council votes, with Soviet support, to authorize "all necessary means" to compel compliance with UN resolutions on Kuwait.

December 1 Boris Pugo replaces Vadim Bakatin as USSR Minister of Internal Affairs.

December 20 Shevardnadze resigns, warning that "a dictatorship is coming."

December 25 Prime Minister Ryzhkov is incapacitated by a heart attack.

December 26 The USSR Congress of People's Deputies approves constitutional amendments to restructure the government and give the president more authority.

December 27 Gennady Yanayev is elected vice president by the USSR Congress of People's Deputies on a second round of voting.

1991

January 10 Gorbachev orders the Lithuanian government to restore the "constitutional order" or bear the consequences.

January 11 Formation of a Lithuanian National Salvation Committee is announced.

January 13 The KGB Alpha Detachment takes the television broadcast tower in Vilnius with extensive loss of life.

January 14 Valentin Pavlov is named prime minister of the USSR.

January 15 Operation "Desert Storm" begins in the Persian Gulf region.

January 20 Large demonstrations form in Moscow and Leningrad to protest the repression in Lithuania.

January 24 The American ambassador delivers a letter from Bush to Gorbachev that threatens to sever economic ties if violence continues in Lithuania. Gorbachev insists he is acting to avoid civil war.

January 29 Gorbachev issues a decree legalizing joint military-police patrols despite the opposition of republic and local leaders.

January 30 Gorbachev is severely criticized at a plenum of the CPSU Central Committee.

February 1 Georgia imposes an economic blockade on South Ossetia.

February 9 In a referendum, more than 90 percent of Lithuanian voters favor independence.

February 19 Yeltsin calls for Gorbachev's resignation.

February 24 The U.S.-led ground offensive begins against Iraq.

February 26 Gorbachev attacks the democrats in a speech in Minsk.

February 28 Allied military operations against Iraq are suspended.

March 1 A strike by coal miners begins in the Donbas region, then spreads to other areas.

March 3 Referendums on independence are conducted in Estonia and Latvia. In Estonia, 78 percent vote "yes," while 74 percent vote for independence in Latvia.

March 14–16 Secretary of State Baker visits Moscow, meets with Baltic leaders and some republic leaders.

March 17 A majority of participants in the unionwide referendum vote in favor of a voluntary union, but the referendum is not conducted everywhere and the proposition loses in some areas.

March 28 Troops are brought into Moscow to prevent a large pro-Yeltsin demonstration, but it takes place anyway. The troops are removed the following day at the demand of the RSFSR Congress of People's Deputies.

March 31 The Warsaw Pact is officially dissolved.

April 1 Retail prices are raised in the USSR.

April 4 The RSFSR Supreme Soviet votes sweeping powers to Yeltsin.

April 4 Strikes begin in Minsk.

April 9 Georgia declares independence.

April 22 Prime Minister Pavlov presents an "anticrisis program" to the USSR Supreme Soviet.

April 23 Nine republic leaders reach agreement with Gorbachev over Union Treaty (Nine Plus One agreement).

April 24 The RSFSR Supreme Soviet approves a law on the election of a president.

April 24–25 Gorbachev threatens to resign at a CPSU Central Committee plenum.

May 20 The USSR Supreme Soviet passes a law guaranteeing the right to travel abroad and emigrate.

June 12 Yeltsin is elected president of the RSFSR by 57.3 percent of the vote in a general election.

June 17 Pavlov asks the USSR Supreme Soviet for special powers without Gorbachev's approval and is supported in closed testimony by Yazov, Kryuchkov, and Pugo.

June 20 The U.S. ambassador warns Gorbachev of a conspiracy to remove him.

June 21 The Supreme Soviet rejects Pavlov's request for special powers.

June 30 The last Soviet troops leave Czechoslovakia.

July 10 Yeltsin is inaugurated president of the RSFSR.

July 12 The USSR Supreme Soviet approves the union treaty in principle, but suggests changes.

July 17 Gorbachev meets with the Group of Seven in London but receives little economic assistance.

July 20 Yeltsin issues a decree forbidding political activity in state institutions; seen as mortal threat by Communist Party officials.

July 28 Gorbachev informs Yeltsin and Nazarbayev that he will remove Kryuchkov and Pavlov after the union treaty is signed on August 20.

July 30–31 President Bush visits Moscow, meets with Gorbachev and Nazarbayev, and pays a separate call on Yeltsin.

August 1 President Bush visits Kiev and meets privately with Kravchuk.

August 2 Gorbachev announces that the union treaty is "open for signing."

August 4 Gorbachev leaves for vacation in the Crimea.

August 17 Kryuchkov, Pavlov, and Yazov agree with several senior Party officials to demand that Gorbachev relinquish power to them temporarily and if he should refuse, to isolate him and take control.

August 18 Gorbachev rejects the demands of a delegation sent to persuade him to authorize a crackdown. Shortly before midnight, Vice President Yanayev agrees to support the takeover, signing a decree to assume the powers of the presidency.

August 19 Emergency committee announces that it has assumed power. Yeltsin declares the takeover an illegal coup d'état.

August 21 The coup attempt fails; Gorbachev returns to Moscow.

August 24 Gorbachev suspends Communist Party activities and resigns as general secretary of the CPSU.

August 24 Ukraine declares independence, subject to a referendum on December 1, 1991.

August 25 The Belorussian Supreme Soviet declares "political and economic independence."

August 27 Moldova declares independence.

August 30 Azerbaijan declares independence.

August 31 Uzbekistan and Kyrgyzstan declare independence.

September 6 Georgia announces a break in all ties with the USSR.

September 6 The USSR State Council formally recognizes independence of Estonia, Latvia, and Lithuania and supports their membership in the UN and CSCE.

September 6 Residents of Leningrad vote to restore the city's original name, Saint Petersburg.

September 9 Tajikistan declares independence.

September 21 Armenia declares independence.

October 11 The USSR State Council decides to dismember the KGB and change its name.

October 19 The Treaty on an Economic Community of Sovereign States is signed by eight republics.

October 28 The RSFSR Congress of People's Deputies grants Yeltsin the power to implement economic reform by decree for one year.

November 4 Republic leaders meeting in the USSR State Council agree to abolish all USSR ministries except those for defense, foreign affairs, railways, electric power, and nuclear power. Yeltsin tells the meeting that Russia does not intend to form its own army.

November 6 Yeltsin appoints himself RSFSR prime minister and names Gennady Burbulis, Yegor Gaidar, and Alexander Shokhin deputy prime ministers.

November 6 Yeltsin bans the CPSU and Russian Communist Party.

November 14 Yeltsin and other republic leaders in the USSR State Council agree that the new state should be a confederation.

November 15 Yeltsin issues ten decrees to take control over virtually all financial and economic activity in the territory of the RSFSR.

November 22 The RSFSR Supreme Soviet assumes control of the USSR State Bank.

November 25 Yeltsin and Shushkevich of Belarus refuse to initial the treaty of confederation that had been negotiated.

December 1 Citizens of Ukraine vote overwhelmingly for independence and elect Leonid Kravchuk president.

December 5 The Ukrainian parliament formally revokes Ukraine's accession to the treaty that created the USSR.

December 7–8 Yeltsin, Kravchuk, and Shushkevich meet at a hunting lodge near Brest. They decide to end the Soviet Union and create a Commonwealth of Independent States (CIS).

December 10 Belarus and Ukraine ratify the CIS agreement.

December 11 The Russian parliament ratifies the CIS agreement.

December 12 Central Asian leaders meeting in Ashkhabad request membership in CIS as founding members.

December 22 Leaders of eleven republics (all but Georgia) sign the Commonwealth Declaration in Alma Ata.

December 25 Gorbachev makes his resignation speech on television and the Russian flag replaces the Soviet flag over the Kremlin.

Dramatis Personae

Persons mentioned in the book from the USSR and its successors.
(*Only those positions and activities relevant to the narrative are listed.*)

Aasmee, Hardo (b. 1951)   Mayor of Tallinn in 1990–91; a leader of the Estonian National Front.

Abalkin, Leonid (b. 1930)   Economist and member of the USSR (Russian) Academy of Sciences. Deputy prime minister in the Ryzhkov government, responsible for economic reform.

Abdurakhmanov, Palat (b. 1940)   Uzbek CPSU official. First secretary of the Samarkand Oblast Party Committee in 1990 and 1991.

Adzhubey, Alexei Ivanovich (d. 1993)   Journalist. Nikita Khrushchev's son-in-law, who edited *Izvestiya* in the 1960s and interviewed President John Kennedy.

Afanasiev, Viktor Grigoryevich (1922–95)   Journalist. Editor of *Pravda* from 1976 to 1989, following a line more cautious than Gorbachev's after 1987; chairman of the Soviet Union of Journalists, 1976–90; member of the USSR Congress of People's Deputies and of the CPSU Central Committee.

Afanasiev, Yuri Nikolayevich (b. 1934)   Historian. Rector of the Moscow State Institute for Historical Archives during the perestroika period. Elected to the USSR Congress of People's Deputies in 1989, he was one of the original leaders of the democratic movement. Now rector of the Moscow State University for the Humanities.

Aganbegyan, Abel Gezevich (b. 1932)   Economist, member of the Academy of Sciences. Head of Economics Department of the USSR Academy of Sciences from 1986; rector of the Academy of the National Economy in the late 1980s and early 1990s; assisted Gorbachev in preparing the compromise draft of Ryzhkov and Shatalin reform plans of 1990.

Aitmatov, Chingiz (b. 1928)   Kyrgyz writer, noted for works challenging complacency and moral corruption of Brezhnev period. Member of the USSR Congress of People's Deputies and of Gorbachev's first Presidential Council. Named USSR ambassador to Luxembourg in 1990.

Akayev, Askar (b. 1944)   Physicist and politician. President of the Academy of Sciences of Kyrgyzstan until 1990, when elected president of Kyrgyzstan.

Akhromeyev, Sergei (1923–91)   Marshal of the Soviet army. Chief of the Soviet General Staff until December 1988, when he was named adviser to Gorbachev. Participated in abortive coup d'état in August 1991, after which he committed suicide.

Alexii II [Ridiger, Alexei Mikhailovich] (b. 1929)   Patriarch of Russian Orthodox Church from 1990.

Alexandrova, Tamara Alexeyevna Assistant to Anatoly Chernyayev.

Aliev, Heidar (b. 1923) Azerbaijani CPSU official. Ousted from the Soviet leadership by Gorbachev in 1987, Aliev made a political comeback in Azerbaijan in 1993 when he became president following Elchibey's flight from Baku. He had been a candidate, then full member of the Politburo, 1976–87; first secretary of the Communist Party of Azerbaijan, 1969–82; and deputy chairman of the USSR Council of Ministers, 1982–87. Before holding senior CPSU positions, he was a career officer in the KGB and its predecessor security agencies.

Alksnis, Viktor Imantovich (b. 1950) Army officer. Member of the USSR Congress of People's Deputies and of the Soyuz faction, which campaigned for imposition of direct presidential rule in 1991.

Andreyeva, Nina Teacher. Author of an article in *Sovetskaya Rossiya* in 1988 opposing Gorbachev's political reforms.

Andropov, Yuri Vladimirovich (1914–84) CPSU official. Chairman of the KGB from 1967, then succeeded Brezhnev as general secretary of the CPSU, 1982–84.

Antanaitis, Vaidotas Vito (b. 1928) Professor of forestry and Lithuanian politician. Member of the USSR Congress of People's Deputies and one of early Sąjūdis leaders.

Antanavičius, Kazimieras Antano (b. 1937) Economist and Lithuanian politician. Member of the USSR Congress of People's Deputies.

Antonovich, Ivan Ivanovich (b. 1937) CPSU official and political scientist. Member of the Politburo of Russian Communist Party, 1990–91. Since 1992 resident in Minsk, Belarus.

Arbatov, Georgy Arkadyevich (b. 1923) Political scientist and historian. Director, USSR (now Russian) USA and Canada Institute. Member of the USSR Congress of People's Deputies and of the CPSU Central Committee.

Aslonov, Kadriddin (b. 1947) Chairman of Council of Ministers of Tajikistan, 1990–91; briefly president of Tajikistan in 1991.

Avturkhanov, Umar (b. 1944) Chechen military and police officer turned politician. A political opponent of Dzhokar Dudayev, Avturkhanov was elected the local leader in one of Chechnya's regions in December 1991, following a career in the Soviet army and the Ministry of Internal Affairs. He immediately began to challenge Dudayev from his regional base. In 1994 his military forces received support from the Russian Counterintelligence Service (successor of the KGB) but despite an initially successful offensive they were defeated by Dudayev's forces in October on the outskirts of Grozny.

Bakatin, Vadim Viktorovich (b. 1937) CPSU official, politician. USSR minister of internal affairs, 1988–90; member of the USSR Security Council, 1990; unsuccessful candidate for president of RSFSR, 1991; last chairman of the KGB, 1991.

Baklanov, Grigory Yakovlevich (b. 1923) Writer. Editor of literary journal *Znamya* (The Banner) from 1986.

Baklanov, Oleg Dmitriyevich (b. 1932) CPSU official. One of the leaders of the attempted coup d'état in August 1991; had been the secretary of the CPSU Central Committee in charge of heavy and defense industry.

Belonogov, Alexander Mikhailovich (b. 1931) Diplomat. USSR deputy minister of foreign affairs, 1990–91.

Bessmertnykh, Alexander Alexandrovich (b. 1933) Diplomat. Succeeded Eduard

Shevardnadze as USSR minister of foreign affairs in 1991; previously Soviet ambassador to the United States and first deputy minister of foreign affairs.

Bičkauskas, Egidijus (b. 1955)   Lithuanian diplomat. Lithuanian representative in Moscow 1990–91, then Lithuanian ambassador to Russia. Elected to the USSR Congress of People's Deputies in 1989 and was one of the organizers and early leaders of Sąjūdis.

Birkavs, Valdis (b. 1942)   Latvian politician. Leader of Latvia's Way party, which won a plurality in the 1993 parliamentary elections, Birkavs became prime minister of Latvia in July 1993 but resigned a year later to become foreign minister.

Bišers, Ilmars (b. 1930)   Latvian lawyer and politician. Member of the USSR Congress of People's Deputies and, in 1990, first deputy chairman of the Latvian Council of Ministers.

Blokhin, Yuri Vitalyevich (b. 1944)   Economist. Member of the USSR Congress of People's Deputies and of the USSR Supreme Soviet. One of the leaders of the Soyuz faction.

Bocharov, Mikhail Alexandrovich (b. 1941)   Industrial manager. Member of the USSR Congress of People's Deputies and of the RSFSR Congress of People's Deputies; author of economic reform plans; unsuccessful candidate for chairman of the RSFSR Council of Ministers in 1990.

Bogomolov, Oleg Timofeyevich (b. 1927)   Economist and member of the Academy of Sciences. Director of the Institute of the Economy of the World Socialist System (subsequently renamed International Political and Economic Research Institute) and member of the USSR Congress of People's Deputies; one of the early leaders of the democratic movement; now associated with Nikolai Travkin in the Democratic Party of Russia; member of the Russian State Duma since 1994.

Boguslavskaya, Zoya Borisovna   Novelist and author. Author of essays, short stories, several novels, and an admiring book on American women.

Boldin, Valery Ivanovich (b. 1935)   Journalist and CPSU official. Gorbachev's chief of staff who joined the coup leaders in August 1991.

Bonner, Yelena Georgiyevna (b. 1922)   Pediatrician and political activist. Andrei Sakharov's wife; active member of democratic movements.

Bovin, Alexander (b. 1930)   Journalist. Author of press commentary sympathetic to reformers; named Soviet ambassador to Israel when diplomatic relations were renewed in 1991.

Brakov, Yevgeny Alexeyevich (b. 1937)   Industrial manager. Director of ZIL Automobile Plant in 1989 when he was the Party's candidate for the Moscow National Territorial District in the new USSR Congress of People's Deputies; received less than 7 percent of the vote and was defeated by Boris Yeltsin.

Brazauskas, Algirdas (b. 1932)   Lithuanian politician. First secretary of the Lithuanian Communist Party that broke away from the CPSU in December, 1990; vice-chairman of the Lithuanian Council of Ministers, 1991–92; chairman of Lithuanian Seimas, October 1992–February 1993; from February 1993, president of Lithuania.

Brezhnev, Leonid Ilyich (1906–82)   CPSU official. First secretary, then general secretary of the CPSU, 1964–82.

Bunich, Pavel Grigoryevich (b. 1929)   Economist. Member of the USSR Congress of People's Deputies active on the economic reform committee.

Burbulis, Gennady Eduardovich (b. 1945)   Philosopher and politician. Elected to the USSR Congress of People's Deputies in 1989 from Sverdlovsk oblast. Close political associate of Boris Yeltsin who was named first deputy chairman of the RSFSR Council of Ministers in 1991 and assisted in drafting the declaration of the Commonwealth of Independent States.

Burlatsky, Fyodor Mikhailovich (b. 1927)   Journalist and editor. Editor of *Literaturnaya gazeta,* 1986–91; member of the USSR Congress of People's Deputies, 1989–91.

Bykov, Vasily Vladimirovich (b. 1924)   Belarusian author and political activist. Member of the USSR Congress of People's Deputies and a leader of the Belarusian National Front.

Čepaitis, Virgilijus (b. 1937)   Lithuanian politician. Secretary-general of Sąjūdis in 1989; elected to the Lithuanian Supreme Council in 1990, where he served as chairman of the council's Commission on Civil Rights and Ethnic Relations.

Chebrikov, Viktor Mikhailovich (b. 1923)   CPSU official. Member of the CPSU Politburo, 1983–89; chairman of the KGB, 1982–88.

Chekhoyev, Anatoly Georgiyevich (b. 1950)   Ossetian CPSU official. Member of Soyuz faction in the USSR Congress of People's Deputies.

Chernenko, Konstantin (1911–85)   CPSU official. Member of the CPSU Politburo, 1978–85; succeeded Andropov as general secretary of the CPSU, 1984–85.

Chernomyrdin, Viktor Stepanovich (b. 1938)   Industrial manager and politician. Russian prime minister since December 1992; previously was USSR minister of the gas industry, 1985–89, and director of Gazprom, the state natural gas monopoly, 1989–92.

Chernichenko, Yuri Dmitrievich (b. 1929)   Writer. Member of democratic movement in the USSR Congress of People's Deputies; from 1992, Chairman of Peasant Party.

Chernyayev, Anatoly Sergeyevich (b. 1921)   CPSU official: Foreign affairs assistant to President Gorbachev, 1986–91; now with the Gorbachev Foundation.

Chikvaidze, David   Diplomat. Served in the Soviet embassy in Washington in the late 1980s, then in the Ministry of Foreign Affairs in Moscow and, in 1991, as protocol officer in the Office of the President of the USSR; currently an officer in the peacekeeping division of the United Nations Secretariat in New York.

Chornovil, Vyacheslav Maximovich (b. 1938)   Journalist. Arrested in 1967 for nationalist activity; following release started issuing samizdat journal *Ukrainian Herald* with news of dissident activity and the suppression of political dissent; arrested again in 1972; released in 1985; cofounder of Ukrainian Helsinki Watch Group; cofounder of Rukh; elected chairman of Lviv Oblast Soviet Executive Committee in 1989; elected to the Ukrainian Supreme Soviet in 1990; unsuccessful candidate for president of Ukraine in December 1991.

Dementei, Nikolai Ivanovich (b. 1937)   Belarusian Party official. Chairman of the Belorussian Supreme Soviet until removed in August 1991.

Dobrynin, Anatoly Fyodorovich (b. 1919)   Diplomat. Soviet ambassador to the United States, 1962–86; chief of the CPSU Central Committee International Department, 1986–88; adviser to President Gorbachev, 1988–91.

Doguzhiev, Vitaly Khusseinovich (b. 1935)   CPSU official. First deputy prime minister of USSR in 1991.

Drach, Ivan (b. 1936)   Ukrainian poet and politician. Head of the Ukrainian Writers' Union in the 1980s; chairman of Rukh from its formation; elected to Ukrainian Supreme Soviet in 1990; member of Executive Committee of Democratic Party of Ukraine.

Dudayev, Dzhokar (b. 1944)   Air force officer, Chechen politician. Then a lieutenant general in the Soviet air force, Dudayev was elected chairman of the unofficial National Congress of the Chechen People in 1990. Following the unsuccessful coup in Moscow in August 1991, he seized power in Grozny, the capital of Chechen-Ingushetia, declared independence from Russia, and refused to allow officially sponsored elections. Grozny became a center of arms and narcotics trade in 1992 and 1993 and many Russian officials considered Dudayev connected with organized crime in Russia and a beneficiary of the illicit trade. Dudayev and his supporters fiercely resisted the Russian invasion of Chechnya, which began in December 1994, inflicting heavy casualties on the Russian forces, and they continued to fight from the mountains and rural areas after the cities in Chechnya were occupied.

Dubinin, Yuri Vladimirovich (b. 1930)   Diplomat. Soviet ambassador to Spain, 1978–86; to the United States, 1986–90; to France, 1990–91.

Dzyuba, Ivan (b. 1931)   Ukrainian philologist. Wrote a report in 1965 entitled "Internationalism or Russification?" After it was published abroad and in samizdat, he was arrested in 1972 and sentenced to five years in prison and five years in exile; released in 1973 when he agreed to renounce his previous writings.

Elchibey, Abulfaz (b. 1938)   Azerbaijani orientalist and politician. Elected president of Azerbaijan in 1992 when he was leader of the Azerbaijan National Front. He was forced to resign in 1993 following military reverses in Nagorny Karabakh.

Falin, Valentin Mikhailovich (b. 1926)   Diplomat and CPSU official. Chief of CC CPSU International Department, 1990–91.

Filshin, Gennady Innokentyevich (b. 1931)   Economist. Member of reform group in the USSR Congress of People's Deputies and the USSR Supreme Soviet. Chairman of the RSFSR State Committee on the Economy in 1990.

Fokin, Vitold Pavlovich (b. 1932)   Economist and politician. Chairman of the Ukrainian Council of Ministers, 1990–92.

Fyodorov, Boris Grigoryevich (b. 1958)   Economist. RSFSR finance minister, 1990; directed Soviet operations for the European Bank for Reconstruction and Development in 1991 and early 1992; deputy prime minister and finance minister of the Russian Federation, 1992–94; one of the leaders of Russia's Choice in the December 1993 election; member of the Russian State Duma from 1994.

Gaidar, Yegor Timurovich (b. 1956)   Economist. First deputy prime minister, then acting prime minister of the Russian Federation, 1992, when he was considered the architect of the initial Russian economic reform. Subsequently, first deputy prime minister again from September 1993 to January 1994. Led Russia's Choice party in the December 1993 elections.

Gailis, Maris   Latvian politician. Prime minister from 1994, he was previously a deputy prime minister and the minister of state reforms.

Gamsakhurdia, Zviad (1939–93)   Georgian dissident who was elected president of Georgia in 1991 but ousted by his opponents in January 1992; lived in exile in Chechnya 1992–93.

Gayer, Yevdokia Alexandrovna (b. 1934)   Ethnographer. Representative of Maritime Province in USSR Congress of People's Deputies where she was a member of the democratic movement and a strong supporter of Andrei Sakharov.

Gdlyan, Telman Khorenovich (b. 1940)   Criminal investigator. Member of the USSR Congress of People's Deputies, 1989 91; earlier had prosecuted corruption cases in Uzbekistan and other republics and, in 1989, publicly accused several senior Soviet officials of corruption. When he and his associate, Nikolai Ivanov, were charged with employing illegal and coercive methods in their investigation, the Supreme Soviet refused to lift their parliamentary immunity to permit prosecution.

Genzėlis, Bronislavas (b. 1934)   Lithuanian philosopher and politician. Member of the USSR Congress of People's Deputies and early supporter of Sąjūdis.

Gerashchenko, Viktor Vladimirovich (b. 1937)   Economist. Chairman of the USSR State Bank, 1989–91; chairman of the Central Bank of Russia, 1992–94.

Girenko, Andrei Nikolayevich (b. 1936)   CPSU official. First secretary of Crimean oblast Party Committee until 1990, when he was named to the CPSU Secretariat in Moscow.

Godmanis, Ivars (b. 1951)   Latvian physicist and politician. Chairman, Latvian Council of Ministers, 1990–93; a deputy chairman of the Latvian People's Front during campaign for independence.

Gorbachev, Mikhail Sergeyevich (b. 1931)   CPSU official and politician. General secretary of the CPSU, 1985–91; chairman of the Presidium of the USSR Supreme Soviet, 1988–89; chairman of the USSR Supreme Soviet, 1989–90; president of the USSR, 1990–91; since December 1991 president of the Foundation for Social and Political Research (Gorbachev Foundation) in Moscow.

Gorbacheva, Raisa Maximovna (b. 1931)   Wife of Mikhail Gorbachev. Sponsored the USSR Cultural Fund from the mid-1980s until the collapse of the USSR in December 1991.

Gorbunovs, Anatolijs (b. 1942)   Latvian politician. Chairman of Latvian parliament, 1988–93; member of the USSR Congress of People's Deputies from 1989.

Goryacheva, Svetlana Petrovna (b. 1947)   Russian politician. The deputy chairman of the RSFSR Supreme Soviet who proposed Yeltsin's impeachment in March 1991.

Grachev, Pavel Sergeyevich (b. 1945)   Army general. Commander of Soviet airborne troops in 1991; from 1992, Russian defense minister.

Gräzin (Gryazin), Igor (b. 1952)   Estonian lawyer and politician. Member of the USSR Congress of People's Deputies and one of the organizers of the Estonian National Front.

Grechko, Georgy   Cosmonaut. The candidate for a seat in the USSR Congress of People's Deputies in the Moscow national-territorial district who withdrew during the nomination meeting in 1989 so that Boris Yeltsin would win a place on the ballot.

Grishin, Viktor Vasiliyevich (1914–92)   CPSU official. Member of the CPSU Politburo, 1971–86; first secretary of Moscow Party Organization, 1967–85; replaced by Boris Yeltsin in December 1985.

Gubenko, Nikolai Nikolayevich (b. 1941)   Actor and theater director. USSR Minister of Culture, 1989–91; also member of Gorbachev's Presidential Council in 1990.

Gurenko (Hurenko), Stanislav Ivanovich (b. 1936)   CPSU official. First secretary of the Ukrainian Communist Party, 1990–91.

Hadîrcă, Ion (b. 1949)   Moldovan writer. Early leader of Moldovan Popular Front and first deputy chairman of the Moldovan Supreme Soviet from 1990.

Harutiunian (Arutyunyan), Suren (b. 1939)   CPSU official. First secretary of Armenian Communist Party, 1988–90.

Horbal (Gorbal), Mykola (b. 1941)   Ukrainian dissident. A member of the Ukrainian Helsinki Watch Group who was sentenced repeatedly in the 1970s and 1980s for his dissident activity.

Horyn (Goryn), Mikhail (b. 1930)   Ukrainian psychologist and educator. Arrested in 1965 for nationalist activity and imprisoned for six years; arrested again in 1981; released in 1987; one of the organizers of Ukrainian Helsinki Watch Group; founding member of Rukh; elected to the Ukrainian Supreme Soviet in 1990.

Igitian, Genrikh (b. 1932)   Armenian museum director. Member of the USSR Congress of People's Deputies and founding member of the Interregional Group of Deputies.

Ignatenko, Vitaly Nikitich (b. 1941)   Journalist. Press spokesman for President Gorbachev, 1990–91.

Ivanov, Nikolai Veniaminovich (b. 1952)   Criminal investigator. As an official in the office of the USSR General Prosecutor, worked with Telman Gdlyan on the "cotton corruption scandal" in Uzbekistan in the mid-1980s; elected to the USSR Congress of People's Deputies in 1989; subsequently accused of abusing authority during investigations but the USSR Supreme Soviet refused to lift his parliamentary immunity to permit a legal prosecution.

Ivans, Dainis (b. 1956)   Latvian politician. Leader of Latvian People's Front; first deputy chairman of the Latvian Supreme Soviet, 1990–92.

Ivashko, Vladimir Antonovich (1932–94)   CPSU official. First secretary of Ukrainian Communist Party, 1989–90; deputy general secretary of the CPSU, 1990–91.

Izkander, Fazil (b. 1929)   Abkhazian writer of satiric prose.

Kabul (Qobul), Nurali   Uzbek writer; founding member of Erk opposition party.

Kalniņš, Ojars (b. 1948)   Diplomat. Public affairs director of the Latvian-American Association, 1985–91; traveled with a Chautauqua group to a conference in Jurmala, Latvia, in 1986; from 1992, Latvian ambassador to the United States.

Kalugin, Oleg Danilovich (b. 1934)   KGB officer who broke with the KGB in 1989 and was elected to the USSR Congress of People's Deputies in 1990.

Karimov, Islam (b. 1938)   Uzbek CPSU official. Communist Party leader in Uzbekistan, elected president in 1990; from December 1991, president of independent Uzbekistan.

Kashubin, Gennady   Soviet general. The USSR Ministry of Defense spokesman who issued the misleading cover story about the January 13, 1991, attack on the television tower in Vilnius.

Kasparov, Gary (b. 1963)   Chess grand master and politician. Won Soviet chess championship in 1981 and 1982, then defeated Anatoly Karpov for the world title in 1985; an early leader in the democratic movement, at first associated with Nikolai Travkin, then with Arkady Murashev.

Kasymov, Gani   Kazakh diplomat. Assistant to President Nursultan Nazarbayev of Kazakhstan.

Kauls, Albert (b. 1938)   Latvian chairman of an agricultural enterprise. Member of the USSR Congress of People's Deputies and of Gorbachev's first Presidential Council.

Kazannik, Alexei Ivanovich (b. 1941)   Lawyer and jurist. Member of USSR Congress of People's Deputies who relinquished his seat on the USSR Supreme Soviet to Boris Yeltsin. Subsequently, prosecutor-general of the Russian Federation, 1993–94.

Kebich, Vyacheslav Frantsevich (b. 1936)   CPSU official. Chairman of Belorussian Council of Ministers before and after independence; political rival of Stanislav Shushkevich; both ran for president of Belarus in 1994 but lost to Alexander Lukashenka.

Khasbulatov, Ruslan Imranovich (b. 1942)   First deputy chairman of the RSFSR Supreme Soviet, 1990–91; chairman of the Russian Supreme Soviet, 1991–93.

Kirill, Archbishop   Russian Orthodox clergyman. Head of external relations for the Russian Orthodox Church in 1990 and 1991.

Kiselev, Valery Vasiliyevich (b. 1940)   Economist. Member of the RSFSR Congress of People's Deputies from Novo-Kuznetsk.

Kitovani, Tengiz   Georgian military officer. The head of the Georgian National Guard in 1991 who cooperated in the overthrow of President Zviad Gamsakhurdia. Subsequently, as Georgian minister of defense, led an unauthorized attack on the parliament building in Sukhumi that resulted in a Georgian defeat. Arrested in January 1995 for plotting to attack Abkhazia with irregular forces.

Kolbin, Gennady Vasiliyevich (b. 1927)   CPSU official. Replaced Kunayev as first secretary of the Kazakhstan Communist Party in December 1986, which precipitated riots. Subsequently (1989–91) served as chairman of the USSR People's Control Committee.

Komar, Dmitri (b. 1991)   Young man killed by tank during coup attempt in August 1991.

Komplektov, Viktor Georgiyevich (b. 1932)   Diplomat. Soviet ambassador to the United States in 1991.

Komplektova, Alla   Head of the American Division of Intourist in the 1980s.

Korotich, Vitaly Alexeyevich (b. 1936)   Ukrainian poet and editor. Editor of *Ogonyok*, 1986–91. Also member of the USSR Congress of People's Deputies and an activist in the democratic movement.

Korzhakov, Alexander Vasiliyevich   Security officer. Boris Yeltsin's personal security guard who subsequently became the chief of presidential security in the Russian Federation and a member of the Russian Security Council.

Kovalev, Anatoly Gavrilovich (b. 1923)   Diplomat and poet. First deputy minister of foreign affairs of the USSR, 1986–91.

Kovalev, Sergei Adamovich (b. 1949)   Human rights activist who was arrested in 1975 and sent to prison for distributing opposition literature. After his release, won election to the RSFSR Congress of People's Deputies and became chairman of the Russian parliament's Committee on Human Rights. An early Yeltsin supporter, he was one of Yeltsin's severest critics after the invasion of Chechnya which began in December 1994.

Kozyrev, Andrei Vladimirovich (b. 1951)   Diplomat. Russian minister of foreign affairs from 1991.

Kravchenko, Leonid Petrovich (b. 1938)   Journalist. Member of the USSR Congress of People's Deputies; placed in charge of central television in late 1990.

Kravchuk, Leonid Makarovich (b. 1934)   CPSU official and Ukrainian politician. Chairman of Ukrainian Supreme Soviet, 1990–91; president of Ukraine, 1991–94.

Krichevsky, Ilya (d. 1991)   One of the three young men killed during the coup attempt in August 1991.

Kuchma, Leonid (b. 1938)   Ukrainian industrial manager and politician. When named prime minister of Ukraine in 1992, Kuchma was the director of a large missile plant in Dnipropetrovsk, where he had worked for most of his career. He stayed in office as prime minister for barely a year, resigning in September 1993. In 1994 he was elected president with an overwhelming vote from eastern Ukraine and embarked on a vigorous program of economic reform.

Kryuchkov, Vladimir Alexandrovich (b. 1924)   Intelligence officer. Chairman of the KGB, 1988–91; previously directed the KGB's foreign intelligence directorate; one of the organizers of the August 1991 coup attempt; arrested in August 1991 but amnestied by the Russian parliament in 1994.

Kunayev, Dinmukhamed (1912–93)   Kazakh CPSU official. First secretary of the Communist Party of Kazakhstan during Brezhnev period; replaced by Gennady Kolbin in December 1986, and removed from Politburo the following year.

Kurashvili, Boris (b. 1925)   Legal scholar. Researcher in the USSR Institute of State and Law who promoted the concept of a multiparty system and suggested the formation of movements to support perestroika.

Kuzmickas, Bronius (b. 1935)   Lithuanian politician. Deputy chairman of the Lithuanian Supreme Council from 1990.

Kuzmin, Fyodor Mikhailovich (b. 1937)   Army general. Commander of Baltic Military District, 1989–91; endorsed the attempted coup against Gorbachev in August 1991.

Kvitsinsky, Yuli Alexandrovich (b. 1936)   Diplomat. Deputy minister of foreign affairs from 1990.

Laar, Mart (b. 1960)   Estonian historian and politician. Prime minister of Estonia, 1992–94; previously had been a founding member of the Estonian Heritage Society (1988) and of the Estonian Christian Democratic Union (1989); since 1992 has been the leader of the Isamaa (Pro Patria, or Fatherland) party.

Landsbergis, Vytautas (b. 1932)   Lithuanian musicologist and politician. Member of the USSR Congress of People's Deputies from 1989; chairman of Sąjūdis; chairman of the Lithuanian Supreme Council, 1990–92.

Laptev, Ivan Dmitriyevich (b. 1934)   Journalist and politician. Editor of *Izvestiya* from 1986 to 1990; member of the USSR Congress of People's Deputies from 1989; chairman of the Council of the Union of the USSR Supreme Soviet, 1990–91.

Lauristin, Marju (b. 1949)   Estonian philologist and politician. Member of the USSR Congress of People's Deputies from 1989 and cofounder of the Estonian National Front; deputy chairman of the Estonian Supreme Soviet from 1990.

Lebed, Alexander Ivanovich   Army general. Commander of Tula Airborne Division, 1989–91; commander of the 14th Russian Army in Moldova from 1992.

Ligachev, Yegor Kuzmich (b. 1920)   CPSU official. First secretary, Tomsk Oblast Party Committee, 1965–83; member of Secretariat, CPSU Central Committee, 1983–90; member of Politburo, 1985–90.

Likachev, Dmitri Sergeyevich (b. 1906)   Philologist and historian. Chairman of the Soviet Cultural Foundation, 1987–90; member of the USSR Congress of People's Deputies from 1989.

Lobzova, Ludmila   Director, Pushkin Museum in Kishinev in 1990.

Lubenchenko, Konstantin Dmitriyevich (b. 1945)   Law professor. Member of the USSR Congress of People's Deputies and USSR Supreme Soviet, 1989–91.

Lucinschi (Luchinsky), Petru (Pyotr) (b. 1940)   CPSU official and Moldovan politician. First secretary of the Moldavian Communist Party, 1989–90; member of the CPSU Politburo, 1990–91; from 1994, chairman of Moldovan parliament.

Lukashenka, Alexander Rygarevich (b. 1954)   Belarusian politician. Elected president of Belarus in 1994; had been a member of the Belarusian Supreme Soviet since 1990 and was the only deputy to vote against Belarusian adherence to the Commonwealth of Independent States in December 1991.

Lukin, Vladimir Petrovich (b. 1937)   Scholar, diplomat, and politician. Member of the RSFSR Congress of People's Deputies from 1990 and head of its committee on international relations; Russian ambassador to the United States, 1992–94; member of Russian State Duma from 1994.

Lukyanenko, Levko Grigoryevich (b. 1927)   Trained as a lawyer. Arrested in 1961 on suspicion of nationalist activity and spent fifteen years in prison camps; released in 1976 after which he helped organize Ukrainian Helsinki Watch Group; arrested again in 1977, sentenced to ten years imprisonment; released in 1988; a cofounder of the revived Ukrainian Helsinki Watch Group and, in 1989, of the Republican Party of Ukraine; elected to Ukrainian Supreme Soviet in 1990; unsuccessful candidate for president of Ukraine in December 1991.

Lukyanov, Anatoly Ivanovich (b. 1930)   Lawyer and CPSU official. Deputy chairman of the USSR Supreme Soviet, 1989–90; chairman of the USSR Supreme Soviet, 1990–91.

Luzhkov, Yuri Mikhailovich   Politician. Luzhkov was an official in the Moscow city administration in 1990 when Gavriil Popov, then mayor, backed his election as chairman of the Moscow City Soviet Executive Committee—the city council. When Popov resigned his office in 1992, Luzhkov succeeded him as mayor. He is a strong executive and, by 1995, was considered one of the most powerful political figures in Russia.

Makashov, Albert Mikhailovich (b. 1938)   Army general. Member of the USSR Congress of People's Deputies, 1989–91; unsuccessful candidate for Russian presidency, 1991.

Makhkamov, Kakhar (b. 1932)   Tajik CPSU official. First secretary, Communist Party of Tajikistan, 1985–91; president of Tajikistan, 1990–91.

Malkina, Tatyana   Journalist who posed sharp questions to coup leaders on August 19, 1991.

Manukian, Vazgen (b. 1946)   Armenian politician. Chairman of the Armenian Council of Ministers, 1990–91.

Marchan, Amman   Uzbek writer. A founding member of the opposition party Erk.

Martynov, Vladlen (b. 1929)   Economist. Director, Institute of the World Economy and International Relations from 1989.

Maslyukov, Yuri (b. 1937)   CPSU official. Chairman of the USSR State Planning Committee (Gosplan), 1987–91.

Medvedev, Nikolai   Ethnic Russian who spoke in favor of Lithuanian independence at a rally in Vilnius during Gorbachev's visit in January 1990.

Medvedev, Roy Alexandrovich (b. 1925)   Writer and historian. Considered a dissident during the Brezhnev period; member of the USSR Congress of People's Deputies, 1989–91

Medvedev, Vadim Andreyevich (b. 1929) Economist and CPSU official. Member of the Politburo, 1988–90, during which time he headed the Party's Ideology Department; member of the USSR Congress of People's Deputies; member of Gorbachev's Presidential Council in 1990.

Meri, Lennart (b. 1929) Estonian filmmaker, novelist, and politician. President of Estonia from 1992; previously Estonian foreign minister, 1990–92.

Mikhailov, Alexei Economist associated with Grigory Yavlinsky in 1991.

Moiseyev, Mikhail Alexeyevich (b. 1939) Army general. Chief of Soviet General Staff, 1989–91.

Motieka, Kazimieras (b. 1929) Lithuanian politician. Member of the USSR Congress of People's Deputies from 1989, and deputy chairman of the Lithuanian Supreme Council in 1990.

Murashev, Arkady Nikolayevich (b. 1950) Physicist and politician. Elected to the USSR Congress of People's Deputies in 1989; one of the organizers of the democratic movement; in 1992, chief of "militia" (police) in Moscow.

Mutalibov, Ayaz (b. 1938) Azerbaijani politician. Chairman of Azerbaijan Council of Ministers, 1989–90; first secretary, Azerbaijan Communist Party, 1990–91; president of Azerbaijan, 1990–92.

Nabiev, Rakhman (b. 1930) Tajik CPSU official. First secretary of the Tajikistan Communist Party, 1982–85; brought back to power in Tajikistan in the fall of 1991, after which he won an election for president; the opposition, however, charged fraud and a civil war broke out in the spring of 1992, which led to Nabiev's resignation a few months later.

Nazarbayev, Nursultan (b. 1940) Kazakh politician. Chairman of Kazakhstan Council of Ministers, 1984–89; first secretary, Communist Party of Kazakhstan, 1989–91; president of Kazakhstan from 1990.

Nenashev, Mikhail Fyodorovich (b. 1925) Media executive. Chairman of state television until 1990, then chairman of the USSR State Committee on the Press, 1990–91.

Nishanov, Rafik (b. 1926) Uzbek CPSU official. First secretary, Uzbek Communist Party, 1988–89; chairman of the USSR Supreme Soviet Council of Nationalities, 1989–91.

Niyazov, Saparmurad (b. 1940) Turkmen Party official. First secretary, Communist Party of Turkmenistan, 1985–91; president of Turkmenistan from 1990.

Novozhilov, Viktor (b. 1939) Army general. Commander of the Far East Military District, 1989–91.

Obolensky, Alexander Mitrofanovich (b. 1943) Mining engineer. Member of the USSR Congress of People's Deputies who ran against Gorbachev for chairman in 1989.

Obukhov, Alexei Alexandrovich (b. 1937) Diplomat. Deputy USSR foreign minister in charge of U.S. affairs, 1990–91; previously was a negotiator on strategic nuclear weapons.

Orlov, Yuri Fyodorovich (b. 1924) Physicist and human rights activist. Organizer of the Moscow Helsinki Watch Group in 1976, he was subsequently arrested and held in prison camps until he was released in 1986 in exchange for a KGB officer arrested in New York.

Osipyan, Yuri Andreyevich (b. 1931) Physicist and member of the USSR Academy of Sciences. Member of the USSR Congress of People's Deputies and of Gorbachev's Presidential Council in 1990.

Oskotsky, Valentin Political activist in the democratic movement.

Ozolas, Romualdas (b. 1939) Lithuanian politician. Member of the USSR Congress of People's Deputies from 1989; one of the founders of Sąjūdis; deputy prime minister of Lithuania in 1990–91.

Palm, Viktor (b. 1926) Chemist and Estonian politician. Member of USSR Congress of People's Deputies from 1989 and one of the founders of the Interregional Group of Deputies.

Pankin, Boris Dmitriyevich (b. 1931) Diplomat. Soviet ambassador to Czechoslovakia, 1990–91; denounced August coup attempt and was named USSR minister of foreign affairs following the coup attempt.

Patiashvili, Dzhumber (b. 1939) CPSU official. First secretary of the Georgian Communist Party in April 1989, when a demonstration was broken up by force and many killed; blamed for calling in troops and was replaced a few days later.

Pavlov, Valentin Sergeyevich (b. 1937) Economist. USSR minister of finance, 1989–91; prime minister, 1991; arrested following attempted coup in August 1991, but amnestied by the Russian State Duma in 1994.

Petrakov, Nikolai Yakovlevich (b. 1937) Economist. Member, USSR Congress of People's Deputies from 1989; director, Institute of the Market, 1990–91; Gorbachev adviser on economic reform, 1990, but resigned in January 1991 with sharp criticism of Gorbachev's policy.

Petrov, Yuri Vladimirovich Chief of staff in office of Russian president, 1991; head of State Investment Corporation since 1993.

Petrushenko, Nikolai Semyonovich (b. 1950) Army officer. Member of the USSR Congress of People's Deputies who adhered to *Soyuz* faction and agitated for imposition of presidential rule.

Piyasheva, Larisa Ivanovna Economist. Active in campaigning for economic reform; from 1992 worked on privatization issues in Moscow city administration.

Plekhanov, Yuri Sergeyevich KGB general. Chief, KGB Personnel Protection Directorate, 1989–91; in August 1991 cooperated with the coup plotters to hold Gorbachev incommunicado in the Crimea.

Polozkov, Ivan Kuzmich (b. 1935) CPSU official. First secretary of the Russian Communist Party, 1990–91.

Poltoranin, Mikhail Nikiforovich (b. 1939) Journalist and editor. Editor of *Moskovskaya Pravda*, 1986–87; member of the USSR Congress of People's Deputies from 1989 and acted as an unofficial political adviser to Boris Yeltsin; RSFSR minister for the press and information media, 1990–91.

Popov, Gavriil Kharitonovich (b. 1936) Economist. Editor of *Voprosy Ekonomiki*; member of the USSR Congress of People's Deputies from 1989 and one of the founders of the democratic movement; elected mayor of Moscow in 1991, but resigned in 1993; now president of the International University in Moscow.

Portnikov, Vitaly Journalist and political observer.

Primakov, Yevgeny Maximovich (b. 1929) Political scientist and CPSU official. Director of the Institute of World Economy and International Relations, 1985–89; member of the USSR Congress of People's Deputies from 1989; chairman of the Council of the Union of the USSR Supreme Soviet, 1990–91; candidate member of the Politburo, 1990–91; member of the USSR Security Council in 1991; from 1992, director of the Russian Foreign Intelligence Service.

Prokhanov, Alexander (b. 1938) Journalist and writer. Writer of polemical articles, particularly from 1990, advocating using force to preserve the USSR; in 1995, editor of right-wing newspaper *Zavtra* (Tomorrow), formerly *Den'* (The Day).

Prunskienė, Kazimiera (b. 1943) Economist and Lithuanian politician. Member of the USSR Congress of People's Deputies from 1989; prime minister of Lithuania, 1990–91; replaced just before the attack on the Vilnius television tower in January 13, 1991.

Pugo, Boris Karlovich (1937–91) CPSU official. First secretary, Latvian Communist Party, 1984–88; chairman, CPSU Party Control Committee, 1988–90; USSR minister of internal affairs, 1990–91; committed suicide following 1991 attempted coup.

Rashidov, Sharaf (d. 1983) Uzbek CPSU official. First secretary of the Uzbekistan Communist Party, 1959–83.

Rasputin, Valentin Grigoryevich (b. 1937) Writer. Member of the USSR Congress of People's Deputies from 1989 and of the Presidential Council in 1990.

Revenko, Grigory Ivanovich (b. 1936) CPSU official. Member of the USSR Congress of People's Deputies from 1989 and adviser to Gorbachev in 1991 with responsibility for negotiating the union treaty.

Rodionov, Igor Nikolayevich Army general. In command of the troops that attacked a peaceful demonstration in Tbilisi in April 1989, with heavy loss of life.

Romanov, Grigory Vasilyevich (b. 1923) CPSU official. First secretary of the Leningrad City Party Organization, 1970–83; secretary of CC CPSU, 1983–85; candidate, then full member of the Politburo, 1973–85. Considered a Gorbachev rival, he was forced to retire shortly after Gorbachev became CPSU general secretary.

Rostropovich, Mstislav Leopoldovich (b. 1927) Conductor and cellist. Exiled in 1974 because of his support for Alexander Solzhenitsyn, Rostropovich became director of the National Symphony Orchestra in Washington; from 1989 he returned occasionally for concerts in Russia, including a dramatic entry during the coup attempt in August 1991 when he rushed to Moscow and played his violoncello for the Yeltsin supporters gathered around the Russian White House.

Rubiks, Alfreds (b. 1935) CPSU official. Hard-line Latvian Communist Party leader who opposed independence movement. Supported attempted coup in August 1991 and subsequently was arrested.

Rutskoy, Alexander Vladimirovich (b. 1947) Air Force general. Elected to the RSFSR Congress of People's Deputies in 1990, where he supported Yeltsin for chairman; elected RSFSR vice president in June 1991, but began to oppose Yeltsin in 1992, and in 1993 attempted to take power in Russia; arrested after the Russian parliament building was stormed in October 1993; amnestied by the Russian State Duma in 1994.

Rüütel, Arnold (b. 1928) Estonian politician. Elected to USSR Congress of People's Deputies in 1989; chairman of the Estonian Supreme Soviet during the struggle for independence and until 1992.

Ryzhkov, Nikolai Ivanovich (b. 1929) Manager and CPSU official. Chairman of the USSR Council of Ministers (prime minister), 1985–90; unsuccessful candidate for president of Russia, 1991.

Ryzhov, Yuri Alexeyevich (b. 1930) Professor. Rector of the Orjonikidze Aviation

Institute in Moscow when elected to the USSR Congress of People's Deputies in 1989; founding member of the Interregional Group of Deputies and early Yeltsin supporter. Since 1992, Russian ambassador to France.

Sagdeyev, Roald Zinnurovich (b. 1932) Space scientist and member of the USSR Academy of Sciences. Director of a space research institute when elected to the USSR Congress of People's Deputies in 1989, he was a close associate of Andrei Sakharov and one of the founders of the democratic movement.

Sakharov, Andrei Dmitriyevich (1922–89) Physicist, human rights activist. Released from his internal exile in Gorky in December 1986, Sakharov played an increasingly active political role before winning election to the USSR Congress of People's Deputies in 1989. He was one of the founders of the Interregional Group of Deputies and an intellectual leader of the democratic movement until his death in December 1989.

Sangheli, Andrei (b. 1944) Moldovan politician. Moldovan minister of agriculture and food, 1990–92; formed a "government of national consensus" in 1992 and has been Moldovan prime minister since then.

Savisaar, Eduard (b. 1950) Estonian philosophy professor and politician. Elected to the USSR Congress of People's Deputies in 1989; chairman of the Estonian Council of Ministers, 1990–92; leader of the Center Party.

Shakhrai, Sergei Mikhailovich (b. 1956) Russian politician. Elected to the RSFSR Congress of People's Deputies in 1990, he was an early Yeltsin supporter; from 1992 a deputy Russian prime minister and, until 1994, chairman of the State Committee on Nationality Policy; from 1993, chairman of the Russian Party of Unity and Accord, which won nineteen seats in the Russian State Duma in the December 1993 elections.

Shaposhnikov, Yevgeny Ivanovich (b. 1942) Air force general. Opposed attempted coup in August 1991 and was subsequently named USSR minister of defense, and then to head the CIS armed forces.

Shatalin, Stanislav Sergeyevich (b. 1934) Economist and member of the Academy of Sciences. Member of the Presidential Council in 1990 and headed commission in August 1991 to draft a plan for economic reform. Broke with Gorbachev and became an adviser to Yeltsin when the plan his commission developed was not adopted.

Shcherbakov, Vladimir Ivanovich (b. 1949) Economist. Deputy USSR prime minister in 1991; accompanied Primakov and Yavlinsky to Washington in June 1991 to explain plans for economic reform.

Shcherbitsky, Vladimir Vasilyevich (1918–90) Ukrainian CPSU official. First secretary of the Communist Party of Ukraine, 1971–89; member of the CPSU Politburo, 1971–89.

Shenin, Oleg Semyonovich (b. 1937) CPSU official. Member of the CPSU Politburo, 1990–91 and secretary of the CPSU Central Committee responsible for personnel. Supported attempted coup in August 1991.

Shevardnadze, Eduard Ambrosiyevich (b. 1928) Georgian politician. Minister of foreign affairs of USSR, 1985–90, then briefly in November–December 1991. From March 1992, chief of state of the Georgian Republic.

Shmelev, Nikolai Petrovich (b. 1936) Economist and writer. Elected to the USSR

Congress of People's Deputies in 1989; took an active part in the democratic movement and in advising on economic reform.

Shokhin, Alexander Nikolayevich (b. 1951) Economist and politician. Deputy prime minister of the Russian government from 1991 in charge of social policy; a leader of the Russian Party of Unity and Accord; member of the Russian State Duma from 1994.

Shostakovsky, Vyacheslav Rector of the Higher Party School in 1989 and an activist in the democratic movement.

Shushkevich, Stanislav Stanislavovich (b. 1934) Belarusian physicist and politician. Elected to the USSR Congress of People's Deputies in 1989, he was also deputy chairman of the Belorussian parliament in 1990–91. Following the attempted coup in August 1991 he was elected chairman of the Belarusian parliament, in which capacity he signed the declaration creating the Commonwealth of Independent States in December 1991 and became the first chief of state of independent Belarus. Forced to resign in early 1994, he ran an unsuccessful campaign for the presidency of Belarus later in the year.

Sigua, Tengiz (b. 1934) Georgian politician. Chairman of Georgian Council of Ministers from November 1990, he was dismissed by Gamsakhurdia in August 1991. Thereafter, he joined the coalition that removed Gamsakhurdia and invited Shevardnadze to return to Georgia.

Silayev, Ivan Stepanovich (b. 1930) Engineer and industrial manager. Chairman of the RSFSR council of ministers (prime minister), 1990–91; after the August coup was placed in charge of the USSR economic ministries and the interrepublic economic coordination committee that existed until December 1991.

Sitaryan, Stepan Aramaisovich (b. 1930) Economist. Deputy chairman of the USSR Council of Ministers, 1989–91, and from 1990 chairman of its foreign economic commission.

Skoryk, Larysa Pavlovna (b. 1939) Ukrainian theater director and political activist. A member of Rukh, she was elected to the Ukrainian parliament from a district in Kiev in 1990; in December 1991 supported Leonid Kravchuk for president instead of Vyacheslav Chornovil, the Rukh leader.

Snegur, Mircea (b. 1940) Moldovan politician. Chairman of the Moldavian parliament when the language law was approved in 1989. Elected president of Moldova in 1990.

Sobchak, Anatoly Alexandrovich (b. 1937) Law professor and politician. Elected to the USSR Congress of People's Deputies in 1989; one of the founders of the Interregional Group of Deputies and the democratic movement; elected Mayor of Saint Petersburg in 1991; cochairman of the Movement for Democratic Reforms (DDR) from 1991.

Sokolov, Sergei Leonidovich (b. 1911) Army general. Relieved as USSR minister of defense after Mathias Rust landed a Cessna on Red Square in 1987.

Solomentsev, Mikhail Sergeyevich (b. 1913) CPSU official. Prime minister of the RSFSR, 1971–83; chairman of the Party Control Committee, 1983–88; candidate, then full member of the CPSU Politburo, 1971–88.

Solovyov, Yuri Filippovich (b. 1925) CPSU official. First secretary of the Leningrad Oblast Party Organization, 1985–89; candidate member of the CPSU Politburo, 1986–89; removed from both positions following his defeat in the elections for the USSR Congress of People's Deputies.

Solzhenitsyn, Alexander Isayevich (b. 1918) Russian writer. Deprived of his Soviet citizenship and forced into exile in 1973 after writing *The Gulag Archipelago,* which blamed Lenin for creating the prison camps filled by Stalin, he lived in the United States from 1976 until his return to Russia in 1994. In 1990 he published an extended essay entitled "Rebuilding Russia," in which he proposed the dissolution of the Soviet Union and the creation of a Slavic state including Russia, Belarus, Ukraine, and northern Kazakhstan.

Stankevich, Sergei Borisovich (b. 1954)   Historian and politician. Elected to the USSR Congress of People's Deputies in 1989; active in organizing the Interregional Group of Deputies and the democratic movement; in 1990–91, deputy chairman of Moscow City Council; from 1992, state secretary in the Russian government and from 1994 a member of the Russian State Duma.

Stankevičius, Česlovas (b. 1937)   Lithuanian politician. Deputy chairman of the Lithuanian Supreme Council, 1990–92.

Starkov, Vladislav Andreyevich (b. 1940)   Journalist. Editor of *Argumenty i Fakty;* elected to the RSFSR Congress of People's Deputies in 1990; strong supporter of freedom of the press.

Starodubtsev, Vasily Alexandrovich (b. 1931)   Agronomist. Chairman of a collective farm in Tula oblast and chairman of the USSR Peasant Union when he joined the emergency committee during the August 1991 coup attempt. He was arrested in August 1991, but released subsequently and amnestied by the Russian State Duma in 1994.

Starovoitova, Galina Vasilyevna (b. 1946)   Ethnographer and politician. Elected to the USSR Congress of People's Deputies in 1989; active in the Interregional Group of Deputies and democratic movement; elected to the RSFSR Congress of People's Deputies in 1990; adviser to Yeltsin on ethnic issues in 1992; head of the Center for Ethno-political Studies at the Institute for the Economy in Transition, and editor of the newspaper *Yevropeyets* (The European).

Stepanov, Teymuraz (b. 1934)   Personal assistant to Eduard Shevardnadze in the USSR Ministry of Foreign Affairs, 1985–90, and since 1992 in the office of the Georgian chief of state.

Sukhodrev, Viktor Mikhailovich (b. 1932)   Diplomat. Senior officer in the U.S. division of the USSR Ministry of Foreign Affairs during most of the 1980s and frequent English interpreter for Soviet leaders from Brezhnev to Gorbachev.

Suleimenov, Olzhas Omarovich (b. 1936)   Kazakh poet. First secretary of the Kazakhstan Union of Writers and member of the USSR Congress of People's Deputies, 1989–91; organized Nevada-Semipalatinsk Society to campaign against nuclear testing in Kazakhstan; considered a potential political rival to President Nazarbayev.

Tarasenko, Sergei Petrovich (b. 1937)   Diplomat. Headed the General Secretariat in the Ministry of Foreign Affairs, 1987–91; acted as a confidential interlocutor for Foreign Minister Shevardnadze.

Ter-Petrosian, Levon (b. 1945)   Armenian politician. Elected chairman of Armenian Supreme Soviet in 1990, then president of Armenia.

Terekhov, Vladislav   Journalist. As representative of Interfax News Agency, he sharply questioned Gorbachev about the future of the Communist Party at a press conference just after the August 1991 coup attempt.

Terelya, Iosyp (b. 1943)   Religious activist. Imprisoned from 1962 on various charges, he organized an Initiative Group to press for legalization of the Ukrainian Catholic (Uniate) Church in the early 1980s; arrested again and sentenced to a prison term.

Tikhonov, Georgy Ivanovich (b. 1934)   Economist. Elected to the USSR Congress of People's Deputies in 1989 from a district in Tajikistan; active member of Soyuz.

Tikhonov, Nikolai (1905–93)   CPSU official. Member of the CPSU Politburo and chairman of the USSR Council of Ministers until replaced by Ryzhkov in 1985. He had been a rival of Gorbachev in the Politburo.

Tizyakov, Alexander Ivanovich (b. 1926)   Industrial manager. In 1991 was general director of the Kalinin Machine-Building Plant in Sverdlovsk and the president of the USSR Association of State Enterprises and Industrial, Construction, and Communications Facilities; joined the attempted coup in August 1991 as a member of the emergency committee; arrested in August 1991 but subsequently released and amnestied by the Russian State Duma in 1994.

Travkin, Nikolai Ilyich (b. 1946)   One of the founders of the Democratic Party of Russia. Elected to the USSR Congress of People's Deputies in March 1989, and served in the USSR Supreme Soviet, 1989–91; elected to the Russian State Duma in December 1993.

Tretyakov, Vitaly   Journalist. Founder and editor of *Nezavisimaya gazeta,* from 1990.

Tsereteli, Zurab Konstantinovich (b. 1934)   Georgian artist and sculptor. A prolific artist, he contributed one of his sculptures to the park near the headquarters building of the United Nations in New York. Many others are in major cities of the former Soviet Union and elsewhere.

Tsipko, Alexander Sergeyevich (b. 1941)   Writer and philosopher. Wrote some of the first published criticisms of Lenin when he was working as a consultant to the CPSU International Department between 1986 and 1990; from 1990–91 was a deputy director in Bogomolov's Institute for the World Socialist Economy; defended the preservation of the Soviet Union in 1991; from 1992 on the staff of the Gorbachev Institute.

Tuleyev, Amangeldy (b. 1944)   Ethnic Kazakh who was chairman of the Kemerovo Oblast Soviet in 1990; elected to the RSFSR Congress of People's Deputies in 1990; ran unsuccessfully for president of the RSFSR in 1991.

Ulmanis, Guntis (b. 1939)   Latvian economist and politician. Elected president of Latvia by the Latvian parliament in July 1993.

Ungureanu, Ion Spiridon (b. 1935)   Moldovan theater director and stage designer. Moldovan minister of culture in 1990 and a leader of the Moldovan National Front.

Usmankhodzhayev, Inamzhon (b. 1930)   Uzbek CPSU official. Followed Rashidov as first secretary of the Uzbekistan Communist Party in 1983, but was removed in January 1988 and subsequently convicted of corruption.

Usov, Vladimir (d. 1991)   Young man killed during the attempted coup in August 1991.

Ustinov, Dmitri (1908–84)   CPSU official. USSR minister of defense, 1976–84, and member of the CPSU Politburo.

Vähi, Tiit (b. 1947)   Estonian factory manager and politician. Estonian minister of transportation, 1989–92; prime minister of Estonia in 1992; became prime minister again in April 1995 after the coalition he headed won the elections to the Estonian parliament.

Vakhidov, Erkin   Uzbek poet. One of the founders of the Erk party in Uzbekistan.

Väljas, Vaino (b. 1931)   Estonian CPSU official. First secretary of the Estonian Communist Party, 1989–91.

Varennikov, Valentin Ivanovich (b. 1923)   Army general. Commander of Soviet ground forces in 1991 when he supported the attempt to remove Gorbachev; was a member of the group that confronted Gorbachev in Foros, Crimea, on August 18, 1991.

Velikhov, Yevgeny Pavlovich (b. 1935)   Physicist and member of the USSR Academy of Sciences. One of Gorbachev's advisers on science policy; member of the USSR Congress of People's Deputies and of the USSR Supreme Soviet, 1989–91.

Vezirov, Abdulrakhman Halil ogly (b. 1930)   Azerbaijani CPSU official. He was the first secretary of the Azerbaijan Communist Party when the National Front seized power in January 1990. Replaced at that time by Ayaz Mutalibov.

Vishnevsky, Sergei (d. ca. 1988)   Journalist. *Pravda* correspondent and political commentator in the 1970s and 1980s.

Vlasov, Alexander Vladimirovich (b. 1932)   CPSU official. Lost the election for chairman of the RSFSR Supreme Soviet to Boris Yeltsin in May 1990. He had been chairman of the RSFSR Council of Ministers since 1988, and before that was USSR minister of internal affairs.

Volkogonov, Dmitri Antonovich (b. 1928)   Army general and historian. Elected to the RSFSR Congress of People's Deputies in 1990 and was the first Soviet general officer to support Yeltsin. After the attempted coup in August 1991, headed a committee to review and open secret archives.

Volkov, Leonid Borisovich (b. 1929)   Political scientist. One of the founders of the Russian Social Democratic Party; elected to the RSFSR Congress of People's Deputies in 1990; member of the Russian Supreme Soviet committee on foreign affairs and international economic ties, 1990–93.

Volsky, Arkady (b. 1932)   CPSU official and politician. Assigned by the USSR Supreme Soviet to administer Nagorny Karabakh, 1989–90; one of the organizers of the Movement of Democratic Reform (DDR) in 1991; president of the Union of Industrialists and Entrepreneurs since 1992 and a leader of the Civic Union political party.

Vorontsov, Nikolai Nikolayevich (b. 1934)   Biologist. When named chairman of the USSR State Committee for Environmental Protection in 1991, he was the only non-Communist member of the USSR Council of Ministers. During the 1991 coup attempt he was the only Cabinet minister to protest the emergency committee's attempt to seize power.

Vorotnikov, Vitaly Ivanovich (b. 1926)   CPSU official. First deputy chairman of the RSFSR Council of Ministers, 1975–79; Soviet ambassador to Cuba, 1979–82; chairman of the RSFSR Council of Ministers, 1983–88; chairman of the RSFSR Supreme Soviet, 1988–90; member of the CPSU Politburo, 1983–90.

Voznesensky, Andrei (b. 1933)   Russian poet. Denounced by Nikita Khrushchev in 1962 as a "bourgeois formalist," he consistently refused to tailor his poetry to the political demands of the day; active supporter of reform in the cultural organizations dominated by the Communist Party.

Vulfsons, Mavriks (b. 1918) Latvian political scientist. Elected to the USSR Congress of People's Deputies in 1989; member of the Latvian National Front.

Yakovlev, Alexander Nikolayevich (b. 1923) CPSU official, diplomat, and philosopher. Soviet ambassador to Canada, 1973–83; director of the Institute for the World Economy and International Relations, 1983–85; secretary of the CPSU Central Committee, 1986–90; member of the CPSU Politburo, 1987–90; member of the Presidential Council in 1990 and adviser to Gorbachev in 1991; one of the founding members of the Movement for Democratic Reforms (DDR) in 1991; director of the Ostankino Television Company from 1993.

Yakovlev, Yegor Vladimirovich (b. 1930) Journalist and editor. Editor of *Moscow News,* 1986–1992; elected to the USSR Congress of People's Deputies in 1989; one of the leaders of the democratic movement; in 1992 headed Central Television.

Yakunin, Gleb Pavlovich (b. 1934) Russian Orthodox priest who was a political prisoner. Elected to the RSFSR Congress of People's Deputies in 1990, where he was an early Yeltsin supporter.

Yanayev, Gennady Ivanovich (b. 1937) CPSU official. Elected USSR vice president in December 1990, following a career in the Komsomol and trade union leadership; joined coup leaders in August 1991, after which he was arrested; amnestied by the Russian State Duma in 1994.

Yarin, Veniamin Alexandrovich (b. 1940) A worker in Nizhny Tagil who won election to the USSR Congress of People's Deputies in 1989. Active member of the USSR Supreme Soviet, 1989–91.

Yaroshenko, Viktor Nikolayevich (b. 1946) Economist. Elected to the USSR Congress of People's Deputies in 1989 and supported Yeltsin for the chairmanship; Russian minister of external economic relations, 1990–92.

Yavlinsky, Grigory (b. 1952) Economist and politician. Worked in the State Committee for Economic Reform, 1989–90; RSFSR deputy prime minister, 1990; deputy chairman of the USSR State Committee on Economic Reform, September–December, 1991; from 1992, chairman of the Center for Economic and Political Studies, Moscow; cofounder of the Yabloko Party in 1993 and a member of the Russian State Duma from 1994.

Yazov, Dmitri Timofeyevich (b. 1923) Army general. USSR minister of defense, 1987–91; member of emergency committee that tried to take power from Gorbachev in August 1991; arrested when the coup attempt failed, but released in 1992; amnestied by the Russian State Duma in 1994.

Yegorov, Alexei KGB officer assigned by Kryuchkov to work on contingency plans for an imposition of martial law, August 1991.

Yeltsin, Boris Nikolayevich (b. 1931) CPSU official, then Russian politician. First secretary, Moscow Party organization, 1985–87; candidate member, CPSU Politburo, 1986–88; elected to the USSR Congress of People's Deputies in March 1989; elected to the RSFSR Congress of People's Deputies in 1990; elected chairman of the RSFSR Supreme Soviet in 1990; elected president of the RSFSR in June 1991.

Yeltsin, Naina Iosifovna Boris Yeltsin's wife.

Yevtushenko, Yevgeny Alexandrovich (b. 1933)   Poet and political activist. Elected to the USSR Congress of People's Deputies in 1989.

Yezhov, Nikolai (1895–1939)   Head of the NKVD, 1936–38, at the height of the Great Purge.

Zadornov, Mikhail   Economist. An associate of Grigory Yavlinski in 1990–91 who coauthored an article with him in January 1991 criticizing Gorbachev's economic policies.

Zagladin, Vadim (b. 1927)   CPSU official. Deputy chief, then first deputy chief of the CPSU International Department, 1967–88; subsequently, foreign affairs adviser to Gorbachev.

Zakharov, Gennady   KGB officer. While an employee of the U.N. Secretariat in New York in 1986 was arrested for espionage.

Zalygin, Sergei Pavlovich (b. 1913)   Writer and editor. Editor of *Novy mir* from 1986; elected to the USSR Congress of People's Deputies in 1989; activist on environmental issues.

Zaslavskaya, Tatyana Ivanovna (b. 1927)   Economist and sociologist. Director of the All-Union Center for the Study of Public Opinion on Social and Economic Questions; elected to the USSR Congress of People's Deputies in 1989.

Zaslavsky, Ilya Iosifovich (b. 1960)   Textile engineer and politician. Elected to the USSR Congress of People's Deputies in 1989; one of the founders of the democratic movement; from 1993 a leader of Russia's Choice. Member of Russian State Duma from 1994.

Zhirinovsky, Vladimir Volfovich (b. 1946)   Russian politician. Founder of the Liberal Democratic Party; unsuccessful candidate for Russian president in 1991, but his party came in second in elections to the Russian State Duma in December 1993.

Zorin, Valentin Sergeyevich (b. 1925)   Journalist. Interviewed Secretary of State George Shultz for Soviet television in 1987 and was the host of a regular television talk show on Moscow Central Television.

Zorkin, Valery Dmitriyevich (b. 1943)   Lawyer and jurist. Chairman of Russian Constitutional Court, 1991–93; resigned the chairmanship following the attack on the Russian White House in October 1993 but remained a member of the panel of judges.

Notes

Chapter One: How Did It Happen?

1. Lecture at Brown University, May 4, 1993. Professor Afanasiev does not claim the saying to be original, but he does not know to whom it should be attributed.

2. Although Yeltsin had agreed that the presidents of the other three republics where nuclear weapons were located would have a say in any decision to use them, it was not clear how their voices could be included if a decision had to be made. In any case, most of the former Soviet nuclear arsenal was located in Russia and was effectively under Russian control.

Chapter Two: The Empire

1. The report on this trip was published as Allen J. Ellender, *A Report of United States Foreign Policy and Operations, 1961: U.S.S.R., Japan, Taiwan, Hong Kong, South Vietnam, Laos, Cambodia, Thailand,* Senate Document no. 73, 87th Congress, 2nd session (Washington, D.C.: U.S. Government Printing Office, 1962).

2. Kazakhstan was an exception. Russians and Ukrainians had poured into the northern plains during Khrushchev's "Virgin Lands" campaign, an effort to increase Soviet wheat production.

3. J. V. Stalin, *Works,* vol. 5 (Moscow: Foreign Languages Publishing House, 1953), pp. 269–270.

4. *KPSS v rezolyutsiyakh i resheniyakh s"yezdov, konferentsii i plenumov TsK,* 7th ed., part I (1898–1925) (Moscow: Gospolitizdat, 1953), p. 443.

5. These events are described in detail in Bohdan Nahaylo and Victor Swoboda, *Soviet Disunion: A History of the Nationalities Problem in the USSR* (New York: The Free Press, 1990).

6. Robert Conquest has provided the most thorough and accurate study of this human catastrophe in his *Harvest of Sorrow* (New York: Oxford University Press, 1986).

7. The text was published by the U.S. government in 1948: R. J. Sontag and J. S. Beddie, eds., *Nazi-Soviet Relations 1939–1941: Documents from the Archives of the German Foreign Office* (Washington, D.C.: U.S. Government Printing Office, 1948). One of the German diplomats who participated in the negotiations described them in his memoirs: Hans von Herwarth, *Against Two Evils* (New York: Rawson, Wade, 1981).

8. This was the case from the late 1930s on. Earlier, it had been permissible to treat the expansion of the Russian empire as an imperialist advance. But once Stalin began to fuse Russian nationalism with Soviet "patriotism" (particularly noticeable during and after World War II), this approach became taboo.

9. Ivan Dzyuba, *Internationalism or Russification? A Study in the Soviet Nationalities Problem,* 2d ed. (London. Weidenfeld and Nicolson, 1970).

10. For example, see Murray Feshbach and Alfred Friendly, Jr., *Ecocide in the USSR: Health and Nature Under Siege* (New York: Basic Books, 1992).

11. Some Western scholars agreed with this analysis. For example, Duke University Professor Jerry Hough wrote in 1989, "It would be a mistake . . . to exaggerate the potential for ethnic instability in the Soviet Union in the near term. . . . The Soviet leadership has long exercised great skill in avoiding this problem"; *Russia and the West: Gorbachev and the Politics of Reform* (New York: Simon and Schuster, 1989), p. 4.

12. Mikhail Gorbachev, *Perestroika* (New York: Harper & Row, 1987), pp. 105, 107.

13. M. S. Gorbachev, "O perestroike i kadrovoy politiki partii. Doklad na Plenume TsK KPSS 27 yanvarya 1987 goda," *Izbrannye rechi i stat'i,* vol. 4 (Moscow: Izdatelstvo politicheskoi literratury, 1987), p. 331.

Chapter Three: The Torch Passes

1. Boris Yeltsin, *Against the Grain: An Autobiography* (New York: Summit Books, 1990), p. 139.

2. M. S. Gorbachev, *Dekabr' 1991: Moya pozitsiya* (Moscow: Novosti, 1992), pp. 140–141.

3. Niccolò Machiavelli, *The Chief Works and Others,* trans. Allan Gilbert (Durham, N.C.: Duke University Press, 1965), p. 26.

4. The playwright Mikhail Shatrov was one of the first to float this report in public, in an interview with Agence France Presse in 1987. Others subsequently picked it up, including the television talk-show host Vladimir Pozner, who repeated it in his memoir of the period, *Eyewitness: A Personal Memoir of the Unraveling of the Soviet Union* (New York: Random House, 1992).

5. The most detailed accounts of the session by participants published to date can be found in Ryzhkov's and Ligachev's memoirs: Nikolai Ryzhkov, *Perestroika: Istoriya predatelstv* (Moscow: Novosti, 1992), and Yegor Ligachev, *Inside Gorbachev's Kremlin* (New York: Pantheon, 1993).

6. As the master of ceremonies commented at the 1985 Gridiron Club dinner in Washington, the vice president's motto seemed to be "You die, I fly."

7. Paraphrased from memory. The thrust and the style of speech are accurate, but the words are not literal.

8. Gorbachev, *Dekabr' 1991,* pp. 140–141.

9. Yeltsin, *Against the Grain,* p. 140.

10. Author's interview with Nikolai Ryzhkov, Mar. 4, 1992.

11. Author's interview with Mikhail Poltoranin, Sept. 23, 1992.

12. Ryzhkov, *Perestroika,* p. 243. The actual figures he quotes for 1986 production as compared to that of 1985 were: vodka and other spirits, 146 million deciliters, down from 280 million; wine, 140 million deciliters, down from 401; beer, 488 million deciliters, down from 718.

13. Quoted from the manuscript of Korotich's unpublished memoir, *Zerkalo.*

14. From his speech to the Central Committee when he accepted the position of general secretary of the CPSU, Mar. 11, 1985; M. S. Gorbachev, "Rech' na vneocherednom plenume TsK KPSS," *Izbrannye rechi i stat'i,* vol. 2 (Moscow: Izdatelstvo politicheskoi literatury, 1987), p. 132.

15. *Pravda,* June 26, 1987.

Chapter Four: Elbow Room for Reform: Easing Pressures from Abroad

1. M. S. Gorbachev, *Izbrannye rechi i stat'i,* vol. 3 (Moscow: Izdatelstvo politicheskoi literatury, 1987), p. 245.

2. Eduard Shevardnadze, *The Future Belongs to Freedom* (New York: The Free Press, 1991), p. 81.

3. The official announcement came on July 3, the day after it was leaked to reporters in Washington; *The New York Times,* July 3, 1985, pp. 1, 6.

4. This was a reference to Oleg Kalugin, who subsequently ran intelligence operations in both Washington and New York. In 1990, after he had attained the rank of major general, Kalugin broke with the KGB, denounced it, entered politics, and won a seat in the Soviet parliament. He published an account of his career in *The First Directorate: My 32 Years in Intelligence and Espionage Against the West* (New York: St. Martin's Press, 1994).

5. Alexander Yakovlev, "Protiv istorizma," *Literaturnaya gazeta,* Nov. 15, 1972; condensed translation in *Current Digest of the Soviet Press,* vol. 24, no. 7 (1972), pp. 1–7. The article also defended the interpretation of history based on the "class struggle"—a position Yakovlev would subsequently reject.

6. Alexander Yakovlev, *Muki prochteniya bytiya* (Moscow: Novosti, 1991), pp. 60–62.

7. Ibid., p. 63.

8. A. N. Yakovlev, *Ot Trumena do Reigana* (Moscow: Molodaya gvardiya, 1984), p. 394.

9. See, for example, Shultz's comments in his memoir *Turmoil and Triumph* (New York: Charles Scribner's Sons, 1993), pp. 166–167.

10. Soviet leaders not only used overt propaganda instruments to vilify Reagan but also ordered the KGB to conduct a covert campaign of forged documents. Some examples of these are reproduced in Christopher Andrew and Oleg Gordievsky, *Comrade Kryuchkov's Instructions: Top Secret Files on KGB Foreign Operations, 1975–1985* (Stanford, Calif: Stanford University Press, 1993), pp. 98–103.

11. Shultz, *Turmoil and Triumph,* pp. 276–280.

12. International practice—and Soviet regulations themselves—required warning an intruding aircraft and making a serious effort to compel it to land before lethal force was used. This was not done in the case of the Korean airliner in 1983, nor in 1978, when an aircraft strayed over the Murmansk area of northern Russia.

13. Placed in quotes because I do not consider these issues exclusively internal; at that time, however, the Soviet authorities did, and they resisted making them a formal topic for negotiation.

14. This section on interrelationships was edited out of the speech before it was delivered, but the same thought was placed in subsequent statements and in the president's letters to the Soviet leaders.

15. The text was published in *Weekly Compilation of Presidential Documents,* Jan. 23, 1984, pp. 40–45.

16. *Weekly Compilation of Presidential Documents,* June 28, 1984, pp. 944–946.

17. These critics of the SDI failed to suggest what incentive the Soviet Union would have to agree to a large reduction of its heavy intercontinental ballistic missiles (ICBMs) in the absence of such a program in the United States.

18. *Weekly Compilation of Presidential Documents,* Oct. 18, 1985, pp. 1291–1296.

19. *Weekly Compilation of Presidential Documents,* Nov. 18, 1985, pp. 1399–1402.

20. The full text was published in *Weekly Compilation of Presidential Documents,* Nov. 25, 1985, pp. 1422–1424.

21. One important exception: In the working group on issues other than arms control, the Soviet delegation accepted language for the joint statement which, for the first time, acknowledged that human rights were an appropriate topic for bilateral attention.

22. Secretary of State Shultz rushed to convene a press conference since he had to fly to Brussels that evening to brief the Allies. His face expressed his disappointment to the assembled journalists, and he failed to stress the many important issues that the meeting had solved. Shevardnadze later told me that the Soviets had been prepared to brief the press in positive terms, but when Shultz had presented the meeting's outcome in a pessimistic light, they had had no choice but to follow suit.

23. Volkogonov, elected to the Russian parliament in 1990, was the only Soviet general who supported Yeltsin before 1991.

24. Author's interview with Dmitri Volkogonov, Sept. 21, 1992.

25. We now know that Gorbachev did not have to depend on Reagan's word regarding Daniloff's innocence. At this time, the KGB had already recruited CIA officer Aldrich Ames, who was regularly supplying them with information about U.S. agents. Daniloff, of course, was not one of them.

26. In *Turmoil and Triumph,* Shultz presents a different view of these events. It is apparent from his account that his staff—probably because of bureaucratic animosities—failed to inform him of a number of pertinent facts.

27. None of this, however, could prevent the damage caused by Aldrich Ames, the KGB's "mole" in the CIA, who had already been recruited and continued to work for Soviet, then Russian, intelligence until his arrest in February 1994.

28. Soviet officials who organized the meeting later informed me that it had been approved by the International Department of the Communist Party Central Committee, which at that time was headed by Anatoly Dobrynin, who had just returned to Moscow from many years as Soviet ambassador to the United States. The KGB, they said, was dubious, as were the Latvian Communist Party leaders, but Dobrynin's view prevailed.

29. Several other Americans who were invited to speak, including Robert McFarlane, Richard Perle, Jeane Kirkpatrick, and Assistant Secretary of State Alan Keyes, declined to go at the last minute.

Chapter Five: A Fateful Rift

1. In answer to Boris Yeltsin's speech at the October 1987 Central Committee of the Communist Party of the Soviet Union plenary meeting; *Izvestiya TsK KPSS,* February 1989, pp. 285–286.

2. From speech in reply to Yeltsin at Party conference; *Pravda,* July 2, 1988.

3. Yegor Ligachev, *Inside Gorbachev's Kremlin* (New York: Pantheon, 1993), p. 105.

4. Based on author's notes taken at the meeting on Apr. 17, 1987.

5. Author's interview with Mikhail Poltoranin, Sept. 23, 1992.

6. Boris Yeltsin, *Against the Grain: An Autobiography* (New York: Summit Books, 1990), pp. 178–181.

7. In an interview on September 23, 1992, Poltoranin told me he was convinced that the attack on Yeltsin was planned in advance and would have occurred even if Yeltsin had not spoken out.

8. Arbatov's account of the session can be found in his book *The System* (New York: Times Books, 1992), p. 330.

9. Yeltsin, *Against the Grain,* pp. 199–202.

10. It finally appeared in the February 1989 issue of the Central Committee monthly bulletin, *Izvestiya TsK KPSS,* pp. 209–287.

11. The article actually appeared the day before Gorbachev departed Moscow, but his absence in Yugoslavia delayed his reaction to it.

12. *Sovetskaya Rossiya,* Mar. 13, 1988, p. 3.

13. Giulietto Chiesa, Moscow correspondent for the Italian Communist Party newspaper *L'Unità,* who had excellent contacts in the CPSU, published a detailed report on how the "letter" had been prepared and published; *L'Unità,* May 23, 1988; an English translation can be found in Foreign Broadcast Information Service, *Daily Report: Soviet Union,* May 31, 1988, pp. 55–58.

14. Ligachev, *Inside Gorbachev's Kremlin,* pp. 301–303.

15. Author's interview with Mikhail Gorbachev, Sept. 30, 1992.

16. Michail S. Gorbatschow, *Gipfelgespräche: Geheime Protokolle aus meiner Amtszeit* (Berlin: Rowholt, 1993), pp. 233–245. At the time of this writing, I am unaware of any Russian or English edition of this book, but a French translation, entitled *Avant-mémoirs,* was published in Paris in 1993 by Éditions Odile Jacob.

17. Author's interview with Arkady Volsky, Sept. 23, 1992.

18. *Weekly Compilation of Presidential Documents,* June 6, 1988, pp. 703–708.

19. The poll results were recorded in the author's journal when they were published, but without an indication of the original source.

20. In theory, he or she. But very few—if any—Party secretaries were women.

21. The telecast contained extensive excerpts from all the speeches. But about half of Yeltsin's was omitted, along with all the applause he evoked, while Ligachev's reply was carried in full, including the outbursts of applause from the audience.

22. Yeltsin, *Against the Grain,* pp. 222–224.

23. The old title was "chairman of the Presidium of the USSR Supreme Soviet."

Chapter Six: "The Common Interests of Mankind"

1. *Pravda,* July 26, 1988.
2. *Pravda,* Aug. 6, 1988.
3. *Pravda,* Dec. 8, 1988.
4. *Krasnaya zvezda,* Aug. 13, 1988.
5. *Pravda,* Aug. 13, 1988.
6. Mikhail Gorbachev, *Izbrannye rechi y stat'i,* vol. 7 (Moscow: Izdatelstvo politicheskoi literatury, 1990), p. 188.

Chapter Seven: Stirrings in the Hinterland

1. Charles F. Furtado and Andrea Chandler, eds., *Perestroika in the Soviet Republics: Documents on the National Question* (Boulder, Colo.: Westview Press, 1992), p. 11.

2. *Pravda,* Jan. 28, 1987.

3. *Pravda,* July 5, 1988.

4. Martha Brill Olcott, "The Collectivization Drive in Kazakhstan," *The Russian Review,* April 1981, p. 136; Robert Conquest, *Harvest of Sorrow* (New York: Oxford University Press, 1986), pp. 192–197.

5. Many biographical facts are presented, in the form of answers to questions, in Nazarbayev's book *Bez pravykh i levykh* (Moscow: Molodaya gvardiya, 1991).

6. He was forty-five years old when he was named chairman of the Kazakhstan Council of Ministers.

7. *Pravda,* March 5, 1986, pp. 4–5.

8. Dinmukhamed Kunayev, *O moem vremeni* (Alma Ata: RGZhI "Deuir," MP "Yntymak," 1992), p. 265.

9. For example, a British journalist in Moscow, Martin Walker, filed a report in *The Guardian* (London) on December 30. Relying on "eyewitness accounts," he wrote that at least 20 people had lost their lives, 200 had been injured, and more than 1,000 had been arrested. Subsequent investigations have concluded that many fewer (three or four people) died, but the numbers cited for those injured and arrested seem nearer the mark.

10. "Soviet Leader Criticizes Rioters," *The Washington Post,* Jan. 9, 1987, p. A-25. Subsequently, in his memoirs, Ryzhkov gave a much more accurate account of the Alma Ata riot and bewailed the lack of attention it had gotten

from the Soviet leadership at the time; Nikolai Ryzhkov, *Perestroika: Istoriya predatelstv* (Moscow: Novosti, 1992), pp. 200–201.

11. For example, at a meeting of journalists in February 1987; *Kazakhstanskaya pravda,* Feb. 19, 1987.

12. TASS, June 29, 1988, as quoted in Bohdan Nahaylo and Victor Swoboda, *Soviet Disunion: A History of the Nationalities Problem in the USSR* (New York: The Free Press, 1990), p. 303.

13. *Izvestiya,* Mar. 29, 1988.

14. Franz Werfel's *The Forty Days of Musa Dagh* is the most famous literary portrayal of this tragedy.

15. An English translation of the text is included in Furtado Chandler, *Perestroika in the Soviet Republics,* pp. 65–66.

16. Nahaylo and Swoboda, *Soviet Disunion,* pp. 297–298, 313.

17. Author's interview with Alexander Yakovlev, Mar. 17, 1992.

18. Mikhail Gorbachev, *Izbrannye rechi i stat'i,* vol. 7 (Moscow: Izdatelstvo politicheskoi literatury, 1990), p. 142.

19. Furtado and Chandler, *Perestroika in the Soviet Republics,* pp. 221–223.

20. Author's interview with Vyacheslav Chornovil, Sept. 29, 1992.

21. *Pravda,* Sept. 11, 1987.

Chapter Eight: Washington Fumbles

1. Statement on ABC's *This Week with David Brinkley,* Jan. 22, 1989.

2. The Carter decision was usually called a "grain embargo," but this was a misnomer. Carter allowed the sale of 8 million tons of grain a year, which the Soviet Union was entitled to buy under our bilateral Long-Term Grain Agreement; however, sale of additional amounts, which the agreement had made contingent on the approval of the U.S. government, was banned. Nevertheless, U.S. farmers thought the ban on additional sales depressed prices at a time when many were struggling to avoid bankruptcy. President Reagan removed the restrictions on sales shortly after he took office in 1981.

3. Some on the right, such as Richard Viguerie, editor of *Conservative Digest,* did in fact accuse Reagan of softness toward the end of his presidency, but these accusations did not have a significant political effect.

4. In their well-informed book on U.S.-Soviet relations during the Bush administration, *At the Highest Levels* (Boston: Little, Brown, 1993), Michael Beschloss and Strobe Talbott report that Bush warned Gorbachev in December 1987, while both were riding in Gorbachev's car from the Soviet Embassy to the White House, that he would have to indulge in anti-Soviet rhetoric from time to time but that this should be disregarded. The Beschloss-Talbott report seems to be based on a memorandum Bush himself wrote on the conversation, since no other American was present (except perhaps a Secret Service guard).

Pavel Palazchenko, Gorbachev's interpreter, however, remembers the conversation differently (interview with author). Bush, he recalled, told Gorbachev that *Reagan* had had to indulge in anti-Soviet rhetoric from time to time but that he had genuinely been interested in accommodation. Not a practiced lip reader, Palazchenko may have missed Bush's intended meaning and thought Bush was talking about Reagan. If so, Gorbachev would have heard and understood what Palazchenko interpreted in Russian, since he did not understand enough English to grasp what Bush was driving at. Bush, of course, would not have understood how his words were being rendered into Russian. In fact, both Gorbachev and Shevardnadze seemed unusually nervous about the continuity of U.S. policy during the spring of 1989.

5. Strangely, many people who argued that Gorbachev was on his way out also used this argument. I had trouble understanding why we should worry about his turning the tables on us if he was certain to be swept from office in a matter of months.

6. In this case, Bush overruled the initial cautious recommendations by the bureaucracy and insisted on a proposal with meaningful reductions.

Chapter Nine: A Vote That Counted

1. Mikhail Gorbachev, *Izbrannye rechi i stat'i,* vol. 7 (Moscow: Izdatelstvo politicheskoi literatury, 1990), p. 558.

2. Nikolai Ryzhkov, *Perestroika: Istoriya predatelstv* (Moscow: Novosti, 1992), p. 284.

3. At Alexander Yakovlev's request, Sakharov went to Azerbaijan and Armenia in December 1988, in an unsuccessful effort to reconcile the parties to the dispute over Nagorny Karabakh. Following the April massacre in Tbilisi, he had rushed to the scene and sought outside help for the injured demonstrators.

4. Ryzhkov, *Perestroika,* p. 284.

5. This was my assumption at the time. Burbulis confirmed to me during a conversation on February 18, 1993, that the nomination and withdrawal had been planned in advance with precisely this purpose in mind.

Chapter Ten: The Balts Take the Lead

1. Charles F. Furtado, Jr., and Andrea Chandler, *Perestroika in the Soviet Republics: Documents on the National Question* (Boulder, Colo.: Westview Press, 1992), p. 11.

2. Ibid., p. 203.

3. Actually, a noticeable number of participants were not ethnic Balts, though they supported Baltic independence; the "Interfronts" did not speak for all the non-Balts in the area.

4. *Pravda,* Aug. 26, 1989.

5. My emphasis; Furtado and Chandler, *Perestroika in the Soviet Republics,* p. 95.

6. *USA Today,* Sept. 16, 1989.

7. Author's interview with Boris Yeltsin, Sept. 19, 1992.

Chapter Eleven: A Pivotal Year

1. *Nashi obshchie problemy vmeste i reshat': Sbornik materialov o poezdki M. S. Gorbacheva v Litovskuyu SSR, 11–13 yanvarya 1990 goda* (Moscow: Politizdat, 1990), p. 12.

2. *Materialy plenuma Tsentralnogo komiteta KPSS, 19–20 sentyabrya 1989 goda* (Moscow: Politizdat, 1989), p. 224.

3. One of these statements turned out to be ironically prophetic. It read: "The guarantee of our federation's durability is the completely voluntary nature of the association of the Soviet republics in a single union state." If *that* was the guarantee, then no guarantee existed!

4. Author's meeting with Valentin Falin, Dec. 21, 1989.

5. The question was asked by Yelizaveta Steiger, who did the interview for *Argumenty i Fakty,* but she asked it on Starkov's explicit instructions.

6. On October 14, *Pravda* reported the fact that the meeting had taken place but did not publish Gorbachev's remarks. A more substantial account subsequently appeared in Yegor Yakovlev's article "Zaderzhat' mayatnik—ostanovit' chasy," *Moskovskie novosti,* no. 43 (Oct. 22, 1989), p. 43.

7. Charles F. Furtado, Jr., and Andrea Chandler, eds., *Perestroika in the Soviet Republics: Documents on the National Question* (Boulder, Colo.: Westview Press, 1989), pp. 134–135.

8. Gorbachev published extensive excerpts from his notes of this meeting in Michail S. Gorbatschow, *Gipfelgespräche: Geheime Protokolle aus meiner Amtszeit* (Berlin: Rowohlt, 1993). The discussion of "Western values" appears on pp. 125–129.

9. Foreign Broadcast Information Service, *Daily Report: Soviet Union,* Dec. 14, 1989, p. 63.

10. Foreign Broadcast Information Service, *Daily Report: Soviet Union,* Dec. 19, 1989, p. 37.

11. Ibid., p. 39.

12. Foreign Broadcast Information Service, *Daily Report: Soviet Union,* Dec. 29, 1989, pp. 38–39.

13. *Pravda,* Dec. 26, 1989.

14. Author's interview with Alexander Rutskoy, Sept. 23, 1992.

15. According to Yeltsin, the original document was found after the Soviet Union collapsed in the papers held personally by Gorbachev as Party general secretary.

16. Author's interview with Leonid Kravchuk, Sept. 28, 1992.

17. *Pravda,* Nov. 26, 1989.

Chapter Twelve: A Winter of Discontents

1. *Pravda,* Jan. 1, 1990.

2. Foreign Broadcast Information Service, *Daily Report: Soviet Union,* Jan. 12, 1990, p. 49.

3. From an interview with René de Bok and William Wansink in *Elseviers* (Amsterdam), quoted from the text subsequently published in *La Stampa* (Turin) on January 24, 1990.

4. Ezio Mauro, *La Repubblica,* Feb. 2, 1990, p. 11.

5. Foreign Broadcast Information Service, *Daily Report: Soviet Union,* Jan 12, 1990, pp. 47–49.

6. Foreign Broadcast Information Service, *Daily Report: Soviet Union,* Jan. 16, 1990, pp. 117–120.

7. The city's original name, Ganje, would soon be restored.

8. Alexander Prokhanov, "Tragediya tsentralizma," *Literaturnaya Rossiya,* no. 1 (1990), p. 1.

9. *Literaturnaya Rossiya,* no. 52 (1989), pp. 2–3.

10. Bernard Guetta, "Des conseillers de M. Gorbatchev le pressent de rompre avec les conservateurs," *Le Monde* (Paris), Jan. 31, 1990, pp. 1–2.

11. *La Repubblica,* Feb. 2, 1990; translated in Foreign Broadcast Information Service, *Daily Report: Soviet Union,* Feb. 7, 1990, pp. 91–92.

12. He had wanted to send the balloon up from Red Square, and, although this was denied, a permit was issued for it to ascend from the bank of the Moscow River near the Mazhdunarodnaya Hotel. Nevertheless, Moscow's weather had the last word and the balloon was unable to fly despite the official permit.

13. *The New York Times,* Feb. 5, 1990, pp. 1, 6.

14. *Pravda,* Jan. 15, 1990.

15. *Materialy plenuma Tsentral'nogo komiteta KPSS, 5–7 fevralya 1990 goda* (Moscow: Politizdat, 1990), p. 9.

16. Ibid., pp. 162–166.

17. Ibid., pp. 67–69.

18. Author's interview with Vadim Bakatin, Oct. 6, 1992.

19. Verkhovny Sovet SSR, Tretya sessiya, *Byulleten' No 8 Sovmestnogo zasedaniya Soveta Soyuza i Soveta Natsional'nostey,* Feb. 27, 1990, pp. 137–139.

20. Ibid., pp. 143–144.

21. Foreign Broadcast Information Service, *Daily Report: Soviet Union,* Feb. 28, 1990, pp. 30–32.

Chapter Thirteen: The Unelected President

1. Foreign Broadcast Information Service, *Daily Report: Soviet Union,* Mar. 13, 1990, p. 57.

2. Foreign Broadcast Information Service, *Daily Report: Soviet Union,* Mar. 15, 1990, p. 44.

3. *Corriere della Sera* (Milan), Mar. 9, 1990, quoted in Foreign Broadcast Information Service, *Daily Report: Soviet Union,* Mar. 13, 1990, p. 76.

4. Ryzhkov told me two years later, in an interview on March 14, 1992, that he had withdrawn only out of a feeling of loyalty to Gorbachev, which he subsequently concluded had been misplaced, and that he was convinced that he would have won the election if he had allowed his name to stay on the ballot. I doubt that he could in fact have won, but given his popularity among industrial managers and the Party *apparat,* he would likely have made a strong showing on a secret ballot.

5. Foreign Broadcast Information Service, *Daily Report: Soviet Union,* Mar. 19, 1990, pp. 44–45.

6. Foreign Broadcast Information Service, *Daily Report: Soviet Union,* Mar. 20, 1990, p. 99.

7. Foreign Broadcast Information Service, *Daily Report: Soviet Union,* Mar. 22, 1990, p. 87.

8. Quoted from the text of the appeal received by the U.S. Embassy in Moscow.

9. Foreign Broadcast Information Service, *Daily Report: Soviet Union,* Apr. 13, 1990, p. 56.

10. The Jackson-Vanik amendment to the Trade Act of 1974 prohibited any trade agreement with the Soviet Union which was not approved by Congress. Therefore, the administration did not have the option of making the treaty an executive agreement not subject to Senate confirmation.

11. Ninety deputies voted in favor and three abstained; Foreign Broadcast Information Service, *Daily Report: Soviet Union,* Apr. 19, 1990, p. 83.

12. Charles F. Furtado, Jr., and Andrea Chandler, eds., *Perestroika in the Soviet Republics: Documents on the National Question* (Boulder, Colo.: Westview Press, 1989), pp. 102–103.

13. Foreign Broadcast Information Service, *Daily Report: Soviet Union,* Apr. 20, 1990, pp. 88–89.

14. Foreign Broadcast Information Service, *Daily Report: Soviet Union,* Apr. 13, 1990, p. 57.

15. *Izvestiya,* Apr. 6, 1990; an English translation of the text can be found in Furtado and Chandler, *Perestroika in the Soviet Republics,* pp. 36–40.

16. *Pravda,* Apr. 11, 1990.

17. Foreign Broadcast Information Service, *Daily Report: Soviet Union,* Apr. 19, 1990, p. 47.

18. *Izvestiya,* Mar. 1, 1990.

19. Foreign Broadcast Information Service, *Daily Report: Soviet Union,* Mar. 16, 1990, p. 60.

20. These were my personal conclusions; they were not shared by all members of our staff, who continued to stimulate my own thinking with challenging observations and information.

Chapter Fourteen: Russia Makes a Choice

1. *Sovetskaya Rossiya,* May 25, 1990.

2. Statement by Boris Yeltsin at a press conference after being elected chairman of the RSFSR Supreme Soviet; *Sovetskaya Rossiya,* May 31, 1990.

3. Article 76, Constitution of the USSR.

4. *Sovetskaya Rossiya,* May 25, 1990.

5. Ibid.

6. The issue was not debated explicitly in these terms, and it is possible that not all the deputies who voted in favor of the sovereignty declaration had thought through all of its implications. There was, however, no other conclusion that one could logically draw from their vote.

7. Author's interview with Ivan Antonovich, Sept. 25, 1992.

8. The meeting was officially called a "conference," but after it convened the delegates voted to convert the assembly into a founding congress.

9. Antonovich also said he believed Gorbachev could have blocked Polozkov's election if he had endorsed a different candidate from the outset; author's interview with Antonovich, Sept. 25, 1992.

10. Foreign Broadcast Information Service, *Daily Report: Soviet Union,* Apr. 19, 1990, p. 24.

11. Ibid., pp. 25–26.

12. This attitude was, of course, an about-face from the traditional Soviet goal of driving the United States out of Europe, but that goal had been quietly dropped along with the "class struggle" theory, and any remaining doubts Gorbachev might have held as to the benefits to the Soviet Union of a U.S. presence in Europe evaporated at the Malta summit in December 1989.

13. The vote was 3,411 to 1,116; *Pravda,* July 11, 1990.

14. Speech by Mikhail Gorbachev of July 7, 1990, as reported in *Pravda,* July 11, 1990.

15. "Moldavia" is derived from the Russian form of the name. "Moldova" is the name of the country in Romanian and has been preferred since independence. Similarly, the name of the capital changed from the Russian "Kishinev" to the Moldovan "Chişinău."

16. The permit was subsequently issued when, following my return to Moscow, I asked the State Committee on Religion officially for the reasons for withholding the import license.

17. A constitution derived in part from the Constitution of the United States was subsequently approved by the Supreme Soviet of Uzbekistan. Unfortunately, this was not enough to guarantee a democratic government.

18. Radio Liberty published a list of these declarations as of October 31, 1990; Ann Sheehy, "Fact Sheet on Declarations of Sovereignty," RFE/RL Research Institute, *Report on the USSR,* Nov. 9, 1990, pp. 23–25.

Chapter Fifteen: The Curse of the Purloined Property

1. Gavriil Popov, *Chto delat'?* (Moscow: Izdanie gazety Pozitsiya, 1990), p. 9.

2. *Moskovski Komsomolets,* Aug. 8, 1990.

3. In an epigram dedicated to Leonid Abalkin, the deputy prime minister responsible for economic reform; *Knizhnoe obozrenie,* Feb. 9, 1990, p. 10.

4. Soviet scholars distinguished between the officials who had made careers in the Party apparatus (such as Gorbachev, Yeltsin, and Ligachev) and those who had risen in the system as managers of plants or farms (such as Ryzhkov). Both groups were made up of Communist Party members, but their psychology differed. Gorbachev's political reforms had affected mainly the "ideological" *nomenklatura,* who no longer had the authority or staff to monitor and second-guess managers. The managers, on the other hand, had gained power with the decline of day-to-day Party tutelage.

5. See, e.g., his statement to the press just after being elected chairman of the RSFSR Supreme Soviet; *Sovetskaya Rossiya,* May 25, 1990.

6. He was, of course, describing the arrangement originally envisioned in the Maastricht Treaty, not that which evolved by 1993.

7. *Izvestiya,* Sept. 4, 1990.

8. Ibid.

9. Ibid.

10. Several of our Great Lakes are larger on the surface, but they are not nearly as deep.

11. *Komsomolskaya Pravda,* Nov. 4, 1990. The letter was signed by Stanislav Shatalin and Nikolai Petrakov of the Presidential Council, Vladlen Martynov of IMEMO, and two senior members of the RSFSR government, Grigory Yavlinsky and Boris Fyodorov.

Chapter Sixteen: Gorbachev Swings to the Right

1. *Pravda,* Dec. 21, 1990.

2. Quoted in *Moscow News,* no. 47 (1990), p. 5.

3. On Sept. 24, 1990; *Izvestiya,* Sept. 25, 1990.

4. Soviet law permitted military personnel elected to legislatures to remain on active duty during their terms in office.

5. *Krasnaya zvezda,* Nov. 15, 1990, pp. 1–4.

6. Foreign Broadcast Information Service, *Daily Report: Soviet Union,* Nov. 19, 1990, p. 15.

7. Author's interview with Vadim Bakatin, Oct. 6, 1992.

8. Nikolai Ryzhkov, *Perestroika: Istoriya predatel'stv* (Moscow: Novosti, 1992), p. 20.

9. *Izvestiya,* Nov. 17, 1990.

10. *Moscow News,* Nov. 16, 1990.

11. Anatoly Chernyayev described Gorbachev's private reaction in his memoir *Shest' let s Gorbachevym* (Moscow: Izdatelskaya Gruppa Progress, Kultura, 1993); German translation: Anatoli Tschernajew, *Die letzten Jahre einer Weltmacht: Der Kreml von Innen* (Stuttgart: Deutsche Verlags-Anstalt, 1993), p. 333.

12. Vadim Bakatin, *Osvobozhdenie ot illyuziy* (Kemerovo: Kemerovskoye knizhnoye izdatelstvo, 1992), p. 90.

13. Ibid., p. 91.

14. Author's interview with Vladimir Ivashko, Nov. 23, 1990.

15. "Hurenko" in Ukrainian.

16. Translated from the broadcast of his speech on Moscow television on December 20, 1990.

17. Moscow television, Dec. 20, 1990.

18. Shevardnadze's personal assistant, Teymuraz Stepanov, in whom he regularly confided, told me in a conversation on Mar. 7, 1994, that sometime before Shevardnadze's resignation Gorbachev had asked him if he would be interested in becoming vice president. Shevardnadze, Stepanov said, had replied

that if Gorbachev wished him to continue on his team, he would prefer to remain as foreign minister. Both Shevardnadze and Stepanov believe that Gorbachev had dropped the idea but mentioned it in his comment to mask what had in fact been flagging support for Shevardnadze's policies.

19. Cases in point were the unannounced movement of military equipment east of the Urals to circumvent some of the quantitative restrictions in the Treaty on Conventional Forces in Europe, an attempt by the Soviet military to exclude from the agreed-upon ceilings certain forces clearly covered by that treaty and to backtrack on some agreements Shevardnadze had made in the negotiations on strategic nuclear weapons.

20. Chernyayev included the text of the letter in *Shest' let s Gorbachevym*, pp. 399–400; German translation: Tschernajew, *Die letzten Jahre einer Weltmacht,* pp. 336–337.

21. Yanayev was not confirmed on the first ballot but passed by a modest margin when Gorbachev resubmitted his name and insisted he be approved.

22. Yeltsin later challenged these figures, pointing out that they had omitted some significant tax categories, including import and export duties collected on products used in or exported from the RSFSR.

23. Chernyayev, *Shest' let s Gorbachevym,* p. 388; German translation: Tschernajew, *Die letzten Jahre einer Weltmacht,* pp. 328–329.

24. Ibid.

25. Ibid., p. 387.

26. Ibid., pp. 404–405; German translation: Tschernajew, *Die letzten Jahre einer Weltmacht,* p. 341.

27. *Moscow News,* Nov. 11, 1990.

28. Alexei Levinson, "Tri cheloveka goda," *Nezavisimaya gazeta,* Feb. 28, 1991, p. 2.

Chapter Seventeen: Rehearsal

1. Quoted from author's journal, as recorded at the time.

2. As recorded in the author's journal from the text of Petrakov's open letter to Gorbachev.

3. Quoted from author's journal, as recorded at the time.

4. Foreign Broadcast Information Service, *Daily Report: Soviet Union,* Jan. 11, 1991, p. 43.

5. It was broadcast on the radio on the program controlled by the RSFSR government; Foreign Broadcast Information Service, *Daily Report: Soviet Union,* Jan. 14, 1991, p. 95.

6. The day before, the Council of Federation had named a commission to visit Lithuania and report back on the situation there.

7. Foreign Broadcast Information Service, *Daily Report: Soviet Union,* Jan. 14, 1991, p. 94.

8. Foreign Broadcast Information Service, *Daily Report: Soviet Union,* Jan. 15, 1991, p. 78.

9. *Komsomolskaya Pravda,* Jan. 16, 1991.

10. "Paralich vlasti ili vlast' paralicha?" *Nezavisimaya gazeta,* Jan. 15, 1991.

11. *Pravda,* Jan. 23, 1991.

12. At that point, the reformers were usually called the "left" and the hard-line Communists the "right." Since these were shifting labels used differently from their meanings in the West—where Communists are usually considered to represent the extreme left—I have usually tried to avoid them except in direct quotes of Soviet commentators and in describing Gorbachev's abandonment of the reform intellectuals in the autumn of 1990.

13. As recorded in the author's journal from the text of Petrakov's open letter to Gorbachev.

14. Chernyayev reproduced portions of his notes on this conversation in his memoir *Shest' let s Gorbachevym* (Moscow: Izdatelskaya Gruppa Progress, Kultura, 1993), pp. 416–418. He omitted most of what I said but gave an extended summary of Gorbachev's remarks, which, however, omitted his initial comment about the country being on the brink of civil war.

15. *Trud,* Feb. 12, 1991.

16. Department of State press briefing, Washington, D.C., Feb. 13, 1991.

17. *The New York Times,* Feb. 15, 1991, p. A-34.

18. *Izvestiya,* Dec. 25, 1990.

19. Other questions were proposed for the ballot, including one on private property, one of no confidence in the president of the USSR, and one to disband the USSR Supreme Soviet, but the one on the presidency was the only one actually included on the March 17 ballot.

20. Press conference held by Boris Yeltsin, Moscow, Feb. 6, 1991. The council included Anatoly Sobchak, Pavel Bunich, Georgy Arbatov, Tatyana Zaslavskaya, Yuri Ryzhov, and other erstwhile Gorbachev supporters; Foreign Broadcast Information Service, *Daily Report: Soviet Union,* Feb. 7, 1991, pp. 66–68.

21. Soviet television, Feb. 21, 1991.

22. Chernyayev, *Shest' let s Gorbachevym,* pp. 408–412.

23. Foreign Broadcast Information Service, *Daily Report: Soviet Union,* Feb. 28, 1991, p. 74.

24. Ibid., p. 76.

25. *Izvestiya,* Mar. 26, 1991.

26. When I discussed this incident with Vadim Bakatin during an interview on October 6, 1992, he remarked that "such a report could have come only from the KGB."

27. *Izvestiya,* Mar. 9, 1991; *Pravda,* Mar. 9, 1991.

28. *Pravda,* Mar. 8, 1991.

29. Chernyayev, *Shest' let s Gorbachevym,* p. 427.

30. On February 15, 1991, Sergei Alekseyev, the committee chairman, issued a statement that concluded that the decree suffered from "substantial gaps and other shortcomings"; *Izvestiya,* Feb. 16, 1991.

31. In a speech to prosecutors in February, Gorbachev stated, "We must have one dictatorship for all—the dictatorship of the law"; Foreign Broadcast Information Service, *Daily Report: Soviet Union,* Feb. 14, 1991, p. 20.

32. *Gazeta wyborcza,* Apr. 6–7, 1991; English translation in Foreign Broadcast Information Service, *Daily Report: Soviet Union,* Apr. 10, 1991, p. 32.

Chapter Eighteen: Gorbachev Looks for Compromise

1. *Pravda,* Apr. 10, 1991.
2. *Moscow News,* no. 16 (1991).
3. *Financial Times,* Apr. 20–21, 1991.
4. The leaders of the three Baltic states, Georgia, and Moldova refused to attend; Yeltsin went on one of his frequent vacations and sent Ruslan Khasbulatov to represent him.
5. Foreign Broadcast Information Service, *Daily Report: Soviet Union, Supplement,* Apr. 11, 1991, pp. 13–15.
6. Foreign Broadcast Information Service, *Daily Report: Soviet Union,* Apr. 23, 1991, p. 23.
7. *Izvestiya,* Apr. 24, 1991.
8. *Izvestiya,* Apr. 9, 1991.
9. We had been told that two members of the Soyuz radical wing, Viktor Alksnis, one of the "black colonels," and Yevgeny Kogan, a Russian speaker of Jewish heritage from Estonia, would also attend the lunch. They did not come, however, and our guests offered no explanation for their absence.
10. Some of the Soyuz leaders not at the lunch were notorious for charging that the CIA was conducting a massive campaign to destroy the Soviet Union.
11. Translated from a videotape recording of the television broadcast of the session.
12. The vote was 588 in favor, 292 opposed, with 75 abstentions.
13. *Komsomolskaya Pravda,* Apr. 5, 1991.
14. Gorbachev said in an interview with a foreign publication in the 1980s that he had been baptized as an infant and that he considered this "completely normal."
15. During an interview in September 1992, Yeltsin told me he had come to believe in God and the value of prayer when his life was spared during the August 1991 coup attempt.
16. *Le Monde,* Apr. 17, 1991, p. 4.
17. The evening news program, *Vremya,* delayed its coverage until the last day of the four-day visit; Foreign Broadcast Information Service, *Daily Report: Soviet Union,* Apr. 18, 1991, pp. 37–38.
18. See, for example, Sylvie Kaufmann's interview with Yeltsin in *Le Monde,* Apr. 17, 1991, p. 4.
19. Foreign Broadcast Information Service, *Daily Report: Soviet Union,* Apr. 18, 1991, pp. 36–37.
20. *Pravda,* Apr. 24, 1991.
21. Delegations headed by USSR First Deputy Prime Minister Vitaly Doguzhiev (who had been in charge of coordinating humanitarian assistance from abroad) and Česlovac Stankevičius, the Landsbergis deputy who had accompanied Lithuanian Prime Minister Kazimiera Prunskienė in her meeting with Secretary of State Baker, met on April 4, 1991, to initiate the negotiations.
22. Roman Solchanyk, "The Draft Union Treaty and the 'Big Five,'" RFE/RL Research Institute, *Report on the USSR,* May 3, 1991, pp. 16–18.

23. Following the Party Congress of 1990, the Central Committee no longer had the power to remove the general secretary, as it had Khrushchev in 1964, since that official was now elected by the Party Congress. It was assumed, however, that Gorbachev would resign if a majority vote should be cast against him.

24. *Pravda,* Apr. 23, 1991.

25. Quoted in Anatoly Chernyaev, *Shest' let s Gorbachevym* (Moscow: Izdatelskaya Gruppa Progress, Kultura, 1993), p. 442.

26. Valentin Stepankov and Yevgeny Lisov, *Kremlyovsky zagovor* (Moscow: Izdatelstvo Ogonyok, 1992), pp. 76–77.

27. Author's interview with Eduard Shevardnadze, Apr. 29, 1991.

28. These laws are covered in Yulia Pospelova and Lev Sigal, "Law on Russian Presidency Breezes Through Parliament," *Commersant,* Apr. 29, 1991, p. 2.

29. Shortly after he recovered from his heart attack, Ryzhkov expressed his resentment of his treatment by Gorbachev in an interview published in the *Sunday Telegraph* (London), Apr. 7, 1991, p. 17.

30. A book he later published revealed that he was an ill-informed, xenophobic populist; Aman Tuleyev, *Dolgoe ekho putcha: Kak zhit' dal'she* (Moscow: Paleye, 1992).

31. *Rossiiskaya gazeta,* July 11, 1991.

Chapter Nineteen: Blindman's Bluff

1. From a speech at a closed session of the USSR Supreme Soviet. The text was later published in *Den,* Dec. 15–21, 1991, and in *Krasnoe ili beloe? Drama Avgust-91: Fakty, Gipotezy, Stolknovenie mnenye* (Moscow: Terra, 1992), pp. 42–45.

2. *Pravda,* June 22, 1991.

3. Author's conversation with Gavriil Popov, July 22, 1991.

4. According to Chernyaev, German Chancellor Helmut Kohl told him at one point that if Gorbachev came to London as a guest in 1991, he would be sure to participate as a full member in 1992; Anatoly Chernyaev, *Shest' let s Gorbachevym* (Moscow: Izdatelskaya Gruppa Progress, Kultura, 1993), p. 445.

5. For example, on May 20, 1991, *The Times* (London) ran a front-page story headlined "Beleaguered President Turns to West: Secret Envoys Sent to Seek Aid for Gorbachev."

6. Foreign Broadcast Information Service, *Daily Report: Soviet Union,* May 24, 1991, pp. 19–22.

7. The phrase in Russian, *shans na soglasie,* means literally "chance for accord," but "window of opportunity" is a more felicitous rendering in English.

8. *Pravda,* June 18, 1991, and *Izvestiya,* June 18, 1991.

9. *Nezavisimaya gazeta,* June 19, 1991.

10. These quotations are based on my memory, since I kept no record. Nevertheless, I am certain that the key elements are correct.

11. In fact, the story must have been distributed more widely than was prudent. Within a few weeks the story had leaked to writer Michael Beschloss and *Time* magazine Washington bureau chief Strobe Talbott, who were collecting

material for a book on U.S.-Soviet relations during the Bush administration. Talbott, already in possession of the basic facts, questioned me about the incident in September 1991, when I was in Washington.

12. Chernyayev, *Shest' let s Gorbachevym,* p. 451.

13. The record of this conversation, which Chernyayev reproduced in his book, contains several inaccuracies, probably because he took few notes as we talked (he observed the whole exchange with some astonishment, only sporadically jotting anything down) and wrote it up later from memory.

For example, he quotes me as saying that "American intelligence has received information that there will be an attempt to remove you tomorrow." In fact, I never referred to an intelligence report but only to "a report based on more than rumor but less than hard information," and also I did not specify that the attempt to remove him would be the next day. Popov had not mentioned a date, though his effort to get a message to Yeltsin implied that the attempt could be imminent.

Many people, particularly Soviets, automatically assume that any reference to a "report" means an intelligence report. In fact, if it is a political topic, it is much more likely to be a diplomatic report. I had foreseen this possible misunderstanding and therefore had consciously tried to use a phrase which would not suggest covert intelligence. Judging from Chernyayev's notes, my effort failed.

Chernyayev also misunderstood another statement I made. Somehow he got the idea that I myself did not believe the content of the message. Actually, all I said was that we could not confirm the information, which was, of course, true; personally, I was convinced that it was probably accurate, but, without naming the persons involved, I was not in a position to explain why; see Chernyayev, *Shest' let s Gorbachevym,* pp. 450–452.

14. Chernyayev, *Shest' let s Gorbachevym,* pp. 452–453.

15. From a statement Bessmertnykh gave to Soviet prosecutors investigating the origin of the August coup attempt; published in V. Stepankov and Ye. Lisov, *Kremlyovski zagovor* (Moscow: Izdatelstvo Ogonyok, 1992), p. 79.

16. Author's conversation with Gavriil Popov, Moscow, March 20, 1992.

17. Michael Beschloss and Strobe Talbott described these meetings in Washington in detail in *At the Highest Levels* (Boston: Little, Brown, 1993), pp. 384–391. Chernyayev discusses his role in the discussions and Gorbachev's attitude in *Shest' let s Gorbachevym,* pp. 448–450.

18. Beschloss and Talbott, *At the Highest Levels,* p. 391.

19. Chernyayev, *Shest' let s Gorbachevym,* p. 450.

20. Based on a discussion with Yavlinsky on June 1, 1994, in Moscow. Yavlinsky also published an account of this experience, "Shans na soglasie," in the Moscow weekly *Ekho Planety,* no. 44 (October–December 1993), pp. 18–21.

21. At that time Burbulis was one of Yeltsin's closest advisers, but he was already pressing for Russia to declare independence rather than sign a union treaty.

22. Yavlinsky, "Shans na soglasie," p. 20. In the autumn of 1990, Gorbachev had given assurances that "all the good parts" of the "500-Day Plan" would be retained when it was reconciled with the government plan.

23. Although the Group of Seven had agreed to grant the Soviet Union associate membership, which would have entitled it to technical assistance, Gorbachev was unwilling to accept what he considered second-rate status in these organizations. Therefore, the formal application for membership, announced on July 23, 1991, was for full membership. Although the principal Western countries felt that the Soviet economy did not yet qualify for full membership, the Soviet application was eventually accepted.

24. The quotations are from Chernyayev, *Shest' let s Gorbachevym,* pp. 455–457.

25. Beschloss and Talbott, *At the Highest Levels,* p. 407.

26. Chernyayev, *Shest' let s Gorbachevym,* p. 457.

27. Chernyayev has described how the phrase "choice of socialism"—thitherto an obligatory part of the Communist Party catechism—was dropped in the final edit; Chernyayev, *Shest' let s Gorbachevym,* pp. 473–475.

28. Foreign Broadcast Information Service, *Daily Report: Soviet Union,* July 22, 1991, p. 71.

29. Chernyayev, *Shest' let s Gorbachevym,* pp. 394–395.

30. Foreign Broadcast Information Service, *Daily Report: Soviet Union,* Aug. 1, 1991, pp. 17–19.

31. The return dinner, which the Bushes hosted at Spaso House, went off more smoothly. The Yeltsins, the Nazarbayevs, and the Ter-Petrosians of Armenia all attended, and during the dinner Nazarbayev, ever the conciliator, went to the tables where Yeltsin and Ter-Petrosian were seated and invited them to go with him to the head table and to offer a collective toast to Bush and Gorbachev.

32. A subsequent investigation by the Lithuanian authorities revealed that the attack had been made by personnel from the Riga OMON unit, the "black beret" forces under the Ministry of Internal Affairs ostensibly organized to conduct antiterrorist operations. Although there had been other attacks on Lithuanian border posts, which Moscow considered illegal, none involved the sorts of brutal murders that occurred on July 31. Investigators assumed that the brutality of the operation had been planned specifically to disrupt the Bush-Gorbachev meeting; "Zagovor protiv Litvy," *Izvestiya,* Dec. 19, 1991, p. 3.

33. We never learned for certain who had authorized the original message, but I suspect it had come directly from Gorbachev. I doubt that an assistant, even one of high rank, would have presumed to offer a trip to Stavropol with Gorbachev without checking with Gorbachev.

34. Besides needling Bush, Safire may have been atoning for an earlier offense against Ukrainian national feelings. While he was speechwriter for President Nixon, he had accepted a suggestion from Soviet Ambassador Anatoly Dobrynin and had had Nixon refer to Kiev as the "mother of Russian cities" upon his arrival. What Dobrynin had failed to explain, and Safire apparently did not know, was that this was a phrase used by Russians to stress the unity of Russian and Ukrainian history. It was abhorred by Ukrainians, who considered it a Russian chauvinist attempt to rob Ukrainians of their distinctiveness. But Safire did not have to deal with the consequences; as director of Soviet affairs in the State Department at that time, I had to answer the mail from indignant Ukrainians.

35. For example, the action of the Ukrainian parliament in July 1991 to take property under Ukrainian government control rather than let it be privatized by Moscow.

36. See Roman Solchanyk, "Ukraine and the Union Treaty," RFE/RL Research Institute, *Report on the USSR,* July 26, 1991, pp. 22–24.

37. Address on Moscow television, August 2, 1991; translation available in Foreign Broadcast Information Service, *Daily Report: Soviet Union,* Aug. 5, 1991, pp. 35–36.

38. The word he used, *obedineniye,* is sometimes translated as "union," but it implies a looser association than *soyuz,* the word used for "union" in "the Soviet Union." His choice of the word was politically significant; the March referendum had been in favor of a *soyuz,* not an *obedineniye.*

39. *Literaturnaya Rossiya,* July 19, 1991.

40. *Nezavisimaya gazeta,* Aug. 8, 1991.

41. For example, Mikhail Poltoranin told me during an interview on September 23, 1992, that he was convinced that Yeltsin would not have signed.

42. On background, you can say "No comment" and not get quoted; on the record, refusal to comment can be cited as implicit confirmation of the question asked.

43. Transcribed from a tape recording of the August 5, 1991, press conference; ellipses indicate indistinct portions.

Chapter 20: Coup Perdu

1. *Pravda,* Aug. 20, 1991.

2. Rossiisky nezavisimy institut sotsialnykh i natsinalnykh problem, *Krasnoe ili Beloe? Drama Avgust-91: Fakty, Gipotezy, Stolknovenie mnenye* (Moscow: Terra, 1992), p. 73.

3. Quoted in Valentin Stepankov and Yevgeny Lisov, *Kremlyovski zagovor* (Moscow: Izdatelstvo Ogonyok, 1992), p. 86.

4. Boris Yeltsin, *The Struggle for Russia* (New York: Random House, 1994), p. 41.

5. Ibid., pp. 38–39.

6. Ibid., p. 39.

7. These and subsequent details of preparations for the attempted coup d'état in August 1991 come from the published records of the investigation conducted after the coup failed; Stepankov and Lisov, *Kremlyovski zagovor.*

8. Ibid., p. 84.

9. Ibid., p. 85.

10. Ibid., pp. 85–86.

11. Recounted in Mikhail Gorbachev, *The August Coup* (New York: HarperCollins, 1991), pp. 18–19.

12. In Gorbachev's words: "Using the strongest language that Russians always use in such circumstances, I told them where to go"; ibid., pp. 19–24.

13. This account of the meeting in the Kremlin, including all direct quotations, is based on Stepankov and Lisov, *Kremlyovski zagovor,* pp. 89–91.

14. Texts of the various announcements, along with the times of transmis-

sion (Greenwich Mean Time) can be found in Foreign Broadcast Information Service, *Daily Report: Soviet Union,* Aug. 19, 1991, pp. 9–13.

15. Foreign Broadcast Information Service, *Daily Report: Soviet Union,* Aug. 19, 1991, pp. 19–20.

16. Although it was dated August 16, *Izvestiya* later reported that the original copy given to TASS was dated August 18. A "correction" was later issued to change the date to August 16 in order to make it appear that the statement had been signed before the Emergency Committee was named.

17. Foreign Broadcast Information Service, *Daily Report: Soviet Union,* Aug. 19, 1991, p. 15.

18. In Latvia, for example, Alfreds Rubiks, the first secretary of the Moscow-oriented Latvian Communist Party, responded by announcing the formation of a local Emergency Committee headed by Fyodor Kuzmin, commander of the Baltic Military District; Foreign Broadcast Information Service, *Daily Report: Soviet Union,* Aug. 19, 1991, p. 34.

19. Author's interview with Nazarbayev staff assistant Gani Kasymov in Almaty, Oct. 1, 1992.

20. Yeltsin himself told me in an interview on September 19, 1992, that the delayed departure had "saved [his] life" since orders had been given to shoot down his plane shortly after departure at 5:00 P.M. According to Yeltsin, when the departure was delayed, the commander of the missile unit was not sure that the order was still in effect; unable to get confirmation from Moscow that it applied to an 8:00 P.M. departure, he did nothing. Aside from this account, however, I have seen no evidence that orders were issued to shoot Yeltsin's plane down; if such orders existed, it is likely they would have surfaced during the investigation following the coup attempt.

21. Stepankov and Lisov, *Kremlyovski zagovor,* pp. 110–111.

22. Yeltsin, *The Struggle for Russia,* p. 57.

23. Testimony by some of the KGB officers in the Alpha Detachment is included in Stepankov and Lisov, *Kremlyovski zagovor,* pp. 117–121.

24. Ibid., p. 132.

25. Michael Beschloss and Strobe Talbott, *At the Highest Levels* (Boston: Little, Brown, 1993), pp. 422–423.

26. Ibid., p. 433.

27. A translation of the text was published in Foreign Broadcast Information Service, *Daily Report: Soviet Union,* Aug. 20, 1991, pp. 2–8. The words, however, fail to convey the hesitant, faltering images captured by the television camera. I based my own judgment on a videotape recording of the television broadcast made at Columbia University.

28. Vadim Bakatin, *Izbavlenie ot KGB* (Moscow: Novosti, 1992), pp. 14–15. Primakov and Bakatin asked Alexander Bessmertnykh, also a member of the Security Council, to join them in this declaration. He refused, citing the need to avoid damage to the Ministry of Foreign Affairs. If he had signed, he might not have been dismissed after Gorbachev's return to Moscow.

29. Bakatin reports that he was called from Rutskoy's office in the White House with the request to use his influence with Yazov to prevent an attack by paratroops. Yazov, however, denied that there was any intent to attack the

White House, and Bakatin thought he was telling the truth; Bakatin, *Izbavlenie ot KGB,* p. 15.

30. James Billington, *Russia Transformed: Breakthrough to Hope* (New York: The Free Press, 1992), pp. 49–59.

31. Ibid., p. 54.

32. Yuri S. Sidorenko, *Tri dnya, kotorye oprokinuli bolshevism* (Rostov-on-Don: Periodika Dona, 1991), p. 30.

33. Some subsequently doubted that Akhromeyev, a proud officer, would have hanged himself. Military tradition had it that the proper instrument for suicide was a pistol. However, it appears that Akhromeyev did not have a pistol in his office, having turned in his service revolver when he retired, and resorted to the rope because he had no choice; Stepankov and Lisov, *Kremlyovski zagovor,* pp. 236–244.

34. An English translation can be found in Foreign Broadcast Information Service, *Daily Report: Soviet Union,* Aug. 23, 1991, pp. 20–30.

35. Foreign Broadcast Information Service, *Daily Report: Soviet Union,* Aug. 23, 1991, p. 28.

36. Ibid., p. 29.

37. Ibid., pp. 30–32.

38. An English translation of the transcript was published in "Gorbachev's Speech to Russians: 'A Major Regrouping of Political Forces,' " *The New York Times,* Aug. 24, 1991, p. 6.

39. The texts of Gorbachev's statement and decrees were published in "Gorbachev's Statement on Party," *The New York Times,* Aug. 25, 1991, p. 14.

40. Bakatin, *Izbavlenie ot KGB,* p. 59.

Chapter Twenty-one: Fatal Blows

1. Foreign Broadcast Information Service, *Daily Report: Soviet Union,* Aug. 27, 1991, p. 3.

2. *Izvestiya,* Sept. 4, 1991.

3. *Izvestiya,* Nov. 15, 1991.

4. *Izvestiya,* Nov. 26, 1991.

5. Earlier declarations had stopped just short of declaring immediate independence. In 1990 Estonia had declared "a period of transition to independence," and earlier in 1991 it had reinstated some articles of its prewar constitution, Latvia had announced that the independent Republic of Latvia was still in existence de jure, but it was prepared to negotiate the terms of de facto independence with Moscow.

6. The treaty was concluded on July 31, 1991, while President Bush was in Moscow; Foreign Broadcast Information Service, *Daily Report: Soviet Union,* July 31, 1991, p. 70.

7. The United States, in deference to Gorbachev's request, delayed recognition for a few days. President Bush was criticized for this at the time, but the short delay was not unreasonable and did no damage to the Baltic governments.

8. The vote was actually 94.39% in favor of independence and 0.46% op-

posed; Elizabeth Fuller, "Armenia Votes Overwhelmingly for Secession," RFE/RL Research Institute, *Report on the USSR,* Sept. 27, 1991, pp. 18–20.

9. Also spelled Dzemyantsei and Dziemianciej, depending on the transliteration from the Belorussian alphabet.

10. Based on author's interviews with Zenon Pazniak, the National Front leader, and Stanislav Shushkevich, the Belarusian parliament chairman, in Minsk, Sept. 24, 1992. The events are covered in detail in Walter Stankievich, "The Events Behind Belorussia's Independence Declaration," RFE/RL Research Institute, *Report on the USSR,* Sept. 20, 1991, pp. 24–26.

11. Author's interview with Shushkevich, Sept. 24, 1992.

12. Kravchuk was accused by some of equivocating, but, if so, he hesitated for only a few hours. On the evening of August 19, he agreed to a statement declaring the emergency committee's decrees inoperative on Ukrainian territory.

13. Ironically, one of the reasons Gamsakhurdia gave for dismissing the foreign minister was that the latter had failed to secure a meeting with President Bush during Bush's trip to Moscow in July. Actually, Bush had refused to meet with Gamsakhurdia because of his flagrant violations of human rights, particularly in South Ossetia.

14. The RSFSR Federal Security Agency was founded by President Yeltsin's decree of November 26, 1991. For Bakatin's role in assisting in its creation and his dealings with other republics as KGB chairman, see Vadim Bakatin, *Izbavlenie ot KGB* (Moscow: Novosti, 1992), pp. 91–128.

15. The senior body in the ministry, made up of the minister and his deputies plus the commanders of military regions.

16. Alexander Rahr offered an excellent analysis of these groups in "Russia's 'Young Turks' in Power," RFE/RL Research Institute, *Report on the USSR,* Nov. 22, 1991, pp. 20–23.

17. *Izvestiya,* Oct. 1, 1991.

18. Gorbachev protested that it was improper to ban the Communist Party as such. However, in an interview on September 30, 1992, in Moscow, he told me that he would have agreed to ban "Party structures," that is, the specific organizational forms it had taken to rule the country.

19. Yeltsin's ban was challenged in the Russian courts, and a year later the Constitutional Court upheld only part of the ban. It ruled that the president could dissolve Communist Party structures but could not forbid organization of a new party with the same name.

20. Chernyayev lists about eighty foreign political figures with whom Gorbachev met during this period, some more than once; Anatoly Chernyayev, *Shest' let s Gorbachevym* (Moscow: Izdatelskaya Gruppa Progress, Kultura, 1993), pp. 496–497.

21. Even though technical means existed to shield the building from listening devices, Congress had for years forbidden the State Department to finish it. The Senate refused to appropriate funds to use it at all but was willing to fund a different building. The House of Representatives, in contrast, refused to authorize a different building unless the unfinished one could be used. As a result, our diplomats had to work in Moscow in a crowded and dangerous firetrap. Unfortunately, even Bakatin's gesture was insufficient to settle the issue.

22. Only Georgia and Moldova refused to attend the first meeting of the new State Council.

23. The negotiations were discussed in detail by M. Berger in *Izvestiya,* Sept. 27, 1991, p. 2, and *Izvestiya,* Sept. 30, 1991, p. 2. English translations can be found in *Current Digest of the Soviet Press,* vol. 43, no. 39 (1991), pp. 5–7.

24. The text of the treaty was published in *Rossiiskaya gazeta,* Oct. 22, 1991. An English translation can be found in *Current Digest of the Soviet Press,* vol. 43, no. 42 (1991), pp. 4–9.

25. Andrei Grachev, *Dalshe bez menya . . . : Ukhod Prezidenta* (Moscow: Izdatelskaya Gruppa Progress, 1994), p. 123.

26. The quotations and description of the scene are from Gorbachev's press secretary, Andrei Grachev, who was present at the meeting and took notes; Grachev, *Dalshe bez menya . . . ,* pp. 123–124.

27. Ibid., p. 145.

28. Ibid., p. 145.

29. Ibid., p. 148.

30. Foreign Broadcast Information Service, *Daily Report: Soviet Union,* Nov. 15, 1991, p. 26.

31. Ibid., p. 27.

32. Since the founding of the United Nations, the Ukrainian and Belorussian SSRs had been granted U.N. membership separately from that of the USSR. The result of a political deal Roosevelt and Churchill struck with Stalin (who had asked for separate U.N. membership for each republic of the Soviet Union), the arrangement worked because the Belorussian and Ukrainian delegations always voted with the USSR. In effect, the arrangement was a device to give Stalin two extra votes in the organization. Aside from this single example, there was no precedent for accepting constituent parts of a member state as full members of the organization.

33. The full text of the draft treaty was carried in *Izvestiya,* Nov. 26, 1991. An English translation is available in Foreign Broadcast Information Service, *Daily Report: Soviet Union,* Nov. 26, 1991, pp. 21–25.

34. Grachev, *Dalshe bez menya . . . ,* pp. 164–165.

35. Mikhail Gorbachev, *Dekabr' 1991: Moya pozitsiya* (Moscow: Novosti, 1992), pp. 11–15; Grachev, *Dalshe bez menya . . . ,* p. 164; Bakatin, *Izbavlenie ot KGB,* pp. 218–219.

36. Author's interview with Stanislav Shushkevich in Minsk, Sept. 24, 1992.

37. Grachev recounted this exchange in his account of the meeting, Grachev, *Dalshe bez menya . . . ,* p. 16.

Chapter Twenty-two: Coup de Grâce

1. Speech at the All-Russian Congress of Judges, Moscow, Oct. 18, 1991; *Rossiiskaya gazeta,* Oct. 19, 1991.

2. Address to the RSFSR Supreme Soviet, Dec. 12, 1991; *Pravda,* Dec. 13, 1991.

3. *Komsomolskaya Pravda,* Dec. 13, 1991.

4. "Ukraine Hears Its President's Oath and Breaks with the Union," *Izvestiya,* Dec. 6, 1991.

5. See, e.g., "Minsk Prepares for a Meeting of Leaders of the Three Slavic Republics," *Izvestiya,* Dec. 5, 1991, p. 1.

6. *Izvestiya,* Dec. 7, 1991, p. 1. "Triple alliance" could also be translated as "triple union."

7. "Conversation of the USSR President and the President of Russia," *Rossiiskaya gazeta,* Dec. 7, 1991.

8. I discussed the meeting with each of them separately in September 1992.

9. "Declaration by the Chiefs of State of Belarus, the RSFSR, and Ukraine," *Rossiiskaya gazeta,* Dec. 10, 1991, p. 1.

10. Author's interview with Stanislav Shushkevich in Minsk, Sept. 24, 1992.

11. Russian texts of the agreement and the other declarations made following the meeting in Bison Forest (all of which indicate that the official place of signature was Minsk) can be found in *Izvestiya,* Dec. 10, 1991, and *Rossiiskaya gazeta,* Dec. 10, 1991. English translations can be found in Foreign Broadcast Information Service, *Daily Report: Soviet Union,* Dec. 10, 1991, pp. 56–57.

12. Foreign Broadcast Information Service, *Daily Report: Soviet Union,* Dec. 9, 1991, p. 32.

13. *Izvestiya,* Dec. 10, 1991, p. 2; English translation in Foreign Broadcast Information Service, *Daily Report: Soviet Union,* Dec. 10, 1991, pp. 15–16.

14. *Izvestiya,* Dec. 10, 1991.

15. Along with the defunct Transcaucasian Soviet Socialist Republic, which was later split into three union republics of Armenia, Azerbaijan, and Georgia.

16. Author's interview with Konstantin Lubenchenko in Moscow, Mar. 13, 1992.

17. See, e.g., "Serious Government Crisis in Russia; Rutskoy Not to Resign, Will Go on the Attack," *Izvestiya,* Dec. 5, 1991.

18. *Izvestiya,* Dec. 19, 1991.

Chapter Twenty-three: Reflections on Some Answers

1. Alexander Herzen, "The Development of Revolutionary Ideas in Russia," *Sobranie sochinenii v 30i tomakh* (Moscow: Izdatelstvo Akademii nauk SSSR, 1964–65), vol. 7, p. 31 (French text) and pp. 160–161 (Russian text).

2. From a speech in Munich, reproduced in Mikhael Gorbachev, *Dekabr' 1991: Moya pozitsiya* (Moscow: Novosti, 1992), pp. 195–196.

3. Boris Yeltsin, *The Struggle for Russia* (New York: Random House, 1994), p. 35.

4. Ibid.

5. Lecture by Levon Ter-Petrosian at Columbia University, New York, Sept. 26, 1994.

6. *Nezavisimaya gazeta,* English ed., vol. 3, no. 6–7 (1992).

7. A phrase used by Vladislav Starkov in an interview with the author Mar. 17, 1992. Starkov explained that Gorbachev had not opposed the Soviet system but "swam in it." He was a product of the system, and it was simply his historical fate to be in power when it collapsed through no personal contribution of his own.

8. This is essentially the judgment of Gorbachev's conservative and reformist critics, although these groups have diametrically opposing views of what he should have done. Conservatives, such as Ligachev and Ryzhkov, hold that he should have stayed with the policies of 1985 and 1986 and not attempted fundamental political changes, especially those which weakened the Communist Party. Yeltsin and other reformers, on the other hand, charge that he was too cautious in pressing for political change, consistently underestimating the degree of support that reform would attract in Soviet society.

9. This, with some individual qualifications, is the view of close Gorbachev associates such as Alexander Yakovlev and Anatoly Chernyayev.

10. Gorbachev, *Dekabr' 1991,* p. 195.

11. Ibid., pp. 195–196.

12. Author's interview with Gorbachev in Moscow, Sept. 30, 1992.

13. Raisa Gorbacheva was not reticent about expressing her opinion of people. Her hostility to Yeltsin in 1987 could well have played a role in the vehemence of her husband's rejection of Yeltsin. Nor was she always discreet when discussing her husband's colleagues. In 1990, just after the Party Congress, she criticized Alexander Yakovlev to foreigners at a diplomatic reception for having suggested that Politburo members should retire at age sixty-five. She apparently felt that Yakovlev was implying that Gorbachev should retire at sixty-five— some six years off—when Yakovlev was simply offering a face-saving explanation for the fact that he had not been reelected to the Politburo.

14. This refers to the period under discussion, up to December 1991. Subsequently, following his struggle with the Russian parliament in 1993, Yeltsin withdrew an offer to hold presidential elections in the spring of 1994.

15. There is circumstantial evidence that Valery Boldin worked as Kryuchkov's agent throughout his tenure as Gorbachev's chief of staff. As early as December 1977, there was a curious incident involving Boldin in one of the meetings during the Washington summit. Although not designated as a participant, Boldin slipped into one of the restricted meetings in the Oval Office, sat at the side, and took notes. The U.S. participants thought little of it; apparently, Gorbachev had asked him to come in after the list was drawn up. Subsequently, however, a member of the Soviet delegation told me that his joining the group had been a surprise to them as well. He was not sent out because they did not want to create a stir, but the Soviet officials wondered how he had gotten past their own security officers. Following the August 1991 coup, the incident seemed to have an explanation other than Boldin's personal curiosity; that is, he must have been sent by Kryuchkov, who was a member of the Soviet delegation but had not been included in the meeting, to report on what Gorbachev said. This would explain why the KGB guards had let him into the room even though his name was not on the list of participants.

The fact that Kryuchkov and Boldin were meeting together in Boldin's office during the attack on the Vilnius television complex in January 1991, and the transcripts of Gorbachev's conversations, which they had monitored, were found in Boldin's office after the coup attempt demonstrate the very close association of the two men.

16. Author's interview with Vadim Bakatin in Moscow, Oct. 6, 1992.

17. A Soviet court later invalidated Gorbachev's decrees. Kalugin himself managed to escape criminal prosecution only by winning election to a seat in the USSR Congress of People's Deputies and thus acquiring parliamentary immunity. Ironically, he was elected in archconservative Ivan Polozkov's district when the latter gave up his seat to take over the leadership of the Russian Communist Party.

Chapter Twenty-four: Epilogue

1. *Nezavisimaya gazeta,* English edition, July 1982.

2. A remark frequently made by Yeltsin; it is repeated in his memoir *The Struggle for Russia* (New York: Random House, 1994), p. 145.

3. *Rossiiskaya gazeta,* December 10, 1991; translated in *The Current Digest of the Soviet Press,* vol. 43, no. 49 (Jan. 8, 1992), pp. 10–11.

4. Soviet naval forces were organized in four fleets: the Northern Fleet, based at Murmansk; the Baltic Fleet, based at Kronstadt; the Pacific Fleet, based at Vladivostok; and the Black Sea Fleet, based at Sevastopol in the Crimea. All except the last were on Russian soil and passed automatically to Russian command.

5. Yeltsin's decree was published in *Krasnaya zvezda* on May 9, 1992. For a discussion of early moves to organize the Russian army, see Stephen Foye, "Post-Soviet Russia: Politics and the New Russian Army," *RFE/RL Research Report,* vol. 1, no. 33 (Aug. 21, 1992), pp. 5–12.

6. Ben Slay, "Rapid Versus Gradual Economic Transition," *RFE/RL Research Report,* vol. 3, no. 31 (Aug. 12, 1994), p. 37.

7. Some political insiders attributed Khasbulatov's estrangement from Yeltsin not to the substantive issues involved but to his disappointment when he was not named Russian prime minister. In fact, Khasbulatov earlier had been a supporter of the very policies he began to condemn in 1992.

8. For example, in November 1992, Arkady Volsky told a forum in Moscow sponsored by the *Financial Times* that the capital flight during the first ten months of the year had been on the order of $16 billion to $18 billion.

9. Author's interview with Boris Yeltsin Sept. 19, 1992.

10. The four questions and the votes were: (1) Do you have confidence in the president of the Russian Federation, Boris Yeltsin? [Yes—58.7%; No—39.2%]; (2) Do you approve of the socioeconomic policies carried out by the president and government since 1992? [Yes—53%; No—44.6%]; (3) Do you consider it necessary to hold early elections for president? [Yes—49.5%; No—47.1%]; (4) Do you consider it necessary to hold early elections for people's deputies? [Yes—62.7%; No—30.1%]. These results implied that Yeltsin's support was almost double that of his opponents in the Russian parliament. See Wendy Slater, "No Victors in the Russian Referendum," *RFE/RL Research Report,* vol. 2, no. 21 (May 21, 1993), pp. 10–19.

11. In terms of total seats, Russia's Choice had 96 to the LDP's 70, but the Communist Party placed third with 65 and the Agrarian Party, dominated by state- and collective-farm managers, held fourth place with 47. See Vera Tolz,

"Russia's Parliamentary Elections: What Happened and Why," *RFE/RL Research Report,* vol. 3, no. 2 (Jan. 14, 1994), p. 3.

12. Ilya Zaslavsky, one of the leaders of Gaidar's Russia's Choice party, told me in January 1994, that he had been so confident of an easy victory that he had not bothered to vote!

13. According to Yeltsin's "state of the nation" address on Feb. 16, 1995, the private sector accounted for 62% of the Russian gross domestic product in 1994; Open Media Research Institute, *Daily Digest,* no. 35, Feb. 17, 1995.

14. For example, the data showed that electricity consumption decreased by 14% from 1990 to late 1994, while industrial production supposedly fell by 44%; Peter Rutland, "A Twisted Path Toward a Market Economy," *Transition,* Feb. 15, 1995, p. 12.

15. *Argumenty i Fakty,* no. 24, June 1994.

16. *Argumenty i Fakty,* no. 31, August 1994.

17. Goskomstat announcement of Feb. 15, 1995, quoted in Open Media Research Institute, *Daily Digest,* Feb. 17, 1995.

18. Ironically, the only Soviet official who ever discussed the subject with me seriously was Oleg Baklanov, the Central Committee secretary for defense and heavy industry, who helped organize the August 1991 attempted coup. In January of that year, he approached me for information about U.S. conflict-of-interest legislation. I obtained a set of relevant laws from Washington and forwarded them to his office but was never aware that anyone made a serious effort to define precisely what a civil servant could or could not do in the growing private sector.

19. The Interfax News Agency, quoting an official in the Interior Ministry, reported on Feb. 26, 1995, that the illegal flight of capital from Russia totaled $50 billion in 1994 and that it was still rising at the rate of $1.5 billion to $2 billion a month; Open Media Research Institute, *Daily Digest,* Feb. 28, 1995.

20. Brazauskas defeated Stasys Lazoraitis, who had lived in emigration for fifty years. The presidential election on Feb. 14, 1993, was the first ever held in Lithuania. Previously, the chief of state had been the chairman of the Seimas.

21. In the presidential election of Sept. 20, 1992, Rüütel had won a plurality, with 42.7% of the vote, but the Estonian Constitution authorized the parliament to select the president if no candidate secured an absolute majority. On Oct. 6, 1992, the Estonian parliament elected Meri, who had received only 28.8% of the vote.

22. Andres Tarand, who had previously been minister of the environment, was named prime minister.

23. "Estonia's Government Is Ousted in Vote Signaling Slower Reform," *The New York Times,* Mar. 7, 1995, p. A-10.

24. Under the agreement, Ukraine would get 164 of the 833 ships in the fleet. See Ustina Markus, "Ukraine: Stability amid Political Turnover," *Transition,* Feb. 15, 1995, p. 69.

25. Operational control of nuclear missiles in Ukraine remained effectively in Russian hands, since only the Russian president had the means of arming and releasing the missiles. However, they could not be moved out of Ukraine without Ukrainian approval.

26. See John W. R. Lepingwell, "The Trilateral Agreement on Nuclear Weapons," *RFE/RL Research Report,* vol. 3, no. 4 (Jan. 28, 1994), pp. 12–20.

27. Suzanne Crow, "Russian Parliament Asserts Control over Sevastopol," *RFE/RL Research Report,* vol. 2, no. 31 (July 30, 1993), pp. 37–41.

28. I have used "Belarus" and "Belarussian" to refer to the country and its nationality after the official change of name in September 1991 but "Belorussia" and "Belorussian" when the reference is to the period before independence.

29. Unlike "right-bank Moldova" to the west of the Dniester, this territory had been part of the USSR from its inception in 1922 and was an autonomous unit within the Ukrainian SSR. When the USSR annexed Bessarabia following the Nazi-Soviet secret protocol in 1939, it combined the two territories to form the Moldavian Soviet Socialist Republic. The rural population in "left-bank Moldova" was largely Moldovan, but the cities were heavily populated by Russians and Ukrainians, most of whom had moved into the area since the 1940s.

30. Sometimes translated as "Trans-Dniester Republic."

31. Rudolf A. Mark, "Progress amid Crisis," *Transition,* Feb. 15, 1995, p. 57.

32. Elizabeth Fuller, "Transcaucasia: Ethnic Strife Threatens Democratization," *RFE/RL Research Report,* vol. 2, no. 1 (Jan. 1, 1993), p. 22.

33. Ethnic Abkhazians made up less than 18% of the population of Abkhazia. They were far outnumbered by Georgians, as well as by Russians. The U.N. High Commission for Refugees has estimated that up to 350,000 of Abkhazia's 540,000 population fled Abkhazia between August 1992 and October 1993; *Refugees,* no. 98 (1994), p. 22. In other areas, "ethnic cleansing" was normally conducted by a local majority or substantial plurality. Abkhazia may be the only place where a small minority of the total population forced everyone else out.

34. Fuller, "Transcaucasia."

35. In 1994, the U.N. High Commission for Refugees estimated "internally displaced Azerbaijanis" at at least 630,000 and refugees who had come from Armenia, mainly in 1988, at 228,000, which together made up more than 10% of the total population of Azerbaijan; *Refugees,* no. 98 (1994), p. 25.

36. Elizabeth Fuller, "The Transcaucasus: War Turmoil, Economic Collapse," *RFE/RL Research Report,* vol. 3, no. 1 (Jan. 7, 1994), p. 54.

37. Elizabeth Fuller, "Between Anarchy and Despotism," *Transition,* Feb. 15, 1995, pp. 60–61.

38. "Kak nam obustroit' Rossiyu? Posil'nye soobrazheniya," *Literaturnaya gazeta,* Sept. 18, 1990 (special supplement of 15 pages).

39. China was the only possible alternative, but Kazakhs feared Chinese hegemony more than Russia's and communication and transportation links with China were meager.

40. *Sevodnya,* Jan. 21, 1995, p. 2; translated in *Current Digest of the Post-Soviet Press,* vol. 47, no. 3 (1995), p. 27.

41. *Sevodnya,* Jan. 21, 1995, p. 2.

42. Bess A. Brown, "Central Asia: Overriding Economics," *Transition,* Feb. 15, 1995, p. 55.

43. They also failed to honor commitments to contribute development funds for the area. During the meeting in 1995, Nazarbayev commented that although

international organizations were making the contributions they had promised, the states in the area were not. Uzbekistan, he said, had paid only 2% of its pledge and Turkmenistan nothing at all; Open Media Research Institute, *Daily Digest,* Mar. 6, 1995.

44. See articles in *Nezavisimaya gazeta* and *Sevodnya* of Feb. 16, 1994, translated in *The Current Digest of the Post-Soviet Press,* vol. 46, no. 7 (Mar. 16, 1994), pp. 11–12.

45. Although Dudayev claimed that 77% of those eligible had voted, and that he had received 85% of the vote, observers reported that most polling stations were not even open, and there was no neutral supervision of the vote count. See Ann Sheehy, "Power Struggle in Checheno-Ingushetia," *Report on the USSR,* vol. 3, no. 46 (Nov. 15, 1991), p. 24.

46. Gorbachev's last press secretary, Andrei Grachev, believes that Yeltsin's anger at this intervention, which occurred between Nov. 9 and 11, 1991, may have fueled his final break with Gorbachev; Andrei Grachev, *Dalshe bez menya . . . : Ukhod Prezidenta* (Moscow: Izdatelskaya Gruppa Progress, 1994), p. 134.

47. *Izvestiya* carried a detailed account of how Dudayev's forces took over the Russian armaments in its Jan. 10, 1995, issue: "Kto vooruzhal Dzhokhara Dudayeva?" by Yuri Bespalov and Valery Yakov, pp. 1–2.

48. In 1991, the Chechens and Ingush, a related people, who, like the Chechens, had been deported by Stalin, were united in the same republic, called Chechen-Ingushetia. However, after Dudayev's seizure of power in Grozny, the capital, the Ingush voted to leave the Chechen-Ingush Republic and form their own republic as a constituent part of the Russian Federation. The federal government approved of the split in 1992, and what had been Chechen-Ingushetia became the separate republics of Chechnya, with about 800,000 people, and Ingushetia, with 500,000.

49. Stephen Handelman, who published a careful study on post-Soviet crime, summed up the Dudayev group's role in all of this as follows:

"Whether or not the Dudayev Government directly profited from the illicit arms trade, it made little effort to stop the business. In Moscow, police traced the Chechens' swift rise to power in the post-Soviet crime world to their profits from the sale of drugs and weapons. Within two years of Dudayev's appearance as president, the Chechens were the premier arms dealers of post-communist society. They owned more than five hundred flats in the capital, as well as an estimated one hundred and forty businesses and joint ventures and half a dozen hotels. Although no one could come up with a conclusive link between the syndicates and the government in Grozny, there was circumstantial proof of their mutual dependence. The timing of the Chechen gangs' transformation from small bands involved in petty extortion and stolen-car rackets into sophisticated crime conglomerates trading in guns and drugs coincided with the rise of Chechnya as a financial and political force." Stephen Handelman, *Comrade Criminal: Russia's New Mafiya* (New Haven: Yale University Press, 1995), p. 220.

50. Surveys by the All-Russian Center for the Study of Public Opinion, reported in the Open Media Research Institute *Daily Digest,* Feb. 24, 1995.

51. *Izvestiya,* Jan. 5 and 6, 1995.

Bibliography

Abalkin, Leonid. *Neispol'zovanny shans: Poltora goda v pravitel'stve.* Moscow: Politizdat, 1991.

Afanasiev, Yuri. *Ya dolzhen eto skazat': Politicheskaya publitsistika vremen perestroiki.* Moscow: PIK, 1991.

Afanasiev, Yuri, ed. *Inogo ne dano: Perestroika: glasnost', demokratiya, sotsializm. Sud'by perestroiki; Vglyadyvayas' v proshloe; Vozvrashchenie k budushchemu.* Moscow: Progress, 1988.

Aganbegyan, Abel. *Inside Perestroika: The Future of the Soviet Economy.* New York: Harper & Row, 1989.

Aganbegyan, Abel, and Timor Timofeyev. *The New Stage of Perestroika.* New York: Institute of East-West Security Studies, 1988.

Allworth, Edward A. *The Modern Uzbeks: From the Fourteenth Century to the Present; a Cultural History.* Stanford: Hoover Institution Press, 1990.

Altstadt, Audrey L. *The Azerbaijani Turks: Power and Identity under Russian Rule.* Stanford: Hoover Institution Press, 1992.

Andrew, Christopher, and Oleg Gordievsky. *Comrade Kryuchkov's Instructions: Top Secret Files on KGB Foreign Operations, 1975–1985.* Stanford: Stanford Univ. Press, 1993.

Arbatov, Georgy A. *Zatyanuvsheesya vyzdorovlenie (1953–1985 gg.): Svidetel'stvo sovremennika.* Moscow: Mezhdunarodnye otnosheniya, 1991. English translation: *The System: An Insider's Life in Soviet Politics.* New York: Times Books, 1992.

Aron, Leon, and Kenneth M. Jensen. The *Emergence of Russian Foreign Policy.* Washington: U.S. Institute of Peace, 1994.

Åslund, Anders. *Gorbachev's Struggle for Economic Reform.* Updated and expanded edition. Ithaca: Cornell Univ. Press, 1991.

Attali, Jacques. *Verbatim: Chronique des années 1981–1986.* Vol. 1. Paris: Fayard, 1993.

Bahry, Donna. *Outside Moscow: Power, Politics, and Budgetary Policy in the Soviet Republics.* New York: Columbia Univ. Press, 1987.

Bakatin, Vadim. *Izbavlenie ot KGB.* Moscow: Novosti, 1992.

———. *Osvobozhdenie ot illyuziy.* Kemerovo: Kemerovskoye knizhnoe izdatelstvo, 1992.

Beschloss, Michael R., and Strobe Talbott. *At the Highest Levels: The Inside Story of the End of the Cold War.* Boston: Little, Brown, 1993.

Bialer, Seweryn, ed. *Politics, Society, and Nationality Inside Gorbachev's Russia.* Boulder: Westview Press, 1989.

Bialer, Seweryn, and Michael Mandelbaum, eds. *Gorbachev's Russia and American Foreign Policy.* Boulder: Westview Press, 1988.

Billington, James H. *Russia Transformed: Breakthrough to Hope: Moscow, August 1991.* New York: The Free Press, 1992.

Blacker, Coit D. *Hostage to Revolution: Gorbachev and Soviet Security Policy, 1985–1991.* New York: Council on Foreign Relations, 1993.

Blaney, John W., ed. *The Successor States to the USSR.* Washington: Congressional Quarterly, 1995.

Boldin, Valery. *Ten Years That Shook the World: The Gorbachev Era as Witnessed by His Chief of Staff.* Translated by Evelyn Rossiter. New York: Basic Books, 1994.

Borisova, N. M., ed. *Glasnost': Mneniya, Poiski, Politika.* Moscow: Yuridicheskaya literatura, 1989.

Brement, Marshall. *Reaching out to Moscow: From Confrontation to Cooperation.* New York: Praeger, 1991.

Bremmer, Ian, and Ray Taras. *Nations and Politics in the Soviet Successor States.* New York: Cambridge University Press, 1993.

Breslauer, George W. *Can Gorbachev's Reforms Succeed?* Berkeley: Univ. of California, 1990.

Brown, Archie, ed. *The Soviet Union: A Biographical Dictionary.* London: Weidenfeld and Nicolson, 1990.

Brumberg, Abraham, ed. *Chronicle of a Revolution: A Western-Soviet Inquiry into Perestroika.* New York: Pantheon Books, 1990.

Brzezinski, Zbigniew. *Game Plan: How to Conduct the U.S.-Soviet Contest.* Boston, New York: The Atlantic Press, 1986.

———. *The Grand Failure: The Birth and Death of Communism in the Twentieth Century.* New York: Charles Scribner's Sons, 1989.

Carpenter, Russell H. *Red Carnations: A Report on the March 1989 Soviet Elections.* Washington: International Human Rights Law Group, 1989.

Carrère d'Encausse, Hélène. *Decline of an Empire: The Soviet Socialist Republics in Revolt.* New York: Newsweek Books, 1979.

Chernyayev, Anatoly S. *Shest' let s Gorbachevym.* Moscow: Izdatelskaya Gruppa Progress, Kultura, 1993. German translation: Anatoli Tschernayew. *Die letzten Jahre einer Weltmacht; Der Kreml von innen.* Stuttgart: Deutsche Verlags-Anstalt, 1993.

Cohen, Stephen F., and Katrina vanden Heuvel. *Voices of Glasnost: Interviews with Gorbachev's Reformers.* New York, London: W. W. Norton & Co., 1989.

Committee on Foreign Affairs, U.S. Congress. *Soviet Diplomacy and Negotiating Behavior, 1988–90; Gorbachev-Reagan-Bush; Meetings at the Summit.* Special Studies Series on Foreign Affairs Issues, vol. 3. Washington: U.S. Government Printing Office, 1991.

Communist Party of the Soviet Union. *XIX Vsesoyuznaya konferentsiya Kommunisticheskoi partii Sovetskogo Soyuza. Stenograficheskii otchet.* Moscow: Politizdat, 1988.

Connor, Walter D. *The Accidental Proletariat: Workers, Politics, and Crisis in Gorbachev's Russia.* Princeton: Princeton Univ. Press, 1991.

Conquest, Robert. *Harvest of Sorrow: Soviet Collectivization and the Terror-Famine.* New York: Oxford Univ. Press, 1986.

Crawshaw, Steve. *Goodbye to the USSR: The Collapse of Soviet Power.* London: Bloomsbury, 1992.

Dallin, Alexander, and Gail W. Lapidus, eds. *The Soviet System: From Crisis to Collapse.* Rev. ed. Boulder: Westview Press, 1995.

Dawisha, Karen, and Bruce Parrott. *Russia and the New States of Eurasia: The Politics of Upheaval.* Cambridge: Cambridge Univ. Press, 1994.

Denber, Rachel, ed. *The Soviet Nationality Reader: The Disintegration in Context.* Boulder: Westview Press, 1992.

Desai, Padma. *Perestroika in Perspective: The Design and Dilemmas of Soviet Reform.* Princeton: Princeton Univ. Press, 1989.

Dyker, David A. *Restructuring the Soviet Economy.* London and New York: Routledge, 1992.

Dzyuba, Ivan. *Internationalism or Russification? A Study in the Soviet Nationalities Problem.* 2nd ed. London: Weidenfeld and Nicolson, 1970.

Falin, Valentin. *Politische Erinnerungen.* Munich: Droemer Knaur, 1993.

Felshman, Neil. *Gorbachev, Yeltsin, and the Last Days of the Soviet Empire.* New York: St. Martin's Press, 1992.

Feshbach, Murray, and Alfred Friendly, Jr. *Ecocide in the USSR: Health and Nature under Siege.* New York: Basic Books, 1992.

Furtado, Charles F., Jr., and Andrea Chandler, eds. *Perestroika in the Soviet Republics: Documents on the National Question.* Boulder: Westview, 1992.

Garthoff, Raymond L. *The Great Transition: American-Soviet Relations and the End of the Cold War.* Washington: Brookings, 1994.

Goldman, Marshall I. *Gorbachev's Challenge: Economic Reform in the Age of High Technology.* New York, London: W. W. Norton & Co., 1987.

———. *What Went Wrong with Perestroika.* New York: W. W. Norton & Co., 1992.

Gorbachev, Mikhail S. *Avgustovskii putch: Prichiny i sledstviya.* Moscow: Novosti, 1991. English translation: *The August Coup: The Truth and the Lessons.* New York: Harper Collins, 1991.

———. *Dekabr' 91: Moya pozitsiya.* Moscow, Novosti, 1992.

———. [Gorbatschow, Michail]. *Gipfelgespräche: Geheime Protokolle aus meiner Amtszeit.* Berlin: Rowohlt, 1993.

———. *Izbrannye rechi i stat'i.* 7 vols. Moscow: Politizdat, 1987–1990.

———. *Perestroika i novoye myshlenie dlya nashei strany i dlya vsego mira.* Moscow: Politizdat, 1987. English translation: *Perestroika: New Thinking for Our Country and the World.* New York: Harper & Row, 1987.

Grachev, Andrei. *Dal'she bez menya . . . : Ukhod prezidenta.* Moscow: Kultura, 1994. English translation: *Final Days: The Inside Story of the Soviet Union.* Boulder: Westview Press, 1995.

Gromyko, Andrei. *Pamyatnoe.* 2 vols. Moscow: Politizdat, 1988. Abridged English translation: *Memoirs.* New York: Doubleday, 1990.

Gwertzman, Bernard, and Michael T. Kaufman, eds. *The Decline and Fall of the Soviet Empire.* New York: Times Books, 1992.

Handelman, Stephen. *Comrade Criminal: Russia's New Mafiya.* New Haven: Yale Univ. Press, 1995.

Hazan, Baruch A. *Gorbachev and His Enemies: The Struggle for Perestroika.* Boulder: Westview Press, 1990.

Hewett, Ed A., and Victor H. Winston. *Milestones in Glasnost and Perestroika: The Economy.* Washington: Brookings, 1991.

Hogan, Michael J., ed. *The End of the Cold War: Its Meaning and Implications.* Cambridge: Cambridge Univ. Press, 1992.

Hosking, Geoffrey. *The Awakening of the Soviet Union.* Cambridge: Harvard Univ. Press, 1990.

Hosking, Geoffrey, Jonathan Aves, and Peter J. S. Duncan. *The Road to Post-Communism: Independent Political Movements in the Soviet Union, 1985–1991.* London and New York: Pinter Publishers, 1992.

Hough, Jerry. *Russia and the West: Gorbachev and the Politics of Reform.* New York: Simon and Schuster, 1988.

Human Rights Watch/Helsinki. *Azerbaijan: Seven Years of Conflict in Nagorno-Karabakh.* New York: Human Rights Watch, 1994.

Hyland, William G. *Mortal Rivals: Superpower Relations from Nixon to Reagan.* New York: Random House, 1987.

Ivashov, L. G. *Marshal Yazov (Rokovoi avgust 91-go).* Moscow: Bib. zhurnala Muzhestvo, 1992.

Kaiser, Robert G. *Why Gorbachev Happened: His Triumphs and His Failure.* New York: Simon & Schuster, 1991.

Kalugin, Oleg. *The First Directorate: My 32 Years in Intelligence and Espionage Against the West.* New York: St. Martin's Press, 1994.

Karaulov, Andrei. *Vokrug Kremlya.* 2nd ed. Moscow: Slovo, 1993.

Karklins, Rasma. *Ethnopolitics and Transition to Democracy: The Collapse of the USSR and Latvia.* Washington: The Woodrow Wilson Center Press, 1994.

Khasbulatov, Ruslan I. *The Struggle for Russia,* edited by Richard Sakwa. London and New York: Routledge, 1993.

Kuleshov, S. V., O. V. Volobuyev, E. I. Pivovar, et al. *Nashe Otechestvo: Opyt politicheskoi istorii.* 2 vols. Moscow: Terra, 1991.

Kunayev, Dinmukhamed. *O moem vermeni.* Alma Ata: RGZhI "Deuir," MP "Yntymak," 1992.

Kutsyllo, Veronika. *Zapiski iz Belogo doma: 21 sentyabrya–4 oktyabrya 1993 g.* Moscow: Izdatelskii Dom Kommersant, 1993.

Kvitsinsky, Yuli [Kwizinskij, Julij]. *Vor dem Sturm: Erinnerungen eines Diplomaten.* Berlin: Siedler Verlag, 1993.

Lapidus, Gail, and Victor Zaslavsky, eds. *From Union to Commonwealth: Nationalism and Separatism in the Soviet Republics.* Cambridge: Cambridge Univ. Press, 1992.

Laqueur, Walter. *Black Hundred: The Rise of the Extreme Right in Russia.* New York: Harper Collins, 1993.

Ligachev, Yegor. *Inside Gorbachev's Kremlin.* New York: Pantheon Books, 1993.

———. *Izbrannye rechi i stat'i.* Moscow: Politizdat, 1989.

Luzhkov, Yuri. *72 chasa agonii: Avgust 1991 g.; Nachalo i konets kommunisticheskogo putcha v Rossii.* Moscow: Magisterium, 1991.

Malia, Martin. *The Soviet Tragedy: A History of Socialism in Russia, 1917–1991.* New York: The Free Press, 1994.

Mandelbaum, Michael, ed. *Central Asia: Kazakhstan, Uzbekistan, Tajikistan, Kyrgyzstan, Turkmenistan, and the World.* New York: Council on Foreign Relations, 1994.

———. *Western Approaches to the Soviet Union.* New York: Council on Foreign Relations, 1988.

McFarlane, Robert C. *Special Trust.* New York: Cadell & Davies, 1994.

McFaul, Michael. *Post-Communist Politics: Democratic Prospects in Russia and Eastern Europe* Washington: Center for Strategic and International Studies, 1993.

Medvedev, Grigori. *The Truth about Chernobyl.* New York: Basic Books, 1991.

Medvedev, Roy, and Giulietto Chiesa. *Time of Change: An Insider's View of Russia's Transformation.* New York: Pantheon Books, 1989.

Medvedev, Zhores. *Gorbachev.* New York: W. W. Norton & Co., 1986.

Menges, Constantine C. *Transitions from Communism in Russia and Eastern Europe.* Lanham, MD: University Press of America, 1994.

Mesbahi, Mohiaddin. *Central Asia and the Caucasus after the Soviet Union: Domestic and International Dynamics.* Gainesville: Univ. Press of Florida, 1994.

Mezhenkov, Vladimir, and Eva Skelley, eds. *One Way Ticket to Democracy.* Moscow: Progress Publishers, 1989.

Morrison, John. *Boris Yeltsin: From Bolshevik to Democrat.* New York: Dutton, 1991.

Motyl, Alexander J. *Dilemmas of Independance: Ukraine after Totalitarianism.* New York: Council on Foreign Relations, 1993.

———. *Sovietology, Rationality, Nationality: Coming to Grips with Nationalism in the USSR.* New York: Columbia Univ. Press, 1990.

———. *Will the Non-Russians Rebel? State, Ethnicity, and Stability in the USSR.* Ithaca: Cornell Univ. Press, 1987.

Nahaylo, Bohdan, and Victor Swoboda. *Soviet Disunion: A History of the Nationalities Problem in the USSR.* New York: The Free Press, 1990.

Nazarbayev, Nursultan. *Bez pravykh i levykh: Stranitsy avtobiografii, razmyshleniya, pozitsiya . . . ; Otvety na voprosy izdatel'stva.* Moscow: Molodaya gvardiya, 1991.

Nenashev, Mikhail F. *Posledneye pravitel'stvo SSSR: Lichnosti; Svidetel'stvo; Dialogi.* Moscow: Krom, 1993.

Nitze, Paul H. *From Hiroshima to Glasnost: At the Center of Decision; A Memoir.* New York: Grove Weidenfeld, 1989.

Oberdorfer, Don. *The Turn: From the Cold War to a New Era: The United States and the Soviet Union, 1983–1990.* New York: Poseidon Press, 1991.

Odom, William E., and Robert Dujarric. *Commonwealth or Empire? Russia, Central Asia, and the Transcaucasus.* Indianapolis: Hudson Institute, 1995.

Olcott, Martha Brill. *The Kazakhs.* Stanford: Hoover Institution Press, 1987.

Parker, John W. *Kremlin in Transition.* 2 vols. Boston: Unwin Hyman, 1991.

Pavlov, Valentin. *Gorbachev-putch: Avgust iznutri.* Moscow: Delovoi Mir, 1993.

Pechnev, Vadim. *Gorbachev: K vershinam vlasti; Iz teoretiko-memuarnykh razmyshlenii.* Moscow: Gospodin Narod, 1991.

Peck, Merton J., and Thomas J. Richardson, eds. *What Is to Be Done? Proposals for the Soviet Transition to the Market.* New Haven: Yale Univ. Press, 1991.

Pipes, Richard. *The Formation of the Soviet Union: Communism and Nationalism, 1917–1923.* Rev. ed. Cambridge, Mass.: Harvard Univ. Press, 1964.

———. *Russia under the Bolshevik Regime.* New York: Knopf, 1993.

———. *The Russian Revolution.* New York: Knopf, 1990.

Piyasheva, Larisa. *Mozhno li byt' nemnozhko beremennoi?* Minsk: Polifakt, 1991.

Popov, Gavriil Kharitonovich. *Chto delat'? O strategii i taktike demokraticheskikh sil na sovremennom etape.* Moscow: Izdanie gazety Pozitsiya, 1991.

———. *Eti chetyre goda.* Moscow: Moskovskiy rabochiy, 1989.

———. *Puti perestroiki: Mnenie ekonomista.* Moscow: Ekonomika, 1989.

Pozner, Vladimir. *Eyewitness: A Personal Account of the Unraveling of the Soviet Union.* New York: Random House, 1992.

———. *Parting with Illusions.* New York: The Atlantic Monthly Press, 1990.

Rahr, Alexander (compiler). *A Biographical Directory of 100 Leading Soviet Officials.* Boulder: Westview Press, 1990.

Raun, Toivo U. *Estonia and the Estonians.* Stanford: Hoover Institution Press, 1987.

Reagan, Ronald. *An American Life.* New York: Simon & Schuster, 1990.

Remnick, David. *Lenin's Tomb: The Last Days of the Soviet Empire.* New York: Random House, 1993.

Rorlich, Azade-Ayşe. *The Volga Tatars: A Profile in National Resistance.* Stanford: Hoover Institution Press, 1986.

RSFSR Congress of People's Deputies. *Chetvertyi S"yezd Narodnykh deputatov RSFSR. Stenograficheskii otchet.* 4 vols. Moscow: Izdanie Verkhovnogo Soveta RSFSR, 1991.

———. *Spisok Narodnykh deputatov RSFSR, na 12 fevralya 1991 g.* Moscow: Izdanie Verkhovnogo Soveta RSFSR, 1991.

Rossiisky nezavisimy institut sotsialnykh i natsionalnykh problem. *Gorbachev-Yeltsin: 1500 dnei politicheskogo protivostoyaniya.* Moscow: Terra, 1992.

———. *Krasnoe ili beloe? Drama Avgust–91; Fakty, Gipotezy, Stolknovenie mneniy.* Moscow: Terra, 1992.

———. *Nesostoyavshiisya yubilei; Pochemu SSSR ne otprazdnoval svoego 70-letiya?* Moscow: Terra, 1992.

Ryzhkov, Nikolai Ivanovich. *Perestroika: Istoriya predatel'stv.* Moscow: Novosti, 1992.

Saikal, Amin, and William Maley. *Russia in Search of Its Future.* Cambridge: Cambridge Univ. Press, 1995.

Sakharov, Andrei. *Memoirs.* Translated by Richard Lourie. New York: Knopf, 1990.

———. *Moscow and Beyond: 1986 to 1989.* New York: Knopf, 1991.

———. *Progress, Coexistence & Intellectual Freedom.* New York: W. W. Norton & Co., 1968.

Senn, Alfred Erich. *Lithuania Awakening.* Berkeley: Univ. of California Press, 1990.

Sestanovich, Stephen, ed. *Rethinking Russia's National Interests.* Washington: Center for Strategic and International Studies, 1994.

Shane, Scott. *Dismantling Utopia: How Information Ended the Soviet Union.* Chicago: Ivan R. Dee, 1994.

Sheehy, Gail. *The Man Who Changed the World: The Lives of Mikhail S. Gorbachev.* New York: Harper Collins, 1990.

Shevardnadze, Eduard. *Moi Vybor: V zashchitu demokratii i svobody.* Moscow:

Novosti, 1991. English translation: *The Future Belongs to Freedom.* Translated by Catherine A. Fitzpatrick. New York: The Free Press, 1991.

Shlapentokh, Vladimir. *Soviet Intellectuals and Political Power: The Post-Stalin Era.* Princeton. Princeton Univ. Press, 1990.

Shultz, George P. *Turmoil and Triumph: My Years as Secretary of State,* New York: Charles Scribner's Sons, 1993.

Shmelev, Nikolai, and Vladimir Popov. *The Turning Point: Revitalizing the Soviet Economy.* New York: Doubleday, 1989.

Sidorenko, Yuri Sergeyevich. *Tri dnya, kotorye oprokinuli Bol'shevizm (Ispoved' svidetelya, pokazaniya ochevidtsa).* Rostov-on-Don: Periodika Dona, 1991.

Simons, Thomas W., Jr. *The End of the Cold War?* New York: St. Martin's Press, 1990.

Sobchak, Anatoly. *Khozhdenie vo vlast'.* Moscow: Novosti, 1991. English translation: *For a New Russia: The Mayor of St. Petersburg's Own Story of the Struggle of Justice and Democracy.* New York: The Free Press, 1992.

Sontag, R. J., and J. S. Beddie. *Nazi-Soviet Relations 1939–1941: Documents from the Archives of the German Foreign Office.* Washington: U.S. Government Printing Office, 1948.

Starr, S. Frederick, ed. *The Legacy of History in Russia and the New States of Eurasia.* Armonk, N.Y.: M. E. Sharpe, 1994.

Stepankov, Valentin, and Yevgeny Lisov. *Kremlyovsky zagovor.* Moscow: Izdatelstvo Ogonyok, 1992.

Sukhanov, Lev. *Tri goda s El'tsinym: Zapiski pervogo pomoshchnika.* Riga: Vaga, 1992.

Suny, Ronald Grigor. *The Revenge of the Past: Nationalism, Revolution, and the Collapse of the Soviet Union.* Stanford: Stanford Univ. Press, 1993.

Szabo, Stephen F. *The Diplomacy of German Unification.* New York: St. Martin's Press, 1992.

Taagepera, Rein. *Estonia: Return to Independence.* Boulder: Westview Press, 1993.

Tatu, Michel. *Gorbatchev: L'URSS va-t-elle changer?* Paris: Le Centurion, 1987.

Thatcher, Margaret. *The Downing Street Years.* New York: Harper Collins, 1993.

Tuleyev, Aman. *Dolgoye ekho putcha: Kak zhit' dal'she?* Moscow: Paleya, 1992.

Urban, George R. *End of Empire: The Demise of the Soviet Union.* Washington: American Univ. Press, 1993.

USSR Congress of People's Deputies. *Chetvertyi S"yezd narodnykh deputatov SSSR; 17–27 dekabrya 1990 g. Stenograficheskii otchet.* 3 vols. Moscow: Izdanie Verkhovnogo Soveta SSSR, 1991.

———. *Narodnye deputaty SSSR, po sostoyaniyu na 1 oktyabrya 1990 g.* Moscow: Izdanie Verkhovnogo Soveta SSSR, 1990.

———. *Pervyi S"yezd narodnykh deputatov SSSR; 25 maya–9 iyunya 1989 g. Stenograficheskii otchet.* 5 vols. Moscow: Izdanie Verkhovnogo Soveta SSSR, 1989.

———. *Vtoroi S"yezd narodnykh deputatov SSSR; 12–24 dekabrya 1989 g. Stenograficheskii otchet.* 6 vols. Moscow: Izdanie Verkhovnogo Soveta SSSR, 1990.

von Herwarth, Hans. *Against Two Evils.* New York: Rawson, Wade, 1981.

Voslensky, Michael. *Nomenklatura: The Soviet Ruling Class.* Garden City, N.Y.: Doubleday, 1984.

Yakovlev, Alexander Nikolayevich. *The Fate of Marxism in Russia.* Translated by Catherine A. Fitzpatrick. New Haven and London: Yale Univ. Press, 1993.

―――. *Muki prochteniya bytiya: Perestroika nadezhdy i real'nosti.* Moscow: Novosti, 1991.

―――. *Ot Trumena do Reigana.* Moscow: Molodaya gvardia, 1984.

―――. *Predislovie; Obval; Posleslovie.* Moscow: Novosti, 1992.

Yeltsin, Boris. *Against the Grain: An Autobiography.* Translated by Michael Glenny. New York: Summit Books, 1990.

―――. *Zapiski Prezidenta.* Moscow: Izd. Ogonyok, 1994. English translation: *The Struggle for Russia.* Translated by Catherine A. Fitzpatrick. New York: Times Books, 1994.

Zaprudnik, Jan. *Belarus: At a Crossroads in History.* Boulder: Westview Press, 1993.

Zinoviev, Aleksandr. *Gorbachevizm.* New York: Liberty Pub. House, 1988.

Index

Note: CP refers to Communist Party; MG refers to Mikhail Gorbachev; CPD refers to Congress of People's Deputies

About the Author

JACK F. MATLOCK is a professor at Columbia University. During a thirty-five-year career in the U.S. Foreign Service, he served four tours at the American Embassy in Moscow and two in senior positions in Washington dealing with the Soviet Union. While on an assignment to the National Security Council staff during the Reagan administration (1983–86) he was responsible for coordinating U.S. policy toward the Soviet Union and drafted key policy papers and much of Reagan's correspondence with the Soviet leaders. Named U.S. Ambassador to the USSR in 1987, he helped negotiate the end of the cold war and witnessed the development of forces in the Soviet Union that brought on its disintegration shortly after his departure in 1991. While on assignment to the embassy in Moscow, he traveled to all the republics of the former Soviet Union and came to know the leaders of the political establishments and of the anticommunist opposition movements in most of them. He lives in New York and Washington with his wife, Rebecca Burrum Matlock.

About the Type

This book was set in Times Roman, designed by Stanley Morison specifically for *The Times* of London. The typeface was introduced in the newspaper in 1932. Times Roman had its greatest success in the United States as a book and commercial typeface, rather than one used in newspapers.

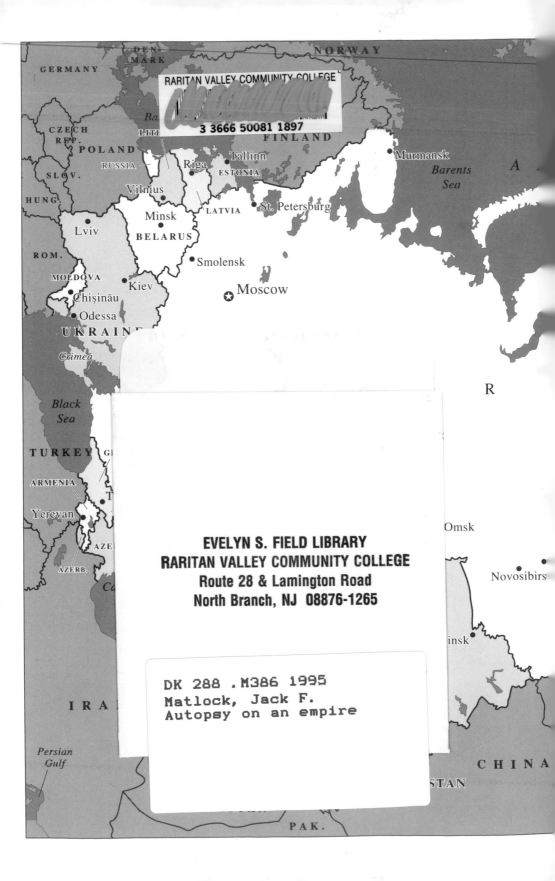